Penguin Books

The Penguin Encyclopedia of Ancient Civilizations

Arthur Cotterell was born in Berkshire in 1942. He was educated at Ashmead School, Reading, and St John's College, Cambridge. Now Principal of Kingston College of Further Education in Surrey, he combines a career in education and training after school with an extensive interest in other civilizations, many of them ancient. His published works include *The Minoan World*, *A Dictionary of World Mythology*, *The First Emperor of China* and *China: A Concise, Cultural History*. At present he is writing a general history of East Asia, an area in which he is well travelled. He is also editor of the new *Penguin Encyclopedia of Classical Civilizations*, due to be published in 1992.

Arthur Cotterell is married with one son and lives in Surrey.

The Encyclopedia of
ANCIENT CIVILIZATIONS

Edited by Arthur Cotterell

Penguin Books

PENGUIN BOOKS

Published by the Penguin Group
Penguin Books Ltd, 27 Wrights Lane, London W8 5TZ, England
Penguin Books USA Inc., 375 Hudson Street, New York, New York 10014, USA
Penguin Books Australia Ltd, Ringwood, Victoria, Australia
Penguin Books Canada Ltd, 10 Alcorn Avenue, Toronto, Ontario, Canada M4V 3B2
Penguin Books (NZ) Ltd, 182-190 Wairau Road, Auckland 10, New Zealand

Penguin Books Ltd, Registered Offices: Harmondsworth, Middlesex, England

First published in Great Britain by Windward, an imprint of W. H. Smith & Son Ltd, Leicester, 1980
First published in the USA by Mayflower Books, Inc., New York, 1980
Published in paperback by Penguin Books, and simultaneously in hardback by Viking 1988
10 9 8 7 6 5 4 3

Printed and bound by Dai Nippon Printing Company Ltd, Tokyo, Japan

Title-page illustrations: Glass masks from Carthage, fourth century BC.
Illustration, page 6: Maya design from a polychrome plate. Probably God K, late classic period
(AD 600-800).

Contributors

A. L. Basham
Professor of Asian Civilizations,
Australian National University, Canberra

Ignacio Bernal
Former Director of the National Museum of
Anthropology, Mexico

Robert Browning
Professor of Classics and Ancient History,
Birkbeck College, University of London

T. R. Bryce
Senior Lecturer in Classics,
University of Queensland

T. Burrow
Boden Professor of Sanskrit (1944–76),
University of Oxford

Geoffrey W. Conrad
Assistant Professor of Anthropology,
Harvard University

Arthur Cotterell
Assistant Principal,
Richmond Upon Thames College, London

William Culican
Reader in Ancient History,
University of Melbourne

Richard A. Diehl
Professor of Anthropology,
University of Missouri

W. G. Forrest
Professor of Ancient History,
University of Oxford

John Gould
Professor of Greek,
University of Bristol

A. K. Grayson
Professor of Near Eastern Studies,
University of Toronto

O. R. Gurney
Emeritus Professor of Assyriology,
University of Oxford

N. G. L. Hammond
Honorary Fellow of Clare College, Cambridge,
and Emeritus Professor of Greek,
University of Bristol

Ho Peng Yoke
Foundation Professor, School of Modern Asian Studies,
Griffith University, Queensland

J. T. Hooker
Lecturer in Greek, University College,
University of London

Thorkild Jacobsen
Emeritus Professor of Assyriology,
Harvard University

E. J. Keall
Associate Curator, West Asian Department,
Royal Ontario Museum and
Associate Professor, Department of Middle East and
Islamic Studies, University of Toronto

David M. Lang
Professor of Caucasian Studies,
University of London

Richard E. Leakey
Director of the National Museums,
Kenya

Wolfgang Liebeschuetz
Professor of Classics,
University of Nottingham

Trevor Ling
Professor of Comparative Religion,
Victoria University of Manchester

R. A. Markus
Professor of Medieval History,
University of Nottingham

H. B. Nicholson
Professor of Anthropology,
University of California, Los Angeles

Wendy D. O'Flaherty
Professor of History of Religions
and Indian Studies, Divinity School,
University of Chicago

R. M. Ogilvie
Professor of Humanity,
University of St Andrews

J. M. Plumley
Emeritus Professor of Egyptology,
University of Cambridge

Kenneth Quinn
Professor of Classics,
University of Toronto

Colin Renfrew
Professor of Archaeology,
University of Southampton

Helmer Ringgren
Professor of Old Testament Studies,
University of Uppsala

N. K. Sandars
Fellow of the Society of Antiquaries,
London

Robert S. Santley
Assistant Professor of Anthropology,
University of New Mexico

Colin Walters
The Griffith Institute,
Ashmolean Museum, Oxford

B. H. Warmington
Reader in Ancient History,
University of Bristol

William Watson
Professor of Chinese Art and Archaeology,
University of London

R. F. Willetts
Professor of Greek,
University of Birmingham

G. R. Willey
Bowditch Professor of Archaeology,
Harvard University

T. Cuyler Young, Jr.
Curator, West Asian Department,
Royal Ontario Museum and
Professor, Department of Near Eastern Studies,
University of Toronto

Contents

Preface

Arthur Cotterell

The past quarter of a century has witnessed a profound change in our approach to the earliest civilizations of man. Archaeologists and ancient historians have turned their attention to uncovering the general processes which underly the formation, maintenance, and breakdown of civilization itself. The new emphasis–'what made this civilization tick'–does not diminish in any way our appreciation of particular achievements but rather it recognizes the remarkable fact that ancient civilizations were the creation of our own ancestors. They were man-made environments. The history of the human species is, as Colin Renfrew points out, primarily the history of the civilized world, and not of man as an organism. The most striking alterations in human behaviour have taken place within 'civilization', which appeared in the Old World around 3000 BC in Sumer and Egypt, as well as the Indus valley (after $c2700$ BC), the Yellow river valley (before $c1500$ BC) and the island of Crete ($c2000$ BC), and in the New World around 1000 BC in Mexico and 900 BC in Peru.

This encyclopedia offers a survey of these first civilizations. It focuses on their emergence, development, interaction, decline; the termination date for the ancient phase of civilization varies from area to area but everywhere it coincides with a definite rupture in the historical pattern. In Europe we stop at the collapse of the western provinces of the Roman empire, in Egypt and West Asia with the Arab conquest, in India at the fall of the Gupta empire, in China at the Tartar partition, and in America with the arrival of the Spaniards.

Our aim has been to provide a comprehensive view of ancient history through the study of its civilizations. An encyclopedia covering such a vast range of human endeavour cannot hope to be more than introductory. Yet there is the possibility that the reader will obtain an overall view as well as the means of pursuing in detail topics of special interest. It is a wish all contributors share.

Time-chart of six areas of ancient civilization covered by the entries in the encyclopedia

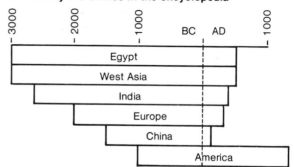

The cradles of ancient civilization.

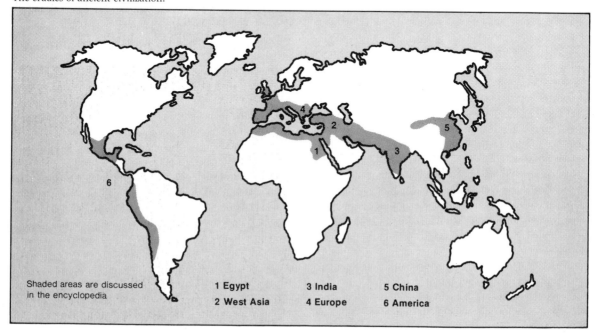

Shaded areas are discussed in the encyclopedia

1 Egypt
2 West Asia
3 India
4 Europe
5 China
6 America

Prehistory

Richard E. Leakey

The age of the planet

Modern scientific awareness of both prehistory and the vast geological age of planet earth is really a result of investigations over the past two hundred years. Although the eighth-century Chinese mathematician and astronomer, I-Hsing, had considered the world to have been in existence for millions of years, it was more than a millennium before such a notion could be entertained in Europe. As late as 1650 the Archbishop of Armagh, James Ussher, calculated from the Old Testament that the date for the creation of the earth was 4004 BC. Dr John Lightfoot, then the Master of St Catherine's College, University of Cambridge, further refined this date and declared that it had taken place on 23 October 4004 BC at nine o'clock in the morning.

The calculation allowed a modest 6000 years for the age of the planet and this was duly printed in the margin of the Authorized Version of the Bible. Despite this, pressure began to build up against the Ussher/Lightfoot proposition, especially during the eighteenth century when fossils began to be widely accepted, together with the growing awareness that the earth's geology was complex in nature. Extinct animals were identified and some scholars put forward the ingenious suggestion that they were remains of creatures drowned in the Flood. As time progressed and the science of geology began to be studied seriously, many more fossil finds were made and, in addition, stone implements were discovered and recognized as being the works of man before the use of metal.

Sequences of fossils were documented and put forward as proof of the length of time represented by the fossil-bearing strata. Opposition to this idea was so strong that a popular contention held that a series of catastrophes must have occurred, each having wrought havoc with the animal and plant life of the planet, thus producing the fossils. After each disaster, God had restocked earth with quite new species. Noah was believed to have built his ark to deal with the last catastrophe.

It was in the early part of the nineteenth century that the immense age of the planet began to be generally accepted. In 1830 Charles Lyell published *The Principles of Geology* which had considerable impact upon scientific thought at the time. Evidence for the long descent of mankind came from the discovery of flint hand axes associated with the remains of extinct mammals. This discovery was first made in 1850 by a French customs official at Abbeville, Jacques Boucher de Crèvecoeur de Perthes. He argued strongly for the great antiquity of his finds. We now know that these artifacts indeed belong to the Old Stone Age of Europe and, since their discovery, many more sites have been found and studied all over the world.

On 24 November 1859, Charles Darwin published *On the Origin of Species* and the first printing of over 1000 copies was sold out the day of publication. Darwin's proposition was that the diversity of species known in the living world was the result of evolution. He put forward the theory that natural selection was the mechanism by which living organisms had gradually adapted to changing environments over many generations. He recognized that, by this process of evolution, a species might change and that an ancestral form might be quite different from its evolutionary descendant.

Origins of mankind

In 1871 Darwin published his *Descent of Man* which firmly placed mankind in the evolutionary scheme and suggested that we had had apelike ancestors. He also suggested that Africa would prove to be the cradle of mankind. Although there was considerable controversy over Darwin's ideas, a significant body of scientific evidence began to be accumulated and the basis of modern biology was firmly established. The evolutionary theory for human origins was in direct contrast with the fundamentalist version of the Creation. In 1856 prehistoric remains of man were found in the Neander Valley in Germany and in 1868 further finds were made in southwestern France at a place called Cro-Magnon, close to Les Eyzies. In the 1890s even more primitive-looking fossils were recovered in central Java, then in China at Chou-k'ou-tien, and in 1924 the first 'ape-man'

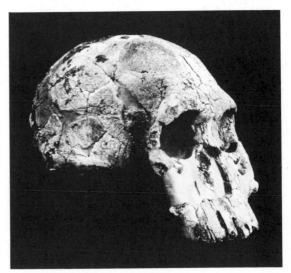

1470, the oldest complete skull discovered in Kenya, reveals a crucial hominid development—an enlarged brain.

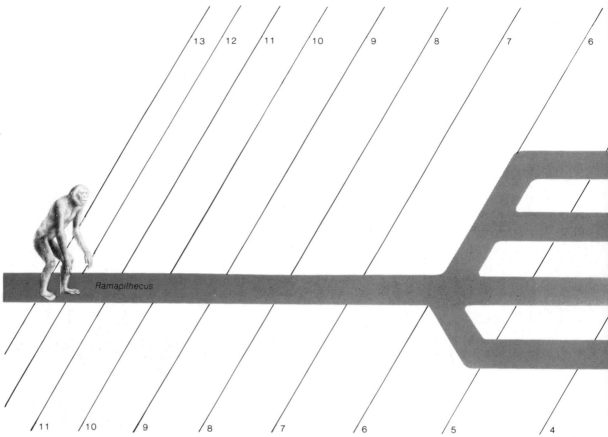

The probable evolutionary path of the hominids. Tool-making among *homo sapiens* led to the 'agricultural revolution' upon which the first civilizations were founded.

skull was discovered in South Africa. All these finds strengthened the evolutionary story of man and led to a great increase in investigations.

Today, the focus of research on human origins is firmly placed in Africa, with special emphasis on the various Rift valley sites in eastern Africa. From the fossil remains of partial skulls and skeletons that have been recovered from sites in Ethiopia, Kenya and Tanzania, it is apparent that the ancestral line leading to us stretches back beyond 4 million years. Furthermore, discoveries have shown that, in addition to our own genus *Homo*, there have been other species of man which became extinct despite their essentially human adaptations.

At the present time, scientific evidence points to a small apelike creature known as *Ramapithecus* as the common ancestor of all the fossil species of mankind and ourselves. Jaws and teeth of *Ramapithecus* have been found in sites ranging from China to Kenya, with the largest collection coming from Pakistan. These fossils range in age from about 8 million years to the older African finds dated at 14 million.

It is presumed that *Ramapithecus* was upright and bipedal, although this essential human adaptation has

yet to be confirmed by the fossil evidence. Modern theories present *Ramapithecus* as the first crucial adaptive stage of man at which the apelike creatures were adapting to an open country habitat and, in so doing, changing diet and locomotion. It is thought that further environmental factors brought about additional evolutionary changes which can be recognized as the various fossil species known during the past 3 million years. Existing fossil evidence indicates that this occurred only in Africa despite the fact that *Ramapithecus* was widespread in late Miocene times. A great deal of additional evidence is required to establish firmly the events leading to later species and the notion of an African genesis.

In Africa, there are fossils that prove that the earliest recognizable form of *Homo*, namely *Homo habilis*, lived alongside a species known as *Australopithecus robustus*. Some theorists have put forward evidence that a third species, *Australopithecus africanus*, was also a contemporary. It is widely agreed that both species of *Australopithecus* became extinct about a million years ago and that the one surviving species, *Homo erectus*, spread across the Old World and provided the widespread stock for the eventual appearance of *Homo sapiens*. The evolutionary relationship between *Homo habilis*, *Homo erectus* and *Homo sapiens* is not fully understood al-

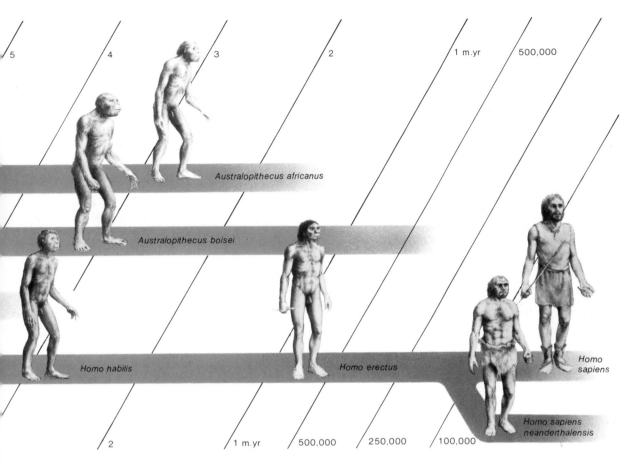

though many scientists today consider all three to be part of a single evolutionary lineage. A conflicting theory has *Homo habilis* as an extinct branch, with *Homo erectus* being derived from an Asiatic source hitherto undiscovered.

The recent discovery of fossils from Hadar in Ethiopia and Laetoli in Tanzania may have bearing on this debate. These finds are being interpreted as a new ancestral species, *Australopithecus afarensis*, providing a link between *Ramapithecus* and the later hominids. The fossils are between 3 and 4 million years of age and are thus of a most interesting evolutionary age.

Early social organization

Regardless of the details of how one fossil species relates to another, there is broad agreement that *Homo* was the line which showed evidence for significant behavioural changes. The fossil skulls demonstrate a change in the shape of the brain as well as an overall increase in volume and this is correlated with the evidence for stone tool making and an ever increasing utilization of meat in the diet. The analysis of the archaeological record indicates that food sharing and the use of a home base became an ever increasing characteristic of early *Homo*, with the development of language and culture as a natural consequence of this unique adaptation.

Homo habilis and the early forms of *Homo erectus* are visualized as having been increasingly dependent on their ability to provide meat for their diet and, from this, the need to fashion sharp cutting tools became paramount. There are important social consequences of a meat-eating economy, and more complex relationships between individuals and especially between the sexes are seen as a result.

Another important consequence would have been the increased versatility of the species in its ability to range into new habitats and environments. The gradual spread of *Homo erectus* either from an African or Asian source is thus explained. Migration would have been a very slow process and probably the result of succeeding generations seeking new hunting grounds. Present-day studies of human societies that exist by hunting and gathering show the importance of maintaining a relatively low population density with groups of between 25 and 50 being the average.

As *Homo erectus* spread through Africa, Europe and Asia, the various populations would have become isolated from one another and so would develop regional characteristics or identity. Some populations were adapting to temperate climates and this perhaps explains the first deliberate use of fire as a source of warmth and perhaps later as a means of preparing food. The

Homo erectus fossils from between 1.5 million years and 0.5 million years show quite distinctive features, but except for the brain size of between 775 cc and 1100 cc, they are not dissimilar to modern humans. The characteristic 'beetle brows' are not considered to have had any adaptive or evolutionary significance.

Early forms of *Homo sapiens* are seen as the evolutionary descendants of *Homo erectus*, but here again, modern science is unable to agree. One postulated theory is that *Homo sapiens* evolved in one place and that this species then spread across the world, eliminating the scattered and less successful populations of *Homo erectus*. The gradual isolation of these *sapiens* populations is represented as the origin of modern racial groups. An alternative theory that is less popular presents *Homo erectus* as merely an evolutionary stage or condition which inevitably evolved into *Homo sapiens* – each broad region of the Old World having the more or less simultaneous development of *sapiens*. For this notion to be accepted, it is essential to represent *Homo erectus* and *Homo sapiens* as one and the same species, being part of a single evolving line which has distinctive early and late stages, simply because of the separation by time.

Neanderthal Man is an example of the early stage of *Homo sapiens* at which there was a significant expansion of brain size. Moreover, extensive studies of Neanderthal sites in Europe and West Asia have demonstrated the much more elaborate culture and complex life style. At Shanidar in Iraq, there is even a suggestion that 60,000 years ago Neanderthal people had religious ideas and a concern for the after-life. Shortly after this period, there is increasing evidence for prehistoric art and the long occupation of sites by hunting bands.

There is a tremendous wealth of evidence for the activities of man in Europe over the past 40,000 years and all of this provides an indication of the essentially modern human condition. For a variety of reasons, considerably more archaeological work has been conducted in Europe for this later period and the paucity of material from Africa, Asia and America should not be interpreted as evidence for a European genesis for modern man.

In relatively recent times, probably during the last 10,000 years, various populations of *Homo sapiens* began to place increasing reliance on the deliberate production of food. There are now many sites that have yielded archaeological evidence for the domestication of plants and animals and this is put forward as the beginning of the so-called 'Agricultural Revolution'. In fact, domestication probably has its origins much further back in time, perhaps related to the first appearance of *sapiens* some 100,000 years ago. The lower density of populations and the greater antiquity has made such evidence very scarce, but it does represent one very important area for continuing prehistoric research.

Successful agriculture enabled populations to remain in one area for long periods and also resulted in the increased size of particular groups. This settled way of life certainly facilitated the dramatic increase of cultural complexity which is a characteristic of this very recent and perhaps final phase of human evolution. So began the period of 'civilization', much of which is now known about through the written records of our immediate forbears.

The Emergence of Civilization

Colin Renfrew

Civilization

Among the organisms that inhabit, or have inhabited, the earth, man is unique in possessing a history. Of course for every species of creature the story of its emergence could be told, recounting some genetic mutation from a kindred form which allowed it in some way to adapt better to its environment, and hence to propagate, according to the Darwinian principle of the 'survival of the fittest'. There would then be the new behaviour to describe, associated with the new form, and the subseqent genetic mutations which made it in turn the progenitor of further related species. And then, for all but a few species, the circumstances of its extinction, as environmental conditions changed or as competitor species proved more successful.

Man is different. Only some 2 or 3 million years have elapsed since he first appeared upon the scene – a short period on the evolutionary time scale, and a bare 40,000 or so years since our own species, *Homo sapiens*, is first attested. Yet in that short space of time man has totally modified his behaviour, from the lifestyle of the early hominid, a gatherer of plants and occasional hunter of animals, to that of the modern world citizen. In doing so he has totally transformed his personal environment into something that is very much his own creation – from the moment of his birth in the hospital maternity ward to his inhumation (or cremation) in accordance with the rites of a religion, itself probably no more than 2000 years old. Genetically, so far as we can tell, this modern man is identical in terms of his physical constitution and abilities to his Stone Age predecessor during the last Ice Age.

This historical process is therefore a unique one. For in a sense man himself, as he comes into the world, is as unchanged, as little different from his remote ancestors, as are the newly born members of the other species which have no history. Today's new-born child and the baby of a palaeolithic cave man cannot be distinguished. Yet they are destined to lead completely different lives, since each is the inheritor of a very different world. The history of the human species is primarily the history of that world, rather than of man as an organism, and over the millennia man's world has undergone some striking, indeed revolutionary transformations. Of these the most radical and arguably the most remarkable is the emergence of civilization.

The emergence of civilization

Tracing human evolution back to our remote African origins, millions of years ago, we come to some significant milestones on the way. Perhaps the most intriguing of them, indicating a process as yet little understood, marks the development of *Homo sapiens sapiens* himself at the onset of the Upper Palaeolithic era some 40,000 years ago. But whereas that crucial development may have occurred in a single area of the earth's surface, a later momentous achievement, the development of food production, seems to have happened independently in a number of different regions in the millennia following the end of the last Ice Age. In each of these regions man domesticated a range of plants and a few animals, thereby transforming and controlling his subsistence base. Naturally these changes took a long time, and several of them have their origins very much earlier: the 'neolithic revolution' did not happen suddenly. Its consequences were fundamental; an expansion of the human species to regions, such as the islands of Polynesia, or the rainless river valleys of Mesopotamia, which had previously been almost uninhabited. This process was accompanied by a marked increase in population, and the development of a settled way of life for the first time in a whole range of environments.

These early farming settlements were, in the main, rather small villages of just one or two hundred people. In favourable circumstances, however, the population could grow to a much larger figure, as at the oasis of Jericho, where the settlement occupied an area of some 74 acres (30 ha) and there was an enclosing fortification wall as early as 7000 BC.

Several thousand years later a further great transformation occurred. In different parts of the world, towns and cities grew up, centres of population with a built-up area ranging from as little as 187 acres (76 ha) for some of the cities of Sumer around 2500 BC, up to 9 sq miles (23 sq km) for the great city of Nineveh almost two thousand years later, or an estimated 8 sq miles (21 sq km) for Teotihuacán in Mexico a further thousand years later, around AD 600.

These new settlements were not simply large agglomerations of population. They were societies of a new kind, displaying a highly organized form of central government. Each polity had a ruler, a central adminis-

Despite extensive fortifications like this tower (c7000 BC), Jericho did not achieve 'civilization'.

tration and a system of ensuring that the wishes of both were carried out within its territories. Such polities are what the anthropologist terms *state* societies. With the city and the state came, nearly always, a series of singular achievements of the human species. There were advances in technology—for instance great advances in metallurgy in the Old World, in chemical techniques and in engineering. There were developments in pure science, notably, the precise and intricate calendar of the Maya of Central America. Systems of recording and writing were developed. Everywhere rulers and priests lived in sumptuous palaces and worshipped in

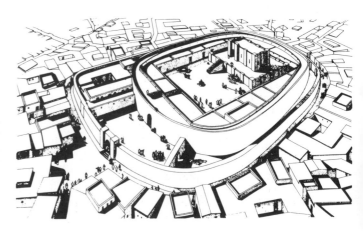

A reconstruction of the 'Oval Temple' at Khafaje, dating from about 2500 BC. This Sumerian site was dug in the 1930s.

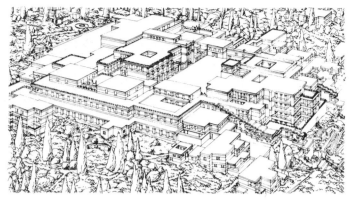

Above: The Palace of Minos at Knossos: an artist's impression.

Right: Egyptian scarabs showing early hieroglyphs. The need to show ownership and maintain records probably caused the development of writing.

impressive temples, in a society with marked distinctions between rich and poor.

Among the great civilizations which appeared early on, their respective continents were those of the Sumerians of Mesopotamia (*c*3000 BC), the Egyptians of the Nile valley (likewise *c*3000 BC), as well as the Indus valley civilization (after *c*2700 BC), the civilization of Shang China (before *c*1500 BC) and of Minoan Crete (*c*2000 BC), while in the New World, the civilization of the Olmecs of Mexico (from *c*1000 BC) and the Chavín of Peru (from *c*900 BC) were among the earliest. In each there are monuments and works of art that far surpass anything hitherto seen in the area. The palaces and frescoes of Minoan Crete, for instance, find no counterpart in the Aegean a millennium earlier, nor can the bronzes and jades of Shang China find a striking early

The multi-plaza 'acropolis' at Copán, a major Maya Classic settlement and religious centre.

precursor. In each region something entirely new, remarkable and unexpected had come into the world.

What is civilization?

This remarkable phenomenon, the emergence of civilization, is at once one of the most momentous episodes in human history and one of the most difficult to explain. Indeed the concept of 'civilization' is perplexingly difficult to define adequately. Geographers naturally think first in terms of settlement patterns, and for them a key problem is the emergence of urban settlements and of cities. Indeed the very term 'civilization' is related to the Latin *civitas* (city), just as 'urban' is derived from the Latin *urbs* (town), and indeed 'political' or 'polity' from the Greek *polis* (city or state). Questions of urban origins are inextricably linked with any discussion of civilization. It is important to realize that many of the features which we think of as typical of civilization, such as the existence of writing, monumental architecture or a

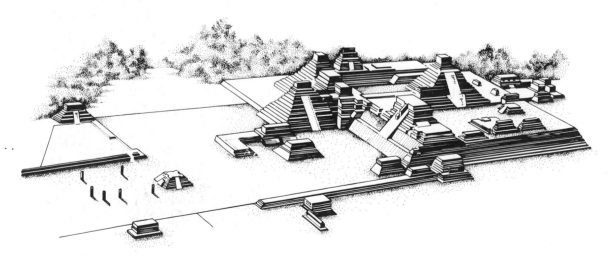

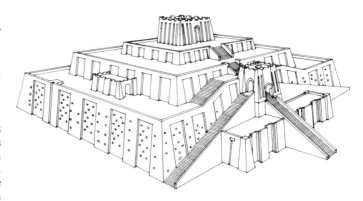

developed art style, do not need to be accompanied by large urban settlements. The culture of the Maya of Mesoamerica, like that of Khmer Cambodia in the eleventh century AD, has sometimes been called a 'civilization without cities'. Conversely early settlements of large size, such as Jericho and Çatal Hüyük, may not show accompanying features such as to justify the term 'civilization'.

Of course geographers are careful not to define cities on the strength of settlement population alone: a city has to fulfil 'central place' functions, offering services to a rural hinterland, before it can qualify for the term. Anthropologists today tend to stress in particular the organization of society, frequently avoiding the term 'civilization' precisely because it is so difficult to define, and speak instead of a 'state level of sociopolitical organization'. Here the defining criterion is a central governmental authority, often accompanied by the division of the population into social and economic classes. In anthropological parlance this is a stratified society rather than a ranked society in which status is often defined primarily by kinship. Sustaining the state authority in such societies, it is suggested, is the legalized use of force: the ruler has rights and obligations which transcend his personal standing. Yet the trouble with definitions of this kind, however appropriate in principle, is that they are difficult to apply to societies long dead for which evidence on such matters is not always readily forthcoming.

It was perhaps for this reason that the anthropologist Clyde Kluckhohn suggested a much simpler, rather unsophisticated but eminently usable definition. His definition of 'city dweller' and 'urban' loosely designates societies characterized by at least two of the following features: towns of upward of, say, 5000 inhabitants, a written language and monumental ceremonial centres.

Perhaps no definition is entirely adequate, although Kluckhohn's is as convenient as any. It is essential to see any 'civilization', 'urban society' or 'early state' as a particular form of human culture. For it is precisely man's 'culture', that is to say, the means he has developed for coping with his environment over and beyond his genetic inheritance, which distinguishes him from other species. Starting with the manufacture and use of tools and with the development of a complex language for communication, man has developed a rich 'culture' over the millennia so that, in this respect (and in this respect only), a child born today comes into a very different world from that of 40,000 years ago. 'Culture', in this sense, is something handed on from generation to generation, shaping the growth and education of the child so that a person in one society develops a very different way of life from one in another cultural environment. We are shaped, therefore, from our earliest days by the culture into which we are born, and it is this which distinguishes us from our ice age ancestors.

Reconstruction of the ziggurat at Ur.

But we also add to that store of human experience, and to the range of adaptive devices which make up our material and spiritual environment, by developing new ways of coping—not only with the material world of nature, but with each other and with the new material world which we are creating. In the words of J. K. Feibleman:

'We are the creatures of the institutions we have made, and this is no less so because we have made them. There is a helix of interaction between man and his works, so that the effects on him of his works spur him to further works which have further effects, and so on until it is impossible to tell which is man *qua* man and which is his work.'

Man has gradually and progressively, although not always irreversibly, created about himself an environment which has increasingly mediated between himself

One of the Amarna tablets. Considerable light is shed on the fourteenth century BC in West Asia by the recovery of the cache of tablets at Amarna in Egypt.

15

Town house at Mallia, clearly the residence of an affluent Minoan family.

and the world of nature. First tools and clothes are interposed between his body and the elements. Then built dwellings create a new, man-made space within which to live and work. The domestication of plants and animals allows a measure of control over his food supply, and indeed he works now with species which are themselves the result of his own activities and in that sense are artifacts. Increasingly his contacts are with this world which he himself created, and with aspects of the social organization which has grown up simultaneously with it. Nor have these simply been changes in his material conditions. Man has the unique ability to use symbols, to think symbolically, and much of his science and technology, as well as most of his social environment (and nearly all of his religious framework), depend on this quality. As the German philosopher, Ernst Cassirer, put it:

'The functional circle of man is not only quantitatively enlarged; it has also undergone a qualitative change. Man has, as it were, discovered a new method of adapting himself to his environment. Between the receptor system and the effector system, which are to be found in all animal species, we find in man a third link which we may describe as the *symbolic system*. This new acquisition transforms the whole of human life. As compared with the other animals man lives not merely in a broader reality; he lives, so to speak, in a new dimension of reality.'

If all this is progressively true for human culture as a whole, it becomes much more emphatically so as the urban transition, the rise of civilization and the formation of the state take place. For now man lives in an environment that is almost entirely man-made. The city is a world of its own, indeed a microcosm of all experience. Through craft production and exchange the specialist obtains the raw materials, including food, which he requires. The specific form of society in which he now lives determines the manner in which he spends

his time, while the religion or philosophical system of the civilization which he shares, conditions his thought. In the words of the American social historian, Lewis Mumford:

'The expansion of human energies, the enlargements of the human ego, perhaps for the first time detached from its immediate communal envelope, the differentiation of common human activities into specialized vocations, and the expression of this expansion and differentiation at many points in the structure of the city, were all aspects of a single transformation: the rise of civilization.'

Civilization, however it may be defined, is something unique to human experience. But it is not a unique event, for civilizations have come about at different times and places over much of the earth's surface. And this is a phenomenon which we have only now begun to understand.

The problems of origins

Early urban societies in different parts of the world frequently show resemblances with one another. The pyramids of Egypt have at times been compared with the pyramidal temples of the Maya, and the rich burials of the princes of early Ur in Mesopotamia, accompanied by wheeled wagons and numerous sacrifices of human retainers, may be compared with those of the early rulers of China at Anyang. Numerous similarities of this kind can be found, and in the early years of this century ingenious theories were constructed around them.

Civilization, it was argued, had a single place of origin. For the Australian anthropologist, Sir Grafton Elliot Smith (1871–1937), this was Egypt, and from there the 'Children of the Sun' were imagined as carrying the basic techniques and ideas of civilized life out into distant lands, crossing continents and oceans until even the Americas felt the civilizing influence of 'heliolithic' culture. Other writers, such as Lord Raglan, stressed the importance of Sumer rather than Egypt, but the underlying idea was the same. Indeed it survives in our own day with the theories of Thor Heyerdahl, who has built craft such as he believes the ancient Egyptians might have used, and navigated the oceans with them himself.

Such theories are not of themselves impossible and exploits such as the *Kon Tiki* expedition have demonstrated this in a graphic way. But in terms of simple logic, if civilization emerged in the valley of the Nile, such a process could have taken place in other areas also. It has sometimes been argued that such a complicated sequence of interlocking events as the rise of civilization could only have taken place once in human history. The same has been asserted for the invention of metallurgy, but there is no conceivable theoretical justification for such a statement, however plausible it may or may not be thought to be. This is a matter for the facts to decide.

Over the past 20 or 30 years the diffusionist view of culture, that most major innovations occur only once and are then spread by contact between the populations of different areas, has not fared well. In particular the 'hyperdiffusionist' view—that all civilization originated in Egypt—looks particularly absurd in the absence of supporting facts and the growing documentation for local developmental processes at work in different areas. Moreover the construction of secure and independent chronologies for the different areas concerned, due mainly to the application of radiocarbon dating and to the tree-ring calibration of radiocarbon dates, has clarified some of the pitfalls of diffusionist thinking. The prehistory of Europe, for instance, can no longer be seen in Gordon Childe's memorable phrase as the story of 'the irradiation of European barbarism by Oriental civilization'.

It is still permissible, of course, to argue about the implications of the evidence, and there remain a few diffusionists who argue for significant influence by the Egyptians upon the emerging cultures of Mesoamerica. But the consensus of scholars now accepts the abundant indications that agriculture developed independently in the Americas and that, on the resulting sure economic base of settled village farming, the foundations of Mesoamerican civilization were laid.

There can only be a single earliest civilization in any area: in Mesoamerica the Olmecs at present win that prize (although the early Maya may soon compete for it), and in the western part of the Old World, the Sumerians. Naturally any subsequent civilization in the area is open to influence from contacts with the local pioneer or with its successors. But increasingly it is appreciated that, to understand the origins and development of any civilization, it is necessary to look at the local conditions of its existence: at its subsistence, at its technology, at the social system, at population pressures, at its ideology, and at its external trade. No longer is it sufficient simply to analyze the contacts which it may have had with earlier civilizations in terms of supposed influences, which are rarely spelled out in detail. The processual approach in archaeology seeks to examine the factors promoting change in terms of these local conditions as well as by considering the consequences for the society of its external trading links. Its methods have therefore begun to make the old division between 'pristine' civilizations and 'secondary' civilizations, argued by anthropologists such as Morton Fried, seem an unacceptably diffusionist one. There is no doubt that contacts between societies and cultures can in certain circumstances be of determining significance. But it is the work of the archaeologist first to document such contacts and then to examine their consequences. A preliminary classification into 'pristine' and 'secondary' sets a facile taxonomy in place of serious analysis.

It is more profitable, instead, to look at the circumstances before the rise of complex society in any given area and to follow the trajectory of development from the origins to agriculture, through the development of ranked society, showing some measure of centralized leadership, and so leading to the formation of state society. A number of recent approaches offer new ways of looking at the problem. It does not follow that the evolution is a steady one, nor that a ranked society such as a chiefdom need develop into a state society. But no civilization has ever developed without the sure base of a prosperous food production, or without some prominent difference in wealth and prestige in the ranked society which it succeeded.

Current approaches

In recent decades we have come to see that there is a general problem here. It is not enough to talk of a single civilization in isolation. We must make the attempt to explain and understand the remarkable general phenomenon of the rise of complex society, taking place altogether independently in different parts of the world and also occurring repeatedly over the centuries and millennia in the same area. Indeed a related problem is that of the not uncommon collapse of early state societies, since in a significant number of cases sophisticated and complex societies have undergone complete and rather sudden breakdown, with an ensuing 'dark age'. The well-known case of the end of the Mycenaean civilization of Greece around 1100 BC has some striking general resemblance to the Classic Maya collapse about AD 900, and other instances of systems collapse can be recognized in a number of early state societies, including the Indus valley civilization (c1900 BC).

Some of the early generalizations about the rise and fall of civilizations, such as those of the English historian, Arnold J. Toynbee (1889–1975), were rather anecdotal; in fact descriptive as much as explanatory. Others have highlighted a single important factor. Karl Wittfogel, for instance, in *Oriental Despotism* (1957) stressed the importance of intensive food production facilitated by irrigation agriculture and suggested some causal links between the kind of social structure necessary to operate a complex irrigational system and the highly centralized, autocratic sort of society implied by the title of his book.

Gordon Childe (1892–1957) was the first archaeologist to consider the evidence in a systematic way, assembling the data in his book *The Most Ancient East* (1928). He outlined his view of the sequence of events in his still very readable book *Man Makes Himself* (1937), and most clearly and concisely in a masterly article entitled 'The urban revolution' (1950). Perhaps the next really interesting investigation after Childe was undertaken by the American anthropologist, Robert Adams, in his Lewis Henry Morgan lectures for 1965, published under the title *The Evolution of Urban Society*. Here, for the first time, the development of civilization in two unrelated areas, namely, early Mesopotamia and prehispanic Mexico, was systematically compared. Morgan himself (1818–81) was one of the founding fathers of evolutionary archaeology. His *Ancient Society* (1877) significantly influenced Karl Marx, whose stress on the relationship between the economic and social structure of early 'pre-capitalist' and subsequent societies, embodied in his concepts of 'mode of production' and 'relations of production', helped to shape Childe's thought and directly or indirectly has had a bearing on most subsequent workers. Indeed a number of scholars have recently returned anew to the original writings of Marx, some of them published for the first time only recently, and have drawn inspiration from them. This neo-Marxist school, exemplified by Maurice Godelier and Jonathan Friedman, highlights the interactions between economic activities and other aspects of society in a manner initiated by Marx and followed by many later writers. To the outside observer, however, the discussion sometimes seems to spend longer on elucidating the *ipsissima verba* of the original Marx, often from the textual analysis of very concise quotations, than in examining the real problems presented by the data after more than a century's subsequent research.

One important recent approach has been spatial: approaching the study of early complex society from the standpoint of its spatial organization. Here much of the inspiration has come from the 'locational analysis' school of modern geography, including the application and investigation of Central-Place theory initiated by W. Christaller (1863–1969). He observed striking regularities in the distribution and spacing of settlements in an urban landscape. Subsequent studies have also emphasized the possible regularities in the size and scale of the various settlements. These ideas have been applied directly to the early period of Mesopotamian civilization by Greg Johnson. Others have indicated the recurrent pattern seen in many early complex societies in which the spatial pattern seems to have existed in the repeated occurrence of an 'early state module'; the civilization in question consisting of a dozen or more independent polities, each with its primary centre, and each with a territorial area of some 580 sq miles (1500 sq km).

Another promising approach is to consider early state societies, not so much as devices for efficient and intensive food production (as Karl Wittfogel stressed), but rather as organizations for the efficient processing of information, facilitating the centralized administration which seems to have been a feature (indeed almost a defining feature) of all early state societies. This perspective has profitably been employed by Kent Flannery in his interesting paper 'The cultural evolution of civilizations' (1972), and Henry Wright and Greg

A clay tablet from the Minoan palace at Phaistos on Crete, with signs for wheat, oil, olives and figs.

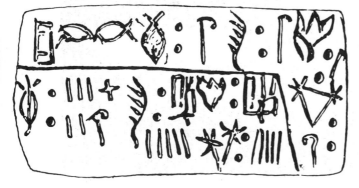

Johnson have also used this approach, coupled with a consideration of the accompanying hierarchy of settlement, in their consideration of state formation in early Iran.

Theoretical explanations of this kind are not mere armchair hypotheses. Increasingly they are shaping the design of programmes of excavation and research, so that it is fortunately becoming less common simply to excavate a promising archaeological site because it is there and offers the hope of some rich finds. Excavations are becoming more and more problem-oriented: the archaeologist initiates his survey or his excavation in order to seek answers to specific questions arising from these more general theoretical considerations. A project design is conceived so that the activities of the project can be used to answer those questions in the most effective and economical way. This may involve the use of probabilistic sampling designs which, like all statistics, can appear rather intimidating to the non-specialist. But when applied intelligently these techniques need not be accused of dehumanizing the study of the past: they are no more than techniques for obtaining specific answers, cheaply and reliably, to well thought out questions.

Most research projects, in response to thinking of this kind, are now interdisciplinary, drawing on a wide range of scientific specialisms to cast light on early food production, technology and trade. The American anthropologist R. K. Braidwood's pioneering project into the origins of food production in West Asia, which involved the excavation of the very early agricultural village at Jarmo (1948–55), was of this kind. Its counterpart in the Tehuacan valley of Mexico was directed by R. S. MacNeish. A comparable approach has been applied to the study of early complex societies in many areas. This is exemplified by the work of Kent Flannery in the Oaxaca region of Mexico, by MacNeish in Peru, by Frank Hole in Iran, by Chet Gorman and his colleagues in Thailand, and by the University of Minnesota's Messenia expedition and the writer's own project on the island of Melos, both in Greece. The study of urban origins in this interdisciplinary way is by no means restricted to prehistoric or early state societies. The development of urban society in Europe during the first millennium AD has been studied in Scandinavia, in north Europe and in Britain, where it is demonstrated by the work of the Winchester Research Unit using a comparable perspective. The study of the formation of early complex society is now a major focus of research on a world wide basis, and our understanding of the nature and origins of civilization is being consequently enlarged.

Prospect

For more than a century, up to the 1950s, the study of early civilization implied essentially the excavation of the great sites of the ancient world, and the careful description and publication of the finds. This allowed an increasingly clear picture of the way of life to be built up for a whole range of early complex societies—such as the Hittites, the Sumerians, the Indus valley civilization, the

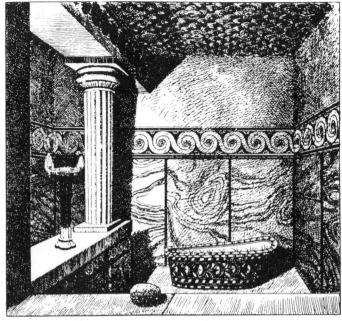

Olmec, the Minoans–whose very existence was entirely unknown before the great discoveries and pioneering excavations of the nineteenth and early twentieth centuries. The work of great pioneers, such as Sir Austen Henry Layard (1817–94) and Sir Leonard Woolley (1880–1960) in Mesopotamia, and Sir Arthur Evans (1851–1941) in Crete, or the early discoveries of pre-Columbian civilization in the Americas, laid the indispensable foundation for our understanding of the early civilizations which they discovered.

Today, however, although much remains to be learned, we do have many of the basic facts and scientific techniques, including the use of chronometric methods, and are rapidly establishing many more. The thrust of current work in some areas is therefore shifting from discovery and reconstruction to understanding and explanation. The systematic comparative study of early civilizations, of which the American authropologist, Julian Steward (1902–72), in his *Theory of Culture Change* (1955) was one of the pioneers, is once again a serious objective. A coherent attempt is now being made to develop explanatory models to try to offer some understanding of how and why civilizations emerged at the different times and places that they did, rather than simply to reconstruct the hard facts of that emergence. It is clear, first of all, that there is no single path to civilization, no pattern of unilineal evolution which all different early complex societies independently follow, just as there is emphatically no single centre of diffusion from which all major advances spread. But simply to advocate multilineal evolution is to say no more than that there are different pathways to civilization, which is now a known fact.

A reconstruction of the Queen's bathroom, the Palace of Minos, at Knossos. Through such drawings *The Illustrated London News* reported the spectacular discoveries of Sir Arthur Evans on the island of Crete.

Some authors have indeed stressed specific causal factors: intensified food production, or developing technology, or pressure to change arising from population increase, or a need to organize brought about by competition for scarce resources. All of these are clearly relevant factors, but it is becoming increasingly clear that no adequate explanation can be formulated, even in

Sir Austen Henry Layard (1817–94) directing his workmen at the site of ancient Nineveh.

Ancient cities compared: the outer city limits of Knossos are probably over generous. Note the extensive fortification of Uruk, a feature of Sumerian cities.

a single case, which relies only on one of them. Several factors must together be considered to arrive at what can

be called a 'multivariate' explanation. One way of formalizing such an approach is to use systems theory. This approach has been outlined for the prehistoric Aegean in the writer's *The Emergence of Civilisation* (1972), involving the use of subsystems to explain the dynamics of change in a civilization's evolution. Sustained growth is seen as arising from a multiplier effect between subsystems, whereby change in one facilitates rather than hampers change in another, i.e. the subsystems act upon each other – as might happen to the agriculture subsystem when influenced by technological advances in the development of tools brought about by increased productivity in the mines subsystem. Thus, growth is achieved which has overcome any anticipated negative feedback (the rise in output of one subsystem reducing the output of another). Dynamic systems modelling, using comparable insights, has been used with actual data to simulate the Maya collapse by Jeremy Sabloff and his colleagues. But these are early attempts, trial runs at theories rather than substantial and satisfying explanations.

What is clear, is that archaeology has over the past three decades moved on from a stage at which it was sufficient to recover the finds and describe them, to one in which we seek, by comparison and generalization, insight into the more general processes which underlie the formation of civilization. While few definitive conclusions can yet be claimed, there is near unanimity that the task is worthwhile and important, not only for the understanding of forgotten civilization, lost and long dead, but also for the insight which it may give to our own world, a world in which changes in technology and in ideology follow one another with bewildering rapidity in a manner we simply do not understand.

The early civilizations of man represent adaptations to, and developments in, his own created environment which were at first brilliantly successful. Many of these changes evidently stopped being successful, and the consequences of their failure were spectacular. While it can sometimes be facile to draw hasty or simplistic conclusions from that record of endeavour, achievement and failure, the study of early civilizations offers the best possibility we have of using the experience of the human past to enrich the human present.

Egypt

Painted scene from the rock-cut tomb of the governor of the Oryx nome, Khnumhotep, *c*1900 BC, at Beni Hasan. Khnumhotep is shown spearing fish from a light skiff.

Ancient Egypt

Colin Walters

Introduction

The period between about 3100 BC, when dynastic history began, and 332 BC, when Egyptian independence was brought to an end by the conquest of Alexander the Great, is normally referred to as Ancient Egypt.

Following the system originally devised by the priestly historian Manetho, who lived during the reigns of the first two Ptolemies, this period is customarily divided between thirty, or sometimes thirty-one, dynasties. Other broader divisions are traditionally recognized, though the system adopted here differs in some respects from the norm.

c3100–2613 BC	The Early Dynastic period	Dynasties 1–3
c2613–2160 BC	The Old Kingdom	Dynasties 4–8
c2160–2040 BC	The First Intermediate period	Dynasty 9 –early Dynasty 11
c2040–1652 BC	The Middle Kingdom	Late Dynasty 11 – Dynasty 13
c1652–1567 BC	The Second Intermediate period	Dynasties 15–17
c1567–1069 BC	The New Kingdom	Dynasties 18–20
c1069–656 BC	The Third Intermediate period	Dynasties 21–25
656–332 BC	The Late period	Dynasties 26–30 (31)

The dates assigned to the dynasties and to individual reigns are calculated by using information from a number of sources. Manetho, in this respect, is unreliable, and of greater value are the lists of kings compiled by the Egyptians themselves. Of these the most important are the *Turin Canon of Kings*, a document composed in the nineteenth dynasty, and the so-called Palermo Stone, of which only fragments survive, which gives details of reigns and events down to the end of the fifth dynasty. The shortcoming of all these sources is their failure to employ a continuous system of dating (which the Egyptians never did), and in order to relate Egyptian history to our chronological system it is necessary to make use of astronomical data and, for the later periods, comparative dating.

The Egyptian calendar consisted of 365 days, divided into three seasons of four months each plus five epagomenal days, whereas the true astronomical year comprises a little more than $365\frac{1}{4}$ days. With no adjustment, therefore, after 4 years New Year's Day would be a whole day ahead of its true position, after 120 years it would be a month ahead, and eventually, after 1460 years, any specific astronomical event would have occurred on every day of the civil calendar, and the process would begin once more.

We are fortunate that the reappearance of the dog-star Sirius, after a period of absence, was treated by the Egyptians as New Year's Day and it is a stroke of even greater good fortune to have it recorded that in AD 139 this heliacal rising of Sirius coincided with the first day of the civil calendar. Armed with this knowledge it is possible to calculate with fair accuracy the dates at which earlier Egyptian references to the event occurred. With these reasonably secure chronological 'pegs' we can use Manetho, the king-lists and secondary sources such as historical inscriptions, family genealogies, and

Pharaonic Egypt.

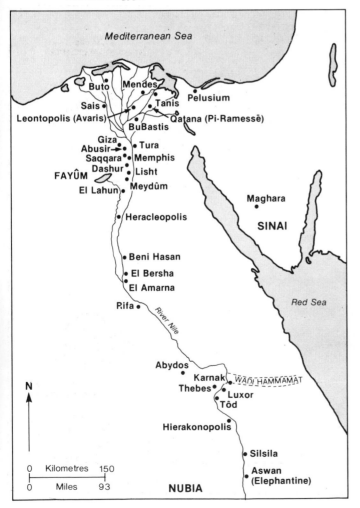

the like, to work out the dynastic chronologies which form the basis for our study of ancient Egypt.

The Early Dynastic period (Dynasties 1 to 3) c3100 to 2613 BC

The crucial event in Egyptian history, of which we are constantly reminded and which the Egyptians symbolized in a number of ways, was the unification of Upper and Lower Egypt under one ruler.

These territories were never clearly defined, though Lower Egypt seems to have consisted essentially of the Delta and perhaps the area immediately to the south of its apex, while Upper Egypt comprised the rest of the country to a point close to, if not at, the first cataract.

The identity of the first king of the newly created state is shrouded in mystery. According to Manetho and certain of the king lists he was Menes. It has been said that behind this name lurks the historically attested figure of Narmer, whose involvement in the events leading up to the unification is clearly established. The Early Dynastic period is calculated as having lasted for nearly 500 years, but the almost total absence of written evidence makes it a dark age for historians, illuminated only infrequently. The country was governed from Memphis, close to modern Cairo, and tradition ascribes its foundation to Menes himself. The royal court was situated here, and the kings of the third dynasty, at least, were buried nearby at Saqqara and elsewhere in the vicinity. The question of where the kings of the first two dynasties were buried has still not been resolved. Funerary monuments belonging to many of them have been discovered at both Saqqara and Abydos, in Upper Egypt, but which were used for the actual burials is a problem not easily solved.

Even in these early days Egypt had trading links with Byblos, situated along the Lebanese coast, and was active in Nubia, south of the first cataract of the Nile, as indicated by the excavations at Buhen near the second cataract. From the beginning of the third dynasty, if not before, the turquoise mines of Wadi Maghara in Sinai were already being worked.

None of these trading expeditions, it seems, was aggressive in character, though the Egyptians occasionally had cause to protect themselves against the local populations. In this respect the policy of these early kings, to respond only when provoked, was that pursued almost without exception by their successors down to the end of the Middle Kingdom. To these shadowy rulers goes the credit for laying down the foundation on which the monolithic civilization of the Old Kingdom was erected. Our knowledge of this formative period conveys a picture of a rapidly maturing culture, with many of its distinctive features already present.

The Old Kingdom (Dynasties 4 to 8) c2613 to 2160 BC

For the student of Egyptian history the Old Kingdom is a period of sharp contrasts. The levels of architectural and artistic achievement are staggering. What was accomplished at this time was in many respects never attempted or rarely equalled later. Gigantic monuments were constructed for pharaohs whose names have become familiar for that very reason; but of those pharaohs, their deeds and the condition of the land they ruled, we know lamentably little. It was only towards the end of the period that autobiographical and other inscriptions began to complete the picture.

The monumental evidence comes largely from the great necropoli at Giza, Saqqara, Meydûm, Dahshur and Abusir. Here were buried the kings, their families, and privileged members of the court circle. The scale on which the fourth dynasty pyramids were conceived bears testimony to the highly efficient utilization of state resources which made their construction possible, and to the all-powerful position enjoyed by their owners in this world. In the fifth and sixth dynasties there was a sharp decline in the size of the royal tombs, but perhaps not too much should be made of this. The successful government of Egypt depended largely on the loyalty and diligence of the provincial governors (nomarchs).

Some idea of the nomarch's importance can be

Nubia.

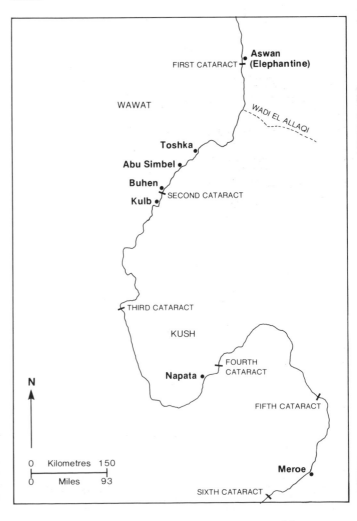

Chronology of Egypt

Pharaonic Period

BC

*c*3100   The pharaoh 'Menes' becomes the first ruler of a unified country

*c*2650   The Step Pyramid, first monumental building in stone, constructed for King Zoser at Saqqara

*c*2575   The Great Pyramid of Khufu built at Giza

*c*2160   Climatic conditions hasten the end of the Old Kingdom

*c*2040   The Middle Kingdom established by the Theban Mentuhotep

*c*1652   Following the end of the Middle Kingdom much of Egypt is taken over by Asiatic rulers known as the Hyksos

*c*1567   Theban forces complete the expulsion of the Hyksos. Dynasty 18 is established

*c*1490   Queen Hashepsowe becomes the only woman to rule Egypt for any length of time

*c*1469   Tuthmosis III becomes king upon the death of Hashepsowe. His reign sees the greatest extension of Egypt's military power

*c*1405   Power and prosperity are merged to bring Egyptian civilization to its apogee under Amenhotep III

*c*1367   Amenhotep's son and successor adopts the name Akhenaten, breaks with the established religion, and sets up a new capital at Amarna

*c*1350   Brief reign of Tutankhamun, whose tomb survived virtually intact until discovered in 1922

*c*1305   Seti I, second king of Dynasty 19, partially restores Egypt's position abroad

*c*1286   Ramesses II narrowly escapes defeat at the hands of the Hittites at the battle of Kadesh

*c*1269   A peace treaty is signed between the Egyptians and Hittites

*c*1218   Merenptah defeats an attempted invasion of Egypt by the Sea Peoples

*c*1182   Ramesses III successfully defends Egypt against a determined land and sea assault by the Sea Peoples

*c*1080   The New Kingdom ends. Rule of the country shared by the High Priest of Amun and two royal houses

*c*945   Kings of Libyan descent establish Dynasty 22

*c*925   King Sheshonq intervenes in Israel and sacks Jerusalem

*c*715   Seizure of power in Egypt by Nubians

663   Assyrians attack Egypt, sack Thebes, and leave vassal rulers in charge. Egypt enjoys a cultural 'Indian Summer'

605   Egyptian force defeated by the Babylonians at Carchemish

525   Persian army, under Cambyses, occupies Egypt

332   Alexander the Great defeats the Persians

Set, an animal manifestation of a deity. By the time of the Old Kingdom, the creature had acquired an almost fabulous form as a recumbent dog with an upright tail, a long neck and squared ears.

Ptolemaic Period

305   The satrap of Egypt, Ptolemy, sets up his own dynasty

30   Cleopatra, last of the Ptolemaic line, commits suicide
Octavian claims Egypt for Rome

Roman and Byzantine Period

BC

23   A Roman force is defeated by, and in turn defeats, the Meroites from Nubia

AD

38   First outbreak of violence between Greeks and Jews in Alexandria

115   Final struggle between the two races. Jewish population decimated

172   Revolt of the Boucholoi in the Delta

*c*180   Catechetical School established at Alexandria

201   Persecution of Christians by Severus – many Egyptians killed

249   Persecution of Decius

270   Palmyran forces invade Egypt and temporarily take control of Alexandria

*c*270   St Antony takes up the eremitical life

303   Great persecution of Diocletian begins – heavy toll in Egypt

*c*320   Pakhome sets up the first cenoebitic community

323   Constantine becomes emperor – triumph of Christianity

325   Council of Nicaea condemns Arianism

431   The First Council of Ephesus (second in 439). The Egyptian Church enjoys a brief triumph in its doctrinal battle with Constantinople

451   Council of Chalcedon: Monophysitism declared a heresy. The Egyptian Church refuses to accept the decision and is cut off from Orthodox Christendom

641   The Arab assault on Egypt begins. In the following year the Byzantine forces capitulate and Egypt becomes a Muslim state

obtained from the impressive rock-cut tombs of the southernmost nome at Elephantine, below the first cataract, most of which date to the sixth dynasty. Like others of their kind these men played an indispensable part in both local and national affairs, looking after the inhabitants of their district and serving their king when called upon.

For the governors at Elephantine this service involved participation in the expeditions which were regularly sent through Nubia to obtain exotic products such as incense, ivory and panther skins. These expeditions were not without incident. An affecting inscription from the tomb of Sabni tells how he recovered the body of his father, who had in some way met his end in Nubia, and during the reign of Snofru (fourth dynasty) a campaign was conducted against the Nubians which resulted in the capture of large numbers of prisoners and cattle. Nubia was exploited in other ways. Although the gold mines, which were so intensively worked in later times, were not yet operating, the diorite quarries north-west of Toshka were in constant use, at least through the fourth and fifth dynasties. At Buhen a colony was established which was involved in the smelting of copper. Other records, from Kulb and the Wadi el Allaqi, show that Egyptian prospectors were scouring the area for mineral deposits. Egyptian exploration and exploitation of Lower Nubia was undertaken energetically through most of the Old Kingdom.

Similarly, the links established with Byblos during the first three dynasties were maintained almost unbroken until the end of the sixth dynasty. For a land like Egypt, almost totally devoid of good timber, the cedarwood from the Lebanese hills was much prized. So, too, were the copper and turquoise of Sinai, where mining operations continued more intensively than ever. In these areas it was sometimes necessary to battle with those who resented the Egyptian presence. During the reign of Pepi I (sixth dynasty) military campaigns were conducted against Palestinian tribesmen, one involving the transportation of troops by ship.

The area to the west of the Nile Valley was largely unproductive and held no attraction for the Egyptians. It was for this reason that they adopted a purely defensive posture in this area. Victories against the 'Libyans' are recorded during the reign of Snofru and later during the reign of Sahure (fifth dynasty), but the need for such action seems to have occurred only sporadically.

According to Manetho, Pepi II ruled for 94 years and, although this figure cannot be verified from Egyptian sources, there is no doubt that he reigned for a very long time. His death effectively brought the sixth dynasty to an end. There followed a period which, though of short duration (approximately 20 years), was, if we are to believe the documentary and other inscriptional evidence, one of crisis and social revolution. The vivid accounts of famine and social disorder cannot be lightly dismissed. They constitute our principal source of information for this unsettled and even anarchic period. Although we have some idea of what happened, it is much more difficult to understand why. Traditionally it

was seen as the natural consequence of declining royal power and a parallel increase in the influence of the provincial nobility and the priesthoods of favoured cults; a state of affairs made worse by the long reign of Pepi II and by external pressures. All this, it is suggested, created conditions which, in the uncertainty following the king's death, resulted in social upheaval.

This interpretation of events takes no account of contrasting evidence of stability and well-being right to the end of the sixth dynasty: the quality of the art, the continuing activity in Nubia, Sinai and Palestine, and the apparent loyalty of the provincial governors. These are not the signs of a crumbling society.

Ultimately, perhaps, a decisive factor was the Egyptian climate which, following fairly moist conditions in predynastic times, became progressively drier during the Old Kingdom, with a significant reduction in the variety of flora and fauna. There are apparent references to low floods and to the famine conditions which resulted. These changes were spread over a considerable period, but at the end of the sixth dynasty, they became severe enough to undermine the stability of the state and provoke the people to rebellion.

The First Intermediate period and the Middle Kingdom (Dynasties 9 to 13) c2160 to 1652 BC

The unfavourable conditions seem to have continued throughout the ninth dynasty, during which the 'kings' ruled from the town of Heracleopolis (Egyptian *neneswet*), some 60 miles (96 kilometres) south of Memphis, which still remained the administrative capital. For nearly 30 years their authority was apparently unchallenged, but the extent of their effective control is uncertain, particularly in the Delta.

During the confusion at the end of the sixth dynasty tribesmen had taken the opportunity to cross the eastern frontier of Egypt and settle in this fertile region. It is unlikely, however, that they ever succeeded in occupying the entire area and the western Delta probably remained independent of Asiatic and Heracleopolitan control.

Eventually the Heracleopolitan claim to the throne of Egypt was challenged by a powerful family in the south, and for the first time in Egyptian history, the name of Thebes (Egyptian *waset*) is heard. For about 90 years these rivals fought an intermittent civil war. Many of the provincial governors were inevitably sucked into the conflict, but their prime concern seems to have been the safeguarding of their own interests and those of their subjects as the battle raged around them.

Around 2040 BC the issue was resolved in favour of the Thebans, led by Nebhepetre Mentuhotep, and the land was once again under the rule of an undisputed king. Nebhepetre ruled for 50 years from his accession in 2060 BC, and during this long reign order was restored within Egypt. The king clearly had to rely upon some of the long-established families of provincial nobility, but he also created a new élite of loyal Thebans.

Internal stability encouraged the revival of activity abroad. Egyptian authority was asserted in Lower Nubia (*wawat*), partly as a result of the king's personal intervention, thus re-opening the southern trading routes. Once the Asiatics had been driven from the eastern Delta; trading expeditions to Syria/Palestine—which had perhaps been continued by the nobility in the western Delta during the Heracleopolitan period—were once again sent out by royal decree.

In the reign of Sankhare Mentuhotep, Nebhepetre's successor, a large expedition travelled across the eastern desert to the Red Sea and on to the land of Punt, situated within the area of modern Ethiopia and the eastern Sudan. This land, with its abundant natural resources, had received Egyptian trading missions from the fifth dynasty, if not earlier. It has been suggested that the end of the eleventh dynasty was precipitated by a brief revisitation of severe climatic conditions, though the evidence on this occasion is rather more ambiguous.

The founder of the twelfth dynasty was probably the vizier (Egyptian *chaty*) Amenemhat, who led a quarrying expedition into the Wadi Hammamat during the reign of Nebtowyre Mentuhotep, the last king of the eleventh dynasty. As Sehetepibre Amenemhat (I) he headed a line of vigorous, able kings who ruled for consistently long periods and under whose direction the prosperity of the country was advanced and new levels of cultural achievement were attained. Although Sehetepibre was, it seems, slain by assassins, the survival of his dynasty had been safeguarded by the appointment some years previously of his son Senwosret as co-regent, a practice adopted by his successors.

It was probably Sehetepibre who took the decision to establish the court at *It-towy*. Its exact location is still unknown although we know it was somewhere between Memphis and Meydûm. It appears to have remained the royal residence throughout the dynasty. From here the elaborate administrative machinery of the country was organized and operated, headed as always by the office of the *chaty*. What part was played by the old provincial nobility is difficult to say. There is some negative evidence that during the reign of Khakaure Senwosret (III) (1878–1843 BC) their powers were curbed, but to what extent and in what way is harder to say. It is clear that during the dynasty, and probably during the reign of Khakaure, a reorganization of the

Fragment of painted decoration, from a New Kingdom noble's tomb at Thebes, showing the owner engaged in the traditional pastime of fowling in the marshes.

administration was carried out which resulted in the establishment of three government departments (Egyptian *warwt*) responsible for looking after the districts into which the country was divided for this purpose.

A significant feature of the times is the amount of activity in the Fayûm, the purpose of which seems to have been to regulate the flow of water entering Lake Moeris and to reclaim land in its vicinity for agricultural purposes. The apportioning of credit for this enterprise is difficult, though it was probably initiated by Sehetepibre and perhaps brought to a successful conclusion by Nymare Amenemhat (III) (1842–1797 BC). It is also possible that during the reign of Nymare the Fayûm basin served as a flood-escape for the waters of a series of exceptionally high inundations which are known to have occurred, thus protecting Lower Egypt from their disastrous effects. Little could have been done, however, to divert the destructive force of the floodwaters in Nubia, where much damage was done to Egyptian installations. The kings of the twelfth dynasty expended much time and effort in controlling the area between the first and second cataracts, both to facilitate trade with the region to the south and to safeguard the mining and quarrying activity within Lower Nubia itself. Under Sehetepibre and his son Kheperkare Senwosret (I) expeditions, that were at least partially military in character, signalled Egypt's determination to assert her dominion in the area. Egyptian authority was given physical expression by the construction of a series of impressive, fortified entrepôts at strategic points between the two cataracts; the greatest concentration being at the second cataract. Two others were established at the entry to the Wadi el Allaqi in the eastern desert and there can be little doubt that their *raison d'être* was the opening up of the gold mines within the Wadi, though the quantities extracted at this time were probably not great. Gold was also apparently obtained from further south, in the land known from this time forward as Kush.

But if Egyptian policy towards Lower Nubia was proprietorial, a different state of affairs existed to the northeast. For the whole of the twelfth dynasty we know of only one overtly military expedition which penetrated any distance into Palestine, during the reign of Khakaure, and its objectives were strictly limited. All other contacts appear to have been commercial and, to judge from the evidence at our disposal, these were extensive and continuous. However, whereas in Palestine they seem to have consisted almost entirely of trading missions, in Syria, and particularly along the coastal strip, a greater effort seems to have been made to establish diplomatic links, though whether of a permanent nature is difficult to say. Certainly the traffic was in both directions. While Egyptians and Egyptian objects, some of royal origin, found their way to Ugarit, Byblos, Qatna and elsewhere on the mainland, as well as indirectly to Crete and Cyprus, Asians and Asiatic gifts also came to Egypt. A collection of objects of Syrian provenance was discovered in caskets bearing the name of Nubkaure Amenemhat (II), at Tôd in Upper Egypt;

while in the tomb of the governor Khnumhotep at Beni Hasan was found a painted scene depicting the visit of an Asiatic chieftain with his retinue during the reign of Khakheperre Senwosret (II) (1897–1878 BC).

By the time the Middle Kingdom drew to its close the relationship had become a very close one. The so-called Execration Texts, which were intended to counteract the threat posed by a variety of hostile agents, displayed a knowledge of Asiatic place names that could only have been acquired by a close acquaintance with the area. At the same time, the evidence builds up of Asiatics in the employ of the Egyptian state: a number of them assisted the mining operations in the Sinai, which greatly increased in frequency during the reign of Nymare, while others were to be found in Egypt herself. The significance of this trend was quickly to become apparent. At the close of the twelfth dynasty, Egypt slipped into another of those poorly documented and confusing periods which punctuate her history. Obscurity does not necessarily indicate decline, however, and for more than 100 years after the death of Sobkkare Sobkneferu, the queen whose reign brought the dynasty to an end, continuity of a sort was maintained by a long line of kings (50 or more). Most of these kings resided at *It-towy* and sustained, for a while at least, an Egyptian presence in *Wawat* and contact with Byblos.

The Second Intermediate period (Dynasties 15 to 17) *c*1652 to 1567 BC

Following the fall of the thirteenth dynasty control of large parts of the country was assumed by Asiatics, whom Manetho called the Hyksos, and to whose leaders the Egyptians applied the nondescript term *heka-ḫaswt*, 'princes of the foreign lands'. These foreign rulers resided in a city called Avaris and form Manetho's fifteenth dynasty. The sixteenth dynasty, in all probability, comprised a number of vassals representing Hyksos interests in the central and southern parts of the country.

The Hyksos retained power for about 100 years. For much of that time a Theban family exercised a degree of independence in the south, and eventually took up arms against the foreigners and drove them from the country, thereby paving the way for the establishment of the eighteenth dynasty. Many of the central issues relating to this period, which was a watershed in Egyptian history, cannot be resolved. Attempts to identify the Hyksos with a specific race fail from lack of evidence. Similarly, the manner in which they seized power in Egypt is uncertain. The Manethonian account suggests an invasion, but according to another theory the takeover was essentially peaceful and was the inevitable outcome of the increasing Asiatic presence in the Delta and the declining authority of the thirteenth dynasty kings. We have no means of knowing at present which interpretation is correct. Another problem is the location of the Hyksos capital, Avaris. That it was somewhere in the eastern Delta seems certain, but precisely where we do not know. The region of Qatana has been suggested as one possibility.

The Hyksos kings adopted the paraphernalia of Egyptian royalty and in general terms left little behind them that is culturally distinct. They are credited with having introduced the Egyptians to new types of weaponry and perhaps also to the potential of the horse as an animal of war, though it can no longer be maintained that prior to their coming it was unknown to the Egyptians, since a skeleton dating to the Middle Kingdom was discovered at Buhen.

The struggle to evict the Asiatic intruders was waged by three successive members of the Theban family. Two of these, Seqenenre Tao (II) and his son Kamose, were assigned to the seventeenth dynasty, while the third, Nebpehtyre Ahmose, a brother of Kamose, was given the honour of heading the most famous dynasty in Egyptian history.

The New Kingdom (Dynasties 18 to 20) c1567 to 1069 BC

This fame derived very largely from the military exploits of four or five kings, which led to a dramatic extension of Egyptian influence in West Asia and the total subjugation of Nubia. This greatly increased the country's wealth, which in turn stimulated her cultural life. Power and prosperity were merged to bring Egyptian civilization to its apogee under Nebmare Amenhotep (III) (1405–1367 BC).

The successors of Ahmose were able to take advantage of the bridgehead which his pursuit of the Hyksos had established in southern Palestine and, although Djeserkare Amenhotep (I) left no record of activity in the area, Akheperkare Tuthmosis (I) apparently took the Egyptian army as far as the Euphrates and there set up a stela. His short-lived successor, Akheperenre Tuthmosis (II), had little time for military adventures, and after his death the throne of Egypt was occupied for 20 years by his widow Makare Hashepsowe (1490–1469 BC), supported by a powerful group of ministers, principal among whom was the chief steward, Senenmut. Unique though this episode was, and remarkable though its leading lady may have been, her reign made little impression in the field of foreign affairs. Her departure, however, left the stage clear for her nephew and stepson Menkheperre Tuthmosis (III) (1490–1436 BC), the legitimate successor of Akheperenre, whose position she had usurped during his infancy and early manhood.

Menkheperre enjoyed an independent reign of 32 years, and during the first 20 of these he led at least seventeen campaigns into Palestine and Syria, bringing him into conflict with Mitanni. This was a Hurrian confederacy occupying an ill-defined kingdom north of the Euphrates, whose influence extended into the area contested by Menkheperre. His eighth campaign culminated in the defeat of a Mitannian force, the crossing of the Euphrates near Carchemish, and the erecting of a stela alongside that of his grandfather. The Egyptian army never campaigned so far from home again. Menkheperre's son, Akheperure Amenhotep (II) (1436–1411 BC), was content to try and hold what his father had won, perhaps not entirely successfully, and under Menkheperure Tuthmosis (IV) (1411–1403 BC) a treaty was concluded between Egypt and Mitanni.

The lands subdued by the Egyptian army were policed by small garrisons, but in general terms Egyptian interests were looked after by civil officials, the most important of whom were the provincial governors (rabisu). Control of the larger centres of population was left in the hands of local princes, whose sons were removed to Egypt as a guarantee of loyalty. A royal messenger acted as an intermediary between the Egyptian court and the Asiatic provinces, from whom annual tribute was assiduously exacted.

During the Hyksos period, the Nubian rulers of Kush appear to have had at least an understanding with the foreigners and to have enjoyed undisputed control of their kingdom. The pharaohs of the eighteenth dynasty, however, swiftly reasserted their claim to the territory, and by the end of Akheperkare's reign the conquest had reached a point between the fourth and fifth cataracts. Behind the soldiers came the administrators, miners, traders and priests: occupying, exploiting and building.

With the elimination of any military threat the Middle Kingdom fortifications declined in importance, to be

The pharaoh Menkheperre Tuthmosis III (1490–1436 BC), under whose rule the Egyptian army came into conflict with Mitanni.

replaced by a series of walled towns, each with its temple, which became the symbol of Egypt's domination: a domination so complete that no identifiable Nubian culture belonging to the period has survived. The gold mines of the Wadi el Allaqi and Kush were now in full production, and everywhere Egyptians and Egyptian customs were to be found. Over this scene of cultural and military conquest presided an official with the ringing title 'King's son of Kush'. Nubia was now, in effect, part of Egypt.

Nebmare was succeeded, perhaps before his death, by Neferkheperure Amenhotep (IV) (1367–1350 BC). The reign of this king is traditionally referred to as the 'Amarna Period', and the king himself is more usually known by the name he later adopted, Akhenaten. El Amarna is the term applied nowadays to the site of the ancient city of Akhetaten, founded by the king himself in the fourth year of his reign, at a previously unoccupied site halfway between Memphis and Thebes. In his choice the king claimed divine guidance from the Aten, or 'sun's disk'. His adoption of, and eventually virtual identification with, this god and his attempt to suppress other cults—especially that of the immensely powerful Theban state god Amun—provoked hostility in his lifetime and caused his name to be anathematized after his death. His city and temples were razed to the ground

and his name and that of his god expunged wherever they could be found. So thorough was this act of revenge that little has survived on which to base a reconstruction of events or to assess the characters and motives of the principal actors in the drama.

In the highly distinctive art of the period the king is depicted with a most peculiar physical appearance which, it has been suggested, might indicate a glandular disorder. This will almost certainly never be proved. Similarly, it is doubtful whether the precise role of his queen, Nefertiti, will ever be fully understood. It has recently been suggested that she, in fact, was the 'Smenkhare' who has always been treated as a young man of unknown parentage who served as Akhenaten's co-regent for three years and died shortly before or after the king. That such a radical suggestion is possible shows how even fundamental questions relating to the period are unresolved, and are likely to remain so. 'Smenkhare' and Akhenaten were succeeded by the young boy Nebkheperure Tutankhaten (soon changed to Tutankhamun) who ruled for nine years (1350–1341 BC) and whose death was probably caused by a head wound. This much has been established by a re-examination of the young king's body, found intact with much treasure in his tomb. It was upon his death, or possibly that of his short-lived successor Ay, that a bereaved queen sent a message to the Hittite king promising the throne of Egypt to one of his princes. The prince, when finally dispatched, was murdered before reaching the Egyptian border.

During the lifetime of Tutankhamun the city of Akhetaten was abandoned by the court, which returned to the ancient city of Memphis. One of the retinue was no doubt the great commander of the army and king's deputy, Horemhab. With the young king's death the great dynastic line came to an end, and following Ay's brief career as pharaoh it was this powerful figure who assumed control of the country.

Details of his reign are sparse, but it would seem that his energies were directed principally towards national rehabilitation following the upheaval caused by Akhenaten's policies. One piece of evidence, which cannot be verified, mentions a campaign which reached Carchemish during the sixteenth year of the king's reign. If true, this would be a remarkable feat, given the political situation at the time.

There are some indications that Egyptians in later times treated Horemhab as the founder of the nineteenth dynasty, though ancient historians normally bestow that privilege upon the ephemeral king, Menpehtyre Ramesses (I).

The early kings of this dynasty gave priority to the restoration of Egyptian influence in Syria/Palestine, which had been allowed to lapse during the reign of Akhenaten and which had clearly not been greatly influenced by Horemhab's mission, if indeed this had

Egyptian relief work from the tomb of Menmare Seti I (1305–1290 BC). Detail showing a priest of Horus—the hairpiece denotes royalty.

29

ever taken place. The initial thrust was made by Menpehtyre's successor, Menmare Seti (I) (1305–1290 BC), in a series of campaigns – probably four. The recovery of Palestine presented relatively few problems, but as they proceeded further north, the Egyptians found themselves disputing the ground with the Hittites, with whom Menmare was directly in conflict at least once. It is difficult to be sure just how successful the king was, or how much he had hoped to achieve, but it would seem that by the end of his reign some sort of understanding had been reached between himself and the Hittite ruler.

This understanding did not survive the death of Menmare. His son, Usermare Ramesses (II) (1290–1223 BC), resumed hostilities with speed and zest, but with little tactical skill. In about 1286 BC the Egyptian army, organized into four divisions, advanced upon the city of Kadesh on the river Orontes. Misled by false information from bogus Hittite 'spies' the Egyptians walked unsuspecting into the Hittite trap, from which they were rescued only by the arrival of reinforcements at a critical stage in the battle. The Hittites were denied the complete victory that was so nearly theirs, while the Egyptians retired to lick their wounds. Usermare's later ventures into the area were less ambitious, and in the 21st year of his reign a treaty was concluded between the two powers. It preserved at least the illusion of Egyptian influence abroad, though in reality her capacity to intervene in the area's affairs was greatly reduced. Usermare's military adventuring came to an end, and the remainder of his 67-year reign was a period of relative peace and prosperity, permitting the nation's energies to be directed towards the fulfilment of the king's building programme, both in Egypt and Nubia.

Nubia remained under strict Egyptian control during the reigns of Menmare and Usermare, although it seems that difficulties were encountered in trying to maintain the levels of gold production reached in the eighteenth dynasty. There are also signs that before Usermare's death, northern Nubia was being abandoned by its population, though the reasons for this are still not clear.

During the reigns of Usermare's successors the fortunes of Egypt underwent a fairly rapid decline. Far from exerting any influence abroad, Egypt herself was now threatened by external forces, and the elimination of these threats became the limit of her ambitions. There are hints of the troubles ahead during Usermare's reign, when it became necessary to establish a series of forts along the Mediterranean coastline, and the king was forced to engage in battle with Libyan tribesmen. The pressures increased dangerously under Baenre Merenptah (1223–1213 BC), the eldest surviving son among Usermare's copious offspring, so much so that a great battle was necessary on the edge of the Delta during the fifth year of his reign to throw back a confederacy of Libyan tribes and northern sea-borne forces intent on establishing themselves within Egypt. One record of the deliverance contains a reference to the state of Israel, suggesting that the Exodus of the Jews from Egypt occurred in the reign of Merenptah's predecessor, Usermare.

Between Merenptah's reign and the end of the nineteenth dynasty, a span of approximately 20 years, three kings reigned in swift succession and were themselves briefly followed by the surviving queen, Sitre Twosre. It was about 1193 BC that Userkhaure Sethnakhte inaugurated the twentieth dynasty, perhaps after a brief interregnum. His reign was short, serving merely to pave the way for the king who, with the benefit of hindsight, we can see was the last great native pharaoh of an independent Egypt – Usermare-meramun Ramesses (III) (1190–1158 BC).

The victory won by Merenptah had only given Egypt a breathing space, and the new king swiftly found himself confronted by a series of determined assaults on his kingdom from east and west. First, in the fifth year of his reign, the Libyan tribes made another attempt to move into the western Delta. Then, three years later, a confederacy of Sea Peoples, as they were known to the Egyptians, swept through Syria and Palestine and attempted, by land and sea, to invade and occupy Egypt. The assault was thrown back only after a desperate battle (1182 BC). Finally, in the eleventh year of his reign, another campaign was necessary against the Libyans, bringing some degree of peace to the Egyptians. However, the sun was rapidly setting. Before the end of Ramesses' reign, there was unrest in the village on the west bank at Thebes occupied by the workmen engaged on the royal tomb, and the king himself was the subject of an unsuccessful assassination plot hatched in the royal harem.

After the great king's death, eight more bearing the name Ramesses followed one another, mostly in swift succession, and the indications of decline multiply. The many papyri from the period contain cases of dishonesty and corruption that paint a gloomy picture of the ethical standards of the time, though the element of chance that is always present in the survival of documents may have exaggerated the situation. The most dramatic evidence is to be found in the record of investigations into alleged (and partially proven) violation of royal tombs, conducted during the reign of Neferkare Ramesses (IX).

Sinai and Palestine were abandoned, and even in Nubia control was slackened. Steadily Egypt withdrew upon herself, trying to grapple with a faltering economy, harassment from increasingly bold tribesmen on the western edge of the Valley and fragmentation of the nation's very unity.

Finally, c1080 BC, this fragmentation was formally acknowledged, and while Neferkare remained titular head of state, effective governance of the country passed into the hands of the high priest of Amun and viceroy of Nubia, Herihor, at Thebes. A newcomer, Nesbanebded, was given control in the north of Egypt at Pi-Ramessē. For the next 11 years, until the death of Neferkare, this triple division of authority continued, and in this way ended the New Kingdom.

The Third Intermediate period (Dynasties 21 to 25) c1069 to 656 BC

In the centuries that followed, the lean years increasingly outnumbered the fat for Egypt. The continuity of her culture, which survived political upheaval and military defeat, conveys a misleading impression of stability and pharaonic might. Behind this façade, however, the reality was very different. Unable to respond as once she had done, she now found herself threatened by powers greater than her own, and control of her affairs was successively assumed by Libyans (or men of Libyan descent), Nubians, Assyrians, Persians and, finally and irrevocably, Macedonians. The gloom was relieved when in the twenty-sixth dynasty, a brief renaissance rekindled the flame; but history was fast catching up with Egypt and could not be gainsaid.

For about 130 years the kings at Tanis and the high priests of Amun at Thebes ruled the country between them, their alliance strengthened by marriage ties. It was, it seems, an uneventful interlude. The intervention in Palestinian affairs that resulted in the capture of the town of Gezer, during the reign of Siamun, was an isolated act of aggression. Near the end of the twentieth dynasty a line of Libyan chiefs had become established at Bubastis, halfway between Memphis and Tanis, probably descendants of captives settled there by Ramesses III. When the last king of the twenty-first dynasty died without heir it was the head of this family, Sheshonq, who by virtue of his close associations with the royal house became the founder of the twenty-second dynasty.

This began auspiciously. Hedjkheperre Sheshonq (945–924 BC) proved himself a strong and able ruler whose authority was accepted throughout the land. He re-established trading with Byblos and renewed Egyptian interest in Nubia, which had become independent during the twenty-first dynasty. His famous intervention in Israel (c925 BC), against Rehoboam, was one of the Egyptian army's last successes on foreign soil.

But the promise of Hedjkheperre's reign was not maintained. As the dynasty proceeded the authority of the king was challenged, first in Thebes and then elsewhere. Less than a century after Hedjkheperre's death civil war broke out and shortly after this the country began to break apart. First of all another dynasty, the twenty-third, set itself up at Leontopolis in the central Delta and, once the precedent had been established, others swiftly followed suit. All over the Delta local chiefs presided over their own 'courts', and the same process was repeated in other parts of country. A period of confusion ensued, and while Egypt thus tore herself apart, a Nubian kingdom centred on Napata, near the fourth cataract, and gradually moved its sphere of influence northwards. While the assorted dynasts vied with each other the Nubian prince, Py, took over Thebes, adopted a pharaonic titulary, and prepared for the achievement of his ultimate ambition – the conquest of all Egypt.

This was soon accomplished. Alerted at Napata of the southward advance of his only serious rival, Tefnakht of Sais (the first of the two kings of the twenty-fourth dynasty), Py came north, crushed all opposition, captured the ancient city of Memphis, and received the recognition of Tefnakht and other local rulers, among them the last sad representatives of the twenty-second and twenty-third dynasties. Py, however, retired to Napata shortly after his victory and it was left to his successor, Shabako, to complete what he had begun.

By 715 BC Shabako was installed in Memphis: a Nubian seated upon the throne of a nation that for so long had controlled the affairs of his people. But their time was short. Far from being able to savour their belated moment of glory, the Nubian pharaohs found themselves constantly looking over their shoulders at the threat posed by the Assyrians. To this Shabako adopted a conciliatory response, but his successor, Shebitku, foolishly joined forces with Palestinian princes when they attempted to throw off the Assyrian yoke. Defeat and retreat were the rewards for this ill-considered venture. The commander of the Egyptian army on this occasion was the crown prince Taharqa, and when he succeeded to the throne his acquaintance with the Assyrian army was renewed with disastrous consequences. First Esarhaddon and then Assurbanipal advanced upon Egypt, driving Taharqa back to Thebes and then to Napata, where he died shortly after. His nephew, Tantamani, reoccupied Egypt and killed the Assyrian vassal-ruler, Necho (I), but his triumph was short-lived. In 663 BC the Assyrians came once more. Tantamani abandoned Egypt and Thebes was sacked of the accumulated treasure of centuries.

The Late period (Dynasties 26 to 30) 656 to 332 BC

The Assyrians left Egypt in the hands of vassal native rulers, and for more than 100 years the country experienced an 'Indian Summer'. The illusory unity of the twenty-fifth dynasty was given real substance by a succession of strong kings, and an artistic revival took place that was characterized by a harking back to ancient traditions; a tendency found in other aspects of the cultural life of the period.

But this return to former ways could not disguise how different a country Egypt now was. Large numbers of foreigners, particularly Greeks, were settling in the country, either as traders or as mercenary troops, making Egypt far more cosmopolitan than before. The experiences of these troops underlined the inescapable reality that no antique cosmetic could disguise, namely, that Egypt could not significantly influence the outcome of the swiftly changing political drama being played out in West Asia.

Yet while other kingdoms fought and passed away, Egypt stubbornly survived. First the Assyrians left the stage, defeated and replaced by the Babylonians. An Egyptian challenge to their power resulted in comprehensive defeat at the battle of Carchemish in 605 BC, and though the Babylonians never succeeded in occupying any part of Egypt, they remained a constant threat until, in turn, they were eclipsed by the growing might of the Persians.

This time Egypt could not escape, and the defeat of her forces at Pelusium in 525 BC by the army of Cambyses ushered in a period of nearly 200 years during which the

Persians either exercised direct control over the country (as in the twenty-seventh dynasty and for 11 years before the coming of Alexander), or strove to reimpose that control when it lapsed.

There is little evidence from Egyptian sources of conditions under Persian rule. Later tradition made it a time of misery and oppression, but perhaps things were not quite as bad as that. During the reign of Darius I (521–486 BC) a canal connecting the Nile with the Red Sea was completed and the same monarch instigated a codification of Egyptian laws–hardly the acts of an oppressor. Nevertheless, for whatever reasons, the native population in the persons of Delta princelings, twice attempted to eject the foreigners; the second time with Athenian assistance. The sole king of the twenty-eighth dynasty, Amyrtaeus, was perhaps a descendant of these rebels. The revolts were put down, but not without some difficulty, and after the reign of Darius II a family, hailing from Mendes in the Delta, regained a measure of independence for the Egyptians. The Persians were never far away, however, and, aware of their inability to counter this threat by themselves, the Egyptian kings contracted a series of unfortunate alliances with partners (Sparta, Athens, Cyprus) who proved themselves of little value when their assistance was sought. An unsuccessul Persian assault during the reign of the first king of the thirtieth dynasty, Nekhtnebef, encouraged his successor, Teos, to undertake an expedition against the Persians in Phoenicia, but this last military venture on foreign soil ended ignominiously and Teos was replaced by Nekhtharehbe, the last king of independent Egypt. In 343 BC the Persians attacked again, this time successfully, and Egypt was once more under their domination. The interlude was brief, however. Eleven years later the irresistible force of Alexander's army reached Egypt and the Persians capitulated without a fight. Alexander the Great conducted the necessary rituals to ensure his acceptance as pharaoh and he departed, leaving behind a land which, although neither he nor anyone else could have known, had been irrevocably changed by his brief visitation.

Egyptian art

To understand Egyptian art it is necessary to abandon all the criteria which we apply when assessing the art of our age and the culture to which we belong, since Egyptian art reflects attitudes and priorities very different from our own.

The art with which we are familiar is essentially an expression of an individual artist's creative instincts, unimpeded by restrictions of any kind. Egyptian art, on the other hand, was almost entirely functional; it was commissioned by the state, the king or favoured members of the nobility, and it imposed on its practitioners rigid conventions which allowed limited scope for originality. The fact that they managed to produce art which we find aesthetically pleasing only means that it satisfies our requirements for acceptance, not that the forces which inspired it were the same.

With very few exceptions the examples of Egyptian art now available to us come, or have come, from either temples or tombs. In neither case was it the intention to beautify or 'decorate'. In temples the mural scenes and sculptured images of gods and kings were all a part of the complex Egyptian thinking on creation, the gods, the temple as the god's abode and the ritual within that temple, its place in the maintenance of a proper order of things and the well-being of Egypt, the concept of divine kingship and the king as an intermediary between the gods and men, and mankind's relationship with the gods.

The 'decoration' in the tombs, and the sculptured figures found within them (normally of the deceased and his immediate family), were intended to assist the passage of the owner into the next world and ensure his well-being once he arrived there. Here the Egyptian's priorities are clearly demonstrated–survival after death, the correct performance of ritual as a guarantee of this, plentiful supplies of food and drink and participation in agreeable pastimes.

Diorite statue of King Khaefre, found in the valley temple of his pyramid at Giza. Khaefre, one of the sons of Khufu, reigned c2550 BC. This magnificent piece of sculpture, one of the masterpieces of Egyptian art, shows the king being protected by the falcon-god, Horus.

Whether religious or funerary, therefore, Egyptian art had well-defined and important functions in matters of great importance—stability in this world and a safe anchorage in the next—and, so that its effectiveness in these eternal tasks could be guaranteed, the figures on the walls and the activities in which they were engaged were endowed with life by the operation of magic and the performance of ritual. To us Egyptian art is a reminder, sometimes charming, sometimes impressive, of an extinct way of life: to the Egyptians it was crucial to the continuation of life itself and central to the nation's survival.

Another adjustment that needs to be made by those who study Egyptian art today is that in those days the population had much more limited access to the temples and tomb-chapels than is permitted to us, and therefore the art was not on general display. Because it was so functional it was inevitable that there would be a good deal of thematic repetition. Scenes of battle, of offering and of festival and procession occur on the temple walls *ad nauseam*, while conventionalized representations of agricultural activities, hunting, and feasting recur in tomb after tomb. Little variation could be expected in the temples, bastions as they were of rigid tradition, but a certain amount was tolerated in the tombs, usually reflecting differences in the worldly duties, life styles, and hopes of the deceased. The royal tombs fall into a distinct category. Since kings were gods rather than men, their expectations were also different. In the next world they would be with the gods in their journeyings and their struggles against the forces of evil, and these are the themes which are therefore depicted on the walls of the tombs in the Valley of the Kings at Thebes.

As well as conformity of subject-matter there were strict canons governing many aspects of form and presentation. While these give Egyptian art its distinctive appearance they also help to bestow on it a somewhat dulling sense of 'sameness'.

In fact, closer examination reveals that Egyptian art is divisible into quite distinct stylistic groups, formed in general by historical (and consequentially geographical) factors. During each of the three major periods of Egyptian history (the Old, Middle and New Kingdoms), artistic fashion was controlled by the court ateliers in the capital city, although there always existed provincial art of a generally less-exalted standard.

Little of the art of the Early Dynastic Period has survived, but an idea of its precocious quality can be obtained from a series of magnificent slate palettes and stone maceheads, some decorated in a manner that suggests foreign influence.

Before the end of the period, however, a distinctive Egyptian style had evolved. Throughout the Old Kingdom the Memphite school dominated, producing work of superb quality. Mastery over even the hardest stones was achieved (for example, the diorite statue of King Khaefre in the Cairo Museum). Private sculpture produced masterpieces of portraiture (Rahotep and his wife Nofret, Hemiunu, Ankh-af, and the so-called 'reserve-heads' which were placed in tombs), and relief work

attained heights not often reached in later times (the tombs of Mereruka, Tiy, Kagemni, and others at Saqqara). Wood as a medium appears to have been more popular than in subsequent periods (panel of Hesy-re, the statue of Ka-aper, otherwise known as the 'Sheikh el-Beled'), and the confident Egyptian craftsman was even prepared to experiment with metals (the copper statues of King Pepi I and the prince Merenre).

The hiatus at the end of the Old Kingdom was more than an historical interlude. When order was restored Memphis had lost its position as the arbiter of taste and there developed in the Middle Kingdom, especially in the twelfth dynasty, an art which, without abandoning all the qualities which distinguished the work of the Old Kingdom, emphasized its independence from the past by taking and refining the technical skills developed during that period and wedding them to greater realism. It was a marriage between Memphis and Thebes, the old and the new, and the results of this fruitful partnership can best be seen in the powerfully impressive set of royal statues from the twelfth dynasty and the superb relief-work in the restored kiosk of Senwosret I at Karnak. At a humbler level, the painted scenes in the provincial tombs at Beni Hasan display a liveliness not always present in the technically superior Old Kingdom relief work.

Sadly, relatively little Middle Kingdom art has survived. Much was destroyed by the building activities of later generations, especially the kings of the New Kingdom, and the art of this period is consequently better represented than any other. Funerary art is particularly plentiful, more commonly painted than carved, though some of the finest relief work ever produced in Egypt is to be found in the tomb of Ramose at Thebes (contemporary with Amenhotep III and Amenhotep IV, in the eighteenth dynasty). Tombs from the latter half of the eighteenth dynasty (post-Menkheperre), with their richer colours and somewhat freer compositions, suggest that the artists were reacting to stimuli from abroad—which would have been a logical consequence of the new, outward-looking Egyptian foreign policy. Royal statuary of the eighteenth dynasty loses the forceful, almost brutal character of that of the twelfth dynasty, but conveys a sense of majesty without quite returning to the remoteness of the Old Kingdom (a splendid example of this is the green schist statue of Menkheperre in the Cairo Museum).

The art of the 'Amarna Period' (1367–1350 BC) is unmistakable. This is largely because of the so-called 'realism' with which the royal family was portrayed, allowing us to intrude on intimate domestic scenes and depicting the king, his queen Nefertiti, and their daughters in a way which makes no concessions to the ravages of time or physical peculiarities. So gross are some of the king's colossi, in particular, that one questions whether artistic truth had not degenerated into caricature. Like so much else connected with this strange interlude, its art poses questions which cannot be satisfactorily answered.

During the reign of Menmare Seti and the early part of the reign of Usermare Ramesses, art of a high quality

Bas relief work from the tomb-chapel of the *chaty* Ramose at Thebes, *c*1365 BC. The two figures here are Ramose's parents, Neby (right) and Apuya.

was still being produced (note especially the raised relief work in the temple of Menmare at Abydos and the Turin statue of a youthful Usermare), and some of the battle-scenes on the temple walls show considerable skill in their composition. Very soon, however, quality was replaced by quantity. The cult of the colossal (not in itself a new thing—see the enormous statues of Nebmare Amenhotep and his queen Tiy) took over, while sunken relief was preferred to raised relief. Though this is sometimes effective *en masse* (for example, the scenes on the walls of the temple of Medinet Habu, dating to the reign of Ramesses III), the fine workmanship of Abydos is missing. Painting in the tombs became more and more garish (the tombs at Deir el Medina).

During the Libyan and especially Nubian dynasties (twenty-second and twenty-fifth dynasties) a return to the artistic traditions of earlier days is apparent, and in the twenty-sixth dynasty this movement reached a glorious climax. Nothing demonstrates the resilience of Egyptian civilization and the skill of her craftsmen better than the splendid sculptured figures and fine relief work produced at this time. Though the inspiration for much of this came from the art of bygone days, it was much more than unimaginative copying. Classical forms and styles were utilized with immense technical skill to render the human features and emotions in a way never quite encountered before. Thus to the end of Egyptian history the artist was still displaying the gifts which had for so long distinguished him from others, and imbuing his work with a freshness that mocked the political decline of the age. When the Egyptian artist set about his work he usually adhered fairly strictly to long-established traditions. In part this was decreed for him by the functional nature of the art, but it also reflects the essentially conservative mentality of the Egyptians.

More distinctive than any other feature of Egyptian art is the manner in which the human figure is portrayed in relief work and painting, combining profile, semi-profile and frontal viewing so as to convey most accurately the true form of each part of the body. As a result, each figure assumes the appearance of an illustration in an anatomist's manual, and important figures (larger than the others), in particular, inevitably acquire a large measure of idealization in their pres-entation. A perfect type replaced the individual, though the method still permitted the representation of distinc-tive features. In addition, a rigid canon of proportion was maintained, according to which a figure (or at least the principal ones) was required to fill a specific number of squares in a grid marked out on the prepared surface.

The underlying principle influencing the form of the human figure–to represent the figure as it actually was and not as it would be seen by the beholder–also governed the way in which other elements of a scene were depicted. A house or shrine might be shown partly in plan and partly in elevation, or a pool surrounded by trees appear as a flat expanse of water viewed from above. Oxen being transported by river were shown *on top of* the shelter *within* which they were clearly travelling. A net used for trapping fowl was laid flat so that the number caught could best be shown.

As a general rule scenes were arranged in a series of horizontal registers. Very little attempt was made to separate the elements of a narrative scene, and thus we find the various stages of, for example, a battle, harvest, or the vintage, represented as a continuous composition. One of the most interesting examples of this is the unique scene on one of the walls of Medinet Habu recording the naval battle between the Sea Peoples and the Egyptians in the reign of Ramesses III. This gives the appearance of being a confused *mêlée* of boats, but in fact the scene is made up of pairs of boats, each pair representing the contending navies, illustrating different stages in the battle and culminating in the Egyptian victory.

Little attention was paid to perspective. Action taking place nearest the beholder was placed at the bottom of the register, and that further away was set progressively higher, with only the most rudimentary indications of landscape and little difference in scale. Again and again we need to remember that the purpose was not to 'paint a picture'. The technical mastery displayed by the Egyptian artists and sculptors is staggering, particularly when it is realized that this was achieved with equipment which would be considered pathetically inadequate today and frequently in conditions which would seem to be quite unsuitable for the production of high quality art.

To look at the superbly finished statues of kings and gods, perhaps in a stone as intractable as granite or diorite, it is difficult to believe that such a level of workmanship could have been achieved with the aid of copper chisels, saws and bow-drills for the softer stones (later also bronze chisels) or, for harder stones, by laborious rubbing and pounding with the aid of an abrasive agent of some kind. The final polishing removed all traces of the working and, so perfect is the finished product, that a conscious effort is required to appreciate the skill, time and patience involved.

By comparison relief work was relatively straightforward, since this was normally done on either limestone (the tombs) or sandstone (the temples), both of which could be cut easily with copper tools. The rough design was outlined on the prepared surface, using register lines and grids where necessary. For raised relief the background was cut away around the figures, which were then modelled, while for bas relief the figures themselves were cut down from the surface.

Since a sufficiently smooth surface for painting was hard to obtain naturally, it was customary for a layer of mud plaster to be applied to the wall, overlaid with a

An example of the distinctive art of the 'Amarna period' (1367–1350 BC). Nefertiti, principal queen of Akhenaten, is accompanied by one of her daughters, who carries a sistrum.

layer of lime plaster. On this the registers and grids were marked out in red paint and the compositions, including the accompanying inscriptions, were roughly sketched out–perhaps by apprentices. During the final painting the figures were given a sharp outline. Shading was hardly ever attempted. A selection of basic colours was employed, obtained either from minerals occurring naturally or prepared artificially. These were ground down, mixed with water and an adhesive added (glue, gum or egg white). The colours were applied with brushes made by fraying the end of a stick or, for delicate work, a single rush. When working near or at the surface, natural or reflected light (using mirrors) was perfectly adequate, but in chambers dug deep into the hills clay lamps were necessary, with salt probably being added to avoid smoke.

Egyptian art contributes much to our understanding of life in those times–the character of the people and of the land which they inhabited. The eye for detail, often inconsequential, the beautifully-observed scenes of natural history, the delightful touches of humour expressed through verbal exchanges between characters in a scene–all this and more helps to bridge the immense gap that separates us from them. It is a matter of regret that almost all Egyptian art is anonymous. It would be

Girl musicians playing at a banquet. From the tomb of Nakht at Thebes, c1400 BC.

nice to be able to pay homage to those to whom we owe so much and whose work attracts such justifiable admiration.

Egyptian architecture

A study of Egyptian architecture confirms in certain respects what we have learned about the people from their art: their unswerving loyalty to established forms and long-held traditions and their readiness to undertake seemingly daunting tasks with 'unsophisticated' techniques and only basic equipment. But alongside this solid, dependable conservatism and this painstaking diligence we find, on occasions, an unexpected fallibility and a failure to learn from mistakes, perhaps also deriving in part from a reluctance to change.

The Egyptians built in stone and brick. As a general rule stone was employed for the construction of temples and tombs, while sun-dried mud brick, the most convenient and comfortable material, was commonly used in houses and even palaces. Prior to the New Kingdom, limestone was favoured for monumental building, the principal source being the Tura quarries to the southeast of modern Cairo, though for the Giza pyramids a certain amount was obtained from the immediate vicinity. The limestone further south, though plentiful, was of poorer quality.

Limestone continued to be used during the eighteenth and nineteenth dynasties (the temples of Menmare and Usermare at Abydos), but it was increasingly replaced during this period by sandstone, which was easily and principally obtained from quarries fronting on to the river on both banks at Silsila, between Edfu and Kôm Ombo. For the widespread building activities of the New Kingdom, pharaohs relied almost entirely upon stone from this source (for example, the temples of Karnak, Luxor, Medinet Habu and the Ramesseum).

The only other stone used at all widely was granite, almost all of which came from the extensive outcrop at Aswan. It was used for the lower facing courses on the pyramid of Khaefre (the second largest at Giza) and for his impressive 'valley temple' at the same site, and formed the greater part of the facing on the third pyramid, that of Menkaure. At Silsila and Aswan good stone was available on or close to the surface, but at Tura (and the neighbouring quarry of Ma'sara) and other smaller quarries, it was frequently necessary to sink galleries into the rock to reach a good stratum. These galleries often stretched for hundreds of yards, and could be more than 20 ft (6 m) high.

Both limestone and sandstone (and bronze from the Middle Kingdom) could be cut easily with copper chisels struck with wooden mallets. The stone was removed by trenching on three sides and detaching it from the base with wooden wedges.

Granite was a much more difficult proposition, and the methods used to remove it from the quarry are still not perfectly understood. Much of the work seems to have involved laborious pounding and wearing away with balls of dolerite, though wedges were also apparently used (whether metal or wood is hard to say). From the quarry the stone had to be transported to the construction site. Since the quarries at Aswan were some distance from the river it was necessary to construct embankments along which the blocks could be hauled, probably on sledges. This in itself would have been a considerable undertaking, particularly in view of the enormous weight of some of the blocks (the famous unfinished obelisk would, it is estimated, have weighed over 1100 tons–100,000 kg).

Once at the river (much closer at Silsila and Tura) the stone was loaded on to boats. For the transportation of very large blocks, such as obelisks, a barge of considerable size was required, this being towed by a flotilla of smaller vessels. The extraction of the rock and its transportation clearly required the efficient organizing of large numbers of men, and this was even more important at the construction site itself.

The conformity of so much building design would have reduced the need for detailed plans, but it is known, from the survival of a small number, that they were employed on some occasions at least.

The chosen site would first of all have been levelled and marked out with measuring cords. The unit of measurement was the Royal Cubit, equivalent to 20.62 in (52.37 cm). Correct orientation, when it was considered necessary, must have been obtained by reference to one or more celestial body. The final act of preparation was the sinking of foundations, and it was here that the Egyptians sometimes fell short of their own high standards. On some surfaces they were hardly required, so firm was the ground, but in other places (such as Karnak) they most certainly were, and yet only the most rudimentary precautions were taken.

Once all the preparations had been made and the workforce assembled, construction could begin. The Egyptians had to manage without pulleys or other lifting tackle, and scaffolding had only very limited employment. Essentially they made do with ramps and embankments for raising the blocks to the required height and levers to ease them into position. When mortar (for the most part gypsum mortar) was used, it was normally less as a binding agent and more as an aid to correct positioning. In the absence of any written or other

Top: The great temple of Amun at Karnak, the ram-headed god of Thebes. His rivalry with the sun-god Re^c eventually led to the composite deity, Amun-Re^c. Below: Luxor, near Karnak, was another cult centre of the Amun.

evidence we must assume that these simple techniques were somehow employed even for the construction of the pyramids. We are just as much in the dark as to how something like the great columned hall at Karnak was built. It is thought that the first course of the perimeter wall and the lowest drums of the columns were placed in position, and the remaining internal space then filled with mud. As the walls and columns rose, so would the working platform be raised. Once the uppermost courses were in position the filling would be gradually removed to ground level.

The facing blocks of a monument were dressed after laying, and the finely finished appearance often masks very inadequate internal construction. This is particularly true of New Kingdom monuments where, presumably because of the haste with which they were built, two parallel facing walls are often found separated only by roughly laid blocks or simply by rubble. The

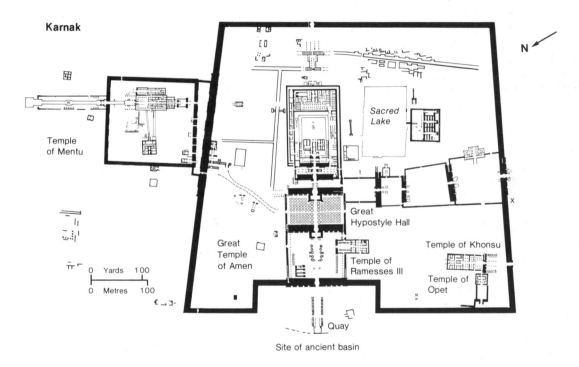

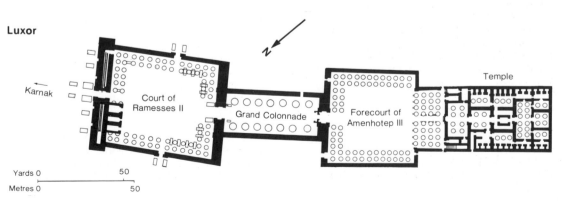

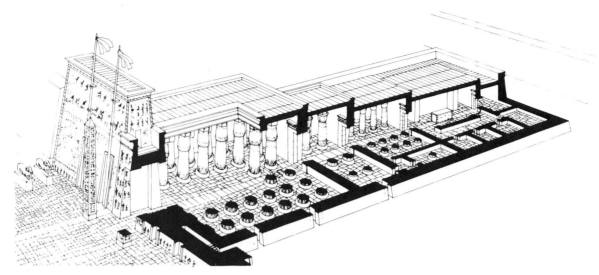

A typical Egyptian temple of the New Kingdom (c1567–1069 BC).

same inattention to detail is also apparent in the construction of some of the roofing, where the architraves linking the columns, and the roofing blocks set upon them, can rest on a dangerously inadequate bedding surface. In contrast, careful provision was made in the design and construction of the roof to draw off rainwater.

Not surprisingly, given the intensity of light and, in summer, the heat, windows were not a prominent feature of Egyptian architecture. In temples, particularly, there was little need for them, since the desired atmosphere of awe and mystery could be best achieved with the minimum of light. Only in the New Kingdom was clerestory lighting used.

The problems encountered in handling such an intractable material as stone were absent with brick architecture. The Nile mud, of which the bricks were made, was shaped in a mould and left to harden in the sun. In addition to palaces, houses and their dependencies, bricks were used in the construction of the walls surrounding temple precincts, towns and fortresses, some of these being of vast dimensions. Some splendidly preserved brick vaulting can be seen today among the buildings attached to the Ramesseum at Thebes.

Few pharaonic towns have survived in anything like their original form. Some have disappeared beneath the rising alluvium, others have been destroyed by the overbuilding of later generations, while those which remained reasonably intact have suffered severely from the depredations of the peasantry looking for sebakh (a fertilizing agent) among the ruins.

The great capitals, Memphis and Thebes, are now as though they never were. Only a small number of less important towns (or villages) survive to give us some

Exceptionally well-preserved mud-brick magazines attached to the mortuary temple of Ramesses II at Thebes (c1250 BC).

idea of what 'urban' life was like. The most interesting of these is undoubtedly Akhetaten (Amarna) which, since it was occupied for such a short period, has retained its original form. The evidence coming from this site suggests that it was constructed according to a fairly well-defined plan, the central sector containing the 'official' buildings including the great temple and a palace, the southern suburb the impressive houses of the more important persons, and the northern suburb the dwellings of the humbler classes. Even here, however, there are signs that the 'blueprint', if such there was, was not always being followed, and the probability must be that in towns with a longer life than Akhetaten any original scheme was soon abandoned. One factor which commonly influenced the siting and spread of a town was the impracticability of building on arable land.

Apart from Akhetaten, only the Nubian fortresses and the villages of el Lahun and Deir el Medina present anything like a coherent picture and, since all were built for specific purposes, they need not be typical of settlement planning. The latter two housed the workmen engaged on royal funerary monuments (el Lahun during the reign of Senwosret II and Deir el Medina through most of the New Kingdom). Both were walled settlements. At el Lahun there was a clear distinction between the houses of the senior officials, which were elaborate in design, and those of the workers themselves, which were small and crowded together. At Deir el Medina the houses were contiguous and fronted on to shared paths. A third workmen's village was established at Akhetaten, in the desert to the east of the town. Excavation of this site is still continuing.

Though houses of all types were built of the same material, the similarity ended there. There was a great difference between the spacious country estates of the wealthy and the crowded multi-storied houses in the towns, and the very basic facilities provided in the workmen's villages were probably those customarily found in the houses of the lower classes.

The suggestion has recently been put forward that Egypt was probably a more 'urban' society than has hitherto been admitted, and that a large proportion of the population lived within walled settlements and worked in the fields by day. Certainly the idea that an agricultural economy vitiates against such a settlement pattern is not necessarily true.

It would be idle to pretend that Egyptian architecture conveys an impression of great beauty. It is, by and large, solid, square and monumental. The effect is often overwhelming; it evokes respect, even awe, rather than delight. In fact, some of the architectural details do have considerable aesthetic appeal, especially the columns and capitals imitating the papyrus, lotus and other plants. The Step Pyramid complex at Saqqara, with its delicate reminders in stone of earlier building materials, is particularly pleasing. But these features are often lost in the mass, leaving us only with size, weight and the impression of massive power. Considering the great emphasis placed by the Egyptian on eternal survival, these qualities are perhaps not surprising.

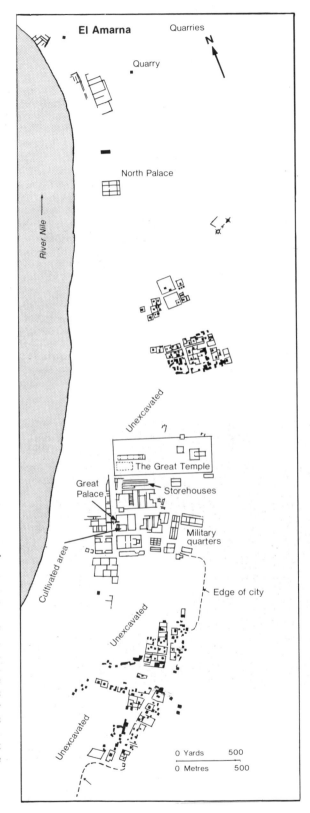

Burial customs

The ancient Egyptians took elaborate precautions in an attempt to ensure that they survived death, reached the next world, and there enjoyed an amenable existence. In saying this, it needs to be emphasized that only the wealthy and powerful have left us their tombs, funerary furnishings, paintings and reliefs, inscriptions and sometimes their bodies. The great majority of the population has left us virtually nothing, and this means that we have little idea of the attitude of the ordinary Egyptians towards the prospect of death and their preparations for the event.

According to Egyptian thinking, the continuation of life beyond the grave depended on the survival of a person's name, the preservation of his body, the provision of regular supplies of food and drink, and the ability to overcome those dangers and trials which might hinder or prevent progress from this world to the next. To meet all these requirements the Egyptians evolved an elaborate web of devices which, taken together, constitute perhaps the most determined attempt in the history of mankind to defeat the physical reality of death. But among all the spells, the incantations, the whole paraphernalia without which no high-born Egyptian could contemplate that journey into the unknown, there is not a hint of spiritual content. It was the reaction of a practical, pragmatic, essentially materialistic people to an inevitable event which, since it could not have been avoided, needed to be prepared for as thoroughly as possible.

What was ideally wanted was a tomb which could function as a 'house' for the *ka* (a sort of *alter ego* which, on death, assumed the dead's personality) and provide a resting-place for the carefully preserved body, and which

could be filled with scenes and objects to serve him in the next world and ensure that he wanted for nothing. On the coffin, on the walls of the tomb, or on papyri placed within the tomb, were texts which would guarantee acceptance by the gods. Many of these preparations could, and would need to have been taken before death. The tomb would have had to be cut or constructed well in advance, and the more ambitious the project the more time would have been required. Very often not enough had been allowed, and the owner had had to be buried in an unfinished tomb.

The style, and to a certain extent the scale, of a tomb were influenced in varying degrees by the class, the age, and the district to which the person belonged. During the first two dynasties the kings and their nobles were buried in the same type of tomb. This consisted essentially of a burial chamber at the bottom of a shaft, with a brick superstructure which might be solid or contain a number of rooms. Because of their external appearance these tombs are commonly referred to as *mastabas*, from the Arabic word for 'bench'.

At the beginning of the third dynasty occurred that architectural 'leap in the dark' which proclaimed the growing authority of the king and thereafter distinguished his funerary monument from that of lesser mortals. King Zoser's original intention was to be buried in a *mastaba* like his predecessors, but the genius of his chief minister, Imhotep, inspired a radical change of plan and the construction of a 200 ft (61 m) high pyramid rising in a series of six steps. Around this within a great perimeter wall, was set a complex of buildings the precise purpose of which is not clear, but which seem to have been connected with the performance of rituals by the king in his role as king of Upper and then of Lower Egypt.

Until comparatively recent times the Step Pyramid appeared to be architecturally unique. Then, in the early 1950s, an Egyptian archaeologist, Zakkaria Goneim, uncovered the remains of a similar monument close-by belonging to a hitherto unsuspected successor of Zoser, Sekhemkhet. The discovery of a sealed but empty sarcophagus in a roughly hewn chamber beneath this pyramid stimulated much discussion, and has yet to be satisfactorily explained.

Throughout the remainder of the Old Kingdom the pyramid continued in vogue for royal burials. The evolution from the stepped pyramid to the true pyramid can be clearly traced. At Meydûm, south of Saqqara, stand the remains of a monument which was probably built for Uni, last king of the third dynasty. This, too, was originally a stepped pyramid, but by filling in the steps and facing the entire monument it was turned into a true pyramid. The transition was completed at Dahshur, a site lying between Saqqara and Meydûm, where two pyramids were built, both apparently for Snofru, first king of the fourth dynasty. One of these is variously termed the 'bent' or 'rhomboidal' pyramid, because its

The Step Pyramid of King Zoser at Saqqara. The first monumental building in stone, dating to *c*2650 BC.

angle of incline is sharply reduced over the last third of its height. Alongside stands the first true pyramid to be designed and constructed as such. It is, however, of relatively humble proportions, and is dwarfed by comparison with the two larger pyramids at Giza, those of Khufu and Khaefre, which reach a height of about 450 ft (137 m).

The complex arrangement of buildings attached to the pyramids of Zoser and Sekhemkhet was afterwards greatly simplified, and it became customary for each monument to consist of four principal elements, of which the pyramid was the focal point. Abutting on to the east side of the pyramid (which was always built on the west bank of the Nile) was a mortuary temple, in which the last rites were conducted prior to burial and where the cult of the dead king was perpetuated after his death. Leading from the mortuary temple towards the Valley of the Kings was a roofed causeway, and on the edge of the Valley itself was another 'temple'. Here, rituals of purification and resuscitation were performed over the body of the dead king before it was taken up the causeway and laid to rest in its pyramid. It was common practice to bury a number of boats close to the pyramid. These were usually called 'solar boats', because it is thought that they may have been intended to allow the king to accompany the sun-god on his journeyings, though whether this is the entire explanation for their presence is hard to say.

After the fourth dynasty, indeed before its end, the size of pyramids declined dramatically. Those belonging to the kings of the fifth dynasty (mostly at Abusir) and the sixth dynasty (Saqqara) are now barely recognizable as such. Clustered around them, as around all the pyramids, are the *mastaba* tombs of nobles who had been given permission to be buried near the kings whom they had served.

The pyramid form was retained for the tombs of the twelfth dynasty kings (at Dahshur and in the Fayûm), but in spite of the great power of the monarchy at this time no attempt was made to return to the gigantic scale of the fourth dynasty monuments.

The shift of the capital (or court residence) in the Middle Kingdom meant that rock-cut tombs, popular with the provincial nobility even during the Old Kingdom, now became far more common than *mastabas*. In accordance with common practice these tombs (at Beni Hasan, Rifa, el Bersha and Elephantine especially) mirrored in their design the basic house plan of the period, with an entrance courtyard or vestibule, a large central chamber and, often, smaller rooms at the rear.

It was also, no doubt, the fact that they came from a region (Thebes) where rock-cut tombs had always been favoured, that prompted the kings of the eighteenth dynasty to abandon the pyramid, but much more important was the desire for security in an attempt to defeat the tomb-robber. Deep corridors and vast chambers were cut from the cliffs of a remote valley in western Thebes, and various devices introduced to baffle or thwart the robber. Almost without exception these proved unsuccessful, and eventually, in a desperate

attempt to preserve at least the bodies of the long-deceased kings, the high priest at Thebes had them moved secretly to a communal tomb high up in the cliffs at Deir el Bahari in the twenty-first dynasty, where they remained undisturbed until AD 1881.

The whole object of cutting the tombs in the Valley of the Kings would have been defeated by constructing mortuary temples in their vicinity, and so these were strung out along the edge of the cultivation on the west bank. Some, if not all of these, also contained within their precincts a palace for use during the king's lifetime (the Ramesseum, belonging to Usermare Ramesses, and the temple of Medinet Habu, built for Ramesses III, are good examples).

During the Late period the centre of events shifted back to the Delta, and for this reason very few royal tombs have survived. It is clear, however, that at this time powerful individuals were having tombs built on an almost royal scale (a very good example is the tomb of Montemhat at Thebes).

One interesting feature of some twenty-seventh dynasty tombs at Saqqara is that, at long last, a method had been devised which defeated the tomb-robber. The burial chamber was set at the bottom of an enormous shaft, 30–50 ft (9–15 m) deep. This chamber was roofed, and a pot with its top broken built into the roof. The shaft was then filled with sand. On the burial day the coffin was introduced into the chamber via a smaller shaft alongside. After installation the pot in the roof of the burial chamber was broken from beneath and sand allowed to fill the chamber. Any attempt by the robbers to clear the chamber from below merely resulted in more sand flowing in from the great shaft.

The preparation of a tomb was not the only provision that a prudent man might make before death. It was, sadly, not wise to trust to the family devotion in the matter of the all-important daily offerings at the tomb. It was far better to enter into a business arrangement with a 'mortuary priest', who would undertake this duty in return for payment. Arrangements would also have to be made with the embalmers. Preservation of the body was absolutely crucial to continued existence. It was essential that its constituent parts remained in working order so that the dead person might have total freedom of movement in the next world. It was also extremely important that it should retain as lifelike an appearance as possible, since this meant that the ba (which left the body at death but returned each evening) would have no difficulty in identifying its owner. If the body were destroyed, the ba would be doomed to search eternally in vain.

The artificial preservation of the body became necessary when the building of ambitious tombs removed it from the curative qualities of the hot sand. The most effective method took a long time to evolve, and it is not until the New Kingdom that we find bodies being treated in a way which accords closely with the description left us by Herodotus.

Firstly, the brain and the contents of the body cavity were removed, the former through the nose and the

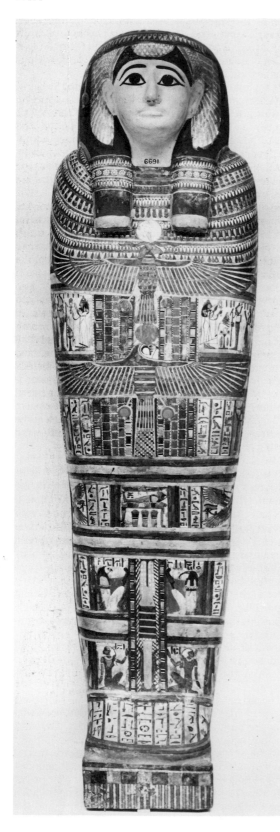

latter via an incision in the left side, usually near the groin. The heart was left *in situ* because, to the Egyptians, it was the seat of understanding and therefore of immense importance. The body was then treated with natron, probably in solid form. This assisted the dehydration of the body but left the skin supple. The body cavity and skull were then packed, most commonly with linen and resin. Artificial eyes were sometimes inserted, and the nose and ears often plugged. The body was then bandaged, in the course of which protective amulets were inserted between the wrappings, the most important being the heart scarab.

Since the Egyptians could not imagine a body functioning without its internal organs, these were themselves carefully preserved after removal, and stored in separate containers. Eventually these were given stoppers representing the heads of the Four Sons of Horus, and are usually referred to as Canopic Jars.

In the twenty-first dynasty a new practice was adopted whereby the viscera were wrapped and returned to the body. At the same time a further refinement was added to the embalming process, involving the subcutaneous packing of the limbs with a malleable substance, the purpose being to preserve the outward form of the body more successfully than hitherto.

Only the royal family and very high members of the nobility were buried in sarcophagi, others made do with wooden coffins. Prior to the New Kingdom these were normally rectangular boxes with flat lids, the sides of the box often painted to represent the façade of a building. From the New Kingdom onwards anthropoid coffins were the norm, the lids on these taking the form of a mummified figure and the decoration being much more elaborate.

Quite clearly many of the objects placed in the tomb had belonged to the dead person in his lifetime. Others, however, were manufactured for the occasion. These included the simple, often crudely-made, models of familiar activities such as brewing, baking, etc., which were intended to complement or replace the painted and carved scenes. Like these, the models were endowed with a life of their own by the recitation of spells. Another very important class of objects were the small figurines known as *shabti* or *ushabti* figures (perhaps from the Egyptian word meaning 'to answer'), which were intended to take the place of the dead person in the next world whenever he might be called upon to undertake physical labour. Eventually there was one *shabti* for each day of the year, with overseer figures to keep an eye on them.

It is evident that the Egyptians tried to anticipate and counter in advance every eventuality which might occur after death. Even the ultimate test of fitness to pass on to the 'promised land', judgment before Osiris, was prepared for by the insertion somewhere in the tomb of

Inner coffin of the 'Lady of the House' Takhebkhenem (450 BC). In one of the vignettes Takhebkenem carries a sistrum before Osiris, a strange hawkheaded kneeling figure.

the so-called 'negative confession'–that denial of wrong-doing in this world that would have to be uttered by the dead person while his heart was weighed against the 'feather of truth'.

In spite of everything, the Egyptians had ample reason to doubt whether their striving after immortality would ever be successful. The plundered tombs, the dismembered bodies, the abandoned offerings; all these signs of failure lay around them. But still they tried, sustained presumably by the hope that their fate would be different from so many others.

Egyptian language and literature

The Egyptian language has affinities with both the Semitic and Hamitic linguistic systems, particularly with regard to vocabulary. Precisely how this fusion occurred is now extremely difficult to determine, though it is presumed to have involved racial intermingling at some point. The art of writing was almost certainly brought from Sumer, probably in the Late Predynastic period, when it is known that Egypt received other cultural stimuli from Mesopotamia. As in other respects, however, what Egypt borrowed she quickly turned into something uniquely her own.

The basis of the language was an alphabet of 24 symbols. These were all consonants or semi-consonants, and one of the distinguishing features of the Egyptian language is that it has no way of expressing vowel sounds. There were, all together, over 700 hieroglyphic signs representing different phonetic combinations. As such, they could be used independently or, more commonly, in conjunction, to form words. Many words were followed by a sign or signs which had no phonetic value but which were used solely as a guide to the general meaning of the word. These are usually called determinatives.

In the history of the language four distinct scripts can be distinguished, of which three were in use during pharaonic times. The hieroglyphic system was employed throughout, and survived until the end of the third century AD. It was the script always chosen for monumental texts. Two of the other scripts, termed hieratic and demotic, were simply abbreviated forms of the hieroglyphic. Hieratic was already in use in the Old Kingdom, and in the New Kingdom was widely employed for literary compositions and business documents. Demotic was an even more cursive script which developed during the twenty-sixth dynasty and continued in use until the fifth century AD. The fourth script, Coptic, became the language of the Egyptian Christians.

The commonest writing material was obtained from the papyrus plant, which grew freely in Egypt in ancient times, but which is now virtually extinct there. A sheet of papyrus provided an excellent writing surface, and its manufacture was quick and easy. The inner pith of the stalk was cut into strips, which were placed side by side

in two superimposed layers, one vertical and the other horizontal. These were pressed together, and the natural juices within the plant served as a binding agent. The ability to write in a generally illiterate society places the individual among a privileged élite, and such was the position of the scribe in ancient Egypt. A number of texts extol the virtues of the scribe's profession. Admission into its ranks involved attendance at a scribal school, where pupils gained proficiency by copying an assortment of standardized texts. A fully qualified scribe carried with him the equipment of his trade–a wooden palette in which he would have kept his brushes (made from a single rush stem frayed at the tip) and inks (black from carbon, and red from red ochre).

Conditions in Egypt are highly favourable to the survival of even the most perishable materials (save in the Delta), and this has meant that a great deal of textual matter is available for study today. Almost every type of text is represented. The great historical inscriptions, being official records for posterity, were reserved for a monumental setting, normally a temple wall. Their reliability as sober accounts cannot be guaranteed. Other formal inscriptions include those with a religious

The *Story of Sinuhe*, set in the twelfth dynasty, was one of the most popular of its kind. This hieratic script tablet was made in Ramesside times on a large piece of limestone.

theme, also found on temple walls as well as in royal tombs, and funerary texts in private tombs.

Valuable though all these are in their different ways, much more interesting, and frequently more informative, are the 'informal' texts, often on humdrum subjects, written on a variety of materials – papyrus, pottery, limestone flakes, and so on.

Particularly engaging are the 'stories' which vary from simple, unsophisticated tales (*The Shipwrecked Sailor, The Doomed Prince*), through longer 'epics' (*The Tale of the Two Brothers*) to weightier stories with a serious theme and sometimes an historical basis (*The Story of Sinube, The Adventures of Wenamun*). Not all these were intended simply to entertain. In the Middle Kingdom, particularly, literature was clearly used for propaganda purposes (as in *The Story of Sinube*), with the god-like figure of the king featuring largely as the benevolent shepherd of his flock.

Another important body of literature concerns what are usually referred to as 'Wisdom Texts', since they contain advice from the venerable and experienced to the young. This advice often stresses the benefits which will accrue from the recommended mode of behaviour; which is thus simply a means to an end rather than desirable for its own sake. One such text, *The Teaching of Amenemope*, has many clear points of contact with the Book of Proverbs, whose authors it perhaps influenced.

The Egyptian preoccupation with material well-being and advancement crops up frequently in the texts. A markedly different attitude to life (and death) is encountered in a smaller body of texts, usually called 'pessimistic', which, because of the conditions they describe, are thought of as coming from that disturbed period at the end of the Old Kingdom, though this is not always provable. They certainly express ideas which are out of keeping with normal Egyptian thinking, either advocating self-indulgence (as in the *Song of the Harper*) or even welcoming death (as in *A Dialogue of a Pessimist with his Soul*) as a means of escaping from reality.

Some compositions, by virtue of their content, structure, and lyrical mode of expression, accord closely with our idea of poetry. Almost certainly some of these, at least, were sung to musical accompaniment. They consist largely of love poems and hymns to various gods, of which the most famous is undoubtedly that addressed to the god Aten, and some also contain passages of great beauty. Much simpler, but even more moving, is a prayer couched in poetic terms, addressed to the god Ptah by one of the workmen at Deir el Medina who had been struck blind. Hardly literature, but containing a mass of information, are the business documents, the legal records (such as the record of the trial of the tomb-robbers in the twentieth dynasty and that of the conspirators in the assassination plot against Ramesses III), the mathematical treatises and the astronomical texts. Particularly important are the medical texts, revealing as they do a strange mixture of magical mumbo-jumbo and acute observation.

Ultimately, though, perhaps the most fascinating documents of all are the letters, partly for their content, but even more because they enable us to intrude on private lives and encounter people behaving naturally and not posturing for effect. Reading the letters sent by the mortuary priest Hekhanakhte, during the reign of Mentuhotep III in the eleventh dynasty, in which he instructs, scolds and lectures his eldest son who has been left in charge of the estate in his absence, gives an unattractive picture of a pompous, cantankerous old man. More important, the ancient no longer seems as remote.

The Sea Peoples

N. K. Sandars

The name

The name 'Sea Peoples' or 'Peoples of the Sea' has been given to the perpetrators of widespread destruction in the eastern Mediterranean in the later thirteenth and early twelfth centuries BC. The Egyptians gave an account of enemies coming 'from the midst of the sea' and 'the countries of the sea' who attacked their lands in *c*1218 and again in *c*1182 BC. The established centres of civilization, especially Egypt, were rich and tempting prizes for land-hungry settlers and war-like raiders from the north, among whom the so-called Sea Peoples were the most active. Both invasions were repelled, but they were only part of a more extensive and prolonged movement which coincided with the destruction of Mycenaean society in the Aegean, the overthrow of the late Hittite empire in Anatolia, and great alterations of population in the Levant and around the Aegean and Anatolian coasts.

Our knowledge of the Sea Peoples comes from contemporary Egyptian inscriptions, from reliefs showing many of the attackers, and, less directly, from Hittite and Ugaritic cuneiform texts (Ugarit being a small but important state on the north Syrian coast); also from archaeologically recorded destruction levels throughout the whole area.

The background

A long period of prosperity in the eastern Mediterranean, during which trade flourished, came to an end in the last decades of the thirteenth century BC. This equilibrium

The second attack of the Sea Peoples on Egypt in 1182 BC.
This relief celebrated the victory of Ramesses III.

had depended on the stability of the two major powers: the Egyptians and the Hittites. In spite of occasional wars they maintained an order from which independent and client states grew rich; but the complex trading and exchange systems they encouraged depended on safe communications. In the Levant there were predatory nomads and, piracy being a way of life for many coastal people for centuries, the balance was always uncertain and peace was a fragile commodity. There was too great dependence on foreign troops or over-powerful subjects, and the client states strained for real independence. There were also increasing attacks from new and old enemies such as Assyria and the Kaska of northern Anatolia. In the Aegean, where northern mercenaries were probably employed by Mycenaean princes, there was pressure from the Balkans.

The Sea Peoples and Egypt

The attack of c1218 BC on Pharaoh Merenptah (1223–1213 BC) was from Libya and its northern allies. Inscriptions at Karnak name several tribes of Sea Peoples: the Shardana, some of whom had served as the bodyguard for an earlier pharaoh (Ramesses II, 1290–1223 BC), but whose homeland is unknown; the Lukka, known as pirates and raiders in the eastern Mediterranean since the fourteenth century and who Hittite annals place in southwest Anatolia. There were also the Teresh, Shekelesh and Ekwesh, also probably from Anatolia. The Teresh have been linked with the Etruscans, and the Shekelesh with the Sikels who gave their name to Sicily; while the Ekwesh, who appear only once in the Egyptian records, are usually identified with people known to the Hittites as Ahhiyawa, and at a

further remove with Homer's Achaeans. After the Libyans, theirs was the largest contingent; they came either from western Anatolia, from the islands, or from mainland Greece. After a six-hour battle in the desert, the attackers were defeated and large numbers of prisoners taken.

A second attack of concerted northerners, without the Libyans, was defeated in 1182 BC, by Ramesses III (1190–1158 BC). Inscriptions at Medinet Habu describe the northern lands (Anatolia and north Syria) as forming a conspiracy 'in their islands. All at once on the move, scattered in war'. With the exception of the Shardana, the Shekelesh, and possibly the Teresh, the enemy had new names: Tjeker perhaps from the Troad, Denyen from southern Anatolia or north Syria, Peleset and Weshesh whose homeland is unknown. They were defeated in a land battle, probably on the borders of Egypt and Palestine. The Egyptian reliefs portray the attackers on foot and in chariots, their ox-carts loaded with women and children. This was followed by a naval battle in the Nile Delta in which the characteristic boats of the Sea Peoples, their bow and stern posts ending in the heads of water-birds, were rammed and capsized. Many of the attackers in the boats wore horned helmets, as had the Shardana bodyguard of Ramesses II, while others, including most in the land battle, wore a stiff headdress of feathers, some stiff material or possibly their own treated hair. They carried round shields, fought with swords and spears, and wore short kilts like Mycenaean fighters.

The Sea Peoples in Palestine

After their defeat some of the attackers stayed in Egypt, while more settled in Palestine. The Tjeker, who established themselves on the coast around Haifa, were still

45

Captives taken by Ramesses III after the repulse of the Sea Peoples.

known as a seafaring people around 1100 BC. The Danuna, long known to the Egyptians, at least by name, in the eighth century BC were settled in southern Anatolia with a capital at Adana which was probably not far from their earlier homeland. After the retreat from Egypt, they may have split up, some entering the Jordan valley which, according to one argument, identifies them with the Israelite tribe of Dan. They then settled on the coast around Jaffa. Further south again lie the biblical Philistine cities: Ashkalon, Ashdod, Gaza, and these were probably settled by the Peleset. The Peleset and the Philistines can be identified linguisti-

cally, but by few other means. Since in Jewish history the Philistines alone of the Sea Peoples were distinctly remembered, they must have absorbed the remains of the other contingents. Although the homeland of the Philistines, like the Peleset, is unknown, they had various characteristics of dress, customs and language that may suggest Anatolia, and to a lesser extent the Aegean. Pottery found in Palestine from the twelfth and eleventh centuries BC has patterns derived from Mycenaean wares transferred to local fabric in local matt paint, the so-called 'Philistine pottery'.

The diaspora

The rest of the raiders scattered further afield. Some probably made a stay in Cyprus, where a number of destructions of important sites such as Enkomi and Kition may mark their arrival. In particular the Shardana, who gave their name to Sardinia, probably took this route. Small bronze figures found in Sardinia several centuries later represent armed warriors very like the Shardana with horned helmets, round shields and greaves. Other groups may have reached Corsica as well as south Italy and Sicily. Soon after the mid-twelfth century BC the Sea Peoples disappeared, but the dire events of which they were part cause and part consequence, inaugurated a long Dark Age in the Aegean and in Anatolia. The fall of Troy in the early twelfth century BC (Troy VIIb1) was one among many disasters that overtook Mycenaean centres in Greece, as well as the Hittites, and other states in Anatolia, while echoes of these times seem to survive in the *Iliad*.

Ptolemaic Egypt

Colin Walters

Egypt, an Hellenistic kingdom

Upon the death of Alexander in 323 BC his successor and half-brother, Philip Arrhidaeus, appointed Ptolemy son of Lagus—a distinguished commander in Alexander's army—to the satrapy of Egypt. Following the assassination of Philip (in 317 BC) and of Alexander IV (in 310–309 BC), the unity of the Macedonian empire was broken—and in 305 BC Ptolemy declared himself what he had effectively been for some time – king of Egypt. Ptolemy I Soter, 'the Saviour' as he called himself, thus established a dynasty which ruled Egypt until the death of Cleopatra in 30 BC, when the country passed into the hands of the Romans.

Outwardly the fabric of Egyptian life during this period remained much as it had been in pharaonic times. The agricultural economy, revolving around the annual inundation of the Nile, was controlled by factors beyond the powers of man to influence, and the political significance of Alexander's conquest could not, and did not, disturb the foundations of such a long-established way of life.

But this apparent continuity is illusory, for in certain important respects Egypt under the Ptolemies was fundamentally different from the Egypt which the pharaohs had bequeathed to them. For this the replacement of a native ruler with a representative of a foreign power was directly responsible. It meant, first of all, that from then on there could be no such thing as an 'Egyptian' foreign policy, or 'Egyptian' involvement in international affairs, except indirectly. The political history of the period concerns Egypt only in so far as it concerns the interests and ambitions of the Ptolemies.

In more general terms, the period as a whole was one in which the interests of the indigenous population were subordinated to those of their new masters. The exploitation of Egypt's natural resources was now intended to benefit not the Egyptians, but an alien ruling class.

During the first hundred years of Ptolemaic rule the influence of the Egyptians on the affairs of their own country was negligible. An early attempt by the Ptolemies to employ them in an administrative capacity had not been successful, and Macedonians, Greeks and

Ptolemy I Soter, the first Macedonian king of Egypt, who established a dynasty which ruled Egypt for nearly 300 years, until the death of Cleopatra in 30 BC.

Hellenized Semites were imported to take their place. At the same time, because it was considered too risky to recruit Egyptians into the army, Macedonians and Greek soldiers arrived in large numbers and were garrisoned strategically throughout the country. In this way, in spite of the employment of some Egyptians in the lower strata of the administration and the appearance of a very few higher up (perhaps descendants of the ancient nobility), the tendency was towards a civil and military structure in which the mass of the population had virtually no representation.

The only sphere of national life in which the Egyptians retained their status was religion. In their relationship with the temples and their priesthoods the Ptolemies adopted a cautious policy, clearly appreciating the need to establish an understanding with this most jealously cherished feature of Egyptian life. There was no sweeping secularization of temple property, and grants of all kinds, including land, continued to be made. The priests themselves were treated as a privileged élite among the natives, enjoying, in theory at least, freedom from compulsory labour, a large degree of control over their professional duties and a right to a limited amount of income from the management of temple property. The temples thus survived as a focus for the ancient beliefs of the indigenous population, but only under the watchful eyes of the authorities. They also served as places of refuge for Egyptians escaping from the harsh realities of life. *Anachoresis*, as it was termed, was one of the few ways in which they could express opposition or despair. Constitutionally they had no status at all and, though granted protection within the law, were totally dependent on the government for their subsistence. The only way of breaking free from that dependence was to abandon hope and resort to *anachoresis*. The harsh truth was that with the coming of the Ptolemies the position of the Egyptians *vis-à-vis* the foreigners in the country had undergone a marked deterioration.

The Ptolemies themselves, by adopting pharaonic titulary and paying due homage to the gods, won acceptance as rightful heirs to the throne of Egypt, but such acceptance did not automatically extend to their officers with whom the Egyptians had dealings, and it was the behaviour of these which created friction and resulted in a loss of good will and cooperation.

Although some foreigners were to be found in the lower strata of society, in general terms they were separated from the Egyptians by several rungs of the social ladder. They were also separated in a more literal sense, for the large numbers who entered Egypt in the third century BC on the whole kept themselves to themselves in their own settlements or quarters of towns, and any mingling of the racial groups, particularly in the early days, was limited and not officially approved.

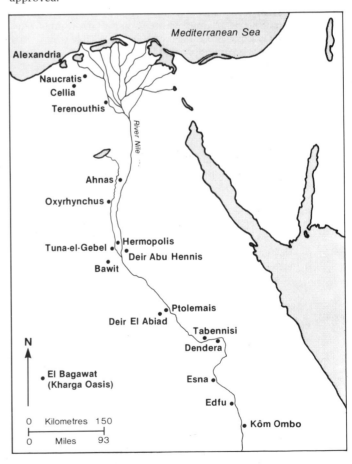

Ptolemaic, Roman and Byzantine Egypt.

There was some intermarrying at the lowest level between Egyptians and members of other races, but there is no evidence that the practice was anything but a rarity among the middle and upper classes, at least for a considerable time. The Greeks and their kin set up communities along familiar Hellenic lines, centring their social life on the local *gymnasium*, employing Hellenic laws, maintaining the cults of their own gods, and enjoying all the advantages that accrue from belonging to the ruling race.

Equally exclusive was the Jewish population, which had been swelled considerably by the large numbers of prisoners of war brought back to Egypt from Syria by Ptolemy I. The level of immigration was maintained, even after the Ptolemies lost control of Syria in 198 BC, by the arrival of refugees fleeing from the upheavals in Judaea and by the markedly pro-Jewish sentiments of Ptolemy VI (180–145 BC). These newcomers dispersed themselves throughout the country, though the Fayûm and, particularly, Alexandria were favoured. By the end of the Ptolemaic period two of the five quarters into which the city was divided were inhabited (though not perhaps exclusively) by Jews.

In their new homeland the Jews were inevitably brought into contact with both Greeks and Egyptians, and the practical requirements of their day-to-day existence meant that some concessions had to be made. Those who, by reason of their social status or because of where they lived, dealt principally with Greeks, adopted Greek names and used the Greek language rather than Aramaic for business transactions. On the other hand, those living in the rural districts, and therefore having more to do with the Egyptians, took Egyptian names and used Egyptian. But these concessions did not destroy their Jewish identity, which was assiduously preserved. The *Torah* remained the fundamental law governing all Jewish communities in Egypt, Hebrew was used among themselves, and the exclusiveness of their faith set them apart from their fellows and made intermarrying all the more difficult. Thus, although they contributed significantly to the economic life of the country, the Jews, by the overt assertion of their difference from others, remained aloof and, although there is only the slenderest evidence for persecution towards the close of the Ptolemaic period, anti-Semitism had found expression in Greek literature for some time before this, and the events of the Roman period were anticipated by attitudes prevailing long before they took over the country.

The revival of Egyptian resistance

In 217 BC, during the reign of Ptolemy IV Philopator (222–205 BC), the Ptolemaic army defeated the Seleucid Syrians at the battle of Raphia (217 BC). The victory was won with the assistance of Egyptian troops, and the historian Polybius (second century BC) later suggested that it was this that awakened within the native population a sense of its own power, and was directly responsible for the outbreak of civil strife that followed. This might well have been the essential truth of the matter, but the simmering discontent of the Egyptians

had erupted into open violence before this, during the reign of Ptolemy III Euergertes (246–222 BC). It is also doubtful whether this and the post-Raphia revolt were uprisings inspired by a nationalistic surge against alien rulers. More probably they were expressions of resentment by the Egyptians against those responsible for their unhappy condition, who happened to be foreigners but might just as well have been their own kind.

A marked and continuing increase in the influence of the native Egyptians and, resulting from this resurgence, greater belligerence in their attitude towards authority, is one of the characteristics of the period from 222–30 BC. The other noticeable feature is the realignment of social groupings. Whereas hitherto the divisions had largely been on racial lines, the social structure now evolving was based much more on class. In so far as the upper classes were still largely alien and the lower classes indigenous, a racial element was inevitably present, but this seems to have become less and less important than a philosophy based on 'us against them'.

As the period progresses it becomes increasingly difficult to distinguish 'revolts' from the generally lawless state of affairs prevailing throughout the country. At the heart of the matter, as always, was the rural economy and its state of health. Here, an interlocking series of developments created a dire situation. Inflation, burdensome taxation and the excesses of the king's agents alienated the people who really mattered–those who cultivated the fields–and their response, on an ever-increasing scale, was flight and abandonment of their land. The reaction of the authorities alternated between conciliation and compulsion. More land came into the hands of the Egyptians, temples increased their holdings, rents were sometimes reduced, and similar inducements introduced to encourage the reclamation of land. At the same time the government attempted to curb the abuses of its officials, as the decree of Ptolemy VIII Euergertes II (170–116 BC) makes clear. But the stick was never far behind the carrot, and as the situation deteriorated so compulsion became more common, which in turn only accentuated the unrest and accelerated the depopulation of the land.

In the end the government found itself in an impossible position, from which it twisted this way and that to extricate itself. Concession merely encouraged the demand for more, and compulsion made worse the condition it was meant to cure. The ordinary citizens found themselves at the mercy of the king's deputies, and extortion, accompanied by violence and torture, became commonplace. In these circumstances it is scarcely surprising that the persecuted should have sought the protection of powerful landowners, even though by so doing they were surrendering what little independence they had.

Politically the Egyptians were still excluded from the hierarchical structure, but there is evidence that in other

The pyramids of Khaefre and Menkhaure at Giza, dating from the Old Kingdom (c2500 BC).

respects the natives were assuming greater responsibilities and infiltrating sections of the administration hitherto closed to them. The virtual cessation of Greek immigration during the second century BC forced the Ptolemies to rely more and more on Egyptian talent.

Thus the Ptolemaic period staggered towards an inglorious close, presided over by an enfeebled monarchy and with an increasingly hostile population governed by a corrupt and incompetent administration. The economy was crumbling, and national unity was non-existent. For periods at a time the Thebaid was virtually independent, and eventually, in 85 BC, Ptolemy IX Soter II found it necessary to destroy Thebes before some sort of order could be restored. As always in desperate times, society fragmented into a collection of groups and individuals intent only on self-preservation. Established interests sought to entrench their positions while the less fortunate strove by whatever means they could to ride out the storm.

Greek and Egyptian cultures

Ptolemaic Egypt presents the intriguing picture of two quite distinct cultures coming into contact and co-existing for a considerable period. The question is, to what extent did each culture retain its essential individuality and to what extent did one absorb the other?

Unfortunately the answer has to be based on material that is both meagre and comes from a restricted milieu. There is virtually nothing from which to assess the cultural allegiances of the lower classes. The strong assumption, and it can be nothing more, must be that the Egyptian peasantry, those most reluctant betrayers of tradition, remained loyal to their way of life, speaking their ancient tongue, worshipping their familiar, popular deities and being buried according to time-honoured practices. All who shared such an environment, heavy with the memories of ages, would have found it hard to resist its pressures, and the probability is that those Greeks (and others) who married into, or lived among, the Egyptian peasantry would soon have lost their old cultural ties.

It was a different matter in the three towns (Alexandria, Naucratis and Ptolemais) and in the other exclusively Greek communities scattered throughout the *chora*. Here a conscious effort was made to preserve an Hellenic identity. The inhabitants of these enclaves retained their native tongue and read and composed their own literature. They brought with them their Olympian cults and, although archaeological evidence is virtually non-existent, are known to have built temples of a traditional kind. Their tombs and houses were constructed according to the traditions of their homeland. In other words, throughout the Ptolemaic period there existed within Egypt large pockets of population which deliberately recreated the culture of the society

Temple of Ramesses III at Medinet Habu, Thebes (c1190–1160 BC). On the north side of the first court of the temple, colossal statues of the king as Osiris stand against the pillars.

from which they had come.

On the other hand, they made no attempt to convert the native population to their way of life. It was neither their purpose nor desire that this should happen, and in many ways they deliberately set out to exclude them.

The Egyptians would, in any case, have been hard to wean from their own customs, and left to their own devices, it is scarcely surprising that in all important respects they retained their individuality. Whether as monumental hieroglyphic or as cursive demotic the Egyptian language flourished. People lived in the same types of houses and were buried in the same kinds of tombs. The state religion flourished, managed by long-established priesthoods with the aid of ancient rituals in temples of changeless form. What we have of Egyptian art in the Ptolemaic period (some sculpture in the round and much more relief work) conforms almost without exception in both subject-matter and style to ancient traditions.

There was, inevitably, cultural interaction at many points in the course of 300 years, but such evidence as there is demonstrates that among the upper classes (particularly the Greek) interest in the other's culture was principally the curiosity of enquiring minds coming into contact with something new, and in no way, constituted conversion to another way of life. What contact there was between the Egyptian and Greek religions, for example, was almost entirely brought about by Greek initiative, and was a product of their fascination in the antiquity of Egyptian religious life. They identified Egyptian gods and goddesses with their own, and formulated and championed the cult of Serapis, a form of the Egyptian deity Osorapis. But there is no evidence that purely Greek cults ever found favour with the Egyptian population as a whole.

Similarly, in the decoration of their tombs and other buildings, the Greeks often made use of typically Egyptian elements and motifs, such as the obelisk, sphinx, solar disc, but all these signify nothing more than a taste for something a little exotic and did not in any way make the monuments themselves 'Egyptian'.

There existed, side by side, quite distinct Greek and Egyptian schools of art, the former represented by sculpture in the round, terracottas, bronzes, and the painted decoration from the Alexandrian tombs, the latter by the relief work on the walls of temples such as Kôm Ombo, Dendera and Edfu, a small collection of private and royal statuary, and plentiful funerary stelae. There are also examples of an art that is sometimes taken as demonstrating a fusion of the two schools, where subject, technique or treatment has been borrowed by one from the other. This 'fusion' consisted almost entirely of the adoption of alien elements, often of a very superficial nature, which did not affect the character of the whole.

Only very occasionally do we encounter something which seems to go deeper. Such is the tomb of the Egyptian priest Petosiris at Tuna el Gebel, who lived during the second period of Persian occupation and survived until the reign of Ptolemy I Soter. His tomb (or rather family vault) is decorated partly in traditional Egyptian style and partly in a manner which treats Egyptian themes in a rather indifferent 'Hellenic' fashion. This attempted marriage of styles is clearly studied, and is not so much the standard-bearer for a Graeco-Egyptian artistic movement as a curiosity, never apparently repeated, inspired by a mind receptive to the new ideas recently arrived in the country.

There must also have existed, in time, a section of the population (the products of mixed marriages) which lacked a clear cultural identity and compensated for this by adopting elements of both the Greek and Egyptian (for example, the tomb designated to Anfushy II on the island of Pharos at Alexandria, dated to the first half of the second century BC).

In summary, there is little evidence that there ever existed a 'Graeco-Egyptian' culture. The Egyptians made few concessions, the Greeks made many, though among the urban élite these amounted to little more than cultural experimentation.

In broad terms, the Ptolemaic period was one of flux. The introduction of large numbers of foreigners subjected Egyptian civilization to unfamiliar pressures. But it survived, by clinging tenaciously to what it had always had. The way of life which the Greeks brought with them was never anything more than an alien skin grafted on to parts of the Egyptian body. Beneath, and all around, life continued as before in all essentials. The Egyptians might no longer have been masters of their own destiny, and politically and commercially their country might have become part of the Mediterranean world, but socially and culturally they remained true to themselves, never profoundly affected by the customs and attitudes of their new rulers.

But powerful new forces were about to shape the life of the country. In 30 BC, following the death of Antony after the battle of Actium, the shrewd and scheming Cleopatra died by her own hand; the triumphant Octavian marched in, and Egypt became a Roman province.

Early Roman Egypt

Colin Walters

Egypt, a Roman province (30 BC to AD 200)

The Roman hold on Egypt was swiftly and ruthlessly tightened. Disturbances in the Thebaid and the eastern Delta, provoked, it seems, by the appearance of tax collectors, were speedily put down. Perhaps because of this immediate demonstration of Egyptian recalcitrance Augustus (ruled as emperor 27 BC–AD 14) stationed three legions in the country, backed up by auxiliary troops. These were distributed in some strength throughout the Nile valley and in the Delta, with the headquarters at Alexandria. Here was also based a naval squadron, which policed the southeastern Mediterranean, while river patrols, introduced by the Ptolemies, were continued. All this amounted to an impressive show of strength, much greater in scale than anything attempted by the Ptolemies, and so effective that it was soon possible to withdraw one of the three legions. The troops that were left were more than adequate to cope with a thoroughly cowed native population.

To the south the Romans were called upon to deal with a rather more serious threat. During the last centuries of pharaonic rule Nubia had been more or less left to its own devices. The Ptolemies, however, re-established a presence in Lower Nubia, even reopening the gold mines in the Wadi Allaqi. The prosecution of this policy involved reaching an understanding with the kingdom of Meroe, the capital of which lay far to the south between the fifth and sixth cataracts. Whatever form this understanding took, it seems to have survived until the end of the Ptolemaic Dynasty, but the Romans aroused the hostility of the Meroites by re-dictating the

terms to their own advantage. In 23 BC a Meroite army of 30,000 men attacked and defeated three cohorts of Roman troops at Syene (modern Aswan). The Roman response was swift. Petronius, at the head of 11,000 troops, came south, defeated the Meroites, and pursued them as far as Napata. Following this victory, Lower Nubia (known as the Dodekaschoinos) became a buffer zone between Egypt and Meroe, colonized and exploited energetically by the Romans, with military camps scattered throughout the area but, save for an expedition during the reign of Nero, their interest in the region further south ended, and the Meroites were left in control of their kingdom.

The swift assertion of military power both within Egypt and on her southern border was accompanied by a reorganization of the country's administration. Three districts were established, the Thebaid, the Delta and Middle Egypt, each under the control of an *epistrategos*. Within these areas the ancient division into *nomes* was retained. The result of this and other reforms was to give a far greater degree of centralization to the governmental structure. At its head was set a prefect of equestrian rank who, as the representative of absentee emperors, inherited the pharaonic role.

This appointment symbolized the difference between Egypt and other Roman provinces, which were presided over by men of senatorial rank, and emphasized the importance they attached to their latest acquisition. Egypt was to be the granary of Rome, and to this end her new rulers applied their genius for administrative efficiency.

Economic recovery

The decay of the agricultural system during the final stages of the Ptolemaic period had been alarming, and Augustus wasted no time in taking steps to rectify the situation. Troops were employed to assist in the restoration of the irrigation network, an indication of the urgency with which the task was undertaken. Thereafter the essential work was carried out by native corvée labour. In this way the productive capacity of the land was dramatically restored. Indeed, the advent of Roman rule, bringing as it did peace, security, firm government and efficient organization, produced a remarkable recovery in the Egyptian economy and allowed commerce to flourish. Alexandria became the most important trading centre in the eastern Mediterranean, its business life stimulated by the settled conditions, the Red Sea was opened up to facilitate trade with the East, and a wide range of Egyptian products was exported.

But this prosperity, which lasted into the second century AD, was not a shared prosperity. To a much greater extent than in Ptolemaic times Egypt was now nothing more than a vassal state, the possession of foreigners for whose benefit her great natural wealth was to be ruthlessly exploited, and the Egyptians themselves were merely the instruments by which this was to be achieved.

During the first two centuries of Roman rule the Egyptian section of the population almost disappears from our field of vision. Native cultural traditions showed increasing signs of stagnation, either reduced to the lowest level of survival or maintained only in a very restricted milieu. The Romans cared nothing for Egyptian susceptibilities, and while the ancient cults were maintained and temple building continued with state support, much temple land was confiscated and the administration of the temples themselves overhauled. A single 'High Priest of Alexandria and all Egypt' was installed, who was no priest but a Roman civil official. Thus the Romans brought the temples and their affairs within the sphere of direct governmental control, ensuring that their resources could be utilized as the state wished and frustrating the political ambitions of their clergy.

The emasculation of the temples, for so long strongholds of ancient tradition and a vital source of national inspiration, contributed much to, and itself symbolized, the declining fortunes of the Egyptian people.

The position of non-Egyptian residents

The fortunes of the Greeks and Jews had also been affected by the arrival of the Romans, who themselves never formed a significant proportion of the population. The status and function of the Greeks within Egyptian society remained the same, and their power and privileges survived largely intact. At the same time, they now had to get used to the fact that they no longer belonged to the ruling race and were thus in a significantly more vulnerable position, though they were secure so long as the Romans needed them as much as they needed the Romans.

For the Jewish community, on the other hand, Roman rule was an unmitigated disaster. The introduction of the poll tax by Augustus led to the fundamental distinction between Greeks and non-Greeks, with Jews being included in the second category. The financial burden of the new tax was thus made worse by the social stigma attached to its payment, since it bracketed together the wealthiest Alexandrian Jew and the lowliest Egyptian peasant. This indignity and the resentment it caused, coupled with the anti-Semitic prejudices of the Alexandrian Greeks, provided all the ingredients for violent conflict. This duly occurred at regular intervals, first in AD 38, then in 41, again in 66, and

Coffin portrait from a Roman cemetery in the Fayûm, Egypt, second century AD.

finally and decisively in 115, when the struggle spread beyond the confines of Alexandria. The outcome was the virtual elimination of the Jews as a distinctive community capable of performing an important function in Egyptian society.

This protracted and bloody conflict, and its outcome, contributed significantly to the deteriorating economic situation during the second century. The more difficult the country found it to meet Roman demands, the more the screw was turned. Philo, writing in the middle of the first century AD, speaks of the barbaric behaviour of tax-collectors, and documentary evidence bears him out. Compulsory service and collective responsibility were more and more widely applied, and requisitioning by the state became commonplace.

Unrest among the Egyptian peasants

Under these pressures many, and not only among the peasantry, abandoned their responsibilities and, with the temples no longer a safe refuge, either joined the growing number of robber bands operating from marsh or desert or sought anonymity in the teeming streets of Alexandria, from where the authorities periodically attempted to flush them out.

As the second century drew to its close Egypt presented a contradictory picture. The larger towns, particularly Alexandria, were flourishing, but in the countryside the situation was deteriorating rapidly. Archaeological and documentary evidence suggest that many settlements (for example, Kerkenouphis, Medinet Habu, Naucratis, Edfu, Tanis) suffered at least partial destruction and were in some cases abandoned al-together. The so-called 'revolt of the Boucholoi', which broke out in the Delta in 172–3, was probably no more than a particularly serious and prolonged outbreak of lawlessness in an area that had suffered from the effects of brigandage for many years. Whatever its origins, it is noteworthy as being the only recorded instance of open and determined rebellion by the native Egyptians in the second century.

These people were about to discover a new identity. The bases of their culture, which had served them for so long, were at last weakening. Demotic might still have been employed as the medium in which literary works (some of considerable merit) were composed, and hieroglyphic texts might still have been carved on temple walls and elsewhere, but in the community as a whole the ancient script had become an anachronism in a changing world, and by the end of the second century had been virtually abandoned. In the same way the ancient artistic traditions had lost their vigour. What is still recognizably Egyptian in subject and style is either of crude workmanship or is, as on the walls of the Upper Egyptian temples, stilted reproduction of time-honoured models. Almost without exception the outstanding artistic productions of the period came from the non-Egyptian community, and represented either non-Egyptian themes in non-Egyptian styles (as with most of the sculpture) or non-Egyptian art in an Egyptian setting (the portrait-masks placed on the bodies of the deceased members of the Hellenic community).

From this cultural, political and social limbo the Egyptian population was now to be rescued by its sudden and enthusiastic adoption of Christianity.

Late Roman and Byzantine Egypt

Colin Walters

Christian Egypt (AD 200 to 641)

The strength of the Christian challenge to established paganism during the first two centuries AD is difficult to gauge. It is not known how and when the new faith was introduced into the country, nor how far and how quickly it spread. There is no corroboration of the tradition, first reported by the Greek Church historian, Eusebius (265–339), in the fourth century, linking the Evangelist Saint Mark with the Egyptian mission, and a search for clear indications of Christian allegiance among the letter writers of the period is unproductive. Were it not for a small collection of biblical papyri, almost all of the Old Testament, which have been assigned to the second century, the silence would be deafening.

What seems beyond doubt is that the word was first brought to Alexandria, very probably to the Jewish population in that city, and that during the first two centuries converts came very largely from the non-Egyptian communities, both in Alexandria and the *chora*.

By the beginning of the third century, they were numerous enough to make a contribution to the cultural life of the community and to bring upon themselves the unwelcome attentions of the authorities. The Catecheti-cal School, one of the great centres of Christian scholarship, was established in Alexandria c180, and at the turn of the century was presided over by Clement (c150–216) who, like his successor Origen (c185–254), was one of the leading figures of the early Church. In 201 he was forced into exile by the persecution instigated by the Emperor Septimius Severus (ruled 193–211), in the course of which many Christians from all parts of the country sacrificed their lives.

It was to be more than a century before those who survived could feel secure enough to declare their faith openly. That century was, in Egypt as in other parts of the Roman empire, a period of hardship and unrest. The state, beset by problems largely of its own making, reacted by making heavier demands of its subjects. Compulsion became the keystone of government policy. The wealthy landowners and the impoverished peasantry, though not immune, suffered less than the moderately well-to-do. Among this class ruin was widespread. More and more land was abandoned and the irrigation system neglected. Inflation soared to unprecedented levels. These sombre developments took place against a background of lawlessness, outbreaks of violence in the streets of Alexandria, and threats to the very security of Egypt. In the south a belligerent tribe occupying the eastern desert and hills of Lower Nubia, the Blemmyes (otherwise known as the Beja), constantly harassed Upper Egypt and, on two occasions, appear to have joined forces with rebellious elements within Egypt. Although defeated they continued to be a thorn in the flesh of the authorities for a long time to come. More serious was the threat posed in the north by the forces of Palmyra, a city state situated between the Orontes and Euphrates rivers. In 270, when their leader was the remarkable Queen Zenobia, they succeeded in defeating a Roman force and gaining some measure of temporary control in Alexandria before being driven out by the general, Probus.

These revolts, invasions and incursions were a symptom of, and themselves contributed to, the malaise affecting the Roman empire at this time. The presence among its subjects of a growing number whose loyalty was reserved for a higher authority than the emperor was not calculated to improve matters, but as conditions deteriorated the Christians became a convenient scapegoat for all manner of wrongs and misfortunes and suffered both official and unofficial persecution.

Persecution of Christians

During the reigns of Decius (249–251) and later Valerian (252–260) all adults were called upon to make offerings as a token of allegiance to the emperor, and for their opposition to this Christians were tortured and put to death. The victims included many Egyptians. At about this time, during the patriarchate of Dionysius (d. 264), the first serious attempt seems to have been made to convert this section of the population. This would probably have made little headway without a means by which the missionaries could explain the message in intelligible terms to people unable to understand Greek. For this they used the Coptic language, which had developed among the pagan population during the first two centuries but which now began an association with Christianity which it retains to this day. This language utilized the Greek alphabet but added a number of letters taken from Demotic to render sounds not catered for in Greek. In this way the Egyptian language, now well over 3000 years old, attained its final form, and as such still survives in the Church liturgy.

The departure of Valerian ushered in a period of relative calm for the Christian community, but the greatest trial was yet to come. In 284 Diocletian became emperor. His radical administrative and fiscal reforms did much to restore unity to the empire and helped to make possible the economic recovery of the fourth century, from which Egypt benefited as much as any other part of the empire. He is, however, remembered less for this than for the brutal persecution of Christians which began in 303 and which was particularly severe in Egypt. In all probability Diocletian's colleague Galerius was at least as much to blame and, after Diocletian's death, he enthusiastically continued the persecution, but it is the former whose name will ever be associated with this doleful episode.

The annals of the Egyptian Church are full of stories of defiance and heroic martyrdom, and these, together with the account of Bishop Eusebius, graphically illustrate the full horror of what took place. It left such an impression that the calendar of the Egyptian Christians dates from Diocletian's accession.

Gallienus (253–68) called off the persecution, but it was the accession of Constantine to the imperial throne in 323 that ensured the triumph of Christianity.

Eusebius was himself in Egypt during the persecution, and his description of the country as one where Christians formed the majority is therefore of particular interest. It was probably not much of an exaggeration, if at all, and this state of affairs clearly owed much to the successful mission among the Egyptians. The result of this was to modify fundamentally the character of Egyptian Christianity. Hitherto this had been dominated by the philosophic intellectual school of Greek-speaking and Greek-thinking theologians in Alexandria, and by the pseudo-philosophical fantasies of Gnosticism, which, in its Christian form, drew heavily upon contemporary pagan ideas.

To the large number of illiterate peasants now being recruited all this can have meant very little. They found, instead, another outlet for their newly acquired faith, and by so doing not only made a profound contribution to Christian culture but also provided the Egyptian race with a new focus for its national pride.

The Egyptians took to monasticism like ducks to water. We do not know precisely how or when it started, but its impact and appeal were immediate and immense, and its growth rapid. In the beginning it lacked organization. Individual hermits detached themselves from the community and lived lives of severe simplicity. Such a man was Saint Anthony (c 251–356), who took to the desert in the last quarter of the third century. Though one among many, and certainly not the first, he is traditionally looked upon as the man whose example inspired the multitudes who followed.

It was not long, however, before the solitary hermit became a rarity, even though he remained the ideal. First of all, individuals joined together to form loosely knit groups, and then c320, the first coenobitic community was established at Tabennisi by Pakhome (St Pachomius, c290–346). In this, and the many which were subsequently founded, the monks lived according to a precise set of rules and code of discipline.

The monastery of Epiphanius which is situated in the western desert at Thebes. This reconstruction shows the original monastery as it must have appeared at the beginning of the seventh century AD. The *kasr* (tower of refuge) is the dominant feature.

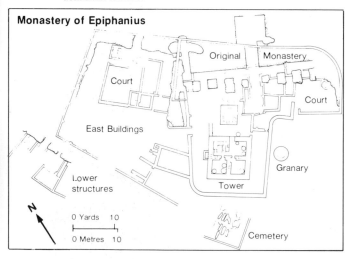

Monastery of Epiphanius

Original Monastery

Court

Court

East Buildings

Granary

Lower structures

Tower

N

0 Yards 10

0 Metres 10

Cemetery

In the centuries that followed, the monasteries and their inmates played an important role in events at home and abroad. In many respects they seem to have filled the gap left by the ancient temples in national life. Physically they dominated the horizon just as those had done. They cultivated their own land, the extent of which steadily increased as time passed, and employed hired labour. They sold the products of their handiwork, and in return purchased what they needed. They protected the local inhabitants against the excesses of the authorities and gave succour to the needy and those made homeless by the depredations of the Blemmyes and their kind. And all the while they did battle with the demonic forces of darkness and rooted out paganism where it might be found.

But it was not only pagans who were now the enemy. During the days of danger and persecution Christians had, on the whole, been united in adversity; but, once their religion became the universal faith, sanctioned by imperial decree, this bond was broken and doctrinal

differences came to the surface. These soon became an expression of political rivalry, particularly between Alexandria and the new capital Constantinople, which had been established in 330. In the period up to the middle of the fifth century, council succeeded chaotic council as intimidation, mob rule and subterfuge were employed by the two sides to assert the rightness of their beliefs. The Egyptian patriarch could always count upon the unquestioning support of his monastic legions, whether in the streets of Alexandria or in the council chambers, for were not Egyptian pride and Egyptian interests under threat?

Theological controversies

The first great controversy erupted *c*318, when Arius propounded a doctrine denying the divinity of Christ and the concept of the Trinity. He was vigorously opposed by Athanasius, patriarch (328–373), and at the Council of Nicaea in 325 Arianism was rejected and the Nicene Creed became the expression of fundamental Christian belief. The subsequent career of Athanasius illustrates the uncertainty of the times. A champion of orthodoxy, his fortunes fluctuated depending upon the doctrinal allegiance of the current emperor, and his patriarchate was punctuated by periods of enforced exile.

The inevitable showdown between Alexandria and Constantinople took place at the Council of Chalcedon in 451, called to debate the vexed question of Christ's single or dual natures (human and divine). Egypt was the principal proponent of the doctrine of a single nature (monophysitism), while Constantinople and the majority of the delegates favoured the concept of duality (diophysitism). At two earlier Councils, held at Ephesus in 431 and 449, the Egyptian viewpoint had won the day, thanks largely to unscrupulous and reprehensible tactics. The Council of Chalcedon now reversed the decisions of Ephesus. Monophysitism was declared a heresy and the Egyptian patriarch, Dioscorus, was sent into an exile from which he never returned. The man sent to replace him, Proterius, was murdered by the Alexandrian mob, and one of their own kind put in his place.

The decisions of Chalcedon were never accepted by the Egyptian Church. Attempts to force them to do so proved fruitless, as did the occasional search for some form of compromise. Only when an emperor shared the same monophysite beliefs as the Egyptians was there any rest from the constant bickering and bloodshed that characterized the second half of the fifth and much of the sixth centuries. In this way the Egyptian Church, largely from its own choosing, drifted into a backwater, cut off from the mainstream of orthodox Christendom, and its institutions and rituals became fossilized, a process hastened by the Arab invasion in 641–2.

With the benefit of hindsight we can see that the last two centuries of Byzantine rule in Egypt formed a bridge linking the fast-fading world of paganism and the rise of Islam. This brief period of Christianity rampant was, for Egypt, one almost of marking time. It was, so far as we can tell, neither as gloomy as the third century nor as encouraging as the fourth. The Blemmyes still gave trouble in the south, the Sasanid Persians threatened, and eventually invaded, in the north. Lawlessness was rife, but when had it not been so? The life of the peasant was hard, but so it always was. Often he was put upon by those above him, but this was nothing new. He might abandon his land, but this was hardly a fresh development. Egypt was now a land dominated by powerful landowners with large estates, and by the new power of the Church and the monastic establishments. Christian now persecuted the pagan, and in Alexandria Christian fought Christian. The Arab invasion exposed the futility of it all. With no protection from a decaying imperial power Egypt and her Church subsided beneath the Islamic wave. The link with the past was finally severed, and she moved into a new world.

The final phase of Egyptian culture

The culture of late Roman and Byzantine Egypt reflects the fascinating admixture of influences and traditions at work in this period of transition. Paganism was a long time a-dying. State worship of the ancient Egyptian gods did not formally end until the temple of Isis at Philae was closed by imperial decree in the sixth century. Hieroglyphs were still being carved at the end of the fourth century, and demotic stubbornly survived until the middle of the fifth. But it was among the non-Egyptian population that paganism endured the longest. A collection of stelae found at Kom Abou Billou (ancient Terenouthis) in the western Delta shows that at the very time when Eusebius was describing Egypt as a Christian country, and for some time after, people in that community were being buried according to ancient rites and having carved on their tombstones the figures of Anubis and Horus.

Later, during the fifth and sixth centuries, figure sculpture that was almost wholly pagan in subject was still being produced at Oxyrhynchus and Ahnas, in Middle Egypt. But the sculptors busy at these sites were among the last practitioners of their kind, for all around them a new art and a new architecture were taking shape.

It was unusual for Christians to adapt pagan monuments to their own uses. Hermits might take up residence in tombs, churches might be built within the precincts of temples, as at Dendera, Luxor and Esna, or, as at Medinet Habu (Coptic *Djeme*) a settlement be established within the protection of the perimeter wall. But more commonly the churches and monasteries, though they might use stone from existing monuments, were constructed on fresh sites.

Most of the monastic communities were established at no great distance from the Nile valley. The semi-anchoretic conformed to a loose pattern, with the dwellings of the individual monks scattered around a small number of common buildings, such as a church and refectory. But even this scheme of things was liable to variation and, over a period of time, to change. In the desert close to Esna was recently discovered a number of large, subterranean cells, each housing only one or two people, apparently occupied during the sixth century. No communal buildings were found here, but at Cellia, another recently-excavated site in the western desert north of Cairo, these had in fact been provided, though at what stage of the site's long occupation it is difficult to say. Much later, probably not before the ninth century, those communities which survived were fortified in an attempt to combat the constant harassment from desert tribes, but long before this it was customary to construct a defensible nucleus which could provide some protection in an emergency. The most prominent feature of this nucleus was a *kasr*, or tower of refuge.

The coenobitic establishments, unlike the semi-anchoretic, were surrounded by a perimeter wall from their very founding, though its defensive capability was probably limited. These communities, because of their organization, must have conformed to a much more standardized arrangement of buildings, and from the rules of their founder, Saint Pakhome, and contemporary descriptions left by visitors, we can see that this was so. Not one of these monasteries has survived in a remotely complete form, but the fifth century church belonging to Deir el Abiad (the White Monastery) at Sohag is, by its setting and scale, one of the most impressive monuments in Egypt from any age.

From the same century, though non-monastic in character, is the ruined 'cathedral' at Hermopolis. This site was particularly revered by the early Christians as being, according to tradition, the southernmost point reached by the Holy Family on its flight into Egypt.

Above: The church of Deir el Abiad, the 'White Monastery', built CAD 440. Below: Plan of the church of Deir el Abiad showing a western narthex, southern narthex and trefoil sanctuary.

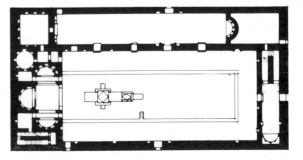

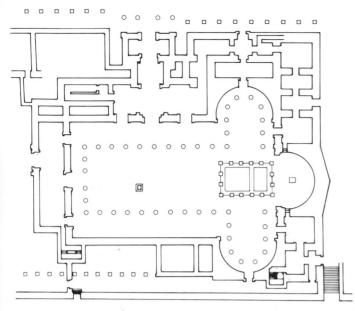

.Plan of the church of el Adra (the Virgin), cAD 450.

Slightly to the south of Hermopolis lies Bawit, the site of a thriving monastery during the fourth to twelfth centuries. Here were discovered, during excavations in the early part of this century, paintings which make a major contribution to the somewhat meagre repertoire of early Christian art in Egypt. Not all of these can be dated with certainty, though it is generally agreed that the majority were probably produced between the fifth and seventh centuries. The figures of Christ and the Virgin feature prominently in these paintings, usually set within a niche in the monk's devotional room, but by far the greater proportion represents warrior saints or monastic figures. There are also a number of Old Testament themes, in particular a series involving David, which are illustrative of a dependence on this book in the early days of Christian art and which, in Egypt particularly, might well reflect a debt to Jewish influences.

This is further evidenced by the earliest Christian frescoes to be found in Egypt, in two of the funerary chapels at the necropolis of el Bagawat in Kharga Oasis, dating probably to the fourth century. Here also Old Testament themes predominate, and include an ambitious rendering of the Exodus.

Apart from Bawit, most examples of early Christian art in Egypt occur piecemeal. The monastery of Apa Jeremias at Saqqara retained a few, more limited in theme than Bawit, and an underground church at Deir Abu Hennes contained scenes depicting episodes in the life of Christ, dating perhaps to the fifth century.

The comparative poverty of the artistic heritage is partially due, almost certainly, to later destruction and insufficient excavation. The small amount of Coptic literature from the period, on the other hand, probably reflects accurately its limited scope and production. Among the native, Coptic-speaking population, only one outstanding figure emerges. Shenute (c334–452) became the archimandrite of Deir el Abiad during the last quarter of the fourth century, and accompanied Cyril (patriarch 412–44) to the first Council at Ephesus. He has left behind a considerable number of sermons and the like which show him to have been a man whose fiery personality was matched by the incendiary quality of his prose. In many ways he typifies the age, symbolizing the resurgence of Egyptian nationalism and helping to give Egyptian Christianity its distinctive, monastically influenced character. He was an Egyptian patriot, suspicious of the Greek-speaking community and its ways, ever ready to defend his monks or the local population against the representatives of a government he clearly detested. He was a staunch upholder of the Egyptian position on doctrinal issues, and a scourge of pagans, ready to kill and burn to eradicate darkness and establish light. In his own community he wielded a stern authority, demanding obedience and punishing severely any breach of discipline. In Shenute the native population found a champion who spoke for a people long suppressed and without a voice. Reading him, echoes are heard from the distant past, long, long ago, from a time when Egyptians were masters of more than their own country. After he had gone there was no one to replace him. Shenute was, perhaps, the last great Egyptian, of a line that had begun more than 3500 years before with Menes.

The Religion of Ancient Egypt

J. M. Plumley

In presenting an overall view of the religion of ancient Egypt it is important to realize that the extant evidence does not permit the creation of a systematic picture. The words written at the beginning of the twentieth century by the German Egyptologist Adolf Erman in the introduction to his *Handbook of Egyptian Religion* still hold good in spite of many significant advances in Egyptology since his time:

'Of all the religions of the ancient world there is perhaps no other for which we possess such an amount of material, so endless and impossible to grasp, as we do for this. It is in fact too great, and in addition to this our comprehension of the ancient religious writings is still very incomplete. All the insight and labour devoted . . . to the investigation of Egyptian religion, or to its description, have hitherto resulted in little more than the preliminary orientation of this intricate domain, and it will require many more decades of hard work before we shall be able to obtain a clear view.'

Formative factors in Egyptian religion

The extent and complexity of the material being such, the problem must be approached initially by the way of other factors. These can be summed up as temporal, geographical and political.

Though the unification of the dual kingdom of Upper and Lower Egypt occurred some 33 centuries before the Christian era, the origins of the beliefs and practices of the founders of the united kingdom lie much further back in time. Thus, when in considering the Pyramid Texts of the Old Kingdom, inscribed during a period round about 2500 BC, it must be remembered that they are immeasurably older than the men who carved them on the walls of the royal burial chambers. Furthermore it would be a mistake to suppose that these texts represent the sum of contemporary religious belief and practice. That there were contributions by many over countless years is therefore a primary consideration in assessing what is meant by the religion of ancient Egypt.

Geographically Egypt was to all intents and purposes isolated from ancient West Asia. Bounded on the east and west by vast inhospitable deserts, with a cataract difficult to navigate in the south, and in the north the Mediterranean Sea, the Nile valley was secure from all but the most determined invasion from outside. This isolation, though never absolutely complete (even in the earliest times there were trading contacts with Asia by way of tracks across the Sinai peninsula and from the interior of Africa down the Nile), deeply influenced the Egyptians. For not only were they able in relatively untroubled seclusion to preserve the past, but because of isolation they tended to be content with the practical achievements of the past and less moved to seek new ideas. This long-engendered conservatism is a further factor in accounting for an often grotesque syncretism of beliefs, exhibiting both patent contradiction and undisguised absurdity.

So long an isolation also bred in the people of Egypt a conception that they were men *par excellence*, applying to themselves the title *romet*, a title which they did not use of foreigners. At a later period this conception was destined to lead to a dangerous consequence, a fierce nationalistic spirit. Nor is it surprising that, believing themselves to hold a privileged place among humanity, the Egyptians should have claimed for themselves other privileges, the favour of the gods, and for their rulers a share in their divinity.

The physical character and the climatic conditions of the Nile valley also reacted on the religious beliefs of the Egyptians as well as on all their secular activities. In contrast to the luxuriance and fatness of the river verges and marshes, to the east and west lay waterless wastes of sand, regions dreaded as the domains of burning heat by day and chilling cold by night, of parching thirst, of blinding, suffocating sandstorms, and the haunt of malevolent demons and strange monsters. This physical reminder of the contrast between life and death influenced them to formulate, in a way which no other people of antiquity ever did, belief in the possibility of life after death.

An ever recurring cycle of life in the Nile valley, demonstrated by the annual growth and dying down of vegetation made possible by the yearly rise and fall of the level of the Nile and aided by the equitable and rarely changing climate, tended to breed in the Egyptian mind a belief that the distinguishing feature of the world in which he lived was continuity and permanence. 'As it was in the beginning, is now, and ever shall be' is an apt verdict on the Egyptians' conception of the physical world. Further, the rich rewards offered in a land that for long periods was undisturbed by war or civil upheavals, tended to colour men's ideas about the hereafter. It is for this reason that in some accounts of the next world the dead were thought of as living in a counterpart of the world of the living, but one that was immeasurably better.

Though Egypt was effectively isolated from ancient West Asia for a great part of its history, this did not prevent political changes in the Nile valley. Over the course of the years settlements united, either as the result of conquest or as the result of a mutual union, to resist conquest by some other group. The union of groups eventually gave rise to the creation of larger units or small kingdoms that, in their turn, led to the formation of larger royal jurisdictions, culminating in the union of the two kingdoms of Upper and Lower Egypt in the last quarter of the fourth millennium BC.

Whether by conquest or by peaceful fusion, in addition to a blending of blood, there would have been a blending of religious beliefs. Those deities which were alike tended to fuse with one another, the only evidence of their independence being in their bearing compound names. In some instances the god of one group might be wedded to the goddess of another. The taking in of a third deity might be achieved by representing him or her as the child of the married gods. It is therefore not surprising that the resulting mixture, caused by the compounding of names, the forming of triads and the inevitable acceptance of seemingly incompatible beliefs, has led some scholars to despair of getting any order or system out of the chaotic mass of contradictions—subject to change and liable to differing interpretation in each new age, each district, and less frequently by individuals.

Any intelligent understanding of the religion of ancient Egypt must not only take into consideration the factors of time, geography and political change, but must attempt so far as is possible to see it through the eyes of the Egyptians themselves and not merely from a Western standpoint. For these reasons it is important not to be content with a scientific but inhuman catalogue of deities and practices, nor to be led into assuming that the wisdom of the Egyptians means an apprehension of religious truth engendered by creeds which they never knew and modes of thought foreign to them.

Physical conditions

The essential physical features of the land in which the Egyptians lived have not significantly changed except that, since the building of the dams at Aswan, the annual inundation no longer occurs and the former extensive marshes have disappeared. It is still possible to see the world of the river valley much as the Egyptians saw it during the formative years of their religious beliefs. Above the solid earth stretched the broad expanse of heaven. To the Egyptians it appeared like a great blue canopy. To them it seemed logical to suppose that at some points upon the earth, either far out into the deserts or beyond the seas, there existed four supports, immovable and everlasting. The colour of the sky, for the greater part of the year unbroken by clouds, became associated with those celestial beings who it was thought inhabited the sky, and for this reason later representations of the high gods often show their flesh as blue in colour. The appearance of the night sky, splendid with its myriad of stars in the clear air, was a cause for wonder. Observed movements of the sun and moon, the planets and the slow shift of the fixed constellations led to speculation that life existed in the sky. Quite early these observations were to provide the basis for a more practical purpose, the demarcation of time and the establishing of a calendar.

The movements of the sun and the moon were patent to all. It was seen that it was a daily event that the sun rose in the east and, passing high over the river valley, set in the west. With the setting of the sun, darkness fell and the cold wind came in from the rapidly cooling deserts. The Egyptians must have concluded very early that the sun was the source of life, for without its light and warmth death followed. A more difficult problem was how to account for the daily reappearance of the sun in the east. The logical solution was to conclude that, after setting in the west, the sun travelled underground during the hours of darkness. It is not hard to see how such a solution would have led to the conclusion that during the hours of darkness on earth the sun was illuminating another world, underground, but essentially similar in character to the world above.

Observation of the moon presented greater problems. In the first place it was a lesser light and it provided no warmth. Not only was its position in the sky constantly shifting, but its disc waxed and waned. Sometimes it did not appear at all, and at times it appeared in the day sky. Its seemingly erratic movement, its growth and decrease, suggested that it was a living being, but unlike the sun it was not constant, suggesting weakness rather than strength in the sky. There is little doubt that these characteristics caused it to be observed in the earliest times, allowing its phases to be plotted so as to anticipate with some exactness its movement. The birth of a lunar calendar must be reckoned to have happened at a very early period in the history of man in Egypt, though probably the first explanations advanced to account for its movements and phases preceded its use as a time reckoner, and passed in various forms into the religious lore of the sky.

From daily experience the early Egyptians learned that land, though bountiful and rewarding, was not entirely friendly, and that what at one moment might be regarded as friendly could become hostile. The warmth of the sun could turn to burning heat. The cool winds from the north could veer round to the south, bringing choking-hot sandstorms. On occasions the river might not rise to water and fertilize its lands. To explain this in a world that seemed so constant, the early Egyptians began to assume that there were invisible forces, normally beneficent, but which could become hostile, or that there were other forces which were always ill disposed.

The fauna as an influence on Egyptian religion

They began to observe some of these forces in the fauna of the land. Some of the animals, especially those they could domesticate, could be regarded as beneficent. On the other hand there were those both hostile and dangerous. In distinguishing between friendly and hostile creatures, they would have observed certain characteristics or qualities belonging to them. Thus the strength of the ox, the speed of the gazelle, the devotion of the dog were qualities to be admired, whereas the ferocity of the lion, the cunning of the hyena, the fury of the crocodile, the lightning strike of the poisonous snake were to be feared and avoided. It is not difficult to see how such animals would come to be regarded as living embodiments of good and evil. It is, however, important to recognize that the ancient Egyptians did not think of these creatures as being just symbols. Probably manifestations is a better term. It seems that the ancient Egyptians grouped the living into gods, men and animals, and that the animals held a special place in the economy of the world by virtue of the fact that on occasions they stood, as it were, between the gods and men to manifest divinity.

A further important factor must also be borne in mind. For the Egyptians the whole world was a living entity. In no way could any part of it be considered as neutral. Every part of the world was alive, partaking of a common life in which men, animals and gods shared. In common with other ancient languages there is no neuter gender in the ancient Egyptian language since it was concerned with a world that was entirely animate. The application of masculine or feminine to one thing or another did not necessarily imply a manifestation of what might be described as physical sexual distinctions but rather underlying conceptions of gender, that is qualities, characteristics, tendencies.

While the Egyptians thought of the world as a living unity, they were aware that a great part of it was subject to growth and decay, that there was a coming into being and a passing out of being—a birth and a death. At the same time there were parts which appeared to be indestructible, eternal, never dying. As a result a great part of the interest of the ancient Egyptian religion was devoted to the problem of how this indestructibility could be induced into what was perishable and how what was mortal could become immortal. In seeking the answers they were essentially concerned with finding practical solutions, as the evidence is that they were concrete in their thinking and did not attain to what might be termed philosophical or metaphysical thought.

Nevertheless it would not have been long before early men asked how the world came into being. For just as continual beginnings and births were about them, so at some time and in some manner there must have been a primeval birth of the universe.

Creation stories

'In the very earliest times there were many accounts of how the creation of the world came about. Of the vast majority of these only the barest fragments appear here and there in various religious writings, and many of these may be in themselves the welding together of older accounts. However, three reasonably coherent accounts can be distinguished, even though they undoubtedly contain within themselves elements from sources then long lost. These accounts or cosmogonies are those associated with the religious centres of Hermopolis, Heliopolis and Memphis.

Differing from one another widely, they are at one in their starting point: the existence before creation of a state so nebulous as to be hardly considered even as a state, when there was no sky, no earth, no air, no Nile, no gods, no men, not even the name of a thing. This inconceivable precursor of state, which it was argued could come into being by incepted action, was described as the Primeval Waters. This primordial abyss without limit, unlike a sea in that it possessed no surface, no up, no down, no side to side, endless, deep, dark and invisible, was personified as Nun, a name which was carried on into Christian times to represent the depth of the sea, of the earth or the abyss of hell. At Hermopolis an attempt to describe Nun was made by stating what it was not: 'in the infinity, the nothingness, the nowhere, and the dark.' Though personified as Nun, there is no evidence that any temple or shrine was ever dedicated to this primordial being. There is a representation of Nun in one copy of the Book of the Dead, a collection of funerary texts from the New Kingdom, which shows him as a man rising from the waters to hold above his head the sacred boat of the sun god. It would seem that at all times Nun remained a shadowy figure.

Just as Nun personified the Primeval Waters, so in the cosmogony of Hermopolis the characters of the waters were personified. The characteristics of depth, endlessness, darkness and invisibility were each given masculine and feminine forms: Nau and Naunet, Huh and Hauhet, Kuk and Kakuet, and Amun and Amaunet. Worshipped at Hermopolis as eight genii with the heads of frogs and serpents, they gave the name of Khnum (Eight Town) to the city of their worship. These genii were believed to have swum together and formed an egg in the darkness of Father Nun. From the egg burst forth the bird of light. Other versions of the myth relate that the primeval egg contained not light but air. In another version from Thebes of the egg origin of the world, the egg was laid by a goose, the Great Primeval Spirit, called Ken-Ken Ur 'The Great Cackler, whose voice broke the silence while the world was still flooded in silence,' (Book of the Dead, chapter 54).

The Greeks called the city Hermopolis, since they identified the chief deity of the place, the ibis-headed Thoth, with their own god Hermes. Thoth was regarded as the head over the eight genii, but it is possible that in earlier times he was a creator-god in his own right. By the dynastic period he had become the inventor of the hieroglyphic system of writing, the original lawgiver, and, as the repository of all learning both sacred and profane, a master of enchantment (hika).

During the First Intermediate period (ninth dynasty to early eleventh) the cosmogony of Hermopolis became mingled with that of Heliopolis with the result that many of its original concepts were lost. The creator-god who held pride of place in the Heliopolitan cosmogony was Atum whose name possibly means 'The Complete One'. The earliest information about this deity occurs in the Pyramid Texts, large parts of which may have originated in Heliopolis. Later Atum became associated with the sun-god Re^c. According to the Heliopolitan account of creation Atum emerged out of Nun either in the form of a hill or on a hill. There is little doubt that observance of the emergence of hills or small islands in the Nile, after the waters of the inundation began to subside, influenced this idea. There was no fixed form for the Primeval Hill, but an early formalizing of it into an eminence with sloping sides or ascending steps may have some bearing on the form of the pyramids. While the priesthood of Heliopolis claimed that it was in the locality of Heliopolis that this event took place, other religious centres made the same claims. Thus at Hermopolis, in the midst of a rectangular space surrounded by a high wall, lay a pool of water known as 'The Lake of the Two Knives' symbolizing Nun. In the middle of the lake was an island 'The Island of Flames' with a small hill, on which it was claimed the light first appeared. Similarly at Memphis the whole district around the city was called Tarjenen 'The Land of Rising' and at Thebes it was claimed that the Primordial Hill was situated near the temple of Medinet Habu.

Atum's emerging was an act of self-volition which resulted in a state of being. Thus in the Heliopolitan theology he is known as Khopri 'The One who Becomes'. In chapter 85 of the Book of the Dead Atum says of himself, 'I came into being of myself in the midst of the Primeval Waters in this my name of Khopri.' A manifestation of Atum, the scarabeus beetle, was partly due to the fact that its name was similar in sound to Khopri, for the ancient Egyptians paid special attention to such phonetic similarities in their religious literature, thereby perpetrating what to modern ears would be regarded as outrageous puns.

In the beginning Atum was alone in the Universe, but he contained all things in himself. Though spoken of as male, he was really bisexual. Indeed in the Coffin Texts he was called 'The Great He-She'. In order to bring all things into being, he had to create them out of himself. The way in which this was achieved was explained, as another account puts it, in terms of natural functions, either mating with his own hand or by expectorating. Thus in the Pyramid Text 600: 'You spat forth as Shu, you expectorated as Tefnut. You put your arms around them in the act of giving the Ka so that your Ka might be in them.' It is to be noted that the names of the two created beings are puns on the verbs meaning to spit and to expectorate. In one case the act leading to the creation belongs to a later age. In fact this second explanation was to lead to a surprisingly developed conception in the Memphite cosmogony, in which the mouth was thought of as the vehicle for the word. It should be noted that for the Egyptians of a later age all the explanations were seen not as alternatives but as complementary.

Atum's two children, Shu and Tefnut, were personifications of air and moisture. Shu, as the air, represented the light cavity in the midst of the primordial darkness and the upholder of the vault of the sky. His sister Tefnut was associated with damp, mist, dew and rain. One problem seems to have exercised the ancient Egyptian mind. Who was the oldest of the beings, Nun or Atum or even Shu and Tefnut? One conclusion was that Atum was always immanent in Nun and that Shu came into being at the same time as Atum. The result of this conclusion was the formation of a trinity: Atum, Shu and Tefnut.

From the mating of Shu and Tefnut were born Geb and Nut. In the beginning both were locked together in close embrace, but their father Shu separated them, lifting Nut above him to form the arch of heaven while Geb lay beneath to form the earth. Thus in many representations of the world Nut is seen with her body painted blue and encrusted with stars, bending over her brother. His body is usually painted green to represent vegetation. Sometimes the figure of Nut is replaced by that of a cow, who is normally associated with the goddess Hathor, and sometimes representations of other goddesses. Geb and Nut were, according to one account, the parents of Osiris, Horus, Set, Isis and Nephthys.

Two versions of the creation of the world according to the Heliopolitan theology are contained in a papyrus in the British Museum entitled *The Book of Knowing how Re^c came into Being and of overthrowing Apepi*. One of the versions is interesting in that it contains a reference to the creation of mankind. It is stated that mankind arose from the tears of the creator, but here it is to be noted that there is a play on the Egyptian word for 'man' and the root 'to weep'.

At some time between the third and fifth dynasties, when Memphis was the capital of Egypt, it seems that the need arose to effect a reconciliation between the cosmogony of Heliopolis, in which Atum was the creator, and that of Memphis, in which Ptah was the creator. An account of this reconciliation is preserved on a slab of black basalt, now in the British Museum. Made at the orders of Pharaoh Shabaka in the eighth century BC it is a copy of a much older monument. For many years it defied all attempts at translation, but by the turn of the nineteenth century its contents were recognized, and in 1928 the German Egyptologist Kurt Sethe (1869–1934), published an authoritative edition of the text with a translation, notes and an important introduction. He was able to show that the text was a libretto of a drama which was acted at certain festivals at Memphis. From the speeches of various deities and explanatory remarks here and there it has been possible to see what were the fundamental beliefs of the Memphite cosmogony. They reveal that in the Old Kingdom one priesthood came as near to promulgating a philosophical approach to the creation story as was ever achieved in Egypt.

As in the Hermopolitan and Heliopolitan cosmogonies there is an ancient abyss-god Nun, but unlike those cosmogonies the theologians of Memphis postulated

Gods and goddesses (from left to right): Osiris as a mummified man; Harpocrates (Horus the child) wearing the double crown of Egypt; Isis; Hathor, goddess of happiness, music and dancing; Khnum, god of the cataract; Khonsu, god of the moon; Serapis, bull-headed god with Hellenistic attributes; Hathor with head of a cow; Sobek crocodile-headed god; Sekhmet, lioness-headed goddess of Sudanese origin; Selket, the scorpion goddess; Khopri, the rising sun, symbolized by

that he was the product of the eternal mind Ptah, who manifested himself in many ways and under many aspects. The creation was thought of as a combination of conceiving through the heart (considered by the Egyptians to be the seat of intelligent thought) and creating through the tongue (the agent of the spoken word or command). The other gods were considered to be no more than the heart or tongue and the lips and teeth of Ptah.

No other similar body of religious teaching has come down from ancient Egypt. Even if none formerly existed, the Memphite inscription at least demonstrates that there were some who could depart from the concrete and naturalistic modes of thinking which are a common feature of the rest of the extant religious writings.

The sky-gods

It has been frequently observed in studies of religion that a form or forms of a sky-god can be found at the base of all the systems of the religion of Classical and West Asian civilizations, in the systems of the rest of Asia and in the semi-civilized religions of pre-Columbian America. It is a fact which suggests that the concept of the sky-god belongs to the most ancient period in the history of religion. In the records of ancient Egypt it is clear that not only were the phenomena of the sky observed and noted, but that the same phenomena were ascribed to a being living in the sky. The evidence, both extensive and incomplete, does not provide a clear picture, for the many variations are due not only to geographical and climatic conditions, but also to the careful preservation of a patchwork of ancient local beliefs mingled together as the result of political changes. It is therefore not surprising that the sky-god appears under many forms and with many different names.

A very ancient tradition is that in which the sky-god appears in the form of a falcon or hawk, bearing the name Hor. This Hor is not to be confused with Horus, the son of Osiris and Isis, though in later times he was so confused. An ancient name for this form of the sky-god was Hor-Wer, 'Horus the Great' or 'Horus the Aged'. The basic meaning of Hor is 'The Lofty One', a suitable name for a high flying bird of prey. The falcon manifestation of the sky-god was worshipped in many parts of Upper Egypt.

Celestial bodies, the sun, moon and stars

The sun and the moon became very early the subjects of religious worship. The sun, being the greater and more powerful, attained greater importance than the moon. The daily passage of the sun across the sky gave rise to a multiplicity of ideas about it. In one instance it was regarded as a newborn child issuing forth at dawn from the womb of Nut, or sometimes as a calf when the sky was thought of as a great celestial cow. At midday the sun soared triumphantly like a glittering falcon, or sailed serenely as if in a great boat upon the blue sea of heaven. In the evening it was an old man who went down in the west into the abode of the dead. In another account it was the great eye of the sky-god beaming down on the earth. In yet another it was, to use an earthy simile, a great celestial beetle rolling the fiery ball of the sun before it just as the scarab rolls its ball of dung along. Certain names were applied to the sun in the various stages of its progress across the sky. Thus under the name Khopri the sun came forth at dawn. Under the name Re^c it was the sun at noon. As Atum it was the sun setting at the end of the day.

Such names are also probable indicators of stages in the development of the religion of most ancient Egypt, when various deities were assimilated to lose their former independence. It is not impossible that Hor himself might have been a form of the sun-god as well as the sky-god, and this may be the reason why, when at the end of the fourth dynasty the theological school of Heliopolis came into prominence, it was not felt impossible for the pharaoh who bore the title of the sun-god Re^c to continue to bear the more ancient Horus title. To the very end of the history of ancient Egypt, worship of the sun-god Re^c in one form or another permeated the whole of religious thought and practice.

the scarabeus beetle; Re^c the sun-god: as Re^c, the sun at noon, and as Atum, the setting sun; Ptah, chief god of Memphis; Thoth, ibis-headed god of Hermopolis; Neith, ancient god of Sais in the Nile Delta; Amun-Re^c, supreme state god; Bes, the most popular and widely worshipped of the southern deities; Anubis, god associated with the cult of the dead.

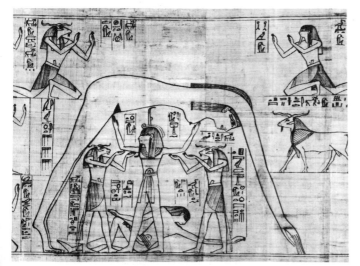

Nut, the Egyptian sky-goddess, supported by the air-god Shu. The sun was a child who entered the mouth of Nut in the evening, passed during the night through her body, and was born from her womb again in the morning.

Though the moon did not rival the sun in importance, it was worshipped widely under a number of forms and names, for it was believed that under its influence women conceived, cattle multiplied their young, the germ grew in the egg, and all throats were filled with fresh air. As the full moon, the moon was known as 'Khonsu the Strong Youth'. Among the explanations for the monthly waxing and waning of the moon's disc was one stating that it was one of the eyes of Horus damaged in a conflict with Set, the rival of Horus, and restored by the goddess Isis.

From very early times the ancient Egyptians had observed the stars, for the Pyramid Texts, embodying much earlier material, indicate that the Egyptians possessed at least an elementary knowledge of astronomy and had given names to the more prominent stars, dividing them into two great groups: *ihmw skw* (not knowing destruction), the circumpolar stars, and *ihmw wrd* (not knowing weariness), the southern stars.

The circumpolar stars towed the boat of the sun through the underworld during the night, paying constant homage to the god of heaven. They were also considered to be the ministers and followers of Osiris.

The patterns of the sky forming the constellations were seen by the ancient Egyptians as celestial manifestations of various figures in their mythology. Orion was known as *S3h* 'the fleetfooted, long striding god, who looks behind him' and as such was considered to be the celestial ferryman. The constellation of the Great Bear was identified with Set, and possessed various names, 'the Thigh (of the Bull)' and 'the Adze'. While it is not surprising that the great stars should have come to be regarded as divinities living in the sky, the innumerable host of nameless stars which surrounded the great stars were considered to be the dead, who had found their way to heaven to wander in eternal glory with the gods.

Special importance was attached to one of the fixed stars, *spdt*, 'Sirius, the Dog Star' called by the Greeks 'Sothis'. Identified with the goddess Hathor, it is often shown as a cow with a star between its horns, lying in a boat. Besides being an object of worship, observation of Sirius had important practical bearing on the regulation of the calendar. Very early it had been noted that, when the star rose helically on 19 or 20 July (Julian Calendar), the inundation of the Nile began. The importance of this observation for regulating the calendar in ancient times is only surpassed by its importance for modern scholars in fixing the main dates of Egyptian chronology.

Chthonic gods

Numerous as were the celestial-gods, the number of known chthonic deities was far greater. Even so they represented only a fraction of local deities, which in the course of time disappeared or are only represented by their names, sometimes singly, sometimes in compound titles, sometimes by fetishes or symbolic figures taken over by another god. The fortunes of the chthonic gods were largely determined by political factors, for the rise in power of a particular locality meant the ascent of the patron deity. Likewise the diminution in importance of a locality naturally affected the stature of its god.

Because of their numbers, it is only possible to comment on a few of the more important of the chthonic deities. One of the oldest and most popular of these, whose worship flourished right down to the Christian period in Egypt, was Min, the great god of Coptos and Akhmin. Min is the earliest attested god, for his symbolic artifact has been found in first dynasty inscriptions. The hieroglyphic form of his symbol ◄Оⵙⵙ▷ has been explained as representing two fossil belemnites, though the earliest examples of the sign resemble a double-headed arrow ⟵⟶. He was the tutelary god of nomads and hunters and his domain was the whole of the eastern desert. Three statues of Min from the first dynasty show him as a man standing upright, holding a whip in his right hand and a phallus in his left. The antiquity of these statues, originally painted black, is shown by the fact that the legs of each are not separate but close together. Later Min appears in the same archaic form, but as an ithyphallic man, indicating that he was considered as being a god of procreation and fertility. In his special character as a god of virility and generation, the cult of Min was widespread. Several 'comings forth of Min' were celebrated throughout the land, the most important festivals taking place at the beginning of harvest. In procession his statue was carried on poles by his priests, all of whom were wrapped in a large canopy, allowing only their heads and feet to be seen. Groups of priests carried bundles of plants sacred to Min, a white bull was led in the procession, accompanied by the images of kings and ensigns of gods, carried on staffs. There is little doubt that among the lower classes the festivals of Min were made the occasions of orgies and debauchery, and it is possible that his festivals were more popular than those of another widely worshipped deity, Osiris.

Ptah, the god of Memphis, is a very ancient deity, for representation of him in the same archaic mode as Min is attested to the reign of the fifth king of the first dynasty. It is probable that like Min he was originally a fertility god, for the *menat* amulet which hangs from the back of his neck has been thought to be a fertility symbol. It is not impossible that his name may share the same origin as the Semitic root *pth* 'to open' and that it may imply, like Hebrew, the notion 'to open the womb' (i.e. to cause to give birth to). Later, when the influence of Memphis declined, Ptah was associated with other deities, especially those concerned with the dead. Thus he appears as Ptah-Seker, Seker being the ancient god of the dead at Memphis and Sakkara. Sometimes he is named Ptah-Asar or Ptah-Osiris, sometimes in a triune form, Ptah-Seker-Asar, Ptah-Seker-Tem or Ptah-Seker and the Setting Sun. Tem (or Atum) the last element in the triune name was the ancient god of Heliopolis. Since he always appears in human form as a man walking naturally and not in the archaic form of Min and Ptah, and, though he is attested to the Old Kingdom, it is possible that he was a creation of the priesthood of Heliopolis and not strictly a local god at all.

Thoth the ibis-headed god of Hermopolis, as has been observed, was associated with the creation account of that city. But he was also associated with the moon. In the person of Thoth the moon possessed such titles as 'Ruler of the Years', 'Computer of the Time of Life', 'Ruler of the Living Stars'. It is not difficult to see how Thoth came to be associated with reckoning and thus to be regarded as the scribe of the gods. Further he was regarded as the judge in heaven who gave speech and writing, the god of all wisdom and learning and the one who discovered the 'divine words'. Originating as a purely local deity, Thoth by a process of assimilation assumed new qualities and aspects until he became a deity universally recognized throughout Egypt.

The Lower Egyptian goddess Neith who had her original centre of worship at Sais, the capital of the fourth and fifth nomes in the western Delta, was a very ancient deity. In dynastic times her symbolic artifact was two arrows crossed over a shield, but the oldest form of this is represented in the Pyramid Texts by a sign which is thought by some scholars to be a shuttle. If this is so then there may be some connection with the verb *ntt* to weave, suggesting that she may have woven spells as well as flax and as such would have been a goddess of magic. Since Neith was also associated with the goddesses Hathor and Isis, she is often manifested in the form of a cow. After the union of the two kingdoms of Upper and Lower Egypt she became an object of popular worship in Upper Egypt. Finally in the seventh century BC in the time of Pharaoh Psammetichus I, who originated from Sais, Neith was exalted to the rank of a state deity.

State gods

A similar rise in rank is also to be seen in the history of two local gods from Upper Egypt. During the eleventh dynasty, when Thebes began its rise to power, Montu, a falcon-headed deity originally a local god at neighbouring Armant, was adopted by the kings of that dynasty as the paramount god of Thebes. Later, while the dynasty lasted, Montu was further exalted to become the state god of Egypt. However Montu's ascendancy was short-lived, for with a change of dynasty he was supplanted by another deity, who had no more been the original local god of Thebes than he had. The newcomer was Amun, who was destined to rise from being the chief local god of Thebes to becoming the greatest of the state gods of ancient Egypt. As a local god, Amun's history can be traced back to the time of one of the early kings of the eleventh dynasty, but in fact he really originated from Hermopolis, where he and his female counterpart were numbered among the eight genii of Hermopolitan cosmogony. Though intended by the pharaohs of the twelfth dynasty that he should become the supreme state god of Egypt, Amun's rise to this position was interrupted by the termination of the dynasty and a period of anarchy in Egypt, during which the country was divided, the northern part being ruled by a line of foreign kings. The real ascendancy of Amun only began with the complete victory of the pharaohs of the eighteenth dynasty over the foreign rulers, and a succession of conquests by Egyptian arms in Palestine and Syria. To obviate any rivalry between Amun and the long established sun-god Re^c, both deities were assimilated to form a composite unity Amun-Re^c. As such this new state god was worshipped as the king of the gods. In his name and with his help, the pharaohs of the eighteenth dynasty founded the New Kingdom and waged their campaigns in Palestine and Syria and in northern Sudan. Out of the tribute won in these wars the pharaohs raised great temples in his honour, especially at Luxor and Karnak.

Funerary gods

Anubis, who became associated with the funerary cult and was represented either as a wild black dog or as a man with a wild dog's head, was honoured in many places. Before the rise to prominence of Osiris, the other great god of the dead, Anubis was considered as the chief deity to whom mortuary prayers were to be made. His principal centre of worship was at the city which the Greeks appropriately called Cynopolis (Dog City). Dogs were also the manifestations of other local deities. Thus at Abydos the original god was Khenti-Amentiu 'Foremost of the Westerners', whose manifestation was a recumbent dog. Later this deity was destined to be merged with Osiris. Another dog-manifested god was Wepwawet 'the Opener of the Ways' who, though later associated with the worship of Osiris at Abydos, originated from the city of Siut, where he had supplanted an earlier deity, Sed. From prehistoric times onwards the standard of Wepwawet was always carried before the king into battle and afterwards during victory celebrations.

Animal manifestations

Manifestations of the gods in the form of animals, birds,

reptiles and, in one case, the scorpion were common throughout the long history of Egypt. The type of creature intended is in most cases easy to identify because the Egyptian artists were both good observers and accurate recorders in their drawing and colouring. Both domesticated and wild animals appear in their work and, in the case of one breed of sheep which died out in the Middle Kingdom, their representations provide the only evidence for the actual appearance of this long-lost breed. But one animal manifestation of a deity remains and will probably remain a mystery as to what it is supposed to represent. This is the so-called 'Set animal'. Many suggestions have been made as to what animal was intended, including the donkey, the okapi, the camel, the jerboa, the pig and the wart-hog. It is possible that the original was a now extinct hunting dog like the saluki. By the Old Kingdom the creature, if it ever existed, had been transformed into an almost fabulous form combining the appearance of a recumbent dog with an upright tail, a long neck, squared ears and a long curved muzzle.

In later times Set appears as the rival of Horus and as the god of evil. His centre of worship was at Enboyet (the Greek Ombos) in Upper Egypt, a very important place in the period just prior to the first dynasty. After the founding of the dynasty the worship of Set spread beyond his locality, and he was recognized by some as 'the Lord of Upper Egypt'. As such he became a dangerous rival to Horus and it was this rivalry that shaped the conception of the nature of Set and his subsequent destiny. It has been thought that Set was one of the original gods of the aboriginal people of the Nile valley, conquered by a later people, who were worshippers of Horus. A revival of the struggle between the two cultures may have taken place during the second dynasty, when the Set faction seems to have triumphed for a short time. It is possible this ancient political struggle was the reason for the later introduction of Set into the myths of Osiris and Horus as their enemy and rival.

Local gods

Not all the local gods rose to importance. By far the majority of them remained almost unknown outside their own localities. One reason for this is that both the deity and his or her worshippers were closely related or even bound to the land by their occupation. While the authority of the deity might have extended over all his worshippers, it did not necessarily extend beyond the recognized limits of the territory of his worshippers. Political events might bring about change, the authority of the god might be enlarged, but by and large the underlying conception that men were bound to the land they inhabited meant that they continued to be under the authority of the deity whom they believed to be the god of the locality. When a man left his district he left his god. He had no right to expect the favour of some other god into whose territory he might have ventured.

One possible solution to the problem was to carry some measure of the authority and protection of the god with him. This could be achieved by carrying on his person a replica of the god or an amulet which could be associated with the god. One of the features of ancient Egypt is the vast quantity of amulets and protective charms of all kinds, made in a wide variety of materials, ranging from gold down to poor pottery. Likewise the number of different deities invoked is as astonishing to modern minds as it was to the men of the Classical World, who were no monotheists when they first came into contact with Egypt.

Foreign gods

Numerous as were the native gods of the land, during the course of history the Egyptians admitted a number of foreign deities. In the earliest times these would have been very few so far as northern contacts with the outside world were concerned. But in the south there had been contacts with Nubia at least as early as the first dynasty. It is not surprising that a number of Nubian or Sudanese gods were brought into Egypt and worshipped. It is possible that more of those deities which are generally regarded as being indigenous to Egypt originally came from the south, but have been so Egyptianized over the years as to conceal their real identity. Thus it is probable that a number of deities manifested as lionesses, such as Sekhmet, Menhèyet and Tefnut, may have had their origins in Nubia and northern Sudan.

The most popular and widely worshipped of the southern deities was Bes, who is mentioned in the Pyramid Texts. He is usually depicted as a dwarf with a large bearded face, shaggy eyebrows and long hair, large projecting ears, a flat nose and protruding tongue. His arms are long and thick, his legs bowed and he wears a tail. Sometimes he appears naked; at other times he wears about his body an animal skin and on his head a crown of high plumes. Unlike the other Egyptian gods, who in two-dimensional pictures are always shown in profile, Bes appears full face, a form of representation which is otherwise only found in pictures of the foreign goddess, Qedesh. Bes was a dancer and a musician playing a stringed instrument. He was probably also a singer. Sometimes he is seen in military guise wearing a short belted tunic, and carrying a sword in one hand and a shield in the other. Being connected with mirth and laughter Bes was also regarded as a guard against evil spirits, a slayer of snakes and other noxious creatures. It seems, too, that he was a patron deity of children, for he is found in association with the hippopotamus goddess, Tawert, who traditionally helped mothers in childbirth.

As a result of the Egyptian conquests in Palestine and Syria during the New Kingdom considerable numbers of foreign craftsmen, servants and slaves were brought into the Nile valley. Such foreigners introduced their own gods, some of which enjoyed widespread popularity as long as Egypt's hold over Palestine and Syria continued.

Among the most important gods of Palestine and

Alabaster head, probably of Queen Tiy, principal queen of Nebmare Amenhotep III (c1375 BC). This head, and three others, served as the stoppers for four Canopic Jars.

Syria, accepted by the Egyptians, was Ershop (Reshpu), a god of lightning, fire and pestilence, who followed in the train of war. It seems that the martial pharaohs of the New Kingdom saw in him and other deities like him a god of war. Further, since there was an ancient tradition that after the rivalry between Horus and Set the whole of the ,Black Land (Egypt) was given to Horus and the whole of the Red Land (foreign lands) was given to Set, it followed that Ershop could be taken into the Egyptian pantheon.

Sharing the war-like properties of Ershop were two foreign goddesses, who attained popularity in the New Kingdom. Anat was represented as wearing the crown of Upper Egypt, often with plumes, armed with spear and shield and carrying a mace. In a number of instances she is shown seated on horseback. Astharte, widely worshipped throughout the ancient West Asia, also appears armed like Anat, and riding on horseback. At a later period she appears as a lioness–headed deity, with a disc on her head, holding a whip (?) in her right hand, and driving a four-horse chariot over prostrate foes.

Qedesh, on the other hand, a Syro-Pheonician goddess, was the personification of love and beauty, and as such was identified with Isis and Hathor. She is represented as a naked woman, standing full face on a lion, holding a bunch of flowers in one hand and a snake in the other. It seems that she was thought of as the mistress of the gods.

Osiris and the cult of the dead

One deity which may have had a foreign origin in very remote times, but became so Egyptianized as to appear a truly native god, was Osiris, who was both a nature deity and a god of the dead.

Two annual events in the Nile valley profoundly influenced the Ancient Egyptian's conceptions about Osiris. The annual inundation and the yearly growth and decline of vegetation not only emphasized to an agricultural people the contrasting facts of life and death, but by their annual regularity suggested the existence of a controlling force behind these events, which out of death could bring life. However, certain traditions about Osiris, most fully stated by the Greek writer Plutarch and supported by numerous, though less explicit references in Egyptian religious writings, have led some scholars to see in Osiris a human king who in the remote past once reigned over Egypt from his capital in the eastern Delta. His traditional death at the hands of his brother Set has been interpreted as his death during a rebellion led by the city of Ombos, the seat of Set worship. The consequence of the death of Osiris was the division of Egypt into two kingdoms, though these were later re-united by a victorious campaign led by Horus, the son of Osiris. The dead Osiris was then deified, and a personal creed attached to his life and death. Under this creed Osiris, risen from the dead, was assigned to rule

Persepolis, the great Persian ceremonial city founded by Darius I (522–486 BC). This is the gateway of his son, Xerxes I (486–465 BC).

over the world of the dead. A further extension of this creed was to see in the resurrection of Osiris and the defeat of Set the eventual triumph of good and justice over evil.

Though it is not possible to state exactly where the Osiris myth took its origin, the Egyptian texts claim that he came from Djedu, the capital of the ninth nome of Lower Egypt. The lord of Djedu is his title. Later the name of the city was changed to Per-Asar, from which derives the Greek, Busiris. It is clear, however, that the original god of Djedu was Andjeti, who is represented in human form as a ruler with a crooked sceptre in one hand and a whip in the other, wearing two feathers on his head. This local deity was very early absorbed by Osiris and his name became an epithet of Osiris. The difference between Andjeti and Osiris is that the former represents a living king, while the latter is always shown as a dead man wrapped in white and holding in his hands the royal insignia.

Very early in the historic period of Egypt, the cult of Osiris was transferred to Abydos in Upper Egypt, where the kings of the first and second dynasties had their royal cemeteries. During the fourth dynasty Osiris became identified with and eventually superseded the local deity Khenti-Amenti, the god of the dead and cemeteries. The tomb of one of the first dynasty kings was traditionally associated with the burial place of his head and quickly became the focal point of pilgrimage. Worshippers of Osiris sought to be buried near his tomb, or, if this was not possible, arranged to have their embalmed bodies conveyed to Abydos to rest there for a period before burial in their home district. A third means by which the favour of the god could be obtained was by visiting his tomb in lifetime and leaving some inscribed votive offering there. The worship of Osiris was widespread in Egypt and especially so since his cult introduced in religion an element which was lacking in the cults of the other gods. This element was the belief that men could as individuals become identified with Osiris and enter into an afterlife which was open to all. However, entry into the other world was conditional on proof of proper observance of morality. It should be noted that what would be regarded in modern times as morality was not the same as that understood by the vast majority of the Egyptians. For them there was no clear-cut distinction between intellectual and moral qualities, such as good behaviour and virtue, respect for the outward practices of religion and genuine piety, or unquestioning obedience to the king and submission to the divine will. The idea of a divine judgment awaiting the deceased had already appeared in the Old Kingdom, but it is most strikingly presented in the New Kingdom in scenes reproduced in many papyri of the Book of the Dead. In these pictorial representations the judge seated on a throne is Osiris, generally attended by the goddesses Isis and Nephthys. The dead person is led in by Anubis and his heart is placed in a balance to be weighed against the feather of Ma'at. Thoth, the divine scribe, stands at one side to record the result of the weighing. Near the balance lurks the fearful Devourer of the Dead, awaiting the outcome of the weighing and poised to fall upon the deceased if judgment should go against him.

During the Classical Period the mysteries of Osiris were transplanted to other Mediterranean lands, but it was the cult of his wife Isis which gained the greatest following outside Egypt, especially in the first years of the Roman empire. No doubt her cult underwent many changes, but in essence it was an Egyptian–inspired worship and the only Egyptian cult to gain widespread allegiance outside the Nile valley.

It is to be recognized that the cults of the many deities of Egypt did not transplant successfully to other countries and other people. They were essentially gods of the Nile valley, conceived and born there, and so deeply rooted there that outside of Egypt they withered and died.

Deified men

Deification of mortal men as objects of worship occurred in Ancient Egypt, but the number of such created deities was small in comparison with the host of other gods. A few pharaohs–such as Snefru of the Old Kingdom, Sesostris III and Amenemhet III of the Middle Kingdom, and Amenhotpe I and his mother Ahmes-Nefertari of the New Kingdom–were worshipped in various localities. Others who were deified, but long after their deaths, were Imhotep, the architect of the step pyramid complex at Sakkarah, and Amenhotep, son of Hapu, who had been the architect of Pharaoh Amenhotep III. In later times both deified persons became gods of healing. Such deified men, rather than the great state gods, were the objects of worship of the common people, who rarely ventured, even when allowed, into the temples. The temples were not places to which men resorted to make individual prayers, rather they existed to serve the gods, providing them with daily sustenance and necessities in return for which the gods would maintain world order. While daily offerings of food and clothing were made to them, the one essential offering was that of the presentation of the emblem of Ma'at, who personified the balance or equilibrium of the creation. Depicted as a goddess wearing an ostrich feather, by her association with equal balance she also came to personify order, justice, and eventually truth. In theory her offering had to be made by the pharaoh but, as the number of temples made this impossible, what was regarded as the special duty of the pharaoh was carried out by his deputies, the high priests.

The pharaoh, the child of the gods

That the pharaoh was looked on as the highest person to make the offerings was due to the belief that, unlike the deified men mentioned above, he was deified at birth–being of divine generation, the actual child of the supreme god. In the Old Kingdom he was regarded as the son of Re^c. In the New Kingdom, when the great state god Amun was in the ascendant, he was thought to be issue of Amun himself. Reliefs on the walls of the temples

Deir el Baheri and Luxor show how the birth of the pharaoh is the birth of a god. Amun assumes the form of the reigning pharaoh and unites with the queen mother to achieve the miraculous birth. A divine origin meant that the pharaoh stood in much closer relation to the gods and as such could more effectively represent the world of men. Further, the harmony of the world depended on the pharaoh's health. To assure his continued vitality each ruler celebrated, usually at the end of 30 years' reign, the festival of the jubilee (the *heb-sed*) in which his vital force was renewed. Often referred to as the good god during his lifetime, at death he was raised to the sky, united with the solar disc and his body absorbed by his creator. The earthly remains of the man-god were then interred in a sumptuous tomb. It can be stated that the mass of funerary beliefs which owe their origins to royal burials were based for their theological justification on the divine nature of the former kings. Though other factors entered into the eventual demise of the Ancient Egyptian religion, there is little doubt that the end of the line of resident pharaohs in Egypt contributed significantly to the end of the old faith and its increasing replacement by Christianity during the third century AD.

Akhenaten and Aton worship

During the long history of Egyptian religion only once did a break with the old traditions occur. This was the short episode called the 'Amarna Period', especially associated with Pharaoh Akhenaten, who withdrew himself from the centre of the state worship of Amun-Re^c at Thebes and established a new capital for himself at Tell el-Amarna in Middle Egypt. Here he promulgated the worship of Aton, the sun disc, at the same time proscribing the worship of Amun-Re^c. Opinions about Akhenaten have ranged between the one extreme of seeing him as a great religious reformer, some crediting him with being the first monotheist, and the other extreme of concluding that he was an eccentric materialist, most dangerous because, as pharaoh, his power was absolute. His religious beliefs were not entirely original, for Aton had long been regarded as the visible and positive experience of the sun-god. Further, certain elements had begun to be added during the reign of his father, Amenhotep III, when foreign influences from Syria and Mitanni penetrated Egypt. The short ascendancy of Atonism was entirely due to Akhenaten himself. His break with tradition affected not only religion but also artistic styles long associated with religion. Liberalism in this field produced some splendid naturalistic art, but it often reflected its inspirer in producing works which are disturbing if not repulsive. However Akhenaten's religious innovations are viewed, as a ruler he was a disaster, most of Palestine and Syria being lost. After his death his capital city was deserted and his successor, the youthful Tutankhamun, returned to Thebes to the allegiance of Amun-Re^c. Among later generations Akhenaten, alone of all the pharaohs, was remembered with opprobrium as 'the Great Criminal' and 'The Conquered One of Amarna'.

West Asia

Statue of Ashurnasirpal II (AD 884–859) from Nimrud, bearing an inscription with his name, title and victorious campaigns. It is one of the few known examples of Assyrian statuary.

Sumer

Thorkild Jacobsen

Country and settlement

Sumer, pronounced 'Shoomer', is the ancient name for a region, in southern Iraq (Mesopotamia) corresponding essentially to the modern administrative *liwas* of Diwaniyah and Nāsiriyah.

The region is part of the alluvial plain laid down by the Euphrates and the Tigris but, as these rivers have changed their course considerably since antiquity, the results of archaeological ground survey need to be combined with a study of the data provided by ancient texts before the ancient topographical setting can be uncovered.

The climate of the region is semi-arid with insufficient rainfall for sustaining a crop of cereals, or an orchard or garden. Artificial irrigation by canals was therefore essential from the first, and gradually small local efforts at canalization grew to a large interdependent system needing constant supervision, dredging and repair of breaches in the dikes to keep it functioning.

The earliest settlements in Sumer proper lie along the edge of the marshes and date from approximately 4500 BC (this and all following dates given are highly tentative). It is possible that still earlier settlements once existed further to the south when the sea level was lower than it is now. As the level rose in the Persian Gulf due to the melting of the snows of the Ice Age, these early settlers would have been forced slowly northward with the coastline.

Who they were, and where they came from, are questions that cannot be answered with any certainty.

Ancient Mesopotamia.

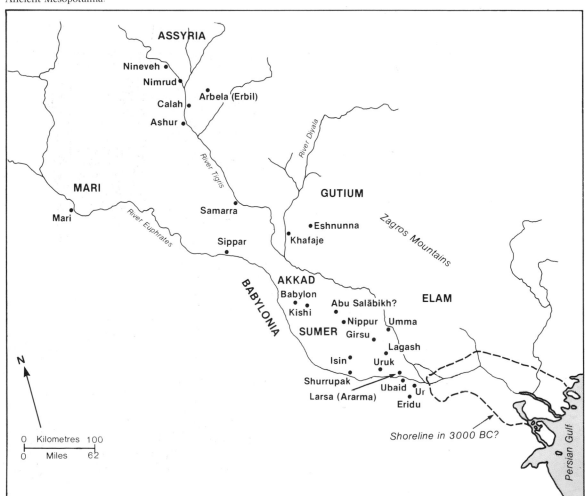

Most likely they were simply ancestors of the people who inhabited the region in historical times, the Sumerians. The distinctive pottery that they used has connections with Iran to the east, but has also been found on the Arabian side of the Persian Gulf. It eventually spread north into what is now northern Iraq and Syria, yet that may well represent a spread of a style in pottery-making only, rather than a movement of populations.

The material culture characteristic of the early settlements is called Ubaidian from the site where it was first found. It has three subperiods: Ubaid I, also called the Eridu period, Ubaid II, also called the Haji Mohammed period, and Ubaid III or Late Ubaid. Their main difference is in the style and colouring of the painted pottery.

The characteristic settlement form of the Ubaid people was the small village. Probably there were also camp-sites of nomadic and semi-nomadic groups. The villages had huts built with mats and clay, houses of sun-dried bricks. The economies that sustained these settlements were fishing, attested by fishbones, net sinkers and clay models of boats; and hoe agriculture, indicated by flint hoe blades, baked-clay sickles, and impressions of kernels of wheat and six-row barley. Plentiful finds of date pits confirm date cultivation, and clay models of sheep and oxen attest to herding. Presumably there were also seasonal hunting and fowling in the marshes.

While villages and campsites were the typical settlement forms of the Ubaid period, they were not the only ones. Here and there, isolated settlements of town or city-like character are found, such as Eridu (about 29

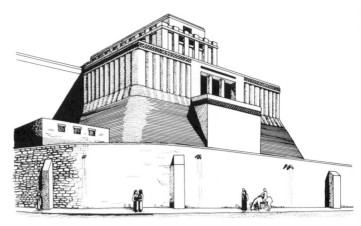

The temple at Eridu: an impression of the stately structure as it was rebuilt in the Proto-literate period. Such shrines formed the nuclei of Sumerian cities.

acres; 12 ha), Ur (about 25 acres; 10 ha) and Uruk (about 173 acres; 70 ha). They stand apart not only by the area they cover and the close massing of people it suggests, but by the truly amazing monumentality of

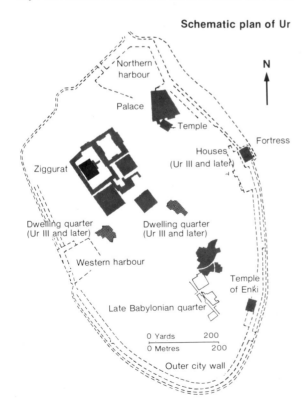

Schematic plan of Ur

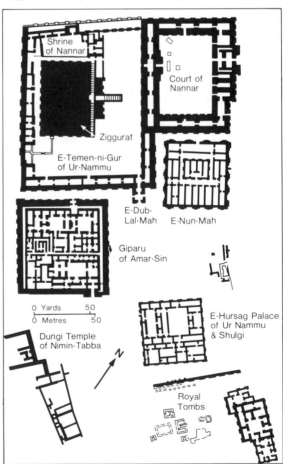

The great lintel from the temple of Nin-khursag at Al ʿUbaid. It represents Imdugud, the benevolent lion-headed eagle of Sumerian mythology, protecting two stags (c2500 BC).

their public buildings and temples. One example is the temple in Eridu, which grew from a small one-room hovel at the beginning of the period to a stately structure measuring 25 × 14 yd (23.5 × 13.5 m) and standing on a 28 × 17 yd (26.5 × 16 m) terrace. The factors that made such striking growth of a settlement possible, and continued to sustain it, are probably intimately connected with the function and prestige of its sanctuary.

Nomadic tribes usually have a stationary storehouse in which the tribe's valuables, especially its sacred objects of worship but also its surplus stores, are kept since it is inconvenient to carry them along on the tribe's wanderings. Such a storehouse, because of its sacred objects, becomes a religious centre at which people gather from afar for religious festivals and–as usual on such occasions–for barter and exchange of goods. Such a role, that of religious centres into which flowed votive offerings from a large region as well as profits from markets held there, could well explain how these larger settlements arose and flourished. Lagash meant 'treasury' in Sumerian, *Urim*, the full form of Ur, denoted 'doorpost', the emblem of a treasury since it held up the mat with which the door opening could be sealed. The fact that so many of the earliest cities had names with good Sumerian etymologies is one more reason to assume that there was continuity of population through to historical times.

The Ubaid period was followed by the Warka period (also called Uruk, levels XIV–IX), which saw the introduction of a new type of pottery–greyware–but otherwise differed little from the preceding Ubaid period. One significant technical achievement must be mentioned, the introduction of the potter's wheel. The Warka greyware was wheelmade.

Beginnings of civilization: Proto-literate

The Proto-literate period (that is Uruk, archaic levels VIII–IV and III = Jemdet Naṣr) following the Warka period was characterized by a burst of creativity and growth unmatched by any other period in Mesopotamian history.

The beginning of the period saw a massive settling of the northern regions of Sumer around Abu Ṣalābikh and Nippur, which had been almost empty before. Since these regions were dependent in the main on grain agriculture, it may be assumed that they introduced the animal-drawn plough, attested in the script of this period. It made it possible to cultivate far larger areas than could be done with the hoe alone. It is also significant that in Nippur (the only pre-Uruk settlement in the region) Enlil, god of the older, sacred parts of the site, was god of the hoe; while his son Ninurta, god of the city area itself, was god of the plough.

The general pattern of settlement in the Early Uruk period was, as in the Ubaid period, one of relatively dispersed small villages with occasional larger settlements. In Middle and Late Uruk, however, significant changes seem to have occured. In the south, around Ur and Eridu, the smaller settlements of the Ubaid period were apparently abandoned. Further north, in the Abu Ṣalābikh-Nippur area, the main course of the ancient Euphrates similarly shows only large settlements with no villages between them. In late Uruk this pattern whereby only larger settlements persisted also came to predominate in the Euphrates branch from Abu Ṣalābikh down towards Adab – forming roughly the northeast border of Sumer. As the smaller villages disappeared from the western and northern edges of Sumer, the heartland around Uruk seemed to crowd up on them – until the following Early Dynastic period, when they disappeared there too. The explanation for these developments seems clear. A growing threat of raids and attacks, against which a small village was helpless, forced the villagers into the larger settlements for protection, or made them move to less exposed regions in the heartland of Sumer. Apparently the raiding began along the borders–conceivably nomads from the surrounding desert areas found tempting loot in the settled areas–eventually forcing almost all of the population into the now greatly expanded cities. It is estimated, for instance, that Uruk grew from about 173 acres (70 ha) at the beginning of the period to some 248 acres (100 ha) at its end. Very likely the threat to life and property posed by pillaging nomadic bands was significantly aggravated by a foreshadowing of the wars between the city states that were to characterize the following Early Dynastic period.

In spite of such harassment as the settlement patterns bear witness to, the achievements of the period were remarkable. Perhaps 'in spite of' is not quite appropriate, since great cultural innovations do not as a rule come from villages but arise in the more complex environment of town or city. The massing of the population in larger cities–even if forced–may thus have contributed to the innovative climate of the period.

In architecture the tradition of monumental temples continued. Now the temples could be decorated with huge pillars into which were set clay nails with differently coloured heads to form geometric designs. Inside, the walls seem in many cases to have been decorated with murals. Although only fragments have survived, we can fortunately form a fair idea of what they were like because the seal-cutters of the time, working with cylinder seals which replaced the earlier stamp seals, appear to have taken them as models and reproduced them faithfully in miniature. The designs fall into two groups: scenes from the cult, such as adoration of divine symbols or the cult-drama of the Sacred Marriage; and scenes of a war-like nature, such as the wholesale killing of unarmed captives after a victory, known later as *karāshum*. While these latter motifs, like the cult motifs, may well have been copied from the walls of temples, it is perhaps as likely that they originally decorated the wall of the *ĝiparu*, the abode of the priest king leader of the community, the *en*, whose religious and civil duties more and more came to include leadership in war.

In addition to glyptic, the period pioneered in relief carving and sculpture in the round. An example of the

former is the famous Uruk vase depicting the yearly rite of the Sacred Marriage between the goddess Inanna and her consort Ama-Ushumgal-anna. The high point of sculpture in the round is exemplified by a woman's face carved in alabaster and of supreme beauty. It is generally thought to represent Inanna.

Great as were the achievements of the Proto-literate period in architecture and art, even more so was the invention, or rather gradual development, of writing, attested here for the first time. By means of writing, man is able to overcome time, space and complexity. Written documents hand down the knowledge of earlier ages, building a rich and substantial intellectual heritage far beyond what oral tradition can do. Letters overcome distance in space and allow central control of far-flung dependencies; and writing serves to organize and retain myriads of detailed facts, for example, in accounting, essential to effective administration of a large temple or other estate.

So far as we can see, accounting was the main purpose for which writing was developed. As represented in the earliest inscriptions it was a picture script, the signs of which were incised or impressed on tablets of wet clay which were then dried. The writing had a highly developed system of numerical denotations, so it seems likely that numbers and pictures were what it began with: dents made in a lump of clay, one for each object or animal counted, and a simplified drawing of what was counted next to them.

Writing in the Proto-literate period was as yet little more than a mnemonic device. Its two major genres were lists of signs, helping the scribe recall what he had memorized; and accounts, which gave him new information, but within a fixed scheme so that he knew what to expect. The original pictorial character of the signs was in many cases lost by the time of our earliest documents. In time successive generations of scribes abbreviated and stylized the signs more and more until at last they were entirely abstract collocations of wedge-shaped impressions.

By the end of the Proto-literate period the inherent limitations of a pure picture writing had already been mitigated by the development of purely phonetic values for some signs. This was a great help in identifying the intended reading of a pictorial word sign or ideogram, which in itself might be capable of a great many different renderings.

The writing was early borrowed by the neighbours of the Sumerians, the Akkadians, and adjusted to fit their very different Semitic language. Early Akkadian orthography suggests that it was borrowed in the form it had assumed in the final stage of Proto-literate.

Two signs occurring in the early writing can claim particular interest: the one for *en*, 'lord', 'priest king' or more precisely 'charismatic productive manager and

The earliest written Mesopotamian documents (third millennium BC), found in the great Sumerian city of Uruk. Documented history began in Early Dynastic III.

leader', and the one for *unkin*, 'folkmoot' or 'general assembly'. These are key terms in the political pattern in the Sumerian myths, which probably took form very early. Highest authority under this pattern was vested in a folkmoot or general assembly, which met when a major crisis threatened, to elect a war leader (*lugal*), or a peace leader (*en*), or to sit in judgment on crimes. The pattern seems to be in origin a local one, suited to a village community or a small tribe, and it has numerous close parallels in tribal and village government all over the world. In the Proto-literate period of Mesopotamia, however, it seems to have been extended to serve larger settlements and their dependent areas. The most significant such extension, the Nippur League, went even further: it was an alliance of all the major cities in Sumer, which met in assembly at Nippur for consultation and concerted action. Expenses of the league were met by the members jointly, and we have seals from the period immediately following Early Dynastic I with seal impressions of groups of such cities jointly guaranteeing that the sealed goods were intact.

That an alliance such as this could only have been formed under pressure of a very serious, patent, and all-embracing danger stands to reason. Offhand the evidence of growing hostile pressure all along the western and northern borders of Sumer, of which we have spoken above, would seem to fit the case. Who exerted the pressure is of course a moot question, but the fact that the western and northern borders were involved clearly suggests desert nomads: later Mesopotamian history offers plentiful parallels for this. Going a step further, these nomads can be identified with the Akkadians, or Proto-Akkadians, for we know that early in the following Early Dynastic period the areas north of Sumer, the Diyala region, and the part of the alluvium from Abu-Ṣalābikh northward, had been taken over by Akkadian-speaking invaders, leaving only city names, temple names and names of city gods in the original Sumerian (for example, *Išnunak* 'Hill of the prince' and the temple *É-sikil*, 'pure house', for *Nin-a-sú*, 'the water sprinkler', a rain god).

Transition to history: Early Dynastic

The Early Dynastic period, which followed Proto-literate, has three subperiods: Early Dynastic I, II, III. Only in the last of these had writing progressed sufficiently for anything like historical records to be kept. The preceding Early Dynastic II was a twilight zone of epic and heroic tales, Sumer's 'heroic age'. Early Dynastic I still lies fully in prehistory, but stands apart from the preceding Proto-literate by distinctive changes in the style of architecture and art, such as the introduction of the plano-convex brick and the defensive 'ovals'.

Early Dynastic I (2750 to 2650 BC)

The disappearing of villages and corresponding growth of the larger settlements in Early Dynastic I affected even the heartland of Sumer around Uruk, which had been a last resort for village settlement. It is possible, of course, that this was a final and decisive stage in the outside pressure, but it seems more probable to assume that the formation of the Kingir League succeeded in stemming that pressure, and that the lack of internal security to which the disappearing of the villages bears witness was due to inner Sumerian rivalries, a war of all against all, which accounts for the appearance of the massive city walls that ring all large cities of this period.

The motivation for these internecine wars was probably complex and varied: competition for a fertile border territory between neighbouring city states, lust for booty and domination in an ambitious war lord, or a growing desire for internal peace and security, distant goals which only a vigorously maintained hegemony could hope to attain. The memories of the hegemony achieved by Kishi in Early Dynastic I, and maintained over a remarkably long period, would have served as an ideal and a spur.

Heroic Age: Early Dynastic II (2650 to 2550 BC)

The early traditions contained in the Sumerian king list began with the first dynasty of Kishi, and the earliest ruler of that dynasty of whom it can safely be said that original inscriptions clearly establish his historicity was En-men-barage-si; or since *en* is a title, Men-barage-si (2630–2600 BC). Two fragments of votive bowls are known that designated him as king of Kishi. Tradition credits him with the disarmament of Elam to the east. He is said to have carried its weapons away, perhaps to pacify it, perhaps merely to prevent it from raiding Sumer.

Other traditions tell that he was vanquished by Gilgamesh of Uruk who 'led out his arms against Kishi, captured the bodies of its seven heroes, and stamped on Lord Men-barage-si's head as on a snake's'. Older tradition, the epic tale of *Gilgamesh and Agga*, has it that it was Men-barage-si's son Agga, not himself, whom Gilgamesh vanquished, and this version has the support of the Sumerian king list which ends the first dynasty of Kishi with Agga, and has its kingship passed to Uruk. As far as can be gathered from hints in the tale, Gilgamesh had earlier been hospitably received by Agga in Kishi when he sought refuge there as a fugitive, and it was probably Agga who installed him in Uruk, only to have him eventually rebel.

The epic tales of the heroes of the period depict political forms that differ in several respects from those of the earlier world of the myths. Notable is the effect of extreme and persistent war-like conditions, such as were testified to by the disappearance of small open villages and the growth of larger, massively walled cities. The war leader or 'king' (*lugal*), who in the myths was chosen for the term of an emergency only, became a permanent office with the lasting state of war emergency. Basis for the king's power was a large retinue of unfree retainers, in part recruited from captives whose life the king had spared. The king thus owned them body and soul, and it is significant that Sumerian had no other term for owner, whether of slaves or goods, than *lugal*. Apparently the very concept of ownership, which implies the right to destroy, only arose within that relationship.

The king's retainers ate with him in his palace (é-gal) and were given fiefs to support them. They served the king as soldiers in war and as workers on public projects in peace.

The king guarded his newly won permanence jealously, sought his authority more and more in divine choice rather than in choice by a human assembly; dynasties began to appear and the king broadened his concerns from leadership in war to leadership in peace. His forces were used in peacetime, not only for building and maintaining the city walls, but also for digging and cleaning major irrigation canals and the building of temples. He also sought a broad basis of support by making his power available to the underprivileged in society, seeing to it that they were not deprived of their rights. Specifically he would ensure that the courts accepted their cases by guaranteeing execution of the courts' verdicts, even if they went against the rich and the powerful.

In addition to all this there was the responsibility for maintaining good relations with the gods, to ensure economic well-being and good harvests for the community, duties that had earlier devolved upon the priest king, the en. Correspondingly, in the city states where the priest king maintained himself in power, the constant war-like conditions forced him to take on the duties of a warrior king. A striking example of this fusion of originally distinct offices is Men-barage-si, with whose name the title en 'priest king' became so closely associated that later tradition knows him only as En-men-barage-si even though he is remembered simply as a warrior king.

As far as can be seen, priest king and warrior king seem to have been titles for rulers of major cities dominating larger, relatively loosely federated territories. For the rulers of smaller independent cities and city states a new title, ensi (more exactly ensiak, Akkadian iššiakkum) came into use. It meant 'productive manager (en) of (ak) the tillage (si)' and designated originally the organizer of the community's ploughing teams. As such – since the asses that pulled the ploughs would also have been used to draw the war chariots – he would have been the natural organizer of the community for war or, in fact, for any other major public task. The use of the term as a political title for an independent city ruler was current only in the third millennium BC. At its end, under the Third Dynasty of Ur, ensi came to denote 'provincial governor' under the suzerainty of the king of Ur; after that it reverted to its original meaning, head of a ploughing team, a sense which it never lost entirely, and which persisted in the title ensi (.ak)-gal 'chief manager of the ploughing'.

History: Early Dynastic III (2550 to 2335 BC)
Documented history began in Early Dynastic III, as writing, by then, had developed enough to be able to convey new information coherently, and so lent itself to the perpetuation of political achievement. Probably the survival of oral traditions of the preceding 'heroic age' was also due to the new possibilities of fixing these traditions in writing.

Settlement in Early Dynastic III followed the three major branches of the Euphrates. The main course was the one furthest to the west. From it, at Sippar, high up at the head of the alluvium, the second major stream, the Iturungal, branched off from the left bank, while a third branch forked from the left bank of the Iturungal at Zabalam to flow down through the Lagash region: for the sake of convenience we may call it the Lagash-branch. Settlement thus did not form a continuum. The central grasslands, the edin, which separated the courses of the Euphrates proper and the Iturungal, acted as a fairly effective buffer. The Euphrates cities interacted mainly with each other, while the Iturungal and the Lagash-branch cities, which shared a common boundary in fertile agricultural lands, were constantly vying with each other for control of it. Only by the later half of Early Dynastic did all of Sumer become a single political arena.

The Euphrates cities
There can be little doubt that the cities along the main course of the Euphrates represented the central and most powerful region of Sumer, where the country's political fortunes were determined. Unfortunately, however, the rulers there have left us only brief votive inscriptions with scant reference to political events, so that a consistent and connected historical account is hard to come by. The cities in question are: Mari, far north, then Sippar, and then Kishi, all north of Sumer; south of Kishi was Abu Ṣalābikh, as yet unidentified, Nippur, Shuruppak, Eresh, Uruk and Ur. A canal branched off after Uruk westward to Eridu.

With the fall of the First Dynasty of Kishi political power shifted down river to Uruk, where Gilgamesh was succeeded by his son Ur-lugal and six further rulers; none of them, however, left any inscriptions.

A serious rival of Uruk in riches and power must have been its neighbour to the south, Ur, where the famous Royal Cemetery has yielded treasures of gold and semi-precious stone fashioned with consummate craftsmanship. The kings and queens buried with this wealth were also in many cases accompanied in death by servants and attendants. Their names are in some cases known from inscriptions on cylinder seals or other objects. The best known are those of Queen Shudi-ad (.anâk) 'Praying for her father' (not Shub-ad or Pu-abī) whose tomb is famous for its rich content, and of King Mes-kalam-shar (or Mes-kalamdug) 'Hero enlarging the country'.

Shortly after these rulers Mes-Ane-pada (2480–2461 BC) founded the First Dynasty of Ur. He claims the title 'King of Kishi', so he must have enjoyed hegemony over all of Sumer. As for his successors, tradition seems to have been garbled, but a likely sequence is Mes-kiaǧ-nuna (2460–2441 BC), A-Ane-pada (2440–2431 BC), both sons of Mes-Ane-pada, then Mes-kiaǧ-Nanna (2460–2441 BC), son of A-Ane-pada. None of them claim the title 'King of Kishi', so hegemony had apparently passed from Ur to some other city.

Ur continued to be important, however, during the

Akkadian period and its capture by Sargon in about 2340 BC was a vital step in that king's acquiring suzerainty over the region. Our knowledge is scant of subsequent history until about 2060 BC, when it flourished under Ur-Nammu who established the city state's Third Dynasty and built the great ziggurat (temple), the remains of which have survived. The fall of Ur in about 2000 BC to the Amorites marked the beginning of the Babylonian era. The most likely successor to Ur would seem to be Mari where the king list locates a dynasty founded by a certain Ilshu (c2450 BC); for an inscription of Ilshu's daughter has been found in Ur. Another tie with Mari is perhaps Mes-kiaĝ-nuna's queen, whose name comprises the name of the god Šamkan, popular in Mari royal circles, and who wrote in Akkadian, the language of Mari at the time.

The Iturungal and Lagash-branch cities
Along the Iturungal lay the cities Adab, Umma, Kidingir, Pa-tibira and Ararma (in Akkadian: Larsa). On the Lagash-branch lay Zabalam, still within Umma's sphere of interest, then Girsu, Lagash, and Ninâ.

Adab was at the beginnning of Early Dynastic III ruled by an *ensi*, Nin-kisal-si whose suzerain was Mesalim, king of Kishi (2550 BC). Later it became independent: two of its rulers, Me-durba and Lugalda-lu styled themselves king; a third, É-igi-nim-pa-è, claimed only the title *ensi*. Mesalim's actual capital is not known, but it is likely to have been on the Iturungal, for he was active on it and on the Lagash-branch. In Girsu he was mentioned as suzerain of the local *ensi* Lugal-shag-engur, and later tradition had him build a temple for the sun-god Utu in Ararma. In Girsu Mesalim not only built a temple for the city-god Ningirsu, but intervened actively in its border dispute with the neighbouring Umma, compelling the two cities to accept judgment by the highest Sumerian god, Enlil, in Nippur. He himself implemented the decision by measuring out and marking the boundary line.

Enlil's decision, unfortunately, did not settle matters. Umma seems to have been economically and militarily stronger than Lagash, and so under constant temptation to get its way by force. In the long drawn-out conflict that followed it was usually the aggressor. Lagash attacked only once, when Umma was temporarily paralyzed by inner strife. Mostly it tried to avoid open war.

The first attempt by Umma to set aside Mesalim's boundary took place in the reign of Ur-Nanshe, king of Lagash (2494–2465 BC), who seems to have lived some two or three generations after Mesalim. His opponent was Pa-bil-gal-tuk, *ensi* of Umma, whom he took captive, and an unknown ruler of Ur. This setback did not, however, discourage Umma for long. A new *ensi*, Ush, invaded Lagash, destroyed Mesalim's stele and adjusted the border in Umma's favour. Akurgal (2466–2455 BC), Ur-Nanshe's son, sent envoys repeatedly to Umma to protest, only to have them abused by Ush. Not until the reign of Akurgal's son, Eannatum (2454–2425 BC), did things look up again for Lagash. A rebellion in Umma in

which Ush was killed—according to Eannatum's scribes, it had been fomented by their city-god Ningirsu—gave Eannatum the opening for a victorious attack, after which he redrew the boundary with the new *ensi* of Umma, Enakalli, restoring it to where Mesalim had it but allowing Umma to retain the 'leasehold' of certain fields. Eannatum also fought many other victorious engagements, all of them defensive: against attacks from Elam and other city states in the east, and against attacks from the north by Subartu (the territory of later Assyria), by Kishi and by Akshak. Noteworthy is the mention of an attack by Mari, since it was most naturally seen as part of the thrust into Sumer which brought Ur under its sway.

Under Eannatum's brother and successor, Enannatum I (2424–2405 BC), Umma had recovered sufficiently to attempt a new takeover of the Lagash borderlands. After first systematically depriving the boundary canal of water, so that fields where a share of the yield had to be paid to Lagash could not be cultivated, the new *ensi* of Umma, Ur-Lumma, hired mercenaries and invaded Lagash. The attack was met by the then crown prince of Lagash, Entemena, who routed the Ummean forces. Ur-Lumma seems to have been killed and his nephew Il, who had fled with him in the rout, took over as *ensi* of Umma. He proved as difficult as his uncle, allowing breaches to open in the boundary canal to prevent cultivation of the fields leased from Lagash. Entemena (2404–2375 BC), seeking to avoid war, decided to have a feeder dug from the Tigris, further east, to supply the needed water. That solution, innocent enough it would seem, was to prove fatal. In time this canal became a major branch of the Tigris and its plentiful waters tempted southern Sumer into over-irrigation with consequent silting up of the field and severe decrease in yield.

Unification trends
Il was followed in Umma by a short-lived son, GISH-SHAG-ki-dùg (2400–2391 BC), after whom came the remarkable Lugal-kinishe-dudu (2380–2361 BC) who apparently was able to break free of the provincial fixation with the Lagash boundary and see the far greater possibilities in the west. He was able to make himself ruler of Uruk and Ur on the Euphrates. Here Mes-kiaĝ-Nanna of the First Dynasty of Ur had been followed by Elulu (2421–2410 BC) and Balulu (2410–2401 BC); the former was probably the father of En-shagkush-anna (2400–2391 BC), who according to his title 'Priest king of Sumer and king of the nation' had apparently managed to unite in personal union the independent city states of Uruk and Ur, an achievement momentous enough to be remembered for centuries in Sumerian royal titularies. En-shagkush-anna also boasted of a victory over Kishi and Akshak and of capturing Enbi-Eshtar, king of Kishi. From the union established by En-shagkush-anna, his successor, Lugal-kinishe-dudu, was able to move on to even more ambitious goals. He eventually won the coveted title of 'King of Kishi' with its implication of hegemony over all of Sumer. While

pursuing these goals he wanted peace and so he concluded a non-aggression pact, or 'brotherhood', with Entemena.

In Lagash Entemena was followed by a number of short-lived rulers, after whom came Uru-inim-gina (or Uru-KA-gina, 2351–2340 BC) who was chosen by Ningirsu out of 3600 persons. This presumably means that he was a usurper. He is known for reforms issued in his first year as king, after his brief rule as *ensi*. During his reign, Lagash was crippled by a destructive raid by a new ruler of Umma, Lugal-zage-si (2340–2316 BC), who eventually, like Lugal-kinishe-dudu, became ruler of all Sumer. Uru-inim-gina continued to rule as king of Girsu, but eventually it seems he was taken prisoner when the kings of Akkadê overran his realm, and he ended his days in Akkadê. That city also caused the downfall of Lugal-zage-si. During a campaign against it, he was most unexpectedly routed by its young king, Sargon. Following his victory Sargon took over rule in Sumer as 'King of Kishi'.

Achievements

The flight from the small, open villages into large walled cities continued in Early Dynastic III, spurred on by the continuous wars between the city states.

Economically the cities depended on agriculture, horticulture, herding and fishing. Trade was mostly in luxury goods. The details of city government are little known; great differences in wealth and power apparently developed with abuse of the poor by the rich. Houses ranging from hovels to mansions with large estates were privately owned. The households, besides free citizens, included a limited number of domestic slaves.

Originally the core and kernel of the city was the temple of the city-god or goddess, harking back (as suggested above) to a 'central place' functioning as a tribal store for sacred and secular assets and as a meeting place for religious festivals and exchange of goods. The communities forming around them were regulated by custom with traditional offices and services. The organization of the temple and its estate was thus in essence a managerial one, rooted in traditional rights to its various offices and functions. At the head of administration of

the temple of the city god stood the city ruler, the *ensi*, a position that was probably his as successor to the *en*, charismatic leader of the temple's economy, whose residence, the *ĝiparu*, was part of the temple complex. As the *ensi* headed the temple of the city god, so his wife headed that of the city god's consort, and their children those of the children of the city god and goddess. Other temples were headed by an official called *sangu*, which seems to have meant simply 'accountant'.

The mainstay of the temple was agriculture. The temple worked some of its lands for its own immediate needs, and these were known as *niĝ-en-na*; some, the *shukum* or 'maintenance lot' fields, were held as fiefs by temple employees and private citizens alike, and others were rented out on a sharecropping basis–these were called *apin-lal* 'plough hitcher' fields. Generally the temple was an economically self-sufficient unit with its own granaries, mills and bakeries as well as herds of donkeys, cattle and sheep; it employed carders, spinners and weavers for the wool. Much the same pattern, aimed at self-sufficiency, seems to have served for other great estates, whether privately owned or not.

A special, and in some ways quite different, major unit was the palace. Originally there was no room in the economy for captives: they were killed. In time, however, the kings found a use for them and would spare many, organizing them into teams, *erín*, to serve as soldiers or workers. As such they continued, however, to be entirely at his mercy; he retained the right to destroy them, that is to say, he 'owned' them.

The king's role as defender, guardian of justice and controller of public works, such as the digging of canals, building of defences and of temples, continued. Of special interest was the king's right to issue in his first year a series of decrees of equity and easement. Uru-inim-gina's famous reforms were such decrees. It stood at the head of a long series among which were the famous 'code' of Ur-Nammu and 'code' of Hammurapi.

Uru-inim-gina's reforms aimed primarily at ensuring social justice, protecting the weak in society, the poor,

Stele of Ur-Nammu (2112–2095 BC), a Sumerian king who rebuilt temples throughout the country and laid the foundations for a centralized administrative system.

the widows and the orphans, against misuse by the rich and the powerful. They also cancelled debts in which the poorer people were hopelessly bogged down, and they looked to effective policing to ensure personal safety. A special interest of Uru-inim-gina's was introducing the new 'ownership' concept into the temple administration, withdrawing the temple's assets from the traditional managerial control and asserting ownership of them by the god, thus centralizing the administration.

Beyond the constant local wars of city state against city state loomed for the ambitious ruler the concept of 'King of Kishi'-hegemony over the whole country. When achieved, as it sometimes was, it brought internal peace, with political conflicts adjudicated rather than decided by brute force. On the debit side was forced corvée labour by the cities for the king. Generally-since based on force only-hegemony, when achieved, did not last.

In literature the period made great strides. The writing began under Eannatum to stress the phonetic aspect. Syllabic signs became more frequently used and the signs, which up to then had been written in arbitrary order, now adopted the order in which the corresponding syllables followed each other in speech. Even earlier, at the beginning of Early Dynastic III, literary texts had been committed to writing. Thus a variety of oral genres, literary and practical-legal, economic, epistolary and so on-were given written form.

In art the growing importance of the king brought the motif of 'the king at war and feasting at peace' into prominence. Sometimes the king's role as temple builder inspired the artist. In Lagash the advance in simple craftsmanship from the reliefs of Ur-Nanshe to those of Eannatum is striking.

Akkadê and Gutium

The unification of the south, achieved by Lugal-zage-si, was maintained only with considerable difficulty by Sargon and his successors on the throne of Akkadê. It was imposed by force, and attempts by the city states to regain their old independence were constant. Sargon (2334–2279 BC), had to deal with a rebellion late in his reign, and his successor Rīmush (2315–2307 BC) has left a particularly brutal record of suppression of similar uprisings. Manishtusu (2306–2292 BC) seems to have given up the attempt to control the south, and also in the early part of Narām-Suen's reign (2291–2255 BC), it seems to have been free. Narām-Suen reconquered it and his son and successor Shar-kali-sharri (2217–2203 BC) appears to have held on to it. As did probably the two last kings of the dynasty, Dudu (2189–2169 BC) and Shu-Turul (2168–2154 BC).

During the latter half of the dynasty a dangerous enemy arose in the mountains northeast of the Diyala region, the Gutians, barbarous tribesmen raiding the rich Mesopotamian plain. Their incursions were difficult to guard against: unpredictable hit-and-run affairs, the raiders long gone before regular troops could arrive on the scene. This extreme mobility earned for Gutium its characteristic epithet, 'fleet snake of the mountains'.

The dynasty of Gutium, as we know it, seems to have begun at some time in Narām-Suen's reign. Its fourth king, Sharlag, was defeated and captured by Shar-kali-sharri and its sixth, Elulu, appears to have contended unsuccessfully for the throne of Akkadê in the interregnum after Shar-kali-sharri's death. At the time the Akkadê dynasty came to an end, however, the incessant Gutian raids seem to have sapped all power for serious resistance. Akkadê's northern location made it particularly prone to raiding, and its character as a trade centre rendered it particularly vulnerable. Tradition has it that all travel, overland or by boat, ceased because of the threat of attacks and that work in the fields became too hazardous, so that all of economic life was permanently disrupted and the country suffered dire famine.

Under such conditions it is understandable that the Gutian rulers could renew their bid for supremacy in Akkadê, this time successfully. The king of Gutium at the time seems to have been a certain Habil-kên, or perhaps his successor, La'arab (2148–2147 BC), whose name boasts military prowess: 'Not to be fought'. La'arab used Narām-Suen's title 'The Mighty one' and possibly added-the only inscription we have is broken at this point-'King of the four quarters'. In its full form Narām-Suen's title, with the inclusion of a mention of Gutium, was taken in a now lost inscription by a king by the curious name of E'erred-upizer ('The spider is descending', 2146–2145 BC) who styled himself 'The Mighty one, king of Gutium and the four quarters'. He should accordingly belong near La'arab. Perhaps the name of La'arab's successor, Irarum, is a corruption of a shortened form of his name.

Two further Gutian rulers are known from contemporary inscriptions, Yarlagan (2134–2133 BC), and Si'um (2132–2131 BC). Both are mentioned in datings by vassal rulers in Umma and belong towards the end of the dynasty.

Umma, which had emerged as a powerful southern city state in the struggle against Akkadê, seems to have fallen upon evil times at some date in Shu-Turul's reign, its inhabitants leaving it and dispersing. The cause may have been the Gutian raids: these may have halted once the city submitted to Gutium, for by the end of the Gutian dynasty Umma had sufficiently recovered to begin the rebuilding of its major temples.

South of Umma, in the Girsu-Lagash region, there are no signs of Gutian presence; a series of independent rulers followed each other from the time of Akkadê. Noteworthy among them is Ur-Baba (2155–2142 BC), who rebuilt the temple of the city god of Girsu, Nin-girsu. Even better known is his son-in-law and successor Gudea (2141–2122 BC), who found it necessary to do Ur-Baba's work over again. His building activities and his appointments of divine staff who oversaw the temple's functions are described in detail in a classic eulogistic hymn in three parts, of which the last two, the so-called 'Cylinders' of Gudea, are preserved. As famous as the cylinders are a number of almost lifesize statues of Gudea in hard black dolerite, beautifully carved and destined for the temple.

Gudea was followed by his son Ur-Ningirsu and grandson Pirig̃-me, whose reigns, apparently, were both very short.

On the Euphrates the Gutians controlled Nippur, but to the south was an independent kingdom at Uruk, which apparently had made itself free during the reign of the last ruler of Akkadê, Shu-Turul (2168–2154 BC). It also included Ur to the south of it, the two city states having formed a unit since the time of Enshakushanna.

Little of any consequence is known of the rulers who made up the Uruk dynasty until the last of them, Utu-hegal (2133–2113 BC). He was charged by the chief god of Sumer, Enlil, with freeing the country of its barbaric oppressors and used the opportunity of the death of Sium and the accession of a new unproved Gutian king, Tirigan (2130), to launch an attack. Moving his troops up a canal connecting Uruk with Naksu on the Iturungal north of Umma, he managed to intercept two of Tirigan's generals sent south to alert the forces in Umma and thus prevented an attack from the rear. On the sixth day, at a place called Ka-Muruki, he engaged the Gutian forces under Tirigan and decisively defeated them. Tirigan fled north with his family, but the city of Dubrum, in which he sought asylum, looked to its own advantage and delivered him up to Utu-hegal's messenger when he arrived. Tirigan was brought in fetters to Utu-hegal, who proudly put his foot on his neck.

Utu-hegal's victory was a decisive and important one. With it the whole of southern Mesopotamia revived politically and economically from the state of near paralysis caused by the Gutian depredations. Utu-hegal tersely said of it: 'Gutium, the fleet serpent of the mountains, the gods' arm for executing (their) decrees, who had filled Sumer with iniquity, had robbed him who had a wife of his wife, him who had a child of his child, who had set up iniquity and hostility in the land.' All of this was now ended. Utu-hegal removed from the borders of the country the 'long boats' in which the Gutians had made their swift raids downstream on rivers and canals. As his victory thus brought security internally, it opened up communications with the outside world. 'Tirigan, the king of Gutium' said Utu-hegal 'held both banks of the Tigris; southward, in Sumer he barred [access to] the fields, northward he barred the road, the country's roads he made grow long grass.' The resumption of communications and trade that followed the victory was dramatically exemplified in the worldwide procurement of building materials for Ningirsu's temple in Girsu recorded by Utu-hegal's contemporary there, Gudea, although Gudea–with local patriotism – gives credit for it to his city god Ningirsu rather than to Utu-hegal.

The resurgence of national pride that accompanied Utu-hegal's victory, by which he 'returned the kingship of Sumer into its own hand' found suitable literary expression in a notable historical work, the Sumerian king list, which traces that kingship and the cities and rulers who held it, back into legendary times. The work was apparently completed only a few years after Utu-

Votive statue of Gudea (2141–2122 BC), an independent Sumerian king of Lagash, whose rule is described in the Cylinders of Gudea.

hegal's victory and the reign it lists for him, 7 years, 6 months and 15 days, probably represents the time he had ruled when the author finished the list, not his complete reign.

From the Gutians Utu-hegal took over Narām-Suen's old title, 'King of the four quarters'. He intervened in the old border dispute between Lagash and Ur and reclaimed from Ur a boundary district, returning it to its rightful owners, Ningirsu, god of Girsu, and Nanshe, goddess of Ninā. Why Utu-hegal sided with Lagash, which presumably at that time was independent, and dealt such a stinging rebuke to his vassal in Ur is not clear. Ur at the time was under the military governor, Ur-Nammu, who seems to have been born there–he called himself houseborn (slave) of Ekishnugal, the main temple of the city–but was of Urukian extraction since his and his family's personal gods were the Urukian deities Ninsûn and Lugalbanda. Possibly Ur-Nammu had shown too much aggressiveness and independence, and needed to be put in his place.

Utu-hegal was followed by Ur-Nammu (2112–2095 BC) who, in his first year resumed the conflict with Lagash, attacking and killing its new ruler, Nam-mah-ni (2113–2111 BC), who had followed Pirig̃-mé. Consequent upon this victory Ur-Nammu took over the Lagash area, installing his own governors. He also undertook a new border regulation presumably favouring Ur, and dug a boundary canal, Nanna-gú-gal, claiming that 'Through a just judgement by Utu [the god of righteousness] he cleared up the underlying facts and confirmed the testimony [about the boundary].'

Ur-Nammu also availed himself of the right of a king to issue in his first year a series of legal easements in cases where customary law had come to be felt as too severe. Like Uru-inim-gina, Ur-Nammu sought to protect the weak in society, widows and orphans, and like him, he dispossessed the traditional administrators of basic economic activities, shipping, herding and so on, of their hold on the means of production. New areas of regulation were assault and battery for which graduated fines were instituted—presumably as substitutes for violent retribution—and divorce and rape.

The major part of Ur-Nammu's reign seems to have been peaceful so that he could devote his time to rebuilding temples throughout the country. They had suffered badly from Gutian neglect. The most important such task was rebuilding Enlil's temple in Nippur, Ekur. He also laid the foundations for a new and effective centralized administrative system in which the cities were put under provincial governors appointed by, and sometimes moved from post to post by, the king. They kept the title *ensi*, but its old connotation of independence was gone. In accord with this emphasis on close central control was a realistic limiting of territorial goals to the southern Mesopotamian heartland itself. Ur-Nammu discarded the ambitious 'King of the four quarters' and substituted for it 'King of Ur, King of Kiengir and Ki-Uri', that is, of southern Mesopotamia: not because he was unaware of the importance of foreign trade, but rather because he refused to let it involve him in far-flung military ventures. Where trade could be protected locally, he did so. Thus, at the very beginning of his reign, he established a 'place of registry' on the seashore for ships trading with Makkan so that they would be safe from attack by marauders in the southern marshes.

Ur-Nammu was succeeded by his son Shulgi (2094–2047 BC) who, for the first half of an unusually long reign, continued the peaceful traditions of his father, whose title with its limited claims he retained. Where the kings of the four quarters had attempted the herculean task of pacifying all major trade routes from the Mediterranean in the northwest to Elam and Parahsum in the southeast, Shulgi was content to look after the security of communication within the heartland itself. He had the roads measured in double miles and set up rest houses in which travellers could spend the night in safety. Eventually, however, after years of internal consolidation, the old ambitious policies of policing trade routes reasserted their hold on the imagination. Shulgi adopted them and the title that went with them, 'King of the four quarters', and, like Narām-Suen, had himself deified.

The first indication of these new, wider ambitions was a political marriage arranged in Shulgi's eighteenth year between his daughter and the ruler of Marhashi (the old Barahshum), clearly indicating that Marhashi and the trade route east, which it controlled, now were spheres of interest for Ur. A similar marriage to the ruler of Anshan, likewise on that route, was negotiated in Shulgi's thirtieth year. Unfortunately that did not work out as intended; only four years later Shulgi had to sack Anshan. Shortly after the first of these two marriages Shulgi also turned his attention to the important road north along the mountains to Erbil, and Nineveh, and from there westward toward the Mediterranean. This road was subject to attack from raiding mountain tribes all the way up to Erbil, and seeking to pacify it involved Shulgi in a frustrating series of campaigns. Localities between the Diyala and Erbil occur again and again in the year-name formulas as having been captured and sacked, but apparently with little lasting effect, so that a new capture and sack soon became necessary. One year, for instance, is named after the sacking of Simurrum and Lulubum for the ninth time.

Toward the end of Shulgi's reign a new threat arose, rather like that posed by the Gutians in earlier times. The nomadic tribes in the west, chief among them the Dedānum, pressed on the border of the cultivated area, raiding and pillaging. To protect the settled population Shulgi built and manned a defensive wall along the northwest border. The wall was known variously as 'The wall in front of the mountains', 'The Wall of the land' and, after Shulgi's time, as 'Keeping Dedānum away'.

Shulgi was succeeded by his son, Amar-suena (2046–2038 BC), not Būr-Sin, who retained the divine status and the title 'King of the four quarters' of his father. He also continued the campaigns along the road to Erbil. He was followed, after a reign of only nine years, by his brother, Shu-Suen (2037–2029 BC), who continued the old patterns and sent his daughter to Simānum to be married to a son of the local ruler. This did not work out: Simānum soon turned hostile and drove Shu-Suen's daughter from her residence, and it took an armed intervention by her father to reinstate her. On the western border work on the wall continued and reached completion, so that Shu-Suen took credit for having excluded the Mardu (Amorite) Bedouin away from the country.

When Shu-Suen died, his young son Ibbi-Suen (2028–2004 BC) succeeded to the throne, entering on a long and fateful reign. At first, though, everything seemed serene. The old experienced ministers continued to guide affairs and their policies continued unchanged.

The new king's third year was named after the sacking of Simurrum in the eastern mountains, and the fifth from the marriage of his daughter to the ruler of Marhashi. By now, however, Ur's luck had run out. Through years of over-irrigation (made possible by the new course of the Tigris initiated by Entemena) the fields in the south had been spoiled and, by the time of the Third Dynasty, Ur must have been dangerously dependent on imports of grain from the north. On top of this, around Ibbi-Suen's fifth year, there was an unexpected and catastrophic breakthrough into the country by the nomadic Mardu tribes – the very thing the great wall had been built to prevent. The result was chaos, suspension of communication and all normal activities, much as had been the case with the Gutian invasion earlier on. Ibbi-Suen had sent a general, Ishbi-Erra, north to buy grain to feed his army and the city of Ur, but Ishbi-Erra, hearing about the Mardu, decided to bring the grain into Isin for safe-keeping and now offered it at twice the price he had bought it for. He also asked to be appointed guardian of Isin and Nippur. Ibbi-Suen, according to what seems the best version of our source, had to accept the outrageous offer, but whether the grain eventually got to Ur at all is not clear. Meanwhile at Ur, serious shortage had developed into catastrophic famine with prices of grain soaring to sixty times the normal.

The cutting off of all communications necessarily made central control of outlying provinces impossible and encouraged ever-present trends to independence. The country largely fell apart, with only the region around Ur itself in Ibbi-Suen's hands. Nippur held out to his eleventh year, when it was forcibly appropriated by its supposed guardian Ishbi-Erra; only Kazallu remained loyal to Ur, at least nominally, to just before the fall of the city.

The Mardu inroads made repair of defences, even of cities in the very heart of the country, mandatory, and two years took their names from the rebuilding of the city walls of Nippur and Ur. The disturbed conditions seem to have encouraged Elam to begin hostilities, for Ishbi-Erra, in his report about the grain, rather insolently advised his king against fighting Elam and thus using up too quickly his sparse grain rations for the army—nor did he need promise to become Elam's vassal or follower, as Ishbi-Erra had enough grain to supply him for years to come.

While Ishbi-Erra's tone was hardly that of a loyal subject, he still avoided an open break. One cause may have been Ibbi-Suen's spectacular military successes in the very campaigns in the east that Ishbi-Erra had warned against; for it was at this time that he probably gained a victory over Huhunuri on the border of Elam.

After some years, however, probably around Ibbi-Suen's twelfth or thirteenth year, Ishbi-Erra began in earnest to work at taking Ibbi-Suen's realm away from him. In this he was encouraged and greatly helped by an omen given by Enlil, which promised him the kingship over the country; so, after a series of military campaigns along the western and northern borders, Ishbi-Erra successfully sent emissaries to all the provincial governors in the north, inviting them to submit to him, and

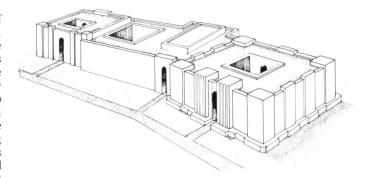

The palace of a Sumerian governor at Eshnunna. On the right is a temple dedicated to the deified king, Shu-Suen, who reigned 2037–2029 BC.

quoting Enlil's decision. Most of the north, Eshnunna, Kishi and Borsippa, defected and Ibbi-Suen could only hope that Enlil might yet change his mind. That, however, was not to be.

At some time toward the end of his reign, Ibbi-Suen was victorious in a campaign against Susa, the capital of Elam, and the neighbouring Adamdun and Awan, taking their rulers captive. His success may have incited Elam to retaliation and, in a letter to his last loyal adherent in the north, the *ensi* of Kazallu, Ibbi-Suen mentioned threats on two fronts: from Elam in the east and Ishbi-Erra in the north. He took courage though, from a favourable omen from Enlil and hoped that the Amorites, with whom he had earlier established friendly relations, would defeat Elam and also capture Ishbi-Erra. None of this came to pass.

Elam, helped by the neighbouring Sua people, launched a devastating attack on all of southern Mesopotamia, and the Mardu, far from coming to Ibbi-Suen's aid, joined in the fray, looting and pillaging the western regions of his paralysed country. The enemy, probably led by the Elamite king, Kindattu, laid siege to Ur itself but was unable to take it by assault. As time went on, however, severe famine assailed the beleagured defenders and eventually, in despair, they opened the gate to the enemy. If they had hoped for lenient treatment, they were rudely disappointed. The mountaineers massacred everybody ruthlessly, and pillaged and despoiled dwellings and temples. The old king was taken captive and led off in a neckstock on the long trek through the mountains to Anshan, south of Elam.

Ishbi-Erra, meanwhile, had weathered the storm behind newly built walls in Isin, emerged with his forces as the Elamites withdrew, and took over the territory and city of Ur as they were abandoned. The acropolis of the city, in which an Elamite garrison had been stationed, was left alone until almost ten years later when he finally drove out the troops occupying it.

The gods had enforced their incomprehensible decision 'to change the times, destroy the established patterns ... and exchange for other ways the ways of Sumer', as one of the laments dealing with these events had it. It spelled the end of Sumer.

Akkad (Akkadê)

Thorkild Jacobsen

The name

Akkad was the name of an ancient city in northern Babylonia (present-day southern Iraq). The term is also used by modern writers to designate northern Babylonia as a whole. The form Akkad reflects Neo-Babylonian writings of the name as *uru-Ak-kad* and the biblical Akkad (Accad in Gen. 10:10). The older form of the name was Akkadê or, in Sumerian, Akkedê with vowel assimilation. It is most often quoted as Agade, a form based on a provisional reading of the standard writing *A-(k)kà-dè* as *A-ga-dè*.

Location and trade routes

The exact location of Akkadê is as yet unknown. All that can be said with certainty is that it was somewhere between Baghdad and Babylon, where the Euphrates and the Tigris rivers come close together and where most of the great southern Mesopotamian capitals throughout history were situated: Kishi, Akkadê, Babylon, Seleucia, Ktesiphon and Baghdad.

Besides being capitals, these cities were also great centres of trade, for the narrow area in which they lay was a crossroad of the great trade routes of antiquity, linking east and west. Like other capitals, Akkadê, too, was a thriving mercantile centre as is clear from later historical tradition. A Sumerian composition from the time of the Third Dynasty of Ur, known as *The Cursing of Akkadê*, tells us of Inanna, the goddess of the city, that 'to have monkeys, huge elephants, water buffaloes, beasts of faraway regions jostle each other in the broad avenues, to have noble dogs, lions, mountain ibexes and alum sheep with long wool, did holy Inanna not allow herself to sleep.' We hear further that 'its harbour, where the ships moored, astonished and astounded' and that 'holy Inanna opened up the gateways of its gates as if for the Tigris going into the sea. Sumer pulled its own goods hither on boats, the Amorites of the mountains, people who know not grain, brought in for her perfect bulls together with perfect billy goats, the Meluhhans, people of the black mountains, brought down for her all kinds of strange things, Elam and Shubartu carried things to her like pack asses.'

The importance of trade for the city and the need to keep the trade routes open was not lost on the rulers of Akkadê. It called for policing the routes, restraining the local rulers from exacting tolls, and keeping highwaymen and wild mountain tribes from robbing the heavily loaded caravans. The need for such a policy was realised by Sargon, the first king of the city, as is obvious from the pattern of his campaigns, and from later tradition about them. Thus an Akkadian heroic epic from the middle of the second millennium BC, *The King of Battle*, dealt with a victorious campaign by Sargon into central Anatolia. An appeal for help by merchants figured as the incentive for Sargon to undertake that far-off dangerous venture.

Sargon I (tentatively ruled 2340 to 2315 BC)

According to a tradition preserved in the Sumerian king list, Akkadê was founded by its first king. Sargon, who had begun life as a fruit grower but rose to become cup-bearer to the king of Kishi, Ur-Zababa. How he escaped the destruction of Kishi shortly afterwards at the hand of Lugal-zage-si of Uruk is not known; perhaps he was warned by the goddess Inanna, who appeared to him in a dream according to another, only partly preserved tradition. A third tradition had a messenger report to Lugal-zage-si that Sargon had lain with his wife and renamed her as his concubine, whereupon Lugal-zage-si apparently attempted to lure Sargon to Uruk by pretending not to be angry.

How much of all this, if any, preserves a historical kernel is hard to say. Sargon's name, which means 'the king is just', is a typical flattering courtier's name, which lends some credence to his having been a royal cup-bearer; his queen's name, known from a contemporary inscription, was Ashluĺtum, which apparently is an abbreviated sentence-name meaning, 'I took (you/her) as spoil'. It could fit a renaming such as the one told in the story.

Totally legendary is the late *Birth Legend of Sargon*, which hints at divine extraction by making Sargon's mother a high priestess and human consort of a god, and his father unknown. When he was born his mother placed him in a box of reeds caulked with bitumen and set him adrift on the river, where he was caught in the pail of a fruit grower who was drawing water, and was adopted by him.

Reliable historical information about Sargon comes mainly from his own inscriptions set up in the temple of Enlil in Nippur after he had conquered that city. We know them from careful copies made by Old Babylonian scribes. How they followed each other in time is suggested by changes in the titles Sargon took in them. The earliest of these, 'King of Akkadê', never occurred as sole title in any of the inscriptions and would seem to have been superseded, as early as the composition of our earliest preserved inscription, by the more grandiose 'King of Kishi'. Last comes the title 'King of the Nation', which was usually listed after the other two and appears to have been assumed last.

In the inscription that seems to have been the earliest one preserved, Sargon told that he had defeated the forces of Uruk in a place called Ugbanda(?) located in the commons of Akkadê itself. Thus it would seem that this, Sargon's first great victory, was a defensive one warding

Babylonian clay tablet (third millennium BC) showing the regions of the world, with a text relating to the conquests of Sargon of Akkad.

off an attack on Akkadè by Lugal-zage-si and his followers, who had already come dangerously near. Lugal-zage-si's defeat proved a total one. Not only was he himself taken captive; the same fate befell fifty of the *iššiakkus*, that is, city rulers, who with their following made up his forces. Sargon quickly followed up the victory. In a place called Nagurzam(?) he defeated the retreating remnants of the enemy, and a third time, at the city of Ur, he fought and was victorious. From Ur he went back upriver into the Iturungal branch of the Euphrates to Umma—in a land criss-crossed by canals like southern Mesopotamia the only effective way to move an army was by boat—and, after subduing Lugal-zage-si's major stronghold he moved southeast down the Lagash river to Lagash, which he likewise defeated, and then on to the sea, where he and his army washed their bloodied weapons in the salt water. This triumphant campaign earned him the proud title of 'King of Kishi' with its venerable implication of suzerainty over all of southern Mesopotamia.

To the time when Sargon used 'King of Kishi' as sole title belong inscriptions telling about successful campaigns in the southeast against Elam and Parahshum, in what is now Iran, and in the northwest up the Euphrates over Mari (Abu Kemal), Iarmutium and Ebla (Tel Mardikh) to the Cedar Forest (Lebanon) and the Silver Mountain (the Taurus). The reason for these far-flung military expeditions could hardly have been desire for territorial aggrandizement; rather, they would have been aimed at securing the great overland trade routes that passed through Akkadè to make them safe for caravans. The Euphrates route was an important link with the Mediterranean, and with Anatolia and Egypt. To the east the major trade route led from Akkadè through the gates of the Zagros down to Susa in Elam and from there east over Kermanshah towards India.

Sargon's concern for trade also shows in his making it possible for sea-going cargo vessels to sail all the way up to moor in the harbour of Akkadè. He mentions ships from as far away as Tilmun (Bahrein), Makkan (Egypt?) and Meluhha (Ethiopia?). That sea trade with India was carried on in the Akkadè period is clear from archaeological evidence.

The far-flung realm Sargon had won was held together, it would seem, mainly by the threat his armies posed, and internal administration was left in local hands. His armies were indeed formidable; in Akkadè alone '5,400 men eat bread daily before him'. However, naked force never was the most secure basis of power, and later tradition was to have it that in his old age all lands revolted against him and beleaguered him in Akkadè. He, however, made a successful sortie and utterly routed them all. To this event the last group of Sargon's inscriptions apparently belongs, the one in which he added 'King of the Nation' to his earlier titles. The campaign recorded there was similar to his first, except that this time he went from Ur to the sea over Eninmar and Lagash, and dealt with Umma on the return march. The temper of the campaign was, however, very different from the earlier one, harsh and clearly aimed at deterring from further rebellion. City walls were razed, leaving the cities vulnerable, and instead of local *iššiakkus*, citizens of Akkadè, on whom Sargon could rely, were installed. Correspondingly Sargon's new titles proclaimed his will—and his god-given right—to rule the south. They were 'King of the Nation' and, as religious corollary, 'Enlil's chief plough-man'. Both had been held by Lugal-zage-si before, and both were granted by Enlil in Nippur. The 'Nation' was accordingly Enlil's domain, Sumer, the south and, in one of the inscriptions, Sargon specified that Enlil 'judged his case' and gave him victory over Uruk.

That Sargon thus took over Lugal-zage-si's titles raised the question of what role that ruler can have played in the events recorded in these inscriptions. Oddly enough it was only in these, not when he was first defeated, that he was mentioned by name and that we are told how he was taken in a neck stock to be exhibited at the gate of Enlil. Did the composer of the inscription include an earlier event for effect? Or had Sargon in fact run the risk of reinstating Lugal-zage-si in Uruk as vassal ruler, only to have him eventually lead the rebellion? We must hope for more evidence.

The last recorded achievement of Sargon was a peaceful one. He rebuilt the destroyed city of Kishi and brought back and resettled its scattered population back.

Rīmush (tentatively 2315 to 2307 BC)

Sargon had two sons, Rīmush and Manishtusu, who each in their turn followed him on the throne. A daughter, famous as a great poet, was appointed high priestess and human consort of the moon god Nanna, city god of Ur. The two sons, if we may judge by their names, were twins, with Rīmush, whose name means 'his [the god's] gift' born first, and Manishtusu, whose name means 'who is with him?' born second and named from a surprised exclamation of the midwife at discovering a twin.

The elder brother of Rīmush came to power first. He found, apparently, that Sargon's measures to discourage further rebellion, razing city walls and replacing local rulers with citizens of Akkadè, had not been effective, the south was determined not to submit. More force was therefore indicated, and Rīmush seems to have thought that a rule of terror would be the answer. Not satisfied with merely defeating rebels and razing their city walls, he revived the old custom of wholesale massacre of prisoners, the *karāshum*, as a punitive measure. If we may believe his figures he began modestly, having by his third year killed or captured only 9624 men. Then, however, we are told that after killing 8724 men in battle in Sumer, capturing Kaku, king of Ur, and the *iššiakkus* allied with him, together with 5862 other prisoners, he led out 5700 men from the cities of Sumer and massacred them. On his return march he found that the city state of Kazallu had turned hostile, so he defeated it, killed 12,652 men in battle, and took the *iššiakku*, Asharid, and 5864 men prisoners. In a separate campaign against the cities along the Iturungal–Adab, Zabalam, Umma and Ki-dingir–he indulged in similar wholesale slaughter, listing 15,718 men killed and 14,576 taken captive in battle with Adab and Zabalam. Afterwards he massacred an unknown number. In the battle with Umma and Ki-dingir 8900 were killed, 3540 captured and 3600 massacred later.

Although these grisly statistics may not in all respects be accurate–they seem to vary somewhat for the same battle from one inscription to another–the general tenor is unmistakable, and when one of the inscriptions sums up his victims killed, captured or massacred as totalling 54,016, it may not be too far off the mark.

In spite of the seemingly constant need for repressing rebellions in Sumer, Rīmush found time in his short reign of nine years to campaign also in the east. Here he defeated Abalgamash, King of Parahshum, killing 16,212 men and taking 4216 prisoners. The victory made him ruler of Elam having 'weeded out' Parahshum, from it.

Rīmush's bloodthirsty policies may not have been wholeheartedly endorsed by everybody around him. They were costly and hardly productive of any solid gains. It seems likely, therefore, that many would have preferred attention to be paid to the northern and eastern trade routes, with Sumer left more or less alone. Whether these or other considerations led to growing dissatisfaction with the king is not known. All we are told–by traditions preserved by experts in foretelling the future from signs in the livers of sacrificial kids–is that Rīmush's courtiers killed him with their cylinder seals, which probably means that they stabbed him to death with the long copper pins–almost like stilettos–that could be passed through the central hole in the cylinder seal and so served both to carry the seal and to pin their garments together.

Manishtusu (tentatively 2306 to 2292 BC)

Rīmush was followed on the throne by Manishtusu, who was to rule 15 years before he too suffered his brother's fate and was killed by his courtiers. To judge from his inscriptions he discontinued his brother's policy of killing and massacring, and since he made no mention of campaigns in the south he may well have relinquished attempts to hold on to it altogether. Nippur, though, seems to have remained under his sway since he was able to set up his inscriptions and statues in Enlil's temple there. The military undertakings he told of took him south from Elam in Anshan and Shirihum, which he defeated. Elam itself seems to have been securely in his hands and there still exists a bust of him with a dedicatory inscription by its *iššiakku*, his servant Eshba. Having subdued Anshan and Shirihum, Manishtusu embarked his troops in ships on the coast of the Persian Gulf to fight 32 cities 'beyond the sea', wherever that may have been. He was victorious and, with an Akkadite's eye for mercantile possibilities, continued his march to visit silver mines. He also quarried black stone, which he freighted back to the harbour at Akkadè. Otherwise Manishtusu is best known for a monument called the 'Obelisk of Manishtusu' which records extensive purchases of land by the king. The lands were intended for settling soldiers of Akkadè's vast army.

As mentioned, Manishtusu found his death in a palace revolution, but no reason for it is preserved in our material.

Narām-Suen (tentatively 2291 to 2255 BC)

Kishi, which Sargon had rebuilt, must have hankered after its old independence, for it quickly seized the opportunity offered by the confusion and temporary paralysis of the central government attendant upon the palace revolution in Akkadè to make itself free. It met in assembly and chose its own king, who took the name Iphur-Kishi, 'Kishi assembled'.

The new king of Akkadè, Manishtusu's son, Narām-Suen, who must have had his hands full at home with establishing himself and purging dissidents, apparently did not feel strong enough to hold Kishi by force of arms and contented himself with having it conclude a non-aggression treaty of 'brotherhood' with him.

The defection of Kishi left almost all of Mesopotamia south of Akkadè independent. Besides Kishi there was a kingdom of Umma under Urdu-Enlila, and one of Uruk and Ur under Lugal-Ane. Lugal-Ane had even had the effrontery to oust Sargon's daughter Enheduana from her position as high priestess in Ur, a telling indication of how low Akkadè's prestige had dipped.

With Kishi now independent, the title 'King of Kishi',

which Narām-Suen's predecessors had all held, became unsuitable, and Narām-Suen reverted to a simple 'King of Akkadè'. It is probable that to the years when this was his main title belongs a victorious campaign against Elam, which apparently had tried to follow the example of Kishi. Its position commanding the eastern trade route however, made control of it imperative for Akkadè; it could not be allowed to go as Kishi had done. In replacing the ruler of Elam, Narām-Suen took over his title 'the Mighty one' to precede his own title 'King of Akkadè' and give it lustre.

For unknown reasons—perhaps fear of its military potential, perhaps lust for its riches—an immense alliance against Akkadè was formed some years into Narām-Suen's reign. It comprised Kishi, Umma and Uruk, Nippur to the south, Simurrum and Nawar to the northeast, and Mari to the northwest. The location of two further countries, Mardaman (unless a metathesis for *mada Arman*, 'the Aleppo plain') and Makkan (unless, as later, Egypt), is unknown.

The attack, when it came, was spearheaded by three kings, who were naturally Iphur-Kishi, Urdu-Enlila and Lugal-Ane. With them may have marched Amar-Enlila, king of Nippur. Narām-Suen had only the forces of Akkadè itself to fall back on, but with them he performed wonders. In nine engagements during a single year he routed his enemies and gained full control of the south down to the sea. Out of gratitude to Enlil, who 'judged his case and gave the reins of the people into his hands and let him have no opponent', Narām-Suen '[broke] the fetters of [the troops of] Nippur', that is, freed them from military and labour service. He also began rebuilding Enlil's temple, Ekur.

Further campaigns took him up into Shubartu, the later Assyria, and west to the Cedar Forest (Lebanon). He also—perhaps on his return march—took Talhatum in the upper reaches of the Habur. A relief of him in the rocks at Diarbekir (further north) could have been cut on this occasion.

At about this time Narām-Suen assumed the new title 'King of the four quarters' or, more literally, 'of the four [world] shores', for the world was thought to be an island surrounded by the 'bitter' (that is, 'salt') sea. The title celebrated his prowess when 'the four quarters' turned hostile against him and he subdued them.

To fellow citizens the prowess shown on that momentous occasion seemed to prove him more than human, a god, and so they wanted to have their saviour made their city god. They accordingly made inquiry of all the major gods in the country and upon receiving favourable answers went ahead and built a temple for Narām-Suen in Akkadè. From then on Narām-Suen's name was regularly written with the determinative for divinity.

Just before he assumed divine status there was apparently a victory over Manium of Makkan; later there were campaigns in the northeast with victories over Simurrum and Arame south of the lower Zab, and against Lulubum further north, a success celebrated on the stele of victory. On this campaign he seems to have brought back a number of notables who had fled

Shubartu before the advancing Akkadite army. Near Lulubum and not too far from modern Kirkūk he subdued a country called Hurshammadki and killed with his own hand a wild bull in the Tibar mountain. Raids from all of these tribes apparently imperilled the winter road up to Nineveh and westward from there.

Narām-Suen's most impressive later feat was a new campaign in Syria where he took Armānum (Aleppo?) and Ebla (Tel Mardikh). Rid-Adad, the ruler of Armānum, was captured and tied to the crossbeams in his entryway. Narām-Suen also gained full control over the Amānus range and imposed corvée on a city, Ulishum, probably for the building of an Akkadite army post at Shikumānum. On this campaign he reached the Mediterranean. One further campaign is known, though only from later tradition, that against Apishal, which Narām-Suen took by sapping its walls. Its location is not known.

The rebuilding of Enlil's temple in Nippur seems to have been planned and undertaken by Narām-Suen as a very thorough renewal, involving the complete demolition of the extant structure, for a year was named from the laying of new foundations. The work may not have progressed beyond that. Bricks with Narām-Suen's name as builder have been found, but they may well have been made under him and only laid later by his son Shar-kali-sharri, who finished the work.

In the composition *The Cursing of Akkadè*, perhaps for didactic reasons and prompted by traditions about wilfulness in Narām-Suen, his rebuilding is presented as an act of impiety, which can hardly be historically true.

Shar-kali-sharri (tentatively 2217 to 2193 BC)

Narām-Suen was followed by his son Shar-kali-sharri, who reverted to the simple title 'King of Akkadè'. Presumably, therefore, he did not quite succeed in keeping his father's realm intact. Significant here is what happened with Elam on the major trade route eastward. We hear, it is true, that Shar-kali-sharri was victorious in battle with Elam and Zahara, but the site where the battle was fought tells its own story. The enemy forces were halted in front of Akshak, a city on the Tigris, not very far north of Akkadè itself. It is thus clear that Elam had become free, and strong enough to challenge Akkadè. Its ruler, Puzur-Inshushinak, even aspired to taking over her empire as he showed by arrogating to himself Narām-Suen's title, 'King of the four quarters'.

In the west Shar-kali-sharri was more successful. He defeated the Amorites in Bashar (Mount Bishri) in Syria and in the northeast he was victorious against the Gutians and took their king, Sharlak, captive. The campaign was very likely an effort to check the Gutian raids down into the fertile Mesopotamian plain, raids that were becoming more and more disruptive.

Shar-kali-sharri also found time for the rebuilding of temples. The most important of these was Ekur, where Narām-Suen had only managed to lay some of the foundations for a new structure. Shar-kali-sharri went on from there and finished the work. One of his years is dated from laying foundations, another from the appointment of the general Puzur-Eshtar to supervise the work of building.

Shar-kali-sharri's death—according to a late tradition he, too, was killed by his courtiers—brought about a three-year interregnum during which four kings, Igigi, Nanum, Imi and Elulu, aspired unsuccessfully to the throne. 'Who was king? Who was not king?' asks the bewildered Sumerian king list.

Eventually Dudu (tentatively 2189–2169 BC) took over, styling himself 'the Mighty one, king of Akkadê'. He in turn was followed by his son, Shu-Turul (tentatively 2168–2154 BC), who kept his father's titles and so probably held on in some measure to his realm. That realm, however, is likely to have been a greatly reduced one.

Shu-Turul was the last of the kings of Akkadê, and shortly after his death Akkadê itself seems to have perished. Such traditions as we have suggest that more and more frequent raids by the Gutian mountaineers eventually managed to disrupt normal economic functions entirely, making roads and canals unsafe for trade caravans, and normal work in the fields impossible, so that economic decline and eventually famine drove people away. The Gutians, who had thus completely overrun southern Mesopotamia, became its nominal kings. They controlled the country as far down as Umma on the Iturungal, but hardly the Girsu-Lagash region and the Euphrates down to Nippur, and certainly not Uruk and Ur south of it.

Government

The Akkadê rulers provided a central authority strong enough to prevent internecine wars among the city states and to make them submit their differences to court decision instead. They likewise pacified trade routes and created safer conditions, which brought back the small agricultural villages that the preceeding Early Dynastic period had wiped off the map in the south. To achieve this, Akkadite garrisons were placed in major cities and army posts set up at strategic points along the great trade routes to police them. One such has been excavated in Tell Brak on the upper Habur.

The Akkadê kings also extended their readiness and ability to apply sanctions to private agreements, as long as they were concluded with solemn invocation of the king. Thus due performance of obligations was stimulated; an obvious boon to commerce.

The realm was held together by force or threat of force

Victory stele of Narām-Suen, king of Akkad (c2291–2255 BC). Hard-pressed by an alliance of enemies, he won a tremendous victory and went on to rebuild votive temples in several cities.

only: integrated administrative control was still in the future. A gradual intensification of violent measures—razing city walls, installing Akkadite *iššiakkus* supported by Akkadite garrisons, and revival of the *karāshum* under Rīmush—failed to stem stubborn separatist tendencies.

Religion

The immense power of the king tended to put him on a par with the gods to many of his subjects, as evidenced

Akkadian seal of deities including the mother **goddess Ishtar**, who derived from the Sumerian Inanna, goddess of fertility and love.

by the unabashed request that the major gods of the country sanction Narām-Suen's deification. A reaction in priestly circles, seeing him as sacrilegiously challenging divine authority, may underlie the picture of him given in *The Cursing of Akkadê*. There Enlil withheld permission for the rebuilding of Ekur, whereupon Narām-Suen, after brooding for seven years, attacked Nippur, despoiling and demolishing Ekur with fateful consequences. And in the later epic, misnamed *The King of Cutha*, he served as a warning against impious wilfulness. In that composition he refused to obey divine orders given through omens not to fight an eerie horde of mountaineers overrunning the then known world, saying to himself 'What lion ever looked at omens? What wolf asked a seeress? Let me go as does the freebooter, as my heart listeth!' The result was predictably disastrous.

Art

The art of Akkadê clearly continued a northern tradition, characteristic of which was a preference for slenderness of the human figure in sculpture and glyptic, and in the cuneiform signs in calligraphy. It came fully into its own under Narām-Suen, freeing itself of any awkward stiffness and achieving easy elegance. No other work equalled Narām-Suen's stele of victory for beauty of composition and ability to convey a mood – in this case glory in superhuman kingly power.

The motifs preferred in the official monuments were all military: the king victorious; the soldiers marching or carrying loot; naked captives in neck stocks, and their massacre in the *karāshum*. In contrast scenes with a mythological reference were prefered in glyptic.

Literature

During the Akkadê period the south continued the transmission and enrichment of the body of Sumerian literary compositions of preceeding ages. Of new achievements the most notable are by Sargon's daughter, Enheduana, a very accomplished poet. She wrote in Sumerian and entirely within traditional Sumerian literary forms. One of her works is a cycle of short hymns to temples, 42 in all. Impressive also is an address to the goddess Inanna in the grand style in which Enheduana appealed to the goddess to redress the wrongs done her – she had been driven from office and had to flee Ur.

Of literary works in Akkadian little is known so far. It is clear, though, that an independent Akkadian literary tradition existed before the Akkadê period and was continued during it. Thus, the royal inscriptions in Akkadian have their own pattern and phraseology and are not simply translations from Sumerian.

Of the other genres a few are known from fragments of compositions that can be assigned to them. Hymns to gods and eulogistic-hymns to rulers are exemplified. One rather grotesque short piece deals with a lover's quarrel to which the god Enki is a party.

Babylonia

A. K. Grayson

The modern recovery of the history of Babylonia began in the nineteenth century, following in the wake of the great archaeological discoveries in Assyria. Although initially the finds were not as spectacular as those in the northern region, the gradual exploration of Babylonia and awakening knowledge of its great civilization, which has developed during this last century, have revealed a highly sophisticated and cosmopolitan society whose cultural attainments were outstanding.

Geography

Babylonia consists of a flat plain through which flow two large rivers, the Tigris and Euphrates (thus the name Mesopotamia 'Between the rivers'), on their courses from Anatolia and Syria to the Persian Gulf. To the east and north the plain is bounded by mountains, the Zagros chain and Kurdistan; to the west and south by the Syrian and Arabian deserts. The climate is hot and dry in summer, cold and wet in winter and in the spring the Tigris and Euphrates overflow their banks, flooding vast parts of the plain. Proper control of this natural water supply enabled man in very ancient times to produce abundant crops, mainly barley and sesame, while cattle, sheep and goats grazed in the verdant meadows. The date palm was cultivated in the south where the hot dry south wind could be relied on to ripen the fruit. The abundant clay was formed into bricks to build houses and monumental structures, and also provided clay tablets for writing purposes.

Given the total lack of other natural resources (petroleum, for which the area has become a major source, was known but virtually useless to ancient man), the inhabitants engaged in foreign trade in order to acquire precious metals, stones and sturdy timber. Both the physical and climatic features of the region have remained relatively constant since Babylonian times and the Marsh Arabs, inhabitants of the marshes on the edge of the Persian Gulf, still live in a manner very similar to that of their ancient predecessors.

The Old Babylonian period (*c*2000 to 1595 BC)

The beginning of the history of Babylonia is traditionally dated to the fall of the Third Dynasty of Ur, *c*2000 BC, and the catalyst in this was the migration of the Amorites from the desert into Mesopotamia. The Amorites, a large group of Semitic-speaking semi-nomads, captured a number of city states where they established new dynasties and then gradually settled down and adapted to the civilization of the Babylonian plain. Internecine warfare between these various dynasties, the previous inhabitants and new immigrants, caused considerable confusion during the early period (c2000–1763 BC) but two cities, Isin and Larsa, successively dominated the scene so that the era has been called the Isin-Larsa period.

The city state of Larsa was eventually captured by an Amorite chieftain, Kudur-mabug, who installed his two sons, Warad-Sin and Rim-Sin, as successive rulers of Larsa while he continued his military activities. Rim-Sin

(c1822–1763 BC) continued the expansion of the mini-empire which his father had won and ultimately captured Larsa's ancient rival, Isin, in his thirtieth year. This was the end, however, of Larsa's glorious period and 30 years later (c1763 BC) Larsa was conquered by Hammurapi of Babylon, thus ushering in a new era.

The remainder of Old Babylonian history (c1763–1595 BC) was characterized by a shift of power further north with Hammurapi of Babylon (c1792–1750 BC) as the focal point. Hammurapi was the sixth member of the first dynasty of Babylon and he inherited a secure, albeit modest city state. During his reign he conducted a series of diplomatic and military exchanges with rival city states, chiefly with Larsa, Eshnunna, Mari and Shamshi-Adad I of Assyria (c1813–1781 BC). Hammurapi was brilliantly success-

Chronology of Babylonia, Assyria and Mitanni

BC	Assyria	Babylonia	Mitanni
2000	Merchant colony in Cappadocia	Fall of Ur III	
	Shamshi-Adad I (1813–1781)	Rim-Sin of Larsa (1822–1763)	
	Ishme-Dagan I (1780–1741)	Hammurapi (1792–1750)	
		Samsuiluna (1749–1712)	
		Fall of Babylon I (1595)	
1500			Parattarna
	Ashur-uballit I (1363–1328)	Kadashman-Enlil I (1374–1360)	Artatama
		Burnaburiash II (1359–1333)	Shuttarna
		Kurigalzu II (1332–1308)	Tushratta
			Mattiwaza
	Shalmaneser I (1273–1244)		
	Tukulti-Ninurta I (1243–1207)		
		Fall of Kassite Dynasty (1155)	
	Tiglath-pileser I (1114–1076)	Nebuchadnezzar I (1125–1104)	
1000			
	Ashur-dan II (934–912)		
	Adad-nerari II (911–891)		
	Tukulti-Ninurta II (890–884)		
	Ashurnasirpal II (883–859)		
	Shalmaneser III (858–824)		
	Shamshi-Adad V (823–811)		
	Adad-nerari III (810–783)		
	Tiglath-pileser III (744–727)	Nabu-nasir (747–734)	
	Sargon II (721–705)		
	Sennacherib (704–681)	Destruction of Babylon (689)	
	Esarhaddon (680–669)		
	Ashurbanipal (668–627)	Shamash-shuma-ukin (667–648)	
	Fall of Nineveh (612)	Nabopolassar (625–605)	
		Battle of Carchemish (605)	
		Nebuchadnezzar II (604–562)	
		Fall of Jerusalem (587)	
		Nabonidus (555–539)	
		Cyrus the Great captures Babylon (539)	

The Old Babylonian period and especially the Hammurapi Age is generally regarded as the classical period in Babylonian civilization, for it witnessed the first flowering of a distinctive culture now called Babylonian. The culture was the product of a conglomeration of various ethnic strains, chief among them being the earlier Sumero-Akkadian civilization which had flourished in the Babylonian plain during the third millennium BC. The Babylonian language was a dialect of Akkadian, a Semitic tongue, and written with the cuneiform script which was originally invented to express Sumerian. The political and economic structure at the beginning was basically the same as that during the third millennium, a number of small autonomous city states ruled by local dynasties and this gradually developed, as it had done earlier, into an imperial structure.

In religion, law, science and the arts there was a clear continuum from the previous civilization with gradual alteration brought about by new political realities. The pantheon of gods was headed by the trinity, An, Enlil and Enki (Ea in Akkadian) but, with the rise of the first dynasty of Babylon, the chief god of that city, Marduk, gained a promotion in status close to Enki, who was said to be his father. Legal practice was basically the same, with a few intrusions such as the *lex talionis* ('an eye for eye, a tooth for a tooth') which came from the Amorites.

The code of Hammurapi of Babylon (*c*1792–1750 BC). It includes the Amorite notion of 'an eye for an eye'.

ful so that at his death the first dynasty at Babylon claimed suzerainty over all of the Babylonian plain and regions north as far as Mari and Ashur.

The political intricacies of the Hammurapi Age were revealed by the discovery at Mari in the 1930s of a vast archive of clay tablets inscribed in cuneiform. These documents, mainly letters and business documents, provide details about the manoeuvres of Hammurapi and his rivals which are far more interesting than the official versions found in royal inscriptions and related sources. Ambassadors from Hammurapi's court resided in Mari, and vice versa, and each sent back reports to his respective king about the activities of his rival monarch. Externally, relations between Mari and Babylon were friendly but, when Hammurapi had finally conquered Rim-Sin of Larsa, he turned on his old ally at Mari and added this city state to his expanding empire.

The Ishtar Gate of Babylon, built during the reign of Nebuchadnezzar II (604–562 BC). The brick-and-bitumen walls were decorated with glazed tiles in brilliant colours.

Legal formulas continued to be phrased in the Sumerian language although legal contracts and the 'law codes' were now written in Akkadian. The literature of the Sumerians was sedulously copied out and studied during the Isin-Larsa period at the same time as in the north an Akkadian literature was beginning to appear. Sumerian, although it died as a spoken language, continued to be used throughout Babylonian civilization for liturgical and scholarly purposes.

There were, nonetheless, some major departures which marked Babylonian civilization as a distinctive development. The shift of power to the north was one of these and it was conditioned by a serious agricultural problem in the south where the salt table of the subsoil had risen through over-irrigation and poor drainage, to such a point that crop yields had gradually diminished and could no longer support the population. Another distinctive feature was the emergence of the Babylonian dialect of Akkadian which replaced, over a period of time, the Sumerian language and Old Akkadian dialect of the third millennium, both in spoken and written communication. Finally, the central role played by the city state of Babylon in all these developments, especially under the leadership of Hammurapi, left an indelible stamp on subsequent history, for thereafter Babylon was regarded as the natural capital, even in periods when the actual capital was elsewhere.

After Hammurapi's death, severe pressures were brought to bear upon the imperial structure which he had founded. These pressures were external foreign peoples and powers and, while each movement was independent of the other, the fact that they all emerged during the same general period placed an unbearable strain upon Hammurapi's successors. One of these forces was the Kassites. The origin and early history of the Kassites are obscure since, before entering Mesopotamia, they were illiterate mountain people and virtually nothing is known of their language. They first appear in the historical record as an invading military force in the time of Samsuiluna (c1749–1712 BC), Hammurapi's successor, but nothing more has been recovered about them until they established a dynasty in Babylonia, c1595 BC.

A second formidable force was the people of the Sealand, a kingdom in the extreme south of Babylonia along the Persian Gulf. Apart from the names of the kings of the Sealand little is known about these people for no native sources have been discovered. Nevertheless, it was a powerful nation which made serious inroads into the holdings of Hammurapi's successors and for a time controlled Nippur in the centre of the plain. The Sealand was eventually conquered by the Kassites. Because of its location in the south, the Sealand was strongly Sumerian in character and preserved Sumerian learning for a long time. During these troubled times Larsa made a short-lived bid to regain its freedom.

The external power that brought to an end the first dynasty of Babylon was the Hittite kingdom in Anatolia. Mursilis I, king of the Hittites, invaded Babylonia and sacked Babylon. Curiously, he immediately withdrew from the area after his success and the Kassites took advantage of the power vacuum to seize control.

The Middle Babylonian period (c1595 to 1000 BC)

The Kassite Dynasty was founded in Babylonia c1595 BC and, while there is a list of the names of the kings of this dynasty, very little is known about the early members some of whom were, in fact, probably rulers of these people before the conquest. One of the early kings after 1595 BC was Agum-kakrime, who boasted that he controlled most of Babylonia and that he brought back the statue of the god Marduk, which had been carried off by the Hittites at the time they looted Babylon. That the statue was retrieved is corroborated by a literary composition in which Marduk himself described his sojourn in the land of the Hittites. The date of these events and of Agum-kakrime's reign is unknown.

The next period of Babylonian history for which there is some coherent information is the fourteenth century BC. A fortuitous discovery at Amarna in Egypt of a cache of clay tablets inscribed in cuneiform has shed considerable light on a brief time span in the history of ancient West Asia, for these tablets contain letters to the Egyptian pharaohs (Tuthmosis III to Amenophis IV) from various parts of the Fertile Crescent, including Babylonia. The letters were written in Akkadian, which by this time had become the language of international relations. Two Kassite kings in particular were represented in the correspondence, Kadashman-Enlil I (c1374–1360 BC) and Burnaburiash II (c1359–1333 BC). These letters reveal an intensive interchange between the two courts, the Egyptians sending gold, and the Babylonians precious gifts and princesses to enter the pharaoh's harem. This exchange was clearly both commercial and diplomatic in nature for the intermarriage of ancient oriental royal families inevitably took place as part of the conclusion of a treaty or mutual agreement of some kind. The exact nature of the cordial relationship between Babylonia and Egypt is unknown.

At the end of the reign of Burnaburiash II there was an upheaval which resulted in the Assyrians interfering in Babylonian affairs and putting Kurigalzu II (c1332–1308 BC) on the throne. This inaugurated a brilliant period in Kassite history, for Kurigalzu led his army on successful campaigns against various enemies including the Elamites and Assyrians.

Little is known of the history of Babylonia after the Amarna Age until we reach the latter days of the Kassite dynasty. The period was characterized by a continuous series of clashes between Babylonia and two of her closest neighbours, Elam and Assyria. Babylonia was invaded and the city Babylon captured by one Assyrian king, Tukulti-Ninurta I (c1243–1207 BC), who carried off the image of the god Marduk to Assyria. Assyrian occupation of Babylonia was short-lived and eventually the Babylonians regained both their independence and the statue of their tutelary deity. Hostilities with Assyria and Elam continued for decades until two attacks by these same powers in one year brought to an end the Kassite dynasty (c1155 BC).

A Babylonian boundary stone. Mesopotamian kings placed such 'divine' markers on their frontiers in order to prevent terrestrial encroachment.

The Kassite period is a poorly documented part of Babylonian history, but what information is available indicates that it was certainly not a culturally deprived era. A new capital was created and called Dur-Kurigalzu (modern Aqar Quf near Baghdad), after King Kurigalzu, and was the focus of great building projects and artistic achievement. The Kassite rulers had the highest regard for Babylonian civilization and so adapted themselves to it that very few traces of anything distinctively Kassite were left. One curious feature that appeared during this time is an object called a *kudurru*. This was a large stone upon which were inscribed details regarding grants of land or grants of tax exemption on land. Many of these objects were actually large boundary stones and bore incised symbols of the deities which were invoked in the text to guard the legal stipulations.

Out of the ashes of the conflagration grew a new line of rulers which originally came from Isin and which is thus known as the second dynasty of Isin. Eventually the capital was shifted to Babylon where the most important of all the members of this dynasty, Nebuchadnezzar I (1125–1104 BC), reigned. This reign was such a memorable one that Nebuchadnezzar became a legend in Babylonian tradition and an interesting group of literary texts date from this period. This phenomenon was occasioned by a successful war with Elam which resulted in bringing back the divine image of Marduk from the Elamites who had carried it off at the fall of the Kassite dynasty. Marduk was installed once again in his temple in Babylon and for the first time publicly acknowledged as king of all gods, thus supplanting the ancient god An of the Sumerians.

Nebuchadnezzar also carried out border raids against Assyria and did a great deal of building, not only in Babylon but in many other Babylonian cities. This prosperous and enlightened era continued during the time of Nebuchadnezzar's immediate successors. Toward the end of the millennium, however, Babylonia was subjected to more and more raids by an invading force of Semitic-speaking semi-nomads, the Aramaeans. Gradually these people spread across the Babylonian plain creating chaos and confusion and so Babylonia entered another dark phase in her history.

Sources for the period of the second dynasty of Isin are rather sparse, but evidence from later Babylonian history indicates that the time of Nebuchadnezzar I was a very important one culturally. It has already been noted that there was a major religious development in connection with the god Marduk. In the literary sphere, there was an important movement to edit and, in a sense, canonize the literature which had been passed on from the Old Babylonian and earlier periods. New literary compositions were created and similar activity in the plastic arts and architecture can be observed.

The Neo-Babylonian period (c1000 to 539 BC)

The effects of the Aramaean invasion continued to be felt in Babylonia for a very long time with the result that little is known about events during the early centuries of the first millennium. The Armaeans were a distinctive and disruptive element in Babylonia during these dark days but gradually they settled down and blended into Babylonian society. Their presence did bring about a major change, however, for the Aramaic language slowly replaced Babylonian as the common tongue although it continued to be written and spoken by the educated classes.

During the ninth century Babylonia's neighbour, Assyria, enjoyed a revival of political power but refrained from encroaching upon Babylonia. Treaties of mutual respect were signed ,between Assyrian and Babylonian kings and when a revolution occurred in the reign of Marduk-zakir-shumi I, Shalmaneser III of Assyria (858–824 BC) stepped in to put it down and help Marduk-zakir-shumi regain his throne. Toward the end of the century hostilities broke out between the neighbours and continued sporadically into the eighth century. Babylonia was the stronger party during this time for Assyria was going through a temporary period of weakness.

A new era dawned in Babylonian history with the reign of Nabu-nasir (747–734 BC) and the systematic observation and compilation of astronomical phenomena and historical events began in his reign. This development was related to the practice of astrology, which was now in vogue, and fortunately for modern historians produced, among other things, the Babylonian Chronicle Series, a continuous chronicle of events in Babylonia for the remainder of her history. A portion of this history has been recovered.

Throughout the remainder of the eighth century BC Babylonian political life was disturbed by the Chaldaeans, a Semitic-speaking group of people who had entered the plain earlier and who were now settled along the coast of the Persian Gulf. One tribe of Chaldaeans, Yakin, produced an eminently capable leader called Merodach-baladan II, who with Elamite support made numerous attempts to seize the Babylonian crown and actually succeeded on two occasions, 721–710 and 703 BC. The Babylonians were divided in their loyalties during these chaotic times while the Assyrians made every effort to defeat and capture Merodach-baladan and his troops. He was too clever for them, however, and whenever the Assyrians were pressing close he withdrew into the marshes of the southern plain which the northern armies found almost impenetrable. Thus political power in Babylonia passed back and forth like a football from the Chaldaeans to the Assyrians and the unfortunate victims were the Babylonians themselves.

The Assyrians, for their part, tried different methods of controlling Babylonia. In Nabu-nasir's time they respected his right to rule but, when the Chaldaeans gained control after his death, the Assyrian king Tiglath-pileser III (744–727 BC) marched into Babylonia and took the Babylonian crown for himself. This practice of an Assyrian king assuming Babylonian sovereignty continued, with the exception of the periods when Merodach-baladan ruled, until the time of the Assyrian Sennacherib (704–681 BC) who attempted to rule Babylonia through a series of puppet kings. This system

came dramatically to an end when one of these kings, Sennacherib's own son, was seized by the Babylonians and handed over to an Elamite army to be carried back to Elam. Sennacherib, enraged by the treachery, led a series of fierce campaigns against the Elamites and Babylonians which ended in the capture and destruction of Babylon in 689 BC.

The sack of Babylon appalled Babylonians and Assyrians alike and while Sennacherib's successors attempted to make amends by a gigantic rebuilding programme, hatred seethed in Babylonian breasts and ultimately sparked a major rebellion which lasted for four years (652–648 BC). At the time the rebellion erupted, Babylonia was ruled by Shamash-shuma-ukin (667–648 BC), the brother of the reigning Assyrian monarch, Ashurbanipal (668–627 BC). Ashurbanipal was the victor in the end, defeating not only Shamash-shuma-ukin but also his Elamite and Arab allies. The hardship and famine which the Babylonians suffered from this prolonged war resulted in a short period of total inactivity.

About twenty years after the suppression of the rebellion, the Chaldaeans made a new effort to gain control of the Babylonian plain and were successful in establishing a dynasty which became the most powerful in Babylonian history. The leader of this movement and founder of the Chaldaean dynasty was Nabopolassar (625–605 BC). Through a series of offensives against the Assyrians, Nabopolassar gained control of the entire Babylonian plain and was crowned king in Babylon. The momentum of the offensive continued after his coronation and he, in league with the Medes, pushed into Assyrian territory and made steady gains. The Assyrian cities fell one after the other and the capital, Nineveh, was taken after a three-month siege in 612 BC. Assyrian power was still not broken, however, for a rump dynasty emerged in the west at Harran, bolstered by Egypt. Nabopolassar's armies took Harran and later, in 605 BC, inflicted a decisive defeat upon the Egyptian army at Carchemish. By this victory Babylonia won not only control over Assyria proper but became heir to her empire, for the Medes restricted their claims to regions further east and north.

During the latter years of Nabopolassar's reign his son, Nebuchadnezzar II (604–562 BC), led the Babylonian army on campaign and it was he who actually achieved the victory at Carchemish in 605 BC where he received word that his father had died. He rushed back to Babylon and was crowned king, inaugurating one of the most brilliant periods in Babylonian history. Nebuchadnezzar continued the vigorous campaigns to which he had become accustomed, concentrating on the west which he effectively brought under his control. The kingdom of Judah, relying upon Egyptian assistance, resisted the Babylonian advance and on two occasions Nebuchadnezzar II captured the city. The second conquest, 587 BC, brought to an end the dynasty at Jerusalem and was accompanied by the massive transportation of Judaeans to Babylon remembered ever after in Jewish history as 'the Exile'. With Jerusalem destroyed, Nebuchadnezzar pressed on to invade Egypt in 668 BC. There is no detailed account of this invasion but it was, at best, an ephemeral success for no subsequent Chaldaean king claimed suzerainty over Egypt.

After Nebuchadnezzar's death there was a short period of rather obscure sovereigns and then Nabonidus (555–539 BC), the last of the dynasty, ascended the throne. Nabonidus is an intriguing figure for, not only did he have a tragic role to play in the fall of Babylon, but he behaved in a very curious fashion throughout his life. He came from a family closely connected with the city of Harran and his mother, who lived to the grand age of 95, boasted of having been a loyal subject of the last Assyrian kings. How he came to be king at Babylon is unknown. Both mother and son were zealous devotees of the moon-god Sin, tutelary deity of Harran, but when Nabonidus tried to promote this cult in Babylonia, the native priests, and especially those of Marduk, were enraged. The religious controversy split the state into factions and a little of the literary propaganda of the time has been recovered.

The most curious feature of Nabonidus's reign, however, is the fact that for ten of the seventeen years he ruled he lived at an Arab desert oasis, Tema, a vast distance from Babylon. In Babylon he left his son, Belshazzar, to rule on his behalf. This unparalleled circumstance has piqued the imagination of ancients and moderns alike so that many different versions of and reasons for this exile have been offered. The fact that the moon-god was highly regarded among pre-Islamic Arabs is certainly relevant and, while Nabonidus may have gone to Tema for a variety of political, economic and personal reasons, his devotion to the cult of the moon would have been a major consideration. When Cyrus the Great of Persia threatened invasion of Babylonia, Nabonidus, now back in Babylonia, staunchly defended his kingdom, but ultimately Babylon was taken in 539 BC.

Babylonian culture flourished during the *pax Assyriaca* of the seventh century BC and again under the Chaldaean dynasty of the sixth century BC. The god Nabu, son of Marduk and god of writing and learning, gained in popularity throughout the period. The practice of astrology permeated society and the nightly watch of the astrologers throughout the kingdom resulted in the massive corpus of detailed records of the movements of heavenly bodies which has been recovered in modern times. Literature was sedulously copied and studied and from time to time new compositions were created. In art and architecture the most impressive remains that have been unearthed by archaeologists are in Nebuchadnezzar's Babylon, a city that obviously had not changed much when Herodotus wrote about it less than a century later and called its Hanging Gardens one of the seven wonders of the world.

Literature

Babylonian literature has its origin in Sumerian literature of the third millennium BC and, like most features of Babylonian civilization, always retained a definite affinity with the earlier culture. When Babylonian literature was first emerging in the Old Babylonian period, scribes were busily translating compositions from Sumerian into Babylonian or writing new versions of such compositions in their own tongue. Thus some portion of Babylonian literature consists of Sumerian works rendered into Akkadian either through direct translation or through editing and reworking. From earliest times, however, there were also original creations in the Babylonian language and throughout Babylonian history the number of these slowly increased and each age, the Old, Middle, and Neo-Babylonian periods, made a contribution.

Intensive editing and selection of literary works occurred during the latter part of the second millennium BC. There were schools of scribes, each under a leading figure, which concerned themselves with these matters. Literary compositions which had been passed down for centuries were reworked, rewritten and their form standardized into a certain number of tablets per composition with a specific number of lines to each tablet. Catalogues of the works were compiled and the names of the editors, the heads of scribal schools, entered. Thus the *Gilgamesh Epic* was worked into a twelve-tablet version, the number of a given tablet and the number of lines thereon being recorded in a colophon, and its editor's name given as Sin-liqi-unninni.

There is no doubt that an oral tradition of tales and legends existed simultaneously with the literary tradition of the Babylonians, but an oral background to their literature was relatively remote, given the fact that so much came by way of the Sumerians. Literary works were probably read or recited to the illiterate public for entertainment and edification. Long after the fall of Babylon in 539 BC, Babylonian literature continued to be copied, studied and created in the plain, although by this time foreign tongues, Aramaic and Greek, had become the everyday means of communication.

Babylonian literature consists of both prose and poetry. The chief characteristic of the poetry is parallelism, the rendition of an idea in two different ways side by side. Thus the passage from the *Atra-hasis Epic* in which the god Enlil complains:

> 'The clamour of mankind oppresses me,
> By their tumult I am deprived of sleep.'

Poetic lines are commonly grouped in couplets, as here, although singlets and triplets do occur. The line ends in a trochee and usually divides into two stichoi, each of which commonly has two beats. Rhyme was unknown but whether or not metre was present cannot now be determined with certainty.

In native tradition, literary compositions are commonly entitled by the first few words of the text and so one finds such titles as *When Above* (*Enuma Elish*) and *He Who Saw the Abyss* (*Gilgamesh Epic*). Formal division of literature according to genres was not explicitly recognized by the ancient Babylonians although modern scholars can, in fact, divide the literature into a number

A lyre with the head of a bearded bull in gold and ornament of other materials. An instrument of this sort appears in the 'peace' scene on the Royal Standard of Ur.

of categories. These are epics and myths, prayers and hymns, wisdom literature and historiography. Certain motifs and stories were popular among the ancient Babylonians and reappear in more than one composition. So, for example, the story of the flood is known both from a version in the *Gilgamesh Epic* and from one in the *Atra-hasis Epic*. The most famous epics and myths are *Gilgamesh, Atra-hasis, Adapa, Nergal and Ereshkigal, When Above, Descent of Ishtar into Hades, Anzu, Etana and Era*. A sub-genre is the historical epic of which two examples are the *King of Battle* and *Tukulti-Ninurta I. Gilgamesh* is by far the longest of all these compositions. Its titular hero was the ruler of Uruk during the middle of the third millennium. Tales were told and written about him in Sumerian but no connected epic has ever been recovered from that early period. There are several compositions about Gilgamesh from the Babylonian periods but the classic text is the twelve-tablet epic which became the canonical version.

Huwawa. The semi-legendary king of Uruk, Gilgamesh, killed the fire-breathing giant Huwawa in the Cedar Forest with the assistance of fierce winds provided by the sun-god Shamash.

According to the epic, Gilgamesh, who was one-third god and two-thirds man, was in his city Uruk when he heard of a strange man, Enkidu, living in the steppes with the wild beasts. He persuaded a prostitute to lure Enkidu to Uruk, where Gilgamesh wrestled with him to try his strength. The two became fast friends and went off on a variety of adventurous expeditions which included the conquest of the monster Humbaba in the cedar forest in the west. Enkidu, however, eventually died and Gilgamesh, sick with grief, set out to discover the secret of immortality from the one man who had survived the ancient flood, Ut-napishtim. After hearing the story of the deluge, Gilgamesh sought, found, but then tragically lost the plant of life.

The prayers and hymns were commonly part of the ritual of a particular cult and, while some are of no special literary merit, others are great pieces of literature. Such, for example, is the *Hymn to Shamash*, the sun-god, a 200-line composition from which the following is quoted:

'The far mountains are capped by thy brilliance,
Thy glow fills the entirety of lands.
Thou dost ascend the highlands to view the earth,
The perimeter of lands in the heavens thou dost
    weigh.
All the peoples of the lands thou dost supervise,
What divine Ea, king of counsellors, created thou
    dost control entirely.'

The term 'wisdom literature' is borrowed from biblical terminology where it is used to describe such works as the Book of Job and the Book of Proverbs, and in Babylonian literature there are similar compositions. Among the more important wisdom pieces are *I Will Praise the Lord of Wisdom, The Theodicy, The Dialogue of Pessimism*, fables and debates, and various collections of proverbs. Several of these works are concerned with the problem of evil and suffering and the case of the good

and pious man who has fallen upon evil days is used as a basis for profound observations upon religion and morality. Cynicism is apparent in one text, *The Dialogue of Pessimism*, wherein, through an amusing sequence of discussions between master and slave, it is illustrated how any activity can lead to success or failure, according to the chance of fortune, and the conclusion is that death is the only dependable thing in life.

The Babylonians were steeped in their own history and wrote many literary compositions which reflect this interest. One of the interesting types of historiographical works was the prophecy. This was a literary text which described past events in prophetic terms as though the author had predicted these before they happened. Having thereby established his credibility, he proceeded to make real prophecies which had a variety of forms according to the particular purpose he wished to achieve. The Babylonian prophecy was a forerunner of apocalyptic literature, a genre to which the Book of Revelation belongs.

Religion

The state religion of Babylonia involved large cults with big temples and numerous personnel while the religion of the private individual was involved with magic and sorcery. The state religion revolved around the great gods of the cities who were ranked in an order corresponding more or less to the political status of their cities. Thus by the first millennium BC, Marduk, god of Babylon, was king of the gods and his son, Nabu of Borsippa, was right next to him. The multitude of cities and pantheons in Babylonia and the waxing and waning of the political fortunes of the various cities throughout Babylonian history resulted in a great deal of conflict and confusion among the numerous cults.

The problem was further compounded by the fact that each god had his own particular sphere of activity. The sun-god Shamash was in charge of justice while the goddess Ishtar embraced both love and war. But inevitably there was considerable overlapping among the pantheons of the many cities. The theologians made gargantuan efforts to systematize the hierarchy and functions of the gods. They drew up long lists of the numerous god names and, in a parallel column, equated the numerous lesser gods with one of the greater and better known deities. These syncretic lists became a literary tradition and were passed on from century to century with revisions and additions.

The care and feeding of the gods in the great temples was a matter of daily concern. Elaborate rituals requiring the participation and support of numbers of temple personnel evolved around the daily presentation of offerings, the cleaning of the divine statues' garments, and the purification of the temples. Offerings were provided from the temple's land holdings, endowments by royal and wealthy people, and from occasional gifts such as war booty. The offerings were consumed by the temple personnel. Special festivals were celebrated by every cult, the chief being the *Akitu* or New Year's Festival of the god Marduk at Babylon. This stretched over a number of days and included a stately procession of neighbouring gods, such as Nabu to Babylon, and a formal parade of Marduk escorted by the king from his temple to the New Year's house outside the city wall. Failure to celebrate the festival because of political turmoil or other causes was a grave matter and, whenever this happened, it was recorded with great concern in the native histories.

The private Babylonian had little to do with the great state cults, other than witnessing the processions at festival time, and he found religious fulfilment in other

Reconstruction of the great temple of Marduk at Babylon.

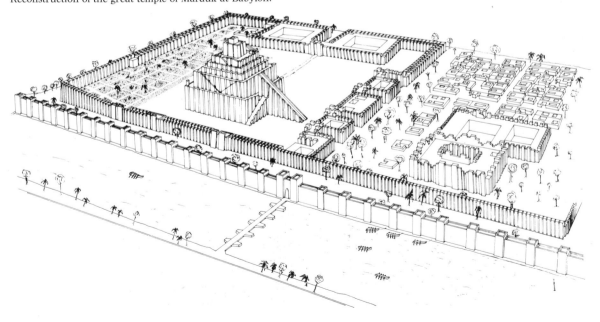

ways. Each Babylonian had a personal god whom he provided with regular offerings and to whom he made special requests, such as for relief from illness. The personal god was expected to mediate upon his devotee's behalf with higher gods who could provide the necessary benefaction. There was a business-like attitude on the part of the Babylonian in this relationship for, if the worshipper felt he was not getting sufficient benefits in return for his offerings, he would threaten to abandon his god and seek another. Indeed, one ancient cynic commented: 'Thou canst teach thy god to run like a dog after thee.' Magic and sorcery were universally popular and there were spells and counter-spells ('releases') for every aspect of life. Black magic was greatly feared and experts in sorcery were sought out to counteract the witchcraft which was believed to have brought trouble or misfortune to an individual.

The practice of divination is one of the most distinctive features of Babylonian civilization and must be fully studied by any who would gain an appreciation of Babylonian thought. The Babylonian believed that the gods communicated their intentions to mankind by means of signs in natural phenomena and worldly events and that it was possible to learn to read these signs through prolonged observation and deep study. The absence of determinism here should be noted; the gods could change their minds at any time and often did so, but they would notify mankind of this. The vehicle of communication could be anything in earth or heaven and omens could be seen in the way smoke rose from a fire, abnormal births among humans or animals, the sudden appearance of a lion in a city street, an eclipse of the moon, or an unusual dream. The Babylonian was surrounded by ominous happenings.

Certain types of divination were more common than others and the two most popular were the observation of the stars and planets, astrology and the observation of

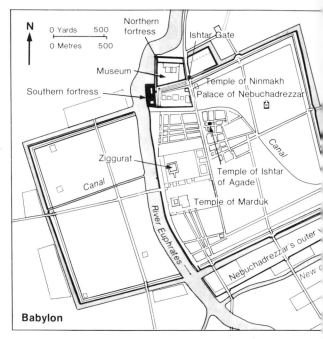

the entrails of sacrificial animals, extispicy. In the latter type of divination the foci of concern were the liver and lungs and the diviners drew up long lists of possible malformations and discolorations in every minute part. They even went so far as to make models of the livers in clay and mark the various parts with appropriate cuneiform inscriptions. The variations and possible combinations of formations were almost endless. But each had an interpretation. For example:

> 'If there is a "weapon-mark" on the ṣibtu (liver part) and it rises from right to left: the army will enjoy the spoil of the enemy army.'

The interpretation, which is often expressed in historical terms as here, was not taken literally but simply as 'good' or 'bad'. In this case the enemy army suffers and so the meaning is good. A number of observations could be gleaned from any given animal and the interpretations, good, bad or confused, tabulated to determine the response.

There was a moral aspect to Babylonian religion for it was generally believed that good behaviour, which included worship of and offerings to the gods, would win divine favour although some, as noted above in the discussion of wisdom literature, questioned this idea. Many of the gods did not behave in a very upright or sober manner, however, and there is the intriguing case of the goddess Ishtar who tried to seduce Gilgamesh. The hero rejected her erotic advances, denouncing her for the evil fate that she had inflicted upon all her previous lovers.

Clay model of a liver, marked with cuneiform inscriptions. Mesopotamian diviners foretold events by the examination of livers from sacrificial animals.

Law

A number of documents from Babylonia called Law Codes have been recovered and the fact that these contain parallels with biblical and modern law has evoked considerable interest in modern scholarship. The documents in question are: *The Laws of Urukagina* (Sumerian, *c*2350 BC), *The Laws of Ur-Nammu* (Sumerian, *c*2112–2095 BC), *The Laws of Lipit-Ishtar* (Sumerian *c*1934–1924 BC), *The Laws of Eshnunna* (Babylonian, *c*1900 BC), and *The Code of Hammurapi* (Babylonian, *c*1792–1750 BC). Although three of the texts are in Sumerian there is a clear relationship and frequently verbal agreement among all of them, reflecting a continuous literary tradition. With the exception of the *Laws of Eshnunna*, they are all written in the form of a royal inscription. This fact indicates that they are not legal codes at all and this observation is corroborated by other features, namely the lack of consistency and the fact that the documents are neither comprehensive nor are they ever referred to in the abundant records of actual legal proceedings of the time. Rather, they are collections, within the framework of royal inscriptions, of independent legal decrees issued by various kings to meet specific problems. Collections of these, of which the *Laws of Eshnunna* is one example, were continuously copied, added to, and elaborated upon. From time to time these were put into royal inscriptions as a boast by the king that he had fulfilled his divine mission to administer his people justly and fairly.

The so-called Law Codes provide a wealth of information not only about legal practice in Babylonia but also about political, social, economic and religious institutions and customs. One of the more interesting facts learned therefrom is in the matter of punishment for bodily injury. In the early codes, if a man injured someone physically he was required to pay a fine, the amount varying according to the gravity of the injury. But in the *Code of Hammurapi* provision is made for retaliation in kind. Thus, if a man broke another man's arm, his arm would be broken. This principle of *lex talionis* appears simultaneously with the ascendance of the Amorites in Babylonia and has its origin with these people.

In actual legal practice, precedent and custom were the guiding rules and there was no codified statement of the law of the land to which reference could be made in a legal dispute. Disputes between two or more parties were commonly settled privately, either directly or through the mediation of a neutral outsider. On occasion a settlement could not be reached in this way and then the disputants would go to court. The court consisted of an assembly of people which included judges and elders. Each side would present its case and usually take an oath by the god or gods that he or she was speaking the truth. Witnesses would present their testimony and similarly swear to the veracity of their words. When all testimony had been heard, the assembly would deliberate and the judges pronounce their decision. The case was recorded on a clay tablet which contained the names of the judges and witnesses and the private seals of the participants impressed in the clay.

Disputes were private affairs and the state did not act as a prosecuting body. While prisons existed, they seem to have been used largely for political purposes. Debtors who could not pay their creditors became debt slaves. In some instances ordeals were used to determine the guilt or innocence of an accused person. Thus a man accused of sorcery was forced to jump into the river; if he drowned he was guilty but if he survived he was innocent and, in the latter eventuality, his accuser was put to death. Women had equal rights with men before the law and even debt slaves had legal rights.

There was a variety of legal transactions which were carefully recorded on clay tablets and a vast multitude of these have been recovered from the Old and Neo-Babylonian periods. These documents are concerned with marriage, adoption, inheritance, sale, exchange, hire, lease, loans and receipts, as well as with court proceedings as already mentioned. Closely related to the legal documents were the administrative accounts of palace, temple and private business, and large numbers of these have also been found. Records of this kind were stored in large clay jars with a seal on top and a brief statement as to the contents of the jar. Before the records were placed in the jar, a catalogue of its contents was prepared so that a particular document could be located when it was required in a dispute.

King and state

The Babylonian political structure was a monarchy. The king ruled through a number of officials who were directly under and responsible to him but he could intervene personally at any level of government and administration. Thus Hammurapi (*c*1792–1750 BC) took a direct hand in dealing with property claims in Larsa after he had captured that city state. The monarchy was hereditary and male primogeniture seems to have been the guiding principle. Babylonian historians designated a continuous line of kings a 'dynasty' (*palû*), but the criterion here was not blood relationship between the members of the dynasty, although they might be related, but lack of serious interruption through war or revolution.

The king was an absolute monarch and in the very early period there were a few checks to his authority in that he had to respect custom and tradition, private property, the sensibilities of the nobles, religion and divination. The king was the ultimate authority in all areas except religion where he was subject to the dictates of the chief god as represented by his chief priest. Thus in the New Year's festival the king's role included being slapped in the face by the chief priest and pulled by the ears as a sign of his subservience to the god.

The king resided in a palace, the size and magnificence of which would depend upon the fortunes of the time, the palace of Nebuchadnezzar II (604–562 BC) probably having been the most splendid. The monarch was surrounded by his court, a body which embraced his highest officials, with the exception of provincial governors who resided in their capitals. The harem was the focus of the king's family life and privacy was rigidly maintained by a guard of eunuchs.

Efficient administration of the country depended upon good communications through a system of roads and relay stations for messengers. Written communications passed back and forth in great number and required a large body of trained scribes. Most people, including the king and his officials, were illiterate so that they were heavily dependent upon the scribes both to write and interpret their commands and reports in an appropriate manner. Many of these letters have been discovered in modern times and they provide a fascinating glimpse of the real events and human relationships of the day, in contrast to the official versions found in royal inscriptions.

Economy and social structure

Babylonian economy was based upon agriculture, animal husbandry, manufactured goods (chiefly textiles) and foreign trade. The chief economic institutions were the palace and temples which owned large areas of land and were also involved in manufacturing and trade. There were in addition private land-holders and business firms, and goods were exchanged on a barter system with silver as the standard of exchange. Payment was in kind and silver did not normally change hands. There was a standard system of weights and measures controlled by the crown and many metal and stone weights, often in the shape of ducks, can now be seen in modern museums. The king could and did decree the price of certain goods at certain times but in general the price of items was allowed to fluctuate according to supply and demand.

There were several levels in the social hierarchy with the king at the top and the slaves at the bottom. In between, in descending order, were the nobles, the free citizens and those in military and civil service. The class structure was generally rigid although some mobility from one level to another was possible. The debt slave had the possibility of paying his debts and regaining his freedom but the only hope for the foreign captive was escape or death.

The basic units in Babylonian society were the family and tribe. An individual's class and station were determined by that of his family and a Babylonian without a family was a rare and miserable creature. Widows and orphans were the responsibility of the state, specifically the king, and adoption was very common. Urban communities formed a salient characteristic of Babylonian civilization and the plain was dotted with cities, notably Babylon, Sippar, Kish, Nippur and Ur. Residents of a particular city were very conscious of being citizens of that city and jealous of any special rights and privileges which they enjoyed either by tradition or royal decree. The Babylonian social structure was shaken fairly often by the influx of new people, such as the Kassites and Aramaeans, but eventually each new group was absorbed and altered the general pattern of society only slightly.

Science

Babylonian civilization has in recent decades become renowned for its scientific achievements, as study of the cuneiform records has revealed how much had been known and passed on to Europe during the Hellenistic era and not, as believed earlier, discovered first by the Egyptians or Greeks. Recognition of Babylonian scientific knowledge has been hampered by the fact that much of it involved the practice of divination and it is not always possible to draw a line between observed fact and logical deduction on the one hand and religious belief on the other. Nevertheless, the observations of the astrologers, which were meticulously recorded on a nightly basis over many centuries, led to accurate predictions of various astronomical phenomena and the correct calculation of the solar and lunar year. The Babylonian calendar was based upon the lunar year but, thanks to the astrologer's knowledge, could be reconciled with the solar year by means of intercalary months.

Medicine was practised by two kinds of experts, the physician (*asû*) and the exorcist (*āšipu*) and the talents of either or both might be demanded at the sick bed. There was a whole set of diagnostic texts in which a multitude of possible symptoms was listed and the diagnosis, prognosis and treatment given. Surgery was known and even delicate operations on the eye were performed. The Babylonians had a superb knowledge of human and animal anatomy and physiology and were aware, for example, of the circulation of the blood and the pulse.

Babylonian mathematical tablet. Study of the cuneiform records in recent decades has revealed a society with outstanding attainments in science and mathematics.

Mathematics was another sphere in which the Babylonians excelled. Theoretical mathematics intrigued them and a large number of texts involving geometry and algebra of a quite sophisticated sort has been preserved. The theorems of Euclid and Pythagoras were already known in the Old Babylonian period. The Babylonians were intimate with the variety of stones, metals, trees, plants, animals, birds and fish which existed in their world and left for posterity a multitude of lists of their names and texts about them.

Assyria

A. K. Grayson

The modern recovery of the history of Assyria ranks as one of the great achievements in archaeology. The spectacular finds at the ancient sites of Nineveh, Calah and Dur-Sharrukin by Paul Emile Bottá (1802–70) and Sir Austen Henry Layard (1817–94), to mention only the two most outstanding figures, excited the imagination of nineteenth-century Europe and North America and prompted even more intensive excavation and study which gradually produced a picture of one of the world's lost civilizations.

Geography

The Assyrian heartland is roughly an inverted triangle with its apex at the city Ashur and the other two points at the cities of Nineveh and Arbela. This area embraces the Tigris river and one of its major tributaries, the Greater Zab. To the east and north of Assyria are the mountains of Kurdistan, to the south the Babylonian plain and to the west the semi-desert area of Syria called the Jezirah. The rolling hills of the Assyrian heartland have a luxuriant growth thanks to the abundant and regular rains which this region enjoys. The crops grown in ancient times were largely barley and sesame and the animals bred were sheep, goats and cattle. Unlike

The Assyrian empire.

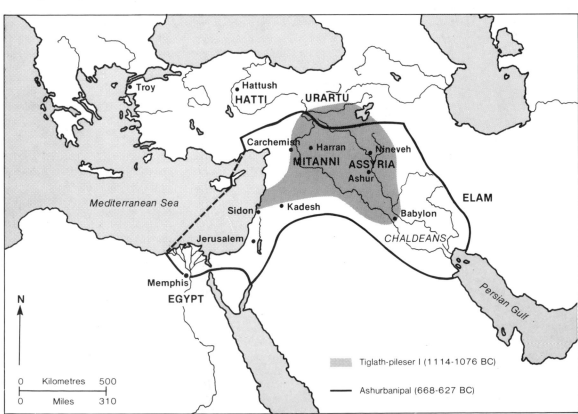

Tiglath-pileser I (1114-1076 BC)

Ashurbanipal (668-627 BC)

Babylonia, dates cannot be grown but grapes were known and used to make wine. The summers are warm and dry and the winters cool and rainy. In the mountains the winters are very cold with ice and snow.

The city state of Ashur was located on the west bank of the Tigris at the point where the Jebel Hamrin fades into the desert and was, therefore, the fording point for caravans on the east-west route. Traffic also flowed up and down the Tigris through the entire length of the Assyrian triangle. Apart from stone (alabaster and limestone) the area was poor in natural resources although today it is one of the world's richest oil fields. Timber, precious metals and stones were imported in vast quantities during the heyday of the Assyrian empire.

The Old Assyrian period (c2000 to 1363 BC)
At the dawn of history in the Assyrian heartland there were three significant city states, Ashur, Nineveh, and Arbela. These were autonomous and controlled only their immediate environs. Almost nothing is known of the early history of Nineveh or Arbela but there is a little information about that of Ashur. It was ruled by a series of leaders called vice regents of the god Ashur who were actively engaged in building projects in their city and over the centuries a maze of palaces, temples and walls was erected.

A profitable trade in copper was carried on during this time with Anatolia and this was done through a large merchant colony established in eastern Anatolia, in Cappadocia, at a city called Kanesh. A great many of the records of this flourishing colony of Assyrian merchants

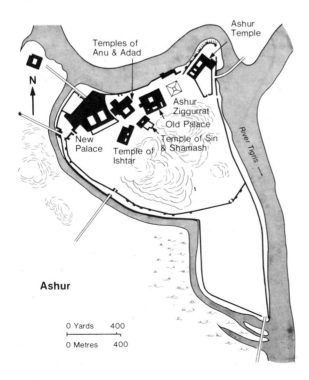

Ashur

0 Yards 400

0 Metres 400

have been discovered and provide considerable information, not only about the trade itself, but also about the ethnic, social and religious complexities of eastern Anatolia at that early period.

The Amorite invasion of Mesopotamia in about 2000 BC resulted in the foundation of a number of Amorite dynasties in the whole region, of which that of Shamshi-Adad I (c1813–1781 BC) at Ashur was one. The reign of Shamshi-Adad marks the first attempt to bring the entire region under one authority and, at the height of his power, he controlled an area stretching from Assyria to Babylonia in the south and Mari to the west. Hammurapi captured Ashur after Shamshi-Adad's death and the region entered a long period of political obscurity during which it came under the control of the kingdom of Mitanni to the west.

The Middle Assyrian period (c1363 to 1000 BC)
The reign of Ashur-uballit I (1363–1328 BC) witnessed not only the recovery of independence for the area but the foundation of the Assyrian Empire. The long war with the kingdom of Mitanni had begun and was not finally completed until the reign of the Assyrian, Shalmaneser I (1273–1244 BC), who incorporated the eastern half of Mitannian territory as the Assyrian province of Hanigalbat. Returning to Ashur-uballit, he had a marriage alliance with the Babylonian royal line and, when a revolution removed the legitimate king there, the Assyrian marched south to restore order and re-establish the line.

After Ashur-uballit's death a prolonged war with Babylonia was waged, mainly in the east Tigris region, with both sides experiencing gains and losses. This war was part and parcel of the constant conflict that prevailed in Assyro-Babylonian relations throughout the history of the two nations. This rivalry can be traced back to the early Amorite dynasties of Hammurapi and Shamshi-Adad I which were ethnically related. The Assyrians were superior in military skills but the Babylonians had a much more highly developed culture. The war with Babylonia was only one of the military occupations of Assyria during this period, for successive kings were slowly building the size and might of the nation through campaigns in the mountains to the east and north against various hostile peoples which had in earlier days harassed their borders.

The reign of Tukulti-Ninurta I (1243–1207 BC) brought the Assyrian empire to unprecedented power but, at the same time, saw the end of the first phase of the Middle Assyrian period. Tukulti-Ninurta was a vigorous fighter who conducted campaigns against the mountain tribes to the north and east, against the Hittites to the west, and into Babylonia to the south. On the last-mentioned expedition he captured and plundered the city of Babylon, carrying off much booty to Assyria. Tukulti-Ninurta was also a great builder and created an entirely new city across the river from Ashur which he named Kar-Tukulti-Ninurta. He met a tragic end. His son led a revolution in which the father was killed and the son gained the throne.

A short period of obscurity, occasioned by the mass movement of various peoples including the Phrygians on Assyria's borders, was followed by the most brilliant period of the Middle Assyrian empire and its final phase. The greatest king of this era was Tiglath-pileser I (1114–1076 BC) who emulated and surpassed the achievements of Tukulti-Ninurta I. The most pressing problem for this monarch was the Phrygians (the Assyrians called them Mushku), whose attack on Assyria at Tiglath-pileser's accession the new monarch successfully repelled. In subsequent years he campaig-

ned against them in eastern Anatolia. The Aramaean invasion was another concern of Tiglath-pileser. The campaigns against them were successful but rigorous and the Assyrian boasts that in pursuit of the Aramaeans he crossed the Euphrates no less than 28 times and on one occasion defeated a total of 6 Aramaean tribes at Jebel Bishri. These endeavours brought him to the Mediterranean where he symbolically washed his weapons in the sea. Tiglath-pileser also found time to conduct a campaign south on which he seized and looted important Babylonian cities. The Aramaean pressure did not let up and during the final years of the first millennium increased to the point where they had captured all Assyrian holdings in the west and were threatening to overrun Assyria itself.

The three reigns which have been highlighted in this survey of political events were also of cultural significance. Babylonian influence in Assyrian civilization was of great importance in all periods and the time of Ashur-uballit I was no exception. The cult of the Babylonian god Marduk is first attested at Ashur at this time. Babylonian religious rituals and literature were imported into Assyria as a direct result of the capture of Babylon by Tukulti-Ninurta I and, in the time of Tiglath-pileser I, the calendar and system of weights and measures were changed to the Babylonian system. As the power and extent of the empire increased, so did the might and authority of its sovereign. These found expression in the development of the Assyrian court and harem which can be traced in a series of texts from the time of Ashur-uballit I to that of Tiglath-pileser I. The king was surrounded by an increasing number of courtiers and protocol which isolated him more and more from his subjects.

The military might of Assyria was transformed at the beginning of the period by the introduction into the Fertile Crescent of the horse-drawn chariot and in the time of Tiglath-pileser I iron smeltering became more common, with a gradual improvement of the quality and efficiency of weapons and equipment.

The Neo-Assyrian period (c1000 to 612 BC)

At the beginning of the millennium, the Aramaeans dominated the scene and almost nothing is known of Assyria apart from the name of her kings. By the ninth century, however, Assyrian power had reappeared and a series of vigorous monarchs led numerous campaigns to the west against the Aramaeans, regaining lost lands. These kings were Ashur-dan II (934–912 BC), Adad-nerari II (911–891 BC), Tukulti-Ninurta II (890–884 BC) and Ashurnasirpal II (883–859 BC).

The Assyrian armies as they pushed westwards reached first the Habur, then the Balih, the Euphrates and finally the Mediterranean Sea. The long and arduous campaigns were much like one another. The royal armies marched ever further west conquering and plundering Aramaean tribes and states. Each campaign first traversed regions previously subdued and, as it did so, the local people produced tribute in the form of food and animals for the troops and luxury items such as gold

Nimrud ivory, eighth century BC. Delicate ivory carving from the Assyrian city of Nimrud.

and silver utensils for the king to take back. From time to time a king led a campaign solely through territory which had already been conquered, collecting his tribute in this manner and keeping a strong Assyrian presence evident in the territory. By the reign of Ashurnasirpal II the conquests had become so extensive that the Assyrians began to create local depots far from Assyria where they stored the grain collected from the surrounding regions and built fortresses to guard them. These then became stages on future military expeditions. It was from these depots of the ninth century that provincial capitals developed and the Assyrian provincial administration of the eighth and seventh centuries BC was formed.

Although the west was the chief goal of the Assyrians in this period, campaigns were launched in other directions. Ashurnasirpal II carried out a series of raids to the east in a region in the Zagros mountains called Zamua. He also pushed down the Euphrates to the edge of Babylonian territory although he did not invade Babylonia. In fact, there was probably a treaty between Assyria and Babylonia whereby the king of each state declared respect for the other and promised to help in case of need. Ashurnasirpal was one of the great builders in Assyrian history. He took over Calah and by a massive construction programme completely transformed it to become the leading metropolis in Assyria.

Ashurnasirpal II was succeeded by his son Shalmaneser III (858–824 BC) who concentrated his military endeavours on two fronts, the west and the north.

Detail from obelisk of Shalmaneser III (858–824 BC), who greatly extended Assyrian power in the west during his long and successful reign.

Shalmaneser went further westwards than any of his predecessors, pushing down into Syria as far as Palestine and up into the Taurus range. The northern campaigns were against a new kingdom, Urartu, which was now becoming a serious threat to Assyria. Above and beyond these major undertakings, Shalmaneser became embroiled in Babylonian affairs for, in accordance with a treaty, he entered Babylonia to put down a rebellion and restore the kingdom to its rightful monarch. This long and successful reign ended in obscurity with internal dissension and a revolution. The immediate successors of Shalmaneser, Shamshi-Adad V (823–811 BC) and Adad-nerari III (810–783 BC), managed to restore some order to the state and even to conduct profitable campaigns on most fronts but a gradual decline became apparent.

This was the period when the kingdom of Urartu was rapidly on the rise and encroaching more and more upon Assyrian territory. Babylonia took advantage of Assyria's trouble to make gains against her ancient rival and, on top of these troubles or as a result of them, domestic strife became more common within Assyria. Some Assyrian nobles became extremely powerful and behaved in some respects as war lords, ruling vast territories and conducting private campaigns as powers responsible only to themselves.

Ethnically Assyria was undergoing a major change during this period in that the Aramaic element in the population was increasing dramatically. This was brought about, not only by the peaceful infiltration of Aramaeans into the state, but also by the Assyrian practice of transporting gigantic numbers of conquered foreigners, most of whom were Aramaeans, to Assyria to work on the enormous building projects of the day. Over many generations this new element, or at least a

proportion of it, slowly worked its way up the social and economic scale, so that by the eighth century BC there were Aramaeans at a very high level in the civil service and army, and the Aramaic language had virtually replaced Assyrian as the everyday tongue.

Assyria's fortunes revived in the middle of the eighth century BC with the accession of Tiglath-pileser III (744–727 BC). A vigorous campaigner in the true tradition of the Assyrian royal line, although he seems to have been a usurper, this king restored internal order and then proceeded to deal effectively with external enemies. He drove the Urartian people from holdings they had gained in Syria and extended Assyria's domain in that region from the Taurus in the north to the Sinai desert in the south. He crowned his successes against Urartu by leading an expedition right up to the gates of the Urartian capital, Teushpa, where he erected a commemorative stele. To the south he tried to maintain peace with Babylonia, but when the Chaldaeans made a bid for power there, he defeated them and ascended the Babylonian throne himself, thus creating a dual monarchy.

The success of the campaigns of Tiglath-pileser III was accompanied and made possible by major improvements in military organization and provincial administration. During this reign a standing army was formed and the practice of transporting recalcitrant people from their homelands pursued with great rigour. The empire was systematically organized into provinces and put under the authority of properly-appointed governors and military commanders.

The successor of Tiglath-pileser III, Sargon II (721–705 BC), was also probably a usurper but he carried on the work begun by his predecessor and added much territory to the empire. He gained more effective control of Syria-Palestine (Samaria fell just before his reign began) and pushed into Anatolia against Midas of Phrygia. To the north and east he led a series of campaigns against Urartu and severely crippled that kingdom's strength. Babylonia was a sore spot during his reign for the Chaldaean, Merodach-baladan II, had seized the Babylonian throne at Sargon's accession and remained in control for twelve years. Eventually Sargon drove him out and ascended the throne himself, thus re-establishing the dual monarchy. Sargon's building enterprises were noteworthy in that he created a new city, Dur-Sharrukin, just north of Nineveh, but this metropolis was abandoned after his death.

Sennacherib (704–681 BC) initially carried on the policies and practices established by his predecessors but eventually became embroiled in a vicious war with Babylonia. In the west he laid siege to Jerusalem and, although the city did not fall, its position as a serious obstacle on the road to Egypt was removed. Elam was now actively cooperating with the Chaldaeans and Babylonia against the Assyrians and the climax came when Sennacherib's son, who sat on the Babylonian throne, was handed over to the Elamites by the Babylonians. The enraged father, Sennacherib, launched a series of fierce attacks upon both states which ended in the capture and sack of Babylon in 689 BC. The destruction of Babylon was a sacriligious act not only in the eyes of the Babylonians but also in the eyes of most Assyrians, and the assassination of Sennacherib a few years later by one or more of his sons may have been a delayed result of this deed. Sennacherib chose Nineveh as his favourite city. Here he carried out extensive building and urban renewal and Nineveh remained the centre of Assyria thereafter.

Esarhaddon (680–669 BC), son and successor of Sennacherib, had two main concerns in his reign: the penetration of Egypt and the appeasement of Babylonia. Egypt was invaded and local people appointed as rulers on Assyria's behalf with Assyrian garrisons to support their authority. This was the crowning achievement in the expansion of the Assyrian empire although the hold over Egypt was rather ephemeral. In Babylonia, Esarhaddon inaugurated a major rebuilding programme in which he sought to heal the horrible wound inflicted by his father and in particular to restore the shrines and cult of Marduk, chief god of Babylon, in a splendid fashion. This monarch was concerned about the succession and stipulated well before his death that one of his sons, Ashurbanipal, would take the Assyrian throne while another, Shamash-shuma-ukin, would have the Babylonian. His concern was well advised for, when he died prematurely, the succession followed just as he had prescribed.

Ashurbanipal (668–627 BC) continued to try and control Egypt but ultimately this latest addition to the empire was lost as Ashurbanipal became more engrossed in Babylonian affairs. The fact that two sons were on rival thrones led to a war between Assyria and Babylonia (652–648 BC) around which various neighbours including the Arabs and Elamites were entwined. The result was a victory for Ashurbanipal and the subsequent punishment of Babylonia's allies. But Assyria's last days were upon her.

On the eastern frontiers of Assyria new groups of people including the Medes and Scythians had for some time been occupying the mountainous terrain and impeding Assyrian control of the region. Toward the end of the seventh century BC, some of these peoples cooperated with the newly founded Chaldaean dynasty in Babylonia to attack Assyria. Assyria's vulnerability was augmented during these days by the reappearance of powerful individual nobles who seem to have been more concerned about their private holdings and revenues than about the defence of the state. Assyrian cities fell one by one to the invaders until Nineveh was taken and destroyed in 612 BC. While a remnant of the Assyrian royal line struggled on with Egyptian support at Harran for a few years, the fall of Nineveh marked the end of the Assyrian empire.

The character of the last kings of Assyria is intriguing. Thanks to various kinds of sources preserved from the seventh century BC, a glimpse can be had of the personal traits and behaviour of these monarchs and this sheds some light on events of the time. Sennacherib shunned the memory of his father, Sargon II, who had died ominously on the battlefield and, in turn, Sennacherib's own close attachment to his son, who was carried off by the Elamites, led him to destroy Babylon. Esarhaddon and Ashurbanipal were highly religious, indeed superstitious, monarchs who constantly sought divine guidance and reassurance and kept the priests and diviners at court excessively busy.

Warfare and hunting

Assyria was a militaristic state and in its great days the most successful imperial power the world had ever seen. The development of military might went back to the time when Ashur as a small city state had either to defend itself or succumb to the surrounding belligerent peoples. In those early days defensive forays against Ashur's enemies won her wealth and through the centuries the raids remained basically the same, so that as late as the ninth century BC, the military campaigns of the Assyrian armies were essentially gigantic razzias. By the ninth century BC the concept of an annual royal campaign had developed. During this century, and particularly during the time of Ashurnasirpal II, the nature of campaigns was gradually altered. They were more effectively organized, the troops better equipped, cavalry used for the first time, and siege engines and engineering techniques became more common. The nature of Assyrian warfare also altered during this century. Whereas previously the campaigns were really just plundering expeditions, in the ninth century BC the idea of an annual tribute from conquered regions appeared and campaigns through areas previously subdued were intended primarily to collect that tribute rather than to wage war.

Until the eighth century BC there was no standing army in Assyria but every male was in theory required to perform military and civil service. In practice, the wealthier and more influential men met this state obligation by other means, such as providing slaves from their estates in lieu of their own service or making an outright payment. The king was the commander-in-chief of the army and, surrounded by his bodyguard, often led campaigns in person. There was a high-ranking officer called the *turtānu* who was in effect the field marshal and often conducted campaigns on the king's behalf. The army was divided into a number of units of decreasing size, each with its own officer, and the basic unit was the 'company' (*kiṣru*) of fifty men under a captain (*rab kiṣri*). When troops were mustered it was each captain's duty to round up his company and lead them to the assembly point.

The beginning of a campaign was a very formal affair. In the spring, the normal season for campaigning, the king or his *turtānu* inspected the main body of troops at the starting point and the priests and diviners performed the appropriate rites. The march then began, led by the standard bearers, priests and diviners, king and bodyguard—in that order. Thereafter came in order the chariots, cavalry, infantry and impedimenta. As the army proceeded through Assyrian territory and possessions, further levies, waiting at various assembly points, were added. The ruler or governor of each district or province traversed was required to provision the troops and animals, for the army carried very little in the way of supplies.

The bulk of the army consisted of infantry and it was the footmen who did most of the fighting. The infantry used as weapons the bow, sling, sword, dagger, spear, battleaxe and mace and for protection troops wore leather and carried shields. The foot archer, who used a bow as tall as himself, was protected by two companions, one carrying an enormous shield and the other a spear. In addition to the infantry there were the chariotry and the cavalry. Many different types of chariot were known but basically they were two-wheeled open-backed vehicles drawn by one or more horses. Each chariot had both a driver and an archer and sometimes one or two shield bearers. Cavalry did not appear until the ninth century BC. The cavalry used a short bow and each bowman was protected by a second mounted man who carried a shield.

Siege techniques involved the use of a variety of methods and machines. The Assyrians camped close to the city which was to be assaulted, and posted redoubts at strategic points around the city to prevent traffic from entering or leaving. An assault involved all bowmen in the army keeping the defenders on the walls under constant fire while the engineers attempted to penetrate the city by means of sapping, scaling and ramming the gates and walls. The battering rams were carried and protected by ingenious cars on wheels which contained several men including archers in turrets who shot at potential attackers.

Siege warfare was costly in terms of manpower and time and the Assyrians were selective in their use of it. Normally they would attempt to win the submission of a target area through propaganda and threats but, if this failed, then they would select one city and lay siege to it. When the city fell, the wall and buildings were destroyed and burned, and the people massacred in horrible ways and hung on poles around the city's periphery. This brutality was calculated to frighten the surrounding regions so that they would give in without further resistance, as they usually did.

The Assyrians loved to hunt and, when an Assyrian king was not on campaign or directing a building project, he was usually in the field hunting animals. The larger and more dangerous animals were the favourite prey, although almost any beast, bird or fish of any size was fair game. Elephants, lions and wild bulls roamed the Syrian plain in the Assyrian period and this was a favoured district for the Assyrian royal hunt. Wild beasts were also brought back to Assyria, where they were kept in zoological gardens, some lions being so tame as to be allowed to roam at will. Captured animals were also used for more formal hunts which were staged outside the city walls. Lions were released in the king's presence and he shot at them with a bow or charged them with dagger in hand. Such formal hunts ended with a religious ceremony in which the king poured a libation over a dead lion.

Relief of Ashurbanipal (668–627 BC) spearing a lion, the imperial beast. The more dangerous animals were the favourite prey of the Assyrians.

Religion

Religion was an integral part of any Assyrian's life and it permeated all aspects of the civilization. There was a great difference between the official cults of the state and the private religious beliefs and practices of humble individuals and most information that has been recovered concerns the state cults. Chief of all gods was Ashur who was called 'king of the gods' and 'father of the gods'. He was a state god and does not appear in popular mythology and literature. His chief shrine was the temple Ehursaggalkurra ('Temple of the Great Mountain of the Lands') in the city of Ashur. Ishtar was a very prominent deity in Assyria, there actually being three goddesses of this name, one at Nineveh, one at Arbela, and one at Ashur. She was responsible both for love and war. Ninurta, first-born son of Ashur, was the god of Calah and he was god both of war and of the hunt. The sun-god Shamash, who was responsible for justice, and the storm-god Adad were joint patrons of divination. The cult of the moon-god Sin at Harran came to be very important in Assyria and, after the fall of Nineveh, the last Assyrian king spent his final days at Harran.

The chief temples in the cities were enormous and complex structures. Each was dedicated to a particular deity but other gods were honoured by smaller shrines within the complex. A large staff of priests under a high priest was responsible for the various rites, and festival days were frequent. Rituals covered all aspects of the daily temple routine including the cleaning of the shrines and the care and feeding of the gods. The images were redecorated from time to time and the garments washed regularly. The food and drink offerings presented to the god were consumed by the temple personnel. By the Neo-Assyrian period the temple buildings and staffs had become so large that the income from temple lands and traditional offerings was inadequate so that major cults were largely dependent upon royal favour for extra revenues and the upkeep of the building. The Assyrian king, as vice regent of the god Ashur, was the chief priest of the state and his presence at various rituals was required although he could send a piece of his clothing as a substitute. Despite the fact that he was head of the official religion, he was subject to various taboos and was compelled to fast on certain occasions.

Divination was popular among the Assyrians and ominous signs were read in every event and phenomenon in earth and sky. In the Neo-Assyrian period the most popular forms of divination were extispicy, the examination of animal entrails, and astrology. The king's actions were governed by the word of the diviners and certain kings such as Esarhaddon were particularly concerned with divination.

107

Babylonian influence on Assyrian religion was immense and two gods from the south, Marduk and Nabu, were very popular in Assyria. Their influence was also felt in the nature of the festivals and the manner in which they were celebrated and Babylonia's chief festival, the Akitu or New Year, had a counterpart in Assyria from a very early period. In the late period a reaction against Babylonian religion set in and found support from the palace during the reign of Sennacherib.

Popular religion took the form of magic and sorcery and the literature which has been discovered in Assyrian libraries contains numerous collections of incantations. There were spells and counter-spells for virtually every aspect of life from conception to death.

Law

In Assyria law was essentially a matter of custom and precedent although there is a document called the *Middle Assyrian Laws*. This text is a collection of articles concerning various offences and their punishment, and the parts that are preserved are concerned with women and sexual offences. The document has a definite affinity with the earlier Babylonian law codes and it is probably more a literary text than an actual codification of laws. The punishments prescribed are extremely harsh, involving beatings, mutilation and gruesome executions.

Legal disputes were normally settled privately by the parties involved but, when such a settlement could not be reached, the disputants went before an officer of the administration who was asked to mediate and, if necessary, proclaim a settlement. There were no courts or judges *per se*. If even the administrative officer could not resolve the dispute, he would send the litigants to the ordeal, and the god of the ordeal would decree his decision. The proceedings of cases handled by the administration were carefully recorded and the names of witnesses and seals of relevant participants placed on the document.

In addition to the court documents there was a variety of legal records kept, many of which have been recovered, and these can be grouped under the general headings of conveyances, contracts, receipts, marriage and adoption documents. Fixed formulae were followed in each type and the penalties prescribed for attempting to violate a legal agreement were sometimes bizarre. The offender could be told to present ten white horses to a god, to burn his eldest son, or even to swallow a bundle of wool.

King and state

Assyria was governed by an absolute monarch who was head of the administration, army, religion and court, and who in theory owned all the land on behalf of the god. In practice there were checks to his authority in that he had to respect custom and precedent, in particular as they related to the upper classes, temples and cities. He was also subject to religious taboos and practices, and the pronouncements of the diviners. Under the king was a descending hierarchy of officials whose offices were both civil and military since Assyria was a militaristic state. Eunuchs were highly prized as trustworthy officers and were present at all the upper levels of the bureaucracy.

Male primogeniture was the hereditary principle for the monarch. The king was surrounded by a large group of courtiers and a harem, and access to his person was difficult, being controlled by one official, the major-domo. The harem was ruled by the king's mother until she was replaced by the first wife to give the monarch a son and heir. The crown prince was raised in the harem until old enough to move to the House of Succession (*bīt redûti*) where he had his own court, like the king's, and was taught to ride and shoot. Only one king, Ashurbanipal, was taught as a youth to read and write.

The favour of the king was jealously sought, for patronage was the order of the day and no one could gain high office without an influential patron. Slander was common and many an officer was brought low by the gossip of his enemies. Bribes were an accepted means of getting things done, for the officials were poorly paid, or at least so they complained. Nonetheless the system worked and the provincial administration created by the Assyrians was the basis for the administrative system used in the later Persian empire.

Economy and social structure

The Assyrian economy was based upon agriculture, animal husbandry and foreign trade. The lush hills and meadows of the Assyrian heartland provided sufficient crops and pasturage and its geographical position was on the crossroads of both the east-west and north-south trade routes. The exchange of goods was by barter with different metals—silver, tin and copper—being used as a standard of exchange at differnt times. Exports included manufactured goods, especially textiles, produced in palaces, temples and large private villas. The chief imports were timber, wine, precious metals and stones, horses and camels.

The development of the empire considerably altered the economic structure of Assyria for it saw growth of large cities in the heartland with fewer and fewer people involved in food production. The heartland, therefore, came to rely upon food imports from the provinces and these, in turn, came to be economically depressed areas. Thus Assryian imperialism was economically oppressive and subject states were ready to withhold annual tribute at the slightest sign of weakness in the Assyrian capital.

The basic social unit in Assyria was the family and, above that, the tribe. Most of the population lived in cities and were very conscious of their rights as citizens of their particular metropolis. A man's family decided his social rank and the kinds of positions open to him although a particularly ambitious individual might move the whole family up the scale. Women were lower in status than men and completely subservient to their father, brothers or husband. At the top of the social hierarchy was the king and at the bottom were the slaves, the debt slave being above the captive taken on a foreign campaign. Assyrian society was a conservative and solid element in Assyrian civilization.

Mitanni

A. K. Grayson

Discovery

The kingdom of Mitanni was completely forgotten for millennia until discoveries in the nineteenth century revealed its name and existence. After a century of modern research, fascinating insights into the nature of this unusual kingdom have been achieved, although a great deal has yet to be learned through further excavation and study in western Syria where Mitanni once flourished. The civilization of Mitanni was the product of two ethnic strains, the Hurrians and the Indo-Aryans, and attention must be given to both these groups in an investigation of this lost kingdom.

The people known as the Hurrians (in the Bible they are called 'Horites') spoke a language which has no recognized affinity with any other language except Urartian. They were immigrants to the Fertile Crescent, making sporadic appearances in the third millennium BC and in the second millennium BC coming in much larger numbers and settling over extensive areas. Their place of origin is not precisely known although they probably came from or by way of the Trans-Caucasian region. When evidence of their presence first appears, in the form of personal names, in the written sources of Mesopotamia the Hurrians are mainly restricted to the east Tigris region and the Zagros and this continued to be true in the early centuries of the second millennium BC. Many Hurrian names appear among the members of the Turukku tribe which lived in the Zagros and brought to an end the rule of the Assyrian Ishme-Dagan I (c1780–1741 BC). While Hurrian personal names are the main source for these people in the early period a few religious texts in the Hurrian language, written in the cuneiform script, were found at Mari (eighteenth century BC).

The establishment of the kingdom

Toward the end of the first dynasty of Babylon (c1595 BC) the Hurrians pushed into upper Mesopotamia and eastern Syria in force, with the result that chaos reigned for some time in these areas. When written sources are again available, the Hurrians are well established in wide parts of Assyria and Syria and a Hurrian presence is evident throughout the Fertile Crescent and Anatolia. The political centre was the newly formed kingdom of Mitanni which ruled over a region which formerly had been Amorite. Although there were still Amorites present at Mitanni, the chief ethnic element was Hurrian, with some evidence of an Indo-Aryan language and culture. The evidence for the presence of Hurrians and Indo-Aryans at Mitanni is almost exclusively linguistic. In fact it consists largely of personal names and it is dangerous to draw too many conclusions from such limited evidence.

The great majority of the personal names are Hurrian and thus one may conclude that most of the population at Mitanni was Hurrian. A small but significant portion of the personal names is Indo-Aryan and these can be recognized by the fact that they are compounded with the names of Indo-Aryan deities or by their concern for horses and horse-racing. Some of the deities mentioned are Indra, Vayu, Svar, Soma, the Devas and Ṛta. Two examples of the interest in horses are the names Biridašwa 'Possessing great horses' and Sattawaza 'He who has won seven prizes [at the horse races]'. Further indication of Indo-Aryan presence is found in the technical terms used in connection with horse breeding, for such terms are Indo-Aryan. This evidence comes from a horse-training manual written by Kikkuli of Mitanni. The text, which was actually found at the ancient Hittite capital, Hattusha, is written on four tablets in the Hittite language. The more technical terms (for example, the numerals 1, 3, 5, 7, 9) are not Hittite, however, but related to the Indic family of languages. There is no doubt, then, that there was an Indo-Aryan presence in the Fertile Crescent by the time of the formation of the kingdom of Mitanni, and this presence was closely associated with the breeding and training of horses. For this reason the Indo-Aryans are generally

A light horse-drawn chariot, one of the revolutionary instruments of West Asian warfare.

credited with the introduction of the efficient and widespread use of the horse, especially in warfare, into this area. One final piece of evidence regarding Indo-Aryans is a social class at Mitanni called *maryannu*, an Indo-Aryan word meaning young man or warrior.

The relative proportions of Hurrian and Indo-Aryan personal names in the kingdom of Mitanni indicates that the Indo-Aryan element was on a small scale. The people were basically Hurrian although at some time they had come into contact with an Indo-Aryan group. The contact was peaceful, involving intermarriage and a general mixing of the two groups. The best evidence for this is the fact that at Nuzi, a site in Assyria which has yielded a cache of cuneiform tablets shedding light upon the Hurrians, people bearing Hurrian and Indo-Aryan names were often related to one another. Peaceful as the intermingling was, the Hurrians learned from the Indo-Aryans the art of breeding and training horses, and their use in drawing a light chariot during the invasion of the Fertile Crescent gave them the superiority in warfare which brought them to power.

There is a theory in modern scholarship that the Indo-Aryans formed a ruling class at Mitanni and that the Hurrians were ruled and oppressed by them. The major piece of evidence in support of this theory is that many of the rulers including governors and family members had Indo-Aryan names. However, while this is true of all the kings of Mitanni, some of the members of the royal family and some of the governors had Hurrian names. The fact that there was a social class called *maryannu* does not necessarily mean that all the members of this warrior class were Indo-Aryans.

The lack of Mitannian records

Any attempt to write the history of the kingdom of Mitanni is frustrated by the almost total lack of indigenous sources. The location of the ancient capital, Washukanni, is unknown, although it must have been in the general area of the Habur river. Even the nature of the few native sources extant is decidedly unhelpful with regard to political history. There is a Hurrian letter found at Amarna in Egypt from the Mitannian king Tushratta to the pharaoh Amenophis III. A Hurrian religious text was found at Ugarit (modern Ras Shamra on the Syrian coast near Latakia) where some Hurrian dictionaries (with Sumerian, Akkadian and Ugaritic equivalents) were also excavated. A number of Hurrian religious texts were unearthed in Anatolia at Hattusha, the capital of the Hittites, and an Akkado-Hurrian royal inscription of Tishari of Urkish in Syria is known. There are also the religious texts at Mari mentioned earlier.

Almost all that is known of the history of the kingdom of Mitanni is known from foreign sources and, as prejudiced and incomplete as such information is, it still illustrates that Mitanni was one of the great powers of ancient West Asia in the second millennium BC. The first king of Mitanni attested in the sources is Parattarna (*fl. c*1500 BC). His name is known from an inscription in Akkadian found at Alalah, modern Atshana near the Gulf of Alexandretta. Idrimi, the king of Alalah and

Idrimi, king of Alalah and a vassal of Parattarna (*fl. c*1500 BC), who is believed to have been the first king of Mitanni.

author of the inscription, was a vassal of Parattarna, king of Mitanni. Thus during this period the influence of Mitanni spread as far west as the Mediterranean, and from Hittite sources it is known that the early Hittite kings waged a long war with the Hurrians and Mitanni over possession of northern Syria and the Taurus mountains. In these sources the term Hanigalbat, rather than Mitanni or Hurrian, is used, and the Assyrians also used this name. The Assyrians for their part were vassals of Mitanni at this time.

The dawn of the 'Amarna Age' in the Fertile Crescent in the fourteenth century BC marked the welcome addition of important information regarding international relations in the entire region. The term Amarna comes from the name of a village in Upper Egypt where several hundred clay tablets inscribed in the cuneiform script were discovered in the nineteenth century. These letters were sent to the Egyptian pharaohs (Tuthmosis III to Amenophis IV) from all parts of West Asia, including

Mitanni, and many of them are from kings. With regard to Mitanni the letters, which include a Hurrian letter from Tushratta as mentioned earlier, show that relations with Egypt were excellent at the beginning of this period and under a series of kings, Artatama, Shuttarna and later Tushratta, Mitanni was at the height of her power. The Egyptian pharaoh Amenophis III married a princess of Mitanni and, on another occasion, when he was ill, Shuttarna sent the statue of Ishtar of Nineveh from Assyria to help heal him.

The fall of Mitanni

The rise of two great powers in the fourteenth century BC, the Hittite and the Assyrian, prepared the way for Mitanni's downfall for she was caught between them. Assyria under Ashur-uballit I (1363–1328 BC) regained her independence and began a long series of campaigns against Mitanni itself. Egypt's friendly attitude toward Mitanni cooled and the pharaoh entertained Assyrian ambassadors at his court. To the west, the Hittite king

Suppiluliumas I (1375–1334 BC) began harassing the Mitannian border. Suppiluliumas kept up the pressure on Mitanni and eventually led a campaign against its capital, Washukanni. Tushratta was murdered in a rebellion and his son, Mattiwaza, fled to Suppiluliumas for asylum. The Hittite married the crown prince to one of his daughters, thus confirming a treaty between them, and set him on the Mitannian throne. Thus Mitanni became a puppet state and buffer zone for the Hittites against the rising Assyrian power.

After Mattiwaza, Mitanni was no longer a major power and Mattiwaza's three successors were not even independent kings. Assyria advanced further and further west into Mitannian territory until Shalmaneser I (1273–1244 BC) incorporated the eastern part of the region as the Assyrian province of Hanigalbat. The remaining portions, which were initially under Hittite control, eventually disintegrated into a large conglomeration of tiny independent states as the power of the Hittites declined.

The Hittites

O. R. Gurney

The name

The name 'Hittite' comes from the Old Testament, in which the Hittites (Hebrew *ḥittîm*) figure in two different roles: first, as one of the pre-Israelite nations of the Land of Canaan to which certain individuals, such as Ephron, Uriah and Abimelech, are said to belong; and secondly, as a group of kingdoms situated to the north of Israel in what is now Syria, whose kings entered into relations with Solomon and the pharaohs of Egypt. Late Assyrian records called the whole of this area 'Hatti', clearly the same word, but its inhabitants were not at that time a single nation and were of mixed origin and speech. They had in fact inherited the name and much of their civilization from the earlier kingdom of Hatti, known to the Egyptians as 'Kheta', far to the north in Asia Minor (Anatolia), a kingdom which flourished for some 500 years (c1700–1190 BC), and became one of the great powers of ancient West Asia. Because of its paramount historical importance, the subjects of this great kingdom are today referred to, first and foremost, as 'the Hittites'. They must not be thought of, however, as a single tribe or nation, for they too were of mixed ethnic and linguistic origin. Thus their identity is political and cultural.

Hatti seems to have been in origin a very ancient name for the district around the city Hattush (about 100 miles east of the modern Ankara) near the Turkish village of Boghazköy. The inhabitants of this district in the third millennium BC spoke *hattili* and would therefore have had first right to the name of 'Hittite' if they had not

been pre-empted by the people of the later kingdom, of which Hattush was the capital. The people of the kingdom, however, spoke *našili* or *nešumnili* (in the language of [the town of] Nesa). This 'Nesian' language is today known as Hittite, the *hattili* language, its speakers being termed Hattian. Hittite or Nesian is a language of Indo-European structure and must have been introduced into Asia Minor by an influx of Indo-European people, probably at the end of the third millennium BC. These Indo-Europeans evidently settled down in considerable numbers among the Hattian population and so dominated them that, by the time of the rise of the dynasty that founded the kingdom of Hattush (c1750 BC), the Hattian language had largely died out, surviving only in the cult of certain gods. Hittite in turn absorbed into its vocabulary a large number of indigenous substantives and names, declining them by means of the grammatical elements of Indo-European.

Historical outline

Among their royal archives, the Hittites preserved memories of a time when their kings had ruled from a city called Kussara which has not been located. From here one of the early kings, Anittas, began to extend his dominion by conquering first the city of Kanesh (probably the Nesa which gave its name to the Hittite language), then Hattush, the later capital. He seems to have transferred his government to Kanesh, the site of which is the mound called Kültepe near modern Kayseri;

Hattush, on the other hand, was destroyed and declared accursed. Between Anittas and the foundation of the Hittite kingdom there is a gap of several generations. Then the policy of expansion was continued by another king of Kussara, Labarnas, whose son, another Labarnas, decided to rebuild and occupy Hattush – a natural stronghold dominating the northern valleys. The city was thereafter known as Hattusha or Hattusas, and in honour of the event the king changed his name to Hattus-il-is ('man of Hattusha').

This king, Hattusilis I, was the true founder of the Hittite kingdom. After consolidating his rule over neighbouring cities of the plateau to the south of Hattusha, he set out on an ambitious programme of conquest. His army crossed the barrier of the Taurus mountains, sighting the Mediterranean for the first time, an adventure celebrated in an early text in highly poetic imagery. Advancing eastwards Hattusilis overran the northern parts of Syria, then ruled by the kings of Aleppo, and brought back scribes to start a school of cuneiform writing in the Hittite capital. But he failed to conquer Aleppo, and the end of his reign was clouded by disloyalty among members of his own family.

His successor, Mursilis I, took up the challenge and succeeded in overthrowing the powerful kingdom of Aleppo. Then, finding the way open before him, he pressed on down the Euphrates and fell upon the kingdom of Babylon itself, a feat of arms always remembered with pride by later generations.

However, the Hittites had far outrun their resources. On their way home they were attacked by the Hurrians, a nation recently settled in the mountainous regions of the upper Euphrates and Tigris and, though they beat off this attack, the kingdom had been fatally weakened by the king's long absence – some time after his return Mursilis was assassinated by his brother-in-law. This crime ushered in a sorry period of palace murders and intrigues during which the Hittites were unable to maintain their conquests. The destruction of Aleppo had created a political vacuum and Syria with most of Cilicia fell to the Hurrians.

Stability was restored about 1525 BC by King Telipinus who promulgated a strict law of succession and took firm measures to suppress violence. In foreign relations he inaugurated a policy of peaceful coexistence, entering into a treaty relationship with the recently-founded Cilician kingdom of Kizzuwadna.

The reign of Telipinus was followed by an obscure period of some 60 years. Then about 1450 BC a new dynasty came to power, in which the names Tudhaliyas and Arnuwandas recur. The first Tudhaliyas conducted victorious campaigns to east and west, but his successes were short-lived. Under his son, Arnuwandas, the kingdom was faced with a new menace, an influx of barbarians or 'Kaska' from the north. Other enemies pressed in from all sides until the kingdom was brought to the verge of extinction.

At this moment (c1380 BC) a king of supreme genius came to the throne. Under the leadership of Suppiluliumas I, the Hittites emerged from the catastrophe and built up in little more than 100 years an empire which, for a short period, made their kingdom the rival of Egypt and Babylon.

First the Kaska, then the kingdom of Arzawa which had occupied Tuwanuwa (Tyana), were forced back and order was restored in the homeland. Only then, after some 20 years, was Suppiluliumas able to turn eastwards and settle accounts with the Hurrians. But the Hurrian king avoided battle, and Suppiluliumas was able to advance southwards into Syria unopposed and recover for Hatti the whole of that territory as far south as Damascus. After a show of resistance at Carchemish Hurrian resistance collapsed following the murder of King Tushratta, and the Hittites were able to install on the Hurrian throne a fugitive prince who became a Hittite vassal and was married to a Hittite princess. In

Part of the defences of Hattush, the Hittite capital. In the foreground is an underground sally-port.

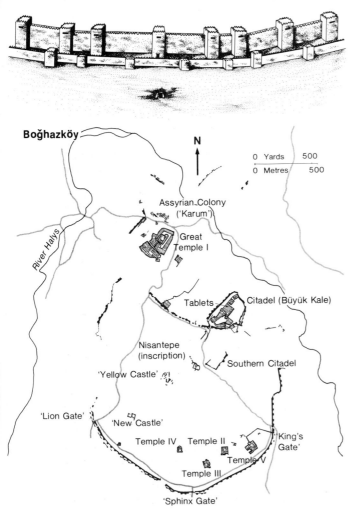

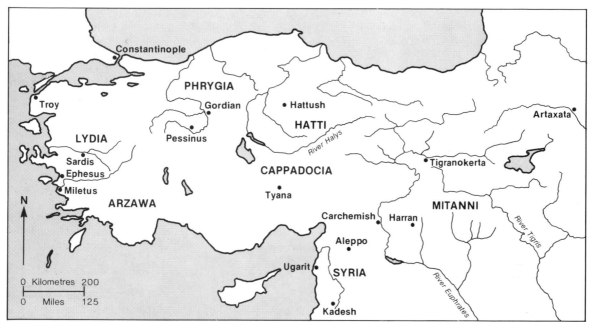

Asia Minor and surrounding areas.

the same way the local rulers of the Syrian cities either paid homage to Suppiluliumas, or were replaced by others who were prepared to do so and whose position was defined by a treaty of vassalage. In this way was created the Hittite empire, a confederation bound together by oaths of fealty, symbolized by the annual payment of tribute and often cemented by diplomatic marriages.

Suppiluliumas' son and successor, Mursilis II, completed his father's work by subjugating the western kingdom of Arzawa. Here, too, there were fugitive princes who could be installed as vassals and married to Hittite princesses. The geography is, as yet, uncertain, but if Apasas, the Arzawan capital, is indeed to be identified with Ephesus, then the Hittite empire under Mursilis II had reached the coast of the Aegean Sea.

The system of vassal kingdoms was reinforced, especially in the north, by Hittite military garrisons and, in Syria, by a Hittite viceroy who ruled at the key point of Carchemish. None the less it proved unstable, and there were frequent rebellions which required the king's active intervention.

The reign of the next king, Muwatallis, was dominated by a trial of strength with the Egyptians who, under Ramesses II, were ambitious to recover their lost Syrian possessions. The Hittite king called on all his vassals to fulfil their military obligations and then, concealing his great army behind the city of Kadesh on the Orontes, fell upon the unsuspecting Egyptian column as it was entering the city from the south. The Egyptians managed to extricate themselves, but the battle of Kadesh (c1285 BC) confirmed the Hittites in their control of Syria and established an equilibrium between the two powers.

When Muwatallis died, leaving a young son by a secondary wife as his sole heir, his brother Hattusilis, who had ruled as viceroy in the homeland during Muwatallis' absence on the Egyptian campaign, became a powerful rival for the throne. Friction between uncle and nephew became acute and, after seven years, Hattusilis carried out a *coup d'état*, sending the young man into exile. Once on the throne, Hattusilis III entered into friendly relations with his Egyptian and Babylonian counterparts, and sharing much of his power with his queen, Puduhepa, brought the kingdom to its highest point of prosperity. Peace with Egypt was sealed by the marriage of a Hittite princess to Ramesses II.

Peace and prosperity continued under his son Tudhaliyas and the Syrian empire remained firmly in Hittite hands. The rising power of Assyria was a potential threat, but outwardly at least friendly relations were maintained. For the west little evidence remains but there is nothing to suggest a major threat. Tudhaliyas was able to devote much attention to a religious reform and it was probably he who ordered the carving of the sculptures of Yazilikaya, an open-air shrine near the capital, and one of the most impressive monuments of Hittite artistic genius.

His son, Arnuwandas III, died after a short reign and was succeeded by his brother, Suppiluliumas II. The few texts from his reign show no lack of confidence; one even records a unique event, a naval victory over an enemy based on Alasia (Cyprus). Yet this is the last of all the historical texts in the Hittite archives. Egyptian records of the reign of Ramesses III tell how the 'Peoples of the Sea' and their allies poured down through Syria and were brought to a halt on the very frontiers of Egypt in 1182 BC. The Hittite kingdom must have been suddenly overwhelmed. Only a few decades later, an Assyrian king, campaigning along the upper Tigris, encountered hordes of Kaska and Muski, the latter probably the

Hittite seals showing hieroglyphs. In the imperial archive at Hattush more than five languages were used.

Mysians and Phrygians, invaders from the west. The reference to the Kaska suggests that this old enemy had made common cause with them in the destruction of the land of Hatti.

In the following centuries the regions of Syria once dominated by the Hittite kings became divided into separate kingdoms, in which the Hittite tradition was diluted by an influx of Aramaeans from the eastern steppe lands. These princelings set up monuments in the 'hieroglyphic' script invented by the Hittites but in a form of the 'Luwian' language formerly spoken in south-western Asia Minor, another Indo-European language, closely related to Hittite. The Hittite heritage for these kingdoms comprised, besides the hieroglyphic writing, a strong artistic tradition and the continuance of royal names, such as Lubarna, Sapalulme, Mutallu and Katuzili. Their inscriptions, however, contain little historical information. One by one they succumbed to the powerful Assyrian war machine and by 700 BC all had been incorporated into the Assyrian empire. It is the rulers of these kingdoms who appear in the Bible as the 'Kings of the Hittites'.

Civilization

The Hittite homeland is a high plateau, dry in summer but with a plentiful rainfall in spring and snow in winter. The Hittite population would largely have constituted peasants, cultivating barley and wheat, tending vines and fruit trees, and pasturing herds of cattle and sheep. There was a recognized class of craftsmen, especially potters, cobblers, carpenters and smiths, and though the metal principally worked was bronze, the smelting of iron was already understood and a high value was set on this metal. The medium of exchange was silver, of which the Taurus Mountains contained an abundant supply, but it is not known how this potential source of wealth was controlled by the Hittite kings.

The king was supreme ruler, military commander, judicial authority and high priest. Surrounding him was a large class of nobles and dignitaries who, especially in earlier centuries, evidently possessed considerable power and were to a large extent his blood relations. Throughout, the government of the most important cities and provinces was assigned by the king to members of his own family, each bound to him by ties of homage and fealty. In later centuries, as already mentioned, the same principle was extended to native vassals who became members of the royal family by marriage. The oath of fealty was a personal matter and so it was necessary, on the death of the king, for all vassal treaties to be renewed by his successor. This feudal principle was in fact the basis of Hittite society as a whole. The nobles possessed large manors, each with its contingent of peasants and artisans, who held their tenements on condition of payment of rent in kind or performance of appropriate services. A peasant could leave his holding to his son; a craftsman could sell it, with the obligation passing to the buyer; but the lord had the right to choose or approve the new feudatory and invest him with the fief.

A notable characteristic of the Hittite state is the prominent part played by women, especially the queen. Puduhepa was regularly associated with her husband Hattusilis III in treaties and documents of state and she even carried on a lively correspondence with foreign kings and queens in her own right. Both she and the last queen of Suppiluliumas I remained in office after their husband's death and it is usually inferred that the Hittite queen held the office for life. There is some reason to believe that a matrilineal system once prevailed in Anatolia and the independent position of the Hittite queen could be a vestige of this, although there is little trace of it in Hittite society as revealed in the laws. The Hittite family was of the normal patriarchal type: the father gave his daughter away in marriage; the bridegroom paid him the bride-price and thereafter 'took' his bride and 'possessed' her; if she was taken in adultery he had the right to decide her fate.

The collection of roughly 200 Hittite laws, though compiled as a single 'work' in two tablets, contains laws of different periods showing a constant development towards milder and more humane punishment. The most primitive clause prescribes drawing and quartering for an agricultural offence. Other capital crimes are bestiality and rape or, in the case of a slave, disobedience and sorcery. But in most of these cases it is stated that 'now' either an animal has been substituted for the man or the penalty has been converted into a form of compensation, either in kind (in cases of theft) or in money (silver), and that a further reform has in many instances drastically reduced the amount to be paid. It is noteworthy that the penalty for a slave and the compensation for injury of a slave are regularly exactly half that for a freeman. The dates of these progressive reforms can only be conjectured. One of them is usually ascribed to King Telipinus on account of the similarity in style to parts of this king's Edict. In their final reliance on the principle of reparation, to the exclusion of capital or corporal punishment, these laws follow the much earlier Sumerian practice, in contrast to that of the Babylonians and Assyrians.

Hittite prowess in warfare was largely due to their exploitation of the chariotry arm. The light, horse-drawn chariot was an invention of the second millennium BC and was rapidly adopted by the armies of the Hittites and their contemporaries. Chariots are already mentioned in the earliest accounts of Hittite wars, but it was in the later empire that this section of the army was brought to a high degree of efficiency by an elaborate system of horse training and by the introduction of a third member of the chariot's crew.

Hittite religion

The religion of the Hittite people was concerned primarily with ensuring the favour of the local deity, whose character was in most cases that of a fertility god controlling the weather. In most shrines he was credited with a wife and family, and the prominence of mother-goddesses is another indication suggesting an early matrilineal society. With the unification of the country under the kings of Hattusha, a centralized religion developed in which the numerous local deities were combined into a complicated pantheon, and it became the king's duty to tour the country and officiate at the most important festivals, chiefly during the winter months when the campaigning season came to an end. A king who allowed his military duties to override his obligations as a priest might provoke the wrath of the gods, with dire consequences for the Hittite state. Mursilis II is particularly notable for his piety and there exist several heart-searching prayers which he addressed to the gods at a time when the nation was afflicted with a serious plague or epidemic. He pleaded that he himself had given no cause for divine anger and, though he confessed that his father had committed several offences, he begged the gods to relent and not to punish the innocent with the guilty.

The names of the deities reflect the ethnic diversity of the Hittite kingdom. The oldest stratum was that of the Hattians, who worshipped a weather-god named Taru and a sun-goddess named Estan. Their ruler of the underworld was Lelwani, and among their lesser deities were the goddesses Istustaya and Papaya, who spun the threads of fate, and Hasammeli, the smith. The incoming Indo-Europeans named their weather-god Tarhu or Tarhunnas, probably meaning 'conquering hero'. In the state cult of the empire this weather-god, Tarhunnas, took first place, with the title 'Weather-god of Hatti', but his spouse was usually known by the title 'Sun-goddess of Arinna' and bore the Hattian name Wurusemu. In some contexts this goddess was more prominent than the god and it was she who led the king to victory in battle. Later, especially in the thirteenth century BC under the influence of Queen Puduhepa, Hurrian deities entered the pantheon and the leading Hurrian pair, Teshub and Hebat, were identified with their Hittite counterparts, the goddess taking a subordinate place.

A common theme of Hittite mythology was the 'disappearing god'. A god absented himself, either in anger or in pursuit of some private occupation such as hunting, and in consequence a blight afflicted the earth. The other gods searched high and low for him; he was eventually found—in one version by a bee—and pros-perity was restored. Another primitive myth tells of a struggle between the weather-god and a dragon in which the god was defeated, losing his heart and his eyes, which were later recovered by his son. This was the cult-myth of a local festival. Another tale, of Hattian origin, tells how the moon once fell from heaven. But the

A Hittite borrowing from the Hurrians, the thunder-god Teshub.

Reconstruction of a Hittite shrine.

more elaborate myths in literary form were of Hurrian origin and concerned Hurrian gods, especially Teshub and Hebat; one succession myth describes struggles between successive generations of gods, culminating in the final victory of Teshub; another describes a life and death struggle between the gods and a monstrous rock in the sea called Ullikummi. Here again Teshub was finally victorious.

Hittite art

Hittite art and architecture were closely connected with religion. The temples excavated at the capital were elaborate complexes constructed of massive polygonal masonry around a central courtyard. The shrine containing the cult statue illuminated by deep windows was approached indirectly from the courtyard and in the main temple stood twin shrines for a divine couple. A typical feature of Hittite religion is the representation of deities in bas relief on rock faces, often in association with a spring, and in many of these reliefs the king, sometimes accompanied by the queen, is shown in an attitude of worship. In such cases the king is dressed in his long priestly robe and skull-cap and carries a symbolic staff in the form of a crook; the god is distinguished by a tall horned head-dress and usually wears a short kilt. Usually each deity is shown in a conventional attitude with one foot advanced as if walking and one hand stretched forward carrying the hieroglyphic sign representing his or her name.

The crowning achievement in this style is the open-air

Sculptured warrior at the King's Gate, Hattush, the Hittite capital.

shrine of Yazilikaya near the capital where, on a natural outcrop of rock forming an enclosed chamber, the whole official pantheon is depicted, gods and goddesses on opposite sides, with the leading divine family meeting in the centre and a colossal figure of Tudhaliyas IV confronting them on a projecting buttress. This is a late monument of the empire and the names and arrangements of the deities are those of the Hurrian pantheon which by then had largely replaced the native Hattian cult. A more versatile style in bas-relief is illustrated on the walls flanking the gate at Alaca Hüyük. Here the king is shown worshipping the weather-god in the form of a bull on an altar, while the queen worships behind him, and there are scenes of hunting (on foot) and of musicians and jugglers in a religious procession. The main city gates, both at the capital and at Alaca Hüyük, were adorned with sculptures in very high relief: two have sphinxes, one the heavy protomes of lions, one a divine figure carrying an elaborate battle-axe.

The successor kingdoms of Syria, especially Malatya, maintained the tradition of divine figures and scenes of worship, but this art fell increasingly under the influence of Assyria, both in style and in subject, with representations of chariots in hunting scenes and in warfare. However, massive gate lions, usually of basalt, and now in the round, remained a typical feature of this art.

The art of the seal-cutter was also well developed. The king and queen of Hattusha used royal stamp-seals, some of which show religious figures similar to those of the bas-reliefs, while the rarer Anatolian cylinder-seals have more elaborate scenes. However, the Syrian kingdoms used cylinder-seals exclusively in the Mesopotamian tradition.

Thus in art, as in history, the Hittites played a major role in ancient West Asia. The recovery of Hittite and Luwian, the earliest known Indo-European languages, has moreover been of special importance and has solved many long-standing philological problems.

Urartu and Armenia

David M. Lang

Introduction

Although five centuries separate the fall of the Urartian state c600 BC from the accession of Tigranes the Great of Armenia in 95 BC, it is logical and convenient to treat the history of Urartu and ancient Armenia jointly, since they represent successive phases of the social, political and cultural development of the region which now forms eastern Anatolia (eastern Turkey) and the Armenian Soviet Socialist Republic. 'Urartu' is the Assyrian name for the Armenian province and lofty mountain which we call 'Ararat'–the Armenians themselves call Mount Ararat 'Masis'.

The Armenians speak an Indo-European language of the so-called 'Satem' division, but there is little doubt of their ethnic affinity to ancient Anatolian population groups, notably the Hurrians, of whom the Urartians are a branch. Furthermore, there existed a flourishing Bronze Age civilization on the territory of present-day Armenia from about 3000 BC onwards–long before either the Urartians or the Armenians appeared in history.

It is interesting that Moses Khorenatsi, writing in the eighth century AD and regarded as the father of Armenian history, indicates his awareness of elements of continuity between Urartian and Armenian history. Moses Khorenatsi's account of the reigns of the Armenian rulers Aram and his son Ara the Fair echoes the exploits of King Aramu of Urartu and his battles against Assyrian invaders, during the ninth century BC.

Topography and climate

The core of both Urartu and ancient Armenia takes in the Lake Van area, the middle Araxes valley, and also the mighty double peak of Mount Ararat and the upper reaches of the rivers Tigris and Euphrates.

Most of the area is high plateau or table land, cut up by enormous mountains, many being extinct volcanoes more than 10,000 ft (3048 m) high. Great Armenia of the classical and medieval periods takes in all land between longitudes 37° and 49° East, and latitudes 37.5° and 41.5° North. It covered a vast expanse estimated at 115,000 sq miles (298,000 sq km). Due to the genocide policy pursued by the last Ottoman governments, the Armenian population was exterminated over 90 per cent of this area, so that modern Soviet Armenia has a territory of only 12,000 sq miles (31,080 sq km).

Parts of Armenia, notably the Araxes valley and the Van region, are incredibly beautiful and fertile. This gives some encouragement to the view that Armenia was the site of the biblical Garden of Eden. Certainly it can be said that the story of Noah's Ark landing on Mount Ararat has some historical justification of a symbolic kind, since a number of animals, birds, and useful plants, including the vine, developed from species still extant in Armenia and the Caucasus. The apricot tree, for example, was taken to Italy from Armenia about 67 BC by the Roman general and gourmet Lucullus.

However, only about a quarter of Armenia's overall territory could be described as a 'land of milk and honey'. Much of the highland zone of Armenia is virtually uninhabitable, except by nomad shepherds seeking summer pasture for their flocks and herds. This windswept region, mostly over 5000 ft (1524 m) above sea level, has a harsh climate, and snow lies there for seven

117

The bare and savagely impressive Mount Ararat, the dominant feature of the Armenian plateau.

or eight months of the year. Some upland Armenian towns have an average winter temperature as low as 12° F (−11° C). The findings of archaeology indicate that the climate was milder and moister, and the vegetation in upland zones more abundant in ancient and medieval times, than today.

The country is often shaken by destructive earthquakes. The subsoil is rich in metals and minerals, including gold, silver, copper and iron, and there are important salt mines. The Lake Van region produces borax and arsenic. There are large supplies of a hard volcanic rock called obsidian, formed from dark vitreous lava, and much used by Stone Age man for making implements. The local tufa or tuff stone is excellent for building.

A notable geographical feature in northeastern Armenia is the enormous alpine Lake Sevan, surrounded by a ring of mountains, and lying some 6000 ft (1828 m) above sea level. It produces a delicious fish called the 'ishkhan' or 'prince' fish. Its present area of 340 sq miles (880.60 sq km) is smaller than in medieval times, as a result of hydroelectric works along the river Hrazdan during the Soviet period.

Among valuable livestock found in Armenia from ancient times are horses and mules, also many kinds of birds, including falcons and eagles. An unusual and valuable insect is the 'kermes'—an aphis found in springtime in the roots of a plant growing on the foothills of Mount Ararat; from this insect is made a special red dye long used in the Armenian textile industry.

Historical outline

Finds of obsidian implements fashioned by primitive man indicate human settlement in Armenia from the Old Stone Age (Abbevillian culture) onwards. Thus human beings have lived there for at least 500,000 years.

During the early Bronze Age, from around 3000 BC, Armenia was inhabited by the people of the 'Kuro-Araxes' culture, so-called from the rivers Kura and Araxes close to which they originated. These people, probably of Hurrian stock, designed beautiful black (occasionally red) burnished pottery with stylized ornamentation. They also ranged as far afield as Syria and Palestine—pottery similar to Kuro-Araxes ware known to West Asian archaeologists as Khirbet-Kerak ware, was being made there around 2500 BC.

The first written records relating to the ancestors of the Armenians were recovered from the Hittite royal archives at Boghazköy in Turkey. They date from about 1350 BC, and refer to wars against local kings of Hayasa-Azzi and other districts situated between the Hittite empire and the territory which was to form Greater Armenia.

After the fall of the Hittite empire, the tale is taken up by the Assyrian annals, which refer to a coalition of minor kings ruling over the district of Nairi, south of Lake Van. Between 1255 and 1114 BC, these local potentates were attacked several times by the Assyrians, led successively by Tukulti-Ninurta I and Tiglath-pileser I, and then again by Ashurnasirpal II in the ninth century BC.

This relentless Assyrian pressure from the south forced the local dynasts around Lake Van to band together in self-defence. The first known king of united Urartu was Aramu or Aramé (880–844 BC) whose exploits are attributed in Armenian tradition to Aram and his son, Ara the Fair.

Following the sack of Arzashkun, Aramu's capital, by the Assyrian king, Shalmaneser III (858–824 BC), the Urartian capital was moved to Tushpa, modern Van, the building of which Armenian legend (following Moses Khorenatsi) fancifully ascribes to the Assyrian queen Semiramis.

During the eighth century BC, under such outstanding rulers as Menua, Argishti I and Sarduri II, the Urartian kingdom became the largest state in West Asia. Its frontiers extended to Colchis and the land of the Georgians in the north, and to Syria in the west. Colossal irrigation works and fortifications bear witness to the power and resources of the Urartian rulers, who assumed the title of 'King of kings'.

The Urartian kings erected two large castles on the outskirts of what is now Erevan, capital of Soviet Armenia. The city itself is really an Urartian foundation–its Urartian name was Erebuni, and it was established by Argishti I (785–760 BC) in 782 BC. The second castle at Erevan–Karmir-Blur or Teishebaini – was founded by Rusa II (685–645 BC).

By the reign of Rusa II, decline had already begun. In 714 BC, Sargon II of Assyria (721–705 BC) invaded Urartu, marching round the northern shores of Lake Van and inflicting widespread destruction.

Urartu finally collapsed about 600 BC, under the blows of the invading Cimmerians and Scythians from the north, and pressure from the Iranian Medes. The country was then partly occupied by Hayasa people coming from the direction of the old Hittite lands, and by speakers of the Indo-European language which we now know as Armenian. These elements gradually merged with survivors of the old Urartian population, who lived on for a period under the name of Chaldians or Alarodians.

The first mention of the Armenians as a nation occurs in the Behistun inscription of Darius the Great of Persia (522–486 BC), and then in early Greek writers including Herodotus. Armenia formed a satrapy or province of the Persian empire of the Achaemenids, though the local people enjoyed considerable freedom under their clan chiefs. The Armenian dynasty of the Orontids ruled independently after 331 BC, following the conquest of Persia by Alexander the Great.

Armenia's political prominence developed under the Artaxiad dynasty, named after Artaxias or Artashes I (190–159 BC), a friend of the celebrated Hannibal of Carthage, who allegedly spent his retirement in Armenia. These two rulers jointly founded a new Armenian capital at Artashat – 'the joy of Artashes' – situated at the confluence of the river Araxes and the river Metsamor.

Armenia became a world power under a descendant of Artaxias, Tigranes II the Great (95–56 BC), who married the daughter of Mithradates Eupator of Pontus (120–63 BC). (As well as being an arch-enemy of the Romans, Mithradates is the hero of a tragedy by Racine, and an opera by Mozart!) Tigranes invaded Mesopotamia, Syria and Phoenicia, and created a short-lived West Asian empire, the extent of which almost precisely matched that of Urartu in the eighth century BC. He built a lavish new capital at Tigranokerta, at the foot of the Taurus mountains, on the north bank of the Tigris, peopled his empire with deportees from Syria and Cilicia, and became immensely rich and despotic.

The ramshackle realm of Tigranes was not built on solid foundations, and was overthrown between 69 and 66 BC by the Roman generals, Lucullus and Pompey, although Tigranes retained suzerainty over most of eastern Armenia. He was succeeded by his son, Artavazd II (56–34 BC), a cultured ruler and a great patron of the theatre. Artavazd was deposed and kidnapped by Antony and Cleopatra (34 BC), and then cruelly murdered with his family.

The Romans eventually tired of trying to rule the rebellious Armenians. The emperor Nero came to an agreement with the Parthian ruling house in Persia, whereby a Parthian royal prince named Trdat or Tiridates was appointed king of Armenia. Nero then invited Trdat to visit Rome in AD 66, and solemnly crowned him in the Forum.

Trdat or Tiridates I founded the distinguished dynasty of the Armenian Arsacids, which ruled until its last representative, Artaxias IV, was deposed in AD 428. The overthrow of the Parthian dynasty in Iran by the Sasanian aristocratic house in AD 226 was a bitter blow for the Parthians' royal cousins in Armenia. The Sasanians were, logically enough, bitterly hostile to all survivors of the Arsacid dynasty in both Iran and Armenia. Eventually the Sasanians partitioned Armenia under an agreement with Constantinople in AD 387.

Meanwhile the Armenians had adopted Christianity as their state religion, probably in AD 301–thus making Armenia the oldest Christian nation to survive into modern times. The Persians staged a full-scale assault on Armenia, with the aim of forcing the people to adopt the Zoroastrian faith once more (battle of Avarayr, AD 451). Although defeated, the Armenians resisted the fire-worshippers until the Sasanian 'Great Kings' were themselves overthrown by the Muslim Arabs in AD 642.

Following the victory of the Arab Caliphs, an Arab viceroy was appointed to rule over Armenia, his capital being the city of Dvin. Beautiful coins with Arabic inscriptions were struck there in vast numbers, and Dvin became an important international trading centre.

Urartian fortress near Lake Van, part of the defensive network organized against invaders.

Social organization and economic life

The findings of archaeology and later travellers' reports and other literary sources give ample evidence about living conditions in Armenia in ancient times. Excavations show that the transition from food-gathering to systematic food production took place in the Ararat valley and adjoining plains not later than 6000 BC. Armenia had a fully-fledged neolithic culture, with permanent settlements surrounded by stone walls. The craft of the potter was practised in Armenia from the Neolithic Age onwards, the manufacture of cooking pots and other useful domestic utensils contributing to a rapid advance in dietary standards.

About 3000 BC, Armenia helped to foster the 'Kuro-Araxes' or early Bronze Age Transcaucasian culture. The local inhabitants dwelt in small beehive-shaped houses with walls of wattle and daub; sometimes the dwellings were rectangular in ground plan.

Only during the early Urartian period, from 900 BC, did the people pass from a patriarchal clan structure to a centralized system of government. The Urartian kings were autocratic in their style of rule, though they were usually supported by a loyal population. The local people benefited from extensive public works (particularly irrigation) and from the defensive network organized against barbarian invaders from the north (Scythians and Cimmerians) and against the Assyrians living immediately to the south. The Urartians were small in stature, but tough, athletic and great horsemen.

Besides gold and silver, Urartu possessed rich deposits of iron, copper and tin. The agricultural wealth of the valleys was fully exploited: their excellent wines not only kept up the morale of Urartian military garrisons but also graced the royal tables of Assyrian and Babylonian monarchs; and rich pastures on the lower slopes of the mountains provided grazing land for cattle, sheep and horses. Manpower for public works was supplied by prisoners of war taken in battle against both rival states and rebellious local tribes.

Following the collapse of Urartu in about 600 BC and the influx of the earliest Armenian-speaking communities, the land reverted to its old patriarchal clan structure. We learn from Xenophon's book, *The Anabasis*, that the common people enjoyed a high standard of living, with plenty of meat and strong barley wine. Around 400 BC they lived in partly subterranean houses, cleverly designed to exclude the winter frost and snow.

From this period dates the growth of a proud and powerful local aristocracy, comprising the hereditary princes and nobles who were later to oppose the central power of the kings. Armenia's rugged terrain favoured strong local dynasts, and made it difficult for the Armenian kings to unify the country. Many feudal princes and dignitaries became very rich, living in impregnable castles and surrounded by squires and vassals. The chief princes wore a special cloak made from the expensive wool of a rare bivalve called a pinnos, which grows a silky beard. This cloak was fastened with a golden brooch, and the princes also wore red boots reaching to the knees, of a type usually reserved for royal personages.

The squirearchy and minor nobility, classed as *azats* or freemen, were exempt from corporal punishment, though subject to taxation. They held small fiefs and formed cavalry troops for the king or leading princes. They also constituted a class of officials and administrators.

Even before the time of Alexander the Great, Armenians kept inns along the main post roads linking Iran with Asia Minor and, later, Byzantine sources referred to the Armenians' business ability. Speaking of the city of Dvin, Procopius remarked: 'From India and the neighbouring regions of Georgia and from practically all the nations of Persia and some of those under Roman sway, they bring in merchandise and carry on their dealings with each other there.'

During the Middle Ages, the common people—serfs and artisans—led an increasingly miserable existence, dwelling in hovels and even holes in the ground. This

Urartian helmet (repoussé bronze). The first written records relating to the ancestors of the Armenians date from about 1350 BC and refer to wars against local kings.

was largely due to the concentration of wealth in the hands of the Church and the feudal nobility.

Armenians were also renowned as brave and tough soldiers, furnishing both cavalry and infantry to their sovereigns. When life was peaceful at home, they served as mercenaries abroad, particularly in the Byzantine empire. Many Byzantine emperors were wholly or partly of Armenian origin.

Religion

Objects of worship, including statuettes and portable hearths or miniature altars decorated with animal figures, have been excavated in Armenia in large quantities. These finds show that primitive religious cults were practised in Armenia from the early Bronze Age up to 5000 years ago.

Later, the Urartians had a highly developed pantheon of gods and goddesses. The chief deity was Khaldi, a Zeus-like figure; Khaldi's consort was named Arubani. Teisheba (the Hurrian Teshub) was god of war. The various gods and goddesses were arranged in a fixed order of seniority, and each one was entitled to a specific amount of rations in the form of animal sacrifices. Lofty temples were erected in honour of Khaldi in the principal cities and castles of the Urartian state. This cult of Khaldi explains why the Urartians were sometimes known to ancient writers as Chaldians, who had no connection with the Chaldaeans of Babylonia.

Following the downfall of Urartu, the Armenians adopted a very different system of religion, largely impregnated with Iranian elements. The chief god was Aramazd, the Armenian embodiment of Ahura-Mazda; the Iranian deity Verethragna, god of war and victory, was called in Armenian Vahagn—he was later considered the equivalent of the Roman god Mars; Anahita, goddess of fertility and mother of all wisdom, was the protectress of the Armenian nation. Temples adorned with magnificent golden statues were erected in the honour of these deities. In classical antiquity, these Armenian gods and goddesses tended to become identified with kindred deities of the Greek pantheon. The cosmopolitan cult of Mithra was also popular in Armenia. His name became enshrined in national mythology in the form Mihr or Meherr.

Christianity was established as the state religion in Armenia by St Gregory the Illuminator in or about AD 301. The Armenians refused to subscribe to the formulation of Christian dogma adopted at the Council of Chalcedon in AD 451. This led to accusations of heresy being levelled at the Armenians by the Byzantine Church authorities. However, the doctrines of the Armenian Church evolved outside the frontiers of Byzantium, and are firmly rooted in the ancient apostolic tradition of eastern Christendom.

Popular religion, much of it pagan in origin, has always played a great part in Armenian daily life. Evil spirits, monsters and dragons abound in ancient Armenian folklore. Acute dread was inspired by the *vishaps* or serpent monsters, whose effigies are carved on megalithic standing stones found on hills in Armenia.

The stone *vishaps* are thought to have been conceived of originally as guardian deities of ancient irrigation systems, but popular superstition ascribed to them a sinister role: they were able to enter into human beings and haunt them; their breath was poisonous; they could ride and hunt on horseback, or fly in the air; they liked sucking milk from cows, and carrying off grain from the threshing floor.

The allies of the *vishaps* were the *nhangs*, portrayed in the guise of alligators or crocodiles. These *nhangs* lurked in rivers, and often took on the appearance of harmless seals, or alluring mermaids. They would catch swimmers by the feet, and drag them to the bottom of the stream. Then they would use their victims to satisfy their own sexual lust, suck their blood, and leave them dead on the river bank.

Also very potent and dangerous were the *devs*, portrayed as seven-headed tyrants. When they wrestled, it was like the shock of mountains clashing together, and lava poured forth from volcanoes. They could hurl enormous rocks a great distance, and dwelt in deep caverns or thick forests. Female *devs* were about the size of a hill; they threw their pendulous left breast over their right shoulder, and their right breast over their left shoulder, lest they made deep holes in the ground. In view of the forbidding aspect of their own females, the male *devs* much preferred girls of the human race, to whom they granted anything they asked, in return for sexual intercourse.

From ancient times, Armenians have believed in witches, also in 'spirits of disease'. These were small in stature, and wore triangular hats. They held in their hands a white, a red and a black branch. If they struck anyone with the white branch, he would fall mildly ill but soon recover; if with the red one, then he would have to stay in bed a long time before getting well; but if the spirit struck with the black branch, the victim was doomed to die and nothing could save him.

Not all supernatural beings were unfriendly, and we find reference to benevolent *shahapets* or protectors of the homestead, who would shield the olive trees and vineyards from frosts and other evil forces. It is also an ancient Armenian belief that every child had from its birth a guardian angel who protected it against evil spirits. The angel's duties included cutting the child's nails, and amusing it with the golden apple which the angel held in his hand. When the child was old enough, the guardian angel returned to heaven, while the child smiled at him and stretched out its little arms.

Art and culture

From the early Bronze Age onwards, the inhabitants of the Armenian lands placed themselves at the forefront of ancient technological development, notably in the fields of ceramics and metallurgy. The burnished pottery of the 'Kuro-Araxes' culture (from 3000 BC onwards) is decorated with imaginative motifs, in the form of spirals and other geometric designs.

The middle Bronze Age, between 2000 and 1500 BC, produced the 'Kurgan' or 'Barrow' culture known from excavations at Lchashen on the shore of Lake Sevan, also from Trialeti in southern Georgia. The bearers of this culture may have been Indo-European invaders from the north, whose chieftains were men of wealth and power. The great 'Barrow' graves of these local rulers have yielded up carts and chariots of sophisticated design, which were buried to ensure transportation for the dead lords in the world beyond the grave.

By 1500 BC, many branches of advanced metal processing were practised with success in Armenia, including forging, chasing, cutting, stamping, grinding and polishing, as well as jewelry inlaying. The Urartians further developed these useful decorative arts and were famous for their unusual bronze shields, decorated with animal figures, and for their cauldrons with distinctive handles, which were sought after by many peoples of the ancient world, including the Etruscans. The Urartians were adept as goldsmiths and workers in ivory and they manufactured furniture of sophisticated design.

Urartian architecture was highly inventive. Much of it was military in character, but there were elaborate temple buildings dedicated to the chief gods. The Urartians were expert at carving large blocks of stone which could be fitted neatly together, even without the use of mortar.

An important contribution to architectural science was the sloping roof with triangular pediment and surrounding colonnade which were used in the Urartian temple of Musasir–a shrine looted and destroyed by the Assyrian king, Sargon II, in 714 BC, and then depicted in the Assyrian reliefs of Khorsabad palace. This design was extensively employed in classical Greece and Rome and more recently, for the main façade of the British Museum, London. The interior walls of many Urartian public buildings were adorned with coloured frescoes.

Between the fall of Urartu about 600 BC, and the conversion of Armenia to Christianity in AD 301, art in Armenia had a somewhat derivative, provincial character. However, we find beautiful silver and gilt rhytons or drinking horns, while the silver coins of Tigranes the Great (95–56 BC) are masterpieces of numismatic art and the classical temple at Garni, recently restored by Professor A. Sahinian, is admired for its harmonious and imposing outline.

The architects of early Christian Armenia took over the classical basilica, perhaps via Syria, and created original variants, such as the Ereruk basilica (fifth-sixth century AD). Armenian master masons were also great experts in the construction of domes; the seventh-century AD circular cathedral at Zvartnotz near Holy Echmiadzin (now in ruins) was one of the architectural marvels of early Christendom.

The Armenians were also highly skilled in the art of manuscript illumination. Sometimes stylized, sometimes naturalistic, but always colourful and graphic, the miniatures in medieval Armenian manuscripts form part of the major treasures of the Christian world.

Both instrumental and vocal music have a long history in Armenia; five thousand years ago, simple melodies were being played on pipes and flutes fashioned from bone and horn. The Urartians are known to have sung cheerful songs to keep up their morale. In early medieval Armenia, *gusans* or minstrels played a central part in social life, and at important feasts these minstrels were accompanied by drummers, pipers, trumpeters and harpists.

Literature and learning

Pictorial writing in Armenia goes back to very early times, perhaps to the New Stone Age. We find pictograms or petroglyphs carved on rocks and cliff faces, depicting stylized human and animal figures. These served as a means of communication, as well as of ritual and artistic expression.

The Urartians developed hieroglyphic writing into a coherent system, used largely for commercial and administrative purposes. This was soon replaced by cuneiform characters modelled on Assyrian prototypes. Urartian literature, however, was extremely scanty, consisting largely of stereotyped royal inscriptions and laconic religious formulae.

Since there was no pre-Christian Armenian alphabet, pagan Armenia had no literature written in the vernacular. Greek and Middle Iranian (written in Aramaic characters) served as literary media, though minstrels composed and handed down orally various love songs and heroic ballads. Artavazd II (56–34 BC) composed original plays in Greek and staged them at his court theatre. An Armenian named Tiran, captured by the Roman general Lucullus, was taken to Rome, where he achieved fame as an orator and grammarian, became a friend of Cicero, and founded a library.

The adoption of Christianity in AD 301 was followed a century later by the invention of the Armenian national alphabet, pioneered by St Mesrop-Mashtotz, who completed the alphabet at Samosata between AD 404 and 406. The characters are written from left to right as in Greek, though the shape of the letters only very rarely resembles that of the corresponding Greek ones; many new letters had to be devised to represent sounds which do not occur in Greek at all.

Mesrop's initiative was followed up by a brilliant school of disciples who set out to create a new Christian literature, covering all the main fields of knowledge–including theology, philosophy, geography and astronomy. The Holy Scriptures, as well as a large corpus of writings of the Church Fathers, were among the first works to be translated into Armenian.

Early original writers include the fifth-century AD Eznik of Kolb, who wrote a polemical treatise entitled *Against the Sects*, vigorously attacking the Zoroastrians and other pagans and heretics. The neo-Platonist philosopher David the Invincible was an expert on the works of Aristotle and was never known to be defeated in argument–hence his nickname.

The foundations of Armenian historiography were laid in the fifth and sixth centuries AD. Armenia made a great contribution to early medieval geography and astronomy through the writings of Anania Shirakatsi, who lived in the seventh century AD.

Syria

William Culican

Syria is an open-sided land, a conglomeration of different environments and resources with few unifying factors except for that part of the Euphrates river system which lies within modern Syrian territory. Its openness to the urban civilizations that evolved in the Euphrates-Tigris system (Sumerians and Akkadians), the agricultural prospects of the Turkish foothills and north Syrian plains, attractive alike to the Mesopotamians, eastern Anatolians and the Semitic tribes originating in Arabia; the fertile coastal strip and the access in the northwest to the mineral resources of the Taurus – all these made Syria a corridor of civilizations without engendering a strong comprehensive statehood in anyway coextensive with modern Syrian boundaries.

In the second millennium BC Syria was placed between superpowers – Egypt, Babylonia and the Hittites – and in the first millennium BC became the prime area of Assyrian expansion. To none of these powers was control of Syria economically or politically vital; but strategically the control of Syria and its important 'international' caravan routes, north-south along the river Orontes, east-west by way of Harran and Damascus-Palmyra, with the Aleppo-Euphrates route running between, meant the security of the national boundaries, as well as control of the threat posed by the nomadic element in Syria's ethnic cauldron. The great powers were certainly not blind to the economic advantages of the control of the Syrian caravan trade or to the many resources Syria had to offer (timber, wool, oil, wine); but it was mainly its shifting expansiveness that provoked their fear.

Beginnings

The outline of the Syrian Neolithic, established from a number of sites, reveals that the dark-faced burnished ware typical of the sixth millennium BC was a ceramic independent of Mesopotamian tradition. Yet the beginning of village settlement in Syria, whether of permanent or semi-permanent dwellings, appears to have received at least some of its initial impetus from the Epi-Palaeolithic hunter-gatherer 'Natufian' communities of Palestine, forced to move northwards perhaps by climatic change, bringing about the movement of game. Situated about 47 miles (76 km) east of Aleppo, Mureybat is the site of the earliest of the 'Natufian-tradition' settlements in Syria and follows the Palestinian tradition of circular houses of stamped clay. The economy of Mureybat I, the earliest level, which ended about 8500 BC, was largely dependent on wild barley as a foodgrain and fully exploited the river and marsh environment for birds, fish and mussels. Its meat came mainly from wild aurochs, ass and gazelle. Subsequent Mureybat II and III continued this basic economy into the eighth millennium BC but with greater dependence on wild grains, to a degree that suggests cultivation (and indeed importation of some grains from a considerable distance), but in no stage at Mureybat, despite the highly developed rectangular houses of Mureybat III, is there evidence of either domesticated grains or animals. A variety of stone and plaster vessels, baskets and wooden containers served for domestic purposes in the complete absence of pottery.

At nearby Tell Abu Hureyra there was a village of over 28 acres (11 ha), thus making it the largest-known early Neolithic settlement in West Asia. The houses were rectangular structures of mud brick divided into rooms with black burnished plaster floors. While pottery was still unknown, extensive use was made of plaster vessels, as elsewhere in the 'aceramic Neolithic' of the Levant. In the upper level, when Hureyra had contracted in size, a little dark burnished pottery was used, probably the earliest of its type in Syria.

Phoenician mother-goddess. Ivory from Ras Shamra, ancient Ugarit. Phoenicians were expert at bas relief, openwork ivory carving and at glass and gilt inlay.

Chronology of Syria, Phoenicia and Israel

BC	Syria	Phoenicia	Israel
1500	Ugarit (Ras Shamra) at its richest (after 1400)		
	PERIOD OF EGYPTIAN DOMINANCE (15TH–13TH CENTURIES)		
	Battle of Kadesh (c1286)		Arrival of Hebrews from Egypt (c1200)
	SEA PEOPLES SETTLE AFTER ABORTIVE ATTACKS ON EGYPT (FROM 1100)		
1000			Saul (1020–1000)
			David (c1000–960)
		Phoenician colonization overseas (900–600)	Solomon (c960–922)
			Separation of Israel and Judah (922)
	Assyrians conquer Damascus (732)	Assyrians reduce Tyre (666)	Sargon II annexes Israel (721)
			Fall of Jerusalem (587)
	INCORPORATED IN PERSIAN EMPIRE (539)		Return of exiles (538)
500			Temple reconsecrated (515)
	ALEXANDER THE GREAT: HIS DOMINIONS (333–323)		
	Antiochus IV (175–163)		Judas Maccabaeus (165–160)
	ROME THE DOMINANT POWER		Herod the Great (34–4)
AD 100			Life of Jesus Temple burned by Romans (70)

Both Mureybat and Hureyra were situated between the Syrian steppe and the Euphrates flood plain and drew upon the resources of game and wild plants provided by both ecologies. The steppe provided the game and the alluvium probably artificially propagated stands of wild grains (at Hureyra) and cultivated forms of wheat, barley and lentils in the later stages. Food plant resources were tapped at considerable distances from these sites and it is remarkable that obsidian, shells and other select raw materials came from as far away as Anatolia and the Red Sea, thus placing Syria centrally in the far-flung trade network that we know to have existed by early Neolithic times.

The full Neolithic appears to have been brought into Syria from the northern Tigris and Euphrates region. The type-site, Tell Halaf, lies on a northern tributary of the Euphrates. The brilliant tradition of painted pottery, first found there, forms an important horizon across West Asia from Choga Mish in southwestern Iran to the sites of the south Konya plain. In Syria Halaf preference was for sites in the low foothills bordering Turkey; by the middle period, Halaf pottery had reached northern Syria (for example, Ras Shamra).

Presumably it was successful agriculture that enabled this expansion of Halaf culture, but very little is known about Halaf economy. At Ras Shamra domestic sheep, dog and pig are associated with the Halaf levels. Extensive trade in raw materials, the export of the beautiful painted pottery and the trade in gaily woven textiles (flax or wool—whose minute designs may be reflected in the pottery painting) have all been suggested as partial reasons for Halaf success. It was not until the Late Halaf period that metals were known. Lead and copper were used for amulets, indicative of the unimportance of metals for practical purposes.

The reasons for the sudden end of Halaf culture in Syria about 4500 BC are unknown and the ensuing period in Syria appears impoverished and piecemeal. It also witnessed the arrival of groups of people from the west and the south, and the beginning of copper metallurgy.

Western Semites

Fear of the expansion of the Martu (the 'Westerners', whose concentration was then probably west of the middle Euphrates) is firmly established in the earliest Sumerian literature. In the usage of the Sargonid and Ur III dynasties (late third millennium BC) the Akkadian *Amurrum* became interchangeable with Sumerian *Martu* and clearly the Amurru in Ur III texts bear West Semitic personal names close in structure to the attested Amorite names of the Old Babylonian period some four centuries later. Though the Martu were known to Sumerians well before Ur III times—their names can be found in the Fara text of 2700 BC—there is no earlier corpus of Martu names surviving; but new evidence from Ebla suggests that the earliest known Martu were Western Semites of already advanced urban status by the mid-third millennium BC.

While certainly to Sumerians the Martu appeared as tent-dwelling nomads, it is too simple a view that nomads entering Syria from the south fanned out in repeating waves in search of a secure agricultural life, thereby causing continual social upheaval. For long periods, a symbiosis of settled urban Amorites and contemporary nomads provided the basis of economic balance, with desert families taking seasonal work in the cities and members of city families returning temporarily to pastoral life. Furthermore, much nomadism was probably controlled by the necessity to seek city markets for selling livestock and crafts. More acceptable than the theory of the coming of the Amorites to Syria about 2000 BC is that of the longer existence of Semitic dimorphic nomadic and urban groups, basically identical in race and language, established in Syria early in the third millennium BC. Thus the Syrian cities, the cities of the 'Upper Land' listed in the Akkadian texts of Sargon I (c2334–2279 BC) and Narām-Suen (c2291–2255 BC) (in order from the Euphrates to the Mediterranean), were either East Semitic (Akkadian) or West Semitic (Amorite) foundations. They are Tuttul, Mari, Iarmuti, Ebla and Arman (closely associated with Ebla and whose king Rish-Adad bore an Amorite name), and on to the Cedar Forest (Amanus?) and the 'Mountain of Silver' (Taurus?). Sumerian cultural influence in statuary and minor arts certainly extended to Mari, but it is not conspicuous in the West Semitic towns to the northwest.

The most important city in this region was Ebla (Tell Mardikh, 24 miles (38 km) south of Aleppo). In the mid-third millennium BC Ebla was a prosperous trading centre of about 250,000 inhabitants administered by a bureaucracy, which according to the huge archive of tablets found there, numbered over 1100 men. Some of this archive is written in cuneiform 'Eblaite' (also called 'Palaeo-Canaanite'), the earliest form of written West Semitic, which perhaps slightly preceded the earliest written Akkadian of Mesopotamia and used the common heritage of Sumerian script rather differently. Clearly Ebla was the contemporary equivalent of the great trading cities of Mesopotamia and from the evidence of the tablets had cast a network of trade over much of West Asia (though not so much over southern Mesopotamia). In trading connections with east and central Anatolia, Ebla was the forerunner of Ashur in the second millennium BC.

Ebla's early rulers, Igrish, Khalam and Ar-Ennum are difficult to date but Ebrum, their successor, defeated Iblul-il of Mari and there is one reference to Sargon of Akkad (Akkadê) in a tablet of his reign. While Ebrum therefore was contemporary with Sargon, it is uncertain how far back the earlier Ebla rulers stretch: probably not significantly before 2400 BC.

At Ebla a Semitic population long precedes the traditional earliest Semites, the Amurru (Amorites) who appear to have come at the end of the third millennium BC and who spoke a Semitic dialect different from Eblaite, which at present has its nearest equivalent in the later version of Akkadian used at Mari about 2000 BC.

While the precise date of the Ebla archive is not determinable, on both historical and palaeographical grounds it either precedes the reign of Sargon or overlaps it. On present theory it was Narām-Suen, Sargon's grandson, who first destroyed Ebla and thereby accidentally preserved the main archive in the palace G of Ebla

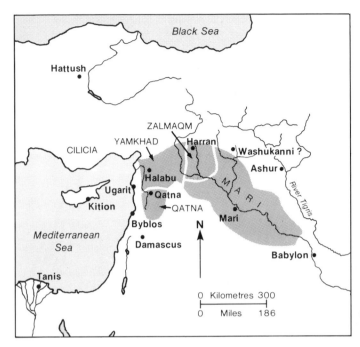

Syria: the states existing at the accession of Hammurapi of Babylon in 1792 BC.

IIB. Ebla lived on for about 600 years: it never regained its political importance: about 2000 BC it was sacked by the Amorites and was later incorporated into the Amorite kingdom of Yamkhad.

Mari

The Akkadian city of Mari (Tell Hariri on the middle Euphrates) rose to wealth and prominence by its control of the main caravan route from Syria to the Persian Gulf. The Sumerian king list assigned to Mari a kingship of 136 years; though none of its royal names survived, kings Lamgi-Mari, Ebih-Il and Idi-Narum have been found in Mari inscriptions of pre-Sargonid date, and these may have been of the dynasty that obtained suzerainty over Sumer as recorded in the king list. Mari next rose to importance in the nineteenth century BC, now as an Amorite town ruled by a short succession of powerful kings, Iakhdun-Lim, Iasmakh-Addu and Zimri-Lim, the latter a contemporary of Hammurapi of Babylon (1792–1750 BC), who eventually destroyed Mari. The archive found in Zimri-Lim's palace is the major source for contemporary Syria, even though Mari's 'foreign affairs' were more concerned with Mesopotamia.

Iakhdun-Lim had expanded Mari's influence westwards by making expeditions to the 'Cedar Forest' and for some time resisted the expansionism of the powerful Shamshi-Adad of Ashur. It is from the letters of Zimri-Lim that we learn the political structure of Syria, with Amorite kingdoms established at Yamkhad, with its capital at Halabu (Aleppo), Zalmaqum (Harran) and Qatna (Mishrifeh). Only two cities of the coast are mentioned–Byblos, whose ruler Yantin-'ammu bears an Amorite name (as did his predecessors whose tomb furniture is inscribed with their names in Egyptian hieroglyphs)–and Ugarit, the name of whose ruler is not given.

Entrance

Royal
residence

Throne
room

Throne
room

Yards 0   20
Metres 0   20

N

Palace at Mari

Golden eagle from the palace at Mari. Before defeat at the hands of Hammurapi of Babylon, the king at Mari ruled a wealthy and powerful state.

Alalakh

The vacuum left by the eclipse of Mari was briefly filled by the kingdom of the Hana (Hanaeans), nomadic Semites who had long existed on the fringes of Mari society and who now formed a short dynasty of six princes at Terqa (Tell Ashara 43 miles (70 km) north of Mari). But in the west Yamkhad retained its power. Yarim-Lim and Ammitaqum, the two rulers of Alalakh (Tell Atshanah on the lower Orontes) whose reigns are covered by the tablets from Alalakh VII, were subject to the kings of Yamkhad, and confusing though the Yamkhad dynasty is, there is no doubt that its geographical extent and political control were paramount in Syria during the eighteenth and seventeenth centuries BC and effectively prevented the designs of first Ashur and then Babylon on west Syrian territory.

After a mixed political history in Levels VI–V, Alalakh IV is shown from its rich archive to have been the capital of Mukish. Of the four known rulers of this later period, Idrimi (1480–1450 BC) has left an autobiography written on a portrait statue, in which he names Parattarna, the first Mitanni king, as overlord. Tablets from Alalakh IV belong mostly to the reign of Idrimi's son Niqmepa, a vassal of Shuttarna of Mitanni and an ally of the nearly princedom of Tunip. Besides their value for such synchronisms the tablets provide an important social picture of a north Syrian city and the basis for reconstructing Syrian political geography in the sixteenth century BC. In the reign of Niqmepa's son, Ilimilimma, Alalakh fell to the Hittites, probably in Suppululiumas' campaign of 1370 BC.

Egyptian relations

One of the most important problems about Syria in the first half of the second millennium BC is the nature and purpose of Egyptian interest in it. Numerous Egyptian monuments leave no doubt about the physical presence of Egyptians in Palestine and Syria during the twelfth dynasty. Evidence starts in the reign of Senusset I (1971–1928 BC) and, continues under Amenemhat II (1929–1895 BC) whose monuments are found at Ugarit and Qatna. In the royal tombs of the Amorite princes of Byblos, gifts from Amenemhat III and IV were prominent treasures. The Egyptian Execration Texts of the twelfth dynasty and the *Story of Sinuhe* show how detailed the Egyptian 'intelligence' of northern Syria ('Retenu') was, but no sources tell us how it was acquired or what purpose it served. Certainly Egypt derived great benefit from Syria's natural resources, timber especially; quite possibly this commerce depended on the maintenance of political stability. Later in the millennium the Egyptian Tell el-Amarna texts make it clear that the petty states of Syria and Palestine looked to the pharaohs to maintain the urban against the nomadic element in southern Syria. In northern Syria Egypt's concordat with Mitanni kept Egypt's interests secure until, after Mitanni's defeat, they were brought face-to-face with Hittite expansion.

Hurri-Mitanni

During the Amorite expansion in the first quarter of the second millennium BC, the Hurrians, a non-Semitic people of probably east Anatolian origin, established themselves on the upper Tigris and in pockets across northern Syria at least as far as Alalakh. Two stray inscriptions written in Akkadian script, but in the Hurrian language, indicated the existence of a Hurrian realm at Urkish, east of Harran, in the late third millennium BC; the Ebla archives now confirm the presence of Hurrians in western Syria at that date, but in general there is a long gap between these early appearances and the full Hurrian impact. Although no material culture or art style can be firmly equated with Hurrians, their influence on the mythology and religion of Syria and the Hittite lands was very great. Though some places seem much more Hurrian than others (Tukrish, for instance, north of Carchemish) it cannot be said that there was a Hurrian 'invasion' or a centralized Hurrian state—at least not the latter, until the sixteenth century BC when a fresh wave of Hurrians formed, by migration and vassalage, the kingdom of Mitanni, stretching from east of the Tigris to Cilicia, and as far south as Kadesh on the river Orontes. Although there are some business archives from Nuzi (Jorgan Tepe) on the river Tigris, all information on the Hurrians and Mitannians comes indirectly. Growth in their influence can be traced, for instance, in the increase in Hurrian personal names between the archives of Alalakh VII and IV in which Hurrian practices were also dominant. Above all Hurrian influence is manifest in literary texts from Ugarit and Hittite liturgical texts.

The most elusive aspect of Mitanni culture is its Indo-Aryan connection. Royal names (Shuttarna, Artatama, Tushratta) as well as certain deities mentioned in treaties are purely Aryan. Furthermore, the presence in Mitanni society of a 'warrior caste' of charioteers (*maryanni*, itself an Aryan word) suggests a feudal system. It must be pointed out, however, that Indo-Aryan names were not confined to Mitanni in the Levant—Hani rulers also had them—so both the origins and contexts of the Aryan strains cannot be elucidated.

The Mitanni kingdom acted as a buffer between the Hittites and Assyria. The height of Hittite power under Suppiluliumas (1380–1346 BC) coincided with the reign of Tushratta of Mitanni (1390–1355 BC), who had married his daughter into the Egyptian royal house of Amenophis IV. Suppiluliumas' first expedition against him ended in defeat, but during the decline of Egyptian influence in Syria in Amenophis' reign, Suppiluliumas was able to put an end to the Mitanni of Washukkani, as well as their vassal-kingdoms of Aleppo and Alalakh.

Ugarit

The Hattush archives of Mursilis II, Suppiluliumas' son, extend Hittite suzerainty deeper into Syria. Carchemish was now ruled by Mursilis' brother and was to remain Hittite. Treaties were made with Amurru, now stretching inland north of Ugarit; and Mursilis' seals from Ugarit itself imply the recognition of his overlordship. His achievements were brought to an end by the Egyptian determination to restore their Asiatic sphere. The inevitable clash came between Muwattalis (Mursilis' son, 1315–1290 BC) and Ramesses II at the battle of Kadesh in about 1286 BC, one of the best documented battles in

Baal, meaning 'lord': in Syria and Canaan the old title of local fertility gods. Relief found at Ras Shamra, and dating from about 1800 BC.

127

ancient history, except for information on the outcome. The fact that Benteshina of Amurru was replaced by a pro-Hittite prince and Hittite treaties were made with Rimisarma of Aleppo and with Kizzuwatna, suggests a Hittite victory. Certainly Ugarit was afterwards subject to Hittite Carchemish and in the second half of the thirteenth century BC the number of sealings of Tuthalias IV found at Ugarit suggests that there may have been a permanent Hittite embassy there. By the end of the eleventh century BC, the area from Cilicia (Que) into northwestern Syria (now 'Hatti' or 'Great Hatti' in Assyrian annals) contained a number of small Hittite states—Carchemish, Arpad, Hama, Hattena, Unqi, Kummuhi—but their main population remained Semitic and Hurrian.

Initially it was the peaceful relations between Egypt and Mitanni that fostered the growth of Syria's main port Ugarit, on the headland of Ras Shamra south of Lattakia. In the Amarna period under Ammishtamru I and Niqmadu II, Ugarit was a vassal of Egypt, but was drawn even closer by diplomacy and intermarriage to the nearby state of Ammuru—both recognized Suppiluliumas and later Mursilis II. Under terms of a treaty made between Ammishtamru II (Ammishtamru's son) and the Hittite king Hattusilis III, a Hittite chamber of commerce was established in Ugarit, though without the right of acquiring property in the city. Later, Ugarit passed under the direct control of the Hittite king of Carchemish Ini-Teshub, but essentially remained autonomous until its eventual destruction about 1190 BC.

The recovery of large numbers of administrative, legal, lexical and literary tablets from Ugarit makes it the most important source for Canaanite social and intellectual life. The Ugaritic myths and epics are our only major source for Canaanite literature and religion. The Ugaritic script, a highly simplified cuneiform used alphabetically, was almost certainly invented there since only few Ugaritic tablets have been found outside it.

Ugarit was also a major channel of Aegean influence. Mycenaeans were established there in number and, before then, Minoans had built a set of chamber tombs of Aegean type. Though there is very little Minoan pottery, Mycenaean and Cypro-Mycenaean are well represented. Indeed there is other evidence from scattered finds elsewhere of gold work and cylinder seals of mixed Minoan and Mitannian themes that Cretans had cultural contact with the Syrian coast before the first Mycenaean impact about 1500 BC. The Mycenaeans especially seized the trading opportunities with the Levant coast in Syria and, besides Ras Shamra, Mycenaean III A and III B pottery has been found at Atshana, Byblos, Tell Kazel and Tell es-Salihiyeh near Damascus, and at Tel Sukas III C as well. In the first half of the second millennium BC objects from Alalakh and Byblos clearly reflected Minoan influence.

In certain local crafts, Aegean themes made deep impact, spreading into inland Syria on the elegant black goblets of 'Nuzi', on 'Mitanni ware' and on Mitannian cylinder seals (which were also strongly Egyptianizing); but at Ugarit it is ivory work that shows the strongest artistic interchange, one ivory goat-goddess plaque found at Ugarit being purely Mycenaean. Ivory was certainly among the commodities sought by the Mycenaeans at Ugarit; the Syrian elephant might have been the source.

Aramaeans

The next ethnic change was brought about by the infiltration into Syria of Semitic groups from the Middle Euphrates whom we call Aramaeans after the then current geographical term for the north Syrian plain *Aram Naharain*, 'the field of the Rivers'.

The Aramaeans rose to prominence in Syria at the end of the second millennium BC and formed a group of small independent states mostly known to us from the Assyrian annals. Bit-Adini (Beth-Eden of Amos I. 5), located in the region of Til-Barsip (Tell Ahmar) north of the bend of the Euphrates, was the most important of these and noted as the seat of military government during the period of Assyrian control. Another state, Bit-Bahyan, had its centre around the modern site of Tell Halaf (biblical Gozan on the upper Khabur) which has yielded the most important set of sculptures in 'Aramaean' style dating to the reign of King Kapara in the ninth century BC. Bit-Halupe was an Aramaean state on the lower Khabur: others are known on the middle Euphrates (Laqe, Hindan and Sukhu) and to the north, Bit-Zamani in the modern Diyarbekir region. Halab (Aleppo), Arpad (modern Tell Refad), 18 miles (30 km) to the north also controlled considerable territory.

Bypassing Hittite Carchemish, which remained Hittite in language and culture, the Aramaeans founded states in the foothills around the Cilician plain, of which Sam'al (modern Senjirli) is the best known.

These northern states seldom acted in any political or military unity or in combination with the most powerful Aramaean group we call Aram-Damascus, which provided under a series of able 'kings of Aram' during the ninth and eighth centuries BC, the greatest political threat to the divided kingdom of Israel and Judah.

Before the rise of Damascus, the small Aramaean principality of Aram Zobah situated in the northern part of the Bekaa between the Lebanon and Antilebanon, rivalled Hebrew territorial ambitions especially in the time of Saul (c1020–1000 BC). David defeated Hadadezer, the Aramaean king of Zobah, thereby probably gaining access to sources of copper in this region. Nothing of importance is known from archaeological sources of either Damascus or Zobah, but there is a strong possibility that both regions gained their wealth from the copper ore within their territories.

Ben-Hadad II of Damascus (about 879–842 BC) forced both Israel and Judah and persuaded several other states, both Phoenician and Aramaean, into one of the first great coalitions of Syrian history to combat the Assyrian threat. Their battle with the army of Shalmaneser III at Qarqar on the Orontes river (853 BC) was indecisive, but it was only the prelude to a century of intermittent attacks from the Assyrians, until Tiglath-pileser III (about 732 BC) conquered and divided its territory into six provinces—Damascus in the centre, Hauran, Qarnini and Gilead in the south; Mansuate (the Bekaa) in the west and Subatu in the north.

The Assyrians governed Syria in their usual fashion, establishing a military garrison or two, but without 'occupation' of the land. Instead they established or advanced local pro-Assyrian rulers over the principalities, deported populations likely to be refractory and policed this structure by annual expeditions for intimidation and collection of tribute, and for quelling the numerous revolts against Assyrian rule. The hold on Syria was vital, for by the time of Sargon II (721–705 BC) greater enemies threatened Assyria beyond the Syrian horizon—the Urartians of Armenia and the Mushki (Phrygians) of central Anatolia.

After the destruction of the Assyrian capital Nineveh in 612 BC by a Median and Babylonian coalition, Assyria's western empire passed under Babylonian rule.

For Syria this had the important consequence of elevating Harran to the 'Western capital' and an important cult centre of the god Sin. Government of the Babylonian possessions was in turn inherited by the Persians on their conquest of Babylon in 539 BC. Technically both Syria and Palestine lay within the Persian satrapy of Athura (Assyria) but epigraphic evidence suggests, by the end of the fifth century BC, a separately governed province 'Beyond the River' (*eber nari* – the Euphrates), mainly Syria and Phoenicia. Remains of both Neo-Babylonian and Persian periods are exceedingly scarce in Syria. There are graves of Achaemenian soldiers at Deve Hüyük and Perso-Babylonian remains at Neirab, Tanjara and Tell Nebi Mend. This situation contrasts markedly with the archaeological evidence for a 'Persian period' in adjacent Palestine, and it is not known if the Persians maintained garrisons in Syria, though presumably they did so in Damascus, which was the capital when Alexander the Great conquered it.

Phoenicia

William Culican

The name

Phoenicia was the name given by Greeks in the first millennium BC to the coastal strip of modern Lebanon and northern Israel from the region of Tripoli in the north to Akko (Acre) in the south, though occasionally the term appears to have been extended to cover the entire coast of Syria and Palestine. Since Phoenicia was thought of as a chain of coastal cities rather than as a 'nation', ancient sources give little idea about either its ethnic composition or territorial extent. Basically the population was descended from the coastal Canaanites of the Bronze Age, though the admixture of more northerly Semitic groups (particularly Amorites), of Aegeans and Cypriots as well as 'Sea Peoples', probably brought about considerable admixture to the basic Semitic stock by the beginning of the first millennium BC, when the Phoenician cities of Tyre and Sidon began their important historical role as the nuclei of Phoenicia. The origin of the name is unknown: the Phoenicians themselves cannot be shown to have used it; though the older Egyptian name *Fenkhw* for part of the Syrian coast might be related. The earliest clear use of it is in Homer (who also used 'Tyrians' and 'Sidonians'), but there are claims that the adjective *po-ni-ki-jo* in Mycenaean Linear B describes spices and other commodities imported from the Levant coast. To the Greeks the word 'Phoenix' had connotations of 'red', but whether referring to the skins of the Phoenicians or the reddish colour of much of the soil of Lebanon, it is almost certainly a false etymology when applied to the people themselves.

In late Bronze Age times the coastal Canaanites had

extended further north to Ugarit and her dependencies, but the onslaught of the Sea Peoples destroyed Ugarit for good and was as severe in the north as it was in coastal Palestine to the south. For some unknown reason

Ancient Syria and Phoenicia.

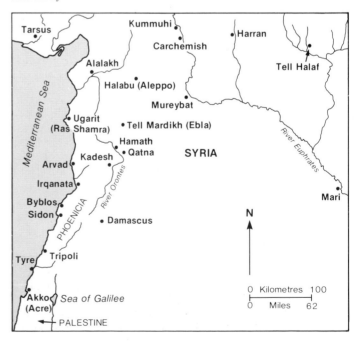

Byblos, Tyre and Sidon appear to have survived to become 'Phoenicia', the main centre of political and commercial power on the entire Levant coast. Independence was another factor for, between the decline of Egyptian domination under Ramesses III in the twelfth century BC and the beginnings of Assyrian pressure in the ninth century BC, these coastal cities developed without harassment.

Egyptian literature has left us one important story which relates to Phoenicia in this period. About 1080 BC the Egyptian Wen-Amun was sent from Tanis to Byblos on an official religious mission. He put in at Dor, then in the hands of the Tjeker branch of the Sea Peoples, and proceeded to Byblos by way of Tyre. Zakarbaal of Byblos stressed to Wen-Amun his independence from Egypt and yet could not provide any escort or protection for his guest, who was travelling in a non-Egyptian ship. It appears that 50 ships of Sidon were doing business with Wereket-El, a Phoenician merchant resident in Tanis. The implications of the Wen-Amun story are that not only had the Egyptian sea patrol of the Levant coast (as in Amarna times) ended but also that the initiation of trade with Egypt had come from the individual and disunited coastal cities of Phoenicia.

Byblos (modern Jebail) provides primary evidence by reviving her age-old links with Egypt. Statues of pharaohs of the Bubastis dynasty (945–842 BC) –Hedjkheperre Sheshonq, Osorkon I and Osorkon II–have been found in the ruins, two superinscribed in Phoenician by local kings named Abibaal and Elibaal. There is also an inscription of Shipitbaal on a separate slab and, most important, the inscribed sarcophagus of Ahiram who appears to have been the head of the dynasty, and whose inscription, the earliest substantial piece of Phoenician writing, is usually dated to the first half of the tenth century BC, slightly predated perhaps by an inscribed bronze spatula from Byblos naming Azarbaal, the earliest Phoenician king known to us.

Commercial enterprise

Commerce (and in its wake colonization) was the best known characteristic of Phoenicia in antiquity, for she not only possessed one outstanding natural resource in her extensive forest, but also stood at the head of important inland routes from southern Syria, central Palestine and northern Arabia. The coastal trade with Egypt, flourishing in the Bronze Age and now revived, was aided in the first millennium BC by the construction of double (north and south) harbours at both Tyre and Sidon. Byblos too had an important small harbour, while the tiny island of Aradus (Arvad), somewhat to the north of metropolitan Phoenicia, continued to act as an important island harbour on the route to the Aegean and southern Anatolia. Tyre and Arvad were virtually impregnable island fortresses: both looked to the sea for their livelihood, but it is important to stress that in the lament on Tyre in Ezekiel's chapter 27, her trade routes ranged over both land and sea, so that the urge to settle abroad was probably not limited to the founding of colonies overseas. Tyrians and Sidonians were certainly settled at Memphis in Egypt in Herodotus' time (probably involved with the shipyards), but these were probably the latest survivors of emporia established at Tarsus, Damascus, Elath, Hama and elsewhere.

Behind such enterprise abroad lay nature's benefice at home. Though but a narrow coastal strip, Phoenicia was intensely fertile and well-watered with rivers and springs. Behind her in the Bekaa lay a substantial granary whose resources could be drawn on, even though we cannot be sure that the Phoenician cities always controlled it. Offshore lay some of the best shallow fishing beds in the Mediterranean.

Tyre and Israel

The conquest of the Palestinian highlands by the Hebrews and the consolidation of Hebrew territory under David (c1000–960 BC), who extended it to control Edom and Moab in the south and Aram Zobah in the north, left Phoenicia somewhat isolated from her Semitic neighbours. David's subsequent treaty with Hiram of Tyre seems to have been part of this consolidation (as were those with Geshur and Hamath) and appears to have allowed Tyre access to the inland trade routes extending to Transjordan and the Gulf of Aqabah. While David thus gained Phoenician neutrality during his wars with the Philistines, it is likely that Tyre in return gained commercial advantages from the treaty. It was renewed under Solomon (c960–922 BC), who supported Phoenicia with foodstuffs whilst Hiram undertook to supply materials and craftsmen to build the Jerusalem temple, providing a new version of the temple of El or Baal-Shamem at Tyre. The biblical evidence (I Kings, 7; II Chronicles, 2) makes it clear that the Tyrians were expert bronze workers and in Homer (*Odyssey* 15, 425) Sidon is said to be 'rich in bronze'. Babylonian docu-

Ruins of the Phoenician temple at Byblos (second millennium BC). Byblos, Tyre and Sidon survived the onslaught of the Sea Peoples to become 'Phoenicia'.

ments of Nabonidus' reign indicate Lebanon as a source of iron, but the origin of these ores is unknown: it was certainly not local and probably the main clue to Tyre's commercial success was her seizure of mining resources, either by taking over the Mycenaean mining heritage of Cyprus or exploiting some inland source unknown to us. It was a problem already seen in the Bronze Age, for Byblos, equally without ores, provided more metal-workers' moulds than any other ancient site. It is certain therefore that Tyre, which did not engage in land battles, not only lay beyond Hebrew aggression but had sources of wealth and expertise that the Philistine cities had not. Some Hebrews did, of course, settle in Phoenicia, part of the tribes of Dan and Asher south of Sidon, but they appear to have made little impression on the maritime situation on the coast or to have bothered Sidon at all.

Besides that of David and Hiram I, a further synchronism can be calculated on biblical chronology. Ithobaal of Tyre married his daughter Jezebel to Ahab of Israel, the son of Omri. Ithobaal in turn was followed in Josephus' account by a Baalezoros, who is certainly the Baalmanzer mentioned in an inscription of the Assyrian ruler Shalmaneser III, dated 842 BC. He was also probably the Belus (Baal) of classical tradition, whose daughter Elissa and son Pygmalion are credited with the foundation of Carthage, traditionally in 814 BC.

Archaeological discoveries

Previously known from a few scattered deposits and a few tombs mainly in the Sidon region, the material culture of metropolitan Phoenicia before the Persian period has become better known in recent years because of a deep trench cut at Tyre, an important necropolis discovered at Khaldé (Beirut), an extensive excavation at Sarepta (modern Sarafand near Sidon) and the gradual publication of rich tomb material from Akhziv, north of Akko. While as yet the late Bronze Age pottery is little known, certain pottery types appear distinctive of Phoenician culture in Iron Age I (1000–850 BC) and even slightly influenced the post-Mycenaean pottery of Cyprus. Representing the beginning of this distinctive Iron Age tradition are strainer-spouted jugs and round-bodied flasks in bichrome painted ware; the former having some relation to the contemporary Philistine 'beer jugs'. These are followed by a 'Red-slip' burnished ware beginning in late Iron I and lasting through Iron II, disc-top and pear-shaped jugs especially, which run parallel to a later series of bichrome flasks and krater urns. While the bichrome tradition has relations elsewhere in Syria, Palestine and Cyprus, the 'Red-Slip' fabric and shapes are highly characteristic of the Tyre and Sidon region. It was carried to Cyprus (where both imports and local versions are found) and to the colonies in the western Mediterranean, where it was imitated and debased. It is rare in inland and coastal Palestine and absent from Syria north of the Tripoli region, except for Al Mina at the mouth of the river Orontes, which may have been a combined Phoenician and Greek trading station, settled by Phoenicians from the central coast. A number of contemporary 'Red-Slip' wares have been found in the Levant in the Iron I–II periods, at Ashdod, Hama Zinjirli and Tarsus, but at none of these sites are the fabrics and shapes similar to Phoenician 'Red-Slip'. It is especially the rich Akhziv tomb material that establishes the homogeneity and distinctiveness of Phoenician Red-Slip pottery.

While Akhziv is certainly the largest and wealthiest Phoenician necropolis of the Iron II period (850–650 BC), others are known in the escarpment behind Sarafand, and in the cliffs at Byblos. Some of the Sarafand tombs extend into the Persian period and link with tombs found previously at 'Atlit. An even earlier record of chamber tombs at Tell er-Rechidiyeh south of Tyre must be added. From these and scattered tombs the pottery of the Iron II and Persian periods is well understood, but Khaldé remains the only Iron I site, though its pottery can be supplemented by finds from Dor, and exported Phoenician pottery at Megiddo particularly.

Both at Khaldé and Akhziv the earliest tombs are cists containing single inhumations with fibulas and weapons, but burial urns of cremated bones placed inside cists or crude stone structures soon make their appearance. Inhumation in rock-cut chamber tombs is usual in Iron II, but many such tombs contain urns of cremated bones as well as skeletons. Exactly such mixed burial customs are found in the western Phoenician colonies. There are also unpublished parallels to the built and gabled tombs of Carthage found at the Sheikh Abaroh site near Sidon.

Assyrian domination

Although earlier Assyrian kings had made expeditions to north Phoenicia extracting tribute from Tyre and Sidon, as did Ashurnasirpal II in 868 BC, it was during the campaign of Shalmaneser III in 854 BC against the Syrian coalition led by Irhuleni of Hamath that we learn of certain northern Phoenician cities that joined Hamath against the Assyrians: Byblos, Irqanata, Arvad, Usanata and Shiana. They are the only ones named of 'twelve kings of the seacoast', but it is uncertain whether the southern Phoenician cities were involved at this date; though Shalmaneser later collected tribute from Tyre. In 738 BC, Tiglath-pileser III in defeating another Hamath-centred coalition punished the seacoast towns of Usnu and Sianu, which centuries earlier lay in the political sphere of Ugarit. These and other towns, namely Simirra, Arqa and Kashpuna, were formed into an Assyrian province centred on Simirra, which lay east of modern Tripoli. Byblos to the south and Arvad offshore are not mentioned. Soon Tiglath-pileser came into open conflict with Tyre during his campaigns of 734–732 BC, for Hiram II of Tyre was in alliance with Resin of Damascus, the Assyrians' chief adversary in Syria. Tyre was captured and tribute exacted but no attempt was made to turn central Phoenicia into an Assyrian province, though occasional tribute was exacted from Byblos, Arvad and Tyre during Tiglath-pileser's reign.

In 701 BC Sennacherib invaded Phoenicia. The

Phoenician bust unearthed in Spain, once an outpost of the Carthaginian empire.

Assyrian king was facing a serious rebellion of Philistia, Judah and Phoenicia which ended in the expulsion from Tyre of the Sidonian king Luli, who sought refuge in Cyprus. This event is recorded in valuable detail in the extant wall reliefs of Sennacherib's palace at Nineveh. It is the fullest surviving representation of the Phoenician navy—waiting offshore while Luli was lowered into a waiting ship on the quay of the burning city. Having taken Sidon ('Great Sidon' and 'Little Sidon') as well as Bit-Zitti (Ain-ez-Zeitun?), Sarepta (modern Sarafand), Mahalliba (Khirbet el-Mahallib?), Ushu (mainland Tyre), Ekdippa (Akhziv) and Akko (Acre), Sennacherib placed Tabalu on the Tyrian throne and, in return for favour, exacted a high tribute from him.

Tabulu was succeeded by Abdimilkuti some time before Sennacherib's death. His revolt from Esarhaddon, Sennacherib's successor, brought unprecedented severity from Assyria in 677 BC. Abdimilkuti was executed and Sidon destroyed. The treasures of his palaces were carried off to Assyria, and a military garrison set up near Sidon. In 671 BC Esarhaddon celebrated his cruel victory over Baalu of Tyre and pharaoh Taharqa of Egypt. But Tyre was not taken. Unlike Sidon, Tyre on her offshore island presented too great a problem for Assyrian siegecraft. Assurbanibal besieged it unsuccessfully in 668 BC, but after the Babylonians had succeeded to the Assyrian empire, Tyre was captured after a long siege by Nebuchadnezzar in 587 BC, who successfully weaned Phoenicia from new Egyptian alliances. Half a century later Phoenicia passed under Persian rule.

Relations with Cyprus

An outstanding feature of Phoenician culture in the Iron Age is its close relationship with Cyprus. This is intense in the Iron II period, large amounts of Bichrome III–IV pottery of Cypriot style having been found both in Phoenicia and the Syrian coast. Some of this pottery was undoubtedly made locally, so that it may indeed be questioned whether the Cypriot bichrome style itself is not mainland in origin. Whatever the case, such is the degree of commonalty that the answer to the problem of the date of the earliest Phoenician colonization of Cyprus is unlikely to be indicated by the simple invasion of mainland pottery. Mainland pottery types can be seen already in the latest Mycenaean tombs at Salamis. During Cypro-Geometric I and II (1025–800 BC) mainland vessels, including the 'Red-Slip' ware not native to Cyprus (though imitated there) makes an increasing appearance, and predominates at Kition. On the other hand, a Cypro-Geometric II tomb that contained a Phoenician epitaph had no mainland pieces among its tomb furniture.

Kition (modern Larnaca) has presented the clearest evidence for Phoenician occupation. After the abandonment of the important Mycenaean site, the Mycenaean temple underwent a series of reconstructions and enlargements. It remains doubtful to whom the earliest post-Mycenaean reconstruction should be attributed, but by 850 BC it had been turned into a great temple to the goddess Astarte, constructed on Phoenician lines and providing ample evidence from its votive pits of Phoenician cult practices. It has also provided the earliest Phoenician inscription yet found in Cyprus, of about 850 BC.

Export arts and crafts

The cedars and junipers that clothed the Lebanon hills were Phoenicia's chief indigenous resource, sought by Egyptians and Assyrians alike. Byblos and an unknown port called Arké seem to have been the main shipping centres, but Phoenicia seems also to have been an exporter of timber from Cyprus, Antilebanon and 'oaks of Bashan' (Ezekiel 27, 5–6). Phoenicia's experience in the timber trade went hand-in-hand with proficiency in shipbuilding. Her ships were not only the bearers of her commerce, but an industry in themselves. Lesser revenue still came from the important by-products of the timber trade, cedar and juniper oils, mentioned in documents from the city of Sippar in the Old Babylonian period.

Phoenician cloth must be mentioned for two reasons: it featured largely in lists of booty taken by the Assyrians; and Phoenicians were renowned in antiquity for their purple-dyed cloth, already mentioned in Ugaritic documents. The obtaining of purple dye from the murex shell was not a Phoenician secret, but knowledge of the chemistry of producing various shades reproduced in recent experiments might well have been their preserve. In any case, their access to large beds of *murex brandaris* is attested by the heaps of these shells still visible at Sidon.

The pre-eminence of Phoenicia in craftsmanship as well as commerce is attested both in the Bible and in Homer, where Sidonians feature as traders in small luxury items. No discoveries within the bounds of Phoenicia throw much light on this tradition, nor do luxury items appear conspicuously in the western Phoenician colonies, with the exception of the colonial area of Spain, which provides a rather different cultural problem. Phoenician art therefore has been recognized in works found elsewhere, ivory and bronze work particularly, which have a certain artistic unity in a rather forced style consisting of borrowings from Egyptian, Syrian and Assyrian art reworked, in a distinctive manner or with characteristic mannerisms. While themes were most often borrowed, details of pattern and decoration were often originally Phoenician, that is, survivals of Canaanite art. Above all Phoenician art was minor and applied: it had little originality, but it was its very decorativeness and craftmanship that sold it to the ancients. The beds, chairs and chests into which the ivories were inlaid, and which, of course, have not survived, were also, it must be remembered, part of the overall production, as were the sets of leather harness from which the Phoenician bronze blinkers and headpieces have survived in the Royal Tombs of Salamis (Cyprus), in Rhodes and Samos. Much orientalized metalwork in the Mediterranean has been attributed to north Syrian workshops, on grounds of style rather than archaeological evidence; but the Salamis tomb discoveries provide firm ground for attributing at least some of it to metropolitan Phoenicia.

The view that northern Syria was one of the main channels of an 'Orientalizing' influence on the Aegean world, though not here denied, is partly coloured by the importance of Al Mina and the growing realization that Greeks established themselves in small colonies in the eighth century BC at Ras el-Basit, Tell Sukas and elsewhere on the north Syrian coast. There appears no parallel situation on the coast of Lebanon—perhaps, it was thought, the Phoenicians did not want them—but now the publication of the Tyre excavations, and sherds from Khaldé as well, show that Greek contact with Phoenicia was as strong as with Syria, and at Tyre went back earlier, to Proto-geometric times. The Al Mina connection must certainly now be qualified.

Ivories and bowls

Until recently 'Phoenician Ivories' had been found everywhere but in Phoenicia—Nimrud, Khorsabad, Arslan Tash, Gordium, Samos, Crete, Samaria and even Hasanlu in Iran. But now a few have been excavated at Sarafand, so Phoenicia at last is on the map. None has been found in the western Phoenician world, though there are relatives from Carmona (Seville), Tharros (Sardinia), and Praeneste (Etruria). While sharing a common corpus of themes, their styles vary considerably, some 'Syrianizing' some 'Egyptianizing' and so on. All graffiti on Phoenician ivories are in either

Phoenician gold crown, a piece of exquisite workmanship, dating from the eleventh to the ninth centuries BC.

Phoenician or Aramaean script, but we cannot answer the question as to whether they were made in one centre, using a range of pattern books, or whether ivory workers, settled in foreign bazaars, adapted these patterns to local taste, or whether a wealthy patron commissioned a local Phoenician-trained ivory worker to decorate his house. All that is certain in that the Phoenicians were expert at bas relief and openwork ivory carving (at which latter, for instance, the Etruscan ivory workers were not) and at inlaying the surface detail with coloured glass pastes and gilt.

The problem is similar with the engraved metal bowls. The archaic (c800 BC) examples from the Kerameikos in Athens and Francavilla Marittima in Calabria have static engraved themes, either Syrian or Egyptian in style. A later group (about 650 BC) combining engraving with repoussé, are mostly silver, sometimes gilded. Their themes are military, mostly lively and occasionally narrative. Bowls of this class come mostly from Etruscan tombs, but there is an important example from Curium (Cyprus) and a forerunner from Idalion. Between these two groups are many bowls difficult to classify. The bowls from Nimrud have two main groupings; one related to the bold-style, high-repoussé bronze work from Salamis, the other, in contrast with well-spaced friezes of minute Egyptian designs, not found outside Nimrud. All probably date to about 750 BC. Bowls from Crete (Fortetsa, Arkades, the Mt Ida cave) have unique designs, yet draw on the same corpus of imagery as the Nimrud bowls. In short, no one workshop seems likely at any period between 800 and 650 BC, and the possibility must be kept open that some bowls found in Italy and Iran were locally made by immigrant Phoenician craftsmen catering to local taste. The influence of both bowls and ivories was far deeper among the Etruscans than any Mediterranean people, except perhaps the inhabitants of Spain.

Figure sculpture is best instanced in pieces from Amrit, the Phoenician settlement made on the coast across from Arvad. It was in a style heavily influenced by the fourth century BC style of Cyprus, but not without some originality.

The Phoenician fleet played a vital role for the Persians in the war against Greece and its threat to Samos probably changed the whole course of Athenian politics in the mid-fifth century BC. The site of the palace of the High Admiral was at Sidon near the Eshmun temple. From here and from the centre of Sidon itself have come parts of Achaemenian double-bull pillars specifically in a Babylonian-Persian style. There are the remains of a large Persian fortress on the acropolis of Byblos, while Sidonian (and other Phoenician coinages in the Persian period) flourished, at least those of Sidon with Persian designs. Apart from the desirability of the Sidonian harbours it is difficult to explain the special relationship that existed between Sidon and the Persians. It began probably in the reign of Eshmunazar, contemporary of Xerxes (486–465 BC), who reports on his sarcophagus inscription that the Great King had given him Dor and Jaffa. Whether a reward for favours received or an initial bribe, Sidon remained loyal to the Persians until twenty years before its capture by Alexander the Great in 332 BC.

Greeks and Persians

It was during the period of official hostility between Phoenicia and Greece during the Persian wars that, paradoxically, cultural relations became strong. The sarcophagi of the two Sidonian kings Tabnit and Eshmunazar found in Sidon in 1872 are black basalt Egyptian sarcophagi of a restricted but well-known type: they represent Phoenicia's last glance towards Egypt. Finds of Attic red-figure are numerous in the Lebanon and especially fourth century BC black glaze. A large group of white marble anthropoid sarcophagi found in great numbers in the hypogea of Sidon (and also in Cyprus, Sicily and Cadiz) have heads carved in a stagnant version of fifth century BC Attic. In the fourth century BC, Sidon developed commercial relations with Athens and by then there were probably many Greeks permanently settled in the Phoenician cities. But it was exactly at this time that Phoenician art had a renaissance. The great and complex Temple of Eshmun outside Sidon was probably begun in the seventh century BC but underwent, in Classical and Hellenistic times, a vast expansion turning it into a kind of spa or Greek Aesculapium. At Umm el-'Amed a complete Hellenistic Greek temple was built plus several sacerdotal dwellings with lintels carved with liturgical scenes in purely Phoenician style. At both sites there is a sharp contrast between the crude, almost megalithic, Phoenician masonry and the reliefs in classical tradition. From Umm el-'Amed and other sites in the Lebanon come a series of votive stelae showing a priest offering sacrifice. He is shown in profile wearing a full robe, not unlike Persian dress, but in fact Phoenician, as we can show from some of the votive terracottas found in a deposit at Kharayeb near Sidon. But the realism in the portraiture of these officiants is of Hellenistic origin. There are several other pieces of Phoenician sculpture that fit into this period, mainly 'empty thrones' or pieces of sphinxes; but there was also a unique tradition of limestone cult stones that help to illustrate some of the Phoenician cults depicted on the Roman coinage of Tyre and Sidon.

Israel

Helmer Ringgren

Beginnings

According to the Bible the history of Israel began when Abraham was called by Yahweh to leave his family and his country to go and settle in Canaan. His son, Isaac, and his grandson, Jacob, lived there until Jacob was forced by a famine to seek his living with his twelve sons in Egypt, where one of his sons, Joseph, had already reached a high position.

After some time, the descendants of Jacob became slave workers in Egypt. Yahweh, however, appeared to Moses and charged him with the deliverance of his people. After some time he achieved this, with the aid of Yahweh, who dried up the 'Sea of Reeds' so that the Israelites could march through. The Egyptian army which pursued the escaping Israelites was drowned in the sea. Moses and his people continued to Mount Sinai, where a covenant was concluded between Yahweh and the people establishing Yahweh as the god of his chosen people, Israel. The conditions of the covenant were laid down in a law including the Ten Commandments. Because of the people's disobedience, however, their march toward the promised country was delayed, and they had to remain in the wilderness for forty years. Finally, after the death of Moses, the people of Israel entered Canaan from the east, crossing the river of Jordan. Under the leadership of Joshua they conquered Jericho, the city walls of which fell in a miraculous way. In a well-planned campaign they then conquered the whole country and settled there.

Few, if any, details of this account can be verified by other sources. On the other hand, the general picture must contain some historical truth. Abraham's immigration probably reflects the movements of Amorite and Aramaean tribes in the first half of the second millennium BC. The reference to God as 'the god of Abraham, Isaac and Jacob' seems to reflect the Sumero-Akkadian idea of the 'personal god' of the individual, while the use of divine names such as El Elyon, El Shaddai, El Berith reflects an older stage in Israelite, or rather, pre-Israelite religion. Certain religious customs, such as the erection of stone pillars (maṣṣebah, Genesis 28.10), were later considered to be pagan.

The entrance of the family of Jacob into Egypt cannot be verified by Egyptian sources, but we do know that groups of Bedouin entered Egypt on several occasions and were granted permission to stay there. Slave workers called '*aperu* (possibly Hebrews) are also attested in Egyptian sources. Exodus 1.11 reports that the Israelites built the cities of Pitom and Raamses, which brings us to the time of Ramesses II (1290–1223 BC). Not surprisingly, the Egyptian sources are silent about the exodus of the Israelites. The birth story of Moses is legendary and contains a motif, which is also connected with Sargon of Akkad, Cyrus, and Romulus and Remus. His name is obviously of Egyptian origin (*mśw*, 'son'). The appearance of Yahweh takes place in the land of the tribe of Midian; strangely enough Egyptian sources mention the name *yhw* in connection with certain Bedouin tribes. The exact geographical location of the exodus and the Sinai events is a matter of dispute, but it is probable that there is some historical truth behind the stories. At least some of the campsites of the Israelites in the wilderness can be identified. A certain difficulty is created by the fact that Ramesses II's successor Mernenptah (1223–1213 BC) mentions the Israelites as already living in Canaan. As a consequence, the date of the exodus cannot be ascertained; though a date in the latter half of the thirteenth century BC remains the most probable, voices have been raised for the sixteenth century BC. A further complication is the fact that Jericho was destroyed several centuries earlier and was hardly inhabited at the time of Joshua.

Several theories have been suggested to harmonize the Biblical account with these and other historical facts known from other sources. The most likely assumption is that only some of the people of Israel were in Egypt and that the group coming from Egypt then joined other groups to form what was to be known as Israel. The Jericho story probably reflects an earlier event. The conquest of Canaan was certainly a gradual process, as even the first chapter of the Book of Judges admits.

The origin of the Yahweh religion is obscure, but certain facts point to the tribe of Midian or the related Kenite tribe. However, it must have received its characteristic form through Moses in the context of one of the early Israelite groups. Typical of this form is the claim of Yahweh to be the exclusive God of his people. This is not yet pure monotheism, since the existence of other gods is not denied; rather it should be termed monolatry. Another characteristic that seems to be original is the emphasis on ethical behaviour as expressed, for instance, in the Decalogue or Ten Commandments, even if it cannot definitely be proved that they are of Mosaic origin. In early documents (Exodus 15, Judges 5) the war-like character of Yahweh is prominent; his association with thunder and storms–like other storm-gods in ancient West Asia–is also emphasized (Exodus 19:16; Judges 5:4). Other sources mention him as the origin of life and death, wealth and poverty, good and evil (1 Samuel 2:6); this monistic outlook, which characterizes many of the high gods of primitive peoples, remains through the ages and is found as late as Isaiah 45:7.

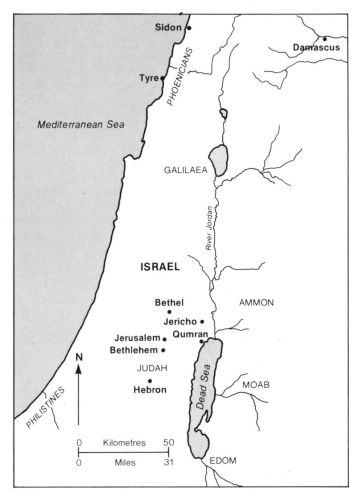

Israel.

The period of the judges

It would seem that Israel as a nation originated only on the soil of Canaan, and that the organization into twelve tribes did not exist before the conquest. Joshua 24 relates a renewal of the convenant at Shechem and, historically speaking, it is possible that this reflects the establishment of some kind of treaty between the various groups of 'Israelites' pledging themselves to serve Yahweh as their god. It has been suggested that this organization was comparable to the Greek amphictyonies, the members of which were each responsible for the service of a sanctuary one month in a year, but this theory has been contested.

The period immediately following the conquest is dealt with in the Book of Judges in which the wars of Israel with various neighbouring tribes are described. As the stories are told, it appears that the battles affected only one or a few of the tribes and may in part have been contemporary with each other. However, they have been fitted into a redactional framework so as to suggest a chronological sequence: every time the Israelites defected from Yahweh they were punished by the attack of enemies, but as they repented Yahweh sent 'judges' to 'save' them. The historical value of the stories varies considerably: the story of Barak and Deborah in Judges 4 and 5 as well as the story of Gideon (Judges 6–8) obviously contain valuable historical material, while the story of Samson (Judges 13–16) has a strongly legendary flavour.

The entrance into Canaan also meant a confrontation with Canaanite religion, as reflected in the story of Gideon's struggles with the cult of Baal. Though Gideon's other name, Jerubbaal (Judges 6:32), contains the name of that god, we are told that he destroyed the altar of Baal and built an altar to Yahweh in its place (Judges 6). We may assume that Baal as a fertility god appealed to the nomadic Israelites when they settled in Canaan and began to practise agriculture (the situation is reflected much later in Hosea 2:8).

The Samson traditions reflect heavy struggles with the Philistines, one of the 'Sea Peoples', who had invaded the southern coast of Palestine (which derives its name from them).

The introduction of monarchy

Under the pressure of the continued struggle with the Philistines, and with other enemies, the Israelites decided to elect a king, 'as all other peoples have' (1 Samuel 8:20). Their choice fell on Saul from the tribe of Benjamin (c1020–1000 BC) who was anointed king by Samuel (1 Samuel 10:1). Saul first defeated the Ammonites and then fought the Philistines with varying success. In these wars a young man of Judah by the name of David distinguished himself and was taken to the king's court. Soon, however, serious conflicts arose between Saul and David, aggravated by some kind of mental illness in Saul. According to one tradition, David had been anointed king by Samuel in advance (1 Samuel 16). The contradictory traditions are difficult to harmonize and the exact course of events cannot be established. In any case, Saul was defeated in a war with the Philistines and took his life on Mount Gilboa.

It seems that this period coincides with the end of the Bronze Age and the introduction of iron. There is a report in 1 Samuel 13:19–22 that the Israelites had to get their iron tools from the Philistines, which may reflect real conditions.

It is from this period that we have the earliest evidence of ecstatic prophets, nabhi', (pl. nebhi'im), living in guilds under a leader and obviously functioning as soothsayers. Samuel was such a prophet (1 Samuel 9 and 10:1).

David

David (c1000–960 BC) established himself as king over Judah with residence in Hebron, while northern Israel recognized Saul's son Ishbaal as Saul's successor. After the assassination of Ishbaal, however, David through skilful manoeuvering was also recognized as king of northern Israel. This was hardly more than a personal union, and a certain tension between the two parts of the united kingdom remained. David won a decisive victory over the Philistines and expanded his kingdom

by subduing the Aramaeans of Damascus, Ammon, Moab, and Edom. Israel had become a great power. David also conquered Jerusalem, held by the Jebusites, and made it the capital of his kingdom.

The reign of David marks a decisive change in the history of Israel in several respects. Firstly, the monarchy was finally established, and a royal ideology, modelled on the pattern of other kingdoms of West Asia, was developed. The king was 'the anointed one' (mashiakh), regarded as the son of Yahweh (2 Samuel 7:14; Psalms 2:7) and ruling on his behalf. In Psalm 110, 4 he is called 'a priest after the order of Melchizedek', that is, a true heir of Melchizedek of Shalem (Jerusalem) who was the priest of El Elyon (Genesis 14).

Secondly, the kingdom chose a capital on neutral ground, not belonging to any of the twelve tribes. David brought the ark, the national palladium of Israel, to Jerusalem, thus making this city the religious centre of the people. The ark was a wooden box, symbolizing the presence of Yahweh, and was also carried with the Israelite armies on their expeditions in order to secure divine assistance. According to later traditions the tablets containing the ten commandments were kept in the ark; it was obviously also considered to be the empty throne of Yahweh.

Thirdly, it seems that a certain syncretism developed between Yahweh and the god of Jerusalem, El Elyon. The biblical sources give the impression that, while Baal was discarded, El Elyon was merged with Yahweh so that El Elyon, 'God the Most High', became one of the epithets of Yahweh. Details of this syncretism remain obscure, but it must have been of decisive importance for the further development of the religion of Israel. For instance, the celebration of Yahweh as king, reflected in the so-called 'enthronement' psalms (47, 93, 95–99), is probably a Canaanite heritage received in Jerusalem. Another feature, which is found in these psalms as well as in other texts, is Yahweh's struggle with and victory over a monster called Leviathan, Rahab, or the Dragon (tannin), personifying the sea as a hostile force (Psalms 74:13 and 89:10; Job 26:12; Isaiah 27:1 and 51:9). Since the struggle of Baal with Prince Sea (Yam) is known from Ugarit, it is probable that this motif, too, is of Canaanite origin. The occurrence of the same motif in the Babylonian Epic of Creation is possibly due to West Semitic influence. In Israel Yahweh's victory is sometimes combined with creation, and other features such as the battle motif, linked up with Baal, are also ascribed to Yahweh. Psalms 29, for instance, describes Yahweh as appearing in a thunderstorm, using a terminology and style that betray characteristics of the Canaanite Baal.

Solomon

David was succeeded by his son Solomon (c960–922 BC). His reign was not altogether successful politically, in that Edom and Damascus were lost, but in other respects he managed to retain good relations with his neighbours. He married an Egyptian princess, and concluded a treaty with Hiram of Tyre. He also developed good

mercantile connections with other countries, which seem to have brought a certain wealth to the country. Court life in Jerusalem developed in the style of other West Asian kingdoms. In the Bible, Solomon is famous for his wisdom, and it is very likely that the teachings of international (especially Egyptian) wisdom were introduced into Israel in his time; the Book of Proverbs is ascribed to Solomon. It is also generally assumed that the first attempt to collect Israel's historical traditions was made under Solomon, resulting in the oldest document of the Pentateuch, generally called J, or the Yahwist source. However, Solomon is best known for his building activities: cities, fortifications, and, above all, the temple at Jerusalem.

The temple of Solomon was a sumptuous but not large building, constructed according to the usual ground-plan of Canaanite temples. It was built as a royal sanctuary and was not meant to replace the other cult places of the country. The local sanctuaries (such as Bethel, Gilgal, Gibeah, and Beersheba) obviously remained; a Yahweh temple at Arad has recently been excavated. In the cella of the temple, 'the Holy of Holies', was deposited the ark of Yahweh, overshadowed by two winged cherubs in animal form. In the temple sacrifices were offered regularly, and religious festivals (Passover with Unleavened Bread, the Festivals of Weeks and of Booths) were celebrated. It is interesting that these festivals seem originally to have been agrarian festivals of the Canaanites, which have since been reinterpreted as commemorating crucial events such as the Exodus, and living in booths in the wilderness, in the history of Israel. The hierarchy of the temple priests, singers, and other functionaries must have developed gradually, though the Books of Chronicles ascribe its organization to David.

The divided monarchy

On the death of Solomon in about 922 BC the tension between the northern and the southern tribes, perhaps combined with widespread discontent with heavy taxes,

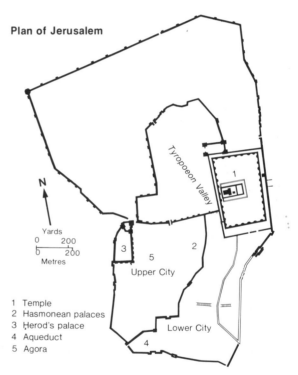

Plan of Jerusalem

Yards
0   200
0   200
Metres

Upper City

Lower City

1 Temple
2 Hasmonean palaces
3 Herod's palace
4 Aqueduct
5 Agora

Top: Reconstruction of the temple built in Jerusalem by Solomon (c960–922 BC), constructed according to the usual ground-plan of Canaanite temples.

led to open conflict and resulted in the establishment of two separate kingdoms, Judah in the south under Solomon's son Rehoboam, and Israel (sometimes also called Ephraim) in the north under Jeroboam, one of Solomon's former officials. Thus Judah remained a hereditary kingdom under the Davidic dynasty, while the king of the northern kingdom was elected, even if short-lived dynastics did occasionally develop.

Jeroboam established two national sanctuaries for his

kingdom at Bethel and Dan, where Yahweh is said to have been worshipped in the figure of a bull (1 Kings 12:26). While the southern kingdom had a certain stability in its dynasty, the northern kingdom soon fell into a period of political unrest, during which a general by the name of Omri seized the throne (876 BC).

Omri was a forceful ruler, which is reflected by the fact that Israel is often referred to in Assyrian sources as 'the house of Omri'. Omri's son Ahab married a Phoenician princess, Jezebel, who is said to have introduced the cult of Baal to Israel. This, as well as certain social evils, drew forth the fierce opposition of the prophet Elijah (1 Kings 17–19, 21; 2 Kings 1–2). He was followed by Elisha who also engaged in politics and made a certain general, Jehu, king (842–815 BC). These are the first two instances of a new development in Israelite prophecy, especially as far as Elijah is concerned.

Jehu's revolution, which was probably religiously motivated and which involved the killing of many worshippers of Baal, including Jezebel, was not a political success. Relations with Phoenicia were strained because of the killing of Jezebel; following a conflict with the Aramaeans Jehu had to pay tribute to Assyria; and finally, the Aramaeans took possession of the whole Trans-Jordanian area. The reign of Jeroboam II (786–746 BC) finally brought about better conditions, politically as well as economically, and Israel regained much of its political power. But at the same time this meant the establishment of an upper class which exploited the poor.

In the meantime Judah continued to exist under the Davidic dynasty. Under Jeroboam II's contemporary, Azariah, also called Uzziah (783–742 BC), Judah, too, had a period of success. But after the death of Jeroboam II northern Israel experienced a period of internal political instability combined with increasing pressure from Assyria; Menahem (745–738 BC) had to pay a heavy tribute to Tiglath-pileser III (744–727 BC); Pekah (737–732 BC) sought support from the Aramaeans to rebel against Assyria, but when Ahas of Judah (735–715 BC) refused to join the allies, they declared war on him (the so-called Syro-Ephraimite war). In spite of the protests of the prophet Isaiah, Ahas turned to Assyria for help. Tiglath-pileser III intervened, defeated the Aramaeans and conquered a considerable part of the northern kingdom. Only the area around Samaria remained under the new king, Hosea, and when he tried to rebel in 721 BC, the successor of Tiglath-pileser, Sargon II, put an end to the entire kingdom. Hezekiah, the new king of Judah (715–687 BC), sought support from Egypt to counterbalance the Assyrian pressure. In the Old Testament he is best known for his attempt at a religious reform.

In the religion of the divided kingdom, a strong syncretistic tendency comes to the fore. Yahweh was the god of a nomadic or semi-nomadic people, while the Israelites obviously regarded Baal as a suitable patron for their agricultural activities. As we have seen, Yahweh was identified with the Canaanite high god, El, or El Elyon, while Baal and his consort, Asherah, were worshipped as deities of fertility.

The biblical writers, who judged the religious conditions according to the ideals of the later Deuteronomic reform, reported on the canaanizing cult on the 'high places' (bamah) with the maṣṣebah, or stone pillar, and the asherah, or wooden pole, as the symbols of the male and the female deities, respectively. A recently found inscription from Kuntillat Ajrud even mentions 'the asherah of Yahweh'.

The official religion–as practised primarily in Judah and Jerusalem–is reflected in many of the Psalms. Here we find a high esteem of Zion as the earthly dwelling of Yahweh, defended by him against hostile attacks ('Zion hymns', like Psalms 46; 48). Besides the sacrificial cult, there are hints at other celebrations, in which the deeds of Yahweh were represented in dramatic or symbolic form ('Come and see', Psalms 46:9 and 48:9). These include a celebration of Yahweh's kingship, also called the enthronement festival (Psalms 24; 47; 93; 96), and a renewal of the covenant, including allusions to the Decalogue (Psalms 50, 81). Several psalms describe the king as Yahweh's son and the guarantor of righteousness (Psalms 2, 72, and 110).

The great prophets

The already-mentioned opposition of the prophets Elijah and Elisha against the worship of Baal continued under Jeroboam II when Amos, coming from Judah, preached against social injustice, syncretistic worship and lack of righteousness. Hosea, who was of northern origin, turned fiercely against the worship of Baal and emphasized that it was Yahweh and not Baal who was the giver of fertility. Taking his example from his own marriage with a certain Gomer, Hosea describes the relationship between Yahweh and Israel as a marriage, Israel being the unfaithful wife, whom Yahweh rejected but then took back. Hosea thus became the prophet of love. In his description of the reconciliation (Hosea 14) he used partly the language of the fertility religion which he condemned.

A little later, two prophets appeared in Judah, namely Isaiah and Micah. Isaiah's preaching was based on two presuppositions, both rooted in Jerusalemite traditions: the inviolability of Zion as the earthly dwelling of Yahweh, and the eternal character of the Davidic dynasty in accordance with Yahweh's promises. Consequently he pleaded for confidence in Yahweh instead of seeking support through political alliances. From the Davidic tradition he developed the hope for a future king who would realize all the expectations connected with an ideal king (Isaiah 7, 9 and perhaps 11). These oracles formed the basis of the later Messianic expectations in Israel. In addition, Isaiah criticized syncretistic practices, reliance on outward cult ceremonies, and social evils.

Micah, on the other hand, concentrated his attack against the oppression of the poor and faithless religious leadership, and predicted the destruction of Jerusalem as a consequence of this. But there is also in his book a prediction of a new ruler coming from Bethlehem, that is, out of the Davidic dynasty (Micah 5).

The last days of Judah

At the death of Hezekiah, Assyria was at the height of its power, extending even into Egypt (an echo of this is found in Nahum 3, 8), and Judah obviously had to pay tribute in order to achieve peace. Under Menasseh (687–642 BC) Judah's dependence on Assyria also seems to have influenced its religion; for in the biblical account Menasseh stands out as a great syncretist (2 Kings 21:1–16). Later, Josiah (640–609 BC) carried out religious reform, abolishing all local cult places and syncretistic practices and centralizing the cult on Jerusalem. It is probable that the Book of Deuteronomy had some connection with his reform since such centralization can be found in Deuteronomy 12.

In this period Assyria fell to the Neo-Babylonian empire (612 BC). Josiah himself died at Megiddo in a fruitless attempt to counter an Egyptian expedition into Mesopotamia (609 BC). Judah became an Egyptian vassal state, but Babylonia soon made its influence felt in Palestine also, and in 597 BC Judah became tributary to Babylon. In the struggle between Babylon and Egypt, Zedekiah (597–587 BC) took sides with the latter. The result was a Babylonian expedition which ended in the capture and destruction of Jerusalem in 587 BC. The leaders and upper classes were deported to Babylonia ('the exile'), and Judah became a Babylonian province.

In the last days of Judah the prophet Jeremiah was active in Jerusalem. He decried the religious apostasy of the people, he blamed their reliance on the temple without appropriate moral conduct, he criticized the rulers, and finally he took sides with the Babylonian party and pleaded for submission. After the fall of Jerusalem he was carried to Egypt, where he probably died. He is especially known for his prophecy of a new covenant (Jeremiah 31:31), and for his personal laments, in which he gives us unique insight into his personal feelings.

'The exile'

The Babylonian captivity was of the utmost importance for the development of the Israelite religion. The fall of Jerusalem was a serious blow to Israel as a nation. It was felt that Yahweh had either abandoned his people or was too weak to protect it. On the other hand, the exiled leaders were obviously determined to save what they could of Israelite traditions. It is probable that much of the material in the Pentateuch was collected and edited during the exile. The so-called Deuteronomic historical work (Joshua, Judges, Samuel and Kings) bears traces of having been composed in the same period. In addition, two of Israel's greatest prophets, Ezekiel and Deutero-Isaiah, were active in the exile.

Ezekiel, a priest who was deported to Babylon in 597 BC, was called to be a prophet in a grandiose vision in which he saw Yahweh seated on a fiery throne-wagon. His earliest oracles, directed to those remaining in Judah, criticized their sins and especially their syncretistic practices. After the fall of Jerusalem, which he described in terms of Yahweh's 'glory' leaving the city, he became a prophet of salvation. He predicted the return of the exiles and the restoration of the nation and drew a sketch of the new temple, to which Yahweh's 'glory' was to return. Ezekiel is known for his strange symbolic actions and for his insistence on individual responsibility (Ezekiel 18).

Deutero-Isaiah is an unknown prophet whose work has been added to the book of Isaiah (40–55). He appeared towards the end of the exile and predicted the fall of Babylon through Kores, or Cyrus, and the return of the exiles to their country. His style was influenced by the Psalms, especially the enthronement psalms. He described the return as a new exodus or as a triumphal procession of the king, Yahweh. Yahweh had not abandoned his people and he was not too weak to help, for he was both Creator and Lord of the whole world. Never before had Israelite monotheism been expressed so clearly. Four passages in the book of Deutero-Isaiah, the so-called 'Songs of Yahweh's Servant' (42:1–4; 49:1–6; 50:4–9, 52:13–53, 12), have become especially famous. Here the prophet depicts Israel as Yahweh's servant, who has failed to become 'a light to the nations' and who is therefore despised and forced to suffer. His suffering, however, is satisfactory for 'the many', and he shall finally be restored to honour. These songs, especially the fourth one, were interpreted in the New Testament as predictions of the coming of Christ.

The Persian period

The prediction of Deutero-Isaiah came true: Cyrus conquered Babylon in 539 BC, and in the next year he gave the Israelite exiles permission to return to their land. At first, however, only one group of exiles seemed ready to do so. A hard task of reconstruction was before them, and several difficulties stood in their way. The temple was rebuilt, to a great extent thanks to the inspiration provided by the prophets Haggai and Zechariah. It was reconsecrated in 415 BC. In the Book of Zechariah, which through its symbolical visions foreshadows later apocalypticism, there are also hints that certain unfulfilled Messianic expectations were attached to a member of the Davidic dynasty called Zerubbabel.

In the reconstruction of Israelite society, two men, Nehemiah and Ezra, played a decisive role. The chronological sequence of the two is a matter of dispute; the Bible puts Ezra before Nehemiah, but several details in the books that bear their names indicate that in reality the order was the reverse. Nehemiah was more concerned with secular matters, such as the rebuilding of the walls of Jerusalem and the organization of the administration. Ezra, on the other hand, devoted himself to religious matters, basing himself on the Law (torah) such as the five Books of Moses, which, according to tradition, he brought with him from Babylon. In order to preserve the purity of the community Ezra rejected mixed marriages. It is from this time that the emphasis on the Law as the norm of Jewish life is derived.

Politically, Judaea was now a Persian province. Unfortunately the sources for this period are sparse, and a reconstruction of the history of the Persian period is impossible. Archaeological evidence shows that the material recovery was very slow; only in the third century BC had the population reached the level of the period before the exile.

Certain biblical books, such as Isaiah 56–66, Haggai, Zechariah, Malachi, and the Book of Esther, reflect religious conditions of the Persian period. There seems to have been a conflict between particularistic and universalistic tendencies, in which the former finally prevailed. There was also a final schism between the Judaean-Jerusalemite community and the population of the former northern kingdom, later known as Samaritans (the exact date of the schism is unknown). While the Judaean community added a number of historical, prophetical, and poetical books to their canon, the Samaritans recognized only the five Books of Moses as holy scripture.

The Hellenistic period

After the battle of Issus in 333 BC, Alexander the Great passed through Palestine on his way to Egypt. The fall of the Persian empire meant that Palestine was incorporated into Alexander's empire. After his death (323 BC), it came first under the Ptolemies in Egypt, and later, in 198 BC, under Seleucid rule. In this period Jews were spread over various parts of the Hellenistic world, and it was in Egypt that the books of the Old Testament were translated into Greek (the Septuagint version).

In Palestine a tension between Hellenistic culture and traditional Judaism developed into open conflict under Antiochus IV Epiphanes (175–164 BC). In 168 BC he abolished the Jewish sacrificial cult in the temple of Jerusalem and introduced the worship of Zeus ('the abomination of desolation', Daniel 11:31). A priest by the name of Mattatias raised the standard of revolt; his son Judas Maccabaeus defeated the Syrians, and in 164 BC, Jerusalem was reconquered and the temple reconsecrated, an event that was later celebrated in the festival of Hanuccah ('consecration').

It was during these difficult years that the Book of Daniel was circulated, instilling hope and courage among the faithful. It represents the apocalyptic genre of literature, characterized by revelations in obscure and symbolic language concerning the end of this world.

The younger brother of Judas Maccabaeus also achieved political independence, and the Maccabaean or Hasmonaean dynasty ruled in Jerusalem till 63 BC, when the Roman general Pompey conquered Jerusalem and placed Palestine under Roman rule. As John Hyrcanus (134–104 BC) combined his royal office with that of the high priest, he met strong opposition in certain circles, and it was probably this that gave rise to the Qumran community, on the shore of the Dead Sea, known to later Jewish writers as the Essenes.

The Roman period

Between 34 and 4 BC a man of Edomite origin, by the name of Herod ('the Great') ruled as vassal king under the Romans. He was known as a tyrant, but he was also famous for his building activities including a new temple in Jerusalem which was completed only after his death (AD 63–64). It was in these years that Jesus was born. Herod was succeeded by his three sons, Archelaus, Herod Antipas and Philippus, who ruled different parts of the kingdom. Archelaus, who got Judaea, was deposed after a few years and replaced by a Roman governor (Pontius Pilate was one of his successors). Herod Antipas, who ruled Galilaea at the time when Jesus preached there, was deposed in AD 39. Philippus was succeeded in AD 34 by Agrippa, who later also received Galilaea. After his death in AD 44 the country became a Roman province. But there was political unrest which finally broke out into open revolt. The emperor Nero sent Vespasian to suppress the revolt, and his son Titus took Jerusalem in AD 70 and burned the temple. Further rebellion in AD 135 caused the emperor Hadrian to establish on the site of ruined Jerusalem the Roman colony of Aelia Capitolina, in which only non-Jews were allowed to live.

Religion

The Hellenistic period coincides largely with what is generally called the 'inter-testamental period', or the period between the canonical writings of the Old Testament and the New Testament. Religious literature from this period includes the Apocrypha, those books included in the Septuagint translation but not in the Hebrew canon; they represent the mainstream of Judaism. Other works, such as the Book of Enoch and 2 Esdras, represent the apocalyptic genre full of visions and revelations. A third group is the Qumran documents, the famous Dead Sea Scrolls (in Hebrew and Aramaic), which were produced by the Essene community.

Several new religious ideas appear in these writings; there was, for instance, a tendency towards dualism in

The Roman despoliation of the Temple in Jerusalem. From the Arch of Titus (AD 79–81). Titus took Jerusalem in AD 70 and burned the temple.

A part of the *Dead Sea Scrolls* found in the caves at Qumran, a product of the Essene community.

that the evil in the world was ascribed not to God but to Satan (or Belial). There are traces of this in the Old Testament (1 Chronicles 21:1) but in its developed form, this dualism was probably influenced by Iranian ideas. It is most prominent in Qumran, where God is said to have created a good and an evil spirit who are rivals in this world.

Apocalypticism was also influenced by Iranian ideas. It was taught that there were two worlds or periods, 'this world' and 'the world to come'. This world would end in catastrophes marking the end of history, and would be replaced by the bliss of the world to come. Sometimes the new world was connected with the 'Son of Man' (the term comes from Daniel 7:13), an eschatological figure sharing some qualities with the political Messiah, who occurs in the so-called Psalms of Solomon. The term Son of Man was taken up by Jesus and used in New Testament christology.

The resurrection of the dead was another new idea, first expressly mentioned in Daniel 12:2. It is foreshadowed by some other passages in the Old Testament (Isaiah 26:19; Psalms 16:10; 49:16), but is again possibly a result of Iranian influence.

The contemporary Jewish historian Josephus reports the existence of three religious parties, namely the Sadducees, the Pharisees (also mentioned in the New Testament), and the Essenes.

The Sadducees are little known. They seem to have been conservative, and rejected certain new doctrines such as the resurrection. At least some of them seem to have been compliant to the political authorities. The Pharisees were interested in the strict and detailed observance of the rules of the Law in order to 'separate' themselves from the 'sinners'. Oral tradition was important for their interpretation of the Law. They accepted the belief in angels and in the resurrection, and cherished Messianic expectations. The Essenes seem to be identical with the community that produced the Dead Sea Scrolls, and formed a kind of monastic community which practised the study of the Law and held the priesthood in high esteem. Their theology was dualistic, with emphasis on God's omnipotence and on predestination. They expected an eschatological war in which the 'sons of light' were to defeat the 'sons of darkness' and thus inaugurate a new era.

Troy

J. T. Hooker

Discovery

Homer's *Iliad* takes its title from Ilios or Ilion, which he used as alternative names for Troy: the *Iliad* being the 'poem about Troy'. Troy was represented by Homer as a great city in the extreme northwest of Asia Minor. Its powerful walls, which precluded the capture of the city by direct assault, enclosed streets, palaces, temples, and the houses of the Trojans and their allies. Convinced that Troy had once existed and was not a mere fantasy of the Greek epic poets, the German archaeologist, Heinrich Schliemann (1822–90), began excavation in 1870 on a hill lying about four miles inland from the Dardanelles. This hill, now named Hissarlik, is generally identified

with ancient Troy; but this identification rests on negative grounds only. No inscription has ever been found at the site, which might throw some light on its ancient name; on the other hand, if Troy was indeed a real place then Hissarlik is the only likely site in the appropriate part of Asia.

Schliemann's excavations at Hissarlik lasted until 1890, and after his death the work was continued by his collaborator, Wilhelm Dörpfeld. From 1932 to 1938 an expedition from Cincinnati, led by William Semple and Carl Blegen, went over the whole ground again and attempted to settle the chronology of the site. Schliemann had found that a number of settlements had

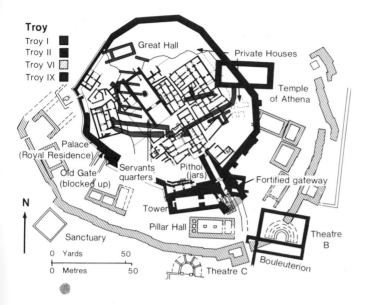

Troy

Troy I ■
Troy II ■
Troy VI ▨
Troy IX ■

Great Hall

Private Houses

Temple
of Athena

Palace
(Royal Residence)

Servants
quarters

Old Gate
(blocked up)

Pithoi
(jars)

Fortified gateway

Tower

Pillar Hall

Sanctuary

Theatre
B

Bouleuterion

Theatre C

N

0 Yards 50
0 Metres 50

occupied the site one after the other, leaving a deposit some fifty feet (16m) deep. Taking into account the refinements introduced by Dörpfeld and the American excavators, we may represent these settlements by roman numerals, beginning with I for the earliest and ending with IX. Within many of these individual settlements sub-phases can be discerned; these are designated by a small letter of the alphabet placed after the roman numeral. So far as can be seen from the excavations, the two most important settlements were Troy II and Troy VI.

Troy II

Troy II belongs to the early Bronze Age (its date is discussed below). Seven sub-phases have been recognized in this settlement: to sub-phase 'c' may be attributed the reconstruction of the site according to a plan which, broadly speaking, was adhered to until the end of Troy II. Troy IIc comprised essentially a squarish, strongly fortified citadel of modest dimensions, measuring scarcely ninety yards from one side to the other. Only a small number of people could have been accommodated within its walls, and so the existence of a 'town' corresponding to this settlement has been postulated; no trace of it, however, has come to light. The fortifications of the citadel were well planned and carefully constructed of brick work and stones. Massive walls, partly incorporating earlier structures, were built to enclose the citadel; and along part of their circuit they were further strengthened by the insertion of rectangular towers. A gateway let into the southwest section of the wall consisted of three small rooms and was approached by a steep ramp paved with stone slabs. A larger gateway, incorporating a square room but not provided

Metalwork from Troy. Bronze and copper were in plentiful supply for the manufacture of weapons and domestic utensils at the time of Troy II.

with a ramp, gave access on the southeast side. Inside the citadel, built along a northwest/southeast axis, stood a large house, more than 30 yds (27 m) long and 10 yds (9 m) wide. A third of its length was occupied by a square vestibule, connected by a door to the main hall. To the floor of this hall was attached a hearth. The entire configuration of square entrance room leading to rectangular hall with hearth is strikingly similar to the *megaron*-complex later known in Mycenaean Greece. The '*megaron*' of Troy II presumably contained the chief ceremonial rooms of the ruler of the place. Several other houses, smaller in size but still following the *megaron*-plan and orientated along the same axis, were found to the south and north of the principal *megaron*. Nothing is known of the religious beliefs or practices of the people who inhabited Troy II: no structures that are obviously temples or cult rooms have come to light. A few graves, containing skeletons in a contracted posture, have been found inside the walls.

The objects recovered from Troy II show that there was no serious cultural break between this and the previous settlement, Troy I; but there were now far greater resources at the disposal of the inhabitants. Bronze and copper were in plentiful supply for the manufacture of weapons and domestic utensils. Most striking of all are the receptacles and ornaments of gold, silver, electron, and other precious or semi-precious materials which made up 'Schliemann's Treasure' (belonging probably to the IIg sub-phase). The Treasure was taken to Berlin, where it disappeared during the Second World War. The descriptions and illustrations of the Treasure still extant show that in its heterogeneity and profusion it resembled the contents of the later Shaft Graves at Mycenae. The delicate workmanship of some of the ornaments, notably that of the elaborate gold necklaces, was especially to be admired. Other substances used for artefacts included carnelian, faience, lapis lazuli and rock-crystal. In pottery manufacture by far the most important innovation was the use of the wheel, which did not, however, entirely drive out the production of hand-made ceramics. Among the characteristic shapes of the pottery from Troy II should be mentioned the tall narrow goblet with long handles, called by Schliemann *depas amphikypellon* in reference to a type of goblet described by Homer.

The most cursory examination of the objects recovered from Troy II makes it plain that the Trojans of that epoch not only had access to great riches but were in contact (directly or indirectly) with many different

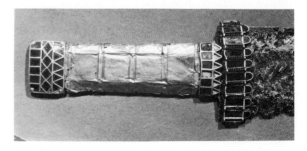

Mrs Schliemann wearing Trojan jewelry. Many of the ornaments which made up 'Schliemann's Treasure' show that it resembled the contents of the later Shaft Graves at Mycenae.

regions. Some of the jewelry, for example, is like that found in Assyrian tombs; while pottery from a very wide region shows traces of Trojan influence: Euboea and other parts of Greece (including the Cyclades), Tarsus (in southeastern Anatolia), Crete, Cyprus, Macedonia, and Thrace.

Like Troy I, Troy II was destroyed in a violent conflagration. The following settlement, Troy III, did not achieve such a high level of culture as Troy II; but it was basically the same culture. The fourth and fifth settlements were also comparatively insignificant. But with Troy VI we come to the most imposing of the settlements, and the longest-lived. It lasted from the middle into the late Bronze Age, and it can be seen to have passed through eight sub-phases (a–h). This settlement presents a number of new elements, which effectively differentiates it from its predecessors.

Troy VI

We may begin with the walls of the citadel and the houses inside them. Powerful though the fortifications of Troy II had been, they were far surpassed by those of Troy VI. As would be expected in a settlement which flourished for several centuries, the walls belong to more than one stage of building. Walls are extant only on the

west, south, and east sides; from these substantial remains it appears that the citadel covered roughly twice the area of the citadel of Troy II. The most arresting features are the five gateways let into the circuit at irregular intervals, the unprecedentedly careful character of much of the masonry, and the great tower built on the east side (probably for the better protection of the water supply). Even when excavated, the tower was 30 ft (9 m) high; and in its original state it had certainly been much higher.

The houses, like the walls, of Troy VI were constructed according to a new plan and were built on terraces ascending from the circuit walls to the centre of the citadel, but only those on the lowest terrace have survived. The ground plans of at least eight of the houses are clearly traceable, and these display a different concept of building: the houses are free-standing and of excellent design and execution. A remarkable example is the so-called Pillar House, near the southern section of the wall. In its final state, the Pillar House comprised three parts: vestibule to the east, main hall in the centre–about 49 ft (15 m) by 26 ft (9 m)–and three small rooms to the west. Notable features (apart from its size) are the two square pillars set in the floor of the main hall (obviously to support the roof) and the three stone steps which lead up from the hall in a northerly direction. These steps presumably mark the principal entrance: the whole cannot therefore be counted as a true *megaron*. Another building (House M, in the southwest of the citadel) is remarkable for its L-shaped plan and the elaborate terrace, more than 13 ft (4 m) high, upon which it stood.

The typical pottery of Troy VI is a species of undecorated grey ware, similar to but not identical with the contemporary 'Grey Minyan' of mainland Greece. It was manufactured by a special method of firing. Matt-painted pottery, also comparable with a Helladic variety, was found as well as the grey ware. The later phases of Troy VI yielded considerable amounts of imported Mycenaean pottery and also imitations of this made locally. Imports and imitations alike attest contact with Greece over a long period; and in fact Troy seems, on present evidence, to have had closer relations with the Mycenaeans than any other Asian site except perhaps Miletus, situated far to the south.

The horse was introduced into the earliest phase of Troy VI, and thereafter it remained in use throughout the life of the settlement. The practice of cremating the dead is found first in VIh; whether this represents an innovation or the continuance of an existing custom is unknown.

After Troy VI

Troy VI was devastated in a great catastrophe, which the American excavators ascribed to the effects of an earthquake. But the settlement was quickly repaired, and the culture of Troy VI survived into the next settlement (Troy VIIa) without perceptible alteration. Collapsed sections of the walls were rebuilt or were incorporated into the structure of new houses. The

Trojan pottery: the grey ware of Troy VI.

houses of Troy VIIa were conspicuous for the quantity of large storage jars found at, or just below, floor level. The grey ware characteristic of Troy VI continued to be made, and there was no falling off in imports of Mycenaean pottery. After a short life Troy VIIa, in its turn, was destroyed by fire.

Settlement VIIb is represented by two strata, known as VIIb1 and VIIb2. Troy VIIb1 seems to have been poorer than VIIa, although culturally no fundamental change had occurred. The local grey pottery was still manufac-tured, and Mycenaean wares were still imported. No destruction took place between VIIb1 and VIIb2, but an important new element is found in the latter stratum: alongside the familiar grey ware and local imitations of Mycenaean imports there appears the so-called *buckelke-ramik* ('knobbed pottery'), a handmade type associated with the civilization of the Danube basin. The settlement of Troy VIIb2 was burned and deserted at time which cannot be determined with any accuracy; perhaps its end should be dated *c*1100 BC.

It is usually thought that Troy was uninhabited for some four centuries after the desertion of the seventh settlement. The settlement now known as Troy VIII (*c*700 BC–*c*340 BC) was a colony planted on the old site by Aeolic Greeks who had migrated from the homeland. Its meagre remains include east Greek pottery and terracottas and also sherds of Attic and Corinthian ware; the native Trojan grey ware is still found as well.

Troy IX (from *c*340 BC) is the name given to the Hellenistic and Roman settlement.

Chronology

A number of problems are presented by the history of Troy. The chronology of the settlements, especially of the earlier ones, has given rise to much dispute: one school, for instance, dates Troy II *c*2500–2200 BC, another *c*2200–1900 BC. The date of the beginning of Troy VI would naturally differ according to the view taken of Troy II; but, whenever Troy VI began, it is shown by the Mycenaean pottery associated with it to have come to an end *c*1300 BC. The grey ware of Troy VI has been accounted for in one of two different ways: either it represents a local ceramic development, having parallels elsewhere in western Anatolia, or it is the pottery of alien intruders who made their way to Troy and dispossessed the previous inhabitants. Finally we have to return to the question posed at the outset: which, if any, of the settlements uncovered at Hissarlik is to be identified with Homer's Troy? Schliemann favoured Troy II; but it is now realized that this settlement was far too early to have been reflected in the Homeric poems. Each of the later settlements Troy VI, Troy VIIa, and Troy VIII has been proposed as the 'Homeric' Troy; at present Troy VIIa is most widely accepted.

Phrygia and Lydia

T. R. Bryce

The early Phrygians

According to ancient Greek tradition, the earliest Phry-gians immigrated to Asia Minor from Macedon and Thrace. To judge from the *Iliad* of Homer, they were already well established in their new homeland at the time of the Trojan War (early 12th century BC). Yet according to Strabo, the Greek geographer, their immi-gration did not take place until after the war. Modern scholars tend to favour this view, and it seems most likely that the tradition of Phrygian migration is to be associated with the appearance of several new popu-lation groups in Asia Minor some time after the collapse of the Hittite New Kingdom (*c*1200 BC). Before the end of the second millennium BC, the Phrygians were firmly established in central Anatolia, in particular within the region enclosed by the Halys (modern Kızıl Irmak) river, the old Hittite homeland.

It has sometimes been suggested that these early Phrygians were the Mushki people who engaged in a series of conflicts with the Assyrian king, Tiglathpileser I (*c*1112–1072 BC) on the upper Tigris. Yet the Mushki of the Assyrian records and the Phrygians of Greek tradition were probably quite separate in origin, amalgamating only towards the end of the eighth century BC. This amalgamation was very likely brought about by the Mushki king Mita, designated in Greek literary sources as Midas.

The kingdom of Midas

In the reign of Midas, Phrygia attained a high level of material prosperity, and by the end of the eighth century BC was a major political power in Asia Minor. The kingdom of Midas extended southwards to the Cilician plain, eastwards towards the Euphrates river, and westwards as far as the coast of the Aegean Sea, and Midas seems also to have been in contact with mainland Greece where he made dedicatory offerings to the sanctuary of Apollo at Delphi.

Midas established the city of Gordion as his capital, the site of which lies about sixty miles (96 km) from modern Ankara. The most outstanding features of Gordion include a monumental entrance gate, an impressive palace complex, and a number of *megaron*-type houses with half-timbered walls. The area outside the city was covered with large mounds, or tumuli, where the Phrygians buried their dead. Of these the most imposing is commonly known as 'The Great Tumulus'. It is still some 58 yds (53 m) high, and the second largest tumulus surviving from the ancient world. Inside was a wooden chamber containing the remains of an elderly man—perhaps Midas himself. The other tumuli were presumably the burial places of various members of the royal family and of the high-ranking Phrygian nobility, overlords of a feudal society whose prosperity rested on a flourishing agricultural basis. Crafts and trades also reached a high level of development in the time of Midas, and Gordion in particular has yielded a fine range of Phrygian artifacts of bronze, wood, and ivory, and the remains of inlaid wooden furniture.

The Cimmerian invasion and its aftermath

Around 695 BC Asia Minor was invaded from the north by a group known as the Cimmerians, who occupied almost the entire country, and in the process destroyed the kingdom of Midas. This invasion meant the end of a united Phrygian empire. Yet a number of Phrygian settlements, including Gordion, recovered from the onslaught, and after the final withdrawal of the invaders, regained some of their former prosperity as small independent principalities subject to the kings of Lydia.

Evidence of this new phase of Phrygian civilization is provided by a number of settlements in the region between the modern towns of Eskisehir and Afyon (west of Gordion). These settlements flourished during the first half of the sixth century BC. A distinctive feature of the new civilization is the impressive array of tombs and monuments which for the most part are carved out of living rock. Their façades represent the front of a gabled building and are generally covered with elaborate geometric patterns. The most imposing of these structures is the 'Midas Monument', which lies on the edge of what is now known as Midas City, a sixth century site near the modern Eskisehir.

The Midas Monument contains a niche where a statue of the goddess Cybele was placed during religious ceremonies. Cybele, the 'Great Mother', was the chief Phrygian deity. With her worship were associated wild orgiastic rites, including self-castration by the goddess's priests. Cybele's chief sanctuary lay in the city of Pessinus, where her cult statue (an unshaped stone) was reputed to have fallen directly from heaven.

Following the collapse of the Lydian kingdom, Phrygia was absorbed into the Persian empire, and in 333 BC fell under the sway of Alexander the Great. After the battle of Ipsos in 301 BC, it became part of the Seleucid empire, and in 133 BC the western part of the country was incorporated into the Roman province of Asia.

The Phrygian language

The Phrygian language survives in two groups of inscriptions which are now only partly intelligible. The first group occurs mainly on the façades of rock-cut

Warriors from Phrygia in Asia Minor, from a terracotta panel of the late sixth century BC.

monuments dating from the eighth to the fourth centuries BC; the second, consisting mainly of curse formulae, dates to the second and third centuries AD. Phrygian belongs to the Indo-European family of languages, and is written in an alphabetic script, almost certainly taken over from the Greeks.

The rise of the kingdom of Lydia

The ancient kingdom of Lydia lay in the far west of Asia Minor, bordering the countries of Mysia in the north, Caria in the south, Phrygia in the east, and the Greek Ionian colonies on the Aegean coast in the west. In a tradition recorded by Herodotus, the first major royal dynasty of Lydia was the Heraclid dynasty, whose members were allegedly descendants of Herakles; this dynasty ruled for 505 years, roughly from the period of the Trojan War to the early seventh century BC.

Around 685 BC a new ruling family known as the Mermnad dynasty arose in Lydia, founded by Gyges, a member of the royal bodyguard, who murdered his predecessor Kandaules, married his wife, and usurped the throne. The new king embarked on a programme of territorial expansion which eventually resulted in Lydia becoming the dominant power in Asia Minor after the collapse of the Phrygian kingdom. At the same time Gyges had to deal with the Cimmerian invaders who had destroyed the kingdom of Midas. The struggles with the Cimmerians continued into the reign of Gyges' successor, Ardys (c651–625 BC), before the invaders were finally and decisively driven from Lydian territory.

Ardys then resumed a series of conflicts begun by Gyges with the Ionian Greek colonies along the Aegean coast. In their attempts to establish control over this coast, the Mermnad kings met with determined resistance from the colonies, especially Miletus which held out against repeated attacks by the Lydian forces. The conflict with Miletus lasted through the reign of Ardys' successor, Sadyattes (c625–610 BC), and ended finally in the reign of Alyattes (c609–560 BC), who drew up a treaty with Miletus acknowledging the colony's independence. Croesus, the last Mermnad king (c560–546 BC), completed the subjugation of the Ionian colonies, with the exception of Miletus, and firmly established Lydian control over much of western Asia Minor.

Under the Mermnad rulers, Lydia developed into a powerful commercial empire, rich in agricultural resources and mineral wealth. The land abounded in flocks and herds, and produced rich harvests of fruit and grain crops; and the mining of precious metals, especially gold and silver, greatly facilitated Lydian commercial enterprise. The greatest and most lasting contribution made by the Lydians in the field of commerce was the invention of coined money. By the sixth century BC the Lydian kings were issuing gold and silver coins, and by the end of the century, coinage was becoming widespread through western Asia and Greece.

Although Lydian control had been imposed upon the Greek Ionian colonies by force, the Greeks seem to have shown no great resentment towards their Lydian overlords. Moreover some of the Lydian kings, Croesus in particular, were held in high regard by the Greeks. An avowed admirer of Greek culture, Croesus adopted many of the trappings of the Greek way of life, assisted in the restoration of the temple of Artemis at Ephesus, and bestowed lavish gifts upon the sanctuary of Apollo at Delphi. At the same time there was much cultural exchange between Greece and Lydia; the Greeks absorbed various Lydian elements into their own culture, especially in the field of music and literature, and according to Herodotus, a number of games invented by the Lydians were taken over by the Greeks.

Lydian culture and civilization were epitomized by the royal city of Sardis, capital of the Lydian empire. Although most of the architectural remains of the city date to periods long after the fall of the empire, the art of the earlier period is well illustrated by a number of beautiful terracottas and relief-sculptured tiles. Not far from Sardis lies the Lydian necropolis now known as Bin Tepe (Thousand Hills). The necropolis consists of enormous tumulus tombs which served as the burial places of the Lydian kings and nobles. The largest of them, designated by Herodotus as the tomb of Alyattes, is 70 yds (64 m) high, and is the largest tumulus known from the ancient world.

The war with Persia and its aftermath

Shortly after the middle of the fifth century BC, the Lydian empire was brought abruptly to an end, as a result of new political developments to the east. A king of Anshan named Cyrus overthrew the Median king Astyages, brother-in-law of Croesus, and established the foundations of what was to become the Persian empire. Alarmed by this newly emerging power, Croesus sought the advice of numerous oracles throughout Greece, and then led an army across the Halys river to forestall the westward advance of the Persians into his own territory (spring of 546 BC). After a heated but indecisive battle, Croesus withdrew to Lydia, but was swiftly pursued by Cyrus. In a pitched battle on the plain of Sardis, Croesus was totally defeated, and his kingdom was absorbed into the Persian empire. Sardis was now established as the Persian administrative centre in the west.

In 334 BC, Alexander the Great liberated Lydia from Persian control, although the country was still subject to payments of tribute and to the administrative control of a local satrap. Following Alexander's death, Lydia was absorbed into the Seleucid kingdom, and after the battle of Magnesia (190 BC) it came under the control of the kingdom of Pergamum. In 133 BC it was incorporated into the Roman province of Asia.

The Lydian language

The Lydian language survives in approximately 64 inscriptions, almost all of which are found on grave stelae from the city of Sardis. These inscriptions date from the sixth to the fourth centuries BC. Our knowledge of the language spoken by the Lydians is still far from complete, although it is clearly Indo-European in origin, and seems to be related to the Hittite and Luwian languages of late Bronze Age Anatolia.

Persia

T. Cuyler Young Jr

The Proto-historic period and the kingdom of the Medes
Throughout the first half of the first millennium BC Medes, Persian, and other Iranian groups gradually moved into and became the dominant force in the western half of the Iranian plateau. Both the Medes and the Persians are mentioned in the Neo-Assyrian cuneiform sources by the ninth century BC. Of the two groups the former were more numerous and important. Early in the millennium the Medes apparently controlled the whole of the eastern Zagros mountain region and were soon pushing westwards, in places to the edge of the Mesopotamian lowlands. The Persians were found in two locations: first, in the central west, later, further south in Fars.

This period is known archaeologically as the Iron Age. The Iron Age I tradition (c1300–1000 BC) represents a major cultural break with the late Bronze Age of western Iran. These new cultural patterns continue in the Iron Age II period (c1000–800/750 BC). The Iron Age III tradition (c750–550 BC) is both a further extension of Iron I and Iron II trends and another important break in cultural continuity in western Iran. Some suggest that the appearance of the Iranians is best associated with the cultural shift at the start of the Iron Age. Others connect the coming of the Iranians with the Iron III period, perhaps now to be dated in the critical region, central western Iran, to as early as the ninth century BC. Most are agreed, however, that the widespread appearance of the Iron III culture over the Zagros after 650 BC probably represents the rapid rise of the Medes to power at that time.

Much of the story of the Medes told by Herodotus is legend; a good deal is accurate history. The first two Median kings, Deioces (728–675 BC) and Phraortes (675–653 BC), probably belong to legend. Deioces supposedly founded the Median kingdom and established its capital at Ecbatana (modern Hamadan). Phraortes, it is said, lost his life attacking the Assyrians, after subjugating the Persians in Fars. While we have no evidence of such an attack on Assyria, we know that the contemporary Assyrian king, Esarhaddon (681–668 BC), was concerned about declining security in the east caused by the raids of a group of Medes, Scythians, Mannaeans, and others led by a local warrior named Kashtariti, whom some would equate with Phraortes. That a Median king of this period asserted his control over the Persians is possible, but unproven.

Tradition holds that at the end of Phraortes' reign there was a major invasion of western Iran by nomadic Scythians, who then held political power in the region from 653 to 625 BC. Herodotus reported that Cyaxares (625–585 BC) drove the Scythians out and re-established Median royal power. Here we are on fairly

Ancient Persia: The Achaemenid empire.

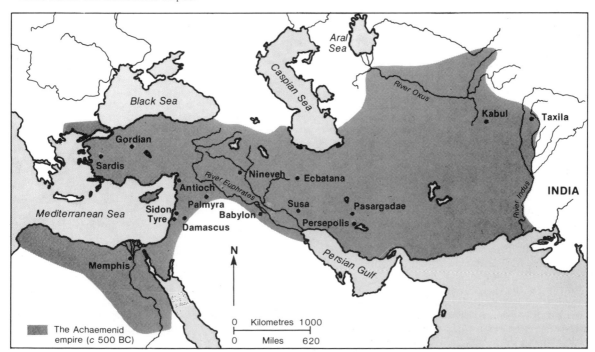

147

The great ceremonial city of Persepolis, founded by Darius I (522–486 BC), was one of the cities in which the Elamite language was used administratively.

firm historical ground; Cyaxares appears in the cuneiform sources as Uvakhshatra. He and the Medes attacked the Assyrian border city of Arrapha in 615 BC, surrounded Nineveh in 614 BC, but were forced to withdraw, and captured instead the Assyrian religious capital, Ashur. The Medes then formed an alliance with the Babylonians and their combined armies captured Nineveh in August of 612 BC. The fleeing Assyrians were chased west into Syria, where their last king, Ashuruballit, disappeared from history in 608 BC.

The conquerors now divided the spoils; the Babylonians controlled the whole of the Fertile Crescent, the Medes, all of the highlands up to central Anatolia. There they clashed, and fought against the Lydians. Peace was established in 585 BC, probably through Babylonian mediation, and the Halys river was established as the Median–Lydian border.

The last Median king, Astyages (585–550 BC), inherited a considerable kingdom from his father, Cyaxares: all of Anatolia up to the Halys, western Iran (perhaps as far east as modern Tehran), and all of southwestern Iran, including Fars–the land of the Persians. Little is known of Astayages' reign. One fact stands out– it was he who was overthrown by the rise to power in the Iranian world of Cyrus II of Persia, an Achaemenid.

The rise of the Persians and Cyrus the Great
The ruling Persian dynasty in Fars (Parsa) traced their ancestry to an eponymous king Hāxamanish or Achaemenes. Three kings succeed Achaemenes: Teispes, Cyrus I, and Cambyses I. We know almost nothing of them except that Cyrus I is probably the Persian who swore allegiance to Ashurbanipal of Assyria shortly after 639 BC. When Cyrus II, justifiably called 'the Great', came to the throne in 559 BC, he may already have been determined to rebel against the control of the Medes and his maternal grandfather, Astyages. He united for the first time several Persian and Iranian groups, initiated diplomatic exchanges with Babylon, and then openly rebelled against Astyages. The war was hard fought, but Cyrus won, and in 550 BC the Median empire became the Persian empire.

Cyrus next attacked Lydia, after lulling the Babylonians into inactivity. An indecisive battle was fought on the Halys river frontier in 547 BC, after which, as it was late in the campaign season, the Lydians retired to Sardis and disbanded the national levy. Cyrus, however, kept coming and captured the capital and Croesus, the Lydian king, in 546 BC. He then sent his army on to subdue the Greek city states of Ionia.

Babylon was next. Cyrus took such good advantage of the unpopularity of the Babylonian king, Nabonidus, much alienated from his people through neglect of local affairs and traditional religion, that the military campaign was almost an anti-climax. To the delight of Second Isaiah and other subjects of Nabonidus, Cyrus marched into Babylon in late summer, 539 BC, and proclaimed himself the tolerant, legitimate ruler of Mesopotamia.

Bearded bull's head on a lyre from Sumer: gold, lapis lazuli and inlaid wood.

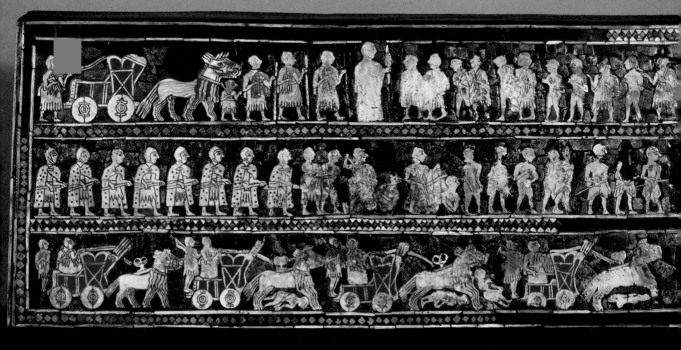

With this conquest the Persian army was brought to the borders of Egypt. But now troubles on the eastern frontier, a recurrent theme in Iranian history, apparently filled the latter part of Cyrus' reign. Here, in the region of the Oxus and Jaxartes rivers, he lost his life in 529 BC.

Cyrus' successors: Cambyses, Darius I and Xerxes I

Cambyses II (529–522 BC) inherited the throne from his father, Cyrus the Great, apparently without trouble. Plans for a campaign against Egypt must have already been well advanced, for Cambyses attacked that country in 525 BC. With Arab help he crossed the dangerous Sinai desert and brought the newly crowned pharaoh, Psammetichus III, to battle at Pelusium. The Egyptians lost, and Memphis fell.

In 522 BC news reached Cambyses of revolt in Persia, perhaps led by his true brother, Bardiya, or perhaps, if we are to believe Darius' story that Cambyses killed his brother before leaving for Egypt, by an impostor, Gaumata. While hastening home to regain control, Cambyses died, possibly by his own hand, possibly from an accidentally self-inflicted wound. Darius, a general in Cambyses' army and a prince of the Achaemenid house, continued homeward to crush the rebellion in a manner profitable to himself.

Darius I told of coming to power and crushing the revolt of Bardiya in his famous Bisitun inscription, just east of modern Kermanshah. Here he proclaimed his blood right to rule through his father, grandfather and great grandfather, Teispes. It would seem, however, that his gaining the throne was more the result of being the leading member of the party of nobles who set themselves against the rebellion, and of having control of key parts of the army.

It took just over a year (522–521 BC) to restore peace. Large parts of the empire joined the revolt, and only through a combination of judicious clemency, ruthless force, clever tactics and sheer willpower did Darius win through. Once in charge, he turned to the task of continuing imperial expansion. Campaigns to the east gained large sections of northern India. In 516 BC Darius moved across the Hellespont in a campaign against the Scythians north of the Black Sea in order to interrupt grain supplies to Greece. Though the Persians were forced to retreat, a bridgehead was maintained in Europe.

Expansion was temporarily halted by a revolt in Ionia in 500 BC. Athens provided some help for the rebels in 498 BC, and the Greeks managed to take the offensive. Persian counter moves were at first feeble, but in 494 BC a renewed Persian offensive was successful. Mardonius, son-in-law of Darius, was put in charge of suppressing local tyrants and restoring democratic government to coastal Asia Minor.

By 492 BC Mardonius had also recovered Persian

The so-called Royal Standard of Ur (c2600 BC) recovered from the Royal Cemetery. The decoration of a wooden box, representing peace and war.

Thrace and Macedonia. From this base Darius invaded Greece proper, only to meet defeat at Marathon on 12 August 490 BC. Forced to retreat, the Great King decided it would take a more coordinated attack to settle this bothersome frontier problem. Planning began, but was interrupted by revolt in Egypt and the death of Darius in 486 BC.

Xerxes (486–465 BC) succeeded his father and quickly crushed rebellion in Egypt in 485 BC. He then began a new Persian policy by ruthlessly ignoring Egyptian forms of rule and imposing his will on the rebellious province. The same policy was used to suppress a revolt in Babylon about 482 BC. Once the rebels were crushed, Xerxes made it clear he would no longer rule as the 'legitimate' king of Mesopotamia, but rather as the Persian conqueror who carried the statue of the Babylonian god, Marduk, off to captivity in Susa. In his Daiva inscription, possibly related to the Babylonian revolt, Xerxes spoke with religious fanaticism of the destruction of false gods and their temples. Here indeed was a new policy, for until then religious tolerance had been the hallmark of Persian rule since Cyrus had allowed the Jews to rebuild the temple in Jerusalem.

The long anticipated invasion of Greece began in 480 BC. The Spartan stand at Thermopylae in August came to naught, and the Persian land forces burned Athens. But their fleet lost the battle of Salamis, and the impetus of the invasion was blunted. Though Xerxes returned home, leaving Mardonius in charge, the war was not really won by the Greeks until after the battle of Plataea, the fall of pro-Persian Thebes, and the Persian naval loss at Mycale in 479 BC. In the decade which followed, the formation of the Delian League, the rise of Athenian imperialism, and troubles in Ionia all marked the decline of Persian ambitions in the Aegean. Xerxes apparently

Tomb of Xerxes I (486–465 BC), the Persian ruler whose policy to destroy 'false gods and their temples' was in marked contrast to the religious tolerance of previous rulers.

lost interest in the west and sank deeper into the comforts of royal life at home. Harem intrigue, which from then onwards would sap the strength of the dynasty, led to his assassination in 465 BC.

The later Achaemenids

The most important event during the reigns of Artaxerxes I (465–425 BC), Xerxes II (425–424 BC), and Darius II (424–405 BC) was the Peloponnesian War between Sparta and Athens, lasting from 460 to 404 BC. Persia favoured one side or the other, as her own interests dictated, influencing events through lavish expenditure of money. At first she supported Athens, gaining in 448 BC the treaty of Callias, in which the Persians agreed to stay out of the Aegean in return for the Athenians leaving Asia Minor to them. Then, after the disastrous Athenian campaign against Sicily in 413 BC, the Persians shifted their support to Sparta. In the treaty of Miletus in 412 BC the Spartans assured Persia of a free hand on the coast of Anatolia in return for money to pay the sailors of the Peloponnesian fleet. Persian gold and Spartan warriors brought Athens to defeat in 404 BC.

During the lengthy reign of Artaxerxes II (405–359 BC) a war with Sparta ended in a favourable peace for Persia; in 405 BC Egypt revolted and, in effect, was lost for good; Cyrus the Younger rebelled, and the so-called Revolt of the Satraps almost destroyed the empire. The last three events revealed to all the unrest which, by the middle of the fourth century BC, pervaded the Achaemenid world.

Sparta, triumphant over Athens, built a small empire of her own, and soon was in conflict with the Persians over the issue of the Ionian cities. Artaxerxes spent gold in Greece to raise rebellion on Sparta's home ground and rebuilt the Persian fleet under the command of Conon, an Athenian admiral. The contest continued from 400 to 387 BC, by which time a revitalized Athens, supported by Persia, created a balance of power in Greece. At Greece's request, Artaxerxes dictated the 'King's Peace' in 387–386 BC in which the Greeks surrendered any claim to Asia Minor and promised to maintain the *status quo* at home.

In 401 BC Cyrus the Younger, brother to the king and satrap of an important Anatolian province, hired ten thousand Greek mercenaries and marched east to contest the throne with Artaxerxes. His rebellion collapsed when he was defeated and killed at the battle of Cunoxa in Mesopotamia. The Greek mercenaries, however, were not broken and, retiring in good order, marched north to the Black Sea and home (as is recorded in Xenephon's *Anabasis*). That so large a body of men could escape from the very centre of the Great King's domain gave witness to the growing weakness of the empire.

In 373 BC Artaxerxes faced yet another rebellion, this time the revolt of a coalition of several satraps, or provincial governors. The rebels were suppressed when efforts to coordinate their attacks failed. Artaxerxes, instead of dealing with the revolt in the ruthless manner of Darius the Great, actually returned most of the rebels to their governorships.

Artaxerxes III (359–338 BC) began his reign by killing off most of his relatives to protect his seizure of the throne. A fresh attempt to regain Egypt failed in 351–50 BC, and a rebellion, which was not put down until 345 BC, then swept through Palestine and Phoenicia and parts of Cilicia. Yet another attempt against Egypt, led by the king himself, was made in 343 BC and succeeded, though the native dynasty withdrew to Nubia, where it kept alive the spirit of revolt and national revival. Persia then made the mistake of refusing help to Athens against Philip of Macedon, who in 338 BC gained control of all Greece at the battle of Chaeronea. A united west proved impervious to Persian gold.

The reign of Arses (338–336 BC) ended as it began, in murder and intrigue. Darius III (336–331 BC) was able to put down yet another rebellion in Egypt in 337–36 BC, but the beginning of the end came soon after with the loss of the battle of Granicus to Alexander in May, 334 BC. Persepolis fell to the Macedonian conquerer in April, 330 BC, and Darius, the last Achaemenid, was murdered in the same year.

Achaemenid language, religion and art

The languages of the empire were as varied as its people. The Persians spoke a southwest dialect of Iranian, Old Persian, which became a written language when Darius

A monumental capital from Persepolis. Ancient peoples revered the strength and virility of the bull.

ordered a script to be developed, so that he could carve the story of his first year of rule at Bisitun. That, and all other royal inscriptions, were tri-lingual in Old Persian, Babylonian, and Elamite. Old Persian, however, was not the working language of the empire. Elamite was used administratively at Persepolis and Susa, but Aramaic was the *lingua franca* of the empire, and was probably the language most used by the government bureaucracy.

In religion, the Iranians were originally polytheists whose gods were associated with natural phenomena, social, military and economic functions, and abstract concepts, such as truth and justice. Some time around 600 BC the great ethical prophet, Zoroaster, preached in northeastern Iran, and his message greatly changed Iranian religion. He upheld the need for men to act righteously, speak the truth and abhor the lie. Indeed, his religion was essentially a dualism in that he stressed the eternal conflict between Truth (*Arta*) and the Lie (*Druj*), abstract conceptions which became almost personifications. The history of Iranian religion throughout the Achaemenid period is that of the struggle between those who tried to follow Zoroaster's teaching and those who held to more traditional Indo-Iranian religious beliefs and practices. Eventually Zoroastrianism emerged triumphant from this contest, but in a much modified form.

In this context, what was the religion of the Achaemenid kings? We know nothing of the beliefs of Cyrus, except that he was religiously tolerant. Darius I was possibly a Zoroastrian, as were almost certainly Xerxes and his successors. Cultic practices attested at the Achaemenid court were, in the main, compatible with what we know of Zoroastrian liturgy of the time: animal sacrifice was avoided, the drinking but not the burning of the intoxicant *haoma* was allowed, and fire, Zoroaster's symbol *par excellence* of the Truth, played a central role in royal worship. There are also religious overtones to Darius' suppression of Bardiya's revolt, and there is a religious as well as a political element in Xerxes' destruction of the Daeva, or devil worshippers, during the Babylonian revolt. Both events may bear witness to religious tensions between early Zoroastrianism and paganism. The adoption of the Zoroastrian calendar by Artaxerxes I on the one hand, and the reintroduction of Mithra and Anahita into the royal pantheon of the ancient deities by Xerxes on the other, illustrates both the gradual acceptance of Zoroastrianism by the Achaemenids and the compromises the new religion was making to gain adherents. What the religion of the common people was is impossible to say; one suspects a variety of ancient and new beliefs and practices held sway. Orthodox Zoroastrianism of later Sasanian times is an amalgam of such popular religions, of the religion of the Achaemenid court, and of the teachings of the prophet Zoroaster.

Achaemenid art, like religion, was a blend of many elements. All the peoples of the empire were marshalled by the Great King to help create an imperial art worthy of Achaemenid power and wealth. Thus tastes, styles, motifs and techniques were blended together in an eclectic art, which itself reflected the Persian concept of an empire in which the individual peoples were generally left to their own beliefs, customs and tastes. For all these foreign elements, however, imperial Achaemenid art remains entirely Persian in conception; the sum of the parts is Persian–not Greek, Babylonian, Elamite or Egyptian. At both Pasargade and Persepolis, the Achaemenid capitals in their homeland Fars, one can trace almost every architectural and decorative detail to a foreign origin, yet the conception and plan of the two sites and their buildings is entirely new in the history of art. Persepolis, primarily the creation of Darius I and Xerxes, remains one of the most remarkable monuments of the ancient West Asia.

The organization and achievements of the Persian empire

At the centre of the empire was the 'King of Kings'. About him was a court of powerful hereditary landholders, the upper echelons of the standing army, the harem, religious functionaries, and the bureaucracy which administered the whole. The provinces, or satrapies, were ruled by governors (satraps) who had their local administrations. In theory, the king controlled all by being the last court of judicial appeal, by commanding the army, and by appointing all officials. He was greatly assisted in his rule by the so-called 'King's Ears', officials sent on regular inspection trips throughout the empire, who reported directly to the king. The system worked well under a strong and conscientious ruler; in

Persepolis

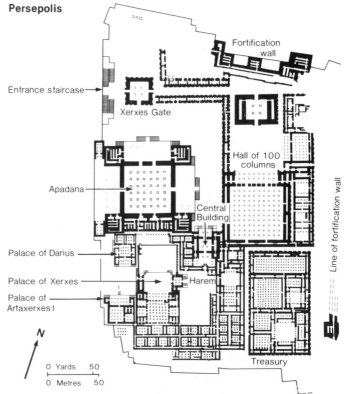

time, given the size of the empire, constant problems of war on the frontiers, rebellions like those in Egypt and weak kings, the system failed. The military and civil authority in the provinces, once strictly separate, merged under the satrap, who himself tended in time to become an hereditary petty king. This, of course, was a formula which produced semi-independent provinces, rivalries, and at times open rebellion.

The army also developed and changed with time. In Cyrus' day it was a tribal levy of all male Persians. Probably under Darius this was replaced by a standing army reinforced in war by a troop levy from the subject peoples. At the core of the standing army were 'the ten thousand immortals', composed of Medes and Persians. The imperial levy fought with the regulars in national units armed according to their own customs, but officered by Iranians. Some troops were permanently stationed at key points throughout the empire. In later years many a Greek mercenary fought faithfully for Persian silver.

On the whole, Persian rule sat lightly on the subject peoples. Conquered nations maintained their own religion, customs, methods of doing business and, to some extent, their forms of government. Law played an important role in keeping the peace, and law reform was a cornerstone of Darius' reorganization of the empire. In each province two courts were in force, one to administer the local laws, the other to deal with matters falling under the imperial or Persian law. With law reform came tax reform. The principal behind taxation was that all land was the king's by right of conquest. Thus, a tax was actually a rent, and the Persians themselves, not being a conquered people, were free of taxes. Each satrapy paid a fixed annual amount. Initially the amount did not take into consideration variations in the size of harvests, but under Darius all land was resurveyed, estimates of yield were made on averages over several years, and taxes were then laid as a percentage of those averages.

Wealth was founded on land and on trade, and the 'King's Peace' encouraged the development of both. The government invested in the construction of irrigation systems and in improvements in horticulture in an effort to strengthen the tax base built on agriculture. Civil and military administration, and trade and commerce were much facilitated by the famous system of royal roads, the most notable of which was the all-weather route from Susa to Sardis. Darius also dug a canal linking the Nile with the Red Sea, and the government further encouraged sea-borne trade by financing voyages of exploration in search of new routes, markets, and raw materials. Port development was encouraged on the Persian Gulf. An imperial standardization of weights and measures, efforts to encourage the use of coinage, and the growth of credit banking, particularly in Mesopotamia, were other measures which much encouraged trade and commerce.

Eventually, however, economic decline sapped the strength of the empire. The main cause of this was increasingly unsettled political conditions from the time of Artaxerxes II onwards. Other factors, however, were involved as well. The removal of too much money in taxes from the economy had a significant inflationary effect as did the payment of large sums to foreign mercenaries and as bribes, for such payments created a most unfavourable balance of payments. Interest rates in Babylon climbed steadily, probably as a result of inflationary pressures. In the end, economic unrest and disruption encouraged political instability and weakness, which in turn caused further economic distress. Alexander attacked a much weakened giant when he crossed into Asia in 334 BC.

The ultimate achievement of the Achaemenids was to have ruled with creative tolerance over disparate peoples and cultures for over 200 years at a time when both West Asia and Europe experienced the end of the ancient and the beginning of the modern world. Some say the ancient world ended when Cyrus marched into Babylon; others argue that it died when Alexander burned Persepolis. In either case, it is clear that the Achaemenid empire was the largest yet known in West Asia and Europe and was a profound force during an important time of change and transition in human history. That period witnessed crucial developments in art, philosophy, literature, religion, historiography, exploration, economics, , science and politics, and those developments—not the least of which was the concept of an empire of many nations—provided the immediate background for the further changes which were to follow in the Hellenistic age.

After Alexander

E. J. Keall

Alexander the Great stands at the beginning of a fresh chapter in world history, with a new phase in the secular contest between East and West. The assassination of the fugitive Achaemenid king of Bactria in 330 BC gave Alexander title to the Persian empire. The next five years witnessed a series of remarkable campaigns and marches by which he subdued the eastern provinces of the Persian empire as far as the Oxus and Jaxartes rivers, and, after penetrating south through the Hindu Kush, conquered the Punjab and traversed the length of the river Indus. At this point, however, the Macedonian soldiers resisted the idea of marching to the Ganges (which for them was a totally unknown world) and the task of subduing the subcontinent of India fell to Candragupta Maurya and his grandson, Aśoka (a convert to Buddhism).

By the spring of 324 BC Alexander was back at Susa, the old Persian administrative capital, after a rigorous march through the Makran desert, while the fleet sailed to the head of the Persian Gulf under the direction of its admiral, Nearchus. Adopting the mantle of the Achaemenids, Alexander planned the organization of his vast new empire, based upon the principle of a fusion of Greek and Persian ideas. But, in the following year he died of a fever at Babylon, and his generals were left to fight for the right of inheritance as his successor.

The Seleucid empire

After an early setback, Seleucus finally entered Babylon in 312 BC, assuming possession of what amounted to the Persian part of Alexander's empire, stretching from Asia Minor to India. But already an inexorable tide had begun to swell as provincial governors and local chieftains took it upon themselves to break away from the remote power base of the Seleucids in Mesopotamia. As individual dynasties were established, causing others to emerge in the same way, the gradual fragmentation of Alexander's empire became inevitable. It took Seleucus eleven years before he was able to put down rival claimants for the control of Syria. The battle of Ipsus in 301 BC put him in

firm possession of that country, but by this time he was already having difficulty controlling areas east of Euphrates.

In spite of these political problems, however, the impact of Alexander's conquests had been enormous, and its effects were to last long after even the Seleucids had faded from the scene. For the Greeks, the Macedonian campaigns had opened up a new world, permitting scholars to absorb the mathematical and astronomical knowledge of Babylonia and India. This impact on western scientific thought was matched by the effect that the Macedonian conquests had upon the east, where the diffusion of Hellenism was to be one of the area's most significant sources of influence for years to come. The most tangible change, following the military victories, stemmed from Alexander's policy of planting new cities peopled with veteran soldiers and other Greek-speaking settlers wherever the conquests occurred. This practice of establishing colonies in strategic positions was continued by Seleucus and his successors. The city of Seleucia on the Tigris replaced Babylon as the administrative capital of Mesopotamia, and numerous other smaller provincial centres were also established.

The important effect that these colonies had upon West Asia, apart from any direct policing role that they may have played, was that abiding centres of Greek culture were left scattered from the Aegean to the Punjab. Their inhabitants were to retain, for centuries at least, some nuances of an earlier Greek ideal which affected the industrial and fine arts, science, and religious and political thought. Greek language and concepts of law were firmly established in the lands of Mesopotamia and Persia. There was, of course, also

Ancient Persia: The Seleucids and the Parthians.

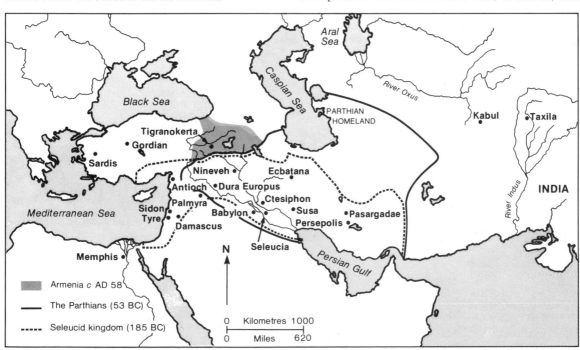

155

Fragment of an Achaemenid seal: a horseman turns in his saddle to shoot with a bow and arrow the so-called Parthian shot at a leaping lion.

much cross-fertilization with local culture, a phenomenon which unfortunately has all too often been regarded as a tragedy by western scholars. For them, Greece represented a 'pure ideal', and the new mixed culture smacked of an 'orientalized and debased form of Hellenism'. Rather, it was a period of dynamic change, when artists and ordinary citizens were exposed to a wealth of ideas which were allowed to develop reasonably freely without marked nationalistic and other orthodox strictures. Such restrictions on expression and ideas were to appear later in West Asia when strong authoritarian regimes took over in the post-Christian era. But for now, the world's inheritance from Alexander was a universality of expression and an interchange that was to remain unmatched until the time of Islam.

The impact of the Macedonian conquest was to be felt for centuries, but the political power of the Seleucids soon came under pressure. The first area to be lost from Alexander's empire was the Punjab, which Seleucus was forced to cede to the rising power of Candragupta Maurya. By the middle of the third century BC, Seleucid authority was being challenged on all sides. While Ptolemy III invaded Syria, states threw off their allegiance in Asia Minor, and the northeast provinces of Parthyene, Bactria and Sogdiana seceded. An Iranian, Arsaces, expelled the rebel governor from Parthyene in 247 BC, founding the Arsacid or Parthian dynasty, which was to last through many vicissitudes for nearly 500 years; in Bactria, the governor, Diodotus, declared himself king in 238 BC.

Desperate attempts followed on the part of the Seleucids to try to retrieve their authority. Antiochus III was partly successful in that endeavour. His campaigns into the east appear to have quietened the Parthians for a while, and the Bactrians were put under severe pressure with a two-year siege of their capital, Bactra, near Balkh. King Euthydemus, the real founder of the Graeco-Bactrian kingdom, was forced to acknowledge Seleucid suzerainty. After this, Antiochus tried his strength in India, too, where the Mauryan empire was collapsing almost as quickly as it had risen. But his efforts had little lasting effect, for he was soon to experience (at Magnesia in 192 BC) a resounding defeat at the hands of republican Rome, which had begun its relentless march towards creating an empire. Seleucid power was lost forever. Without a strong hand at the helm, provinces and kingdoms broke away once and for all, gradually reducing the great empire to the status of a petty principality based in Syria.

In the east, a dramatic chain of events was beginning to unfold. In the early part of the second century BC the Graeco-Bactrian kingdom was subjected to the universal plague of internal dissension. Eucratides appeared as a rebel in c171 BC. It is not clear whether he, or a legitimate member of the royal family of Euthydemus, pushed south of the Hindu Kush into the Punjab. At any rate, a powerful figure emerged around 155 BC in the form of Menander, who forged an extensive (Indo-Bactrian) empire in the once-Greek states that lay on both sides of the Hindu Kush. His extensive holdings, however, were soon to be affected by the arrival of a new force, which was to leave its imprint on the area for the next two centuries.

Chinese sources tell us that events associated with Han activity around the Great Wall of China triggered a move on the part of the Hsiung Nu who, in turn, pressurized another nomadic tribe (the Yüeh-chih) to move westwards. These events occurred in the first half of the second century BC. The exact identification of these tribes is not known, though frequent attempts have been made to link them (without absolute justification) to other names such as Tocharian and Hun. At any rate, around 130 BC, the Yüeh-chih continued their westerly migration and overran Bactria. The Chinese chronicles tell us that the tribe was made up of five groups. Around 35 BC, one of the groups (the Kuei-shuang-wang by name) established a dominant position over the others and, henceforth, the dynasty was known as 'Kushan'.

Before this, the Yüeh-chih had also set into motion another group, the Sakas, better known as one of the many Scythian tribes. The Sakas moved south of the Hindu Kush and infiltrated the Indo-Bactrian kingdom. These fairly ill-defined groups settled in various parts of eastern Iran and northwest India, giving the modern province of Seistan its name (formerly Sakastene). By c97 BC, Maues was minting the first 'Indo-Scythian' coins in India. It was these Sakas who caused the Parthians considerable problems on their eastern border following the death of Mithridates I in 138 BC.

The rise of Parthia

Mithridates had come to power in 171 BC, riding on a wave of Parthian expansion started by his father, Phraates I, during the series of rebellions that were provoked by the weak rule of Antiochus IV. Mithridates had dramatic success in Mesopotamia and southwestern Iran. The most significant event of his career was the capture of the old Seleucid capital of Seleucia on the Tigris in 141 BC. He struck coins there as a sign of his authority and annexed the whole of Babylonia as well. The Seleucids made one more attempt to recover their eastern territories but, with the death of Antiochus VII Sidetes in 129 BC while on campaign in Media, the last Seleucid challenge failed, and the Parthians were left as the main force to be reckoned with in Alexander's eastern domains for the next three centuries.

It would be wrong to speak of the Parthians as heirs of the Achaemenids. Parthia was never an all-powerful empire. Rather, it was a loose union of provinces and principalities, all of which owed varying degrees of respect to the Parthian king. It would be more correct to speak of a Parthian hegemony rather than of a Parthian empire. In reality, Parthia herself had already begun to lose territory to other expansionist movements in the second century BC–notably to Hyspaosines, who founded the kingdom of Characene at the head of the Persian Gulf, and to the Hyrcanians, who represented a permanent threat on Parthia's northern flank. The tide of reversals was stemmed, and even turned back to some extent, by Mithridates II (124–87 BC), under whose rule Parthia witnessed its greatest territorial extent. His campaigns brought him as far west as the Euphrates in Syria, a move which placed him in direct contact with the newly expanding imperial machinery of Rome. To the outsider, as was intended, the adoption by Mithridates II of the title 'King of kings' reflected his widespread territorial domination. But it should also be acknowledged that the use of the title was probably clever propaganda, designed to reinforce the Parthian monarch's claim to be heir.

As it turned out, Parthia was forced to recognize the awesome strength of Rome. The struggle between the two powers was to dominate the political scene for the next 200 years. Following diplomatic talks with the Roman general Sulla in 96–95 BC, the establishment of the Euphrates as the mutually recognized frontier between the two powers marked the end of Parthia's expansionist era. Even before the end of Mithridates' rule, the empire was experiencing internal dissension, with a usurper by the name of Gotarzes declaring himself king in Babylonia. In the east, although they were eventually forced to acknowledge Parthian territorial rights, the Sakas were responsible for causing the Parthians considerable problems, including the death of two kings in battle. On the death of the 'King of kings' in 87 BC, the Parthian royal family had resorted to what later became the standard behaviour following the demise of a monarch, namely, the squabbling over inheritance.

Weaknesses of this kind within Parthia probably encouraged Rome to make inroads, since her solution to the problem of protecting her interests still involved the principle of territorial annexation. But the Romans underestimated the extent to which the Parthian monarch could count upon the nobility to rally troops in time of external threat. Parthia had no standing army and, while her 'volunteer' troops invariably responded with tactical brilliance in the heat of battle, lacked a systematic defensive policy. Rome's greatest mistake was Crassus' abortive invasion and disastrous defeat at Carrhae in northern Syria in 53 BC. The ignominy of defeat, particularly the loss of legionary standards in battle, haunted Roman minds until the emperor Augustus was able to engineer the return of the standards in 20 BC, an event which the poet Horace commemorated in his *Odes*, an indication of how severely the Romans had felt their loss.

The period following Carrhae, however, is one when the Parthians failed to capitalize upon their early military successes. Their hands were tied in the east either by the Kushans or the Scythians. The first great Kushan ruler was Kujula Kadphises; extensive conquests were made in India by his son, Vima Kadphises. Eventually, the greatest extent of Kushan power was to be felt in the late first and early second centuries AD.

In Seistan the Indo-Scythians were replaced by the Pahlava, or Indo-Parthian dynasty, which around the middle of the first century AD included King Gondophares amongst its rulers. Gondophares is the figure known from Christian tradition as Caspar, one of the 'three wise men'. In addition to the impasse on the eastern borders, the country suffered from internal dissension. Potential rival claimants living outside the Parthian realm were often involved. In the intrigues and murders which now became the normal prerequisite for accession to the throne, the Romans were provided with the perfect excuse to interfere in the politics of Parthia without direct military contact. The opportunity came indirectly as a result of the peace treaty concluded between Augustus and Phraates IV. Grateful for the return of the legionary standards, Augustus gave the Parthian monarch an Italian slave girl as a concubine. The girl, Musa, persuaded the king to have her children educated in Rome; then she had him murdered, and placed her son, Phraataces, upon the throne. Later, Phraataces married his mother, and the portraits of the two of them appear side by side on coins, with a circular legend following the Roman style.

Although the period from 20 BC to AD 50 marked a time of maximum contact with Rome, it also saw the gradual decline of the pro-western forces in Parthia. This even applied to the arts; for, owing to the weaknesses of the crown, it is natural to assume that the semi-autonomous city of Seleucia on the Tigris played an important role in catering to and developing the taste for artistic and industrial products. But while that influence from the Greek past was extremely strong, especially at the time that the Parthians were brought into renewed contact with the Classical heritage through their presence in Syria in the first century BC, the first century AD is noteworthy for the emergence of new artistic and cultural trends, which were to last longer than the eventually bankrupt empire.

A Parthian shot: one of the devastatingly effective mounted archers. Parthia had no standing army but 'volunteer' troops showed tactical brilliance in battle.

The political and cultural struggle came to a head when there were two rival claimants, Vonones and Artabanus III, to the throne around AD 12. Vonones was the prince supported by Rome. After the latter had been successfully installed, Tacitus describes the feelings of the Parthians towards their new king: 'Their scorn was intensified because their national habits were alien to Vonones. He rarely hunted and had little interest in horses. When passing through the city he rode in a litter. The traditional banquets disgusted him. Moreover, he was laughed at because his entourage was Greek and because he kept even ordinary household objects locked up.' Artabanus, who presumably liked horses, hunting and Parthian-style banquets, was the rival claimant. He had been raised amongst the Dahae tribes east of the Caspian in the steppe of the real Parthian homeland. Now he was king of Media Atropatene, in northwestern Iran (modern Azerbaijan).

Their respective expressions of victory are highly significant. On one of the coin issues of Vonones, commemorating a temporary victory over Artabanus, the legend carries the words 'King (V) Onones defeating Artabanus'. The formula is faithful to the Roman practice of celebrating such victories. But, after Artabanus' final victory over Vonones, the successful contender from the Parthian homeland deliberately

omitted on his tetradrachm issues some of the previously standardized western imagery. The omission of the customary attribute of 'Philhellene' from the coins can be seen as a confirmation of Artabanus' distaste for Greek ways. A further departure from Greek standards can be seen in the full-face portrait of Artabanus, as opposed to the traditional profile facing to the left. In addition, this was the first time that the king had been shown receiving the palm branch of victory on horseback. Each of these new trends is reflected in the comments of Tacitus, given above, regarding the Parthian king.

It is not surprising to see, therefore, that around AD 35 the city of Seleucia was in open revolt against the Parthian state. In response to this blatant rejection of Greek standards, as well as perhaps more subtle changes in terms of the city's control of its fortunes, Seleucia declared itself independent, maintaining this position under a theoretical state of siege for seven years. Although their declaration of independence lasted that long, it would appear that the actions of the Greeks stemmed from feelings of desperation about their declining influence. It has been suggested that the role of the Greeks was being replaced by Aramaean-speaking groups, the 'native party' of Mesopotamia. Others argue that there was a 'native' reaction stemming from the Iranian plateau, as exemplified by the rude habits of Artabanus III. Of a subtle change there is no doubt. Yet it is questionable whether one could single out one specific reason for it. What is undeniable, though, is that by the middle of the first century AD the political demise of the Greeks of Seleucia was virtually complete.

Parthian culture

Around the middle of the first century AD, Parthia began to demonstrate a remarkable creativity in terms of artistic and cultural expressions. Unfortunately, some of the claims to distinctive differences, which immediately leads to the idea of an Iranian or 'oriental' revival, have been based on extremely fine, if not isolated, points. For instance, the existence of a fire altar on the reverse of an obscure bronze coin of Vologases I, and the introduction of Aramaic lettering on the silver drachms of the same period, are hardly evidence on their own of a national revival. But taken in conjunction with the kinds of statements found in Tacitus, it is apparent that there was a distinct watershed around the middle of the first century AD where one can distinguish on a gross scale between what can be called 'early' and 'late' Parthian culture. Distinctive artistic expressions were developed and, while much of the vocabulary of the language of Parthian art came from the west, it contributed little of its real meaning. 'Oriental' taste pervaded throughout.

It is apparent that the effect of trade upon the arts was more than simply a matter of the importation of goods and the influence that these products may have had upon the artistic taste of the times in general. Economic activity, to which the large number of settlement sites in late Parthia attests, may also have resulted in the acquisition of personal wealth. This would have provided a far wider stimulus to consumer spending and sponsorship of the arts than when power and wealth were in the hands of a relative minority. We may be dealing here with a kind of 'democratization' of the arts, with personal wealth permitting the expanding mercantile class and the proliferating petty nobility to indulge in the cliché formulas of success. The travelling salesman of products and designs would have catered to the grandiose pretensions of the *nouveau riche*. Thus, the individual elements of artistic creation may have been less important than the overall effect, making it difficult for the art historian to trace an orderly development of style. Greek motifs may be found alongside Achaemenid revivalisms and new Roman themes, in what at first may appear to be a confusing eclecticism of subject matter.

It is interesting to observe that while these influential changes in the arts were taking place, the imperial machinery of Parthia itself was suffering. Around AD 40, two brothers, Vardanes and Gotarzes, divided the empire between them. The empire continued to shrink, and there were acute problems stemming from inflation and the subsequent currency debasement. Even the organizational attempts of Vologases I to improve the affairs of the empire seem to have failed in their objective. His foundation of the city of Vologasias as a commercial rival to Seleucia would appear to have been a move designed to reduce further the influence of the Greek mercantile class. These measures were essentially ineffectual, for other middlemen in West Asia, notably the merchants of Palmyra, were beginning to establish their own trade monopolies, and Parthia became isolated.

Trade on a scale to foster such bitter rivalries was generated largely by the huge wealth of the Roman market. Vast sums of money were involved. The Roman emperor, Trajan, took on, as the last venture of his life, the invasion of Parthia in a bold attempt to try to cut out the middlemen and establish direct Roman control over trade. The Roman treasury was suffering from a debilitating loss of gold through the active market in foreign goods. But, although the effects of the Roman invasion were short-lived, Parthia began to suffer on another front as the merchants of Dura-Europos and Palmyra acquired more and more control of the Euphrates caravan traffic. Under Vologases III (IV), Parthia tried to restore the balance in her favour, but the invasion of Syria backfired, and thereafter destructive forces were at work to ensure the eventual downfall of Parthia.

The final blow to the empire can be seen in the aftermath of Lucius Verus' sack of Ctesiphon, the Parthian capital, in AD 165. Dura-Europos was, henceforth, a Roman holding, a striking reflection of the way in which the Parthian territories continued to shrink. Her economy was under even more severe pressure, for disruptions to trade caused by military engagements had had obvious disastrous consequences. This was in addition to the problems of the military engagements themselves, which caused a severe drain on the country's energies and resources. Combined with the internal fragmentation that had been going on for decades, the economic decline spelled the end of the empire. In due course, the vassal kingdom of Persia in southern Iran was to provide the stimulus for dynamic change.

The Sasanian empire

The Sasanian revolution heralded a new era when many of the problems facing the state stayed the same, but some of the lines dividing the various areas of interest were more sharply drawn than before. There was continued confrontation with Rome, often involving a dispute over who had the right to control Armenia. The Huns represented for the Sasanians an even more formidable threat to the eastern borders of their territory than the Scythians had done for the Parthians some centuries earlier; and Zoroastrianism, as a state religion, found itself not only in direct conflict with the Christian Church (which suffered from being associated with imperial Rome), but also with other heterodox beliefs, including Manichaeism, Zurvanism, and the revolutionary dogma of Mazdakism.

To Ardashir belongs the honour of creating the new Sasanian kingdom of Iran around AD 226, following the defeat of the Parthian, Artabanus V. The new dynasty had its origins in the land of Fars which, in a sense, was the spiritual homeland of the Iranians ever since the creation of the capitals of first Pasargadae and then Persepolis by the Achaemenids. Ardashir's forefathers had been connected with Zoroastrian religious cult practices at Istakhr, the city that had developed in the area of Persepolis, so it was natural that the new regime should have strong nationalistic and religious overtones. The Sasanian take-over has been commemorated in literature and embroidered with heroic overtones, often for the specific purpose of establishing legitimacy for the regime. But the precise moments when these legendary events occurred are often disputed by historians. The picture is confused by the fact that the Sasanians rejected the accumulative dating system of the Seleucid era which the Parthians had retained, whereby dates were given in years from the time of Seleucus' accession to power. The Sasanians recorded events according to the number of years of each individual ruler's reign, which can lead to confusion if there is no other frame of reference.

While Ardashir was responsible for the creation of the new kingdom of Iran, it was his son, Shapur I, who expanded the borders to the point where Sasanian possessions included all of modern Iran and parts of Pakistan, Afghanistan, the Soviet Union (on both sides of the Caspian), Iraq, and the Gulf Coast of the Arabian peninsula. In an inscription on the face of an Achaemenid monument near Persepolis, Shapur declared himself the 'King of kings of Iran and non-Iran'. Aside from his role as empire-builder, it was as the enemy of Rome that Shapur is best known to the western world.

Sasanian drinking bowl with applied repoussé, engraved and partly gilded. It probably represents Shapur II dispatching a stag (fourth century AD).

The Romans were the first to make a move, presumably expecting to take advantage of the infancy of the Sasanian empire. They hoped to retain their influence in Armenia, where remnants of the Arsacid dynasty had found refuge from the Sasanian revolution. But the Romans underestimated the military strength of the Sasanians. In 244 BC, the emperor Gordian III lost his life during an abortive invasion along the upper Euphrates, and was replaced by Philip the Arab, who negotiated terms of peace. This triumph, and subsequent similar Roman defeats, were to become the subject of frequent illustration in the form of official commemorative rock reliefs, mostly in the Sasanian homeland of Fars province.

Over a decade later, Shapur went on the offensive himself as a result of a dispute over Armenia. He invaded Syria, capturing its capital, Antioch. Sizable contingents of prisoners were brought back from the Syrian capital and settled in the province of Khuzistan. The prisoners included engineers, and it is said that their skills were put to use in bridge and dam building. The city of Gundeshapur, labelled 'the better Antioch of Shapur', is traditionally held to have been deliberately founded by Shapur to house his prisoners. It established a precedent in urban planning that was to permeate Sasanian history.

The long-term effects of Shapur's second campaign were to be felt long after his death. For the fortified merchant city of Hatra, along with many others such as Dura-Europos in the reaches of the Euphrates, fell to Shapur, putting an end to the pattern of trade that had developed in the Euphrates corridor since Parthian times. The loss of trade may even have affected adversely Hatra's sister Arab city, Palmyra, which was destroyed by the emperor Aurelian in AD 272. But the most

dramatic short-term effect of Shapur's Syrian conquests was the inevitable retaliation on the part of the Romans. This time it was the hapless emperor, Valerian, who marched to the defence of Edessa during Shapur's third Syrian campaign. Valerian's troops were completely routed, and the emperor himself was taken prisoner. Legend has it that he lived out the last days of his ignominious life at Gundeshapur. For all that in the eyes of the west Valerian was a weak and ineffectual leader, his capture for the Sasanians meant an unprecedented opportunity to glorify the new regime. Official rock reliefs depicted a kaleidoscope of events, portraying in a series of scenes the glorious victories of Shapur over Gordian, Philip and Valerian.

Shapur deserves the attention of historians, too, for his successes against the Kushans. The latter had become a dominant force in the area following the decline of Parthian power in the second century AD. With the revolution of Ardashir they had a more formidable opposition to face. But while it seems that it was Ardashir who first defeated the Kushans, it was Shapur who incorporated the realm within the boundaries of the Sasanian empire. From this time must date the appointment of a viceroy, or 'Kushanshah', who was a member of the Sasanian royal family, and ruled on behalf of the 'King of kings' with the assistance of other appointed officials who were also directly responsible to the throne. This arrangement represented a marked change from the way in which the Parthians had organized their empire. Considerable portions of the Parthian empire had been ruled by hereditary dynasties under a loose hegemony of states, which had maintained only a vague allegiance towards the so-called 'King of kings', unless a particularly dynamic and militarily strong figure was in charge. Organization of the empire in Shapur's time, by contrast, depended upon the handing out of provinces as fiefdoms to be ruled by members of the royal family. In this sense his empire represented a radical departure from that of the Parthians, because the power of the feudal lords was considerably weakened.

During 30 years, however, the successors of Shapur I lost nearly all the gains that the illustrious king had made. As a result of the pressure that Bahram II (AD 276–293) came under at the hands of the Kushans, he was forced to cede both northern Mesopotamia and Armenia to the Romans; Narses (AD 293–302) ceded territory west of the Tigris in a move that represented a major Sasanian withdrawal from its occupied territory; and Hormizd II (AD 302–309) married a Kushan princess in a vain attempt to promote peaceful conditions in the east. But out of the chaos emerged one of the most powerful figures of Sasanian history. He was brought to the throne by the nobility—evidence that the monarchy had been weakened and that the great lords were able to manipulate the throne to their liking. Their protégé, however, turned out to be almost overbearingly strong. He was Shapur II, also known as Shapur the Great.

Shapur's military prowess enabled him to re-establish Sasanian domination over areas recently lost. The

Kushans were brought under control, but a new force, the Chionite Huns, was already threatening on the eastern borders. Shapur was obliged to campaign for five years (AD 353–358) before coming to terms with them. Then, as his allies, the Chionites appear with him in the west, when he was able to turn his attention to the Roman conflict. In response to the siege of Amida and Sinjara, Julian 'the Apostate', invaded Mesopotamia in AD 363 but, following his death, his successor, Jovian, was forced to cede all the territories along the Tigris as well as the whole of Armenia. The Armenians put up strong resistance, but without Roman backing they were reduced to the status of a Sasanian province.

Zoroastrianism

The conflict with Rome and the struggle over Armenia had been heightened by the issue of Christianity. The Iranians were Zoroastrians. In fact, by instituting the beliefs of the cult associated with Ahura Mazda as a state religion, the Sasanians had become militant Zoroastrians. As expressed under the regime in the form of orthodox Zoroastrian dualism, the good spirit of light, *Ohrmizd* (Ahura Mazda), was opposed to the demon of evil, *Ahriman*. *Ahriman* was associated with subordinate angels, but these enjoy a position in the official expression of the faith far inferior to that of the holy element of fire. The reverence for fire has given erroneous cause for the belief that the Zoroastrians were fire worshippers. By their insistence upon the orthodox form of dualistic Zoroastrianism and their persecution of heresies and even mildly heterodox cults, the Sasanians were responsible for the increasing formalization of the

faith, for which the tending of the holy fires became one of the most highly prescribed rituals.

Many once-domed structures of the Sasanian era that survive today have been labelled 'fire-temple' without any real justification. Some of the surviving buildings could possibly be associated with secular pavilions or parts of palaces. The fire-temple designation has been applied simply because the tending of the holy fires appears to outsiders as the most exotic aspect of the religion. The Muslim conquerors of the seventh century AD, were struck by the numbers of fire-temples, and some of these buildings were even converted to mosques. The fire-temple structure provided the basis for one of the most distinctive aspects of later Iranian architecture.

There were three categories of fires corresponding to the three original castes of society: priests, warriors, and commoners; and, in addition, there was the king's own royal fire. This was lit at the beginning of his reign and carried around on a portable altar. The fire is illustrated on the reverse of the silver coins. It is also known that there were prescribed rituals for the renewal of the strength of the fire, from parent fire down to that in the private home. Materials used were specially purified for the purpose and, after being brought out into the open for a ceremony, the fire was returned to its sanctuary for further purification. Unfortunately, it is difficult to disentangle the ancient Zoroastrian practices from the way in which customs have developed within the post-Islamic Zoroastrian communities, which are represented in their largest numbers by the Parsees of India. In Sasanian times various popular and philosophic beliefs including magic and demonology were also held by the people, and these attitudes survived in spite of the

Ancient Persia: The Sasanian empire (AD 261).

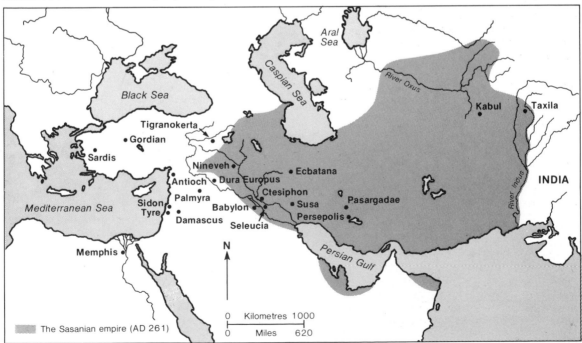

The Sasanian empire (AD 261)

increasingly formalistic expression of the religion and the growth of a rigid caste system for the priesthood.

The person most responsible for the imposition of orthodox practices appears to have been the proselytizing priest, Kartir, who became prominent under Shapur I. His inscriptions on the rock reliefs of Shapur and Bahram II attest to the fact that he was one of the most important figures in the empire, playing an important political, as well as religious, role. The attitudes of Kartir were not original, for Ardashir himself had destroyed pagan monuments and established fire-temples in their place. But Kartir was particularly zealous in that endeavour. He attacked Jews, Buddhists, Hindus, Manichaeans and Christians alike during the reign of five kings, from Shapur I to Narseh.

It is generally thought that Narseh was reasonably tolerant of the Manichaean faith. Mani had preached a syncretistic religion, combining both Christian and Zoroastrian beliefs, and based, to some extent, on the kinds of universalism put forward by other gnostic sects. After preaching in India, Mani returned to Iran, where his ideas received considerable acceptance, even amongst members of the royal family. But he encountered the zeal of Kartir, who pronounced him a heretic, and Mani was executed. After his death, Manichaeism spread in Central Asia, even reaching China. In Iran itself, Narseh favoured the Manichaeans. But in spite of this official tolerance, Manichaean beliefs continued to be regarded as heretical by the clergy. The strict attitudes of Kartir were relaxed, but not overthrown.

Later Islamic scribes wrote of various Zoroastrian sects, though modern commentators argue that it was a question of different schools of philosophical thought rather than different sects as such. For the population as a whole, the problems were likely to have seemed extremely remote from their lives and the way in which they practised their religion. The greatest conflict within Zoroastrianism itself involved the interpretation of the meaning of evil. The Mazdakists believed in the strictly separate origin of good and evil (*Ohrmizd* and *Ahriman* respectively); others, called Zurvanites, believed that *Ohrmizd* and *Ahriman* had their origins from Zurvan, or 'infinite time'. Zurvanite tendencies were widespread in Sasanian times, and some commentators have argued that it actually became the dominant form of Zoroastrianism towards the end of the empire. It does seem that the largely pessimistic attitudes of the Zurvanites were particularly appropriate in that age of speculative gnosticism. But whether it came to dominate Zoroastrianism or not, it is clear that Zurvanism was eliminated as a philosophy amongst the surviving members of the Zoroastrian community, after the conquest of Islam.

A major heretical faith of the fourth century AD was Christianity. According to the Syrian sources, Christianity had gained a foothold in the Aramaic-speaking territories of the Tigris and Euphrates as early as the Parthian period. It is likely that the settlement of prisoners from Antioch may have helped encourage the spread of Christianity in western Iran. In AD 274, King Tiridates of Armenia adopted Christianity. But so long as Rome remained pagan, the Christians experienced no greater persecution than the followers of any other heterodox faith. However, with the conversion of the emperor 'Constantine' and the adoption by Rome of Christianity as the official faith, Christians in Iran now became identified with one of the country's major political enemies. Persecution naturally followed. The first great purge occurred in AD 339, under Shapur II, who was vigorous in the pursuit of orthodox Zoroastrianism. He was responsible for ordering the first compilation of the religious writings of the Avesta. Christians fared a little better under his successors. Yazdigird I (AD 339–421) was extremely tolerant of both Jews and Christians; and, because of his inability to make headway against the Romans, Bahram V was forced to conclude a peace in which he granted freedom of worship to the Christians. But the most important change came in AD 483, when the Christian council of Iran officially adopted the Nestorian doctrine as its dogma. Henceforth, the Christians of Iran did not always need to be identified completely with the power of Rome.

Sasanian decline

Two other formidable adversaries had arisen to challenge the power of the Sasanian monarch. In the years following the strong reign of Shapur II, the power of the nobility was on the increase. Yazdigird I tried unsuccessfully to curb them, and, of his sons, Bahram V had to be brought to the throne against their opposition with the aid of both the Arab (Lakhmid) prince of Hira and Mirh-Narseh, the country's chief minister. Kings were forced to make further concessions to the nobility, especially Peroz (AD 459–484), and the picture changed only with the major reforms introduced by Khusro I, in the sixth century AD.

Sasanian monster in bronze. Most of the bronzes that have been preserved are very late but the Sasanian style persisted long after the fall of the dynasty.

The other great challenge that the Sasanian throne had to face came in the form of renewed pressure from nomadic tribes in the northeast. Towards the end of the fourth century AD, a new ruler, Kidra, had emerged in Kushan territory, south of the Hindu Kush. While the Kidarite Kushans held this southern territory, the land north of the Hindu Kush was occupied by the Chionite Huns. Again, just as the Kushans themselves appear to have emerged as the leaders of the Yüeh-chih hegemony in Parthian times, so the Chionites seem to have become dominated by the Hephthalite group.

Just as the Parthian kings had died fighting the Scythians in defence of the eastern borders, so too did the Sasanians find a new formidable adversary. Peroz was killed in battle against the Hephthalites in AD 484; Valash was forced to pay them tribute and, during this low ebb in the power of the Sasanian monarchy, Kavadh I managed to maintain his throne only with Hephthalite aid. Nevertheless, this particular episode in the endless round of nomadic invasions ceased when Khusro I came to power. He ended the tribute that had been traditionally paid, and then later, allying himself with the newly developing forces of the Turks (an omen for the future), he crushed the Hephthalites completely. While the Western Khanate took possession of the area north of the Amu-Darya (Oxus), the Sasanians re-established their control of the territories south of the river.

Khusrau's predecessor Kavadh I was a vigorous ruler, but his greatest notoriety comes from the fact that he embraced the faith of Mazdakism and introduced social reforms inspired by its tenets. Knowledge of the Mazdakite movement is drawn from outside sources (particularly the Syrian chronicles), from which it can be deduced that Mazdakism was a dualistic religion developed in the fifth century as an offshoot of Manichaeism. According to this new doctrine (apart from the theological stress upon the different nature of Good or Light and Evil or Darkness), man's behaviour was expected to be ascetic and brotherly. To promote this orderliness and moral attitude Mazdak preached what were essentially communistic principles, namely, that property (and, in this case, it included women) should be held in common. This liberalizing doctrine so aroused the hostility of the nobility, as well as of the Zoroastrian clergy in AD 496 that Kavadh was deposed. He regained the throne, but probably because the idealistic grounds on which the religion was based had been abused, with looting and rape taking place, Kavadh nominated to the throne his son, Khusrau, who was an orthodox Zoroastrian.

Khusrau inherited a bankrupt empire in which the nobility had gained power to the detriment of the throne, and where the eastern borders were never secure owing to the constant threat of the Hephthalites. In a sense the real revolution belonged to Khusrau, rather than Mazdak, because the measures the former took to stimulate the economy and to reverse the social trends were to have an effect long after Khusrau's death. Some of the effects of Khusrau's reforms were to be felt even after the introduction of Islam.

Khusrau's first measure was to put down the Mazdakite movement. Its followers were put to death. Then, in order to establish the king at the head of an administrative hierarchy, the army was reorganized under four generals, who were responsible directly to the throne instead of the great lords. A new class of lesser nobility was created, whose numbers further reduced the influence of the great nobles. These were the *dihqans*, or village lords. A fixed income for the treasury was guaranteed by the institution of a new method of taxation based upon a cash assessment of land potential, rather than upon the fickle tithe system. It is apparent from the large number of coins struck that the economy was deliberately stimulated by the circulation of silver derived from taxation. But the relative lack of copper coins and the indications of strict state control, as evidenced by the mint marks, suggest that the centralized tax reforms may have been achieved at the expense of local economies. Sasanian Iran under Khusrau was tax farmed.

Khusrau invested a lot of the revenues in development projects, such as road and bridge building programmes. His income was further supplemented by opportune attacks upon Byzantine possessions in Syria. In spite of the peace treaty concluded with Justinian in AD 532, the city of Antioch was sacked in AD 540, and its inhabitants deported to the Sasanian capital. But his orthodox approach to religion and his centralized approach to government resulted in an excessively bureaucratic system. In effect, the nobility were simply replaced by bureaucrats. Religious rites and practices were standardized to the extent that it put the religion beyond the immediate appeal of the people. The new systems of social stratification tended, in the long run, to fragment society to the advantage of the throne, but it rendered the country vulnerable to attack from outside when the monarchy was weak.

After the death of Khusrau I, the power of the nobility was almost restored by the machinations of one of its kind, Bahram Chobin. He rebelled against Hormizd, who was executed, and then against Khusrau II. Khusrau (later to be called Parviz or Victorious) was forced to flee to Byzantium where he received the support of the emperor, Maurice, with the understanding that Armenia would once again exchange hands. But, with the fortuitous assassination of Maurice, the newly instated Khusrau felt free to attack Byzantium and rampaged throughout West Asia. He reached the shores opposite Constantinople, and sacked Antioch, Damascus and Jerusalem between AD 611 and 614. After carrying off the Holy Cross to Iran, he invaded Egypt in AD 619, and then Yemen.

All this was done while Byzantium was at its lowest ebb, and Khusrau squandered most of his gains on his lavish lifestyle. The riches of the court of Khusrau were proverbial. In fact, for later writers, it was the court of the Khusrau that personified for them the entire history of the Sasanian kings. The great palace at Ctesiphon, for instance, was called by the Arabs the Ayvan Kisra, or Throne Hall of Khusrau. It represented for them the very essence of Sasanian luxury, which could only be reflected in the name of Khusrau. Although the campaigns of Khusrau Parviz brought in great booty, it was also costly to wage these extensive expeditions. The military funding may have been at the expense of the mercantile and working classes.

By the time that Khusrau had returned from his successful Egyptian campaign, the counter-offensive of Emperor Heraclius was already under way. In AD 622 he attacked the Sasanians, and routed the forces in the capital by AD 627. With the assassination of Khusrau II in AD 628, peace was concluded and the Holy Cross returned to Jerusalem. The nobility once more came to the fore and placed on the throne Yazdigird III, who was to be the last of the Sasanian kings.

The Arab conquest

It was an ominous year for the two great world powers. For already Emperor Heraclius and King Kavadh (who reigned for a short time after Khusrau II) had received communications in Arabic from one calling himself Muhammad, the Messenger of God. Muhammad died in AD 632, but his mission was undertaken by his successors, the Caliphs. In AD 633, under the leadership of its generals, the Muslim armies invaded Iraq and Syria. Most of Syria, including Damascus and Jerusalem, was taken in the next five years; in AD 637 the Sasanian capital (Ctesiphon) fell. Thereafter, the Islamic conquest of Iran was inevitable.

The Iranian armies were defeated at Nihavend in AD 641, and a decade later, the fugitive and last Sasanian king was murdered in Khurasan, ending four-and-a-quarter centuries of Sasanian rule. It has sometimes been said that the Muslim conquest was simply the last of a series of Arab migrations into the area of the Fertile Crescent. In many ways there were several groups who would probably have been quite receptive to the new movement. The city of Edessa had been ruled by the Abgar (Arab) kings, and Hatra and Palmyra had both been Arab principalities before being reduced respectively by Iran and Rome. Many of the local population were of Arab origins in later Sasanian times. More significant, however, was the presence of the Monophysite Christian tribe of the Ghassanids in Syria and of the Nestorian Christian group, the Lakhmids in Iraq. They were both Arab and, until defeated and deposed by Khusrau Parviz, they had both acted as buffer states between the two great powers of Byzantium and Iran. Their demise meant that the Sasanians were more easily exposed to the Muslim invasions of the Arabs, while their common ethnic background may have made them receptive to the conquerors' ways.

A better explanation than this, however, is needed to interpret the reasons for the Sasanians' resounding defeat. For Iran itself, the extended wars against Byzantium had sapped the energies of the country, as well as weakened its coffers; for the people themselves, the religion had become so codified under Khusrau Anushirvan that it served only the needs of the priesthood and not those of the people, so there was nothing that they could be called upon to defend in the Zoroastrian faith; and, with the centralization of power achieved by Khusrau, the village lords had no way of combining their efforts in resistance once the royal armies had been defeated. But ironically, while Iran was taken over for the moment by a movement of the Arabs and, while the new faith had an immediate simplicity and appeal, it would not be long before the village lords were again to exert a very strong Persianizing influence upon Islam in that area.

Mesopotamian Religion

Thorkild Jacobsen

General character

Mesopotamian religion was in origin a nature religion with worship of major cosmic phenomena such as the sky, the wind, the mountains, the underground waters surfacing in rivers and marshes, the thundercloud, the moon, the sun and so on. They seem originally to have been worshipped as themselves but experienced and approached in a personal 'I-Thou' mode, or visualized in mythopoetic, ideoplastic variants of their shapes—as when the power in the thundercloud became a huge bird floating on outstretched wings, roaring its thunder from a lion's maw. Very early, the human form became a possible mode of envisaging the powers, often with the features of the earlier non-human one—as when rays pierced the shoulders of the sun-god or branches sprouted from the human bodies of vegetation deities.

In time the human form became the preferred one, and so a rift arose between the power in the natural phenomenon and the phenomenon itself. The power was envisaged in human form, while the phenomenon became a mere thing, owned and operated by the power, as when the goddess 'Foothills' (Hursağ) became 'The Mistress of the Foothills' (Ninhursağa), who received the foothills as a present from her son Ninurta.

As the human form came to dominate religious thought more and more, the gods and their world came to be imagined on the model of the world of men. The gods were seen as an aristocracy of great landowners, the country's all-powerful upper class, dutifully served by the human inhabitants.

Eventually, in around the second and first millennia BC, the gods in their public aspect became more like national gods and were identified with the political aspirations of their nations, so that their relation to nature came to seem more incidental and their share in managing the universe dwindled; the god of the national capital, Marduk or Assur, tended to dominate as the one deciding power. Parallel to this ran, on the private level, a growing closeness between worshipper and god, taking as its point of departure the relation to the personal or family god.

Pantheon

An: ranked as titular head of the pantheon from the third millennium BC onward, An (Akkadian, Anu) whose name means 'sky', was the god of the sky. 'Earth' (*Ki*) whom he impregnated with his sperm, the rain, sometimes appeared as his consort. In the official pantheon, however, as reflected in the great god list An-Anum, his consort is the sky in its female aspect, Sumerian An (Akkadian, Antum) from whose breasts, the clouds, flowed her milk, the rain.

Enlil: more important, or at least more active in human affairs, is En-líl, god of the wind, whose name means 'Lord Wind'. Originally he probably represented the moist winds of spring, encouraging growth. His consort was the grain goddess Ninlil, whom, according to one myth, he raped. After being condemned by the tribunal of gods in Nippur he set out for the Nether World, but Ninlil followed him and on the way he engendered on her a number of chthonic deities so that they might take the place in the Nether World of the first child, the moon-god Suen. Conceivably the myth reflected the wind denuding the grain at winnowing, seen mythopoetically as a rape; the ceasing of the spring winds after harvest is seen as their death, and the storage of the grain underground as its departure also going into the Nether World.

Enlil acted as leader of the divine assembly, which met in a corner of the forecourt of his temple in Nippur called Ub-shu-unkina. He also executed the decisions of the assembly with a destructive storm, which expressed his essence, but which was also often seen as the combined breath expended by the gods in the assembly in saying *heam* ('Amen') to approve a decision.

Ninhursaǧa: third in the triumvirate of great gods was Ninhursaǧa. She was, as mentioned, according to one tradition the consort of Enlil; according to another, represented by the list An-Anum, her husband was the god Shul-pa-è who, like Enlil, was a storm-god. A third tradition makes her the spouse of An.

An important aspect of the goddess, originally probably a separate divinity, was her function as goddess of birth. As Nin-tur(r), 'Lady Birth-hut', she was the power in the hut, fold or pen in which pregnant animals were sheltered while giving birth. Her city was Kesh, not yet identified, and in Adab (Bismayah) she also had a major temple called É-mah, 'The grand house', matching a further name, Nin-mah, 'The Grand Lady'. In Akkadian she was known as Bêlet-ili, 'The Lady of the Gods'.

Enki: in the myths Ninhursaǧa was usually pitted against Enki (Akkadian Ea) the wily god of the fresh waters, who at the beginning of the second millennium BC began to replace her as a member of the ruling triad, under the influence of the increasingly male dominated ethos of those times.

Enki's name, 'Productive Manager of the Soil', characterized him as the one who provided the irrigation waters without which southern Mesopotamia would have been arid desert. His city was Eridu in the south with his temple Apsû, named from the freshwater ocean thought to underlie the earth.

Characteristic of Enki was his cleverness, for in conflicts with other, usually more powerful gods such as Enlil or Ninhursaǧa, he prevailed by his nimble wit, never by recourse to force. An odd, rather ribald story, apparently told at the king's court to entertain rough visiting seafarers from Tilmun, described his seduction of Ninhursaǧa only to be rebuffed until he proposed marriage. He then left her, but returned to seduce their daughter. Her daughter he in turn seduced, when she reached nubile age, and her daughter again. The last girl child was the spider, who had been warned by Ninhursaǧa, but fell for Enki when he proposed, and brought her the wedding gifts she had demanded of him. When he had left, Ninhursaǧa removed his seed from the spider's womb and threw it on the ground. From it various plants grew up, which were later seen, named and eaten by Enki, who then found himself pregnant but, being male, unable to give birth. He thus suffered deadly pain and, only when Ninhursaǧa was persuaded to come and help him in her role as goddess of birth, was he able to be delivered of a number of deities, including the goddess of Tilmun, whose names and functions he then decreed.

Another tale in which Enki was pitted against Ninhursaǧa, who was here called Nin-mah, is 'Enki and Nin-mah'. It told how originally the gods had to toil, performing the hard tasks of irrigation agriculture. They complained, and Enki had his mother Nammu give birth to man to relieve them of this work. At the party to celebrate the birth the gods drank deep and Nin-mah, who had assisted at the birth, boasted that she could make man's form good or bad at will. Enki accepted the challenge, saying that whatever she might do, he would balance it so that the creature could earn his living. Enki did so for all the freaks Nin-mah produced.Then he turned the tables on her and asked her to cope with the creature he would create. He produced man in old age, decrepit in every way, and Nin-mah found herself utterly unable to meet the challenge. She broke into bitter lament, at which point Enki apparently relented, and the story ended on a note of reconciliation.

The older generation of gods are, as will be seen, major elements of the cosmos: sky, winds, foothills, the waters underground, experienced in the personal mode. Younger generations are minor, but distinct, entities such as the moon, the thundercloud, the sun, the morning and evening star, and the rainstorm.

Nanna/(En-)suen. The oldest member of the first

Sumerian seal of the moon-god Nanna, the son of the goddess Ninlil.

younger generation is the god of the moon, Nanna (the full moon), or (En-) sûn (in Akkadian uncontracted Suin, the new moon, without the honorific *en* 'lord'). He was city god of Ur and often envisaged–besides in his human shape–as a bull. His wife was Nin-gal 'The great Lady'.

Ninurta: Nanna's ranking as oldest son of Enlil seems characteristic of a southern, herder tradition. In the agricultural tradition of Nippur that rank belonged to Nin-urta, 'Lord Plough' who in Girsu in the Lagash area was called Nin-ğirsu(k) 'The Lord of Girsu'. He was the personified thunderstorm of spring, which, by the humidity it provided to the air, made the soil easy to plough. His earliest form was that of a huge lion-headed eagle floating on outstretched wings and roaring thunder. Later he was embodied in human form and the thunderbird, Imdugud, became a vanquished enemy serving him. A remarkable cycle of myths about him reflected the hydraulic cycle of the waters rising as steam from the sea and marshes to form rainclouds, which spent themselves over the mountains in the spring, melting the winter snows and with them rushing down the mountain streams to swell the rivers in the yearly floods, which eventually subsided by autumn. In these myths the god played two roles: in his bird form he was thundercloud and enemy, in his human form he was

Assyrian seal showing a sacred tree which was an important symbol in Mesopotamian religion.

flood and friend. In a myth known as 'Ninurta and the Turtle' we are told that the thunderbird stole the emblems of authority over the waters from Enki in the *apsû* and flew away with them to the mountains: as a result the waters rose as vapours from the marshes to become rainclouds. Ninurta, the god in human form, then set out to recapture them, hoping to keep them for himself. However, when he hit the bird with his arrow the pain made it open its claw and the released emblems returned by themselves to Enki. Ninurta, furious, created a floodwave, that is the yearly flood, which pounded against Enki's abode. Enki, however, created the turtle and had it dig a ditch into which Ninurta was thrown: the flood subsided and became a trickle at the bottom of the riverbed as if confined in a pit.

Another myth of the cycle, known as 'Lugal-e', also told of Ninurta's fight in the mountains; there, however, his opponent was Asag, perhaps the fir tree. After his victory he guided the waters of the mountains into the Tigris and created a barrier of foothills, to prevent them from going up there and freezing. This barrier he gave as a present to his mother Ninhursağa, making her 'Queen of the Foothills'. After that he sat in judgment on his foes, the stones, who fought on Asag's side, and his sentences fixed the nature of each stone forever. Some he accepted and blessed; others, who proved vicious, he cursed. Still a third myth about Ninurta, known as 'An-gim' told of his victorious return from battle to Nippur and his gradual calming down.

Utu: The eldest of Nanna's children, the next generation of gods, was the sun-god Utu, in Akkadian Shamash–both names mean 'Sun'–who was also god of justice and fair dealing. His cities were Ararma in the south, Sippar in the north.

Inanna: Utu's sister was the goddess Inanna, Akkadian Ishtar (older Eshtar), who seems to have united in her person a variety of originally distinct goddesses. She was, in one aspect, the goddess of the date storehouse. In another, as goddess of shepherds, she was the power behind the thundershowers of spring that created pasture in the desert. She was also goddess of the Morning and Evening star and, as the latter, protectress and colleague of harlots. One myth, 'Inanna's Descent', tells how, in attempting to wrest rule of the Nether World from her older sister Ereshkigal, she had gained admittance to the city of the dead, but, overpowered and condemned to death, she changed into a slab of rotting meat. Her trusty servant, whom she had previously instructed, then sought help from the great gods, but only Enki responded favourably. He fashioned two creatures who tricked Ereshkigal into promising them whatever they asked for, so when they asked for the slab of meat she had to give it to them. They sprinkled water of life and pasture of life on it, and Inanna rose from it. To be allowed to leave, however, she had to promise to provide a substitute for herself; on her way back she

Shiva Nataraja, 'king of the dancers'. This late bronze (twelfth century) reveals the positive aspects of the fierce god; his hands indicate speech, sustenance, destruction and enlightenment.

Assyrian seal relating to the worship of Ishtar (Inanna), who sprouted a beard in sympathy with her warlike consort Ashur, or Assur.

came upon her young husband, Dumuzi, who seemed to her not to grieve enough at having lost her, so in her jealous rage she delivered him up to the demons who had followed her to see that she kept her word. Dumuzi fled, but was eventually captured. His sister Geshtin-anna searched for him and found him in the Nether World. Inanna then decreed that they could alternate, each spending half a year in the world of the living, while the other remained with the dead.

Ishkur: Ishkur, in Akkadian Adad, brother of Inanna was also a deity of the thundershowers of spring.

Nether World deities: The Nether World was, as mentioned, ruled by Eresh-kigal(.ak) 'Queen of the Underground', whose main function was to weep over children, dead before their time–a distinct kindness to them as the ancients saw things. Her husband was, according to one tradition, Gu(d)-gal-ana(k), 'The Great Bull of Heaven'–presumably an older, non-anthropomorph form of An, the sky, she representing the earth. Another, later tradition pairs her with Nergal of Kutha, who became her husband after he had first offended her by not rising to honour her messenger, and had then visited her and bedded her in the Nether World. He escaped by a ruse, only to be forced finally to return to become its ruler and Ereshkigal's consort. Ereshkigal's son was Ninasu, though according to another tradition he was the son of Enlil and Ninlil; her grandson was Ningishzida.

The Nether World was envisaged as a large city ringed around with walls. It had a king and queen with a staff of administrative officials, notably the adjutant Namtar (Fate), the sheriff Ningishzida, the judges Utu and Gilgamesh, and the gatekeeper Neti. People's fate there depended less upon how they had lived, than upon the care given them by the survivors. As time went on ideas of after-life seem to have become ever gloomier: the dead were covered with feathers like birds, dust lay thick everywhere, and if there was water to drink it was stale and foul.

The destructive aspect of Shiva as Bhairava, 'the joyous devourer'. A late painting suggesting the terror of merciless, inexplicable and unpredictable death.

Marduk: In the second and first millenia BC two city gods rose to prominence as their cities became capitals of nations and even empires; Marduk of Babylon and Assur of Assyria. Marduk, whose name is probably more correctly read as Merodakh, as in the Bible, was originally a god of the rainstorm. His name means 'Son of the Storm' and its extended form Bêl Merodakh shows that he was identified with the West Semitic Baal (*bal*) to which the Akkadian version, Bêl, corresponded. He was early identified with a southern rain-god, Asal-lú-he, 'Asar, the Man-drencher', whose city was Kuar near Eridu, and who was considered a son of Enki. In the Sumerian incantations it was Asal-lú-he, the cloud, who from on high observed attacks on man down on earth by demons of disease and reported them to his father Enki in the deep to learn from him how to counter them.

With time Marduk's function as city god, and later national god, tended to overshadow his earlier nature aspect, politicizing him as, primarily, the bearer of Babylonia's nationalistic aspirations.

Assur: Even more politicized was the city god of Ashur and chief god of Assyria. In him no original characteristics were now traceable. Already, as early as the reign of Shamshi-Adad in Old-Babylonian times, political ambition in that ruler sought to identify Assur with Enlil entirely, and thus to transfer to Assur the authority of Enlil and Nippur. Afterwards Assur simply continued as the national god of Assyria, inciting and aiding Assyrian political aspirations.

Cult: festivals and temples

Two major purposes inform the oldest aspects of Ancient Mesopotamian cult: to make the deity abide with the community, and to help it to function. For both purposes temples were built and festivals celebrated.

The festivals, to begin with the latter, mostly centred around a cult drama which enacted–and thereby magically set going–the desired function of the god. Thus the 'Sacred Marriage' drama of the date-growers in Uruk celebrated the wedding of the power in the date-palm to grow and bear fruit, Ama-ushumgal-ana, with the goddess of the communal storehouse, Inanna, thus having the god with his wedding gifts of abundance enter the house of his bride, the storehouse. With the herders, dependent on pasture and breeding, it was the actual consummation of the marriage that was central and magically caused fertility in nature. In the rite the ruler, priest-king (*en*) or king (*lugal*), not only acted as, but actually became, the god, and his sexual union with the goddess, whose role was taken by a high priestess or perhaps by the queen, fertilized all of nature. Other similar cult dramas were the yearly laments for the death of the god of fertility, who had many locally different forms and names. The one best known was Dumuzi, who died with the withering of pasture as the dry summer set in. There were also festivals centred around divine journeys, such as the one of Ninurta/Nin-girsu to Eridu, bringing with him fertility and abundance. It would seem to represent in drama form the yearly rise of the flood in the rivers. In the early second millennium BC and onwards the cult dramas concerned with fertility in nature were often replaced by, or reinterpreted as, celebrations and magical confirmations of decisive political victories. Most famous of these is the 'New Year Festival' in Babylon, the 'Akitu', which originally was a festival of sowing with the god journeying out into the fields. It was reinterpreted, however, as Marduk issuing out to battle with Tiāmat, who personified Babylon's early foe, the Sealand.

To induce a deity to abide with the community an abode was built for it–a temple, staffed with human servants, the priests. The daily cult was modelled on the running of the household of a great landowner. Meals were prepared and served for the god, at night he was bathed and his bed made ready for him. His lands were looked after by other servants. The god Ningirsu, for example, whose staff of minor gods who oversaw the human workers, described in Gudea's Cylinder B, had a high constable to police the temple, a steward, a chamberlain, two divine musicians, handmaidens–the god's daughters–a counsellor and a secretary who winnowed the unimportant from important in matters submitted to him for decision. For war the god had the assistance of two generals; the animals of his estate were cared for by a divine ass-herd and a divine shepherd, the fields were ploughed by a ploughman, Gishbare; fisheries were taxed by his taxgatherer, Lamar, who sent in reports by a messenger, Inim-sha(g)-tam. A ranger, Dimgal-abzu looked after the protection of the wildlife on the temple estate.

Religion and the economy

The cities grew, as suggested, around temples, sacred treasuries, and the people looked to their temples and gods for prospering their economy. Thus cities along the edge of marshes in the south had city gods connected with fishing, fowling, and the marshman's way of life. Nanshe in Ninâ, was a goddess of fish, Ninmara in Guabba of fowls, Dumuzi-abzu in Kinirsha and Enki in Eridu looked to the prospering of reeds and marsh fauna.

Along the lower Euphrates lay cities of the orchardmen with dendral deities such as Ninasu in Enegir, Ningishzida in Gishbanda and Damu in Girsu on the Euphrates. In Uruk was the date-god Ama-ushumgalanna. Interspersed with these were the cities of cowherds with bovine deities: Ki-abrig with the bull-god Ningublaga, Gaesh and Ur with the moon-god Suen (or En-Sûn in the form of a bull, Ararma (Akkadian, Larsa) with the sun-god Uta, who could be seen as a bison, and Kullab, in or near Uruk, with its bovine pair, Lugalbanda and Ninsûn.

Uruk lay on the edge of the central grasslands, the *edin*, and to the shepherd's pantheon belonged a series of cities with shepherd deities circling it: Uruk and Patibira with Dumuzi the shepherd, and the shepherds' form of Inanna, also the city goddess of Zabalam. Her son Shara was god of Umma. Further north lay Muru with Ishkur, god of the spring rains.

North and east of the *edin*, finally, were the farmers' cities, Eresh and Shuruppak, on the Euphrates with the grain goddesses Nidaba and Sud as city gods; Nippur, to the north, had Enlil, god of the wind and of the hoe, and his son Ninurta, god of rain, and of the plough. Ninurta, under his other name Nin-Girsu, 'Lord of Girsu', was also city god of Girsu in the Lagash region.

Religion and politics

In time, as the gods were no longer simply natural phenomena in the personal mode but became powers in human form controlling their phenomena, their cities cast them in the role of rulers, looking to them for political aid, for protection against external enemies and internal lawlessness. Thus we have a long hymn to Nanshe extolling her concern with social justice, and of Nin-Girsu we are told that he concluded a covenent with Uru-inim-gina that the latter should not allow widows and orphans to be misused by the rich and powerful.

As the gods, while keeping their ties to natural phenomena, were given new roles as city rulers, so also were their mutual relations envisaged in terms of human political forms. The gods constituted a 'Primitive Democracy', met in assembly in Nippur, with An and Enlil presiding, to deliberate on political and other decisions, to choose the city which for a time would be the capital of Sumer and seat of a dynasty, and to decide on when it was to be replaced by a successor. The assembly also sat in judgment on crimes.

With the advent of the second millennium BC, and the rise of the national states of Babylonia and Assyria with their all-powerful monarchs, the concept of the divine assembly tended to become a mere framework for decisions made by Marduk or Assur, and official religion became politicized in the extreme, the god becoming a mere embodiment of the state and its political aims.

For the cities and their human rulers who represented them it was, of course, of the utmost importance to know the will of the city god and to carry it out. To this end the ruler disposed of various approaches: dreams, which might come unbidden, or which might be sought deliberately in a rite of incubation in the temple; omens obtained by reading signs in the livers of sacrificial animals–an extensive literature of handbooks to help the diviners grew up–or in the shape of oil dropped on water, of smoke, and so on. By one method the future was predicted from unusual events of everyday life seen as signs, 'symptoms', of what was to come. If desert plants were found in a city, for example, it was a symptom that desert essence was overcoming city essence, and that the city would become deserted. Important were also signs to be read in the stars, and in many weather phenomena.

Religion and the individual

While religion originally seems to have been a matter for the community as a whole, there also grew up toward the end of the third millennium a private and personal relationship with the divine. It seems to have centred originally on the 'personal god', a personification of a person's luck and efficiency, a role in which any god of the pantheon might serve; but the attitude was soon extended to govern private access to the gods generally. With it went a feeling that if one's luck deserted one, and evils befell one, it must be because one had offended the god who granted it. Thus a sense of 'sin' arose, with attendant rites of confession, penitence and prayer, which in many ways gave greater inwardness to religious experience.

Myths

Curiously enough, the Sumerians have left us only one late, general account of the creation of the world, the Eridu Genesis. It tells of the creation of man and animals, the settling of men in cities, the allotment of the earliest cities to city gods, their early dynasties and the coming of the Flood. The latter occurred because the noise made by proliferating humanity kept Enlil sleepless. Then Enki warned the Sumerian Noah, Zi-ud-sudra, who built a boat in which he saved men and animals. For this he was rewarded by the gods with eternal life.

Fairly systematic, but concerned with the ordering, rather than the creation, of the world is a long composition known as *Enki and the World Order* in which Enki institutes all major economies and crafts and appoints appropriate deities to supervise them.

An Akkadian myth of note is the story of Atra-hasīs, which tells how originally the gods had to toil to maintain the irrigation agriculture which furnished their livelihood, how they resisted, and how Enki solved the problem by creating man in cooperation with the birth goddess. Man soon proliferated, and the noise he made kept Enlil awake. After various unsuccessful attempts to decrease mankind's numbers by famine, for example, Enlil finally decided on the Flood; but Enki frustrated the design by warning Atra-hasīs and having him build an ark and save life. Eventually, to pacify Enlil, Enki and the birth goddess instituted a series of birth-control measures intended to keep man's proliferation within bounds.

While the story of Atra-hasīs deals with the possibility of the extinction of the human race as a whole, the best known of all Mesopotamian tales, the *Gilgamesh Epic*, is concerned with individual extinction, the problem of man's mortality. Gilgamesh, a ruler of Uruk, was a man of excessive vitality. When the people of the city complained, the gods created a companion for him of similar vigour, Enkidu. Together the two performed superhuman heroic deeds, but in so doing offended the gods, who decided that Enkidu must die, as he did. Gilgamesh, horrified, set out to seek eternal life, undismayed by repeated sage advice that his search was futile. At last he reached his ancestor Uta-napishtim, another Akkadian Noah, only to learn that his attainment of eternal life was due to a unique situation. He was told, however, of a rejuvenating plant, which he obtained on his way home, only to have it snatched away from him by a snake while he was bathing in a pool. The snake ate it and promptly sloughed off its skin to emerge young and shiny. Gilgamesh finally realized the futility of his search and returned, sobered, to Uruk.

Somewhat later than the Akkadian *Gilgamesh* epic is the 'Babylonian Creation Story.' It tells of the earliest time, when only the salt waters, Tiāmat, and Apsû, the fresh waters, existed, how generations of gods were engendered, how the movement and the noise they made kept the older powers awake so that first Apsû, then Tiāmat tried to rid themselves of their tormentors. Apsû was killed by Ea, Tiāmat was met in single combat by Marduk, who slew her and then fashioned the visible universe from her body. He also freed the gods who had fought on her side and whom he had captured. Moved by their willingness to undertake the hard task of building Babylon and its temple, he also created man out of the blood of their leader, Kingu, to take over the toil of the gods. The myth seems to embody old nature myths from the west in which the thundercloud fought the sea, but to have been fashioned into a political myth celebrating the unification of Babylonia by Babylon's (Marduk's) victory over the Sealand (Tiāmat) and the effective conciliatory policies that permanently united the country after the victory.

The Evolution of the Alphabet

William Culican

By 'alphabet' we designate a system of writing that expresses the sounds of a language (both vowels and consonants) singly and usually with a single sign. Strictly, the Greeks were the first to do this; but they acknowledged that it was learned by them from the Phoenicians. The truth of this is abundantly testified, not only by the clear derivation of archaic Greek letter forms from Phoenician prototypes, but also by the preservation in Greek of many Phoenician consonants; as well as the same order of letters (*abg, lm, pq* and so on) as in the Phoenician (or West Semitic) alphabet. Even some of the ways employed by the Greeks to indicate vocalic sounds betray the influence of West Semitic sound-making. Since the Phoenicians (like the ancient Egyptians) did not write vowels, the Greeks used signs for Semitic sounds not used in their own language to represent their vowel sounds: *waw* for *u*, *yodh* for *y* or *i*, *he* for *e*. Some West Semitic scripts—Aramaean, Hebrew and Moabite—had used certain consonantal forms vocalically, *álep* for *ā* for instance (hence Greek *alpha*), at first only on the end of words but also in internal positions by the late eighth century BC.

171

Phoenician inscription, 1000 BC. Ahiram sarcophagus. Byblos.

Phoenician

The key date in the history of the Phoenician alphabet is 1000 BC–the date assigned to the inscription on the sarcophagus of King Ahiram of Byblos, the earliest long inscription in systematized alphabetic consonantal script. Typologically the script stands at the head of a small group of inscriptions of Byblian kings, the latest of whom was Shipitbaal, whose father Elibaal was the author of a Phoenician text written on a monument of Pharaoh Osorkon I of the Bubastis dynasty (945–842 BC). For this reason Ahiram's inscription is thought on stylistic grounds to be not more than a century earlier (though the sarcophagus itself might have been re-used). In turn a number of short inscriptions on bronze arrowheads found in Lebanon and Palestine reveal systematic use of more archaic letter forms than Ahiram's: hence our present certainty that the systematized Phoenician alphabet of 22 letters came into use about 1200 BC.

In neighbouring regions the earliest long Palestinian inscription is the Gezer calendar (stylistically dated about 1000 BC) and in Transjordan the stela of King Mesha of Moab at 840 BC. in Syria the long Aramaean inscriptions of Zakir of Hamath at 780 BC and Bar Rekkub of Senjirli at 730 BC, all dated on historical evidence. These and others, together with inscriptions in Punic (West Phoenician) from the western Mediterranean colonies provide a patchy but consistent 'development' of the West Semitic alphabet down to Roman times.

The chief problem in the history of the alphabet lies in the relation of this Phoenician system to its predecessors.

Sinaitic

In origin the idea of one-sign-one-sound was Egyptian, for such were the ambiguities of the hieroglyphic system, in which the signs could indicate either objects or ideas or sounds, that it was often necessary to use an additional symbol to indicate sound alone, to show which way a hieroglyph had to be read. These signs themselves were not originally simple single consonants, but they came to act as such simply because Egyptian had a large number of syllables with single *strong* consonants (often the *acrophon* or first). The main use of this pseudo-alphabet of 24 consonantal signs was to spell out phonetic complements to hieroglyphs; but

more and more it was used for spelling foreign words and names for which no hieroglyphic spelling could be devised. It must be stressed that the Egyptians made very little use of this alphabet: that they never adopted the alphabetic system in principle; and in any case had no vowel signs in it. But it was an important invention, widely considered to have some relation to the two major systems that precede Phoenician alphabetic writing–the script from the Egyptian mines at Serabit el-Khedem in Sinai (Proto-Sinaitic) and that of the Canaanite town of Gebal (modern Jebail) or Byblos (Giblite or Byblian), both of which scripts use a combination of pictographs and linear signs. Both scripts were written by Semites and both appear to be using and developing the alphabetic principle of consonant sign plus vowel; but neither developed a systematized script.

Sinaitic had about 30 signs; too few for a syllabic or pictographic script but, despite the fact that many of them have affinity with Byblian (or even later Phoenician) script, less than three words can be translated. Their importance lies in the theory that the signs cannot be purely acrophonic, that they indicate a mixed principle in the evolution of both Phoenician and South Semitic (Arabian) alphabetic script, that Sinaitic was not a local development, but connected with contemporary (that is early-mid second millennium BC) experiments in Semitic writing at Byblos and elsewhere.

Byblian

The bronze spatula and stone plaque inscriptions from Byblos strongly suggest that a long period of experimentation took place there with some version of the Egyptian

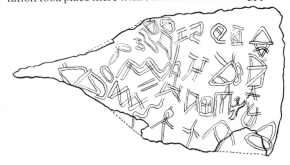

Two sides of a bronze spatula from Byblos. 9.5 cm (4 in) long; (top) with hieroglyphic 'mixed' inscription; (below) with Phoenician linear inscription over erased 'mixed' inscription.

alphabet, already in the early part of the second millennium BC. Acquaintance with the Egyptian system may be expected at Byblos, which had close commercial relations with the Nile Delta. Detailed analysis of the spatula script seems to indicate the use of pictographic and ideographic signs, their more linear stylized counterparts, phonetic indicators and class determinatives, all associated as in the Egyptian system. But the evidence from Byblos poses a basic historical problem in the case of a spatula inscribed on one side in mixed script and, on the other, in linear consonantal Phoenician, one of the earliest Phoenician inscriptions, not far removed in date from that of Ahiram. But even here there are signs that an inscription in mixed script had been erased to make room for the Phoenician linear. This creates the possibility that both scripts were used near contemporaneously, or overlapped. Similarly there are signs that on the Ahiram sarcophagus a mixed 'Byblian' inscription was partly erased before the Ahiram inscription itself was added. It may be observed that already, in writing in Egyptian hieroglyphs the Semitic names of the princes at Byblos during Egypt's twelfth dynasty, certain signs were used alphabetically. Thus it may be taken, with the help of a few early graffiti from the site, that Byblos knew the alphabetic principle early in the second millennium BC.

Palestinian Proto-Canaanite

North of Sinai it is in Palestine particularly that we find a few scattered examples of script with a limited range of signs, some resembling those of Proto-Sinaitic. These occur chiefly on potsherds from Canaanite sites, including Beth Shemesh, Shechem, Gezer, Lachish and Megiddo. Their importance lies not in providing a specific link with either Proto-Sinaitic or Byblian, but in the evidence they provide for widespread attempts at writing in pre-Hebrew Palestine. Dating them is difficult; some like the Lachish dagger and Shechem plaque appear to date to the later part of the Middle Bronze Age (sixteenth or fifteenth century BC) but most are thirteenth or twelfth century BC. None can be read with certainty and none can be proven to be alphabetic, but they most likely are.

Syria and northern Lebanon have provided a few examples of linear writing that diverge from Palestinian experiments. Examples from fourteenth century BC Kamid el-Loz (Bekaa) have longer alphabets with some points of relation to that of south Arabia. Another from El Jish (about 1700 BC) is in a mixture of signs ranging from south Arabian to Minoan Linear A.

Thus while evidence for the systematization of Phoe-

nician increases between 1200 and 1000 BC, it is becoming increasingly difficult to recognize a pre-Phoenician history of 'the alphabet': there appear to have been a number of experiments in alphabetic or partially alphabetic writing in middle and late Bronze Age Canaan. For development into a system, conditions other than purely linguistic ones might have been lacking: trade, religion or 'stimulus diffusion'. However, it is probable that the linguistic economy of the Phoenician 22-letter system was an important factor in its final triumph.

Evidence has recently come to light in an important ostrakon from 'Isbet Sartah near Aphek in Israel that a 22-letter Proto-Canaanite alphabet was in existence about 1200 BC, a date based on both archaeological and epigraphic evidence. It is written from left to right in the Proto-Canaanite tradition and not right to left as in the Phoenician. Earlier Palestinian examples of Proto-Canaanite are written in both directions and vertically, though there appears to have been a growing tendency towards left-to-right direction. Certain details of the letter sequence suggest that its alphabet might have been evolved in Palestine rather than Phoenicia.

Syllabaries and Ugaritic

The Phoenician linear alphabet, which much of the Mediterranean adopted, was long preceded in West Asia by syllabic systems expressed either in cuneiform syllable-signs (Sumerian, Akkadian, Elamite, Urartian and Old Persian) or in hieroglyphs (pictographs) as Egyptian, Hittite and perhaps earliest Urartian; or else in systems of linear symbols like those of Crete, Mycenae and Cyprus.

The earliest known exclusive usage of an alphabetic system of writing was at fourteenth century BC Ras Shamra, ancient Ugarit on the Syrian coast. Its system was a highly simplified 30-sign cuneiform, but it cannot in fact have been derived from the cuneiform syllabary since the pictographic elements, where they remain in the Ugaritic cuneiform signs, are closer to Proto-Canaanite pictographs, and also, the order of letters in the Ugaritic alphabet is that of the later Semitic abecedarium.

All points to Ugarit as one of the many Canaanite experimental systems of alphabetic writing, but one

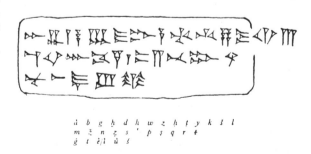

Abecedary from Ugarit, 1400 BC.

'b g d h w ḥ z ṭ y k l 'm' n 'sⁱ p 'ṣ q r š̃ t

Proto-Canaanite abecedary on a potsherd, 16 cm (6¾ in) long; from 'Izbet Sartah, Israel, 1200 BC.

designed to be written on *clay*, for which cuneiform was the accepted form. Even so, the experimental nature of the Ugaritic alphabet is shown by its inclusion of novelties not known in any other Semitic alphabet. Ugaritic itself became simplified: a few texts from Ras Shamra are written in a 22-letter alphabet, as are some six texts found in Canaanite territory. They are all late thirteenth or twelfth century BC and therefore perhaps conform to the shortness of the Phoenician alphabet, for possibly the original Ugaritic alphabet was too large for Canaanite because it was also designed to write Hurrian and other languages spoken at cosmopolitan Ugarit.

The Greek alphabet

Controversy surrounds not only the date at which the Greeks borrowed the Phoenician alphabet but also how and where they borrowed it. There are very many more archaic Greek inscriptions extant than there are Phoenician, so that comparison between a wealth of variants covering a wide area on the one hand (Greek) with a few inscriptions from a limited area on the other (Phoenician) makes conclusions very unreliable.

Many early Greek letters compare with very archaic Phoenician forms ranging from about 1000 to 850 BC (the Ahiram and early Senjirli inscriptions). These strict epigraphic comparisons have led to recent theories that Greeks may have become familiar with the Semitic alphabet as early as 1200 BC and copied Proto-Canaanite forms. Even the arguments that Greek *delta* and *kappa* could not have been borrowed before their Phoenician prototypes of about 850 BC have lost their weight in view of such discoveries as the 'Isbet Sartah ostrakon. But from the Greek side the evidence suggests the mid-eighth century BC for the beginning of writing and it so happens that the course of development of script in Phoenicia between 850–750 BC is so poorly known, especially with regard to archaisms and provincialisms, that form comparisons are in many cases not secure indicators.

A further important factor is historical. While for some years there have been strongly held opinions that the Greeks learned the script (perhaps at one centre or at least with some uniformity) on their trading ventures in Syria, beginning on archaeological evidence in the mid-eighth century BC, the opinion that they learned it from Phoenician traders settled in various parts of Greece (such as Rhodes, Cos, Crete) is now receiving greater consideration, especially since a Phoenician inscription of 900 BC has now been found in a Cretan Geometric tomb at Knossos—the first early inscription to have been found in the Aegean. At present no theory of early borrowing, then later 'reborrowing', seems satisfactory and the answer to 'archaisms' probably lies in regional differences. But other evidence suggests that the Greeks learned the script formally, not only by sporadic contact with merchants. At present the former idea that the Greeks learned the alphabet during the 'Orientalizing' period of their archaic culture (750–650 BC) has become less certain.

Nor is it as evident, as once thought, that the Greeks were responsible for the spread of writing in other areas of the Mediterranean. From its inception Etruscan writing appears to have been only partially alphabetic and in any case the earliest contact with Greek at Ischia is no earlier than Phoenician and Aramaean graffiti now found on that site. In Spain, although there was no slavish borrowing of the Phoenician alphabet, the earliest 'Tartessian' script appears to have begun in a Phoenician ambience about 750 BC.

Sinaitic	Ugaritic	South-Semitic	
			ʼ
			b
			g
			d
			ḥ
			w
			z
			(h)ḥ
			ṭ
			y
			k
			l
			m
			n
			s
			ʿ
			p
			ṣ
			q
			r
			š
			t

Ugarit compared with Sinaitic and South Semitic signs.

India

Mohenjo-daro in Sind, one of the major sites in the Indus valley discovered in the 1920s.

The Indus Civilization

Arthur Cotterell

Discovery and origins

In the 1920s discoveries of mounds in the Indus valley led to the excavation of two large ruined cities of which no mention was to be found in ancient records. These major sites–upwards of three miles (5 km) in circumference during their heyday–were Mohenjo-daro in Sind and Harappa in western Punjab. They were both situated on old river courses and contained many-storeyed, palatial, solidly built houses, which were supplied with excellent wells, drains, bathrooms and toilets. In 1931 another city at Chanhu-daro, closer to the mouth of the Indus river, was dug by the Indian Archaeological Survey and the existence of a pre-Aryan civilization, widely spread over the northwest of the subcontinent, was firmly established. Previous ideas about ancient Indian history had to be revised and with them the world map of ancient civilizations.

Knowledge of the new civilization is still far from complete. Over one hundred sites have been identified of which some five were obviously cities, but to date no scholar has succeeded in the convincing decipherment of the Indus script. The brief legends on seals, potsherds and copper pieces remain a mystery. From archaeological evidence–our sole source of information–it is far from certain who the originators of the Indus civilization were. Systematic excavation has hardly started and the chief site, Harappa, was plundered between 1856 and 1919 for building materials. During the construction of the Lahore-Multan railway line hundreds of thousands of ancient kiln-burned bricks were used to provide a firm footing for the track across muddy lowlands. At Mohenjo-daro deep soundings have recently shown occupation still continuing to great depths in the flood silt. Lower levels at Kalibangan, a city situated to the southeast of Harappa on the now-dry Ghaggar river, indicate a pre-Indus culture of some sophistication. The settlement was fortified from the beginning of the occupation and within the walled area there were mud-brick houses with ovens, water-storage pits, and drains. The inhabitants made a wide range of earthenware vases and bowls as well as bull figurines, beads, and toy cartwheels. They were acquainted with copper, though tiny blades of chalcedony and agate were also used. Their economy depended on agriculture, which would have been assisted by flood irrigation. No cereals were uncovered during excavation but a ploughed field leaves little doubt that farming was combined with animal husbandry. The contrast between this pre-Indus cultural phase and the later Harappan or Indus style lies not only in the pottery forms, the size and materials of blades, the size of bricks and the layout of houses, but more in the scale of urbanization and the advent of literacy. Like Mohenjo-daro and Harappa, the Indus civilization city at Kalibangan seems to have sprung up

Chronology of Ancient India

2500 BC	The Indus Civilization (before 2400–1800)
1500 BC	The Aryan Invasion
	Composition of *Rig Veda* (1300–1100)
1000 BC	
	Aryans in Ganges valley (800)
500 BC	Life of the Buddha (sixth century)
	Darius I annexes Indus valley (c539)
	Alexander in Punjab (326)
	Candragupta founds Mauryan dynasty (324)
	Aśoka (c270–232)
	Accession of Kaniska (78)
	Candra Gupta I founds Gupta dynasty (320)
AD 500	The White Huns start their invasion (450)

fully planned. We have here the superimposition of a complex yet uniform urban culture on a possibly abandoned town. Elsewhere the lack of a break in the occupation of sites underlines the intrusive nature of the Indus civilization.

The explanation for the foundation of the Indus

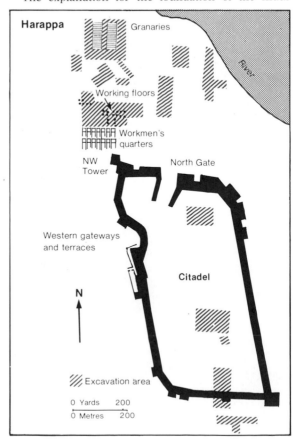

Harappa

Granaries

River

Working floors

Workmen's quarters

NW Tower

North Gate

Western gateways and terraces

Citadel

N

Excavation area

0 Yards 200

0 Metres 200

settlements before 2400 BC is a matter for debate. Diffusionists argue that the idea of civilization arrived from Mesopotamia and facilitated the transformation of the earlier village-towns into full-scale cities. Other theorists contend that they were the culmination of a process of concentration that began with the first semi-permanent villages of the highlands to the north and west of the Indus valley. Population pressure and a growing technological ability are said to have encouraged a shift down on to the flood plain, where people were gathered near citadels because of the opportunities and advantages in the organized exploitation of the environment. A hierarchical society was the solution to the problems of settled life in the valley and the Indus culture was the mature form it assumed.

The sites

Sumer and Egypt had long emerged into a civilized way of living at the time the Indus people built their remarkable cities. Egypt had been unified for seven centuries and the Early Dynastic period in Sumer was over four centuries old. Only China, the isolated centre of development in East Asia, and Minoan Crete and Mycenaean Greece, the genesis of European cultural traditions, were later starters in the Old World. Yet of these four main cradles of civilization the Indus valley was by far the largest in geographical area. It covered more than Egypt and Mesopotamia taken together and its frontiers reached well beyond the watershed of the Indus river. Overall the cultural area was about 1100 miles (1770 km) from east to west and 800 miles (1290 km) from north to south. To the archaeologist the

Ancient India.

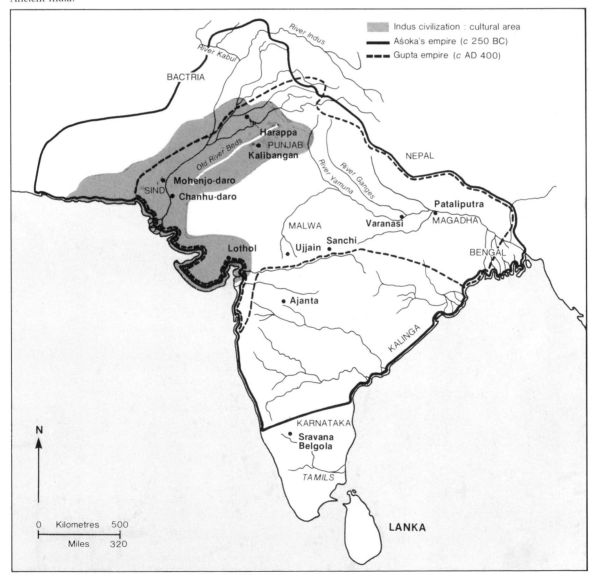

177

Mohenjo-Daro

Citadel

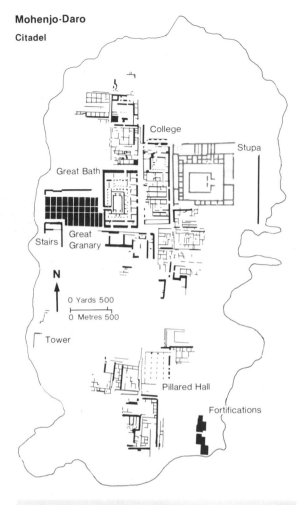

College

Stupa

Great Bath

Great Granary

Stairs

N

0 Yards 500
0 Metres 500

Tower

Pillared Hall

Fortifications

Ruins of Mohenjo-daro, showing the elaborate public drainage system which embraced all parts of the city.

striking feature is its uniformity. There were no great changes between c2400 and c1800BC, the zenith of the cities: the Indus people even outdid the Egyptians in their conservatism.

Indus cities were built on a regular grid plan of straight streets, unlike the older settlements of Egypt and Sumer. The chief thoroughfares ran from north to south and the intersecting streets and lanes ran at right angles to them. At Kalibangan the principal north-south street measured 22 ft (6.7 m) in width, at Mohenjo-daro 30 ft (9.1 m). The cross streets and lanes, half the width of the narrower streets running from north to south, were unpaved and dusty, but a drainage system embraced all parts of the cities. Single-room dwellings at intersections suggest the presence of night watchmen or police. Private houses at Harappa and Mohenjo-daro were constructed with kiln-burned bricks; at Kalibangan and the port of Lothol most residences were built in mud brick and kiln-burned bricks were reserved for drains, wells, baths and quays. Houses were laid out around an inner courtyard; no windows opened on to public places. Staircases and thick ground-floor walls reveal that they had two storeys, possibly three, and it is likely that wooden balconies overhung the courtyard. Each house possessed a well and its bathroom and toilet were connected to the public drains. These brick culverts, as the English archaeologist, Sir Mortimer Wheeler (1890–1976), remarked, were:

'unparalleled in pre-classical times and unapproached in the non-westernized Orient today. At intervals were brick-built manholes where from time to time the municipal sanitary squads cleared the accumulations, in some places leaving an adjacent heap of debris for modern rediscovery. Into the drains, or alternatively into constructed soak-pits or into jars pierced and used for the same purpose, waste was discharged from the houses through earthenware pipes and carefully built chutes, which were sometimes stepped to check the descent and so to prevent overflow and splashing in the public ways.'

Such regulation of city life can only reflect an authoritarian government. And the uniformity of planning in both street layout and drainage systems over so wide a territory must imply a unified state.

Across from the walled residential sections already described, and located invariably to the west, stood fortified citadels. The citadel of Mohenjo-daro, like that of Harappa, is situated on an artificial mound rising to about 40 ft (12 m) in the northwest. Constructed of mud, mud brick and kiln-burned bricks, the mound was once protected against flood by massive embankments and against enemy attack by strongly fortified towers and walls. Even today it is the eroded citadel that catches the visitor's eye. A ruined Buddhist stupa, a reliquary dating from the second century AD, can be seen on its top from miles around. Clearly the public buildings once standing here dominated the city. Of those so far excavated, the most famous is the Great Tank, or Bath. The building consists of an outer series of rooms on three sides and an inner colonnade around the pool itself. From two ends there are steps leading down into the pool, which measures approximately 39 × 23 ft (11.8 × 7 m) and is about 8 ft (2.4 m) deep. Much effort went into making the pool watertight. The kiln-burned bricks of the sides and bottom were set in gypsum mortar, and they were backed by an inch-thick layer of bitumen, a mud-brick wall, a rammed clay filling, and finally an outer wall of kiln-burned bricks. Water was supplied from a brick-lined well dug in one of the outer rooms on the eastern side and removed by means of a drainage hole leading away westward. The corbelled drain, 2 ft (0.6 m) wide and 6 ft (1.8 m) high, had a manhole and was spacious enough to allow cleaners to work inside it. Immediately north of the Great Tank, across a lane, was a structure containing eight bathrooms, measuring about 9 × 6 ft (2.7 × 1.8 m) each, with elaborate drains. The users of these individual baths either lived or worked on the floor above. The arrangement hints strongly of lustration. Quite possibly the users were members of a priesthood, or at least a superior social group, who carried out their ceremonial ablutions in private, whereas the general public was obliged to wash in the Great Tank.

To the north and east of the Great Tank are numerous walls, stairways, passages, courtyards, and drains. As yet, the purpose of the buildings these once formed is still obscure. They may have been occupied by priests, administrators or soldiers. We are better informed about the western area. Here the great granary of Mohenjo-daro was sited. Once a wooden superstructure rested on 27 rectangular brickwork supports, thereby allowing air to circulate freely beneath the stored corn. The importance of this agricultural reserve in the city's economy can be gauged by the position of the granary within the fortified citadel. Food storage was crucial to the social order. The authorities would have paid employees, free or enslaved, in kind. They would have had far-reaching interests in agriculture and commerce. The concentration of surplus food in the granary, like the harbour constructed for trading ships at Lothol, indicates a tightly controlled redistribution system. A trading class doubtless existed in the Indus period, but the archaeological testimony points expressly to the dominance of the state. At Harappa, where the food storage facilities lie to the north of the citadel, excavation has revealed a double granary, five rows of working platforms and two lines of barracklike dwellings. The area, patently designed as a whole, implies that government slaves ground flour for the city's inhabitants.

South of the Mohenjo-daro Great Tank is another striking building, sometimes called the Assembly Hall. It consists of a pillared room almost 90 ft (27 m) square, with an entrance in the middle of the north wall. Twenty rectangular pillars approximately 5 × 3 ft (1.5 × 0.9 m) held up the roof. Associated with this place of assembly are the badly damaged ruins of a finely paved room and a

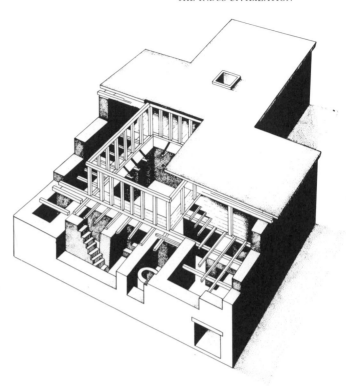

Above: Reconstruction of a house at Mohenjo-daro. Below: Reconstruction of the Great Bath at Mohenjo-daro, stage I.

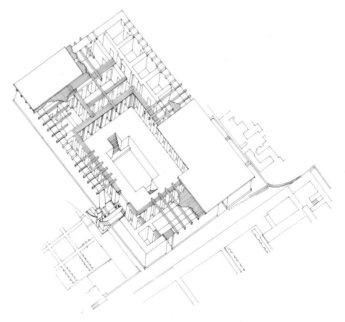

walled courtyard. Possibly the building was an audience chamber.

Equally uncertain is the relationship of the citadel and lower town at Mohenjo-daro. A broad sandy area between them suggests ancient flooding, or another explanation might be the presence of a small lake, deliberately retained in the planning of the settlement. If this were the case, the depression across the lower part of the residential section could have been a canal. The riverside locations of Indus cities bring such arrangements within the bounds of probability.

Economy and society

The Indus civilization relied on agriculture, the majority of the people living in villages clustered around the cities. With the aid of silt-bearing floods and irrigation the farmers cultivated wheat, barley, vegetables, fruit, and sesame as well as mustard for oil. In the vicinity of Lothol rice cultivation had been mastered, a crop of untold significance in the later history of India. Moreover cotton was grown in the Indus valley several centuries before it was in Egypt. Animals included sheep, humped and humpless cattle, buffalo and pigs. Bones and seal engravings point also to the domestication of the cat, dog, camel, horse and elephant.

The farmers most probably handed over to the public granaries a large part of their crops. It is not impossible that ownership of land was restricted, the tillers of soil perhaps being in the direct employ of the city authorities. Public works in the cities and the countryside may have been paid for in wage rations, or have resulted from compulsory labour service. The vagaries of river courses, flooding which could cause famine instead of a bumper harvest, was offset by the storage of cereals. Yet the cutting down of trees for fuel and timber, and the increased grazing of grass may have exacerbated natural conditions. Mohenjo-daro was repaired nine times after flooding.

Craftsmen produced goods for both home markets and foreign trade. Potters turned sturdy red ware, often painted with black floral or geometric designs. Finds of terracotta and stone figurines display the sculptor's remarkable art: human portraiture reached a very high standard in the few surviving pieces. Though the entire range of Bronze Age weapons and tools were cast, metallurgy seems less inspired, and weapons unearthed at Mohenjo-daro are comparatively weak, suggesting that the Indus cities relied on archers firing from the tops of battlements. Baked-clay missiles of two weights, 6 oz (170 g) and 12 oz (340 g) have been found in the citadel at Mohenjo-daro.

Trade was extensive in raw materials and small luxury goods. Lothol had a kiln-burned brick dockyard measuring 730 × 120 ft (222 × 36 m). Merchant ships entered at high tide through a specially designed channel. On the quay stood warehouses ready to discharge export items and store imported goods. From this port high-prowed vessels sailed to the island of Bahrein in the Persian Gulf. This was Tilmun, the legendary Sumerian paradise. Here, at the close of the third millennium BC, a walled trading port exchanged

articles from West Asia and India, but the influence of the Indus merchants was stronger as their system of weights prevailed. The social standing of merchants in the Indus valley civilization is less clear. They dwelled in the excellently constructed houses found in the residential sections of the lower towns of Indus cities, yet they seem to have led unostentatious lives. Both priestly pomp and wealthy display were notably absent. The rulers themselves must have decreed the standardization of daily life. The Indus preoccupation with water

The mother-goddess, precursor of the Hindu Devi, the Indus equivalent of Inanna or Isis.

and personal cleanliness suggests a priest king, or at least a monarchy supported by a priesthood. Not only were Indian kings sprinkled rather than anointed, as in West Asia and Europe, but also the Great Tank of Mohenjo-daro appears to have prefigured the holy bathing places of later Hinduism.

Religious beliefs

The cosmopolitan population of the ancient Indus valley subscribed to a variety of beliefs. The lack of imposing temples supposes worship at family altars, and a number of small images in clay, stone and bronze have been recovered at Mohenjo-daro. Conspicuous among them are representations of a mother goddess, the Indus equivalent of Inanna or Isis. As the universal mother, she bestowed fertility on plants, animals and men. Her cult is especially represented by carved sexual symbols: upright phallic stones, denoting her consort, and circular stones with a hollow centre, representing her own teeming womb. They may be the primitive prototypes of the Hindu symbols of the *lingam* and the *yoni*, which are common today in the temples of Shiva and his goddess Devi. The arch-ascetic of the Hindu pantheon, Shiva himself, would appear to be inscribed on a broken seal found in the lower town. A three-faced god sits on a throne in the attitude of a yogi with legs bent double heel to heel. He is wearing a buffalo-horn headdress, bangles, bracelets, a double belt and a triangular collar. Around him are a tiger, an elephant, a buck and a rhinoceros—Shiva perhaps in the form of Pasupati, lord of the Animals, or Vanaspati, lord of the Wilderness. A second seal engraving shows a figure in a similar posture with kneeling devotees to the right and left, and behind these, two serpent-divinities. In both cases we can assume that depicted is an ascetic ideal, a forerunner of the saints and sages of historic times. Scholars are not agreed that there may have been a resurgence of old beliefs dating from the Indus period in the subsequent displacement of Vedic deities worshipped by the Aryan invaders, and the triumph of Vishnu, Shiva and Devi over Indra, Brahma and their kin. Yet it is generally accepted that in the three-faced Indus god are discernible the attributes of Shiva Mahayogi, prince of the Yogis.

A portrait of a priestly ruler may exist in the famous statuette of stone and paste, recovered from Mohenjo-daro. The impressive figure is draped in a robe that is drawn over the left shoulder but leaves the right bare. Although the decoration on the garment recalls Mesopotamian patterns, the uncovered shoulder was still a way of showing reverence in India during the lifetime of the Buddha. Furthermore, the eyes are half-closed as though in meditation: the priest-like figure has withdrawn his gaze from worldly affairs. The religious ceremonies he would have overseen included sacrifices to the powers within trees, streams and fire. At Lothol and Kalibangan there are examples of fire altars, either round or square in shape, and enclosed by thin mud-brick walls. Presumably he officiated also at the burial of the dead, though at present our knowledge of Indus

The famous statuette of the Mohenjo-daro priest. The uncovered shoulder showed reverence in India during the lifetime of the Buddha.

cemeteries is slight. No evidence of inhumation has been found at either Mohenjo-daro or Chanhu-daro.

The end of the Indus civilization

Radiocarbon dates for the Indus civilization offer a beginning some time before 2400 BC and a termination by 1700 BC.

Although these recent calculations have shortened the 'millennium' of the Indus cities, the unexplored lower levels at Mohenjo-daro may well push back the foundation date again. The decline and disappearance of the civilization is never likely to be so firmly fixed. In approaching the causes of its fall we have to exercise a degree of caution. On the one hand there is archaeological testimony of internal decay; in the final centuries at Mohenjo-daro a marked lowering of civic standards took place. On the other hand, we have the Aryan invaders occupying the Punjab, the land of the Five Rivers, and their traditions of military conquest. They were in control of the Indus valley around 1500 BC. They may have been a source of anxiety to the Indus people from a much earlier date.

Degeneration was in progress at most Indus valley sites after 1900 BC. Houses ceased to be so meticulously planned, and the chief concern was the building up of the city level against renewed flooding. At Mohenjo-daro the number of inhabitants declined from an estimated peak of around 40,000. In the ultimate phase of occupation buildings were of flimsy construction, usually making use of old bricks. Underlying the decline of the city was probably a deterioration of the surrounding landscape. Overgrazing of the grass cover and the clearing of forests could have inaugurated changes in local geography. In addition to these difficulties for the

Indus seal. As yet no scholar has convincingly deciphered the script.

hard-pressed farmer might have been the consequences of neglected irrigation works or an alteration in the flow and course of the river. Certainly the city itself had to cope with a series of abnormally high floods. The picture, however, is not the same for settlements on the eastern and southeastern fringes of the cultural area. Around Lothol and sites near the Jumna river, Indus civilization was transformed into separate regional cultures, presumably as the great cities of the Indus valley lost their influence and dwindled away.

Into the depressed Indus valley poured the fierce Aryans. The date of their first arrival in the Punjab is unknown, but nomad pressure could have been long-standing. The 200 years between the end of the Indus cities and the Aryan invasion is not an immense span of time. Their raids would have been sufficient to complete the ruin of the cities, if the irrigation system was a casualty. They may have shattered dams deliberately. Indra is said to have freed the waters by rolling away stones like wagonwheels. The Aryans would have been more interested in grazing land than in inundated fields for crops. Above all, as Purandara, 'the fort-destroyer', Indra gave them victory over peoples living in strongholds, walled towns and fortified cities. The age of the Indus civilization was truly over.

The Aryan Invasion of India

T. Burrow

The invasion itself

About the middle of the second millennium BC there occurred a major invasion of the Indian subcontinent by tribes calling themselves Arya and speaking an Indo-European language. Their immediate place of origin was eastern Iran, and their closest relatives were the Iranian tribes who later came to occupy the whole of Iran as well as large stretches of central Eurasia. The Aryan invaders of India were responsible for the downfall of the Indus civilization which had previously been in occupation of Sind and the Punjab, and had to some extent extended outside this area. The newcomers colonized and settled the areas that they had conquered on a massive scale, and during the ensuing centuries they progressively extended their dominion towards the east and south. Wherever they settled they imposed their language, and it is probable that by 500 BC Aryan speech had become the predominant language over most of the area in which Indo-Aryan languages are now spoken.

The Aryan homeland

The Aryan invasion of the Indian subcontinent is not recorded in historical documents and it is established as an historical fact primarily by means of linguistic comparison. The discovery that the Sanskrit language was related to most of the languages of Europe formed the starting point for the science of comparative philology, and led ultimately to the development of modern linguistics in general. It also necessitated the conclusion that there had been this Aryan invasion, since at no time could a case be made that the Indo-European languages had originated in India. The question as to where the Indo-Aryans originally came from is bound up with that of the original home of the Indo-European languages. This subject has been under discussion since the western discovery of Sanskrit and the establishment of the Indo-European family of languages, and it will no doubt long continue to be discussed. An earlier theory of a central Asian home has now generally been abandoned in favour of a location in the continent of Europe. Opinions vary between fixing the original homeland in central Europe or in south Russia, north of the Caucasus, the home of the so-called Kurgan culture. The latter location continues to enjoy considerable popularity, but it suffers from the fatal objection that among the manifold languages of the Caucasus region no certain traces of ancient (i.e. pre-Iranian) Indo-European have been established. For this reason the central European theory is to be preferred.

Some indication of the point of departure of the Indo-

Iranians can be gained from the fact that Balto-Slavonic is the branch of Indo-European to which Indo-Iranian appears to be most closely related. This would indicate a somewhat northerly position among the Indo-European dialects existing before the period of the separation of Indo-Iranian from the rest of Indo-European. From this original position wide-ranging migration brought the Indo-Aryans eventually to India, and the closely related Iranians to Iran and to large tracts of central Eurasia. As a result of these migrations, and of the ensuing territorial acquisitions, the Indo-Aryans and the Iranians between them had, by the beginning of the first millennium BC, come to control a territory vastly exceeding in extent that of all the other Indo-European groups combined.

The route to India

The route taken by these migrations has long been a subject of controversy, just as has the location of the original home of Indo-European. One theory takes the Indo-Aryans, and after them the Iranians, over the Caucasus and then eastwards to India and Iran respectively. The other proposes an eastward route across the plains of Eurasia, north of the Caspian sea, followed by a turn to the south, with the Indo-Aryan section moving first, and making its way ultimately to India, followed by the Iranians turning westward to occupy the whole of Iran, but also retaining control of large stretches of Central Asia. There are also combinations of the two theories.

The most significant evidence concerning the migration route is furnished by the existence of Aryan loanwords in the Finno-Ugrian languages. A number of these, for phonological reasons (for example Finnish *sata*, 'hundred', and related words), must be ascribed to the primitive Indo-Iranian period. By general agreement the original homeland of the Finno-Ugrian languages lay in the region of the middle Volga and the Ural mountains, and the presence of such loanwords in them provides conclusive evidence in favour of the northern route. The Indo-Iranians were not the first Indo-Europeans to take this route of migration since they were preceded at an earlier period by the ancestors of the Tocharians who were settled still further to the east in Chinese Turkestan. Certain elements of the Finno-Ugrian vocabulary, which have alternatively been explained either as evidence for the genetic relationship of Indo-European and Finno-Ugrian, or as loanwords into Finno-Ugrian from primitive Indo-European, may on the other hand reflect this earlier eastward migration of Indo-Europeans.

To this extent the prehistoric migrations of the Aryans can be deduced from linguistic relationships. Documentary evidence on this subject first appears in cuneiform tablets from West Asia, notably from records of the kingdom of the Hittites. These provide evidence of an Aryan dynasty ruling over the Hurrian kingdom of Mitanni for a period beginning in the fifteenth century BC. A further extension of Aryan influence is indicated by Aryan proper names occurring in documents over a wider area. This linguistic material is still not very extensive, but this does not detract from its great significance. Apart from proper names it consists of a number of words including some technical terms connected with horse racing, and, of particular significance, the names of certain gods who can be identified with deities of the *Rig Veda* (Indra, Mitra, Varuṇa, Nāsatya). It has now come to be generally agreed that these traces of Aryan language are to be connected, not with primitive Indo-Iranian, nor with Iranian, but quite specifically with Indo-Aryan.

This West Asian evidence has been used to support the theory of an Aryan migration over the Caucasus, and then eastwards over the Iranian plateau in the direction of India. This is not feasible for the simple reason that the Aryans formed the ruling class in a country that was mainly populated by native Hurrians. In this region Aryan manpower did not exist in sufficient quantity to occupy and colonize the extensive areas which eventually came under Aryan rule. Nor is there any evidence of Aryans being settled in that part of south Russia that lies immediately to the north of the Caucasus at this early period. As far as can be ascertained, the first branch of Aryans to appear in this region were the Iranian Scyths in the eighth century BC. The conclusion to be drawn from this West Asian evidence is that instead of there having been, as previously assumed, one Indo-Aryan movement of migration from their intermediate base in eastern Iran, there were two taking place at the same period. While one branch of Proto-Indoaryans was moving eastwards into India, others of the same group were moving westwards across northern Iran in the opposite direction. The furthest point west reached by them was the Hurrian country where for a period they exercised a temporary domination.

The arrival of the Iranians

Thus for a time the area dominated by the Indo-Aryans and the Proto-Indoaryans was a continuous stretch of territory from the Punjab to the frontiers of West Asia. This situation was soon altered by a southward migration of the Iranians, which effectively split in two the area previously occupied by their predecessors. Tension between the two groups found expression in the religious revolution preached by Zoroaster, who is most likely to have lived in the twelfth or eleventh century BC. In the new religion the gods of the Indo-Aryans, known as *daivas*, were declared anathema. There followed a western movement of Iranians into Media and the rest of Iran, which, to judge by our sources, took place about 900 BC. As a result of this, Indo-Aryan territory became confined to the Indian subcontinent.

The settlement of India

The process of Indo-Aryan invasion and settlement has not yet been plotted by archaeological discoveries. On the other hand much can be learned about it from the oldest literary document of India, the *Rig Veda*. This document does not contain any reference showing that the Aryans retained a memory of their migration from a foreign land, but it contains numerous references to the struggles that took place between them and the pre-Aryan inhabitants of the occupied territory, who are known as Dāsa or Dasyu. Such battles, and the destruction of forts or cities, are most frequently mentioned in connection with the god Indra, who, as a result, receives the epithet *Purandara*, 'the destroyer of cities'. The god of fire, Agni, is also prominent in this respect as a result of his part in destroying the cities of the Dasyu. One verse (*Rig Veda*, 7.5.3) is particularly explicit on this point: 'Through fear of you (Agni) the dark people went away, not giving battle, leaving behind their possessions, when, O Vaiśvānara, burning brightly for Pūru, and destroying the cities, you did shine.'

Between the original Aryan invasion and the time of the composition of the Vedic hymns a considerable period must have elapsed. A sign of this is the fact that the terms Dāsa and Daysu, which properly referred to the pre-Aryan inhabitants of the occupied land, are often used to denote demons whom the gods are portrayed as fighting, showing that the recollection of the actual events was becoming blurred. The same conclusion is derived from the fact that the actual migration is no longer remembered.

Linguistic arguments point in the same direction. Important phonetic changes took place in the language between the time of the migration and the composition of the *Rig Veda*. Valuable light is thrown on this point by the Kafiri languages of Afghanistan. These are not, as has sometimes been thought, a third branch of Indo-Iranian, but they descend from the Proto-Indoaryan form of the language as it existed before the changes that took place in the period between the migration and the composition of the *Rig Veda*. Interesting conclusions can also be drawn from the treatment in Vedic and Sanskrit of the consonants *r* and *l*, from which the conclusion can be drawn that there were two main phases of the migration. In the first of these Indo-European *l* was preserved; in the second it had been converted to *r*, a trait shared by Iranian. The latter state of affairs is predominant in the *Rig Veda*, while the later language represents a compromise between the two.

Before the Aryan invasion the territory occupied by them had been inhabited by the creators of the Indus civilization. It is natural to conclude that the Aryan invasion was responsible for the downfall of this civilization, though some scepticism about this has been expressed in various quarters. In spite of this there cannot be much doubt that the Aryan invaders were in fact responsible for the destruction of the previous civilization. There is only a small gap between the date that archaeologists have proposed for the termination of the Indus civilization (c1700 BC) and that suggested above for the Aryan immigration (c1500 BC), but neither of these estimates is sufficiently precise to make this a serious obstacle. The possibility that some other invaders, before the Aryans, destroyed the Indus civilization can be ruled out, since there is no evidence for this whatever.

The destruction of the Indus civilization by the new invaders was remarkably complete, and most of the identified Indus sites ceased to be occupied after this period. The Aryans were aware of the numerous ruined Indus sites among which they lived, and they referred to them by the term *arma, armaka*, 'ruined site, ruins'. Among the references to these the following is of particular significance: 'The people to whom these ruined sites, lacking posts, formerly belonged, these many settlements widely distributed, they, O Vaiśvānara, having been expelled by thee, have migrated to another land.'

Early Imperial India

A. L. Basham

The Mauryas

In 326 BC Alexander of Macedon crossed the Indus in the last stage of his conquest of the Persian empire. He temporarily occupied the Punjab and Sind—most of modern Pakistan—but problems of supply and the failing morale of his troops compelled him to return to Babylon. He left a few garrisons in the conquered provinces, but his death in 323 BC put an end to his ambition of a worldwide Hellenic empire, and by 317 BC the last Greek troops had left the Indian subcontinent, their generals drawn back by the news of the strife between Alexander's ambitious successors.

The invasion of Alexander made so slight an impression upon India that it is not remembered in any Indian source, and its immediate effects may have been very slight on India as a whole, though at a later date they proved considerable. From the historian's point of view, however, the Indian conquests of Alexander throw a little light on an otherwise dark period of the history of the subcontinent, giving us some picture of the state of affairs in northern India at the time. Most of the area of modern Pakistan was divided into numerous small states, some kingdoms, others tribal republics. The most powerful ruler among these was Porus (Sanskrit, Pūru), who fought Alexander bravely, was defeated and became, in the manner of the good *ksatriya* chief, the loyal ally of his conqueror.

Beyond the Punjab to the east, most of the Gangetic basin, and an uncertain area outside it, were in the control of a king of a dynasty called Nanda, who, we are told, was hated by his subjects. Alexander wanted to go on from the Beas river and attack the Nanda, but was dissuaded by his generals. The Nandas, who had their capital at Pāṭaliputra (modern Patna), represented the penultimate phase of a process that had been going on since the time of the Buddha 200 years previously–the steady expansion of the small kingdom of Magadha (southern Bihar) at the expense of numerous other kingdoms and republican oligarchies until it had become the mightiest power in India, the acknowledged overlord of the main area of the subcontinent north of the Vindhya mountains.

A young adventurer of the clan of the Mauryas, named Candragupta, managed to put an end to the Nanda dynasty and gain the throne of Pāṭaliputra. He was known to the Greeks, and according to certain later and rather dubious classical sources he had actually entered the service of Alexander, with whom he quarrelled to become the leader of the resistance movement against the Macedonian garrisons. Even if these stories are exaggerated, it seems that he took advantage of the power vacuum caused by the retreat of Alexander to consolidate his hold on the northwest, whence he marched down the Ganges (Ganga) and overthrew the last Nanda king, whose name is given in classical sources as Agrammes and Xandrames. The exact date of the start of Candragupta's reign is uncertain, but it fell between the years 324 and 317 BC. He reigned for 24 years.

A strong Indian tradition, not confirmed by classical sources, associates Candragupta's accession to power with a brilliant adviser, the brahman Kauṭilya or Cāṇakya, who guided the young man to greatness, and trained him in all the mysteries of politics, becoming his chief minister on his accession to power. Kauṭilya was the reputed author of a book on statecraft, the *Arthaśāstra*, which has survived to this day. Though there is very good evidence that other and later hands helped to write it and it was much edited after the Mauryan period, its kernel may be a text dating back to this time, perhaps composed by Kauṭilya himself. It gives us much insight into the norms of the political life of early India; though it should not be taken as an exact picture of the organization of the Mauryan empire, it no doubt throws some light on it. Another important source is an account of India in Greek, written by a certain Megasthenes, who spent some time at the court of Candragupta, in the latter part of his reign. This account became the standard classical textbook on India and things Indian, and was quoted by many later writers in Greek and Latin. Unfortunately the original text has not survived, but numerous quotations and paraphrases give us some idea of how India appeared about 300 BC to an intelligent Westerner–the first of many foreigners to leave a surviving account of India. With the aid of the fragments of Megasthenes and the *Arthaśāstra* of Kauṭilya we can get a fairly clear picture of the political and social life of this period.

Even in the time of the Buddha the small kingdom of Magadha was beginning to evolve into a kind of bureaucracy, more tightly controlled by the centre than the other states of the time. The stages of its evolution are far from clear, but, by the time of Candragupta, most of north India formed a single empire controlled by a large corps of salaried officials who held office at the king's pleasure. Most of the smaller subordinate kingdoms had disappeared, and had become imperial provinces governed by officers of the Mauryan state. The state was involved in many aspects of industry and trade, and it promoted agriculture by irrigation projects and the planned settlement of uncultivated land. This was not wholly due to a care for the welfare of the people, since the tax on cultivated land, which formed a kind of rent, was at all times the main source of income to the Indian ruler. Thus he took steps to encourage agriculture out of enlightened self-interest, as well as in order to 'please the people', which was theoretically his most important function after his primary one of protection.

Socially, the system of four classes (*varṇa*), which had evolved over the last 600 years, prevailed. It was not, however, as rigid as it later became, and intermarriage still occurred sometimes. The caste system as it existed in later times was only in an incipient stage, and the brahmanical norms of family and social life were by no means universally followed, even among the higher classes. Thus the *Arthaśāstra* allowed the divorce and remarriage of widows, which were not approved of in the later *Dharmaśāstras*, compiled when brahmanic orthodoxy had become more powerful.

The brahmans had dominated the religious life of the western Gangetic area, but they now had many rivals who contended for the support of the laity. An important class of merchants had appeared, and these were the chief patrons of the new ascetic movements, chief of which at this time were Jainism and Ājīvikism. The naked ascetics of these two sects and several others wandered from place to place during most of the year, begging their bread from the laity and teaching their doctrines to all who wanted to listen. The Buddhists may have been less important at this time, though they too were already a significant factor in religious life. All these sects preached *ahiṃsā* or non-violence, with its corollary of vegetarianism, and they opposed the claim of the brahmans to have the monopoly of truth and wisdom. The Maurya rulers, like the Nandas before them, appear to have been favourable to the new sects, and gave them liberal patronage.

Candragupta considerably expanded the empire which he had wrested from the Nandas. Towards the end of his reign he came to blows with Seleucus Nicator (*c*356–281 BC), who had gained control of most of Alexander's Asian possessions; as a result Seleucus recognized him as ruler of all Alexander's Indian conquests (roughly modern Pakistan together with the eastern half of Afghanistan). He was the lord of an immense empire reaching from Kandahar in the west to the mouths of the Ganges in the east; and there is some evidence that his power was also felt in the Deccan. Megasthenes gives us the impression of a strong-willed autocrat, just but stern, living in constant fear of assassination, and keeping a tight finger on the pulse of his ministers, courtiers and subjects through a well-organized system of espionage. The Greek traveller was deeply impressed by the prosperity of India in the latter part of Candragupta's reign, and remarked that the people as a whole were proud, upstanding, healthy folk, of more than average height—a judgment different from that of many later visitors to India.

Archaeology tells us little about the early Mauryan period. In most parts of the Ganges valley good building stone had to be brought from long distances. On the other hand, hard tropical timber was easily available, since the primaeval forest covered a much wider area than at present. Therefore wood was used for almost all building. The splendid wooden palace of Pāṭalipatra, where Candragupta is said to have changed his bedroom every night for fear of assassination, has long since vanished, but some of the massive timber fortifications have been excavated, still in fairly good condition.

According to a strong Jaina tradition there was a great famine at the end of Candragupta's reign. The king, no doubt believing, according to the general view in India at the time, that the famine had been caused by his own sins and shortcomings as a ruler, abdicated the throne, became a Jain, and died in the manner of saintly Jaina monks, by slow self-inflicted starvation, at Sravana Belgola, now in the southern state of Karnataka. The legend of Candragupta's death, whether true or false, gives evidence of the steady penetration of northern influence into the south of India, a development indicated also by numerous brief inscriptions in caves, showing that they were occupied by ascetics of the northern orders.

Candragupta was succeeded by his son Bindusāra, in 300 BC or a little later. We know little of the events of his reign, but it is clear that he kept the Mauryan empire intact and probably expanded it towards the south. By now it was the largest empire in the contemporary world, in touch with the Hellenistic rulers of the Mediterranean and West Asia. This was a time of economic expansion, with constantly increasing areas of land coming under the plough, and the class of merchants growing increasingly influential.

About 270 BC Bindusāra died and a dynastic dispute of some kind followed his death. The throne was seized by his son Aśoka, or Ashoka, who ousted all rival princes and began to reign in the manner of his father and grandfather. According to the Buddhist tradition he began his career as a fierce tyrant, but the account may be exaggerated. In the eighth year after his consecration he put down a revolt in Kalinga (now Orissa) with great bloodshed, and this resulted in a change of heart, announced in inscriptions still to be found carved on rocks from Kandahar in Afghanistan to the southern Deccan and Orissa. He evidently went through an intense spiritual crisis at the thought of the human misery he had caused. This led to his becoming a Buddhist and drastically reforming his administration.

Of all the rulers of ancient India Aśoka is probably the best known in the world at large, and he is the only one

An Aśokan capital (third century BC). Despite Aśoka's pacificism, this carving does reflect Mauryan imperial aims.

to have left us documents reflecting his policy and his personality. These documents consist of inscriptions engraved on rocks, and later on pillars, throughout his kingdom, which included almost the whole of India and Pakistan, except for the southern tip (very roughly the modern states of Tamil Nadu and Kerala) and Assam. The inscriptions are supplemented by legends preserved by the Buddhists, some of which, though exaggerated, seem to contain a kernel of truth.

His reforms were directed at the promotion of the welfare, prosperity and happiness of his subjects, and to achieve this aim he strengthened the central administration, instituting a corps of 'inspectors of morality' (*dharma-mahāmātra*) directly responsible to himself, whose duty it was to ensure that the new policy was being carried out. Much has been said and written about him, some of it hagiological in tone, and we must remember that his pronouncements were intended for public consumption. His real personality is forever lost to us. But surely no kings before Aśoka and very few after him have made public statements such as:

'There is no better work than promoting the welfare of the whole world. Whatever may be my great deeds, I have done them in order to discharge my debt to all beings.'

(Sixth Major Rock Edict)

Many modern specialists consider that Aśoka's new policy of mildness at home and non-aggression abroad was dictated mainly by political considerations, as an attempt to solve the problem of holding together a far-flung empire of many diverse races. There is, however, no doubt that his change of heart was largely motivated by Buddhism, and that he was a very earnest Buddhist, whose faith increased with time. A certain naïvety is evident in some of his inscriptions–he believed that a radical change had taken place not only in himself, but in his subjects at large. In his later years, according to the Buddhist tradition, he became so engrossed in the affairs of the Buddhist *Saṅgha*, or community of 'monks', that the affairs of state were neglected, and ultimately he was ousted in a palace coup. In any case the new policy that he inaugurated did not survive him: on his death in about 232 BC the great empire began to crumble, and the process may have begun even during his lifetime.

As a politician Aśoka may be judged a noble failure, and his memory was only preserved by the Buddhists, but his reign had at least one real and lasting effect. As a result of his patronage the Buddhist church began to expand. Missionary monks were sent out all over India and beyond, and Aśoka himself sent envoys to the Western world, as far as Egypt, Libya and Epirus in Greece, urging the ambitious Hellenistic monarchs to abandon aggression and adopt his new policy of *dharma*. Sri Lanka was evangelized by Mahinda, according to tradition Aśoka's son, and the island never afterwards abandoned the Buddhist faith. It became the centre from which the Doctrine of the Elders (*Theravāda*), the most austere form of Buddhism, spread to southeast Asia, and later, in the last hundred years, back to India itself and to the Western world. Many new monasteries were founded by Aśoka, and innumerable *stūpas* (Buddhist sacred mounds) appeared all over India.

This great advance of Buddhism under Aśoka much encouraged the development of stone architecture. After the fall of the Persian empire, refugee Iranian craftsmen brought to India the art of handling large pieces of stone and imparting a lustrous polish to them. Fine monumental pillars were erected near the *stūpas*, many of them engraved with Aśoka's edicts. Cave hermitages began to be excavated, and the *stūpas* were covered with casings of dressed stone which were plastered and whitewashed. Yet the greatest monuments of Buddhism in India do not come from the time of Aśoka, or that of the Mauryan dynasty, but from the reigns of later kings, none of whom were as powerful as he, and many of whom cared little or nothing for Buddhism.

The age of invasions

The Mauryas were replaced around 186 BC by a new dynasty, that of the Śuṅgas, after a palace revolt. Mauryan power was already much diminished by the breaking away of the more distant provinces, and that of the Śuṅgas did not extend far beyond the Gangetic plain. They were of an orthodox brahman family, and the first ruler of the line, Puṣyamitra, performed the Vedic horse sacrifice, probably in celebration of a victory over marauding Greeks.

Alexander had established a province in Bactria, the area watered by the upper Oxus river. This fell to the Seleucids, who were Alexander's successors in Asia. In the middle of the third century BC, when Aśoka was ruling in India, Diodotus, the Greek governor of the province of Bactria, and Arsaces, a Parthian chieftain who had his headquarters not far from modern Tehran, revolted against their Seleucid overlords at about the same time, and the latter, though they made occasional attempts to regain their power in the east, were quite unable to conquer them. By the beginning of the second century BC the Seleucids, who had now to cope with the rising power of Rome, ceased to trouble themselves over their lost eastern provinces, and the two new states were left to their own devices. The Graeco-Bactrian kingdom soon began to turn its attention to India. Very early in the second century BC its king Euthydemus crossed the Hindu Kush and occupied parts of the Kabul valley. Profiting from the decline of the Mauryas, Graeco-Bactrian armies raided far into India, once, it seems, even reaching the walls of the capital, Pāṭaliputra.

The Śuṅga kings were able to drive back the invaders from most of the Gangetic area, but Greek kingdoms appeared in much of the Punjab, the northwestern area

Coin of a Graeco-Bactrian ruler of northwest India. Graeco-Bactrian armies raided far into India and Greek kingdoms occupied a considerable area in the Punjab but this soon broke up into a complex pattern of smaller kingdoms.

of Pakistan, and the Kabul valley. The Graeco-Bactrian kings of the line of Euthydemus were unable to control this considerable area, and it soon broke up into a complex pattern of smaller kingdoms, attested only by coins. Throughout the second century BC kings of Greek speech and customs controlled most of modern Pakistan, their power sometimes felt as far east as Mathurā. Most important of them was Menander, who, under the name Milinda, is remembered in an important text on Buddhist doctrine as a convert to that religion. His coins are very numerous and widespread, indicating a considerable empire and a long reign, though we have few details of its events.

Divided into several small kingdoms, the Greeks in India slowly gave way to stronger, more united powers. From the steppes to the north of Bactria Śakas, semi-nomadic Iranian tribesmen called Scythians by the Greeks and Romans, pressed upon them constantly, and ultimately drove them out of Bactria, their original headquarters. On their west the Parthian kingdom was an ever-increasing threat to them. In India re-emerging tribal peoples whittled away at their territory. By the middle of the first century BC only a few pockets of Greeks remained in the Punjab and the area of the Kabul valley, then known as Gandhāra.

Much more than Alexander, these Greeks acted as a channel through which ideas from Europe entered India, but Western influence, in the time of the Indo-Greek rulers, was still comparatively slight. It was only later, in the days of the Roman empire, when contact between India and the Western world became closer than ever again for 15 centuries, that there is clear evidence of mutual influence on a large scale.

The invaders made little impact on the Śuṅga and Kāṇva kings in the heartland of India. The Greeks were too busy quarrelling among themselves, and the Indian tribal republics on the borders of their realms increasingly pressed upon them. Puṣyamitra Śuṅga, the founder of the new empire, seems to have consciously reversed the centralizing Maurya policy, and to have returned to the ancient traditions of overlordship that prevailed at the time of the Buddha and before. The Śuṅgas had many subordinate kings, who recognized their suzerainty but were otherwise virtually independent, and issued their own coins. Puṣyamitra is remembered by the Buddhists as their persecutor. Yet the decline and fall of the Mauryas did not mean the decline of Buddhism, which continued to gain support after Aśoka had given it his patronage.

Meanwhile the Greeks gave way to the Śakas. In the first century BC these Scythian nomads occupied the Punjab and penetrated as far as Mathurā, the sacred city about 100 miles (160 km) south of Delhi, where they established a powerful satrapy. At about the same time the Śuṅgas gave way to another short-lived dynasty, the Kāṇvas, after whom that part of northern India that was not controlled by invaders broke up into many petty kingdoms, about which little is known.

The Śakas were a greater threat than the Greeks, for they not only controlled the Punjab and the course of the Yamunā (Jumna) river at least as far as Mathurā, but later they also occupied the Indus valley and thence established themselves in Gujarat, and the region of western Madhya Pradesh formerly known as Mālava or Malwa. Here they established a powerful and prosperous kingdom, based on the ancient city of Ujjain, that lasted until the end of the fourth century AD. The Śakas of the Punjab continued to use Greek on their coins; they were in touch with the Parthian kings of Iran, with whom they had fought, and from whom they had learned much.

An important factor that helped indirectly to bring about the barbarian invasion of India was the unification of China by the emperor Ch'in Shih-huang-ti in 221 BC. The consolidation and expansion of the Chinese empire put pressure on the nomadic peoples of Central Asia, and two of the most important of these, the Hsiung Nu and the Yüeh-chih, waged a fierce war for control of the steppe pasturelands on the western borders of China. The Yüeh-chih were soundly defeated, and in about 165 BC they migrated westwards *en masse*, right across Central Asia to the borders of Bactria. Pressure from these people in turn drove the Śakas to attack Iran and India.

By 129 BC the Yüeh-chih were levying tribute from Bactria, but for over a hundred years after that they left India alone, for they were divided into five tribal groups, which were constantly fighting one with another. Then the chief of the tribe of Kuṣāṇas, Kujūla Kadphises, conquered the other four Yüeh-chih tribes and consolidated them into a single people, who were henceforth known as Kushans (in Sanskrit Kuṣāṇa). Of all the invaders of India of this period, they were the most successful. Kujūla Kadphises carried his power as far as the Indus. His successor, Wīma Kadphises, occupied much of the Punjab. The third great Kuṣāṇa ruler, Kaniṣka, was the most powerful of all, and controlled an immense empire reaching from far into Central Asia to beyond Varanasi in the Ganges valley.

Unfortunately, with the uncertainty typical of much of early Indian history, we have no conclusive evidence as to the date of Kaniṣka, or of the Kuṣāṇa rulers generally. For the past 150 years great efforts have been made to establish their chronology, and whole books have been written on the question. At present most Indian scholars favour AD 78 as the date of Kaniṣka's accession. This is the initial year of the Śaka era, one of the favourite dating systems of later India. Most Western scholars prefer a date early in the second century AD, and a few of them even place Kaniṣka in the third century AD. The evidence is multifarious and self-contradictory, and the problem will never be finally solved unless inscriptional evidence appears, firmly linking a named Kuṣāṇa king with one of the Roman emperors or some other ruler whose date is quite certain.

After Kaniṣka the power of the Kuṣāṇas in the Ganges valley receded, though they held Mathurā for a hundred years. The Śakas of Gujarat and Malwa became independent, and in the third century AD Iran was revitalized under a new dynasty, the Sasanians. The remaining

Kuṣāṇas in the Punjab and eastern Afghanistan became loose vassals of the Persians, and they never again played a major part in the politics of Asia.

Kaniṣka, like Aśoka before him, was remembered by the Buddhists as a great patron of their religion but, whereas Aśoka is recorded in the traditions of both branches of Buddhism, Kaniṣka's memory survives only in that of the *Mahayana* (the 'Great Vehicle'), which was rapidly developing at this time. The Kuṣāṇas formed a bridge between east and west. The Silk Route from China ran through their territory to India and West Asia, and they were contemporary with the high-water mark of Roman power and affluence. Thus through them many aspects of Western culture were transmitted to India, and through their territory the form of Buddhism they favoured was introduced into China.

The age of invasions must have brought much suffering to India, with large armies of alien horsemen raiding far and wide over the plains, ruthless in their warfare and (at least from the point of view of the Indians) barbarous in their customs. Their depredations are reflected in passages in the Hindu scriptures describing the end of the *Kali Yuga*, the present dark age, when impure barbarians slaughter and ravage, when caste and family barriers break down, and when heretics persuade the people to reject the *Vedas* and the brahmans. From the point of view of the times there were phases in the age of invasions that must have seemed very terrible. Yet, viewed from a distance of two thousand years, it was an age of development and progress.

In the first two or three centuries of the Christian era the Roman empire was at its height. In the Mediterranean world there was a great demand for exotic luxuries, and trade across the Indian Ocean from the ports of the Red Sea to the shores of India developed as never before. The spices of India, especially pepper, fine muslins, jewels, ivory and other luxuries, were exported to Europe, and there was little that India wanted in return but gold. The great wealth of western India at the time is indicated by Buddhist monuments, such as those of Sanchi and Bharhut, and numerous artificial cave temples and monasteries in the Western Ghats, beautifully and elaborately carved. Votive inscriptions in these show that their construction was financed not only by kings, but also by many merchants and craftsmen, who must have been comparatively prosperous to be able to make such gifts.

In the western Deccan there arose a long-lasting and powerful dynasty which founded the first important independent state in the southern half of India. This was the Sātavāhana kingdom, which lasted from the first century BC to the third century AD and at its height controlled the whole of modern Maharashtra and Andhra Pradesh. In Tamil Nadu and Kerala we find the first evidence of developed kingdoms in the earliest Tamil literature, which dates from this time. Three little kingdoms, Chola, Chera and Pāṇḍya, divided the area, and three kings constantly fought each other in the hope of obtaining the hegemony. The conventions of these

Kushan statuary representing yakshi or tree spirits, dating from AD *c*100. Graceful figures embodying the ideal of female beauty (full breasts, wide hips and wasp waists) formed part of the decoration of the railings surrounding Buddhist stupas.

early Tamil poems, *The Eight Anthologies*, are different from those of the Sanskritic literature of the north, and reveal a literary culture more secular and more broadly based than that of the Aryans.

The Guptas

The state of things in the Gangetic region at this time, outside the area controlled by the Kuṣāṇas, is obscure, and the small kingdoms that then existed have left us no significant records. Then, in the early fourth century AD, the young king of a minor dynasty began to expand his power. This was Candra Gupta I (c320–335): his name is the same as that of the earlier Maurya Candragupta, but we have separated the two parts as the second element, common to all the Gupta kings, became virtually a surname. When he died, he was in control of the length of the Ganges from Allahabad in the west to the borders of Bengal, the very heartland of India. From this base his son Samudra Gupta (c335–376) expanded his power. Following the Mauryas, he led an expedition into south India and reached Kanchi, the capital of a new dynasty, the Pallavas, exacting tribute and homage from many kings on the way. With the booty gained from this expedition he financed more important campaigns in the north of India, where he 'violently uprooted' numerous small kings and annexed their kingdoms. He reduced the tribal peoples of Rajasthan to vassalage, and his power was felt from eastern Punjab to Bengal and Assam. On his death the only other independent kingdom of northern India of any importance was that of the Śakas of Ujjain.

The next ruler of the dynasty, Samudra's son Candra Gupta II (376–41), was the most powerful of the line. He conquered the Śakas, and seems to have made their capital, Ujjain, his headquarters. Through a dynastic marriage he gained virtual overlordship for a while of the central Indian kingdom of the Vākāṭakas. The area of his kingdom did not equal that of Aśoka, for most of modern Pakistan was still outside it, and his power was not much felt in the Deccan and the south, where the small kingdoms that had submitted to Samudra Gupta were independent again. But he established his hegemony across the whole of northern India from the Arabian Sea to the Bay of Bengal.

Unlike Aśoka, Candra Gupta was remembered in later centuries, under his throne name Vikramāditya, and stories about the exploits of 'Raja Bikram' are still told by the peasants of northern India. Under this name he is associated with the greatest of India's poets and dramatists, Kālidāsa, who is said to have been his court poet, and whose highly polished works reflect the urbane culture of the times. It might be claimed that during this period India was the most highly civilized land on earth, for the Roman empire was staggering under the attacks of the barbarians, and China was in little better state, until the rise of the Sui dynasty (581–618), followed by the T'ang.

The Gupta empire continued to flourish under Candra Gupta II's successor, Kumāra Gupta I (c414–454). There is no record of any important warfare until the very end of his reign, and northern India continued to enjoy peace and prosperity. A decline in overseas trade is indicated by indirect evidence, and this might be expected in view of the difficult times through which the Roman empire was then passing. But cultural activity continued to be vigorous, and this was the time when some of the best painting to have survived in India was produced. This is found in the Buddhist caves of Ajanta, in northern Maharashtra; Ajanta lies outside the confines of the Gupta empire, but it is largely a matter of accident that this is so. In the big cities of the north fine mural painting must also have existed, perhaps finer than anything at Ajanta, but it has long since vanished.

Near the end of Kumāra Gupta I's reign the tide began to turn against the Guptas, whose history had been one of steady expansion for over a hundred years. A Central

A Gupta statue of the Buddha symbolizing meditation and serenity. Originally the Buddhist church eschewed portraits of the Buddha, using symbols such as an empty seat, a footprint or a wheel.

Asian nomadic people, called by Byzantine authors Hephthalites or White Huns and by the Indians Hūṇas, had occupied Bactria in the latter part of the fourth century AD, and thence they gained control of other parts of Central Asia and Afghanistan. No evidence of any threat to the Guptas from these people appears, however, until the middle of the fifth century, when they had occupied most of the Punjab, supplanting local rulers who had been loosely subordinate to the Sasanian kings of Iran.

In or soon after 450 the Hūṇas attacked the Gupta empire. Our knowledge of the course of the war is very fragmentary, depending on brief references in one or two inscriptions, but it is clear that Gupta power was very badly shaken. Matters were made worse by the death of the old emperor Kumāra Gupta in the midst of the war. He was succeeded by his son Skanda Gupta (c454–467), who managed to expel the Hūṇas and to restore the empire to something like its former condition. But soon other threats to its integrity appeared. When Skanda Gupta died after a fairly brief reign the evidence indicates a short period of dynastic disputes, followed by the long reign of Budha Gupta (c475–495). The empire still survived, after a fashion, but it was a mere shadow of its old self. While Budha Gupta controlled the central Gangetic plain directly, beyond this area provincial governors had begun to take royal titles as vassal kings, and they paid scant respect to their imperial overlord. There is no good evidence of further serious attacks from the Hūṇas until the very end of the century, and when they came again the Gupta state had degenerated into a loose feudal-type empire, with the emperor controlling directly only the area of the Gangetic plain that had once formed the kingdom of Candra Gupta I.

For several decades the Hūṇas had been preoccupied with Sasanid Iran, but they had consolidated their hold on the northwest of the subcontinent, and from this vantage point, around the year 500, they attacked in force again. Two Hūṇa warlords, Toramāṇa and his son Mihirakula, terrorized western India for a generation. Mihirakula in particular was remembered in later times as a ferocious and sadistic tyrant and as an inveterate foe of Buddhism.

Mihirakula was ultimately driven out of the Gangetic plain and confined to Kashmir. Independently of each other, different sources ascribe his defeat to two rulers, one the emperor Narasimha Gupta, who expelled him from eastern India, and the other an upstart named Yaśodharman, who, from his headquarters in Mandasor (northwestern Madhya Pradesh), published eulogistic proclamations, engraved on stone, in which he claims the defeat of Mihirakula among numerous other successes. Though the survival of the Gupta empire is attested in northern Bengal, Bihar and eastern Uttar Pradesh until the middle of the sixth century AD, it was now virtually a thing of the past.

Everywhere local kings had arisen, admitting no allegiance to the Guptas. Some of these were of the lines of earlier minor rulers; others were descended from Gupta officials or generals; and yet others were men with strange names, some of whom were descended from martial migrants who had followed in the wake of the Hūṇa invaders and others from tribal chiefs from the hills and forests who took advantage of the anarchy of the times to carve out little kingdoms for themselves. The ancestors of the 36 clans of the medieval Rajputs seem in many cases to have been among these upstarts.

A new era was beginning for India. Though memories of the great empires of the past lingered in the chancelries of local rulers, and for a while Harṣavardhana of Kanauj (606–647) gained the loose hegemony of most of northern India, no king of later times succeeded in achieving what the Mauryas and Guptas had achieved. The pattern of medieval Hindu kingship may be loosely termed feudal, with a number of fairly powerful regional rulers, constantly striving to gain the advantage over their rivals, beneath whom were many subordinate kings, generally ready to change their allegiance or make a bid for complete independence where they thought these steps served their best interests.

Retrospect

During the period of roughly 800 years that we have covered briefly in this article tremendous changes took place in every aspect of Indian life. Though there was obvious continuity between the culture of the time of the Buddha and that of the Gupta period, developments had taken place which had altered the face of Indian civilization, and it was with some reason that Arnold J. Toynbee, in his *Study of History*, found that there had been two civilizations in India, the first ('Indic') culminating in the Mauryas, and then giving way to the second, which survives to this day. Toynbee's analysis is certainly over-simplified, but nevertheless it has a basis of historical truth. In the earlier days of the Mauryas much that now seems typically Indian was either completely absent or hardly to be seen: for example, theistic religious cults, vegetarianism, stone temples and sculpture, a rigid caste system based largely on profession, a developed secular literature, belief in astrology, and advanced systems of medicine and mathematics. These all came in the period we have considered and they still form important aspects of Indian culture. The twentieth-century Indian would hardly have felt at home in the realm of Candragupta Maurya; but in that of Candra Gupta II he would have found much more common ground.

Many complex factors brought about these changes, one of the most important being the series of invasions that took place just before and after the beginning of the Christian era. Another factor was the assimilative character of Indian civilization. Throughout the long course of Indian history many new elements, racial and cultural, have been introduced. At first resented by many Indians, they have slowly found acceptance, and have been given a typically Indian character and absorbed as part of the Indian tradition. The process has continued, over the centuries, and is still going on, as India adopts many of the ways of the Western world, but yet preserves her distinct civilization.

Hinduism

Wendy D. O'Flaherty

Introduction

The early history of Hinduism resembles an Impressionist painting rather than the sharp etching that historians generally aspire to: the colouring is strong and unmistakable, but the outlines are hopelessly blurred. There is no difficulty in telling what is *there*, but every difficulty in telling *where* it is in space or time. What emerges from a study of the ancient texts and archaeological remains is a personality. We can know it with far more intensity and intimacy than there is in our reconstructions of civilizations far closer to us in time or space, but we cannot begin to know precisely where or when such a personality existed.

The religious works that have survived from ancient India are full of vivid trivia that root them squarely in their historical context (information on how to pound spices for curry, how to bribe government officials, how to train an elephant), but we do not know enough about the broader political and chronological framework. The enormous literature that we have from the ancient period is breathtaking in its personal, emotional intensity, but it is entirely anonymous.

Sources

The sources for the study of ancient Hindu religion and mythology are diverse and tantalizing; each tells us a lot, but they never quite overlap. For the Indus civilization (*c*2400–*c*1800 BC), we have pictures without words, rich archaeological sources on both grand and small scale (the foundations of whole cities, hundreds of engraved seals) but a script that we cannot read–and that, in any case, is used only for brief inscriptions on seals that probably do not carry great cultural weight. For the Rig Vedic civilization (*c*1500–1200 BC), on the other hand, we have words without pictures: a magnificent collection of 1028 Sanskrit hymns (each some ten verses long), but almost no useful archaeological re-

mains. In subsequent centuries, we glean increasingly rich supporting material from coins, beginning with the Mauryans in the fourth century BC; inscriptions on stone, notably from the reign of the Mauryan Aśoka; art, beginning with the great carved Buddhist caves and *stūpas*; and the reports of foreign travellers (Greeks from the time of Alexander on, Chinese pilgrims from the early centuries of the Christian era). These materials often supply us with a skeleton of 'hard' facts of time and place. But the overwhelming corpus of information comes from the great literatures in Sanskrit and Pali (and, later, in various vernaculars): works that we can seldom date even within several centuries, because their authors utterly disdained to record their names or venues, and also because so many of these works are oral in origin or transmission, or in both.

The Vedic period (1500 BC to 600 BC)

At some time well before 1200 BC, a branch of migrating Indo-European horsemen and cattle raiders entered northwest India and settled in the Punjab. There they camped rather than built, moving restlessly in search of fresh grazing lands, and there they composed the *Rig Veda*, the oldest religious document of Indo-European civilization, a collection of hymns in an archaic form of Sanskrit that was sung as part of the Vedic ritual. Technically, the religion of the *Vedas* is not Hinduism but Vedism (the former arbitrarily said to begin with the *Epics* in 300 BC), but since the Hindus regard the *Rig Veda* as their canon (and since parts of it do indeed remain an important thread in later Hinduism), the study of Hinduism must begin with the study of the *Vedas*.

The *Rig Veda* is obscure both through its own intention (for the gods love riddles, the sages say) and through our own inadequacy (for the Vedic scholar is constantly stumbling over indecipherable *hapax legomena* and infuriatingly intractable grammatical idiosyncrasies that the later language can shed no light upon). There is, however, so very much of the *Rig Veda* that there are some things about Vedic religion that we can know with some confidence. Many hymns are addressed to Agni, the god of fire (cognate with Latin *ignis*), a god of many forms: natural fire (including lightning in the sky), cultural fire (the hearth), sacred fire (the eater of oblations and the messenger who carries the burnt offering to the gods), and the digestive fire in every belly (perhaps a source of the later concept of the godhead in every body). The other great ritual god is Soma, deification of the sacred drink of immortality, a drink pressed from a plant (also called *soma*–probably a

Badami was the capital of the southern Indian Chalukya empire during the sixth century AD. Three rock-cut Brahman temples were built in that period.

hallucinogen of some kind, perhaps a mushroom) and offered to the gods by the priests who drank it. The third great Vedic god is Indra, phallic god of rain and fertility, great warrior, slayer of demons, king of the gods, wielder of the thunderbolt and lusty drinker of *soma*.

Each of these figures undergoes a major metamorphosis in the transition to later Hinduism. Agni is no longer the object of worship (there are no Hindu temples to Agni), but remains the personification of the priest, pot-bellied, bearded, and pompous, a metaphor rather than a true mythological character. Soma is personified as the moon, the storehouse of the drink of immortality, waning as the gods drink it up each month. Indra is demoted to a buffoon and trickster, a Gargantuan parody of a great king, though he remains a popular figurehead in the mythology. Vishnu and Shiva, who are to become so important in later Hinduism, make brief but significant appearances in the *Rig Veda*: Vishnu as a solar god who strides across space propping it up and helping Indra to kill demons; Shiva (in the form of Rudra) as a sinister outsider who prowls in the mountains among the wild animals and both causes and cures diseases, shooting men and animals with his arrows. These gods, and many others, are worshipped in a kind of serial monogamy that Max Müller termed Kathenotheism: the worship of one god at a time, as if he were the only god.

Though the main thrust of the *Rig Veda* is liturgical, it is possible to reconstruct from numerous half-statements and pregnant asides a dazzlingly rich mythology, from the creation of the universe to the marriages of the gods, their battles and verbal contests. It is also possible to discern, in the later books one and ten (the first and last), the beginnings of abstract speculation about the origins of time and space–'There was neither non-existence nor existence then'; the nature of God–'He who gives life, who gives strength, whose command all the gods obey, his shadow is immortality and death; and the fate of the soul after death–'Beneath the tree with beautiful leaves where Yama drinks with the gods, there our father turns to the ancient ones'.

These concepts, briefly alluded to in the *Rig Veda*, are developed at length in the *Brahmanas*, an enormous group of texts composed by and for priests in Sanskrit in the tenth century BC. Although the ostensible purpose of these texts is to instruct the priests in the precise mechanics of the sacrifice, they constantly veer off into myths describing the origin of the ritual–how the gods obtained immortality, how Indra was restored when his vital fluids left him after he had killed the demon priest Vritra–and the secret meaning of the ritual acts.

This latter concern finally comes into full flower in the *Upanishads* (*c*800–600 BC), where speculations about the unity of the individual soul and the godhead and the transmigration of the soul are the basis of a passionate but carefully traditional mysticism. The *Upanishads*,

roughly contemporaneous with the early teachings of the Buddha (and with remarkably similar philosophical developments in Greece), spring from the Vedic ritual; their meditations on the nature of the cosmos, for example, begin with analogues for the parts of the body of the stallion dismembered in the coronation ceremony. Even the Upanishadic passages dealing with ecstasy (which is likened to the emotions of a man in the embrace of his beloved, or is simply called indescribable–'Not thus, not thus') have precedent in the Rig Vedic hymns composed by poets intoxicated with the *soma* plant ('We have drunk the *soma*; we have become immortal. . . . We have mounted the wind; our bodies are all you mortals can see'). Indeed, the whole of the Upanishadic and Vedantic practice of yoga, the physiological techniques of inducing ecstacy through fasting and breath control, for example, may be viewed as an attempt to recapture the religious vision once opened up by the *soma* plant and subsequently lost when, *c*900 BC, the Indo-Aryans moved down out of the mountains where the plant grows, into the Ganges valley where it was lost to them forever.

Indus valley religion

If an outside, i.e. non-Indo-European, source is sought for the innovations of this period, such as yoga, it is tempting to look to the Indus civilization. This requires a great leap back into history, for that civilization, consisting primarily of two great cities, Harappa and Mohenjo-daro, was destroyed–perhaps by the invading Indo-Aryans, perhaps by its own conservative

Rudra, 'the Howler or Roarer, the Terrible One'. This Vedic god was incorporated as an aspect of Shiva.

entropy–*c*1700 BC. This was well over 1000 years before yoga became highly developed and almost 2000 years before the emergence of other aspects of Hinduism, such as phallic worship and worship of the goddess, that seem not to arise from the Indo-European tradition. The evidence is very slim: a few seals depicting men seated in what may be yogic *asanas* or postures, some phallic stones and ring stones, some crude terracotta statues of goddesses. Only in India might it be thought possible that a cult could remain alive underground for two millennia, and even here it seems hardly possible. Indeed, the cult of the goddess has probably always been important in village culture, but 'high' Hinduism has a deep resistance to it: there are few goddesses mentioned in the *Rig Veda*, only one (Dawn) given any semblance of worship; the *Upanishads* are almost fanatically misogynist; and the cult of the goddess, which plays no part in the *Epics*, only flowers in the *Puranas* well after 455 AD. It is here that a singular, but significant, division is encountered between the 'great' and 'little' Hindu traditions, for it is precisely the interaction between these two layers that has led to the great vitality and richness of the religion. Indeed, this interaction is so ancient and so constant that it is probably only a scholarly convenience to speak of the two categories as separate at all; neither exists in a pure form without any influence from the other.

The Epic period (300 BC to 300 AD)

All the time that the priests were composing the *Vedas*, *Brahmanas* and *Upanishads* in Sanskrit, the rest of the people in India were doubtless doing what they have always done best–telling stories, placating local mischief-makers such as serpents, tigers, and devils, and making images in clay or wood of potentially helpful spirits and divinities. The first time that this rich lode of religion breaks through the Sanskrit surface and is preserved in texts is in the two great epics of India, the *Mahabharata* and the *Ramayana*.

The *Ramayana* is both earlier and later than the *Mahabharata*: it represents a later stage of Hinduism, when the Aryans had moved further east and were living in more elaborate cities, and its present recension was begun later than that of the *Mahabharata* (*c*200 BC to 200 AD), but it is shorter and far more integral, and has not been subjected to the centuries of subsequent accretion that make the dating of the *Mahabharata* such a hopeless task. It is a classic epic: the story of king Rama, whose wife, Sita, was carried off by the demon Ravana to his island fortress (Lanka, much later identified with Sri Lanka) and won back by Rama with the help of the monkey Hanuman. This story was kept alive among the people not only in its Sanskrit form but in translations into vernaculars–the Hindi version of Tulsi Das and the Tamil version of Kamba, as well as dramatic presentations in Indian villages and throughout southeast Asia. It is loved not only for its poetry–the author, Valmiki, is regarded as India's first ornate poet–but for its religious content. For, although in the early layers of the *Ramayana* (preserved in the central books, two to six)

Rama, one of the incarnations of Vishnu, the Hindu god of preservation.

Rama is a mortal prince and not a god, in the later books (one and seven, the first and last) he is an *avatar* or incarnation of the god Vishnu, the object of worship of millions of Hindus, and his cunning ally, Hanuman, is equally popular at the grass-roots level from which his element of the epic almost certainly derives in the first place.

The *Mahabharata* is far longer and more miscellaneous than the *Ramayana* (about 200,000 lines, or roughly ten times the size of the *Odyssey* and *Iliad* combined), an encyclopedia of Hinduism as it developed during the long period of the *Mahabharata*'s recension, sometime between 300 BC and AD 300. Though it contains within it a great epic story–the tale of a long rivalry between the Kauravas and the Pandavas, two closely related families of princes, culminating in a battle in which all are destroyed–it veers off constantly into whole chapters and even books of myths and folk tales, philosophical discourses, treatises on social thought (*dharma*), and hymns of praise to the rising sectarian gods, Vishnu and Shiva. These strands are woven directly into the epic tale: the myths describe divine events that are closely parallel to those happening on earth at the moment in the story when the myths are introduced; the philosophical discourses and social treatises grow directly out of the moral quandaries of the epic heroes; and the hymns of praise turn the plot in new directions as the gods respond and turn the tide of battle. Each of these strands is, in turn, the source of a post-*Epic* aspect of Hinduism worth exploring in its own right.

Myths and folk tales: the Puranas

The tales that first appear in the epic are greatly expanded, codified, and glossed in the great body of Sanskrit literature known as the *Puranas*, the earliest of which are probably roughly coterminous with the *Epics* and the main body of which were composed after AD 455, though all of them draw upon a far more ancient body of folk belief. The basic themes of these *Puranas* are the legends of the kings of the lunar and solar dynasties and the description of the recurrent creation and destruction of the universe. On to this base is grafted a rich mythological treasury, originally non-sectarian or at least indiscriminately Vedic, stories in which the gods as a whole compete with the demons as a whole, or in which gods like Indra and Agni and the Creator (Brahma or Prajapati)–gods no longer actively worshipped in India–act out symbolic cosmic dramas. But in addition to this one encounters a new kind of mythology arising out of the worship of Vishnu and Shiva, through offerings of flowers or fruit to crude images in small domestic shrines, or through more elaborate rituals and sacrifices made in great stone temples.

Vishnu: The *avatars* of Vishnu include not merely the human incarnations of Rama and the prince Krishna (who appears in the *Epics* merely as full-grown man, and who is later depicted in the *Puranas* as a child, the form in which he is most lovingly worshipped by Hindus), but also the animal forms that derive from myths originally associated with other gods in the *Brahmanas* (usually the Creator): the fish who saves the human race from the doomsday flood; the tortoise at the bottom of the cosmic sea on whose back the earth is propped when the gods churn the ocean to obtain the elixir of immortality; the boar who rescues the earth from the bottom of the sea when demons steal it away. These are all variants of a single cosmogonic myth of rescue from the waters of chaos. In addition, Vishnu had semi-human incarnations: the dwarf who becomes a giant and cheats a demon out of the universe by stepping across it in three strides (a development from the Vedic myth of the solar Vishnu); the Buddha, who teaches the 'false' doctrine of Buddhism in order to corrupt the demons so that the gods can conquer them; Kalki, the rider on the white horse, who puts the barbarians to the sword at the end of the Kali Age; and the man-lion (Narasimha), who

disembowels an evil demon in order to rescue and vindicate the demon's son, a devotee of Vishnu.

Though these *avatars* have sometimes been ranked in ascending order, from fish to Buddha, they do not arise historically in that order, nor do they express such a development; they are a group of ancient stories that are applied to Vishnu as his cult gains momentum in the centuries immediately before and after the beginning of the Christian era.

Shiva: Unlike Vishnu, whose mythology is linked with princely human figures central to the two great *Epics*, Shiva has acquired a corpus of myth and ritual arising out of the pre-Aryan and non-Aryan substrata of India as well as out of the *Rig Veda*. His is a mythology of sex and violence, of the worship of the phallus (*linga*) and the terror of merciless, inexplicable and unpredictable death. He appears on earth disguised as an Untouchable or as a filthy, naked yogi; he seduces the wives of the sages in the forest, dancing with them in ithyphallic ecstasy until their aghast husbands castrate him–only to find that the entire universe becomes suspended in impotence until the institution of the worship of the *linga* is established forever. Like Vishnu, Shiva kills demons; his most famous victory (in the *Mahabharata*) is the

Vishnu as *varaha-avatara*, the boar incarnation, saving the goddess earth from the waters of the deep.

destruction of the triple city of demons (cities of gold, silver, and bronze, in heaven, the ether, and on earth) with a single arrow. But, unlike Vishnu's battles, this act is given explicit cosmic overtones: this is the doomsday arrow of fire and flood that destroys the triple world at the end of the aeon. Though Shiva is the god of yogis, philosophers, and brahmans, he is also the outsider who is the enemy of the Vedic sacrifice (in which he is given no share); he destroys a sacrifice to which he has not been invited, but he destroys it by beheading the sacrificial animal—the very act of which the sacrifice itself consists. These ambivalences, which arise out of a particularly strong manifestation of the aspect of the sacred known as the coincidence of opposites, are further echoed in such related ambivalences as his phallic/yogic aspects and his androgyny.

Philosophical discourses: Bhagavad Gita and Vedanta

One entire book of the 18-book *Mahabharata* is devoted to philosophical argument (book 12, the *Shanti Parvan*), and the rest of the epic is strongly laced with it. The *Bhagavad Gita*, part of the sixth book, is probably the best-known religious text in India; it takes the form of a dialogue between the hero Arjuna, who is reluctant to kill his own cousins, and his charioteer, Krishna, who persuades Arjuna to do his duty (*dharma*), to obey caste law and the law of religious action even though these are meaningless in the face of the ultimate unreality of matter.

Treatises on social thought: Dharmashastras

Though Krishna's argument in the *Gita* leads to a discourse on the nature of godhead and the soul, it falls back in the end upon social law (*dharma*) for its moral sanction. This quandary—what is the right thing to do?—is at the heart of the entire epic. One of the heroes, king Yudhishthira, the literal incarnation of the god Dharma (as Arjuna is the incarnation of Indra), wrestles constantly with the tension between 'absolute morality', which can be traced back to the *Upanishads* (the belief in non-injury [*ahimsa*] and in withdrawal from worldly life in order to achieve enlightenment and release from reincarnation [*moksha*] and 'relative morality' (the

teachings of the caste system: that each man must fulfil his own social role even if this involves the taking of human or animal life, that animals must be sacrificed to the Vedic gods, and that every man must beget male children in order that he can be reborn through the offerings such children will make to his ghost in limbo). These values are thoroughly Vedic, though the *Vedas* do not yet treat them in this explicit form, and their interaction with Vedantic philosophical values creates the tension that underlies the *Epics* as well as the later *Puranas*, a tension dealt with in minute juristic detail in the numerous textbooks on social law (*Dharmashastras*).

Hymns of praise: bhakti

The *Mahabharata* and—far more often—the *Puranas* frequently burst into hymns of praise for Vishnu or Shiva, passages quite different in spirit from the dry, formulaic incantations of the *Brahmanas*, the abstract mystic passion of the *Upanishads*, or the wordly myths of the *Epics*. In spirit, they are not unlike the Vedic hymns, though of course their content is almost entirely different. These hymns often consist of the thousand names of God, lists that incorporate many epithets of lesser divinities who have been assimilated to the great sectarian Hindu gods, concise references to mythological accomplishments of the gods ('Slayer of the demon Madhu', 'Beheader of Brahma'); philosophical beliefs ('Unborn', 'Infinite'); or rituals ('He whose phallus is worshipped by gods and mortals'). They sometimes shade off into a more passionate form of devotion (*bhakti*) that is only beginning to gather momentum in this period, deriving from southern Indian Tamil cults of Vishnu and Shiva (the Alvars and Nayanars). This is the final touch in the evolution of full Hinduism, a link both from the vernacular to the Sanskritic (from the Alvars to the *Mahabharata*) and back again, into new forms of the worship of Shiva and Vishnu in vernacular songs, poems, dances, paintings, and every material thing in which hierophany can take place—trees and pots and snakes and rivers and ponds and cows. This constant interaction between majestic, brilliant intellectual speculation and brutal, instinctive worship forms the heart of Hinduism.

Buddhism

Trevor Ling

The historical context

From *c*1000 BC to at least AD 1000 the predominant influence on Indian civilization was Brahmanism. But Buddhism, in certain senses a rival native ideology, also made certain significant contributions; for a short time, during the reign of the emperor Aśoka in the third century BC, there existed what might fairly be called a

Buddhist civilization.

Brahmanism rested upon the assumptions that the brahmans, by their closely guarded possession of knowledge of the sacred Vedic Sanskrit hymns, mantras and sacrificial formulae, were indispensable to Indian society and constituted its highest class, even above the warrior or *ksatriya* class. The sacred lore, which they guarded and transmitted from one generation of brahmans to another, included prescriptions for the ordering of society in four main classes: broadly, *brahmans*, *ksatriyas*, *vaisyas* (or merchants) and *sudras* (or serfs). Membership of these classes was strictly hereditary. Politically, Brahmanical civilization expressed itself in terms of monarchy; in the earlier period there were a number of smaller local rajas or monarchs, but by about the sixth century BC, when the Buddha began to teach, these had been reduced to a few, relatively large monarchies that had absorbed the smaller ones by conquest. Statecraft was an integral feature of brahman tradition.

The absorption of more and more of the people of India into Brahmanical civilization was well advanced by the time of the Buddha. The process also entailed the loss of the sense of membership in small compact local societies, as the older tribal republics were conquered and merged into the expanding monarchies. This appears to have produced a growing psychological malaise as people felt themselves to be adrift in larger, more impersonal political units. As has happened elsewhere in such periods of change and malaise, the sense of *anomie* expressed itself increasingly in the asking of questions concerning the nature of human existence, its purpose, and its destiny. In turn, such questionings gave rise to a number of new philosophies. These opposed the Brahmanical assumptions and were therefore regarded by the brahmans as heretical. One such was the philosophy of the Buddha, also known as Guatama.

The Buddha

The Buddha, himself a member of the *ksatriya* class, born in an area that was on the fringe of Brahmanical civilization, at the foot of the hills of what is now Nepal, challenged the assumptions of the brahmans on a number of matters. In the sixth century BC he made light of the solemn claims of the brahmans regarding the world-upholding nature of their ritual chantings and sacrifices. He questioned the idea that men could know that the world had been created by a supreme divine being, made fun of the alleged characteristics of this being as portrayed by the brahmans and taught instead that a surer basis of knowledge was the careful, disciplined analysis of man's own nature and experience. Such analysis, in Buddhist terms, led to the conclusion that there was nothing in the world or in man himself that was not subject to continual change (*anicca*). Personality was, like everything else, a flux of various constituents, material and mental. The goal of this analysis was the reshaping of the present, characterized as it is by all kinds of ills, unhappiness, and dissatisfaction, into a more wholesome future. The message of this basic Buddhism may be summarized as a demonstration that change is always and everywhere inevitable, however slow it may be, and that what matters is *what kind* of change it will be: whether towards what is more wholesome and free from suffering, or not. The Buddha's teaching consisted to a large degree of the exposition of the method by which such change in human consciousness was to be effected. This had two aspects: first, the observance of certain ethical precepts as an essential basis; and second, a lengthy and sophisticated process of what may, telegraphically, be called mind-training. The ethical precepts covered both personal and social matters: the reciprocal responsibilities of parents and children, pupils and teachers, husbands and wives, friends, employers and employees, householders and monks. Happy would have been the village, it has been truly said, where the people attempted to practise this social ethic. However, in the early period of Indian Buddhism it was not so much in the villages that the new teaching found most of its adherents but in the towns and especially in the larger ones, where urban life had most acutely provoked those personal questionings concerning the meaning and purpose of human life that have just been mentioned. Buddhist civilization was urban in origin and urbane in style. Another aspect of the Buddhist ethic was that it discouraged violence of any sort as a means of solving human problems.

A further important feature of early Buddhism, which had implications for the kind of civilization it would tend to produce, was its rejection of the Brahmanical social system: that is, of the system by which all men were regarded as having received, from birth, a divinely ordained station in life and whereby some were regarded as not fit to receive instruction or education, and not worthy to share in the sacred lore of the brahman class (dire penalties were prescribed under Hindu Brahmanical law for a serf who so much as heard the words of the *Vedas*). According to the early sources, Buddhist teaching and the way of life that it envisaged soon attracted a good deal of attention, so that the Buddha gained a considerable following of disciples, among them men of all classes, high and low.

One of his first followers was a barber, a man whose occupation placed him low in the scale in Brahmanical terms. Another was Bimbisara, the king of Magadha. This was a kingdom that was rising rapidly in importance at that time. Its capital was at Rajagriha, an excellently defendable site surrounded by five steep-sided, forest-covered hills. The natural resources to which the kingdom had access included valuable iron and other minerals in the rugged low hills to the south. The place of the Buddha's enlightenment, Bodh-Gaya, was within Magadhan territory, to the west of the capital. The Buddha and his teaching became known to Bimbisara. He became one of the Buddha's supporters, and sought advice from the Buddha in various matters. The king of Koshala, a neighbouring territory, also became one of the Buddha's friends and supporters, and had lengthy discussions with him. Magadha and Koshala together comprised most of the lower Gangetic plain, from modern Lucknow to Bhagalpur.

The Aśokan Buddhist state

After the Buddha's decease the community of his followers and disciples continued to grow and flourish. The kingdom of Magadha also continued to grow in size and importance, but not all its kings were well disposed

The city gate of Kushinagara, Magadha. The Buddha died in this city at the age of eighty.

towards the Buddhists. In the fifth century BC a new dynasty was established, that of the Mauryas, under whom extensive wars were waged in accordance with Hindu Brahmanical statecraft, in order continually to enlarge the extent of the kingdom. The most famous member of this dynasty was the emperor Aśoka (Ashoka), whose reign began *c*268 BC. He inherited an already vast empire from his father and grandfather. The military campaign by which he extended it to the Bay of Bengal was so bloody that Aśoka himself appears to have recoiled in horror from what had occurred. Possibly already attracted by the Buddhist ethic, he now became its avowed adherent, renounced violence throughout his realm, and began to promulgate this new code by means of inscriptions on rocks and stone pillars in prominent places and on all the frontiers of his kingdom. Many of these have been discovered during the modern period and have enriched historical knowledge of the Aśokan state and of Indian life in the third century BC. (Significantly, the Brahmanical records completely ignore Aśoka until ten or twelve centuries later, when all danger of his influence had passed away.)

The kind of state and the kind of society that Aśoka's various measures and personal example were intended to produce may be characterized in general terms as Buddhist. That is to say, the general intention was to facilitate the pursuit of Buddhist moral principles. Great emphasis was laid upon non-violence at every level, physical, mental and environmental. Aśoka records in one of his inscriptions that, whereas formerly hundreds of animals were killed daily for meat in the royal kitchens, this had now been reduced to only three, and

sometimes two. He records also that he had introduced a ban on the killing of a wide variety of animals, birds and fish throughout his realm. Much attention was given also to the quality of public life and the vigorous encouragement of good behaviour at all levels of social life; towards servants, parents, friends, and others. What Aśoka was seeking to inculcate in all his people, as the inscriptions frequently mention, was *dharma*. This is a word of many shades of meaning, and could be used to refer to the doctrines of the Buddha. But then it would strictly be called 'Buddha-Dharma' (just as there is also a Hindu *dharma*, and so on). The word happens to be cognate with Latin *forma*. The suggestion has been made that Aśoka was seeking to encourage as widely as possible what in modern times has been called 'good form', that is, certain generally acknowledged standards of good behaviour. At least, this gives an idea of what seems to have been the spirit of Ashokan administration.

More specifically, however, Aśoka engaged himself in various measures of a very practical kind to promote better conditions of life and social communication within his realm. For example, provision was made for public medical care, for both humans and animals. Improvements in agriculture and horticulture were introduced. Travel was made easier and safer by the planting of large shady trees along the cross-country roads (a great boon to the traveller under India's fiercely hot sun); wells were dug at regular intervals along these routes and resthouses were provided. The greater ease of travel thus made possible would lead to increased social communication and trade and therefore, especially in more remote areas, better living conditions. Welfare officers were appointed whose task it was generally to ensure that the right conditions, material and social, existed in which *dharma* could be practised.

Another important feature of the Aśokan state was the encouragement of tolerance for and between all religions and philosophies. In this connection *dharma* included strong discouragement of sectarian quarrels and the disparagement of the views of others.

It was during the period of Aśoka's rule (*c*268 to 232 BC) that Buddhism developed a more distinctively religious character. Until then it had been primarily a rule of life based on a philosophical and psychological analysis which could be practised by those who devoted their whole lives to it, and secondarily a social ethic for householders and supporters of the full-time practitioners. It was in connection with those for whom Buddhism was mainly a social ethic that there developed a cult of the veneration of relics of former outstanding and greatly respected Buddhists, including Sakyamuni himself. This had its origin in the practice of venerating the burial mounds, or *stupas*, of such deceased 'saints'. During the Aśokan period large numbers of reliquary shrines were built in what seems to have been a widespread popular movement of a devotional kind. This meant that the householders and their families ('lay' people as they have later come to be called) had a tangible focus for their devotion to the Buddha. The ceremony of offering flowers, incense and lights in honour of the Buddha at such shrines is undoubtedly very old; it has to be remembered that at this period the *Buddharupa*, or image, had not yet been developed as the focus for lay devotion, as it later became. With the development of the cult there went, inevitably it seems, the development also of misconceptions concerning the Buddha and his teaching. Evidence of this is found in the compilation during Aśoka's reign of a Buddhist text called *Kathavathu*, which dealt with points of controversy that had arisen concerning Buddhism, and attempted to correct erroneous ideas. Such controversy, while it was potentially disruptive (and this was the aspect of it that Aśoka discouraged), was also a sign of vigorous life. Another sign of this was the welcome given to Buddhism in Sri Lanka, commended as it was to the Sinhalese king by Aśoka himself through his emissaries. From then onwards it became the major philosophical and religious influence on the civilization of that island.

The position of the 'Sangha'

When Aśoka's reign came to an end, the special position that Buddhism and its representatives in the *Sangha*, or community of 'monks' (*bhikkhus*), had come to occupy in relation to the emperor eventually proved disadvantageous. The rivalry of the orthodox brahmans showed itself increasingly in their antagonism towards a community which, as they saw it, had usurped their special place in the state. But some other brahmans, not directly opposed to Buddhism, entered the ranks of the *Sangha*. This tendency seems to have increased during the Aśokan period, perhaps as a result of the social prestige

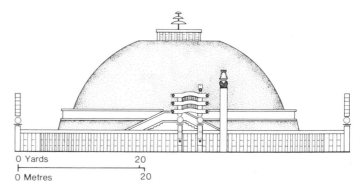

Buddhism now enjoyed within the state. Inevitably, however, brahmans brought with them their hereditary Brahmanical learning, attitudes and ways of thought. This, combined with the increasing devotionalism that has just been noted, meant that Buddhism was now well on the road to new philosophical and religious developments which would radically alter its character.

By the time the Mauryan dynasty came to an end Buddhism had already developed internal divisions in its ideas and practices. This was about 50 years or so after Aśoka's death, and brings us to the early decades of the second century BC. It was a confused period of Indian as well as of Buddhist history, and the quality of Aśokan Buddhist civilization was a thing of the past. During the succeeding centuries Buddhism, in its increasingly varied forms, spread geographically to areas distant from the Gangetic plain; it continued to make its contribution to Indian civilization, though now in a

Top: Reconstruction of the great stupa at Sanchi. Right: One of the many rock-cut shrines and monasteries at Ajanta on the Deccan plateau (second century BC to sixth century AD).

somewhat muted form in most places.

The rise of the 'Great Vehicle'

By about the first century AD a new form of Buddhism had come into being which called itself the *Mahayana*, that is the 'Great Vehicle'; it claimed to be capable of carrying many more Buddhists to the desired destination than the old form could. There was some justification for its criticism of the older, now rather dogmatic *Hinayana*, as it came to be called (the 'Lesser Vehicle'), and one of the effects of the new Buddhism was to stimulate a certain revival within the old. The *Mahayana* doctrine had certain important practical implications. The doctrine centred round the concept of the 'Bodhisattva', or the 'Being who is possessed of the essence of Buddhahood'. Such beings were thought of as Buddhas-to-be, and were located in the heavenly regions, where they were able to exert beneficent influence on behalf of mortals who were much lower on the long path to Buddhahood. They thus came to resemble divine saviours, to whom men could appeal for help, and who could also be regarded as the source of new Buddhist scriptures. One of the important consequences of this was that modifications of the original discipline for monks (attributed to the historical *Sakyamuni* of the sixth century BC) became possible. This had the advantage that the old dietary and clothing rules which, so long as they were strictly adhered to, prevented Buddhist

monks from travelling in cold northern climates, could now be suitably amended. In this way Buddhism, in its later *Mahayana* form, carried by the monks of this more flexible doctrine, found its way from India, through central Asia, to China by about the beginning of the second century AD. In this way one of the most important links between the civilizations of India and China was forged, and the routes between the two countries came to be used not only by Indians travelling north, but also, before long, by Chinese Buddhist pilgrims travelling south to visit the Holy Land of their faith. One of the most notable of these was Fa-hsien, who was in India from about AD 399 to 414, and whose travel diary provides valuable historical information concerning the India of the early fifth century AD. His account makes it clear that by the beginning of the fifth century AD Buddhism was in decline almost everywhere in India. The *Mahayana*, capable of accommodating *many* Buddhists (according to its own claim), had become so accommodating that it ended by accommodating almost none of the people of India. There were brief periods of revival in the one or two strongholds that remained, such as Bengal, but for the most part the great days of Buddhism were now past, so far as India was concerned. In Sri Lanka, however, where the *Mahayana* failed to establish itself securely, Buddhism survived, and the civilization that was associated with it lasted until the coming of the European empire builders.

Jainism

Trevor Ling

Origins

Jainism has been an enduring element of Indian civilization for over 2500 years, Mahatma Gandhi being but one of those who in modern times have come under the influence of its doctrines. The beginnings of its known history are to be found in that period of ferment and change in India that saw also the emergence of Buddhism, that is, the period from about the eighth to the fifth century BC. Like Buddhism it is a system that dispenses with gods and priests. Historically it arose a little earlier than the Buddhist movement, but in approximately the same part of India: in the eastern plains of the lower Ganges valley, in the region that corresponds approximately with modern Bihar.

According to its adherents it is a system of thought and practice whose origins have to be sought in a past so distant as to be virtually beyond the capacity of the human mind to conceive. Traditionally, this inconceivable length of time has produced 24 *Tirthankaras*, or great teachers of Jainism. Of these, the last two are generally regarded as historical figures: Parsva (eighth century BC), and Mahavira (sixth century BC). The latter

was probably a slightly senior contemporary of the Buddha Gautama. He is known also by his personal name, Vardhamāna, Mahavira being more in the nature of a title ('Great-Hero'). His greatness in the eyes of the Jains consisted in his having both recovered and restored the ancient teachings of Parsva, his immediate predecessor in the almost infinitely long line of earlier *Tirthankaras*, and in his own ascetic achievement as one who 'crosses the stream of existence'; this is the meaning of the word *Tirthankara*.

Mahavira's doctrines

The teaching of Mahavira differed fundamentally from that of his fellow countryman, Buddha Gautama, in that the latter taught that what endures is not the 'soul' of the individual. According to Mahavira it is precisely the soul that endures. The whole universe, which is regarded as infinite in time and space, is inhabited by souls (*jiva*) of all kinds: men, animals, plants and the denizens of various heavens and hells. All are subject to the law of *karma*, or activity. In Jain teaching, however (in contrast with Hindu and Buddhist teaching), *karma* is a subtle

Ahimsa is thus the central feature of the Jain way of life, and conditions all characteristically Jain attitudes and practices. By means of *ahimsa* and the austere disciplines of *tapas* the generating of *karma* can be counteracted, and the subtle material 'encrustation' of the *jiva* by such past *karma* can be reduced until, with the absolute purification of *jiva*, salvation (*moksha*) is attained. Each life bears responsibility for its own *karma*, and thus for its own salvation. No god and no saviour are required.

By its very nature Jainism was not likely to become a widespread, popular religious system, but as in the case of Buddhism, the professionals, that is the 'monks' as they are sometimes described in English, received the necessities of life from lay disciples, some of whom were (as in the Buddhist case) local rulers, or *rajas*.

The mission of Mahavira

The story of Mahavira's life is preserved in Jain tradition. He was born in the part of Bihar that lies northwards from Patna across the Ganges. His father was a ruler or warrior, (*ksatriya*), and the Jain tradition is that *Tirthankaras* are always born of *ksatriya*, not of brahman stock. He set out at the age of thirty to follow the religious discipline of his predecessor, Parsva, and wandered fairly widely in Bihar and the western area of neighbouring Bengal, which was then known as Ladha or Radha. The tradition goes that in Bengal he received a hostile reception and was subjected to violent attacks. In the course of a life of austere discipline he attracted a number of followers, both full time and part time, that is, both monks and householders. The monks were formed into a *Sangha*, an assembly or organization, just as were the disciples of the Buddha. After a life of travelling and teaching as one who was *nirgrantha*, that is, without any ties, internal or external, he died at the age of 72, at Pava in Bihar.

His disciples continued to spread Jain doctrine and practice and eventually reached the western side of India, in what is now Gujarat and Rajasthan. Another development carried Jainism towards the south when a number of monks migrated in that direction at a time of famine in Bihar at the beginning of the third century BC. From that time it established itself as a significant minority element in south India, especially in the Tamil country. Wherever it attracted support, Jainism, through its doctrine of *ahimsa* (interpreted as the avoidance of the taking of life of any kind), had the effect of detracting somewhat from the sacrificial system practised by the priests (brahmans) at that time. This principle, so strongly emphasized in Jainism, also made it more suitable, even among lay people, as a way of life for a mercantile class rather than for people engaged in agriculture, since the latter's occupation inevitably entailed destroying the lives of small creatures of various kinds. It was among merchants and traders therefore that Jainism found its chief lay supporters. Nevertheless, the principle of *ahimsa* was not so strictly observed in some cases, notably among some Jain kings and local rulers; generally speaking, however, Jain lay people

Parsva, the twenty-third Jaina *Tirthankara*, reputed to have lived in the eighth century BC.

form of matter, a kind of fine dust, as it were. Every *jiva* or 'unit of life' undergoes continual successive rebirths. The actions it generates (*karmas*) have an effect on the *jiva* which in the case of the majority of beings, is to 'encrust' it, make it gross, and weigh it down. But it is possible to reverse this effect through pursuing a life consisting of actions characterized by *ahimsa*, or non-violence, and through the practice of *tapas* or austerity. (These are the concepts that particularly attracted Mahatma Gandhi.)

Gommatesvara, the Jaina sage. This colossal sculptured figure at Sravana Belgola in southern India is larger than any statue of the Egyptian pharaoh Ramesses III.

have observed the principle, at least in the sense of following a vegetarian diet.

Later developments

As a result of the migration of the monks in different directions, the south and the west, a difference of practice developed in the matter of dress. Those who went south retained the practice of nudity as a symbol of total renunciation of all possessions, while the others, less conservative, took to wearing white clothing. The two wings were therefore known respectively as the 'sky-clad' (*Digambara*) and the 'white-clad' (*Svetambara*). The latter, in the early fifth century AD, held a council and fixed the canon of their scripture; the former, again conservatively, declined to recognize a written canon.

Europe

The massive Lion Gate, the entrance to Mycenae's heavily fortified palace, was built *c*1350 BC.

The Minoans

R. F. Willetts

Introduction

The Minoans created the first major Aegean civilization comparable in its enduring achievements with the older civilizations of the ancient world in Egypt, Mesopotamia and Anatolia. In the process they demonstrated how a small area of the earth's surface, inhabited by inventive people, bounded by the sea and immune from aggressive conquerors for many centuries, could be receptive to, but not dominated by, influences flowing from the vast continents of Asia and Africa. Crete is modest in geographical terms, stretching from west to east for about 170 miles (275 km); its widest points in the centre are about 35 miles (56 km) apart and its narrowest points, in the east, just about 8 miles (13 km) apart. But the island, roughly equidistant from the Greek mainland, the Cycladic islands, Rhodes and Libya, lies across the southern entrance to the basin of the Aegean. It became a familiar anchorage in early prehistoric times for voyagers from the coasts of Asia, Africa and Europe, accepting, adapting and transmitting an adventurous blend of cultural impulses.

The rediscovery of Minoan civilization over the last hundred years, from its origins to its demise, demonstrates a remarkable transition from legend and myth to objective, historical analysis promoted by archaeological exploration combined with literary and linguistic scholarship.

In a famous passage of the nineteenth book of the *Odyssey*, Homer says that there is a land called Crete lying in the midst of the wine-dark deep, which is fair and fertile and girdled by the sea. On that island, he goes on, are countless people and there are 90 cities, with a mixture of languages and peoples, including Achaeans, Eteocretans, Kydonians, Dorians and Pelasgians; and there also is Knossos, mighty city, where Minos used to be king for nine years, familiar of mighty Zeus. In the *Iliad* Homer says that Crete has a hundred towns, and seven from central Crete are mentioned by name: Knossos, Gortyn, Lyktos, Miletos, Lykastos, Phaistos and Rhytion. Again, in the *Iliad*, we learn that 80 ships from Crete participated in the Trojan War, compared with 100 commanded by Agamemnon, leader of the Greek expedition, 60 under his brother Menelaos, 12 under Odysseus from the island of Ithaca.

Assuming that the Trojan War could have occurred in the latter half of the thirteenth century BC, the Homeric record shows what has now become clear from other evidence, that Crete was prestigious, well-populated and prosperous in the later Bronze Age. From the information transmitted by the poets, historians and philosophers of later Classical and Hellenistic times, we gather that the island's past continued to abide in the Greek imagination as a source of haunting legend, religious influence and bygone but memorable social institutions. The historians Herodotus and Thucydides, writing in the fifth century BC, accepted that Crete had once had a great ruler called Minos, with a fleet and dominion overseas. Some modern scholars believe that Plato (*c*430–350 BC) based his report of the lost civilization of Atlantis upon legends about Minoan Crete. Aristotle (384–322 BC), in his *Politics*, discussing the history of the caste system, remarked that it was no original or recent discovery of political philosophy that the state should be divided into classes and that the fighting men should be distinct from the farmers. For, he stated, such a system had continued to the present time in Egypt and in Crete–established in Egypt, according to tradition, by the legislation of Sesostris, and in Crete by that of Minos.

In legend, Minos was husband of Queen Pasiphaë (a daughter of the sun-god), and father of Deucalion, Androgeus, Ariadne and Phaedra. Androgeus emerged superior to his opponents at the games in Athens but his death was contrived by King Aegeus. To avenge his death, Minos made war on the Athenians and they were subsequently compelled to send to Crete, at intervals, a tribute of seven youths and seven maidens, as sacrifice to the Minotaur. The Minotaur was half-man and half-bull, offspring of the intercourse between Pasiphaë and a bull. The monster dwelled in the Labyrinth, constructed by Daedalus. Theseus in due course went to Crete and killed

The West Magazine. Sir Arthur Evans looking at *pithoi* uncovered during early excavations at Knossos.

the Minotaur with the aid of Ariadne, who fell in love with him and gave him the clue of thread that enabled him to find his way out of the Labyrinth.

In antiquity this Labyrinth was considered to be an imitation of the Egyptian Labyrinth which was sacred to the sun. In recent times it has been associated with the 'Theatral Area' at the northwest corner of the palace at Knossos. The myth was celebrated in antiquity in the Crane Dance, which portrayed the windings of the Labyrinth, performed before the horned altar of Apollo at Delos, during the festival commemorating the birth of Apollo and Artemis. It seems that the legends about Daedalus, 'the artist', 'the cunning craftsman', testify to the achievements of the Minoan engineers, builders and

Time-chart of Europe

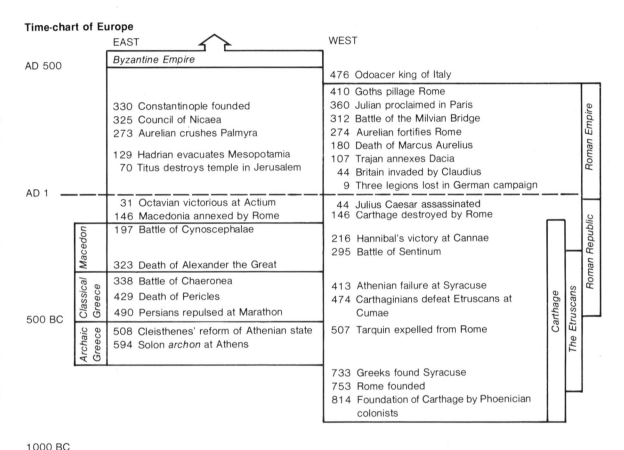

	EAST	WEST	
AD 500	Byzantine Empire	476 Odoacer king of Italy	
		410 Goths pillage Rome	Roman Empire
	330 Constantinople founded	360 Julian proclaimed in Paris	
	325 Council of Nicaea	312 Battle of the Milvian Bridge	
	273 Aurelian crushes Palmyra	274 Aurelian fortifies Rome	
		180 Death of Marcus Aurelius	
	129 Hadrian evacuates Mesopotamia	107 Trajan annexes Dacia	
	70 Titus destroys temple in Jerusalem	44 Britain invaded by Claudius	
		9 Three legions lost in German campaign	
AD 1	31 Octavian victorious at Actium	44 Julius Caesar assassinated	Roman Republic
	146 Macedonia annexed by Rome	146 Carthage destroyed by Rome	
	Macedon — 197 Battle of Cynoscephalae	216 Hannibal's victory at Cannae	
		295 Battle of Sentinum	The Etruscans
	323 Death of Alexander the Great		
	Classical Greece — 338 Battle of Chaeronea	413 Athenian failure at Syracuse	Carthage
	429 Death of Pericles	474 Carthaginians defeat Etruscans at Cumae	
	490 Persians repulsed at Marathon		
	Archaic Greece — 508 Cleisthenes' reform of Athenian state	507 Tarquin expelled from Rome	
500 BC	594 Solon archon at Athens		
		733 Greeks found Syracuse	
		753 Rome founded	
		814 Foundation of Carthage by Phoenician colonists	
1000 BC			
	The Mycenaeans — 1200 Mycenae and Pylos burned		
1500 BC	1500 Thera eruption		
	The Minoans — 1700 New palaces built		
2000 BC			

Agate seal showing an acrobat apparently bull-leaping from a platform or altar.

artisans which the labours of field archaeologists have now revealed.

The discovery of Minoan civilization

Some antiquarian interest in the Cretan past had been stimulated by various reports and descriptions over several centuries before the real work of discovery began in the 1880s. Over the last hundred years since then archaeologists have unearthed monuments from two millennia of the Bronze Age and extended our knowledge far back into the Stone Age. Scholars of several nations have been responsible for this patient, invaluable and often quite spectacular work of discovery; but the names of Heinrich Schliemann (1822–90) and Sir Arthur Evans (1851–1941) as pioneers will always be most prominent in any account of these achievements. Schliemann's excavations at Troy, Mycenae and Tiryns set a precedent to be followed by such successors as

Blegen and Wace, and proved his claim to have found a new world for archaeology.

However, the findings of Evans form a vital focus for Minoan Crete. He first visited Crete in 1893 on a quest for seal stones and the related prehistoric forms of writing. A certain amount of exploring had already been done at Knossos on the site of the Palace of Minos by Kalokairinos in 1878 and also by Schliemann. In 1897 Evans received a permit to excavate some part of the site, but the principal work was to be done over six seasons from 1900 to 1905. His work continued until 1914 and again from 1920 to 1932. His account and interpretation of his discoveries was worthily published in his monumental *The Palace of Minos* in four volumes (1921–35).

By 1905 Evans had decided to arrange the sequence of the Cretan Bronze Age into three periods, Early, Middle and Late Minoan, a division suggested by the legends of

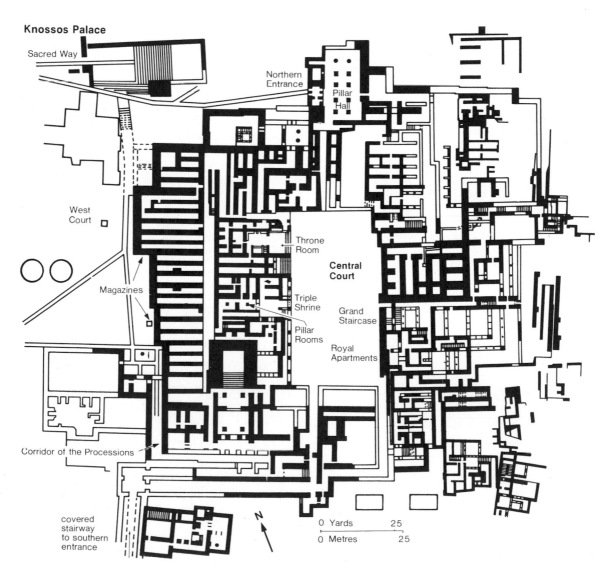

Knossos Palace

Sacred Way

Northern Entrance

Pillar Hall

West Court

Magazines

Throne Room

Central Court

Triple Shrine

Grand Staircase

Pillar Rooms

Royal Apartments

Corridor of the Processions

covered stairway to southern entrance

N

0 Yards 25

0 Metres 25

King Minos and representing a dynastic terminology to be compared with the Egyptian use of 'Pharaoh'. With such a title, Minos could also be regarded as some sort of counterpart of the divine 'Priest-Kings' of Anatolia, representing a god, wearing his clothes, exercising his authority and often bearing his name. The three chronological divisions were subdivided into Early Minoan I, II, III and so on, with still further subdivisions, whenever thought necessary, by means of As and Bs. Schliemann and Evans indeed set the fashion for a new kind of chronology. For, as Minoan remains were to be discovered on Egyptian sites and Egyptian remains on Minoan sites, the prehistory of Crete could be synchronized in some degree with Egyptian records dated by the Egyptian calendar. This chronological system has more recently been considered to involve certain difficulties, in light of other evidence from sites other than Knossos. Hence another descriptive system is sometimes employed. By this alternative means the earlier Bronze Age is typified as Pre-Palatial, the period before the destruction of the first Cretan palaces Proto-Palatial, and the period of the later palaces Neo-Palatial.

While Evans was discovering Knossos in the north, others were exploring the southern area of Crete. The Italian archaeologist Frederico Halbherr began to work in 1900 on the palace site of Phaistos at the eastern end of the ridge closing the central plain of Messara from the sea, in a landscape of great natural beauty. A year later Luigi Pernier took charge of these excavations. A third palace on the north coast, at Mallia, east of Knossos, was first discovered and partly excavated by the Greek archaeologist Joseph Hazzidakis in 1915. At the end of the First World War the work here was continued by French archaeologists. Another Greek archaeologist, Stephanos Xanthoudides, from 1904 onward excavated early circular tombs in the Messara plain. The work of Hazzidakis and Xanthoudides has been continued assiduously by such other members of the Greek Archaeological Service as Marinatos, Platon, Alexiou, Davaras and Sakellarakis. Since the beginning of this century work and publication of finds at Knossos, Phaistos and Mallia has been continuous. The palace at Knossos was restored by Evans on a grand scale, but restoration at Phaistos and Mallia has been more cautiously scientific.

The palaces

The three palaces of Knossos, Phaistos and Mallia had all been subjected to pillage in various ways. The most recently discovered palace, at Zakro in the eastern extremity of Crete, is the only one so far explored that seems not to have been pillaged at all. Preliminary work at the beginning of the century had shown evidence of Minoan buildings, pottery, tools and clay seals. The new excavations have revealed a palace not unlike those of Knossos, Phaistos and Mallia. Except in the northwest at modern Khania (ancient Kydonia) which has not yet been totally investigated, the present opinion is that palaces of the size of Knossos, Phaistos, Mallia and Zakro are not likely to be found. However, smaller yet important conglomerations have already been excavated, among them Ayia Triada close to Phaistos. The large palaces represented the most prominent buildings in large cities, with streets leading up to them from outer perimeters. Though important work is now being done at Knossos, which is bound to yield highly important conclusions, it is still the case that the only extensively explored township of the Bronze Age is at Gournia in eastern Crete on the Gulf of Mirabello, built around a hill, with narrow streets leading to a small palace on the hill top, and with small houses clustered close, in which were found tools and everyday articles of use. This site was excavated between 1901–4 by the American Harriet Boyd; and another American archaeologist, Richard Seager, carried out important excavations on the little island of Mochlos, opposite Ayios Nikolaos on the Gulf of Mirabello, in 1908. Mochlos had probably once been a typical Bronze Age promontory, with harbours either side of an isthmus, until the sea level rose to such an extent that it became separated from the coast.

Monuments of all kinds discovered by archaeology do not deliver statements about the societies that produced them; but they do transmit messages that are subject to different interpretations. Hence the difficulty of offering, even in outline, any precise account of the social organization of the Minoans over a period of two millennia. The special features of the palace centres which have yielded the characteristic glories of the height of Minoan civilization of the second millennium BC have been detected in the influences stimulated by earlier settlements like Vasiliki and Myrtos, rooted in stable social foundations. A prolonged neolithic tradition with a settled agricultural basis was combined with hunting, fishing and stock raising as supplementary features. A simple but firm self-sufficiency was founded upon agrarian techniques in combination with handicraft manufacture, ensuring that a suitable environment for the economic basis of subsequent palatial civilization could be established throughout the centuries of the early Bronze Age.

The flowering of mature Minoan civilization began about 2000 BC and endured for some 600 years, apparently as a process of continuous peaceful development. The Greek Bronze Age as a whole spanned 1700 years, roughly from 2800 to 1100 BC. We may describe the early Bronze Age of Crete (terminating at about 2200 BC) as Pre-Palatial Minoan, the Middle Minoan period (up to about 1700 BC) as Old Palace Minoan, and the ensuing period (up to about 1450 BC) as New Palace Minoan. The Old Palaces were repeatedly damaged and eventually suffered such destruction, perhaps by earthquake, that it became seemingly impossible to reconstruct them on their original plan. Therefore the palaces that have been excavated are the New Palaces, built on similar lines, though some remains of their predecessors have been found at Knossos and Phaistos. Their functional design, with an agglutinative architecture common to smaller palaces, villas and houses, seems suited to a large-sized and close-knit household, with an

Ladies of the Court. A fresco from the palace at Knossos, *c*1600 BC, which was found in the East Hall of the domestic quarters.

abiding tradition of collective social organization. For the skills developed by the neolothic households became differentiated and refined, with a division of labour among specialists, craftsmen and artisans, maintained from the surplus food supply of the farming communities. The Cretan palaces, compared with the Mycenaean, are not like castles, because they had no defensive walling of fortification. The importance of commerce could also imply basic differences between the Cretan palaces and those in Egypt and West Asia. The size and the number of storerooms in Crete support this implication, as does the impressive network of Minoan roadways; and there is no interest in representations of warfare until later times.

The raw materials for the Minoan industrial workshops, such as gold and silver, tin, lead and copper, ivory and lapis lazuli, came by sea transport from neighbouring countries. In the Bronze Age there were many sandy beaches for the reception of ships, and harbour facilities could be provided on either side of small promontories according to the direction of the wind. The craftsmen and artisans who worked with these materials had a favourable status in a society which so successfully exploited natural environmental advantages by encouraging the application of skilled techniques. The planning and building of complex palaces, of paved roads, viaducts, aqueducts, drainage systems, irrigation channels and harbours testify to a remarkable knowledge of engineering.

The splendour of Minoan fresco painting, with the sense of movement as its dominant characteristic, its graceful figures and its decorative designs, is now well known and generally admired. These superb creations often influenced the other arts and crafts in which Minoans also became highly expert. These included the

alloying of metals to great strength; the moulding and hammering of bronze; the dexterous use of filigree, granulation and soldering; the manipulation of gold, silver, ivory and lapis lazuli for inlays; the carving of stone, even rock crystal, basalt and obsidian. Quite apart from its importance in assessing chronology and stratification, Minoan pottery represents a treasured legacy, in its variety and beauty and in the skilful use of colour in its manufacture. Coloured glass was fashioned into jewelry, gold and ivory statues were first made in Minoan times, and a similar originality was applied in the technique of polychrome faience. An astonishing number of Minoan artistic masterpieces have been recovered and miniatures are conspicuous among them.

The scripts of ancient Crete

The technique of Cretan writing in the Bronze Age deserves special mention as a study in itself and for its relationship to the more general investigation of origins and forms of writing among neighbouring civilizations.

The texts discovered by archaeologists were classified by Evans as pictographic or hieroglyphic scripts and linear scripts, the latter being divided into Linear A and Linear B. Early pictographs of the third millennium BC were engraved on seals; more developed forms from about the beginning of the second millennium have survived not only on seals but on tablets and bars, with some resemblances to the Hittite signary and Egyptian hieroglyphs. This kind of writing was apparently discontinued by the end of the Middle Minoan period, to be succeeded by linear scripts with signs composed of simple straight or curved lines–hence their title. Evans applied the term Linear Class A to distinguish earlier scripts from the Linear Class B script in use at Knossos

Linear B tablet. Linear B script was used at Knossos and the Mycenaean citadels in Greece after about 1450 BC.

when the palace was eventually destroyed. Fragments of more than 3000 clay tablets have been found in the ruins of the palace and other buildings destroyed at the same time, about ten times more than the total of Linear A texts so far available.

In 1939 Linear B texts were discovered on the Greek mainland near Messenian Pylos and, since 1945, more have been found at Mycenae, Tiryns and Thebes. The tablets from Knossos were assigned by Evans to the Late Minoan II period terminating about 1400 BC. The mainland tablets mostly belong to the time when Mycenae and Pylos were destroyed about 1200 BC. Despite the gap of two centuries, the writing is virtually identical; and various interpretations and solutions have been offered in explanation. The decipherment of Linear B as an early form of Greek, by Michael Ventris and Dr John Chadwick, was announced in 1953.

Religious beliefs

Minoan Crete has added a special and substantial chapter in the history of world religions. With an emphasis upon natural forces and fertility cults, in certain ways Minoan religion reflects the Cretan landscape, the richness of its plains and the rugged grandeur of its mountain peaks. From the earliest times until late antiquity the island's caves were cult centres. The mystical aspects of Cretan religion which were to have an abiding influence upon the Classical Greek religion of historical times were associated with the concept of a mother-goddess and a dying god, connected with the bull, later celebrated as Zeus Kretagenes ('Cretan-born Zeus'). This god resembled Greek Dionysos, also a bull-god and a dying god. Cretan Zeus, who dies and is born again, differs from the immortal Zeus of the traditional Greek pantheon. The two conceptions of Zeus help us to separate Minoan from Mycenaean phases, the first typified by cults of the mother-goddess in various forms, the second initiating the growing supremacy of the male deities. This male element certainly manifested itself in Minoan times but was apparently stimulated under Mycenaean influence from the mainland in the later Bronze Age, perhaps indeed under the direct influence of Greek-speaking Achaeans, as may be inferred from the traditions of central Crete. Homer and Hesiod, says Herodotus, first fashioned theogonies, gave the gods their epithets, their offices, occupations and their forms: we may infer that the traditional theogonies of Greece derived from the epic tradition with its roots in the Mycenaean world of the later Bronze Age.

The Minoan goddess had no name but the goddesses known to us from later evidence sustained her role in different contexts. They include Demeter and her daughter Persephone, symbol of the seeds which lie on the ground for part of the year, returning as the corn that sustains human beings; Leto, mother of Apollo and Artemis, had definite Minoan associations, markedly in central and eastern Crete in historical times; Britomartis had a Minoan name–'Sweet Maid'; Dictynna, like Artemis, a goddess of the mountains and the countryside, was associated with Britomartis. These compelling influences from prehistoric times are now generally acknowledged as an essential prelude for the proper study and understanding of Greek religion as a whole.

The end of Minoan civilization

The major centres of Minoan civilization suffered catastrophic disaster about the middle of the fifteenth century BC. The cause of this destruction has been the subject of continuous debate. There might have been an invasion and pillage by mainland Mycenaeans; or internal revolt; or a violent natural catastrophe such as earthquake or the explosive volcanic eruption of the nearby island of Santorini (Thera), about 100 miles (160 km) north.

There are some common features in Bronze Age societies such as the Hittites, the Egyptians, the Mycenaeans, even the contemporary Chinese, originating in a monopoly control of bronze by ruling groups in an economy which accumulated wealth for a minority. Specialist craftsmen were supported by tributes from the cultivators, to enable them to produce luxury goods and weapons for administrators, priests, soldiers and merchants. Marked inequalities developed as the constant endeavour to acquire more wealth extended areas of

A snake-priestess, or a snake-goddess, from the Palace of Minos at Knossos.

exploitation by conquest, diplomacy and alliances. As the power and influence of the Mycenaeans expanded in the later Bronze Age, closer contacts between Crete and the mainland must certainly have been established. There are, however, reasons for supposing that Crete in Late Minoan times was undergoing changes typical of other Bronze Age societies, quite apart from the possibility of Mycenaean domination or conquest. Perhaps internal social and economic stresses coincided with an external role of coercion, aided even by colonization.

Such possibilities might account for the Greek traditions of a far from beneficent Minos, with a mighty fleet to sustain dominion overseas. If so, the end of the dominion could have been part of the general collapse of Bronze Age cultures in the later centuries of the second millennium BC.

The causes for the ruin of Minoan civilization are bound to be the subject of continuing speculation. The rich legacies of that civilization in its flourishing heyday survive to be studied and admired.

The Mycenaeans

J. T. Hooker

Mycenaean culture

'Mycenaean' is the name given to the characteristic culture of southern and central Greece in the late Bronze Age (c1600–1100 BC). The earliest manifestations of the culture are found in the Peloponnese in the sixteenth century BC, especially in the northeast (later Argolis) and the southwest (later Messenia). By about 1400 BC the Mycenaean civilization had penetrated the greater part of mainland Greece, extending as far north as Thessaly and the borders of Epirus. From c1400 to c1200 BC two main trends are discernible: the movement towards a remarkable homogeneity of culture over a wide area, and the expansion of the Mycenaeans far beyond the Greek homeland. Excavations have revealed Mycenaean remains in Sicily, southern Italy, Egypt, the Dodecanese, the Cyclades, Cyprus, the Levant, and sites in the west of Asia Minor. There were certainly Mycenaean settlements in Rhodes and in Melos; heavy concentrations of Mycenaean imports elsewhere, for example in Cyprus, may reflect settlement or the establishment of trading posts. The Mycenaeans were thus in direct contact with two of the other 'great powers' in the eastern Mediterranean: Egypt and Ugarit (an important entrepôt on the Syrian coast). Their communication with the Hittite empire was probably indirect. It is a question whether the homogeneous culture of the Mycenaean world reflects a political unity (resembling the Hittite monarchy) or a loose federation of independent states.

Signs of serious trouble become apparent c1250 BC, when some of the major centres of Mycenaean Greece were affected by fires. At the end of the thirteenth century a series of crippling disasters overtook the Mycenaeans, destroying some settlements, severely damaging others, and bringing to an end the unified Mycenaean culture. (The agent, or agents, of this widespread destruction cannot be identified with certainty.) In the undestroyed centres the Mycenaeans continued their way of life, which now showed greater provincialism than in the fourteenth and thirteenth

centuries and was no longer centred upon the imposing palaces. There was some movement of population away from Mycenaean centres to Kephallenia, Achaea, Crete, and Cyprus. An exception to the trend towards provincialism is provided by Perati in eastern Attica, which had links with Egypt and the east. By about 1100 BC the distinctive Mycenaean culture was coming to an end: in the places where it survived it evolved into 'sub-Mycenaean', and Attica replaced Argolis as the main innovative centre of the Greek mainland.

Information about the Mycenaeans is derived from three principal sources. First, and most important, are the reports of the excavations at Mycenaean sites, initiated in a systematic way by Heinrich Schliemann in 1876, and still continuing. Then we have to take account of the allusions to Mycenaean Greece made in the *Iliad* and *Odyssey*. These must obviously be used with great caution, but they do contain some surprisingly accurate descriptions of material objects, topography, and customs. Lastly there are the Mycenaean texts in the so-called Linear B script, which was deciphered in 1952 and shown to be a vehicle for writing the Greek language. The value of these contemporary records needs no emphasis: they have added to our knowledge of the Mycenaean communities (especially of their religious practices and economic structure) in a way that study of the artifacts, by itself, could never have done.

Origins and characteristics of Mycenaean culture

The Mycenaean civilization existed as such in its own right, and it can be defined by its possession of certain clearly marked characteristics. But, before describing the most important of these, we must say something about the origins of the culture now recognized as 'Mycenaean'. The impulses that gave rise to the Mycenaean civilization are imperfectly understood, but one fact can be regarded as certain, namely that 'Mycenaean' does not represent merely a continuation of the 'Helladic' culture of the middle Bronze Age in Greece (c1900–1600 BC). It does incorporate many Helladic features, but it has added to them features derived from the 'Minoan' civilization of Bronze Age Crete. Starting with a fusion of Minoan and Helladic, the mainland Greeks evolved something different from either; and it is this new entity that we now call 'Mycenaean'.

By the sixteenth century BC the Minoans had already had a long and brilliant history. They had traded and colonized extensively abroad, leaving traces of their presence in those areas of the Mediterranean that were later reached by the Mycenaeans. It is remarkable that in the course of this overseas expansion they had little to do with the inhabitants of mainland Greece until about 1600 BC. The influence of the Minoans upon mainland culture was decisive in some fields of activity, for example pottery decoration, fresco painting, and the manufacture of seals and rings. It is impossible to assess to what extent Minoan beliefs and mental attitudes were adopted on the mainland. It does not seem to be the case that Mycenaean civilization arose because of the close contacts with Crete; but it would be true to say that because of these contacts the course of mainland culture was diverted into different channels.

The vigour and independence of Mycenaean culture are displayed to impressive effect in the building types. From their Helladic predecessors the Mycenaeans inherited the concept of the *megaron*, a large squarish room with anteroom and vestibule. The *megaron* formed the centrepiece of the largest Mycenaean palaces: those at Pylos, Tiryns, and Mycenae itself. At these three sites the *megaron* had a circular hearth fixed in the centre of the floor, suggesting the possibility that the room was designed as a place of sacrifice. It was the general practice of the Mycenaeans (a practice quite alien to Minoan habits) to fortify their sites with massive 'Cyclopean' circuit walls, consisting of courses of large roughly dressed boulders, with the interstices filled with small stones and rubble. Pylos is the only major site that has not yielded substantial traces of such walls. All of the known palaces, and some other sites, were decorated with fresco paintings: the Mycenaeans had undoubtedly borrowed from Crete the art of wall painting, and they added to the naturalistic repertory of the Minoan artists scenes involving warfare and the chase.

A good deal is now known about Mycenaean tombs. The most elaborate of these mark an immense advance over anything previously known on the mainland. Prior to the Mycenaean period, the inhabitants of Greece had buried their dead in pits dug out of the ground or in cists (simple rectangular graves lined with stone slabs). These humble burial types never went quite out of use, and they came back into popularity in the depressed conditions at the end of the Mycenaean age. The Shaft Graves at Mycenae (c1600–1500 BC) consist, as their name implies, of shafts sunk into the ground; the floor was lined with pebbles, the sides built up, and the tomb closed by a roof. *Stelai* (stelae: slabs of stone, sometimes decorated with scenes in low relief) were set up over some of the Shaft Graves. In the period following that of the Shaft Graves, important persons at Mycenae were buried in *tholoi*. Nine of these built tombs are known at

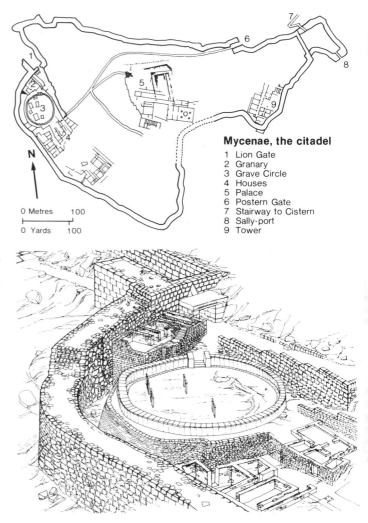

Grave Circle A at Mycenae, as it probably appeared c1200 BC.

Mycenae, the citadel

1 Lion Gate
2 Granary
3 Grave Circle
4 Houses
5 Palace
6 Postern Gate
7 Stairway to Cistern
8 Sally-port
9 Tower

0 Metres 100
0 Yards 100

N

Mycenae, where they were driven into hillsides; but at some other sites they were erected on level terrain. The round burial chamber (the *tholos* proper) was constructed by making each course of stones overlap the one below, until a slightly pointed dome was produced at the top. The *tholos* was approached by a *dromos* (a long, sloping entrance passage) and its mouth was closed by doors. The largest known *tholoi* are the 'Treasury of Atreus' at Mycenae and the great tomb at Orchomenos in Boeotia: both are of massive and careful construction, and both possess a second burial chamber leading out of the *tholos*. Although at Mycenae the *tholos* seems to have been the successor of the shaft for the most important burials, *tholoi* of smaller size were in use much earlier in Messenia, and the practice of building *tholoi* probably originated in that region. At about the time of the first appearance of *tholoi* at Mycenae (c1500 BC) the earliest chamber tombs are found there. Subsequently, down to and later than the era of destruction in 1200 BC, they became the most widespread method of burial in

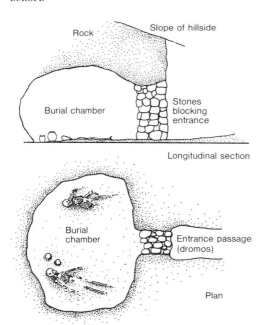

Rock

Slope of hillside

Burial chamber

Stones blocking entrance

Longitudinal section

Burial chamber

Entrance passage (dromos)

Plan

Section and plan of a typical Mycenaean 'chamber-tomb', or *tholos* (*c*1500–1200 BC). A vault was hollowed out in a hillside, closed with stones, and provided with an entrance-passage.

Mycenaean Greece. Whole cemeteries of chamber tombs are known at a number of sites. The chamber tomb consists of a simple vault roughly cut out of a hillside and closed with stones; like the *tholos*, it usually possesses a sloping *dromos*. Mycenaean tombs have a twofold significance for us: on the one hand the burial groups found in many of them display virtuosity in art and craftmanship as practised by the Mycenaeans, the nature of their dependence on other cultures (especially the Minoan), and the extent to which objects were imported from abroad; on the other hand such tombs as the 'Treasury of Atreus', by their very size and elaboration, give a vivid impression of the architectural and engineering expertise at the disposal of the Mycenaeans, especially in the period after 1400 BC. (Mycenaean skill in these fields is further exemplified by roads, bridges, embankments, and the defensive works already mentioned.)

Of the products of Mycenaean civilization, pottery may be considered first, because of its great importance in establishing a chronological framework for the late Bronze Age. A distinctive type of Mycenaean pottery appears first in the sixteenth century BC in Argolid and Messenian tombs. Broadly speaking, it may be said to owe its shapes to the preceding mainland workshops and its decoration to the Minoan culture of Crete. The first experiments at making 'Mycenaean' pottery sometimes led to rather awkward results, but by the second Mycenaean period (fifteenth century BC) the motifs of the Minoan 'marine' and 'vegetable' styles had been absorbed into the mainland repertory with impressive success: this is true especially of the large 'palace-style' jars. After

the destruction of Knossos, the principal Minoan site, in 1375 BC, direct communication between Crete and the mainland was greatly reduced. The Mycenaean potters now went their own way, uninfluenced by developments in Crete, and they manufactured mass-produced ware of high quality, to satisfy the enormous demand in Greece and abroad. The naturalistic motifs taken from the Minoans evolved out of all recognition or were superseded by purely abstract patterns, with frequent use of thick black lines running horizontally round the vessel. The favourite shapes were the 'pilgrim flask' and false-necked jar ('stirrup jar'), both used for transporting liquids, small jugs, and goblets with and without stems. Large bowls ('craters'), decorated with chariots or with stylized animal scenes, stand out as exceptions to the general trend: they were fabricated particularly for the Cypriot market. In pottery, as in other arts, the uniform style of the thirteenth century was abandoned shortly after 1200 BC. The two principal types were then the Close Style, in which the entire surface of the vessel was covered with decoration, and the Granary Style, which reduced painted decoration to a bare minimum, so foreshadowing the sub-Mycenaean ceramic phase.

A typical Mycenaean artifact is the small clay figurine, most often fashioned in the crude shape of a woman but sometimes assuming various animal shapes. Such figurines have been found in very large numbers at Mycenaean sites, especially in tombs; they may have served as votives, but their exact purpose is unknown. Seals and gold rings appear in tombs from the beginning of the

Mycenaean amphora (fourteenth century BC).

Mycenaean terracotta figurines (c1350–1200 BC). Two typical shapes suggesting the female form.

narrower, one shorter and broader) survived into the fifteenth century BC; thereafter two new kinds were developed, of which the more practical and longer-lived had its shoulder extended on both sides in a 'cruciform' shape. Short daggers for hand-to-hand fighting are displayed in Shaft Grave art: actual blades from the Shaft Graves are superbly decorated and are not intended for use. Chariots are depicted in art throughout the Mycenaean age. Their drivers participate in hunting, processional, and funeral scenes; there is no direct evidence that the Mycenaeans ever used their chariots in warfare.

The Linear B texts (especially those from Pylos, c1200 BC) give valuable hints about the economic, political, and social structure of the Mycenaean communities and their religious observances. The Pylos archive attests a complex economic system, with intensive specialization and a high degree of centralized control and inspection. The contents of the most important Pylos tablets are here summarized: the classes being arbitrarily designated by the letters of the alphabet. Aa-Ae texts refer to groups of women (probably slaves), in some cases along with their children, organized in units for the performance of specific tasks; one text speaks of women who look after 'sacred' gold. The An set contains (i) lists of oarsmen from named places and (ii) lists of men at named places, divided into groups and subgroups–the context shows that these are likely to be detachments of soldiers guarding the Messenian coast. On tablets give lists of cattle, sheep, and goats. The E series forms a large and important group. Amounts of grain are recorded together with personal names. The quantities of grain are related to areas of land, which are either owned directly by the persons named or held on a kind of lease from other persons or from the local community (*damos*). One set of plots is situated in *pakijana*, apparently a cult centre near Pylos; we cannot tell whether the other plots mentioned were also at *pakijana*. The Jn texts deal with weights of bronze. Jn 829 lists amounts of bronze that are to be contributed by officials in sixteen places (including *pakijana*) for the manufacture of weapons. Other Jn tablets give details of bronze allotted to smiths

Mycenaean period. Both in execution and in subject matter they owe a great deal to the long-established Minoan schools of miniature art, and it is often impossible to say for certain whether a specific piece found on the mainland was made there or in Crete. The cult scenes and animal representations on the seals are strongly reminiscent of Minoan work; so are the cult scenes on gold rings, but other rings with scenes of warfare or hunting cannot be paralleled in Crete. Striking examples of gold work from the early Mycenaean period are the death masks and ornaments from the Shaft Graves and the two repoussé cups from the Vaphio *tholos* in Laconia. Later in the Mycenaean age (1400–1200 BC) the art of ivory carving reached a high level: boxes, plaques, and free-standing groups exemplify the art at its best.

The evolution of fighting gear may be traced by combining the evidence of fresco painting with that of artifacts recovered from excavations. The chief defensive equipment at the time of the Shaft Graves consisted of a boar's tusk helmet together with one of two kinds of shields: either a tall body-shield or a smaller type in the shape of a figure-of-eight (both types being made of leather stretched on a light frame). By the fourteenth century BC these types had been superseded by a small round shield. Its use presupposes the wearing of body armour, but this is very rarely attested: the best example is provided by the bronze corslet in a Dendra tomb (Argolis) (c1400 BC). Both heavy and light spearheads were found in the Shaft Graves: they seem to belong to thrusting and to throwing weapons respectively. The two sword types of the Shaft Graves (one longer and

One of two gold cups from the Vaphio tomb, Laconia, c1500 BC. The bull-decoying scene is executed in repoussé technique and shows very fine workmanship, perhaps Minoan.

for working: what they were to make with the metal is not specified. The Ma tablets mention assessments of six (unidentified) commodities in named places: these commodities may represent tax or tribute of some kind. The 13 Ta tablets contain an elaborate inventory made on the occasion of an inspection; the contents comprise useless artifacts together with receptacles of the finest workmanship. Another type of inventory (this time of chariot wheels and armour) is given by the S tablets. The texts that convey most information about cult practice belong to the Fr, Tn, and Un classes. They record the disbursement of gold cups and quantities of oil, honey, flour, cheese, and wine as offerings to divinities. The cults and shrines of familiar Hellenic deities are mentioned, notably those of Poseidon, Zeus, Hera, and Hermes. The names of some other gods are certainly Greek but are not known from later times. One important divinity is called simply *potnia*, 'lady'; *potnia* might be the name of one particular goddess or an epithet shared by several deities. The evidence of the Pylos tablets, which give details of offerings to gods at their shrines, is difficult to reconcile with other sources of knowledge about Mycenaean religion. Excavation has revealed small rooms in palaces shown to be cult centres by their benches, libation vessels, and large clay idols. In addition some seals and rings, strongly affected by Minoan influence, vividly represent a kind of vegetation worship sometimes associated with ecstatic dancing.

Linear B inscriptions are much more sparse at other sites. Mycanae itself has yielded some tablets, which are noteworthy for their mention of spices (some of which must have been imported), for instance celery seed, coriander, cumin, fennel, and sesame. One or two fragments of tablets have been found in modern excavations at Tiryns: these form part of an archive similar to the Pylian. A number of tablets from Thebes have helped to clarify some items of Mycenaean vocabulary, especially in the religious sphere. Of considerable importance are the storage jars at Thebes which bear painted Linear B inscriptions; analysis of these indicates that the jars (and their liquid contents) were imported from Crete.

The Mycenaean sites

Only some of the most important sites can be mentioned here; others are described in general works on Mycenaean Greece given in the suggested further reading.

In Argolis the two predominant sites are Mycenae and Tiryns. Mycenae, the settlement from which the entire culture takes its name, occupies a steep hill of modest dimensions about 12 miles (19 km) from the sea. A settlement had been established there long before the beginning of the Mycenaean age, but it first became important c1600 BC. The objects from the two circles of Shaft Graves are among the earliest that can be diagnosed as distinctively 'Mycenaean'. The six graves of Circle A, especially Graves IV and V, contain an unsurpassed profusion of burial gifts, including many of gold and other precious materials. Such gifts attest both the wealth and the artistic resources available at

Mycenae in the sixteenth century BC. It is disputed whether a palace as such existed in the time of the Shaft Graves. The first identifiable circuit walls were built c1400 BC, enclosing the top of the hill. Changes were later made in these walls: the southwest portion was moved outwards so as to include Shaft Grave Circle A, and the whole site was made into a powerful fortress by the addition of a tower, of the Lion Gate (with its massive bastion) at the northwest corner, and of a Postern Gate let into the north wall. Within the walls was the palace with its *megaron*, approached by a ceremonial staircase. To the east and southwest of the palace stood a number of houses, one of which contained the shrine. The walls were further extended to the northeast c1200 BC, so as to protect access to the water supply. The walls thus embraced citadel, palace, and tombs of revered ancestors. The most important structures outside the walls are: Shaft Grave Circle B, the nine *tholoi*, cemeteries of chamber tombs, and houses, some of which have yielded important artifacts and Linear B tablets. Serious destruction is attested at Mycenae c1250 BC, and again c1200 BC and c1150 BC. In the first of these disasters, four houses outside the walls were devastated; another house was destroyed in the second, which affected buildings inside the citadel as well; the third brought to an end the granary inside the citadel. It is uncertain whether the palace was destroyed in the second or the third conflagration. The site of Mycenae continued to be inhabited after the era of destruction, but at a far lower level of culture than in the palatial epoch.

Among the other Mycenaean cities in Argolis, Tiryns deserves special mention because of its size, the formidable strength of its walls, and its functions as an administrative centre. The first phase of excavation, initiated by Schliemann, uncovered a palatial complex, with a larger and a smaller *megaron*, at one end of a low hill; this complex, like that at Mycenae, was approached by a ceremonial gateway and a protecting bastion. The massive walls of the complex, known as the Upper Citadel, had been extended at some time in the history of the site, so taking in the entire hill; but in the early excavations this Lower Citadel received only superficial examination. Renewed excavation, begun in the 1960s and still continuing, has revealed many buildings in the Lower Citadel and also the existence of important houses outside the walls, at least two of which were constructed after the burning of the citadel. *Tholoi* and chamber tombs have been found about a mile from the citadel. Fire devastated the citadel three times in the late Mycenaean period: presumably it was the last of these fires that finally destroyed the palatial complex (c1200 BC?). After the final destruction the palace was not reoccupied, and the surviving inhabitants lived in the houses outside. Other important sites in Argolis were Argos, Asine, Dendra, Berbati, and Prosymna—of which the first three had, or were closely associated with, walled citadels.

No citadels have come to light in the central Peloponnese; but extensive Mycenaean settlements are known in Arcadia (Asea) and in Laconia (Ayios Stephanos and the Menelaion).

In the western part of the Peloponnese the early Mycenaean Age is well represented by a number of *tholoi*, some of which (for example those at Routsi and Peristeria) contained very rich grave goods. With the exception of Nichoria the Messenian sites had dwindled in importance by 1300 BC; and at about that time the great palace of Pylos (some 10 miles (16 km) north of the modern town) was built. The Pylian palace, like the palaces of Mycenae and Tiryns, contained a *megaron*, administrative areas, living quarters, reception rooms, and storage areas; but, unlike them, it did not occupy a naturally defensible position and was not protected by walls. The Linear B texts found at Pylos show that the palace had control over, or at least administrative interest in, large areas of Messenia. The palace was devastated by fire c1200 BC and was not afterwards reoccupied.

Attica has yielded a large number of Mycenaean graves. Besides several cemeteries of chamber tombs there should be mentioned the important *tholoi* at Marathon, Menidi, and Thorikos. There was undoubtedly a Mycenaean citadel on the acropolis of Athens, which offers some points of resemblamce to the Mycenaean citadels in the Peloponnese. More than 40 chamber tombs have been excavated in the region of the Athenian Agora. Both Athens and the ancient site of Lefkandi in Euboea preserved their way of life without serious disruption in the thirteenth or twelfth century BC. (The twelfth-century cemetery of Perati has already been mentioned.)

Three imposing sites are known in Boeotia: Thebes, Orchomenos, and Gla. Thebes had a large walled palace, where artifacts of high quality (including ivory work) have been found, and also seals of Babylonian origin and the objects with Linear B inscriptions described above. The palace was destroyed by fire c1200 BC, being reoccupied subsequently. (The cemetery at Tanagra near Thebes has been found to contain richly decorated coffins or *larnakes:* a method of burial unparalleled in

The palace of Nestor at Pylos, showing the sacrificial hearth (c thirteenth century BC).

Mycenaean Greece.) Northwest of Lake Copais (now drained) is the citadel of Orchomenos, containing a major Mycenaean palace and associated with the large *tholos*. Northeast of the lake rises the hill of Gla, along the top of which the Mycenaeans built a circuit wall nearly 2 miles (3 km) long; within the wall a number of buildings have been partly excavated, but their purpose remains unknown. Both Orchomenos and Gla were violently destroyed, but at what date is not yet certain (1200 BC or later?).

By c1500 BC the Mycenaean civilization had extended into Thessaly. In the later Mycenaean Age the coastal site of Iolkos (Volos) contained a palace which was not destroyed until c1100 BC. Farther north in Thessaly extensive circuit walls with heavy deposits of Mycenaean pottery point to the existence of several flourishing Mycenaean sites. The Mycenaeans made few inroads into Macedonia or Epirus, and their main movements to the Ionian islands did not come until the era of destruction (1200–1100 BC).

Archaic Greece

J. T. Hooker

The Archaic Age of Greece (c700–500 BC), one of the most brilliant and fertile epochs known in the human record, was not recognized as a distinct period by the Greeks themselves. They did not write history, in the true sense, before Herodotus and Thucydides in the second half of the fifth century; and, when those two historians describe persons or events of the Archaic Age, they rely on oral traditions, supplemented by victor lists from Olympia and lists of kings or magistrates kept by some cities. Further information is preserved in later

authors, such as Aristotle (especially important for political developments) and Pausanias (strong on cults and local customs). A good deal of Archaic poetry, though usually in fragmentary form, is extant. Archaic artifacts, especially clay vases, have survived in great numbers.

The Greeks of the Archaic Age were far from forming one Hellenic 'nation'. On the contrary, they were scattered in small settlements throughout mainland Greece (as far north as Thessaly), in Chalcidice, in the

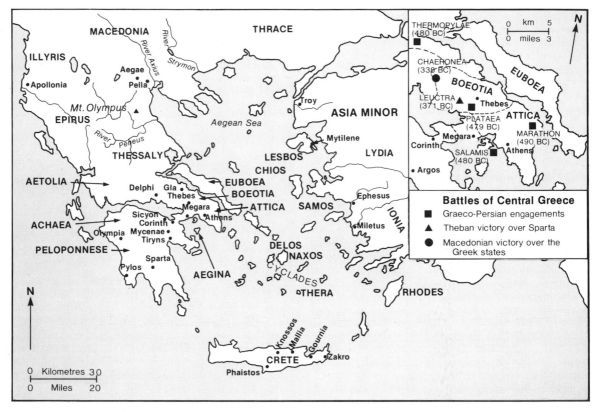

Ancient Greece.

Aegean islands (including Crete), in cities on the west coast of Asia Minor, in islands of the eastern Mediterranean such as Lesbos, Chios, Samos, Rhodes, and Cyprus, and in colonies established in Sicily and southern Italy late in the eighth century BC. Each Greek settlement was, at least in theory, an autonomous state (*polis*); the Greek states (*poleis*) developed in widely different ways during the Archaic period. These strong centrifugal tendencies were balanced by a complex of loyalties, which gave the Greeks a sense of belonging to the same race. Whether they were Dorians (living in the northwest, in the coastal states of the Peloponnese, in Crete, Thera, and Rhodes), Aeolians (in Boeotia, Thessaly, and Lesbos), or Ionians (in Attica and the southwest of Asia Minor), they had in common certain possessions and customs that were distinctively 'Greek' and set them apart from non-Greek peoples (*barbaroi*): (i) the Greek language, spoken in many dialects over a wide area and recorded in writing before 700 BC; (ii) worship of the same gods basically in the same manner, but with local variations in the cults; (iii) participation in three pan-Hellenic cult centres—Olympia (with its Games), Delphi, and Delos; (iv) the *Iliad*, *Odyssey*, and other poems of the 'Epic Cycle', giving the Greeks a glimpse of their heroic past; (v) the veneration of pan-Hellenic heroes, especially Heracles.

Political developments

It is likely that at the outset of the Archaic Age most Greek *poleis* were monarchies, in which the king (*basileus*) belonged to one of the noble families. (Sparta was unique in having two co-regent kings.) In some cities the oligarchic element was stronger, in others the monarchic; but nowhere was the *basileus* an absolute potentate. The ruling aristocrats naturally wanted to keep power in their own hands. In any given *polis* their power might be reduced, or removed altogether, in one of two ways: by the seizure of power by an autocrat (*tyrannos*) or by the extension of political rights to a larger number of citizens. Several *tyrannoi* arose during the Archaic Age by leading a revolt against the aristocratic establishment; and their rule by no means always led to disaster for the cities they governed. Thus under the tyranny of Cypselus and his son Periander (657–585 BC) Corinth clinched her position as the foremost trading nation of continental Greece, sending to Delphi costly tokens of her wealth and artistic achievement and planting colonies along the Corinthian trade routes to the west. In Athens too the cultural life of the city flourished under the tyranny of Pisistratus (546–528 BC) and his son Hippias. Outside the Greek mainland examples of energetic and resourceful *tyrannoi* are provided by Thra-

The Grave Circle at Mycenae. In 1876 Heinrich Schliemann uncovered the Shaft Graves within this cemetery and obliged the academic world to acknowledge Greek prehistory.

sybulus (who at about 610 BC came to power in Miletus, which he skilfully defended against the *barbaroi* to the east) and Polycrates the ruler of Samos from about 532 to about 522 BC–during his tyranny Samos became the major naval power of the eastern Mediterranean and a famous resort of poets from other parts of the Greek world.

As well as the movement towards tyranny, and in direct contrast to it, was the spread of political rights to citizens other than members of noble families. In the Archaic period Greek cities began to trade with one another and with the eastern *barbaroi* on a greatly increased scale. (An important consequence of the increase in trade was the introduction of coinage, probably in the island of Aegina, *c*600 BC.) The mercantile 'middle class' which arose in the seventh century acquired new rights and duties in both the political and the military sphere. The aristocratic cavalry leading retainers into battle was replaced by disciplined ranks of heavy-armed infantry (*hoplitai*): in effect, the middle class at war. Members of the middle class were the principal beneficiaries of political changes in at least some of the *poleis*, for instance Athens and Sparta.

At Athens the *basileus* was no longer a 'king' in a very significant sense. He was mainly concerned with supervising the state religion. His military duties now devolved upon a commander-in-chief (*polemarchos*), while his judicial functions were exercised by an *archon*. *Basileus*, *polemarchos*, and *archon* came from a few noble families and were elected annually. During the seventh century they were joined by six other magistrates, who represented some of the interests of the non-aristocratic classes. On completing his year of office each magistrate joined the Council of the Areopagus, which formed the executive body of the *polis*. The Athenians attributed their first written law code to Dracon (*c*620 BC?): little is known of this except for the articles dealing with homicide. A thorough-going political reform was effected by Solon (*archon* 594 BC). He tried to rectify prevailing economic evils, whereby the rich were oppressing their dependants and debtors, by political means. Economic resources now replaced social status as the test of a man's eligibility for magistracies, and even citizens without property acquired the right of electing magistrates, of sitting in the assembly (*ekklesia*), and of being empanelled as jurors. The *ekklesia* did not yet have the sovereign voice in the state: it merely voted upon measures presented to it on the initiative of the magistrates.

Sparta too, according to Greek tradition, had a great reformer in the person of Lycurgus. Whether there was such a person and, if there was, when he lived have long been matters of dispute. The nature of his reforms too is obscure. What can be said for certain is that by the end of the Archaic period four organs of government exercised authority at Sparta: (i) the two hereditary kings, who

The Athenian acropolis. It was fortified in the late Bronze Age, when a Mycenaean palace may have stood there. The buildings presently visible were erected in the fifth century BC.

were no longer absolute but who retained far more influence that the Athenian *basileus*, especially when they acted in concert; (ii) a council (*gerousia*), consisting of the kings *ex officio* and 28 elders elected for life; (iii) the assembly of citizens; (iv) five ephors elected annually. The interplay of these four organs cannot be grasped with certainty, but in general the executive power in the state was exercised by the ephors, and it was they who presented proposals to the assembly.

Equipped with this constitution (a highly unusual one among Greek states), the Spartans greatly enhanced their standing during the Archaic Age. First they absorbed the neighbouring state of Messenia, enslaving its people (henceforth known as helots) and providing themselves with a source of profit and fear, which was the chief element in Sparta's thinking for the next 350 years. They then set about establishing a hegemony in the Peloponnese by concluding treaties with other cities. Thus arose the so-called Peloponnesian League: by virtue of her leadership of the League Sparta became for a time the leading Greek state and did not shrink from intervening directly in the affairs of other cities, for example by invading their territory and driving out *tyrannoi*. By the end of the Archaic Age there were in existence two powerful confederations of Greek states, the Spartan in the south balancing the Thessalian in the north. The question which of the two confederations Athens would finally join or whether she would create a league of her own was a crucial one and was not decided until the fifth century BC.

While the states of mainland Greece were undergoing the upheavals of the sixth century BC, the Lydian empire in southwest Anatolia enjoyed a brief burst of glory under its quasi-legendary king Croesus. According to Herodotus, Croesus tried to form an alliance with the leading Greek cities, but before he could do so his empire was overwhelmed by the Persians. The latter next advanced to the west coast of Asia, where they annexed the Greek cities and prepared for their next logical step, the attempt to bring the mainland Greeks also into subjection.

Philosophy

By the time of the Persian advance to Ionia, Greek thinkers at Miletus had in effect initiated the entire history of philosophy and speculation, as those terms are understood in the western world. Thales, Anaximander, and Anaximenes all lived at Miletus during the sixth century BC, where they were well placed to become acquainted with the thought of Persia and Babylon. They pondered the nature of the perceptible universe and the way in which the universe is to be related to a supreme being (man's place in the universe they did not consider, so far as we know). Apart from his important astronomical and mathematical discoveries, Thales was known as a sage who had propounded the view that water is the first principle from which the universe is fashioned and from which it takes its life-giving force. Anaximander, another notable astronomer, taught that the primal 'stuff' from which everything had evolved

219

was 'the boundless' (*to apeiron*): out of this, he held, the elements of our world have been produced by the interaction of opposites. Anaximenes too considered the primal stuff to be infinite, but he was prepared to identify it as air, which produces everything else by becoming either denser or more rarified.

Thus the three great Milesians were all dogmatic teachers, each thinking that he had arrived at the ultimate truth about the constitution of matter. A strong reaction against intellectual dogmatism was expressed by the poet Xenophanes of Colophon, who protested also at the nature of the Homeric and Hesiodic gods. Towards the end of the sixth century BC there flourished at Ephesus one of the most enigmatic of all Greek philosophers, Heraclitus. He seems to have believed in a constantly changing universe and an underlying principle (which he called *logos*, but also fire): this principle maintained a balance between opposing forces in the world. The last great philosopher of the Archaic Age was Pythagoras, who was born in Samos during the sixth century BC but spent his mature life in the south of Italy, where he founded a famous school. Pythagoras was as much mystic and visionary as philosopher. The great range of his interests is indicated by some of the doctrines attributed to him, for example the transmigration of souls and the belief that a definite relationship subsists between objects and numbers. He did not simply teach doctrines in the abstract, but used them as the basis of practical instruction; witness his veto on eating flesh, on the ground that all living things were related.

Poetry

Greek poetry of the Archaic Age is rich in variety of theme and of form. We must distinguish between spoken verse (in iambic or trochaic metres or in elegiac couplets, in which each pair of lines consists of a dactylic hexameter + pentameter) and sung, or lyric, verse.

The earliest known writers of elegiacs are Callinus of Ephesus and Tyrtaeus of Sparta, both of whom used poetry for largely practical purposes, to instil patriotic feeling and to encourage the warriors. Mimnermus of Colophon strikes a more personal note, dwelling on the pleasures of youth and the miseries of old age. With these three poets we may contrast Archilochus of Paros, who flourished c650 BC. He too wrote in elegiac couplets but used iambics and trochaics as well. Archilochus is the first wholly cynical poet in European literature, challenging the assumptions and affectations of the aristocratic warrior caste. He scorned the heroic ambition of achieving fame after death and scandalized the Spartans by admitting that he had thrown away his shield at a critical moment. The terseness and force of Archilochus' poetry, admired in antiquity, are attested in the extant remains. His vigour is seen again in his downright sexual allusions: the greater part of a poem describing a sexual encounter was first published in 1974. A younger contemporary of Archilochus, and a more diffuse writer, was Semonides of Amorgos, chiefly known for his satire on women in iambics. The iambic tradition produced in Hipponax (sixth century BC) a master of venom and foul-mouthed abuse: he is credited with the invention of the *skazon* line (iambic trimeter with penultimate syllable long).

Meanwhile the line of elegiac poetry was continued in the verses of Solon. He has already been mentioned as the chief reformer of Athens; he was also the earliest major Athenian poet. He describes the social evils he has tried to cure by his legislation and warns his countrymen against a political danger, that of succumbing to the rule of a *tyrannos*. His impressive poem *On righteousness* has survived in its entirety. The elegiac poet Theognis of Megara was perhaps contemporary with Solon. Nearly 700 couplets have come down under his name: a disputed number are by Theognis himself, while the remainder represent the work of other poets belonging to the sixth and fifth centuries. Many poems in the corpus are purely gnomic but some are more personal, expressing for instance the friendlessness of exile or the plight of a man expropriated from his land; others again exalt homosexual love at the expense of heterosexual.

The metres of lyric poetry, although allied to those of spoken verse, were used in more complex ways. Choral lyric was differentiated from lyric monody. So far as is known, choral lyric began life at Sparta. Terpander and others are said to have initiated a tradition of lyric writing there in the first half of the seventh century. Practically nothing is known of their work, except by reputation, but later in the same century come the choral lyrics of Alcman. These, and all subsequent choral lyrics, consisted of music, dance, and words; only the words have survived, although in a mutilated state. Alcman's maiden songs (*partheneia*) were performed by a chorus of 12 girls including the chorus leader. The performances were given as part of a cult observance, specifically the dedication of offerings to a divinity. The best-preserved of Alcman's poems (often called simply his *Partheneion*) contains allusions to legend, a moral drawn from the legend, and the choral song proper. The last may stand as typical work of a master of the Archaic style. There is little obvious logic in the construction: a series of short, brilliantly expressed, images follow one another in breathless succession, with the poet frequently going off at a tangent in ways baffling to us.

At about the time that Alcman was working at Sparta, different schools of poetry flourished at opposite ends of the Greek world. In Sicily Stesichorus composed choral lyric, but lyric of a very different kind from Alcman's: his poetry has a strongly narrative content, drawing on Theban and Argive saga and Heracles' fight with Geryon. It is to lyric monody that we must turn for personal poetry of a passionate intensity. Terpander had come to Sparta from Lesbos, and in his native island there flourished c600 BC his two most renowned successors, the poetess Sappho and the poet Alcaeus. Sappho expresses the physical and mental effects of love, especially of hopeless love, more poignantly than is done by any other Greek. Her affections, often jealous and frustrated affections, were manifestly concentrated on girls, but there is nothing to indicate whether she was a practising 'Lesbian' in our sense. Little is known of her work apart from love poetry, but we have a piece of narrative on the marriage of Hector and Andromache and some fragmentary epithalamia. The poetry of Alcaeus covered a wider range than Sappho's. Alcaeus speaks scornfully of political opponents; at least once he had to leave Mytilene, and a poem written in exile laments his exclusion from the public life of the capital. His interest in legend is illustrated by hymns to gods and episodes from Trojan saga. The pleasures of wine and gnomic observations are the subjects of other pieces.

Two poets are known to have visited Polycrates' court at Samos *c*530 BC: the Ionian monodist Anacreon and the choral writer Ibycus, who came from Italy. Of Anacreon's genuine work little remains except some bitter-sweet miniatures of erotic and convivial poetry; but the style outlived the master and was perpetuated by generations of versifiers. Ibycus followed the tradition of Stesichorus, but was a much less considerable poet: a long fragment of a piece on the Trojan War survives. Finally we must mention the many-sided genius of Simonides, born in Ceos *c*550 BC and befriended by Pisistratus' son at Athens. Apart from his striking epigrams, he has to his credit the development of two highly important forms of choral lyric, the paean and the *epinikion* (celebrating a victory in one of the pan-Hellenic games): in the latter type, myth, gnomic expressions, and praise of the victor are woven into a brilliant whole. This type of poetry was carried to its consummation in Pindar's *epinikia* in the fifth century BC.

Arts

The arts of the Greek world developed at an astonishing rate during the Archaic Age. Here there is room to mention only three: vase painting, sculpture, and architecture.

The decoration of pottery underwent a profound change early in the seventh century under the impact of the so-called Orientalizing Movement. New themes brought to Greece as a result of the eastern trade led to the disintegration of the Geometric style and the rise of a different concept of the vase painter's role. As would be expected from her commercial importance, Corinth played a decisive part in the transition from Geometric to Orientalizing and remained most influential during the seventh century. Other important schools flourished at Athens, in the Cycladic Islands, and in Asia Minor (including Rhodes). The Corinthian painters liked to distribute their motifs in friezes, ranging from simple repetition of elegant grazing creatures to the complex narrative scenes seen on the Chigi Vase.

A technical innovation made at Corinth in the seventh century was to have far-reaching consequences for the history of vase painting. Artists began to represent figures and objects as areas of black paint, showing details by lines incised before firing. This 'black-figure' technique was introduced to Athens *c*630 BC. Late in the seventh century the Nessos Painter decorated his impressive neck amphora at Athens: Heracles fighting Nessos is shown on the neck, and gorgons on the belly. By 600 BC the Athenian black figure was becoming

Black-figure neck-amphora, signed by Exekias: Achilles prepares to kill the amazon Penthesilea (second half of the sixth century BC).

the leading pottery style of the Greek world. Among its early achievements may be mentioned first the François Vase (*c*565 BC), a tall volute crater with narrative friezes, and second an aryballos by Nearchos (*c*555 BC), displaying on its neck the fight between pygmies and cranes. The acme of black figure was reached in the work of two contrasting masters, the Amasis Painter and Exekias, both of whom flourished from about 550 to about 525 BC. The former executed finely conceived scenes in which Dionysus often plays a part (as on a neck amphora in which the god confronts maenads). The Amasis Painter, however, lacks what can only be called the tragic dimension of Exekias' work. For this quality, and also because of his unsurpassed draughtsmanship, Exekias stands out as the supreme Greek vase painter. The intense concentration his figures can achieve is exemplified by two belly amphorae: one with Ajax about to commit suicide, the other with Ajax and Achilles playing at knucklebones.

The red-figure technique was invented at Athens while Exekias was still working. In this new style of vase painting, the figures were left in the colour of the clay and the rest rendered in black paint; details were added by painted lines rather than by incision. Greater flexibility was now available without loss of the fastidious attention to detail that had marked black figure. At first

Detail from red-figure calyx-crater, signed by Euphronios: the winged figure of death carries off the body of Sarpedon, who had been slain by Patroclus (late sixth century BC).

red figure was used in conjunction with black figure, and a series of vases had a scene painted on one side in the old manner and on the other side in the new. Red figure gradually outstripped black figure in popularity, although the latter was in use down to c450 BC. As a masterpiece of the early red-figure style we may cite a crater signed by Euphronios, who worked at Athens in the last quarter of the sixth century: the corpse of Sarpedon is borne from the battlefield by Sleep and Death.

The increasingly skilful depiction of human and other figures on the surface of vases was accompanied by the rise of monumental sculpture. We have many examples from the seventh century of miniature art in stone, clay, ivory, wood, and bronze; but the first attempts at life-size statuary date from c650 BC. The earliest complete remaining *kouros* (naked youth with one foot forward, intended to be viewed from the front) is Attic work from near the end of the century. It is a funerary statue 77 in (1.96 m) high, expressing to the full the early Archaic concept of large-scale sculpture: powerful, but at the same time heavy and unyielding and set in a stiff, awkward pose. The different parts of the body have not yet been brought into a natural organic relationship with one another. A comparison with a *kouros* from

Anavysos in Attica (of the same height as the last-mentioned) shows the great advance made in the representation of the human body during a period of about 70 years. The pose is formally the same, and the same muscularity is evident in the rendering of the torso, but the various features (especially the head) have achieved more life-like proportions, and above all they are now conceived as parts of a convincing whole. Not far different in date from the Anavysos *kouros* (c530 BC) is a famous statue of a young girl from the Athenian Acropolis known as the Peplos Kore (*peplos* being a kind of woollen jacket worn over the *chiton*). In delicacy of expression and skill at rendering the drapery of women's clothes she is one of the finest of the great series of Attic *korai*: the master who sculpted her was perhaps responsible for the 'Rampin' Horseman, also from the Acropolis. So far we have considered only free-standing figures, but in the sixth century BC and later sculptors achieved a narrative aim as well. For this we may compare the Attic grave reliefs, pedimental compositions at Athens and in Corcyra, and the friezes of treasuries at Olympia and Delphi (of which the Siphnian Treasury at Delphi is outstanding for its rich variety).

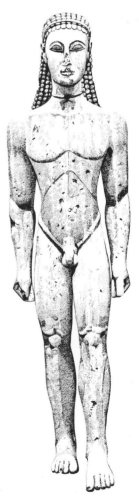

The 'New York kouros': probably Attic work from the beginning of the sixth century BC. Height: 72½ in (183 cm).

Like the vase painters and sculptors, the Greek architects of the seventh century took decisive steps in developing their art. On the mainland, the building of temples in stone was initiated in the second half of the century. One of the earliest experiments is represented by the ground plan of the temple of Apollo at Thermon in Aetolia (*c*620 BC). It is not possible to say exactly when the fully-fledged Doric Order was first applied to the building of mainland temples. The classic configuration of features known as Doric is not attested until the sixth century. The interior of the Doric temple was divided by columns into a wide central area (containing the shrine) and two narrow side aisles. Massive fluted columns sprang straight from the floor along all four sides; they supported an architrave, upon which rested a decorative frieze of alternate triglyphs and metopes; at the ends, the frieze was itself surmounted by a triangular pediment commonly containing sculpted groups. The temple of Hera at Olympia (rebuilt *c*600) was presumably something that would be recognized as fully 'Doric', even though the columns were not made entirely of stone but incorporated some wooden sections. More can be said about the Doric temple of Apollo at Corinth (*c*540 BC): it measures 170×60 ft (52×18 m). Six columns supported each end, and 15 each of the longer sides; 7 monolithic columns, with part of the architrave, are still standing. Ruins of several Doric temples are found in the Greek west: the most important are those at Syracuse and Selinus in Sicily and at Paestum in southern Italy.

Early in the sixth century BC the Ionic Order was developed in the eastern part of the Greek world. It differed in a number of respects from the Doric Order: its delicate columns, with moulded bases and volute capitals, offered a strong contrast to the more austere style of mainland Greece. Two very large temples, each with a double colonnade, belong to this period: one of a

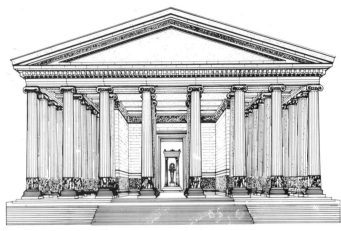

Above: Temple to Artemis, at Ephesus. Below: Temple to Apollo, at Didyma.

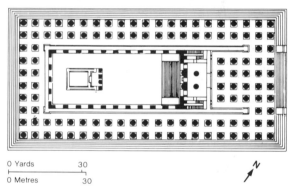

0 Yards   30
0 Metres   30

succession dedicated to Hera in Samos (360×180 ft; 110×55 m), the other (350×170 ft; 107×52 m) dedicated to Artemis at Ephesus.

Classical Greece

W. G. Forrest

Three issues dominate the history of Classical Greece: its relations with Persia; the internal rivalry of Athens and Sparta; and the Athenian achievement, political, literary and artistic.

Persia

The possibility of Persian expansion into the Greek mainland and of a Persian presence in Asia Minor, past, real, imminent or imagined, meant more throughout this period of Greek history than is sometimes thought. In 499 BC many of the cities of the Ionian coast deposed their tyrants, Persian nominees, and tried to break away, with some help from Athens. This messy and not very glorious revolt was squashed in 494 BC and, as a

result, a large Persian fleet crossed the Aegean in 490 BC to punish the Athenians. Few can have been more surprised than the Athenians themselves when victory at Marathon sent the armada scurrying back to Asia. Surprise and jubilation were even greater when an enormous Persian attack in 480–479 BC by land and sea against the whole of Greece was routed after initial success at Thermopylae (though the moral victory lay with the Greeks), at Salamis by sea, due largely to the Athenian navy, at Plataea on land, thanks mainly to the Spartan hoplite, and finally on the coast of Ionia itself, at Mycale.

This great event at once became The Great Event; the distinction between Greek and barbarian, previously little more than a linguistic description, became a distinction between Greek and Barbarian (it was readily forgotten that more Greeks had fought for or sympathized with the Persians than had actively served the loyal cause), and it is very difficult for us to tell how far the myth of the Great Event remained a myth even in the minds of the believers, how far it really affected Greek practice. It offered a ready battle cry for anyone who wanted to argue for cooperation between Athens and Sparta ('Together we beat the Barbarian once, together we can do it again'), an easy theme for a fourth-century rhetorician ('Someone must unite Greeks and lead them against their natural foe'), and, in the end, an excuse for Alexander the Great to march out and tidy up the Barbarian question. But, in fact, the impression remains that Greek politicians for the most part used it rather more often than they were bemused by it.

What we know is that while Persia still posed an active threat to the Greek cities of Asia Minor and even of the Aegean, Athens organized a League of these states under her leadership (founded immediately after the repulse of the invasion, in 478 BC); that this Delian League cleared the Aegean and western Asia Minor of the Persians; that it was maintained even after formal peace was made in 449 BC, that it served Athens' interests but could be justified on the grounds first of a necessary then of a prudential defence against renewed Persian attack, while at the same time it cannot but have helped the general good by controlling piracy, organizing supplies and the like; that when it collapsed in 412 BC the Persians did assert themselves again. On the other hand, although League activity was at first determined by collective decision in theory and for some time also in practice, Athens neither could nor very much wanted to avoid the natural encroachment of an energetic executive (herself) on the deliberative independence of largely compliant and contented allies, in the main quite willing to pay a comparatively light contribution to League funds (the tribute, *phoros*) and to accept the occasional interference of League, i.e. Athenian, officials in exchange for security and a measure of idleness. Some attempts were made to break away, by Naxos *c*471 BC, Thasos 465 BC, Samos 440 BC, Mytilene 427 BC, and more later for different reasons, but they were few and most were engineered by upper-class cliques ('the few'—*oligoi*, 'the rich'—*pacheis*) suspicious and resentful of Athens' democratic inclinations. Such breaches of the oaths of alliance were ruthlessly crushed and later fifth-century Athenian politicians could even describe the League, somewhat hyperbolically, as an Athenian tyranny: but they should have added that the tyranny was a benevolent one.

Athens and Sparta

So Athens had chosen not Thessaly, not Sparta, but independence and, as Thessaly faded somewhat from the scene after her collaboration with the Persian invaders, the relationship between the Spartan and the Athenian Leagues became the overriding issue in interstate politics. Sparta had been given general command of the patriotic struggle in 480–479 BC but afterwards had dithered. Should she exploit that command and continue to rule on land and sea? Should she be satisfied with control of all mainland Greece, either excluding or including Athens? Should she concentrate on security inside the Peloponnese, of her allies and, above all, of her domestic serf (helot) population? Athens had taken advantage of the dithering to form her League, not without some Spartan murmurings, but a serious helot revolt in 465 BC focused Sparta's mind marvellously on the third possibility. Still, when it was put down *c*461 BC there remained hankerings for higher things. In Athens the question was simpler. Should she take positive steps to help the lame dog over a very awkward stile or should she simply sit back and let her captious and rather selfish 'ally' of 480 BC drift into oblivion? In each case opinion fluctuated. There were quite a few 'Boy Scouts' in Athens and Sparta received aid in 463 BC—but four years later there was war, long, desultory, indecisive. There were 'doves' in Sparta as well as 'hawks' and peace was made in 446 BC, largely in Athens' favour. During the next decade, however, the issue clarified itself. Athens was growing fast, economically and in authority, and most Athenians could see no reason artificially to inhibit this growth. But while the growth did not affect Sparta directly it did affect some of Sparta's allies, especially Corinth, and most Spartans could see no reason to resign their role as military 'hit man' of their League merely for the sake of keeping their promises in the treaty of 446 BC. In 431 BC they invaded Attica and the Great Peloponnesian War began.

Athens: constitutional

Lurking behind these two questions, Persia/Greece and Athens/Sparta, was the third, democracy/oligarchy or, more precisely, Athenian democracy/Spartan oligarchy. Sparta had retained her curiously egalitarian, curiously privilege-ridden system unchanged since the days of Lycurgus, the shadowy reformer of Spartan tradition. There were movements inside the straitjacket but the stability of the recognized form was enough to attract the worship of most conservatives in Greece. Athens, on the other hand, offered nothing for a conservative to admire. There, to the outside observer, the theme was adventure, experiment, enterprise.

Solon in 594 BC had first asserted the principle that the law should be above any individual or collection of individuals who might be granted or take upon themselves the right to interpret it. From that moment the story of Athenian political development is the sometimes gentle, sometimes dramatic story of the imposition, the entrenching, the safeguarding of that principle, until by the middle of the fifth century every Athenian male citizen had the same responsibility as any other for the management of his society.

First, in 508 BC, Cleisthenes (*c*570–500 BC) invented a new social and administrative structure which, without destroying the existing familial and consequently conservative system, did make it largely irrelevant by providing Athenians with an alternative that at once satisfied such desire as they already had to control themselves and, of course, in time encouraged a desire and a confidence to control themselves still more. By 462 BC they had reached the point at which no question seemed too important and very few too trivial to be exempt from popular decision, either directly in the assembly, or indirectly in a council (*boule*), developed by Cleisthenes, and chosen annually by lot from the whole citizen body, or in the law courts whose juries were again chosen by lot. The archons (magistrates) and the aristocratic council composed of ex-archons, the Areopagus, became largely decorative, taking the chair in the courts but not affecting the decisions, hearing cases of murder and arson, and, for what it was worth, contemplating the welfare of the sacred olive trees. Already the chief executive power, civil as well as military, had begun to move away from the archons to a body of ten generals (*strategoi*) and these continued in fact to be chosen from traditional ruling families; but there was nothing in the rules to enforce exclusion and even the most aristocratic politician still had to be elected annually and was rigorously judged on his performance by the people as a whole.

Athens: cultural

The measures of 462 BC were the work of an otherwise unknown figure, Ephialtes, assisted in some measure by a grand-nephew of Cleisthenes, Pericles (*c*500–429 BC), who during the years that followed manoeuvred himself up towards a continuous generalship (though still annually elected) from 443 BC and to giving his name to the most stunning decades of intellectual and artistic achievement there has ever been, the Periclean Age. In fairness it should be said that he owed as much or more to Athens, to ordinary Athenians, than Athens did to him. In fairness too, it must be added that it was not only, or even mainly, Athens that produced the artists or the thinkers that made Classical Greece. Many of the names mentioned below will be non-Athenian, from Asia Minor or the islands, now politically as well as intellectually free, or from the Greek cities of southern Italy and Sicily, which had enjoyed their own Great Event in repulsing the Carthaginians in 480 BC and went on to develop their own ideas, against an always shifting background of wealth, splendour, ostentation; of tyranny, oligarchy, democracy–and many other things besides. But most of them visited Athens or even stayed in Athens and, if only because of the nature of our sources, Athens remains for us the focus.

But lest we become too starry-eyed at the outset, it has to be admitted that not all was perfect. For some tastes vase painting took a bit of a tumble in the fifth century. Too great sophistication in technique, the influence of advances in free painting and in sculpture, tempted the painter away from the marvellous balance between potting and painting that marks the sixth century BC and introduced a fussiness, a mannerism, a lack of proportion that can sometimes jar: 'Painted pottery' it has been said, 'now became pottery with painting on it.'

But in sculpture and architecture the story was

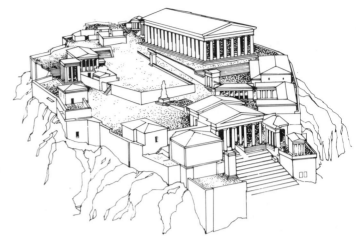

Reconstruction of the Athenian acropolis.

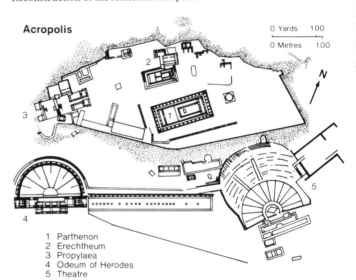

Acropolis

0 Yards 100
0 Metres 100

1 Parthenon
2 Erechtheum
3 Propylaea
4 Odeum of Herodes
5 Theatre

otherwise. The rugged stiffness of the archaic statue, where even the most delicate touches stay superficial, now melts and deepens into a realism in which every muscle, visible or not, seems to be understood, while in buildings sacred and profane, the still slightly gawky proportions of the late sixth century refine themselves to a point at which improvement seems impossible. Let us forget great things that were done outside Attica, the temple of Zeus at Olympia for example, other parts of the building programme in Attica to celebrate formal peace with Persia in 449 BC, at Sunium or Eleusis or elsewhere, and consider only Athena's temple on the Acropolis, the Parthenon, and the sculpture that decorated it. Built between 448 and 438 BC to designs by Ictinus for its structure and Pheidias for its ornament, doric peripteral, some 100×230 ft (30×70 m). The expert is astonished by the subtle tricks of curve and proportion that persuade the viewer of an absolute symmetry; the innocent is content to revel in the symmetry; each has seen something without peer. And meanwhile against

Pericles (*c*500–429 BC), the leading Athenian statesman during the struggle with Sparta.

this apparently stern 'classical' background, the figures of the frieze offer us in the Acropolis Museum or in Lord Elgin's hoard a 'union of common aims and individual freedom ... an order which never breaks down though constantly looking as if it would, which is a perfect illustration of the ideal of democracy ... expressed in the funeral speech of Pericles.'

That speech, coupling a commemoration of the Athenian dead in the first year of the Peloponnesian War with an encomium on Athenian ideals, was recorded by Thucydides (*c*460–400 BC) who, with his older contemporary, Herodotus of Halicarnassus in Asia Minor (*c*485–425 BC), invented the art of history. Records had been kept before, of kings and cabbages, but Herodotus and Thucydides realized that the addition of explanation to a catalogue could both amuse and, especially in the eyes of the somewhat arrogant Thucydides, instruct. It could be said that their achievement was derivative, that they were merely applying Ionian principles to fresher woods or newer pastures; so, it could also be argued, the internal-combustion engine or the atom bomb merely followed from the Renaissance. Whatever the balance of our judgment, the latter part of the fifth century BC saw the creation not only of history but of most of what are regarded as reputable studies today (economics and psychology, are the main exceptions–and some might wish to pause before they blame Classical Greece for ignoring them).

On the Dorian island of Cos, Hippocrates and others around him, created the study of medicine, prognostic, diagnostic, curative, and laid down principles of medical practice that doctors still claim to acknowledge today. At the north end of the Aegean Democritus of Abdera had a far from silly shot at inventing atomic theory; his fellow townsman, Protagoras (born *c*485 BC), had already been thinking about man as a particle in the universe or in a society; in Sicily Gorgias of Leontini addressed himself to the question of how a man could make himself felt in his society and created the art of rhetoric ... the catalogue could continue, but we come back to Athens and a certain Socrates. No one will ever know how much Socrates gave to the creation of philosophy as we understand it, how much was added by his adoring pupil Plato (*c*430–350 BC), but between them they posed many of the questions that have exercised other philosophers since–and quite a few of the better answers were given by Plato's own pupil, Aristotle (384–322 BC).

In literature Athens was even more dominant. In the first half of the century Pindar in Thebes (518–438 BC) had carried the victory ode to its perfection, celebrating the triumphs and glories of Greek aristocrats, kings of Cyrene or tyrants of Sicily with a control of language, metre and construction that is breathtaking even when at its most baffling. But victory in the stadium was an aristocratic or quasi-aristocratic ideal and Athens found another type of festival more congenial to her ways. Twice-yearly orgies of dramatic art, comic and tragic, in honour of Dionysus gave scope for the refinement of crude, simple choral lyrics and dances into performances that still shatter, or paralyse with laughter.

Each of the three tragedians picked out by later Greek critics as the greatest (and by their contemporaries to judge from the awards of prizes), Aeschylus (525–456 BC), Sophocles (495–406 BC) and Euripides (480–406 BC), transformed techniques in style and staging, loosened, opened up the form, humanized the content (though it is a mistake to see any of this as a steady process), but the innocent reader may still be a trifle daunted by the stiffness of the final form. Even the most innocent viewer, however, of a less than competent performance will realize that in the *Prometheus* (Aeschylus), the *Oedipus Rex* (Sophocles) or the *Bacchae* (Euripides) he has been taken, with a directness that makes the formal clutter irrelevant, into touch with issues, old against new, human against divine, human against human, in ways that rule out any judgment except admiration.

These men were concerned passionately with moral and political questions that exercised their audiences (which is not the same as to say that they were political propagandists). Aristophanes (450–385 BC) took a more direct tilt at politics (consequently at politicians) and at any other aspect of Athenian life, literary, social, even philosophical that took his fancy, in his superb manipulations of the curious episodically constructed mixture of exquisite lyrics, bawdy, irreverent slapstick and sophisticated wit which we call Old Comedy.

Neither comedy nor tragedy survived the fifth century BC in their finest form and the reason is not far to seek. It takes confidence as well as courage to ask original questions about gods and men; it takes confidence as well as a sense of humour to give and take uninhibited abuse. The fifth-century Athenian had both, almost to excess. The story ran that a gang of drunken farmers had come to town and sang rude songs outside their enemies' windows. The Athenians laughed so much that they asked them to come again next year—so comedy was born. It is a nice contrast to the priggish, pompous provision in the Twelve Tables at Rome that anyone who wrote an abusive poem was committing a criminal act.

The Peloponnesian War and after

It was this same confidence, as we have seen, that stirred Spartan fear and jealousy and brought a Spartan army across the Attic border in 431 BC. Few Greeks then believed that Athens could survive for more than a year or two a traditional Greek war waged by, traditionally, the finest army. They had failed to see that this would not be a traditional war. With secure access to the sea between long walls connecting city and harbour, with total control of the Aegean and through it of the route to the Black Sea and its grain supply, with largely contented or, even if disaffected, powerless allies, Athens could sit back and watch the invaders devastate the countryside, not without some affront to dignity but with no fear of starvation. Hence ten years of indecisive war ending in a botched-up peace, the Peace of Nicias, in 421 BC. Each side had tried to find ways out of the stalemate, some silly, some clever, some more or less successful, some markedly not, and, as is the way in war, there had been accidents (Athens lost something like a third of her population in a hideous plague between 430 and 427 BC). But stalemate it was and that meant an Athenian victory, for Athens only had to survive, Sparta had to win.

Then came the error. The victory is obvious enough to us, but was perhaps not so clear to Athenians. They decided to remember old interests in the west and, at the request of one Sicilian ally, legitimate enough in itself, to try not only to help but to take control of the whole. This was folly, not only because it produced failure but because it could not conceivably have succeeded. Ridiculous ambition? Some of that there was, but it could be mere frustration at the apparent impasse at home that tipped the scale. Whatever the reason, the great expedition of 415 BC and subsequent reinforcement was lost by 413 BC—half of her forces, her fleet and almost all her money were gone. Moreover, her allies were now more inclined to revolt, though many stayed remarkably loyal. Sparta did not need much prompting to see that she had a second chance. By selling the freedom of Greeks in Asia Minor she got money from the Persians to run a fleet of her own and, although Athens held on for eight more years, few could have been surprised when after a final naval engagement at Aegospotami (405 BC) the Spartans moved into Athens, the walls were pulled down, and victory, real victory, was theirs.

Yet Athens could have made it, even after Sicily, had it not been for internal trouble. Its source was twofold. On the one hand the enormous economic development of the late seventh century onwards was, by the fifth, producing a shift in the distribution of wealth, or rather not so much a shift as a disequilibrium, that began to fray the edges of the accepted aristocratic pattern, while at the same time the complexities of the new society were asking for an expertise that some of the newcomers were better able to provide than the god-blessed nobles of older days. So we find new names appearing in the administration, names more associated with chariot making than chariot racing, not in a flood and not at first at the highest levels, but enough to be noticed and by the traditionalists resented. At the same time, the intellectual revolution described above provided tools for an analysis of these changes which in the hands of the resentful, the unscrupulous or the not-so-clever could be dangerous. Thus there was tension, between the old who suspected new ideas and the young who welcomed them, between the aristocrat who disliked democracy or liked it only when he remained in apparent control and the new-style politician, and this tension became unbearable in the stress of war. There were two very short periods of revolution (in 411 and 404 BC), but more damaging was the general suspicion.

Fortunately democracy was recovered and survived, but the war had been lost and things were never quite the same again. A cynic has said that the only difference between the fourth and the fifth centuries was 10 per cent of cost and poverty, comparative poverty, of course there was. But something else had disappeared as well. As Pericles had said on another occasion, the spring was gone from the year.

Nor, it must be emphasized again, was this true only of Athens. There the spring had been at its brightest, but Corinth, Thebes, Argos, Sicyon and others had had their moments. Now, indeed, in 404, it must have seemed as if Sparta could take over something of Athens' greatness as she certainly took over much of her power. But, as Aristotle sagely remarked, an exclusively military training produces brutes, not men who can control either themselves or other men, and, in the end, even leads to military failure. The squalid story of how Sparta abused her power for the next 30 years shows how right he was. By 371 BC Thebes, which had performed astonishingly well during the Peloponnesian War and had then, unlike Sparta, gone on to develop herself politically and militarily, was able at the battle of Leuctra to end the myth of Spartan invincibility, under two able generals, Pelopidas (c420–364 BC) and Epaminondas (c420–362 BC). But neither new military tactics (chiefly an increased use of cavalry and a more flexible and strengthened phalanx) nor a new political impetus (the freeing of the Peloponnese) could give Thebes a lasting hegemony. Real power, real energy had shifted to other states on Greece's borders, chief among them Macedon, and while the cities squabbled in themselves and between themselves Philip II (b 383, ruled 359–336 BC) schemed and fought his way into central Greece. The oratory of the Athenian Demosthenes (384–322 BC), the finest demagogue of antiquity, contrived some sort of

alliance against him but this was too tardy, may even have been misguided at any date and the story of 'free' Greece ended at Chaeronea in 338 BC.

Macedon

N. G. L. Hammond

Origins of the Macedones and the Temenid dynasty

The surviving words of Macedonian do not show conclusively whether the Macedones spoke Greek or not in early times. But statements by Hesiod and Hellanicus make it virtually certain that they did speak Greek of the Aeolic dialect. The origin of the Greek-speaking peoples was expressed in the form of a genealogy: Deucalion had a son Hellen, whose three sons founded three branches, called 'Hellenes', and a daughter Thyia, who had by Zeus 'two sons, Magnes and Macedon ... dwelling around Pieria and Olympus'. It was these two who founded the Magnesian and the Macedonian branches as cousins of the 'Hellenes'. Hellanicus brought Macedon into the main line by making him a son not of Zeus but of Aeolus, son of Hellen, whose descendants spoke the Aeolic dialect. The sources of Hesiod and Hellanicus himself could not have advanced these genealogies unless they had believed that contemporary Macedonians before and in the fifth century BC were speaking Greek of the Aeolic 'dialect (as the Magnesians demonstrably did).

In Greek tradition the Magnesians were driven out into Thessaly by 'Pierian Thracians'. The Macedones stayed, isolated from other Greeks and neighbours of Mysians, Thracians and Brygi, and their dialect became so idiosyncratic that it was hardly intelligible to southern Greeks. As they practised transhumant pastoralism with summer pastures on Olympus and 'the Macedonian mountain' (north of it) and winter pastures on the Pierian coast, their movements were restricted and like the Vlachs of Olympus today they lost touch with the speakers of their own tongue. A group of small tribes, they formed a tribal state with a royal tribe, the Argeadae, from which their native kings were chosen. It was the arrival of a refugee from Argos in the Peloponnese, Perdiccas, and his winning of the throne c650 BC that brought the Macedonians out of their obscurity. Descended from Zeus through Heracles and Temenus, the conqueror of Argos c1140 BC, he and his descendants were to rule Macedonia for more than three centuries and to call themselves proudly 'Temenidae'. For they were both Macedonians by adoption and Hellenes by origin.

Perdiccas captured a city Edessa and renamed it Aegeae ('Goat-town') because, according to a Delphic oracle, his choice had been determined by the presence of goats. This city, which he made his capital, was at

Vergina just south of the Haliacmon river and on the edge of the coastal plain 'Emathia'. During more than a century of expansion the Macedonians expelled the entire population from neighbouring districts and settled on the land themselves: from Heracleum to the Axius river, and inland to the semi-circle of high mountains (Olympus, Bermium and Barnous) and beyond into the basin of Lake Ostrovo. This was to be the heartland of the Macedonian state throughout its history: its people were all free with no substratum of slaves or serfs, and the mountains and defiles of Tempe (on the Peneus) and Demir Kapu (on the Axius) made it a natural castle.

The growth of the Macedonian state

When the Persians advanced into Europe, they broke the power of the Paeonians c510 BC and this enabled Amyntas I at the head of the Argeadae to occupy Amphaxitis on both sides of the lower Axius. To Persia he submitted. Giving a daughter in marriage to a high-ranking Persian, he obtained Persian favour and added the head of the Thermaic Gulf and Anthemus to his kingdom. His successor, Alexander I (c495–452 BC), with Persian approval and perhaps aid, asserted his authority over 'Upper Macedonia' and made the tribal peoples there–Elimiotae, Orestae, Lyncestae and Pelagones–into Macedones in name, so that they were called, e.g., 'Elimiotae Macedones'. But he was secretly in league with the Greek states that resisted Xerxes, even though he and his subjects had to serve in the Persian forces, and this helped him to take advantage of the defeat of Xerxes. For he annexed the lands between the Axius and the Strymon, and he dedicated gold statues of himself at Delphi and Olympia 'as a first fruit of spoils from captive Medes'.

The tribal peoples of Upper Macedonia had previously belonged to the Molossian group of tribes, to which they were related in dialect and race and their pastoral way of life; but they had Greek speech and some interests in common with the Macedonians. The peoples east of the Axius spoke Thracian and other languages, and although subjects of Alexander they were never called 'Macedones'. In all other respects they seem to have been of the same standing as his other subjects. The resources of the kingdom were now very considerable: great stands of shipbuilding and other timbers, mines of gold, silver, copper and iron, pastoral products, especially from Upper Macedonia, and agricultural products, especially from the coastal plain and the Strymon basin. As the king owned all mineral resources, Alexander issued a fine coinage *c*478 BC and traded into the Aegean.

But Alexander lived in a very competitive world. Athens monopolized sea power, seized Eion at the mouth of the Strymon and acquired mines in Thrace; and the Thracian Edoni held the eastern part of the Strymon basin and even captured Alexander's mines for a time. Thus the blueprint of a greater Macedonian kingdom, which he outlined *c*485–475 BC, was not fully realized. After his death the position worsened, partly because the Greek states and neighbouring Balkan states grew stronger and partly because struggles over the succession weakened Macedon. For a century, *c*452–359 BC, the tribal kingdoms of Upper Macedonia pursued independent policies and often fought against Macedon, and foreign powers–especially Athens–controlled ports on the Thermaic Gulf, held lands in the Strymon basin and supported tribes such as the Pelagones and the Bisaltae against Macedon. The succession troubles arose from the polygamy of the warrior-kings, whose queens and sons were all of equal standing. Alexander left five sons to dispute the succession and similar disputes went on for a century.

The electoral body was a male elite of military qualification, the Macedones proper. In practice they elected only a member of the Temenid house as king or regent, and they conducted and judged all trials for treason. If a man was found guilty, he and his family were executed. Feuds within the royal house led to the extinction of the families of two of Alexander's sons, and then in 400–393 BC there were six successive kings, descended from the other three sons. The last of these, Amyntas III (393–370 BC), left six sons by two wives. When a king came to terms with other members of the royal house, he gave them high positions. Thus in a treaty with Athens *c*415 BC the oaths were taken by the king, Perdiccas son of Alexander, and then by Alcetas, son of Alexander, two sons of Perdiccas, one son of Alcetas, and then by some commoners, the highest among the king's Companions. This treaty mentioned 'kings' of tribes in Upper Macedonia, and one, Arrhabaeus, was entirely independent.

In this period Archelaus (413–399 BC) did most to modernize Macedonia. He built military roads, fortified strongpoints and extended the training of infantry; he brought Euripides to his court and was a patron of the arts; and he planted a new town controlling the defile of the Demir Kapu. Chaos followed in the next decade. The royal household cavalry, trained cuirassiers, were still of the highest quality but the infantry had declined so much by 359 BC that the Illyrians killed 4000 in battle and overran western Macedonia.

The greater state of Macedon
Elected regent to an infant king in 359 BC, Philip, son of Amyntas III, trained his infantry intensively on Theban lines (he had spent three years as a hostage at Thebes) and invented a new weapon, the *sarissa* or pike of some 16 ft (5 m), far outreaching the normal spear of $6\frac{1}{2}$ ft (2 m). In 358 BC he won a decisive battle. At the head of his best infantry on the right wing he broke his way into the front of the Illyrians who had adopted a rectangular formation, and he then brought his cuirassiers through the gap and shattered the Illyrians. Of their army of 10,000 he killed 7000 in the pursuit. At one bound he extended his frontier to the east shore of Lake Ochrid, extended his military road thither over two mountain ranges and fortified a strongpoint facing north. This western frontier of the kingdom was to stand for centuries. Defeating Paeonians and Thracians, he advanced his northern frontier to probably the Kačanik Pass and his eastern frontier to the Nestus, adding great depth to his defences. Meanwhile he repelled an attempt by Athens to impose a pretender by armed force, prevented Athens from combining with the Chalcidian states by his clever diplomacy, and captured the Greek cities on his coast.

Elected king instead of regent, Philip used the almost absolute powers vested in the constitutional monarchy to replan the Macedonian state. He incorporated the hitherto mainly independent cantons of Upper Macedonia. He suppressed their monarchies and made their royal houses serve at his court and in his Companion cavalry. He planted new towns where generally there had been none. Into these he transplanted people from Lower Macedonia, where they had for long been organized in cities, and he mixed them with the local people. The infantry that had won his first battle had come entirely from Lower Macedonia and had earned an honoured title 'Foot-Companions' (*pezetairoi*); and he now drew from his new towns (*astea*) the 'Town-Companions' (*asthetairoi*). This doubled the infantry strength of the field army and fused the Greek-speaking populations. East of the Axius he planted new towns and raised troops from them, especially cavalry; and he levied excellent light cavalry from the Thracians and the Paeonians. Throughout the kingdom he left local administration to the cities, tribes and communes, the king of the Paeonians, for instance, coining as before. At Thebes he had seen flood control and scientific irrigation. By introducing these into Macedonia he revolutionized the economy, increasing the agricultural land and cutting down the amount of transhumant pastoralism. Increasing revenues and better exploitation of the mines enabled him to maintain an almost professional army from his own coffers.

Between 354 and 339 his army subjugated Illyrians, Dardanians, Thracians and Scythians, until his Balkan empire extended from the lower Danube to the Aegean coast and from the Adriatic coast (up to Scodra–modern Scutari) to the Black Sea and the Dardanelles. He enforced peace and order, planted new towns of mixed population (as in Upper Macedonia) and encouraged agriculture and trade; and he left local administration in native hands as far as possible. His fine coinage spread far beyond his empire into central Europe.

He subjugated any Greek cities that opposed him and sometimes transplanted their populations, if they were north of Greece proper. In Greece his policy was different. He won the alliance of Thessaly, defeated the strongest army of any Greek state—20,000 mercenary infantry—and brought to an end in 346 BC a war between coalitions of Greek states for control of Delphi. Elected president of the Pythian Games at Delphi, he made proposals to the Greek city states that were designed to bring general peace, reconciliation and respect for religious practice; and he tried to win the favour of Athens for his policy. He failed. Openly opposed by Thebes, Athens and some other states, he brought his army south—thrice the size of that in 358 BC—and completely defeated a rather larger number at Chaeronea in 338 BC, his superbly drilled pikemen creating a gap in the Greek line into which his son Alexander led the Companion cavalry. His proposal now to create a self-governing League of Greek states and to combine its forces with those of Macedon in a war against Persia was adopted by all mainland states except Sparta. In 336 BC, when about to join his vanguard in Asia Minor, he was assassinated at the age of 44.

Moderns tend to regard Philip's achievement as one of personal genius. It was also the triumph of constitutional monarchy and a remarkable people; for monarchy gave Philip unique, continuous and legitimate powers, unparalleled in any republic, and his people accepted readily infinite dangers in his service. He had secured his monarchy early by disposing of three half-brothers and two cousins in the royal house. He earned the devotion of military people by his audacity in action, and he rewarded his officers and men with estates and remissions of tax and gratuities for gallant service. He was the hub of patronage. He trained the princes and the sons of his officers as royal pages in ceremonial, hunting and war, and he himself punished them for any breach of conduct. Success brought glory, power and wealth to the Macedones, and the pacification and civilizing of a large part of the Balkans. The Macedones expressed their admiration by worshipping him after death as a god, an honour granted only to him and his father Amyntas III. But some hated him and one of them, probably with political backing, killed him at Aegeae.

Some Macedonians certainly disliked his Greek policy. The League of city states rendered neither tribute nor military service to Macedonia, but was left free to make its own policy and rebuild its military and naval strength. Philip created it perhaps in a spirit of optimism, less as a Macedonian king than as a Greek seeking a solution to the troubles of the Greek states. He sought the approval of the Greek states, which he did receive publicly on the day before his death.

The lesson that constitutional monarchy had an immense potential was not lost on Greek thinkers. Already in 346 Isocrates thought Philip capable of ruling the Macedonians as king, uniting the Greeks as a benefactor, and governing many barbarians as emperor. Plato thought that a philosopher made king might change the direction of society in the city state. But the average Greek saw in the Macedonian monarchy the antithesis of republican freedom and in the League a limitation of city state particularism. Demosthenes led the opposition. He dismissed Philip as a 'barbarian from Pella' and Alexander as a mock-heroic 'Margites'. Neither taunt was justified. Philip was a patron of Greek art and promoted Greek culture within his kingdom and empire; and in his settlement he probably had the interests of Greece at heart, at least as he understood them.

Macedon as a world power

The recent discovery of Philip's tomb has shown us how un-Greek the Macedonian monarchy was. The extravagant gifts, the weaponry, the royal accoutrements, the entombment of a young queen, the execution of the assassin's sons and his accomplices on the tumulus and the cremation of horses, weapons and the assassin's corpse were all survivals through almost a millennium from the Heroic Age of the Trojan War. Philip and Alexander were closer to that Heroic Age than to fourth-century Greece in their devotion to heroism, glory and service after the model of Heracles, their ancestor. Alexander aspired to rival his maternal ancestor, Achilles, as portrayed in his favourite book, the *Iliad*, and at 20 he had proved himself a prodigy in battle and administration. The Macedonian assembly under arms elected him king at Aegeae and clashed their pikes on their shields to show they would fight for him to the death. He was their ideal of a king.

The assassination of Philip cast suspicion on some members and connections of the royal house. Execution after trial for treason and killing during arrest removed possible pretenders and their families, including one of Philip's seven or eight wives and her infant child by him. Alexander, however, did not make early marriages as Philip had done to beget heirs. The assassination also shook the authority of Macedon, of which the meteoric rise seemed so much due to Philip. Alexander acted with speed and intelligence. He avoided confrontation with dissidents in Thessaly and Thebes, pardoned acts of rebellion against the Greek League and was elected president of the Thessalian League for life and then commander of the forces of the Greek League for the war against Persia. His charm was backed by the formidable Macedonian army. In 335 BC a brilliant campaign broke the resistance of Thracian rebels on Mount Haemus, Triballians by the Danube, and Dardanians and Illyrians near Lake Little Prespa, all with a minimum of Macedonian casualties. That part of his home base was secure.

While he was near Prespa, he learned that Thebes was in revolt and the Macedonian garrison, placed there by the Greek League, was in danger. By a lightning march along Pindus and west Thessaly he entered Boeotia before news of his approach reached Thebes and before troops intended by Athens, Aetolia and some Peloponnesian states for Thebes were within range. Alexander offered negotiation twice. The rebel leaders responded by acts of war against Alexander's troops and against the garrison. Meanwhile loyalist Greek troops from states

Alexander the Great (ruled 336–323 BC): drawing from the Azara Herm statue, a Roman copy of an original by Lysippus.

armour to the Trojan goddess, Athena, and took her sacred shield, as a Crusader might take a sacred relic, to precede him into battle. The Asian goddess was to give him her land.

He destroyed the military forces of Persia in three pitched battles. In the first he used only his Macedonian troops, the Thessalian cavalry and some specialized units against an army of Persian cavalry and Greek mercenary infantry. In the second his army consisted of Macedonians, Greeks both allied and mercenary, and Balkan troops, and in the third the Macedonians were less than a third of the whole. Alexander himself was the spearpoint and the Macedonians the spearhead in battle, but the other forces both on land and sea were indispensable adjuncts. Persia overthrown, he began to recruit Asians. While he was in the Indus valley his army reached 120,000 men, of whom the Macedonians were one-eighth, the Greeks above a third, and the Balkan and Asian troops more than half. When he intended to conquer Arabia and return to the Mediterranean, he planned to leave a multiracial but primarily Asian army to keep order in the kingdom of Asia; for in infantry of the line one-quarter were to be Macedonians, and in the cavalry and other arms the proportion of Europeans was to be even smaller. For this purpose he had arranged for 30,000 young Persians to be trained in Greek speech and Macedonian weapons so that they could be integrated into the new army, and he recruited 20,000 more Persians. Then, at the age of 32, he died of a violent fever.

The greatest conqueror in history, he used conquest not to create an empire (as Philip had done in the Balkans) but to found a multiracial kingdom with a multiracial army in which every national was judged in terms of worth. Thus there were Asians among his 'Friends', 'Companions' and 'Commanders', and also Asians, especially experienced Persians, among his governors of provinces. Recruitment for the army, which supplied most of his administrators, had to be planned in advance. The soldiers' women and their Eurasian children were made legitimate by Alexander, and the children were educated and trained at his expense; and the sons of the King's Own Guards (the Hypaspists) were trained to be the Guardsmen of the next generation. In order to underline the parity of esteem that he was implementing in the armed and administrative services he and 80 of his Companions married daughters of the Persian and Median aristocracy with a Persian ritual; and on another occasion he held a feast for 9000 Macedonians, Persians and others and prayed for concord and co-partnership in administering the kingdom of Asia. That concept was unprecedented. It is the most original contribution of Macedon to world politics.

The most lasting of Alexander's innovations were his 70 new towns in Asia, many called Alexandria, in which the initial population of 10,000 men was in part Macedonian, Greek and Balkan and in the main Asian. The towns were entirely Macedonian in that they were self-governing but subject to the edicts of the king; the

hostile to Thebes joined Alexander. An action not ordered by Alexander but cleverly developed by him led to the relief of the garrison and then to the capture of the city with much bloodshed, in which the Greek allies played a conspicuous part. What was to be done with the captured population, estimated at 30,000 souls? Alexander referred the decision to the Council of the Greek League, for which he claimed to be operating, and the Council passed sentence of *andrapodismos*, a Greek form of reprisal, which meant enslavement of inhabitants, razing of buildings and distribution of territory. The responsibility lay ultimately with Alexander, who could have guided the Council to a different decision, and the army that carried out the sentence was the Macedonian army. This was the first and perhaps the most striking of the acts that filled the city states with fear and lessened the chances of the symbiosis Philip had envisaged.

To Alexander the crossing from Europe to Asia in 334 BC was of symbolic importance. First to land, he drove his spear into Trojan soil and proclaimed that he accepted Asia as won by the spear, a gift from the gods. It was a proleptic claim. From that moment he was king of Asia. As his subjects, the Asians were to be free and neither part of a Macedonian empire nor slaves to the Greeks, as Aristotle had suggested. It was both belief and propaganda, and it was destined to win many Asian populations to his side. But first he had to defeat the armed forces of Persia. To this end he dedicated his

Elected king, Philip, son of Amyntas III, began to replan the Macedonian state. His fine coinage spread far beyond his empire into central Europe.

'Macedones' were a privileged group of citizens; and the citizens provided recruits for the elite forces of the king's army. They were Macedonian too in choice of site (often low-lying), in size (as compared with a Greek colony) and in economic purpose as centres of capitalistic commerce with coined money inside a vast kingdom. Their political, social and religious life developed mainly on Greek lines. This type of Graeco-Macedonian city with a cosmopolitan population and Greek language was to be the focus of civilization in southeastern Europe and West Asia until the collapse of the Byzantine empire.

At the time a great change came about in a short period. With the prevalence of peace native urbanization began to develop alongside Alexander's new towns, and commercial exchange was encouraged by the release of coined money from Persian hoarded treasure, the improvements of roads and bridges, the opening of sea communication from India to the Persian Gulf, the reclamation of land by drainage and irrigation, and the movement of people and goods between the eastern Mediterranean and Asia. Emigrants from Greece, the Balkans and parts of West Asia to the eastern provinces amounted to many hundreds of thousands. The number of Macedonians was tiny in proportion, but they supplied the leadership and the administrative ability. When we appraise the achievement of Alexander, we must not forget the less than 30,000 Macedonians who were the full citizens of the Macedonian state.

Macedon, the Greek states and Rome

The greatest threat to Alexander had come from the Greeks—50,000 mercenaries in Persian service and 20,000 troops who rose in 331 under Sparta's leadership. Alexander was fortunate enough to defeat the

mercenaries piecemeal, and the half of the field army that he left at home was able to crush the rising. After his death Macedonians in Asia fought against mutinous mercenaries, and in Greece a general rising, led by Athens and Aetolia, defeated Macedonian forces twice and was suppressed only by two armies crossing from Asia. This time the victor, Antipater, employed the usual methods of imperialism: puppet governments, garrisons, war indemnities and execution of the rebel leaders. Demosthenes committed suicide. It was a stage in the breakdown both of Greek freedom and Philip's intentions.

During the struggle for power between the generals from Alexander's death in 323 to 301 BC the last members of the Temenid line were killed and the territories ruled by Alexander split up into a number of kingdoms, each organized on the basis he had made. These kingdoms are called the Hellenistic kingdoms by modern scholars, but almost all the kings and queens were Macedonians down to the last, Cleopatra of Egypt, who committed suicide in 30 BC. All contenders for power coveted the European kingdom, because Macedonia was the legitimate seat of authority and the best troops were recruited in Europe. Their internecine struggles were undisturbed by outside forces in Europe until 279 BC. Then the Gauls invaded. One group overran Macedonia and nearly reached Delphi; another stormed through Thrace; and another broke into Asia Minor. The Gallic menace in Macedonia was arrested by Antigonus Gonatas, who became king of Macedon in 276 BC, defeated the Greek states in 262 BC and ruled Greece through puppet governments. His dynasty lasted until 167 BC.

The Antigonid dynasty in Macedonia was encircled by enemies and constantly at war, whether with dissident Greek states (especially the Aetolian League and the Achaean League), other Hellenistic kings, the northern tribes or later with Rome. Their wars with the first two were inconclusive, except that some of the older states like Athens opted for neutrality. Gains and losses of territory did not affect the general prosperity of the Hellenistic world, which was reflected in a great increase in the number of slaves. The northerners were more damaging; for they looted and killed indiscriminately. The Dardanians, for instance, caused heavy losses in Macedonia in 229 BC, which weakened her for a generation. That happened to be the year in which Rome crossed the Adriatic and established a protectorate over that part of Illyris that extended from Dyrrachium to Apollonia and inland to the sources of the Shkumbi river. Only a narrow corridor separated that protectorate from the kingdom of Macedonia.

Rome disregarded Macedon and (to the south) the Epirote state. This was tantamount to a declaration of hostility, and she went on to open diplomatic relations with the Aetolian League, the Achaean League, Corinth and Athens, all enemies of Macedon. Rome had intervened in the first place to suppress Illyrian piracy and had quickly come to terms with the Illyrians. Rome had then staked out her protectorate. In response Philip V of

Macedon joined the Illyrians and the Epirote League, and in 219 under provocation from the Illyrians Roman troops crossed the Adriatic and reasserted their control of the protectorate. The Second Punic War of Rome against Carthage (218–201 BC) seemed to give Philip a chance of dislodging Rome from her protectorate. He tried twice to capture Apollonia, the second time with the help of the Epirote League, but failed with heavy losses; and the alliance he made with Hannibal brought him nothing but Rome's undying hatred. Hostilities between Rome and Macedon in Illyris ended in 205 BC with a non-aggression pact, when Rome was about to invade Africa.

The almost inevitable clash of two imperialistic powers occurred in 200 BC when Rome attacked without any plausible pretext. Philip had only one army of some 25,000 men, which he dared not expend, whereas Rome had great reserves of manpower and numerous allies. What gave Philip a chance was the quality of his army, the central position of Macedonia and its natural defences in depth. By skilful manoeuvres he kept his enemies apart, defeated the Dardanians and then in 197 BC was drawn from a chance engagement into a pitched battle at Cynoscephalae in Thessaly. The tight-packed phalanx of pikemen was at first successful but lost cohesion, and the Romans, fighting in more mobile units, broke into its flank and rear. At close quarters the pike was useless against the sword and the better defensive armour of the Roman, and Philip withdrew leaving 8000 dead and 5000 captured. Even so he held the strong southern frontier until he obtained a treaty of peace, which cost him his fleet and his possessions in Greece. He kept faith with Rome and rebuilt his strength, leaving to his son Perseus in 179 BC an army of 40,000 trained men.

Rome forced war upon Perseus in 171 BC. The defences held at first but in 168 BC battle ensued at Pydna. When the phalanx attacked, the Romans withdrew to higher ground and attacked in turn when the phalanx lost its cohesion on rough ground. At close quarters some 20,000 Macedonians fell, the 3000 men of the King's Own Guards fighting to the last, and Perseus later gave himself up to grace the victor's march of triumph at Rome and die under harsh conditions in captivity. Macedonia was partitioned into four self-governing republics which paid to Rome half the tax raised by the king; the mines were closed for ten years, and only a few troops were allowed on the frontiers. In 150 BC a pretender, Andriscus, who claimed to be a son of Perseus, raised the standard of revolt, united the four parts and defeated a Roman legion. In 148 BC the rising was suppressed and Macedonia was annexed as a province of Rome under direct rule. The twilight of Macedonian liberty was at an end.

Carthage

B. H. Warmington

The name

Carthage, a Phoenician settlement on the coast of North Africa near Tunis, which became the centre of a powerful empire in the western Mediterranean, and a rival of Rome.

The earliest Phoenician voyages in the west were traditionally dated to the late second millennium BC but no archaeological evidence for them is earlier than the ninth century BC. The cities of Phoenicia, primarily Tyre and Sidon, confined to a narrow strip of land on the Lebanese coast and hemmed in by more powerful neighbours, had a long tradition of trading activity. Their voyages to the west were undertaken in search of sources of metal, especially silver and tin, and these were discovered in southern Spain. Gades (Cadiz), the earliest Phoenician settlement in Spain was said to have been founded in 1101 BC but the first archaeological material is of the eighth century BC. Once the trade with the Iberian tribes had begun it was necessary to protect the trade routes, since Greek voyages to the west were also beginning about the same time, and to discover safe anchorages and watering places. One of the routes followed the southern coast of Sicily, Sardinia and the Balearic Islands, the other the coast of North Africa.

Along the latter route the most important area was the northeast of Tunisia where the Mediterranean reaches its narrowest point. Ancient sources believed that Utica (Utique) was founded long before Carthage, but this seems legendary. Carthage itself was said to have been founded in 814 BC by Tyre and the earliest archaeological evidence from the site is not more than 50 years later than this date.

The name Carthage derives, through Latin, from the Phoenician Kart-Hadasht, meaning 'new city', which might imply that it was deliberately intended to be more than a convenient stopping point on the route to Spain. Nothing can be deduced from the legendary stories of the circumstances of its foundation, which reached their culmination in Virgil's Aeneid. The site offered a sheltered sandy beach on which ships could be drawn up and convenient hills and a promontory for defence. Similar coastal sites were occupied elsewhere along the North African coast slightly later, for example at Hadrumetum (Sousse), Tipasa (near Cherchell) and even on the Atlantic coast of Morocco as far south as Mogador. Phoenician colonies differed from those of the Greeks in two major respects: they almost all remained very small and continued for several centuries to be dependent

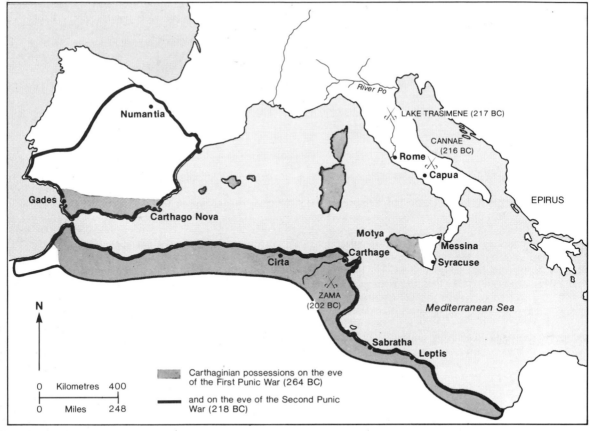

Carthage and Rome.

upon their founders. It would appear that the surplus population of Phoenicia was not large enough to produce a more rapid growth in her settlements except in one or two favoured places like Carthage. On the other hand the settlers do not appear to have had to face much opposition from the indigenous Libyan population of North Africa, which had remained relatively isolated from the cultural developments in Egypt and the eastern Mediterranean world till the arrival of the Phoenicians, and was politically and military weak.

Creation of the Carthaginian empire

The decisive stage in the growth of Carthage as a force in the western Mediterranean occurred in the sixth century. The Phoenician homeland fell under Babylonian rule, Tyre itself suffering a prolonged siege, and subsequently came under the Persians. At the same time the Greek settlements in Sicily attempted to destroy the Phoenician settlements in the west of the island at Motya (Mozia) and Panomus (Palermo) c580 BC. Carthage took the lead in defending the threatened communities and in strengthening the Phoenician position in southern Sardinia, attested archaeologically at Monte Sirai in particular. A further advance in Carthaginian influence was manifested in 535 BC when in alliance with some Etruscan cities she won a naval victory over Greeks from

Phocaea off Corsica that was so decisive that Greeks were effectively prevented from trading with those parts of southern Spain in which the Phoenicians were interested. In 514 BC Carthage prevented an attempt led by a Spartan named Dorieus to found a settlement at the mouth of the Cinyps river in Libya not far from existing Phoenician settlements at Sabratha and Lepcis.

Although details are not otherwise known it is clear that by this date Carthage was effectively an independent city state bound to Tyre only by ties of sentiment and common religion. During the fifth century BC Carthage created an empire that at the time constituted the largest and most powerful political unit in the western Mediterranean world, and included all existing Phoenician settlements together with new ones sent out by Carthage herself. The immediate stimulus for this development may have been provided by a severe defeat in Sicily. Carthage became involved in struggles between the Greek cities in the island and sent a major force, but lost both a fleet and army at Himera in 480 BC. The result of this defeat (which, however, did not result in the loss of the Phoenician settlements in the west of Sicily) forced

Nomadic archer from the Asian steppes, c500 BC. Encroachment by such daring horsemen was a constant threat to the settled agriculturalists who founded the civilizations of the Ancient World.

Carthage to seek to consolidate her leading position among the Phoenicians of the west and to avoid expansion except in North Africa. Here she acquired a substantial territory in the northeastern part of Tunisia, beginning with the peninsula of Cap Bon. This became necessary as the population of Carthage grew probably to equal those of large contemporary Greek cities such as Athens and Syracuse. Later, all the area northeast of a line roughly from Thabraca (Tabarka) to Thaenae (Henchir Thyna) came under Carthaginian control and penetration went on occasion as far as Theveste (Tebessa). Some, though not many, of the other Phoenician settlements also seem to have increased in size: e.g. Lepcis, Hadrumetum and Utica. However, although Carthage exercised firm control over all the coastal settlements, little penetration into the interior took place elsewhere.

Wars in Sicily

During the fifth century Carthage took no part in the politics of Sicily following the disaster of 480 BC. However, in view of the bitter rivalries among the Greek cities of the island it was inevitable that from time to time conflicts should occur into which Carthage could not help being drawn on occasion. In particular, various rulers of the most important city, Syracuse, attempted on several occasions to drive the Carthaginians from their positions in the west of the island. These attempts, even those of the most powerful Dionysius I (398–392, 382–375 and 368 BC) were unsuccessful and the boundary of the Carthaginian area was generally recognized to be the river Halycus (Platani). On one occasion Carthaginian territory in North Africa was invaded. In 331 BC Agathocles of Syracuse landed in Cap Bon and caused much devastation before he was finally defeated.

The Punic Wars

After some three centuries of complete domination in the western Mediterranean and a rather uneasy *modus vivendi* with the Greeks of Sicily, the Carthaginian empire came into conflict with Rome and was eventually destroyed. Treaties dated to 508 and 348 BC involving mutual recognition and the regulation of trade existed between the two powers and there had been little occasion for conflict because the Romans had little interest in Mediterranean trade, and were primarily occupied in expanding their power in Italy. By the early third century they dominated the peninsula and thus began to impinge upon Sicily, so long divided between Carthaginians and Greeks. The three wars between Carthage and Rome are known as the Punic Wars, from the Latin *bella Punica*.

The First Punic War began in 264 BC as a result of Rome's attempt to gain a foothold in Sicily by forming an alliance with Messana against Syracuse, though the

Temple of Castor and Pollux in the Roman Forum. Rebuilt by the emperor Tiberius in AD 8, the three surviving marble columns have splendid Corinthian capitals.

former had previously had a Carthaginian garrison. The Carthaginians appear to have believed that their position in the island would be threatened unless they resisted. The war lasted till 241 BC and was said by the historian Polybius to have been the most destructive in terms of human life of any war up to that date (this would include the wars of Alexander the Great). The war was largely fought out in Sicily and the waters surrounding it. On land the Romans gradually took most of the Carthaginian territory but failed to capture the naval base at Lilybaeum. A Roman invasion of North Africa in 256–255 BC brought Carthage under siege but the invaders were completely destroyed with the aid of experienced Greek mercenaries. In the conflict at sea the Romans, without a seafaring tradition, performed remarkably well, though they suffered heavy losses especially when fleets were lost in storms; nearly 200 ships and 100,000 men are said to have been lost off Camarina in 255 BC. Both sides were able by immense efforts to build new fleets after repeated losses till in 242 BC Carthage lost her fleet off the Aegates Islands and the further defence of Lilybaeum became impossible. In the peace terms she gave up Sicily and surrendered Sardinia to Rome in 238 BC.

Under the determined leadership of Hamilcar Barca, who had defended Lilybaeum, Carthage turned her attention to Spain in order to achieve direct control over the mineral resources and to create an army from the inhabitants to match the Roman legions. The policy was continued by his son Hannibal (247–*c*182 BC) and, when in 219 BC Carthage rejected Rome's threats against further expansion in the Iberian peninsula, two-thirds of it were now under her control. Hannibal led his new army over the Alps and in the Second Punic War inflicted serious defeats on the Romans in Italy, above all at Cannae (216 BC), Rome's worst military disaster. However, his army was not large enough to attempt an attack on Rome itself and though he was able to maintain himself in Italy Rome's manpower gradually told. Spain was lost to Carthage in 206 BC and Hannibal was recalled to Africa in 203 BC. He was defeated by Scipio in 202 BC at Zama Regia. Carthage was forced to surrender her fleet and all overseas territory and in effect became a Roman satellite. During the next 50 years she was frequently under pressure from Masinissa, chieftain of the Numidians, who enjoyed Rome's favour, and in 149 BC Rome began the Third Punic War with the object of destroying Carthage entirely, from irrational fears about her possible revival. The city was razed to the ground in 146 BC.

Carthaginian trade

The Carthaginian empire existed to defend, and was economically dependent on, her commerce. In the ancient world Carthage was the prime example of a city whose wealth was based on trade. Most of this appears to have been in primary products and in perishables and is difficult to trace archaeologically. The most famous and the most profitable were in metals, silver and tin from southern Spain and probably gold from Africa south of the Rio de Oro. The process appears to have involved the acquisition of the metals from indigenous peoples in exchange for trade goods of relatively small value–this at least is attested for the gold trade. In the Spanish area the profitability of Carthaginian trade was maintained by the ruthless exclusion of all Greek competition. Ancient sources record two voyages of exploration and trade in the fifth century BC that were apparently of particular importance. One led by Himilco sailed up the western coast of Spain and France. There is no evidence that Himilco or other Phoenicians ever traded in Britain itself but it is probable that tin from the island reached the Carthaginians by intermediaries along the Atlantic route, which had existed since prehistoric times. The other voyage, led by Hanno, went south along the Atlantic coast of Morocco at least as far as Cape Verde, apparently in search of gold.

Carthage also traded with the Greeks both in the Aegean and in Sicily. Archaeological evidence of substantial imports from the Greek world comes from Carthage itself and a number of settlements within her empire. It is probable that after the acquisition of territory in the interior of Tunisia, which constituted a much larger area than that controlled by most Greek cities, Carthage was a substantial exporter of agricultural products. Carthaginian manufactures of trade goods were apparently substantial but were nondescript in style and not always easily identifiable. It is surprising to find that Carthage did not issue her own coins till the fourth century BC, long after coinage had become established as a medium of exchange in the Greek world. However, the wealth of Carthage derived from her trade and the notoriously harsh exploitation of non-Phoenician subjects was sufficient for her to be able to raise numerous large armies of mercenaries when the need arose.

Carthaginian institutions

The institutions of Carthage went through several changes in the course of her history. In early days a form of kingship existed no doubt derived from the kingship of the Phoenician cities; it appears not to have been strictly hereditary but in practice one family, the Magonids, provided most of the known kings. As in the contemporary Greek cities, and indeed Rome and the Italian cities, kingship soon declined to be replaced by a more broadly based system, in the case of Carthage profoundly oligarchic. In the fifth and subsequent centuries the government was headed by chief magistrates with the title *sufets* or *suffetes*, a word akin to the Hebrew *shofet*, translated as judge in the Old Testament. Two were elected annually and the Romans later considered the *sufets* very similar to their own annually elected consuls. Although the citizen body is said to have elected them they all came from the wealthiest class in the city. Another similarity with the constitution of Rome, and also of many Greek states, was the power of a council of life members from the wealthy class, like the Roman senate, which decided all major matters in consultation with the *sufets*. Only if there was disagreement did the

Carthaginian coin, showing a horse being crowned by 'Victory', from an uncertain mint in Sicily, late fifth century BC.

people have a voice. Unlike the Romans and the Greeks, however, the Carthaginians decided at an early stage to separate military from civil and judicial powers. Even early kings appear to have had military power conferred upon them only for specific occasions and, in later times, generals were always special appointments, though in practice certain families seem to have developed a military tradition that resulted in their obtaining appointments over several generations. Unlike many major Greek cities, and Rome, Carthage never experienced a successful *coup d'état* led by a general. This is the more surprising since Carthage, uniquely in the ancient world, relied very largely on mercenaries. It appears that no general was able to establish firm enough ties with such an army to lead it against the city. The reason for reliance on mercenaries was no doubt that Carthaginian manpower was far too small to control and defend a widely scattered empire and at the same time fight major wars with rival powers. Experience tended to show that armies of experienced mercenaries were as often as not a match for the citizen armies of the Greek enemies of Carthage. The most important source of recruits was in North Africa among the tribes of Numidia and Mauretania (the northern parts of Algeria and Morocco). Iberian and Celtic tribes in Spain were also important sources and in the later period of Carthaginian history, Italians, Gauls and Greeks are also found. Little is known of the navy. It appears that Carthage was able regularly to have fleets of up to 200 ships at sea, this being roughly the size of the largest fleets of the Greek world in the fifth century BC, those of Athens and Syracuse. It is probable that rowers were obtained from Carthage itself and Phoenician settlements. In spite of its reputation it was not markedly superior to its rivals in major encounters.

Religion

Carthaginian religion long retained a number of primitive features, especially the practice of infant sacrifice, which continued long after it had died out in Phoenicia. The polytheistic system was headed by the male deity Baal Hammon (identified by the Romans with Saturn in their system) who had the same function as divine protector of the community as the *baal* of cities of Phoenician and associated culture in the east. Other deities of Phoenician origin attested at Carthage were Melkart and Eshmoun, the equivalents of Heracles and Aesculapius. As contact with the indigenous population increased, the cult of a goddess named Tanit, apparently of Libyan origin, became extremely popular; she seems to have taken over the fertility functions of the Phoenician Astarte. The sacrifice of infant children to Baal Hammon, apparently either as a form of 'first fruits' or in performance of vows, continued, with fluctuations, till the last period of Carthage. The burned bones of infants were buried in urns, the sites frequently being marked by inscribed stelae, in sanctuaries found both at Carthage and elsewhere in her empire in North Africa, Sicily and Sardinia.

During the fourth and subsequent centuries, Carthage experienced a growing amount of influence from the Greek world. Certain Greek religious cults were established (for example Demeter) and in the latest period large temples were built in place of the traditional open sanctuaries. One or two philosphers said to be of Carthaginian origin are known and in the second century we hear of libraries in the city, though we know

of only one work written by a Carthaginian, a treatise on agriculture. The most recent excavations at Carthage indicate that during the period of Greek influence a substantial new area of the city was built near the artificial harbour known as the *cothon*. The harbour, which survives today as two lagoons, was equipped, though probably not before the late third century BC, with the substantial buildings described in an ancient source. An outer rectangular harbour was for merchant ships, and a circular inner harbour could accommodate 220 warships in covered sheds. The city walls are said to have extended for 22 miles (35 km) across the isthmus on which Carthage was situated. Within easy reach of the harbour was the hill known as Byrsa which formed an inner citadel. The location of the earliest city, generally believed to have been in this area, has yet to be proved archaeologically. An ancient figure of 700,000 is given for the total population of Carthage but this probably includes the inhabitants of the surrounding country. However, it would, if correct, fall within the same range as the generally accepted figure for the population of ancient Athens.

Influence of Carthaginian civilization

The role of Carthaginian civilization was in the introduction of many peoples of the western Mediterranean, particularly those of North Africa, to the more advanced civilization of the eastern Mediterranean. Although little stands to her credit in terms of original art, philosophy or political organization, substantial changes occurred in the economy and social structure of the Libyan tribes under her influence. The agricultural resources of northern Tunisia were first exploited by the Carthaginians and this was the foundation of the famous prosperity of the area in the Roman period. Masinissa and other chieftains, in the period of Carthaginian decline and immediately afterwards, encouraged the tendency towards the adoption of a settled agricultural economy by their subjects. The religion of the indigenous peoples was influenced by the Carthaginians, and the Neo-Punic language, a late form of Phoenician, spread widely, especially when many Carthaginians fled from the Romans to Numidian areas. Above all, town life on the Phoenician model began to spread among the Libyans, often under the patronage of chieftains, for instance at Cirta (Constantine, Algeria) Masinissa's capital. It was on this basis that the rapid development of urbanization followed under the Romans: over 30 North African towns still used the term *sufets* for their chief magistrate well into the Roman period. Carthaginian influence on the development of Sardinia and southern Spain is also becoming much better understood as a result of new archaeological evidence.

Glass mask from Carthage (fourth century BC): both glass and glazing were known in ancient West Asia from very early times.

Sicily and Magna Graecia

B. H. Warmington

Greek colonization

Sicily and Magna Graecia were areas that received settlers in large numbers from the Greek world during the period *c*750 to 600 BC and formed an extension of Greek civilization in the west for many centuries following the initial movement. (*Magna Graecia* was the Latin term for southern Italy from the Bay of Naples to the Gulf of Taranto in which Greek settlements were made.) During the eighth century BC Greek explorer-traders had penetrated western Mediterranean waters in search of metals and perhaps other natural products, and the earliest settlements were sited in order to exploit or protect trade routes. The first was on the island of Ischia to be followed (*c*750 BC) by Cumae on the Bay of Naples, from which there was access to Italian metal deposits and also to the Etruscan communities north of the Tiber. These were followed by Zancle (Messana) and Rhegium on the straits of Messina. Initial settlements connected with trade were followed by far more numerous and important foundations sent out from various parts of the Greek world to exploit areas of fertile land discovered in the course of exploration. Traditional or approximate dates established by archaeology for a number of these are, in Sicily: Naxos (734 BC), Syracuse (733 BC), Leontini (729 BC), Catana (729 BC), Gela (688 BC), Himera (649 BC) and Acragas (580 BC); in Italy: Sybaris (720 BC), Croton (708 BC), Taras (706 BC), Poseidonia (Paestum) (700 BC) and Locri (673 BC). Apparently some unspecified combination of land hunger, overpopulation and social tensions lay behind this massive movement, in which many Greek cities were involved, in particular Chalcis, Eretria, Corinth and Rhodes in Sicily and the small communities of Achaea in Magna Graecia.

A significant feature of the whole movement was that apparently without exception, including further settlements made by the early foundations themselves, all formed new and independent communities from the start, retaining only the most formal ties with their founders, which in any case might number several different cities. Thus the Greek way of social organization in independent cities received a massive extension in the western Mediterranean.

The turbulent west

The Sicilian cities were more successful than those in Magna Graecia. The indigenous islanders (Sicels) were relatively weak and most Greek foundations (Syracuse being an exception) appear to have lived in relative peace with them. Wars became frequent with the Carthaginian cities in the western third of the island, the majority, however, being caused by the desire of some of the Greeks to exclude the Carthaginians from the island altogether. In Magna Graecia the cities were more isolated from each other than in Sicily and from the fifth century exposed to overwhelming pressure from Sabellian tribes. During the sixth century a number of cities such as Syracuse, Sybaris, Acragas and Himera came to rival in wealth and size the most important cities of Greece. Substantial public buildings adorned many of them, notable examples being temples that survive at Selinus, Acragas, and Himera in Sicily and Poseidonia (Paestum) in Italy. Economic relations with Greek cities were close and the western communities played a full part in such important Greek festivals as the Olympic games. Sicily appears to have imported manufactured goods from Greece and to have exported foodstuffs, especially wheat, not only to the Greek world but also to North Africa and Italian communities. The western Greeks also played a prominent role in the cultural life of the Greek world. An early and widely acclaimed lyric poet, Stesichorus, lived at Himera, Pythagoras emigrated from Samos to Croton *c*531 BC and his followers

Ancient Italy, before the rise of Rome.

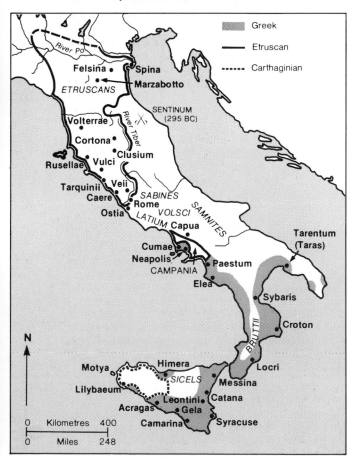

were influential there till 455 BC. Croton was also the site of an important school of Greek medicine. In the fifth century BC the philosopher Empedocles came from Acragas and Gorgias, the earliest 'sophist' and teacher of rhetoric, from Leontini.

Politically most cities went through stages similar to those in Greece, but from early times were notorious for political violence both internal and external. Rivalries were intense and warfare frequent. Syracuse destroyed her own foundation, Camarina, c550 BC, and in 510 BC Croton destroyed Sybaris, the wealthiest city of Magna Graecia. Growth of population, wars and social tensions led to the overthrow of landed aristocracies in the sixth century BC in a number of cities and their replacement by 'tyrants' (autocratic rulers not necessarily tyrannical in their manner of ruling). The most successful early tyrant was Gelon, originally from Gela, who seized control of Syracuse in 485 BC. He introduced a policy of ruthless transfers of population between cities dependent on him which became a characteristic of Sicilian politics, and made Syracuse the most important Greek city in the west. While the Persians were attacking Greece, Gelon defeated a Carthaginian force sent to defend the west of the island, but did not go on to drive it out completely. In the second half of the fifth century BC many cities, including Syracuse, enjoyed a period of relative calm with democratic institutions but the unsuccessful attempt by Athens in 415 BC to add the island to her empire, and intervention by Carthage in 410 BC in defence of her position, put an end to a fragile stability. In Magna Graecia, Cumae, in alliance with Syracuse, defeated the Etruscans in 474 BC but within half a century was conquered by the Sabelli and lost her purely Greek character. About the same time the Lucani followed by the Bruttii exerted increasing pressure on other cities of Magna Graecia till by c300 BC only Taras was still a city of wealth and importance.

The coming of the Romans

The first half of the fourth century BC in Sicily was dominated by Dionysius, who ruled Syracuse for some 30 years and became the most powerful individual Greek of his times. The last Sicilian ruler able to play an independent role in the Mediterranean world at large was Agathocles of Syracuse (the first Sicilian ruler to

Temple at Acragas, Sicily. Acragas was one of the cities to rival the most important cities of Greece in wealth and size during the sixth century AD.

assume the title of king) who at the time of his death (289 BC) ruled two-thirds of Sicily and some of the surviving cities of Magna Graecia. A decade later Pyrrhus, king of Epirus, briefly helped the Sicilians against Carthage. In 269 BC, Hiero of Syracuse took the title of king, and though at first he was friendly to Carthage when Rome intervened in Sicily, in 263 BC he changed sides and remained a loyal client of Rome till his death in 215 BC. Rome had captured Taras in 272 BC at the same time as she completed her control of southern Italy, being less dangerous to the residual Greek position than the Lucani and Bruttii. The most destructive event for Greek culture in the west was the Second Punic War; most of the Greek cities of Magna Graecia were either destroyed or ruined during its course. In Sicily an anti-Roman revolt in Syracuse led to the sack of the city. At the end of the war Sicily became Rome's first overseas province and her whole economy was directed towards Italy rather than Greece and North Africa. Literary sources, and a substantial tribute of corn, testify to the continuing prosperity of Sicilian agriculture but, although Greek language and culture remained dominant in the island for many centuries, Sicily became a relatively unimportant part of the Roman empire.

The Etruscans

R. M. Ogilvie

Origins

The Etruscans (Tyrrhenoi in Greek, Tusci or Etrusci in Latin, or Rasenna in their own language) developed a brief but remarkable civilization in Italy between c800 and 300 BC. Their heartland was the rich area south of the river Arno, north of the Tiber and west of the

Apennine mountains, much of which today is still known as Tuscany.

The question of the origins of the Etruscans is impenetrable. Basically there are only two tenable theories. Either they were an indigenous people who developed their culture as a result of contact with Greek traders and others. Or they (or at least a very small number of them) came from West Asia at some time during the disturbances that followed the collapse of the Hittite and Mycenaean empires and settled in Italy, cross-fertilizing with the native (Villanovan) population already established there. The question cannot yet be solved archaeologically, but, on the whole, the second solution seems more probable: not only because the Etruscan language has close affinities with eastern scripts (such as that found on the island of Lemnos) and features of Etruscan religious ceremony (such as the use of the curved wand or *lituus*) can best be paralleled from eastern sources, but because of the strength of the tradition that there was a migration from Asia Minor. It is not just the legend of Aeneas fleeing from Troy that was to figure so prominently in Etruscan art. More important is the account in the Greek historian Herodotus which, although employing many traditional ethnographical themes, nevertheless may well preserve a folk memory. His account (1.94) is as follows:

> 'There was a great famine in Lydia. King Atys tried to distract the minds of the Lydians from the famine but after 18 years divided the population in two. One half, under his son, Tyrsenos, emigrated. They went first to Smyrna where they built ships which they crowded with provisions. They then set off in search of new lands and eventually settled among the Umbrians, founding the cities they still live in. They called themselves "Tyrsenoi" after their leader.'

Herodotus dates this migration to about 1200 BC but, as is known, his sense of chronology is unreliable beyond two or three generations before his own day.

What is unmistakable is that in the eighth century BC the inhabitants of Tuscany coalesced into a number of urban centres, building cities sometimes on a regular plan, more often taking advantage of local topographical features. In the north these cities seem to have depended primarily on agriculture, working the rich lands that surrounded them. Such were Clusium, Cortona, Per-

usia, Volaterrae, Rusellae, Vetulonia, Volsinii and Populonia: prosperous and determined cities which also knew the secrets of metalwork and could exploit the very considerable bronze and iron deposits that exist on the island of Elba and on the adjoining mainland. To the south was another group of cities–Veii, Tarquinii, Caere, Vulci, Statonia, and others–which although also depending on local agriculture seem to have been far more involved in international trade, importing large quantities of Greek vases and other works of art and exporting bronzes and their own exquisite black 'bucchero' pottery.

Relations with Greek culture

Roman writers refer to a 'council' of 12 Etruscan cities but we know nothing about its organization, if indeed it ever existed. It was probably no more than a formal religious league with no political significance. However, despite their isolated existence, the Etruscans did have a profound effect on Italian history.

In the first place they were attached to Greece and all its culture. The Etruscan alphabet (which was to become the basis of the Latin alphabet) is directly derived from Greek. Etruscan vase painting was inspired by Greek models: indeed there was a tradition that Demaratus, an exile from Corinth, settled in Etruria, bringing with him the technical skills of the Corinthian pottery industry. And much of the metallurgical techniques no doubt also were borrowed from Greece. The contact with Greece resulted in the major phases of expansion. The Greeks had long been settled in southern Italy, especially in Campania in the area around Naples and Cumae. There is a narrow corridor that passes by Rome and links Etruria with Campania. The Etruscans built a road, past Praeneste, down to Campania and founded a number of settlements there, traditionally 12 but probably less. Certainly there were Etruscan communities at Capua, Acerra, Pompeii, Nola, Nocera and Sorrento but they were all short-lived. Founded in the late sixth century BC they were doomed to destruction by the encroachment of the hill peoples (Volsci, Aequi, and Samnites) who threatened their lines of communication as they forced their way down to the coastal plains. One defeat, at Aricia in 504 BC, was a serious blow. The *coup de grâce* came in 474 BC when the Etruscans were defeated in a naval battle at Cumae by the Carthaginians, which crippled their power. The other point of contact with the Greeks was the northern end of the Adriatic. Here again the Etruscans in the sixth and fifth centuries BC had established settlements for commercial purposes. The Adriatic ports of Spina and Adria were constructed and the Po river valley as a whole came under Etruscan control, again according to Etruscan tradition, settled by a federation of 12 cities, of which we can only name Mantua, Bologna (Felsina) and Marzabotto (a unique example of town planning on a grid system). These

One of the frescoes in the tomb of the Triclinium at Tarquinii (*c*500 BC), evidence of the Etruscans' belief in the afterlife.

Etruscan outposts were equally short-lived, but for a different reason. Towards the end of the fifth century various Celtic tribes crossed the Alps from France and settled in northern Italy. Ultimately they were to drift south and to end by capturing Rome itself *c* 386 BC, but their immediate impact was to force the Etruscan colonists to withdraw to Etruria proper.

Etruria and Rome

In the long run the most important act of Etruscan expansion was the settlement of a large number of families, probably from Tarquinii, Caere, Veii and Vulci, in Rome. They became integrated with the local population but made up a dominant section of the governing society (the symbol of absolute power, the *fasces*, was Etruscan as was the magisterial chair, the *sella curulis*) and provided at least three kings: Tarquinius Priscus, Servius Tullius and Tarquinius Superbus. The fusion of Etruscan religion and culture with Roman, the intermarriage of Etruscans and Romans, and the arrival of Etruscan skills (including writing) and technology were the essential ingredients that inspired the growth of Rome. In one of the great Etruscan tombs, the François tomb at Vulci, dating from the fourth or third centuries BC, a fresco depicts the murder of Cneve Tarchunies Romach (that is Cn. Tarquinius of Rome). One of the central social relationships, that between patron and client, seems to have originated in Etruria and so does that of the freedman (freed slave) which was to become so important in the early empire. It is no accident that Augustus' confidential adviser for much of his life, Maecenas, came from an Etruscan family, the Cilnii, descended from a line of kings.

Etruscan institutions

We know very little about how the individual Etruscan cities were run. Most of them during the eighth and seventh centuries BC seem to have been ruled by kings and there was a king at Veii still in the fifth century BC, but inscriptions from several Etruscan cities suggest that from about 550 BC onwards the government lay in the hands of magistrates, presumably elected annually, whose title was *zilath* or *purthane* (perhaps related to the Greek *prytaneus* or president). The precise organization will have varied from city to city and there was no central, federal government linking the individual cities, which seem very rarely to have acted in concert. As late as the first century AD an inscription was set up in Latin at Tarquinii commemorating the achievements of one of the great families at Tarquinii in the sixth and fifth centuries BC, who may even have led an expedition to Syracuse when the Athenians attempted to capture it in 415–413 BC.

The difficulty is one of language. We have thousands of funeral inscriptions that record names and a few personal details and can now be interpreted with some confidence–'Velthur, son of Paris and of Thanchvil Caclni, died aged 25'–but very few extensive documents that would enable us to understand both the semantics and morphology of the Etruscan language. One of the

Ornate black 'bucchero' pottery commonly found in Etruscan tombs, sixth century BC.

longest is written on strips of linen which were used to swathe an Egyptian mummy. It is now in Zagreb and appears to be a religious text. More recently three gold, one bronze and one lead leaf, recording dedications, have been discovered at Pyrgi and Santa Marinella and have enormously increased the body of extensive texts written in Etruscan. Yet despite these and numerous glosses preserved by Roman writers, our knowledge of Etruscan is still pitifully thin, and hence our knowledge of Etruscan life is also very shadowy.

The Etruscan heritage

There are, however, three main areas where the special contribution of the Etruscans can be identified. The first is in the field of religion. Long before the Romans, the Etruscans had evolved a sophisticated anthropomorphic pantheon of deities, presided over by Tinia who employed three kinds of lightning as his special power. The iconography of those gods was influenced by Greek art and sculpture, as can be seen from some fine surviving statues at the shrine of Piazza d'Armi at Veii, but the theology was probably always purely Etruscan.

This is borne out by two particular features. Unlike the Greeks, the Etruscans paid particular attention to the cult of the dead: their necropolises constitute the richest of all their surviving remains. In some cities, tombs are built like underground houses and are decorated with paintings and furnished with all the usual household equipment so that the dead man can simply resume and continue his earthly life. Hundreds of such tombs have been discovered at Caere, Tarquinii, Vulci, Orvieto and elsewhere and give us a vivid picture of everyday life in Etruria–from games to hunting, wrestling to dinner parties. Elsewhere tomb chambers were not built but even so the funeral goods buried with the dead, often comprising articles of great luxury, indicate a deep-

243

seated belief in the afterlife.

Secondly, the Etruscans developed a highly specialized art of divination, by which they were able to foretell the future or, at least, the will of the gods. Sometimes this was done by observing the flight of birds (auspicy, augury), which the Romans inherited. More often they consulted the entrails of sacrificed animals, determining events by the pattern and texture of the liver, which was divided into segments, each of which had its own signification. A model liver made of bronze, dating from the third century BC, was found at Piacenza in 1878 and illustrates the various permutations of explanation. Throughout the Roman republic and empire Etruscans were employed to exercise this skill on behalf of the state. They were known as *haruspices* (literally 'gut-gazers'). Almost all the Etruscan literature of which we know consisted of ritual books concerned with the interpretation of supernatural phenomena such as lightning, augury and the like. It is very doubtful whether there was any non-religious literature, although Latin sources do speak of historical annals. They have not survived and their character is entirely hypothetical, but, as late as the time of Cicero, Etruscan scholars such as P. Nigidius Figulus and A. Caecina were actively involved in the study of Etruscan religion.

The second main contribution that the Etruscans made was in the field of architecture and engineering. The classical Roman temple was mediated through the Etruscans who not only revised the *cella* plan but experimented with local stone and wood in their construction. Much of southern Etruria consists geologically of a tufa which is soft before it is exposed to the air and easily tunnelled into. The Etruscans exploited this not only for chamber tombs but for a huge network of water tunnels which channelled surplus water off the land in order to prevent soil erosion and to stave off the formation of the deep-cut ravines that are such a feature of the modern landscape. Two outstanding examples of this technology were the construction of the Cloaca Maxima, which drained the Forum at Rome (c575 BC)

and the tunnel that stabilized the level of the Alban Lake (c400 BC).

Thirdly, the Etruscans revealed a curious combination of originality and imitation in their art which in its day had no rival outside the Greek world. Etruscan vases, in their design and decoration, are almost indistinguishable from their Greek prototypes; Etruscan sculpture, particularly in terracotta, was admired by contemporaries and can be admired by us. It combined a classicism of techniques with a strange, remote, almost Oriental sense of design. Some of the finest examples are displayed in the Villa Giulia Museum in Rome. But the high point of Etruscan art was its bronzework: mirrors, candelabra, tripods, brooches, cauldrons, all of exquisite workmanship. Certainly for the southern Etruscan cities, metallurgy was a primary source of their prosperity.

The end of Etruscan power

The lack of unity of the Etruscan cities and the fact that Rome enjoyed a unique strategical position— commanding not only Etruria's links with the Greek colonies in southern Italy but also the salt trade up the Tiber that was vital for the economy of inland Etruria in the centre of Italy—meant that, once Veii had been devastated and Caere had been persuaded to ally herself with Rome, the Romans, many of whom, like the Fabii, Licinii and Cassii, derived their ancestry from Etruscan roots, were able gradually to absorb the great Etruscan cities. There was no dramatic confrontation, although a coalition of Gauls, Samnites, Umbrians and Etruscans fought a last-ditch battle against the Romans at Sentinum in 295 BC and lost. Rather it was a gradual process of attrition. Because the Roman nobility was very largely Etruscan by origin, it had links with the upper classes in other Etruscan cities, as we know from the foreign contacts of the Fabii. One by one the Etruscan cities succumbed to Rome—Sutri, Nepi, Falerii and then Arretium in 302 BC, Volsinii in 264 BC, and the rest. There was no war against Etruria as such. The governing classes in Etruscan cities came to realize that their interests were bound up with Rome and made what terms they could. And Rome offered them a flexible series of settlements, so that by 100 BC all the major cities of Etruria had become part of the Roman provincial organization of Italy; and apart from occasional displays of disaffection, as during the conspiracy of Catiline in 63 BC, they settled down to become the network of Italian civilian administration. Rome was indebted to the Etruscans for many of her most imaginative and creative poets and writers—Propertius and, probably, Tibullus among them. Livy, too, had strong Etruscan connections.

Ultimately the Etruscans were integrated into the universal Roman world, but their contribution to the creation of that world cannot be underestimated.

Etruscan terracotta sarcophagus showing the deceased couple, second half of the sixth century BC.

Rome before the Republic

R. M. Ogilvie

Origins and early organization

The success of Rome was in large measure due to its geographical setting. It is situated far enough from the sea to escape both the attentions of pirates and the ravages of malaria. At the same time it commands one of the first practical crossings of the Tiber, the principal river of central Italy. In this way it could control not only the goods and traffic from the north to the south of Italy but also the commerce along the Tiber itself and the roads that bordered it. It also was able in due time to develop a major port, Ostia, from which it could extend its trade throughout the Mediterranean, in very much the same way that the Piraeus was developed as the port of Athens.

Recent excavations have shown that the site of Rome was occupied in Chalcolithic times but the earliest significant habitations belong to the first millennium, the most important being on the Palatine and Esquiline Hills. The absolute dates are still controversial, perhaps *c*850 BC (the traditional Roman date for the founding of Rome is 753 BC), but there is little doubt that the sites were occupied by separate, although related, communities of incomers who had come down from the Danube basin as one of many waves of an Indo-European-speaking people who were to settle not only in Italy and Greece but even to spread as far as Persia and India. At Rome the two communities not only had different pottery styles but also different burial customs, and this is what is behind the traditional legend about Romulus, the king of the Romans, who fought and defeated the Sabines but who in consequence negotiated a settlement whereby the Romans and the Sabines were jointly to colonize this uniquely promising site.

Initially its life was primarily pastoral. There is good archaeological evidence to illustrate the extent to which animal farming, especially pigs, flourished—a fact that again is reflected in legend. But at an early date the importance of the big salt-pan beds at the mouth of the Tiber was recognized. Salt was an essential commodity in the ancient world and as the big communities in central Italy began to grow, Rome was able to monopolize not only the recovery but also the transport of salt, so that the Via Salaria (Salt Road), along the banks of the Tiber, had by the seventh century BC become one of the principal arteries and brought a prosperity to Rome that her neighbours, such as Lavinium or Gabii, could not enjoy.

Of the early history of Rome little is known. Traditionally it was ruled by kings—Romulus, Numa, Tullus Hostilius and Ancus Marcius—and during this period the political and religious institutions, which were to persist for a thousand years, were created. The most important was the Senate, an advisory body chosen by the king from the heads of the principal families that had settled in Rome. Hence their title 'Conscript Fathers' (*patres conscripti*). They enjoyed not only direct political power but also considerable religious responsibility, and their status was hereditary: the descendants of 'Fathers' appointed by the kings were known as patricians and formed a separate class within Roman society. Those who did not belong to this élite were known as the *plebs*: but the plebeians numbered among their ranks not only the poor peasant labourers but also, in increasing numbers, rich merchants and artisans who had settled at Rome. In addition to the Senate there was from very early times an assembly based on *curiae* (wards or parishes). Each *curia* probably represented an ethnic unit, and as the attraction and reputation of Rome grew, so new groups were drawn to it and formed new *curiae*. By the end of the monarchy there were 30 voting units in the Curiate Assembly, which concerned itself not only with family matters such as wills and adoption but also with the bestowal of plenary power (*imperium*) and may have been the basis of a rudimentary militia.

The coming of the Etruscans

Early Rome was, however, essentially a conglomeration of individual communities built on different hills. Traces of these separate communities still survived in classical times, particularly in religious rites such as the Argei procession on 16–17 March which visited 27 different localities before throwing 27 rush dolls (a substitute for humans) into the Tiber. By the mid-seventh century BC some closer cohesion becomes evident and Rome seems to have begun to assert her sovereignty over nearby territory, particularly along the line of the Tiber. Ostia

The she-wolf became for the Romans the symbol of their own greatness. The Capitoline wolf shown here dates from the early fifth century BC.

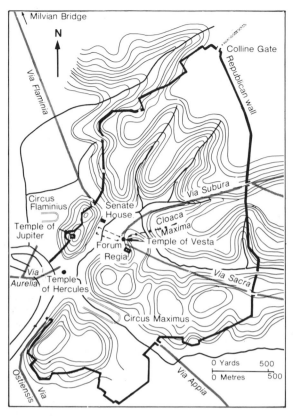

Map of Rome in the time of the republic.

was traditionally founded by Ancus Marcius—a tradition that cannot readily be discounted. The decisive development, however, was the infiltration of the Etruscans. They were essentially city dwellers and they were also fine craftsmen. Rome lies just on the edge of southern Etruria, not far from Tarquinii, Caere and Veii, but the salt trade will also have drawn the attention of the great interior cities, such as Vulci, Clusium and Vetulonia, to her importance. The beginning of Etruscan influence at Rome cannot be precisely dated, but it probably belongs to the last quarter of the seventh century BC. Over a generation the character of Rome was dramatically changed. The Etruscans were great engineers—Etruria is criss-crossed with subterranean water tunnels—and it is to them that the achievement of draining the central area of Rome, the Forum, must be attributed. The Main Drain (*Cloaca Maxima*) dates in its original form from about 600 BC. Once it had been constructed, it became possible for the separate communities to unite in a common marketplace with common temples and places of assembly. The Forum, which previously had been used for burials, was paved and the first public buildings in it, such as the Palace (*Regia*, later, under the republic, the seat of the chief priest) were constructed. Rome had become a town and not a collection of villages.

The archaeological evidence for this, by and large, confirms the historical story which says that the Elder Tarquin came from Etruria and took power at Rome on the death of Ancus Marcius *c*625 BC. Certainly the Etruscan element in Rome is clear from now on, both in the wide spread of Etruscan artifacts, including pottery with inscriptions in the Etruscan language, but also in the emergence of families whose names are distinctively Etruscan: Licinii, Menenii, Sicinii and so on.

The creation of a centralized town also involved major changes to the social organization of Rome. One of the great technological advances that the Etruscans brought to Rome was the heavy-armed infantryman, which they had copied from the Greek hoplite. Their solid ranks were to prove unbeatable against the loose formations of Rome's enemies and were the beginning of a long tradition, refined by experience and training, that was to end with the Roman legion. But such tactics require disciplined practice and also sufficient affluence for citizens to purchase their own heavy armour. The Etruscan kings, therefore, reformed the basic structure of society by creating a new system under which citizens were classified on the basis of their wealth and not by their wards or parishes (*curiae*). Initially there was probably a single class (*classis*) of people whose wealth qualified them for military training and a second class of these who were ineligible (*infra classem*): subsequently the system was modified to comprise five classes with varying income bands. Because the new army was so important for Rome's survival, the membership of the *classis* not only became the criterion of citizenship but also conferred political rights. A new assembly, the Comitia Centuriata, was created which became the main body for public discussion of issues, for the passage of laws and (later) for the election of magistrates. In this assembly the distinction between patrician and plebeian counted for nothing: all who had a stake in the country could have a say in her affairs. Traditionally this reform is ascribed to king Servius Tullius (578–535 BC) and those approximate dates certainly fit the archaeological evidence for the introduction of heavy infantry. Servius is also credited with a reform of the tribal organization, replacing the three Romulean tribes (Ramnes, Tities, Luceres) with four urban tribes and a number of rural tribes, but the authenticity and details of this are buried in obscurity.

The Etruscans were not a small dynasty imposing themselves on a subject population. There was evidently such a sizeable infiltration that the Roman and Etruscan communities seemed to have merged into a homogeneous whole. Long after the Etruscan kings had been expelled, the Romans retained as the symbol of supreme power the Etruscan device of a double-headed axe encased in a bundle of rods—capital and corporal punishment. And Etruscan religion replaced the old, primitive worship of the Romans who had not thought of their gods in anthropomorphic terms or built houses for them. Originally Mars was the chief god of Rome representing those powers that protected the security of the city (war) and agricultural prosperity. Mars was associated with Jupiter, the sky-god, and Quirinus, the god of the Sabines, one of the largest immigrant communities. They were worshipped without statues or temples. The Etruscans replaced this triad with a new one—Jupiter, Juno and Minerva—for whom they built a huge temple on the Capitoline Hill which was dedicated just after the fall of the monarchy in 507 BC and moulded magnificent statues after the Greek fashion. In the same way various practices of divination to secure knowledge of the will of the gods were imparted by the Etruscans to Rome and became permanently established there, such as the consultation of entrails (*haruspicina*) or the flight of birds (augury/auspices).

In the hundred years between 650 and 550 BC Rome had grown both in size and diversification of population. Her rulers were now Etruscans who had contacts far away from Rome throughout the Etruscan and Greek world. Greek vases are found in Rome and there is even a story, not wholly incredible, that Rome consulted the oracle at Delphi before the end of the sixth century BC. This prosperity can be traced in the buildings, temples and houses and also in the level of imported goods. It was based still to a large extent on the importance both of Rome's agricultural economy and of her control of the salt trade, but a new factor was the short-lived expansion of the Etruscans to the south. The Greeks, from about 735 BC onwards, had built a number of colonies in southern Italy, at places such as Cumae, Neapolis (Naples), Sybaris, Croton and Tarentum. They had been founded partly in response to overcrowding in their mother cities and partly with an eye to exploiting the virgin territory of Italy. Two things in particular attracted the colonists—the rich mineral deposits in Campania and on Elba, and the very fertile, in places volcanic, soil. The Greeks colonies increased and prospered, and the Etruscan cities of the north, with their love of Greek art and craftmanship and their affinity to the urbanized civilization of the Greeks, began to extend their influence down to Campania. The Etruscans can be seen to have founded settlements in Capua and Pompeii from the seventh century BC onwards. For these settlements to flourish the Etruscans needed good communications by land to the great cities of the north. Rome commanded one such route: the road that led south from the Tiber through the Alban Hills to the valley of the river Tolerus. Rome was also able to control the other route, which led from Tiber crossings at Crustumeria or Eretum down through the natural gap between the Alban Hills and Praeneste (Palestrina) to join the river Tolerus near Ferentinum. On either route she was able to police and tax the traffic that passed down the coastal plain of western Italy. It was this fact that contributed to her remarkable prosperity in the sixth century BC and it is significant that when Etruscan power in Campania was destroyed as a result of the disastrous naval battle of Cumae in 474 BC, and the inroads of the Samnite hill peoples from c450 BC, Rome's economy also suffered a shattering decline.

The Etruscan kings

According to the historical tradition three Etruscan kings—Tarquinius Priscus, Servius Tullius and Tarquinius Superbus—ruled from c625–c510 BC. The gen-

eration gap looks too large and there were probably other kings as well, but the existence of an Etruscan dynasty is indisputable. After the model of the great Greek tyrants such as Polycrates, Periander and Pisistratus, they devoted themselves not only to great public-building programmes but also to an expansionist policy in international affairs. Rome's whole future depended upon her control of the small plain known as Latium, which was inhabited by 30 or more communities of the same basic ethnic stock and with certain basically similar religious customs as the original Romans themselves. The Etruscan migration to Rome gave a new impetus to the movement which had already been seen in the seventh century under Ancus Marcius. Under the Tarquins the Romans not only conquered a series of key places in the neighbourhood (such as Gabii on the vital north–south trade route) but also formed a historic alliance with the Latin peoples which was commemorated by the foundation of a temple to Diana on the Janiculan hill at Rome by king Servius Tullius c540 BC. A very ancient inscription recording the foundation of this temple was still accessible and legible in classical times but the site of the temple has not yet been excavated to establish its precise date and purpose. It is clear, however, that the kings of Rome intended that it should replace a federal cult of Diana at Aricia, among the Alban Hills, to which many of the Latins paid homage. The Romans were doing no more than asserting their supremacy in Latium.

By c510 BC Rome had become a major power, with a large stretch of territory under her protection. The historical sources say that about this time she made a treaty with Carthage in which their respective spheres of influence were set out. Such a treaty is by no means unlikely, because gold tablets, written in Etruscan and Phoenician/Punic and dating from the same epoch, have recently been discovered at Pyrgi, the port of the Etruscan town of Caere. The temple of Capitoline Jupiter was the biggest temple of its day in Italy, and under the Tarquins her prosperity looked assured. A Roman Tarquin figures on a fine Etruscan wall painting at Vulci. But, probably in 507 BC, the king was expelled and eventually a dual, annual magistracy (the consulship) was set up instead.

The fall of the monarchy

The reasons for this drastic revolution are very unclear. It was certainly not a movement against the Etruscan population of Rome as such: they were already too numerous and too well integrated, and they survived as a dominant element in society. It was perhaps to some extent a social phenomenon. The age of tyrants was over and it is no coincidence that Pisistratus' son was driven out of Athens in 510 BC. There were also internal and external difficulties. Internally there were a growing number of powerful families who were jealous at being excluded from the Senate and, hence, the privileges of being patricians. Externally, the Etruscans were beginning to be threatened, particularly in the south, by the raids which the hill people, such as the Aequi and

Volsci, were making on the coastal plain. This disruption was compounded by the activities of various freelance Etruscans who roamed the country with large bands of 'condottieri': legend preserves the story of Lars Porsenna of Clusium who attacked Rome about this time and the Vulci frescoes commemorate others such as Macstarna and the brothers Vibennae. The revolution, therefore, had no doubt several different inspirations but its effects were momentous. Rome became a democracy but the democratic offices were to be hotly contested by a small group of families whose ambitions and jealousies were to lead to the civil wars of Marius and Sulla, and Caesar and Pompey. Rome without a king had no ultimate source of religious authority and this led to the feuds between patricians and plebeians that were to dominate politics for the next two centuries.

Republican Rome

R. M. Ogilvie

The early years

When the republic was instituted about 507 BC (neither the date nor the precise form of the institutions are wholly certain) Rome, for all her strategic importance and material prosperity, was vulnerable. Power had been transferred to a narrow group of long-established families, the patricians, who had the monopoly of religious authority, and of the annual dual magistracy, the consulship, but who had to live with a much larger group of citizens—some landowners, some artisans, some peasants—who were excluded from any real say in government. At the same time there were other factors changing the face of Italy. Celts had spilled over the Alps into northern Italy and disrupted the Etruscan settlements; roving armies, such as that of Lars Porsenna which captured Rome *c*505 BC, were at large; the hill people of the Apennines, such as the Aequi and Volsci, were pressing down on to the coastal plains; malaria seems to have become endemic in the coastal marshes.

The effect of all this, as can be seen clearly from the archaeological deposits, was that the economy of Rome

suffered a dramatic decline. The import of Greek vases, for instance, was drastically cut and the question of personal debt (*nexum*) became one of the dominant issues reported in our sources. It was no doubt economic factors that led to a substantial portion of the population making a token withdrawal from the city in 494 BC (the first Secession), as a result of which the plebeians secured their own officials, tribunes, and shortly afterwards their own assembly at which plebeian matters could be decided. The friction between the plebeians and patricians caused by these economic and social difficulties did, however, continue and led to the setting up of a Commission of Ten who codified and published the Twelve Tables in 451 BC, which set out for the first time for all to see the rights and privileges of all Roman citizens under the law. The turning point, however, was the defeat of the Etruscans in southern Italy at the battle of Cumae in 474 BC, as a result of which the Etruscans were gradually forced back to their homelands north of the river Tiber, so that the Romans no longer enjoyed the strategic benefits of their situation midway between the rich Etruscan and Greek civilizations in Italy. As early as about 496 BC Rome had to fight a major battle (Lake Regillus) in order to maintain her supremacy even among her Latin neighbours, but on this occasion her superior military technique, in particular the adoption of Greek-style heavy-infantry tactics, proved decisive, and Rome, in consequence, formalized a series of treaty obligations with the Latins that were to be the pattern for all subsequent Roman international relations. In return for military cooperation, various mutual agreements concerning trade, intermarriage, and transfer of domicile were completed.

This cooperation was to be badly needed, because one of Rome's closest neighbours, the Etruscan city of Veii, on the north bank of the Tiber, had been among the earliest cities to feel the economic recession and attempted to compensate for it by an aggressive policy which would have destroyed Rome's monopoly of the lucrative

Bas relief of the Roman army, showing a legionary standard. Augustus recovered lost standards from the Parthians.

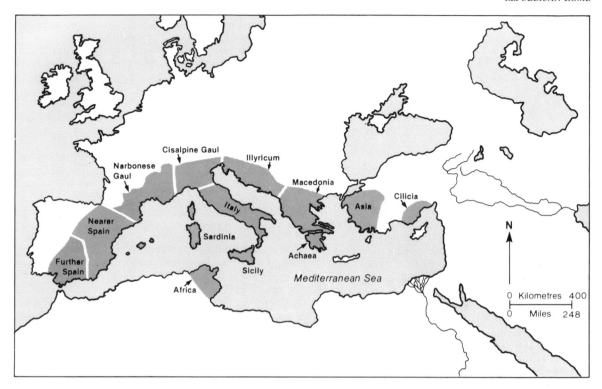

Republican Rome: the provinces in 100 BC.

salt trade up the Tiber. Veii, a very fine natural site, was eventually captured by the Romans about 396 BC after a long and intermittent war, but not before the patricians had been forced in 447 BC to accept another social compromise, the creation of a multiple magistracy (the numbers varied from three to six according to need), 'military tribunes with consular power' to replace on occasion the two consuls. The prime purpose was to create enough generals to take command of whatever front Rome was fighting on, but, more importantly, the new magistracy was open on an equal footing to the plebeians so that not only could new talent be tapped, but a major source of contentious discrimination removed.

The fall of Veii appeared to establish Rome on a stable basis as the major power in central Italy but disaster was to strike only a few years later (traditionally 386 BC) when a force of Celts under Brennus captured and sacked Rome. It took a generation for Rome to recover her prosperity and to reassert her hegemony over the Latins. At first power seems to have reverted to the patrician élite but gradually a new set of plebeian aristocrats emerged who identified their interests with the patricians. In 367 BC the consular tribunate was ended and instead the consulship as such was opened to plebeians as a result of laws passed by Sextius and Licinius. These were later confirmed by a plebiscite (i.e. a bill passed in the plebeian assembly), moved by a tribune L. Genucius in 342 BC and consolidated by a law of Hortensius in 287 BC.

Consolidation of Roman power

The primary task that faced Rome was to re-establish her control over her Latin neighbours and the adjoining parts of Etruria. This she did in a series of campaigns that culminated in a decisive victory over the Latins in 338 BC, after which, whatever the propaganda fictions that may have been disseminated and whatever the mutual rights that the Latins may have still enjoyed, Rome was effectively mistress of the whole of the area from the Tiber to the border of the Greek territory of Campania. And the reality of its growing power is symbolized by a treaty which Rome subscribed with the great North African power of Carthage in 348 BC.

The new patrician-plebeian coalition, headed by a number of outstanding figures such as the Decii and Papirii, was obviously attracted by the great economic and political opportunities open to them. Southern Italy was mainly Greek and was itself in turmoil, partly because of the collapse of the dominant tyranny at Syracuse and partly because of the chaos in mainland Greece, which was only to be resolved by the ambitions of Philip II of Macedon (d. 336 BC) and his son Alexander the Great (d. 323 BC). The Romans, however, were not the only people to recognize this vacuum in Campania (around Naples), which is both rich in fertile, volcanic, agricultural land and in very substantial mineral deposits, and which the Greeks had colonized from the seventh century. The Samnites, a hill people of basically the same ethnic stock as the Romans and Latins, had also begun to encroach on the Campanian plains. They captured the Graeco-Etruscan cities of Capua and Cumae while the Romans were consolidating their position

249

along the river Liris, which marked the recognized frontier with Campania.

War was inescapable but given the elusive nature of the Samnites, who fought on a hit-and-run basis, success was difficult to achieve. Three wars in all were fought against the Samnites (343–341, 326–304, 298–290 BC) and in order to secure final victory (and in the process they also suffered some major reverses, such as the disaster of the Caudine Forks when a whole army was surrounded and forced to surrender under ignominious circumstances) Rome had to win over the surrounding peoples, many of whom were Greek or had long-standing connections with the Greek world. At the same time the continuous emergency united the Romans and under the censor Appius Claudius (312 BC) further steps were taken to improve the disadvantaged position of the plebeians, in particular redistributing the poorer of them among all the tribes instead of only among the few urban tribes, so that their voice became a real force in the tribal assembly.

The struggle with Carthage

Rome's conquest of Campania and Samnium, together with the increasing control of Etruria, confronted her both with the Greek settlements of southern Italy and with the great commercial and military power of Carthage, which had a substantial presence in Sicily and which, even as early as about 500 BC, had had treaty relations with Rome and other cities, such as Caere, as recently excavated gold tablets have revealed. The Greek confrontation, although perilous at the time when Pyrrhus of Epirus in northwestern Greece came over to help the citizens of the Greek city of Tarentum and fought a series of desperate battles against the Romans (280–275 BC), was relatively short-lived. The struggle with Carthage was much more serious and prolonged and resulted in Rome gaining control of the whole of the Mediterranean. The immediate issue was Sicily–historically a Greek island and one whose commercial and agricultural potentialities were enormous (it remained one of the most important corn granaries for Rome down to the late empire), but which the Carthaginians had also attempted to secure for their own interests. Rome was drawn into conflict by an appeal from some Campanian mercenaries who were resisting the attempts of Hiero of Syracuse to capture Messina. In a long war (264–241 BC), despite an ambitious raid on Africa itself under Regulus, Rome was unable to establish her superiority until, with the help of the southern Italians, she developed a powerful fleet which eventually drove the Carthaginians not only from Sicily but also from Sardinia and Corsica, which the Romans annexed as provinces.

Carthage was determined to recover her lost possessions and was alarmed at the growth of Roman influence, particularly in Illyria and Spain. In 218 BC the young general Hannibal led an army overland from southern Spain across the Alps into Italy itself and in a series of brilliant battles from Lake Trasimene to Cannae, defeated the Romans.

Hannibal was helped by being able to open a second front when he secured the alliance of Philip V of Macedon, who, like Pyrrhus before him, was worried by Roman expansion in the Greek world. But Hannibal was fighting far from home, without the possibility of regular supplies or reinforcements, and the Romans, under Q. Fabius Maximus Cunctator, managed to pin him down in Italy while another army was sent to Africa and triumphed at the battle of Zama (202 BC), so forcing the Carthaginians to sue for peace. The consequences of the second Carthaginian war were not only the extension of Roman power to Spain and southern France but also to Greece. Rome had a score to settle and the second Macedonian War (200–196 BC), fought as a reprisal against Philip, was followed by adventure into Asia Minor itself, where Hannibal had taken refuge.

Social and political developments

All of this had very practical effects for the Roman population of Italy. On the one hand large standing armies had to be maintained during the third and second centuries, involving the highest proportion of male citizens conscripts known in history. This is turn, since the economy was largely an agricultural one, led to the ruin of peasant smallholdings, and even when the head of the family did return from the wars, the attractions of the city were liable to prove more alluring than the intermittent labour of the fields. On the other hand, for the patrician-plebeian nobility the opportunities were golden. A series of great families begin to dominate Roman politics: Scipios, Metelli, Claudii, Aemilii, Fabii, Sempronii and so on. The rewards of a successful campaign (especially in Spain or the eastern Mediterranean) could be enormous in terms of booty (bullion, works of art, slaves) and the only practical investment for such wealth was in land. So the *nobiles* bought up or otherwise acquired land in Italy and farmed it, not by inefficient and uneconomic tenant farmers, but by concentrating their holdings into huge multi-purpose units which were worked by slave labourers. Slaves, often prisoners of war, had two great advantages: they did not have families to support and so were more cost-effective and, secondly, they could be used in gangs on different tasks at different times of the year. Roman Italy thus became not only a great military power but also one of the relatively few societies whose economy has depended upon slavery.

The political effects were no less significant. During the second century the successful *nobiles* became richer as the commands available to them became more extensive. Inevitably there was much competition between rival families and also much collaboration, with dynastic marriages, patronage and adoption. But success depended upon the nobleman winning and keeping the goodwill and loyalty of the troops under his command and arranging for their welfare when they were discharged. The seeds were thus sown for the private armies and the civil wars that were to scar the whole of the first century BC. A further consequence was that, whereas previously Roman expansion had largely been undertaken fortuitously and reluctantly, now active politicians were seeking for new fields in which to win glory and wealth. The Third Carthaginian War (149–146 BC) was deliberately provoked and ended with the annexation of a large area of North Africa. Similarly Corinth was captured in 146 BC and the province of Macedonia formed. King Attalus bequeathed his kingdom of Pergamun to the Romans in 133 BC. All the time the Romans were pushing further east and south into the lands that had once formed the empire of Alexander the Great.

Rome and Greece

From the very beginning Rome had been in touch with Greek culture, first through the Etruscans (the Latin alphabet is derived from Greek through the medium of Etruscan) and then through the contacts with southern Italy and Sicily. Her involvement with Greece itself and with the great Hellenistic kingdoms from the mid-third century BC onwards intensified this relationship.

Culturally, it was the Greeks who gave the inspiration for the birth of Latin literature. There was no native Latin literary tradition and the Etruscans seem to have been more concerned with technical writing (especially in the field of augury and other religious subjects). Once the Romans came directly into contact with the Greeks, they admired their achievements and attempted, with brilliant success, to imitate them. A translation of the *Odyssey* by Livius Andronicus (d. *c*204 BC) opened a new era. What the Romans did was to take Greek models and invest them with a specifically original Roman quality. From Fabius Pictor, who was the first Roman to write a history of Rome (*c*200 BC); from Q. Ennius (d. 169 BC) who wrote a Greek-type epic, the *Annales*, which encompassed the most stirring events of Roman history from its foundation down to contemporary times; from Plautus and Terence who adapted for Roman audiences the plays of New Comedy; from the Elder Cato (censor in 184 BC) who, in spite of outspoken criticism of the demoralizing influence of Hellenism, was one of the first to introduce the full technique of Greek oratory into Roman public life, the line was to continue down to Catullus, Horace and Virgil, Sallust, Livy and Tacitus. The originality of Latin literature, like eighteenth-century English literature, lies precisely in its lack of originality. It is interesting that this holds true not only for literature but for art, sculpture and architecture as well, as any visitor to Pompeii, Herculaneum or Delos will immediately recognize.

It was perhaps of more moment that the same contact with the Greek world had a profound effect on Roman religion. Not only were a number of new cults introduced from the east (such as Cybele, Magna Mater, Bacchus, to be followed by Isis, Mithras and others) but the old gods became identified with their Greek counterparts and acquired their iconography and mythology. In primitive times the Roman gods were not thought of anthropomorphically, nor did they have a set of myths associated with them, but gradually Jupiter came to be thought of as Zeus, Mars (who was originally the presiding deity of the community) with Ares, Minerva with Athena and so on. Although this Hellenization enriched art and cult, it tended to diminish the fundamental, peasant piety of the Romans who saw all the natural processes of life as subject to supernatural control.

The breakdown of republican institutions

The immediate problem that fuelled the civil dissensions of the first century BC was the plight of the non-Roman Italians who did not enjoy the privileges of Roman citizenship but had to carry many of the burdens, and were increasingly evicted from their own lands either to make way for ex-soldiers or for the big estates of the *nobiles*. The problem was a real one but was also one that could be and was used for purely political purposes by ambitious men, particularly by exploiting the gulf between the rich, aristocratic élite and the growing number of small landowners, businessmen and traders (*equites*) who prospered with the expansion of the Roman empire, but who were effectively denied any say in its direction. Tiberius Gracchus and his brother Caius, both themselves distinguished *nobiles*, used the office of tribune of the plebs (133 BC; 123–121 BC) to appeal over the heads of the Senate to a wider audience on the emotive issues of land reform and Italian citizenship. The Italian question was not to be solved for another generation, until, after abortive legislation by another *nobilis* tribune, M. Livius Drusus (91 BC) and a bitter 'social' war between Romans and Italians (91–88 BC), the principle that Italians should be entitled to Roman citizenship was conceded. Yet the legacy of bitterness was to linger on for the rest of the century. The only solution to the land problem was the huge extension of settlements of veterans, Italians and others, outside Italy itself, which materially contributed to the spread of Romanization throughout the provinces.

The Gracchi may have been motivated by liberal ideals but at least some of their drive came from seeing that here were new fields which they could work to improve their own political standing and so enhance their prestige (*dignitas*). The rivalry between leading politicians increased as the stakes grew higher and the jealousies more intense. C. Marius, who did not come from an aristocratic background but was taken up by the Metelli, established himself as a formidable figure not

Coin of Mithridates VI of Pontus, defeated by Pompey the Great in 66 BC.

Julius Caesar (*c*100–44 BC).

merely by outstanding military genius, as shown in wars against king Jugurtha in Numidia (112–101 BC) and against the Cimbri, a Celtic marauding force (113–101 BC), but also by popularist measures to reform the army and to expedite resettlement. His position was not allowed to go unchallenged. L. Cornelius Sulla (*c*138–79 BC), a man from an old family who had made a name for himself on Marius' staff in Africa, and was anxious that political power should be retained within the tight circle of *nobiles*, obtained the important command against Mithridates VI of Pontus in 88 BC, which gave him control of an army and opportunities for self-aggrandizement. When Marius' supporters tried to terminate it, Sulla marched on Rome (82 BC) and had himself elected dictator 'for the reform of the constitution' (81–79 BC).

The pattern was thus set. Dominant figures, abetted by their adherents among the *nobiles*, their soldiers, their clients and other groups in Rome and abroad, struggled for power and to maintain their *dignitas*. Sulla had hoped that by an enlarged Senate, which would bring new blood into the ranks of the *nobiles*, a consensus government could be formed. First, Cn. Pompeius Magnus, having proved himself suppressing a revolt in Spain (77–71 BC), and then having eliminated the pirates from the eastern Mediterranean (67 BC) and finally conquered Mithridates (66 BC), returned to Rome only to meet with frustration as other *nobiles* were reluctant to accept his undisputed pre-eminence. And perhaps Pompey himself was uncertain what to do with his power. The immediate problems of settling his veterans and having his actions in the eastern Mediterranean formally approved were difficult enough. In 59 BC he compromised with M. Licinius Crassus, reputedly the richest man in the Roman world, and G. Julius Caesar, who established an

Pompey the Great. After his defeat at Pharsalus by Julius Caesar in 48 BC, he fled to Egypt and was assassinated there. It is an irony of fate that four years later Caesar himself was assassinated in Rome, in Pompey's Theatre.

informal Triumvirate, which lasted until Crassus' death on an ill-fated campaign in West Asia in 53 BC. Part of the agreement was that Caesar should be given command in Gaul, which he held for ten years and succeeded in subduing the whole country. The command not only made Caesar a wealthy man but gave him the backing of an army as formidable and disciplined as any that Marius, Sulla or Pompey had led. The old constitution went on, consuls, praetors, tribunes were elected, the Senate met and debated and the assemblies voted, but more and more power was concentrated into the hands of a very few men. It is not clear just when Caesar decided to follow Sulla's lead and set himself up as sole ruler, but certainly when his opponents in the Senate thwarted his demands in 49 BC he took the decision to cross the river Rubicon and invade Italy, precipitating a civil war which was ended by his defeat of Pompey at Pharsalus in Greece in 48 BC. Although pockets of resistance held out in Spain and Africa, Caesar was supreme. He duly became dictator for life and there is evidence that he intended, as a means of ensuring that his position was unrivalled and unique, of taking the status of king and god.

Autocracy was ultimately to be the only way in which the Roman empire could survive and even in the few years that Caesar had before his assassination in 44 BC it is remarkable how many long-overdue reforms were accomplished, from an overhaul of the calendar to detailed constitutional legislation for colonies abroad, from a massive financial reorganization to moral and social welfare. But the traditions of the republic died hard.

The Early Roman Empire

Wolfgang Liebeschuetz

The work of Augustus

That the empire survived the civil wars that destroyed the republic was largely due to the long life (63 BC–AD 14) and political skill of Gaius Julius Caesar Octavianus, later known as Augustus. In 44 BC Octavian, great-nephew and adopted son of the murdered dictator, rallied Caesar's veterans and used them first against Marc Antony, senior leader of the Caesarians, and then in alliance with Antony and Lepidus (the Second Triumvirate), against the republicans. Proscriptions caused the death of some 300 senators and 2000 knights. Opponents of the triumvirs were cowed, and much property made available with which to reward the troops. After Brutus and Cassius had been defeated at Philippi (42 BC), and Marc Antony and Cleopatra at Actium (31 BC), Octavian was master of the empire. With the settlement of 27 BC he laid the foundations of the 'principate', a system of government that was to give the empire internal peace–with only brief interruptions–for around 250 years.

Essentially this was monarchy modified so as to make it acceptable to men familiar with free republican institutions. The ruler was not king but first citizen (*princeps*). Of his formal titles, Caesar proclaimed that he was a descendant of the dead dictator, and Imperator (hence 'emperor'), that he was commander in chief. The Senate marked the fact that this citizen had unique prestige and influence by conferring the title of Augustus. The *princeps'* power was like that of a king in that it rested on hereditary loyalty, especially of the army, to himself, his family and descendants (whether by birth or adoption). His personality was magnified and publicized through the so-called imperial cult, a complex of ceremonies making use of the forms of religion to express and instil loyalty to the ruler. At the same time Augustus voluntarily restricted his actions within the limits of various constitutional powers conferred by the Senate, for which, taken singly, republican precedent could be found. Moreover, he let his position evolve through a series of settlements, and thus avoided outrage to public and especially senatorial opinion. In 27 BC he was granted a proconsular command, or province including Gaul, Spain and Syria, and by far the greatest part of the Roman army. In 23 BC he received the power of a tribune, and his proconsular authority was made greater than that of any other provincial governor. In 19 BC he received (probably) consular powers that entitled him to introduce administrative reforms in Rome and Italy. This complex of powers remained the constitutional basis of the imperial office and continued to be

Caesar Augustus (63 BC–AD 14), from Prima Porta, near Rome (probably after 13 BC). First of the Roman emperors, he symbolizes Roman power.

granted by the Senate, which thus retained, in theory at least, a share in the appointment of the emperor.

Augustus reduced the huge armies of the civil war to around 300,000 men, made up half of Roman citizens serving in legions and half of provincials in auxiliary units. The army was stationed in frontier provinces. After around 25 years' service legionaries received a lump-sum pension from a military treasury fed by two special taxes. Auxiliaries, on retirement, were given Roman citizenship. Augustus was lucky to have able yet reliable generals, notably his friend Agrippa, and in later years his stepsons Tiberius and Drusus. These and others expanded the empire very considerably until in AD 9 the loss of three legions in the disastrous battle of the Teutoburg Forest ended a sustained attempt to conquer Germany, and reconciled Augustus to frontiers stabilized along the Rhine, Danube and Euphrates. By and large growth of the empire had come to an end. The conquest of Britain, begun under Claudius, was the only major post-Augustan addition to the empire to prove lasting. Suspicion of successful generals, and the strain on the economy of recruiting, paying and pensioning the extra troops required by expansion reconciled most

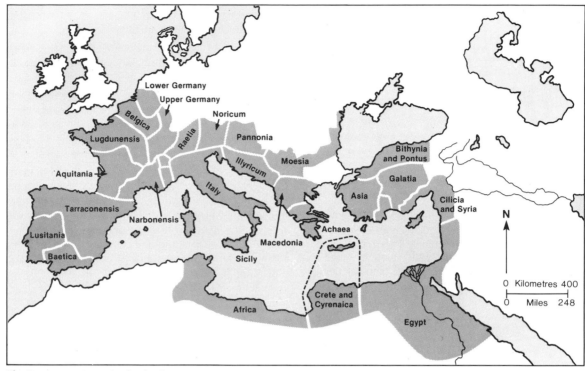

The Roman empire at the death of Augustus (AD 14).

emperors to a basically defensive policy. In time the army had to be enlarged nevertheless—at great social cost.

Augustus reorganized the administration of the whole empire. At Rome he appointed an equestrian *praefectus annonae* to organize supplies for the free issue of corn that was the privilege of the inhabitants of the capital. For the first time the city received a police force, fire brigade and organization for flood control.

After the death of Augustus the public assemblies lost their electoral and legislative functions to the Senate. Public opinion could still find expression in demonstrations in the theatre or circus, where emperors were expected to watch the shows in the midst of huge numbers of their subjects. Numerous colonies were founded for the settlement of veterans, especially in southern France, in Spain and North Africa. In this way the surplus population of Italy, which had contributed to the instability of the late republic, was dispersed, and the raising of revolutionary armies made much more difficult for the future. Appointment of provincial governors was shared between emperor and Senate. Imperial provinces were governed by a *legatus Augusti* of senatorial rank or by an equestrian official. Senatorial provinces were governed by ex-consuls or ex-quaestors, with the title of proconsul. In imperial provinces finance was in the hands of an equestrian procurator, in senatorial provinces of a quaestor. But inhabitants of both kinds of province looked upon the emperor as their head of state. Similarly resolutions of the Senate (*senatus consulta*) had legal force for the whole empire.

Under Augustus literature flourished. The epic of Virgil (70–19 BC), history of Livy (59 BC–AD 17), the personal poetry of Horace (65 BC–8 BC), Propertius (after 16 BC), Tibullus (48–19 BC) and Ovid (43 BC–AD 17?) were soon recognized as Latin classics worthy to be mentioned with those of the Greeks. Among the themes treated most memorably were the history and traditional values of the Roman people and the emotions of personal relations, especially of love.

Imperial Rome

Porta Flaminia
Porta Salaria
Porta Pinciana
Porta Nomentana
Porta Collina
Porta Clausa
Porta Viminalis
Mausoleum of Hadrian
Mausoleum Augusti
Pantheon
Stadium Domitiani
Thermae Diocletiani
Thermae Constantini
Aurelianic Wall
Baths
Portico Octavii
Thermae Traiani
Porta Tiburtina
Circus Flaminius
Capitolium
Pons Aurelius
Roman Forum
Colosseum
Pons Fabricius
Pons Sublicius
Forum Boarium
Porta Praenestina
Porta Aurelia
Pons Probi
Porta Portuensis
Baths of Caracalla
Porta Ostiensis
Porta Appia

The Julio-Claudian emperors

The solidity of Augustus' achievement was demonstrated by the empire's essential stability under his successors. The armies remained remarkably loyal to even the most unmilitary emperors, and the provincial administration functioned well irrespective of scandalous happenings at Rome. The Julio-Claudian emperors feared assassination, and numerous self-interested informers nourished this fear. But the danger, real or imagined, came from intriguing aristocrats. Individuals most likely to be accused of treason were men related to the dynasty, not army commanders. Of the emperors Tiberius (AD 14–37) was able, responsible and experienced, but as he grew old and disillusioned he placed excessive confidence in Sejanus, the praetorian prefect, retiring to Capri in AD 26. The result was a complete breakdown of communications between the emperor and his principal subjects, with results fatal to numerous senators and eventually to Sejanus himself. Tiberius survived, hated but in power. Gaius (AD 37–41), son of Germanicus known as Caligula (Baby-Boots), seems to have aimed at ruling as a Hellenistic monarch rather than as *princeps* in the tradition of Augustus. After a serious illness he became cruel and extravagant to a point suggesting madness. When Gaius had been murdered by officers of the Guard, the Senate debated whether to restore the republic. But the Guard proclaimed Claudius (AD 41–54), brother of Germanicus, whose scholarly hobbies, stammer, undignified appearance and uxoriousness made him a figure of fun. Nevertheless achievements such as the conquest of southern Britain (AD 47), the construction of a new harbour at Ostia, the establishment of a career in the equestrian civil service, generous extensions of Roman citizenship, and a series of statesmanlike solutions to administrative problems, show Claudius to have been an effective emperor.

Nero (AD 54–68), son of Agrippina, fourth wife of Claudius who adopted him, was by temperament an artist rather than a ruler. The empire was ruled well as long as Nero let himself be guided by Seneca (4 BC–AD 65), his former tutor, and Burrus, the praetorian prefect.

The family of Augustus showing the Julio-Claudian dynasty

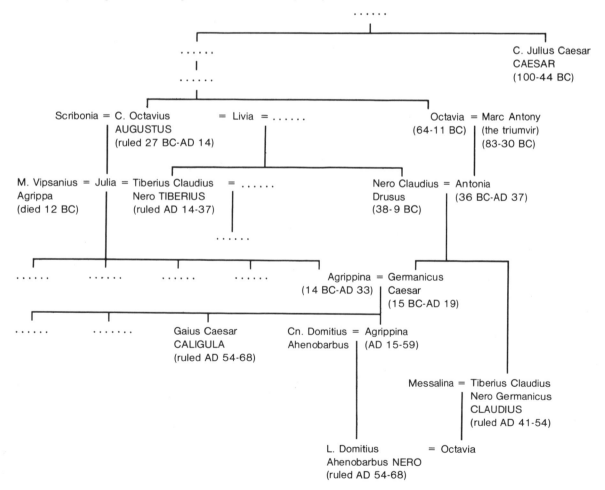

At Rome, Trajan (AD 98–117) built a new forum and shopping centre, one of the marvels of the city.

Eventually the murders of his brother (Britannicus), mother (Agrippina), and wife (Octavia), together with undignified public appearances as charioteer or singer, lost Nero the respect of a large part of his upper class subjects. In AD 64 he was suspected of having caused a disastrous fire at Rome. To clear himself he prosecuted members of a new near-Jewish sect, the Christians, thus initiating the Persecutions. In AD 65 a widespread conspiracy was discovered. It was suppressed, but Nero, panic stricken, resorted to a long series of judicial murders. When revolts broke out in Gaul, Spain, North Africa and Palestine Nero lacked the confidence to appeal to the loyal frontier armies. Eventually he was deserted by the Guard, and outlawed by the Senate. Abandoned by all, as it seemed to him, he committed suicide.

From the Flavians to the Severans

The Julio-Claudian dynasty was now extinct, and dynastic loyalty ceased to restrain the legions. After Galba had been recognized as successor to Nero the Praetorian Guard proclaimed Otho, the army of Lower Germany proclaimed Vitellius, and the army fighting in Palestine Vespasian. The secret was out that an emperor could be made elsewhere than at Rome–and that he need not be a Roman noble. Vespasian (AD 69–79) ended the civil war, restored the imperial finances, filled the depleted Senate with men from Italian or provincial municipalities and colonies. He founded colonies in provinces, and expanded the equestrian civil service. He introduced the imperial cult into provinces that still lacked it, presumably to strengthen the prestige of his new dynasty. He built the Colosseum at Rome. His son Titus had in AD 70 captured Jerusalem and destroyed the Temple. Later

he commanded the Guard and was a virtual partner in empire. During Titus' brief reign (AD 79–81) an eruption of Vesuvius destroyed Pompeii and Herculaneum.

Domitian (AD 81–96), younger son Vespasian, successfully defended the German frontier and advanced it to the river Neckar. He began fortification of the Upper German Limes. Agricola, his governor of Britain, advanced deep into Scotland. At Rome Domitian was an autocrat who had himself addressed as 'lord' (*dominus*) and even 'god' (*deus*). Conflict between the Senate and the Flavian emperors, which had begun under Vespasian, came to a head. There were treason trials, executions of senators and expulsions of philosophers. Domitian was hated as a tyrant. After his murder Nerva (AD 96–98) was proclaimed by the Senate but could only maintain power by adopting Trajan, the commander of Upper Germany and its armies.

Trajan (AD 98–117) was the first of four 'good' emperors who succeeded by adoption, and whose reigns were marked by harmony between emperors and Senate. Trajan annexed Arabia Petraea, conquered Dacia (Rumania) and Mesopotamia. The empire now reached its widest extent. He sent Pliny the Younger (*c*AD 61–*c*112) to Bithynia to supervise the finances of the cities, a symptom of the slow but steady growth of centralization. At Rome Trajan built a new forum and shopping centre, one of the marvels of the city. Hadrian (AD 117–138) evacuated Mesopotamia, and travelled through the empire inspecting armies and reorganizing the frontier defences. The legions were now in the main recruited locally, and losing their mobility. Detachments rather than whole legions were moved to crisis points. In Britain Hadrian was responsible for the building of the frontier wall that bears his name. At Rome freedmen at the head of the palace department were replaced by equestrian officials. It also became possible to enter a civil-service career without first holding an army commission. The Pantheon, the Castel San Angelo (mausoleum) and the vast villa at Tivoli still recall Hadrian's taste as a patron of architecture. Under Hadrian died Tacitus (b. cAD 56), the great historian of the early empire. The conflict of freedom and monarchy is one of his recurring themes. A contemporary, Juvenal (b. between AD 50 and 65), brought the peculiarly Roman literary genre of satire to its highest peak. After these giants the creativity of Latin writers in the traditional forms seems to have gone into rapid decline.

The emperor Antoninus Pius (161–183) was altogether a civilian who ruled in cooperation with the Senate. Some revolts were put down by his generals, but for the most part the empire was at peace. In contrast the reign of Marcus Aurelius (161–180), the Stoic emperor, was filled with war. Verus his brother and co-emperor occupied Mesopotamia and destroyed Seleucia, the last remaining centre of Hellenism in the area. The returning armies brought back the plague. Marcus and his armies defeated a succession of heavy German invasions of the Balkan provinces. In the devastated frontier zones he settled barbarian tribesmen. He was the first of many emperors to adopt this policy.

The death of Marcus was soon seen to have marked the end of a golden age. This age had seen a large increase in the number of Roman citizens as citizenship was conferred on numerous individuals and communities in the provinces. At the same time the value of citizen rights was being eroded by the increasing importance in law of the distinction between an upper class of *honestiores* (senators, knights, decurions and veterans) and a lower class of *humiliores*, with the result that *honestiores* were subjected to milder penalties, and exempted from horrific punishments like crucifixion or being thrown to the beasts. During the second century AD wars had been comparatively few, but they had nevertheless produced stress, indicating that the finances of the empire were inflexible, and depended on an economy scarcely strong enough to support them.

Marcus Aurelius' son, Commodus, was the first emperor since Domitian to succeed by birth (180–192). Unsuited though he was, the dynastic loyalty of the army made his succession inevitable. Commodus gave up Marcus' plan to establish provinces east of the Danube, preferring to control the tribes by treaties and subsidies. He was dependent on his advisers, especially his praetorian prefects. Relations with the Senate deteriorated. Conspiracies were followed by prosecutions and numerous executions. Seemingly convinced that he was an incarnation of Heracles, Commodus wished to present himself on New Year's Day as both consul and gladiator. He was promptly assassinated. His death was followed by a period of civil wars recalling the events of AD 68–69. Septimius Severus (192–211) restored peace with many executions and confiscations. He raised the pay of soldiers and allowed them to contract legal marriages. His son Caracalla (211–217) raised the soldiers' pay once more and promulgated the famous *Constitutio Antoniana*, which conferred Roman citizenship on all inhabitants of the empire. With the murder of

Alexander Severus (220–235) the Severan dynasty ended and with it the early empire.

The influence of empire

The early empire brought the benefits of prolonged peace to the Mediterranean world. In the east the cities recovered from the ravages of republican imperialism, and impressive ruins as well as literary works still bear witness to the prosperity of their upper classes. In the west the Roman way of life was introduced by Roman officials and veterans, and was widely adopted by such natives as could afford it. City life, fine pottery, wine drinking, appreciation of the many uses of olive oil, glass vessels, window glass, artistic bronze ware, came to regions that had not known them before, first as imports,

Above: The Pantheon in Rome. Hadrian's building has proved one of the most durable of Roman temples.

Below: Plan of the Pantheon (AD 120); an absolute circle with an attached portico.

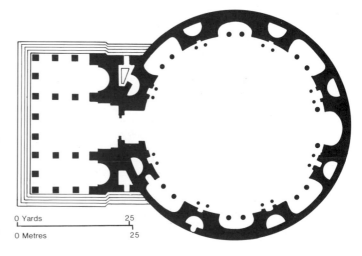

0 Yards 25
0 Metres 25

later, where possible, as local products. Cities with characteristic structures such as markets, basilicas, baths, amphitheatres, colonnades sprang up and brought together the most prominent families of the area in a way that was most convenient for the ruling power. The countryside saw the adoption of the villa system, which was both a way of life and a means of agricultural exploitation. Urbanization and Roman tax demands required a greater farm surplus and encouraged new farming methods. The needs of the armies, and the settlement of veterans, furthered agricultural development of frontier areas. On the whole the Romans helped to spread the technological inventions of others rather than make inventions themselves. But building with concrete was a Roman invention which made possible the vaulting of wide spaces and the creation of dramatic spatial effects unknown before. Technological change spread very slowly. So important a technique as the use of the waterwheel was invented in the Hellenistic period but came to be widely used only in the third and fourth centuries AD. Throughout the Roman period oxen, not horses, were the principal source of animal power.

In the sense that the provinces were taxed to feed the inhabitants of Rome and the army, the Romans exploited their empire. In return the provincials were protected from invasions. In time the difference between Roman citizens and subject peoples disappeared. But when everybody was a Roman the distinction between upper and lower class had taken the place of that between citizens and non-citizens. On the whole the Romans did not meet with persistent and deep-rooted

opposition of the kind that has brought down the European empires in our century. Local patriotisms died remarkably quickly. The exception were the Jews, whose rebellions of AD 66–70, 115–118 and 132–135 were the expression of a combination of nationalism and religion that was unique in the empire. The same spirit maintained the cohesion of the Jews in the Diaspora after the destruction of their state. A similar, and related sense of unity bound together Christian communities, which were to be found in an increasingly large number of cities, particularly in the eastern provinces and North Africa.

The anarchy of the third century and its causes
Up to the end of the Severan dynasty the Roman world seemed to be flourishing. There followed 49 years of extreme internal instability and repeated foreign invasions during which there were about 20 legitimate emperors, not to mention a host of unsuccessful usurpers. Alamanni and Franks broke the Rhine frontier. Goths harried Greece, the Balkans and Asia Minor. The Sassanid dynasty refashioned the Parthian kingdom into an aggressive New Persian Empire which repeatedly invaded Syria and twice sacked Antioch. In desperate straits to pay their troops, emperors reduced the silver content of the currency until the silver *denarius* had become a silver-coated copper coin worth about 0.5% of its value before debasement. As the central authorities were unable to defend the provinces, the empire seemed on the point of breaking up. Odaenatus and his widow, Zenobia, built up an eastern kingdom around Palmyra. A rival line of emperors defended Gaul and maintained

The Roman empire at the death of Trajan (AD 116).

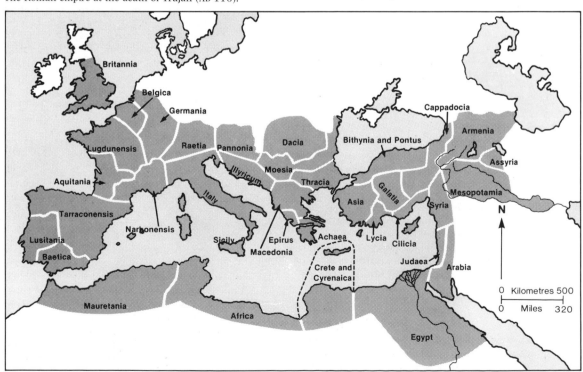

its independence for 15 years (259–74). The forms of urban life were transformed: civic building, the erection of monuments with statues and inscriptions, conspicuous expenditure for the benefit of fellow citizens or gods almost ceased, never to be resumed on anything like their old scale.

The collapse of the third century AD has been explained in terms of a crisis of the slave system of agricultural production, caused by a great reduction in the supply of slaves and weakening of the economic resources of the curial class who had been among the principal supporters of the empire. It is certainly true that the curial class was weakened, and this mattered because the cohesion of the empire depended on the cooperation of these local aristocracies, concentrated in cities, enjoying urban amenities and governing the surrounding countryside, with Roman officials who were few in number, but ultimately backed by the overwhelming force of the Roman army. It is nevertheless not necessary to conclude that change in the slave system was the principal factor responsible for the empire's loss of cohesion. It is impossible to make reliable estimates of numerical trends in rural slavery. Even if tenants replaced slave managers this did not necessarily mean that slaves ceased to do the actual work. There is no dispute that the position of slaves and dependent peasants was becoming more alike, and that there was an ever-increasing concentration of land in the hands of the very rich, at the expense of the medium-sized landowner, including the *curiales*. Undoubtedly some purely political factors were weakening cities, and the class controlling them. While the empire had brought city organization to many regions that had lacked cities before, it eventually tended to cripple cities. The Roman authorities ended popular politics, thus depriving the peasant of a share in the political process. This development, symbolized, among other things, by the distinction between *honestiores* and *humiliores*, undermined the city as an instrument of social organization, and made it incapable of rallying the human resources of the empire against invaders as the peasants of Italy had once been rallied against Hannibal.

The early empire had enjoyed an exceptionally long period of freedom from external pressures. This was now ended for good, and the government was forced to make ever heavier demands on the city councils. As a result the *curiales* were either weakened financially, or given a strong motive to escape from their duties. In either way a basic unit in the organization of the empire was damaged. At the same time the army was tending to fall into regional groups, each liable to make its own commander emperor. This tendency had already shown itself in AD 68–9. It had become stronger since almost all soldiers were locally recruited, often from the sons of veterans and their wives. Moreover control of the army had been assisted by a careful balancing against each other of military grades and classes, such as legionaries and auxiliaries, senatorial officers and equestrian officers, – centurions and other ranks. The extension of Roman citizenship, the gradual withdrawal of senators

A fine example of Roman engineering: the granite bridge at Alcantara in Spain is 630 ft (192 m) long.

from military commands, the increasing proportion of posts filled from the equestrian order, often by men risen from the ranks, upset the balance and made control more difficult, particularly at a time when there was no dynasty that claimed empire-wide loyalty, and when the soldiers' concern for their home province, threatened by invasion, was stronger than patriotism for the empire as a whole. The outcome was anarchy.

The general persecutions
The best-documented events in the otherwise extremely poorly documented middle of the third century AD are two general persecutions of the Christians launched by the emperor Decius in 250 and Valerian in 257. Decius' object was to compel all Christians to perform an act of pagan worship. The context was a sacrifice of all inhabitants of the empire to the gods of the empire. Valerian's attack was directed particularly at bishops and laymen of high standing. He also prohibited meetings for Christian worship. These persecutions produced both apostates and martyrs but completely failed to break the Church. The expansion of Christianity had worried the government since Nero, as Christians persuaded men to abandon ancestral cults for their own new and exclusive worship. Their solidarity too was worrying to an administration that was reluctant to allow its subjects to organize even a fire brigade. In addition Christians were often unpopular. So the government had soon adopted a policy of discouraging Christianity by making it punishable by death. In practice, Christianity was defined as refusal to perform a

pagan rite of worship when ordered by a magistrate.

For many years prosecution had been left to private initiative and as a result 'persecutions' had been local and intermittent. But when Christianity expanded nevertheless, especially in Asia Minor, Egypt and North Africa, and when the calamities of the third century AD showed that the gods were angry, it seemed that the government attack on the Christians might appease them. In the event the failure of the two general persecutions was dramatic; Decius was killed in battle, and Valerian was captured by the Persians. So Gallienus (253–268 AD) ended persecution and for the next 40 years Christianity was tolerated. In fact the discipline and mutual help of the Christian communities proved a great strength in that very disturbed world, and Christianity gained converts year after year while the traditional cults and even the so-called mystery religions were greatly weakened.

The beginnings of recovery

In the course of a terribly troubled reign Gallienus began the process of recovery. He built up a striking force largely composed of cavalry stationed in northern Italy. He also excluded senators from military commands, thus making the leadership more professional and improving the career prospects of officers risen from the ranks or the equestrian order. Provincial governorships too came to be increasingly filled with equestrians. Military recovery was achieved by a series of exceptionally able emperors of Balkan origin. Claudius (268–270) destroyed a huge Gothic invasion force. Aurelian (270–275) first drove various German tribes out of the Balkans, then put an end to Zenobia's empire of Palmyra and finally ended the Gallic secession. After a reign of only five years Aurelian was murdered, but the foundations had been laid on which his successors, especially Diocletian and Constantine, could construct the later empire.

The Later Roman Empire

Robert Browning

The Roman empire in AD 270

When in AD 270 the army of Pannonia proclaimed its commander Aurelian (L. Domitius Aurelianus) emperor in Sirmium, the period of crisis and anarchy in the Roman empire had already lasted for 35 years, and the first signs of recovery from the crisis had been visible since the reign of Gallienus (253–268). Both the crisis and the recovery resulted from the aggravation of trends that had been discernable since the days of Marcus Aurelius. The balance between barbarian pressure and Roman resistance had changed, and the initiative now often lay with the barbarians. Their attacks were no longer isolated, but continuous and ubiquitous. The demands of defence reinforced the military character of imperial power, and the political role and influence of the senatorial aristocracy–but not its wealth–declined.

The Roman fortress of Divitia (Cologne), built to resist barbarian pressure.

Emperors were now created by the army and deposed by the army, and lacked the legitimacy that the compromise of the principate had given them. They sought to compensate for this lack by surrounding their persons with ceremonial, often borrowed from Sasanid Persia. The court became a centre of power and policy making. At the same time the old balance between city and countryside was breaking down. The effects of plague and the drift to the cities reduced the manpower available for agriculture. The patronage of military officers and the growth of large estates with a self-sufficient economy reduced the income of the cities, which became unable to manage their own affairs. Growing contact with the aggressive barbarian world strengthened the sense of Roman solidarity. But that solidarity was often manifested on a regional or local scale in the form of support for 'usurpers', who offered hope of protection for a limited area. Imperial power, though more authoritarian than before, was often divided between several regional rulers.

Aurelian (AD 270 to 275)

Aurelian found a threefold division of power on his accession. He himself held Italy and the central provinces, Tetricus ruled in the west, and the whole of the east was controlled by king Vaballath of Palmyra and his consort Zenobia, who had extended their authority to fill the power vacuum left by Roman weakness. Aurelian's first aim was unification of the empire. It took him two hard-fought campaigns to crush Palmyra in 273, and in 274 he marched west and defeated Tetricus at Châlons. The new unity was symbolized and legitimatized by the

Aurelian (AD 270 to 275), who helped to restore the later Roman empire.

adoption as the official state religion of the cult of Sol Invictus, whose special protection Aurelian claimed to enjoy. Defeated barbarian prisoners were settled in unpopulated regions of the empire, and senators were obliged to bring abandoned land under cultivation. Aurelian sought to revive the economy by issuing new gold coinage and replacing some of the more debased silver coins, as well as by forbidding those who practised certain key trades, such as shipping and baking, from abandoning them. It is symptomatic of the general sense of insecurity that he surrounded Rome itself, for centuries unprotected, with a formidable wall, much of which still stands, and abandoned the province of Dacia, north of the Danube.

In 275 Aurelian was assassinated. After an attempt by the Senate to maintain its candidate on the throne the choice of the army fell on a Pannonian general, M. Aurelius Probus. Probus succeeded in expelling invaders from Gaul, Rhaetia, the Danube frontier zone, Asia Minor and Upper Egypt. But as he was celebrating a triumph in Rome in 281, usurpers were already establishing themselves in Gaul. In 282 Probus was assassinated by his soldiers, who proclaimed as emperor M. Aurelius Carus, the praetorian prefect. Carus was killed by lightning while on an expedition against Persia, and on 20 November 284 the army chose as emperor Diocletian (C. Aurelius Valerius Diocletianus), a soldier from what is now Montenegro. Aurelian's successors had followed his policy of defence and consolidation. Diocletian saw deeper into the malaise of Roman society and sought more radical remedies for it.

The empire on the defensive. Like other cities, Rome had to be fortified in the third century AD. The emperor, Aurelian, surrounded Rome with a formidable wall.

Diocletian's reforms

The first problem he faced was the usual one of invasion along all frontiers, complicated in this case by a widespread revolt of the Gaulish peasants. In a series of campaigns from Britain in the west (where a local commander, Carausius, had proclaimed himself emperor) to Armenia in the east he restored the territorial integrity of the empire and even established a Roman protectorate over Armenia and Iberia. There were more lasting and serious problems. First, that of succession and legitimacy: how to ensure the continuity of imperial power beyond the lifetime of an individual ruler and its universal and unquestioning acceptance. Diocletian's solution was a collegiate exercise of authority, with two Augusti and two Caesars who would automatically succeed the senior emperors on their death or abdication. The junior emperors were bound to the senior by ties of adoption and all four emperors were linked by marriage ties. The senior Augustus and his Caesar were declared to be under the special protection of Jupiter, the junior under that of Hercules. Diocletian chose his fellow Illyrian Maximian (M. Aurelius Valerius Maximianus) as his fellow Augustus in 286, and in 293 Galerius (C. Galerius Valerius Maximianus) and Constantius (Flavius Valerius Constantius) became their respective Caesars. There was no territorial division of the empire between the four; all had authority everywhere. By this arrangement Diocletian hoped to avoid a dangerous interregnum on the death of an emperor and to enhance the prestige and authority of the imperial office.

The next problem was that of building a bridge between a remote, centralized source of decisions and the local officials who had to carry them out. Diocletian's solution was to reduce the size and increase the number of the provinces, to group provinces in dioceses under a *vicarius* (originally a deputy to the praetorian prefect), and to appoint several praetorian prefects, each responsible for a huge region of the empire. The officials in this hierarchy had access not only to their immediate

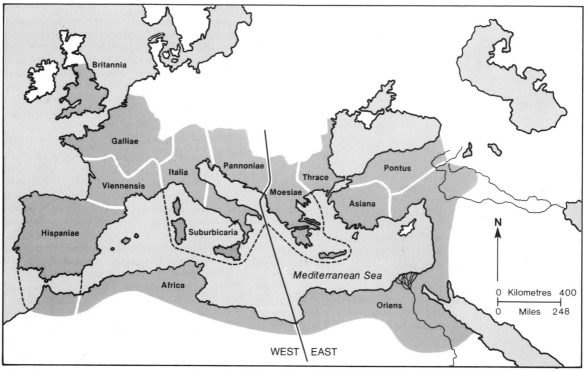

The Roman empire: the administrative dioceses introduced by
Diocletian before AD 300.

superiors, but also in certain cases to the next higher
stage. This greatly inflated civil service was staffed
largely by equestrians of military background.

Inflation and irregularity of revenue from taxation
were long-standing problems. In the early part of
Diocletian's reign inflation became headlong. Diocletian
tried to freeze all prices by an edict in 301, needless to say
in vain. He was much more successful in dealing with
taxation and revenue. The army had long been in the
habit of levying its requirements in kind from the local
population, a levy known as *annona militaris*. Diocletian
developed this practice into a regular system of taxation.
At first he budgeted the state's requirements in advance
and distributed the total roughly between provinces and
cities. From 297 a more sophisticated system was
introduced. A notional unit of taxable wealth, the *caput-
iugum*, which took account of area and quality of land,
livestock, and available manpower, was used to calculate the payments due in kind, and assessments were
made for five-year periods. The details escape us, and the
system was probably not uniform from region to region.
Other taxes, payable in gold, were levied on city dwellers
and on senators and high officials.

Diocletian's reforms left the empire much more tightly
administered and more homogeneous than before. Non-
conforming groups were less tolerable in such a highly
structured society than in the more chaotic world of the
recent past. Religious communities that refused formal
acknowledgment of the divine authority of the emperor,
and whose way of life made them appear something of a

closed group, were particularly liable to persecution. In
302 a persecution of the Christians began which was not
the result of local initiative, as had generally been the
case in the past, but of central direction. It was the most
severe trial that the Church had undergone.

Breakdown of Diocletian's constitutional arrangements

Satisfied that he had set the empire on the right course,
Diocletian abdicated on 1 May 301, and obliged Maximian to abdicate with him. Constantius and Galerius
became the new Augusti, and chose Severus (Flavius
Valerius Severus) and Maximinus (Galerius Valerius
Maximinus Daia) as their Caesars; both were Illyrian
soldiers. The transfer of authority appeared to have been
carried out satisfactorily. In fact the retirement of the
two Augusti opened a period of political crisis and
fragmentation of power which lasted until 324. The
success of the tetrarchy had depended upon the dominant personality of Diocletian. Now that he was gone
it broke down because of the contradictions between the
principles of cooptation, of seniority, and of dynastic
succession, and the difficulty of confining the ambitions
of individuals within so rigid a framework. Constantius
died in 306. His son Constantine (Flavius Valerius
Constantinus) proclaimed himself Caesar (306), then
Augustus (307). Maxentius (M. Aurelius Valerius Maxentius), son of Maximian, had himself proclaimed emperor in Rome in 306, and in 307 his father emerged
from a retirement which he had not wanted and
established himself in Gaul.

Constantine (AD 307 to 337)

The events of the next few years were chaotic. Sometimes there were as many as seven persons exercising imperial power simultaneously, none of them recognized by all his colleagues. For Constantine, however, the unity of the empire was the paramount goal. At first his authority was limited to Britain, where he had first been proclaimed emperor. The death of Maximian in 310 gave Constantine control of Gaul and Spain as well. In 311 the death of Galerius left four claimants to imperial authority: Constantine in the west, Maxentius in Italy and Africa, Licinius (Valerius Licinianus Licinius) in Illyricum, and Maximinus in the east. Constantine allied himself with Licinius against Maxentius. In 312 he invaded Italy and defeated and killed Maxentius outside Rome (battle of the Milvian Bridge, 28 October 312). In the next year Licinius defeated Maximinus, leaving the empire divided between Constantine and himself. Tension soon grew between them, and in 314 Constantine drove Licinius out of Europe except for Thrace. In 324 he finally defeated Licinius' forces and established himself as sole ruler of the empire.

Constantine and Christianity

Constantine, like most of his contemporaries, was alert for signs and messages from the transcendent powers that rule the world. And he was eager to objectify his own driving ambition under the guise of a divine mission. In 310, while still in Gaul, he had a vision of the sun-god Apollo, who promised him 30 years of power. He had been in contact with Christians, and his mother Helena was probably a practising Christian. On the eve of the battle of the Milvian Bridge he had a further vision in which he was told that if he painted a Christian symbol—probably a cross surmounted by a loop—on the shields of his soldiers he would be victorious. He followed the advice, and won the battle. The original story was subsequently embroidered by panegyrists, and Constantine's nocturnal vision turned into a daytime display in the sky witnessed by thousands. The victory at the Milvian Bridge persuaded Constantine that the God of the Christians was powerful and well-disposed to him. But it did not make a Christian of him. The inscription on the triumphal arch which he set up in Rome speaks of his 'divine inspiration', but avoids any mention of Christianity. However, from this moment on Constantine favoured the Christian community more and more, identified himself more closely with it, surrounded himself with Christian advisers. Within a few years the monogram of Christ began to appear—sometimes side by side with pagan symbols—on the coinage. Later Constantine took to calling himself the thirteenth apostle and the bishop of those outside the Church. Finally, on his deathbed in 337, he was baptised. The so-called conversion of Constantine was neither an act of calculated policy nor a blinding moment of enlightenment, but a slow process of growing into community of thought and feeling with a minority group that had a unique sense of mission and an empire-wide organization. By identifying himself with the Church he transformed the Church and drew it into full participation in the public life of the empire. From being a religion largely centred in the lower middle class of the cities Christianity spread upwards to the leading ele-

The family of Diocletian and Constantine

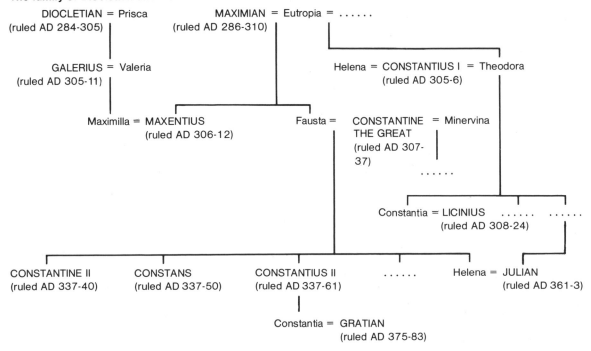

Constantine the Great (AD 307–337): this colossal head symbolizes the eternal authority claimed by the imperial throne.

ments of society and to some extent outwards to the countryside.

In February 313 Constantine and Licinius issued a joint document (the Edict of Milan) proclaiming toleration for all religions and restoration of all property confiscated during persecution. The Christians were almost the sole beneficiaries of this shift in policy. Constantine showered money and privileges on the Church. All clergy were granted immunity from curial charges, distributions in money and kind were made from public funds to churches throughout the empire, new churches of unparalleled magnificence were built at the expense of the emperor, estates producing substantial revenues were granted to the Church. Christian individuals and communities were favoured and promoted. All these measures led to a great expansion of Christianity among strata of society who had previously remained aloof from its influence. But the new religion made little headway among the peasantry, from which the army was mainly recruited. Constantine's army, the ultimate sanction of his power, remained largely pagan.

The privileges accorded to the Church, and

Constantine's conviction that it was his duty to regulate the relations between his subjects and the supreme divinity, inevitably led the emperor to take note of and become involved in disputes within the Church. A problem of church discipline in Africa, and later a theological dispute about the Trinity, called for decision by Constantine, who consulted the bishops. To settle the latter dispute he called a council of bishops in Nicaea in 325, at which he himself presided. In this way the problem of relation of Church and state first presented itself.

Constantine's reforms

Constantine ruled for 30 years, and for 13 as sole emperor. His reign marks the final recovery of Roman society from the third-century crisis. Among his measures of reform were the creation of a mobile reserve army and of a system of frontier defence in depth; the issue of a new stable gold coinage (largely financed by the confiscation of temple treasures in the latter years of his reign); the radical reorganization of the civil service, making still sharper the division between civil and military careers; and the creation of a second capital city, Constantinople, on the site of ancient Byzantium. The new capital lay on the crossing of the military highway from the Rhine to the Euphrates, along which emperors had established their residences for a century, and the sea route linking the Black Sea and the Mediterranean. Begun in 324, and inaugurated on 11 May 330, Constantinople was conceived as a second Rome, with all the privileges of its sister city. And it was from the first a wholly Christian city, with no pagan cult sites.

When Constantine died in 337 he left the Roman empire capable of defending itself, efficiently administered, financially solvent, and more and more animated by a sense of Christian solidarity, which conferred a new legitimacy upon its rulers. It was a society far more authoritarian, more closely administered, more preoccupied with the supernatural, than had been the empire in its heyday. And its political centre had moved to the Greek-speaking eastern provinces, where its economic and cultural centre had long been.

Constantine's successors

Constantine intended his three sons and possibly two of his nephews to exercise collegiate rule after his death. It did not work. By 340 only two were left, Constans in the western two-thirds of the empire, Constantius II in the east. Both were engaged for some years in frontier warfare, Costans in Gaul, Constantius against the Persians. Constans upheld the theology of the Council of Nicaea, while Constantius adhered to the Arian doctrine that the Son was subordinate to the Father. Thus the theological dispute took on a political character. Both closed pagan temples and discriminated against pagans in public life. In 350 an officer of German descent, Flavius Magnus Magnentius, raised a revolt in Gaul, killed Constans, and established himself as ruler in the west. Constantius II marched west to meet him, recovered Italy in 352 and Gaul in 353, in hard-fought campaigns. The Franks and Alamans seized the opportunity to invade and devastate much of Gaul. In 355 Constantius, anxious to continue his Persian war, appointed his cousin Julian (Flavius Claudius Julianus) as Caesar to take charge in Gaul. In a series of brilliant campaigns from 355 to 360 Julian crushed the Franks and Alamans, and stabilized the Rhine frontier.

Julian (AD 361 to 363)

Julian was a committed pagan, an adherent of Neoplatonist philosophy, and a devotee of mystic cults. His father and brother had been murdered in 337 with the permission, if not on the orders, of Constantius II, and he had been kept for many years under house arrest. Not surprisingly his hostility and contempt for Christianity were total. But he had carefully to conceal his views so long as his life depended on Constantius. His victories made him the idol of his soldiers. In February 360 the army proclaimed him emperor in Paris, probably not without some encouragement from Julian himself. At first he tried to come to terms with Constantius II, but in 361 he broke with him and marched east to Illyricum with the cream of the army of Gaul. Constantius II set out from the east to meet him, but died on the way, leaving Julian as sole ruler, but a fanatically pagan ruler, of an empire now largely Christian.

Julian was a strange combination of Roman autocrat and Greek philosopher, of war-hardened general and compulsive communicator, of realist and dreamer. And he was by nature impatient. He longed to wipe out the Christian Roman empire of Constantine and his sons, to sever the links between the Church and public life, and to return to a utopia in which Greek cities ran their own affairs and Roman power was unchallenged. His hero was Marcus Aurelius. He seems to have underestimated the radical changes in Roman society since Marcus Aurelius' day, and in particular the degree to which the urban upper classes had been penetrated by Christianity. Though in his short reign he made a number of minor administrative and fiscal reforms, the realist in him gave way more and more to the dreamer. Discouraged by the cool welcome he received from the very classes upon whose support he counted, he decided in 362 to launch an all-out campaign against Persia. In 363 he led an immense army into Persian Mesopotamia and penetrated as far as the Persian capital of Ctesiphon, which he was unable to take. Thereafter he lost sense of direction and purpose, marched aimlessly northward through Persia, and was mysteriously killed in a skirmish on 26 June 363 at the age of 32. Needless to say, many blamed the Christians for his death.

Julian favoured pagans and discriminated against Christians in public life, but what little persecution of Christians took place depended more on local initiative than on imperial directive. His edict of 363 forbidding Christians to teach classical literature was a shrewd measure aimed at breaking the link between the cultured urban upper classes upon whose support the empire depended and the Christian Church. But it was never widely carried out and lapsed on his death.

The massive stone walls of Constantinople, not breached until AD 1453 when the Turks seized the city.

Impressed by the unity and organization of the Christians, Julian sought to weld the disparate survivals of pagan belief and observance into a coherent whole and establish a kind of pagan church, with a professional priesthood, capable of performing the charitable role which the church had largely taken over from civic organs. But the gulf between Neoplatonist mystics and traditionalist peasants was too great. Paganism was not a unifying principle, as Christianity was; Julian had set himself a task which was impossible, and he did not live long enough to learn the art of compromise. He left little mark upon the Roman world, except by his writings, which were long studied by rhetoricians and philosophers.

The German problem

After Julian's death the army in Persia acclaimed as his successor a young Christian officer, Jovian, who survived only long enough to extricate the army and to sign a peace treaty which ceded much territory to Persia together with the cities of Nisibis and Singara. The long period of peace that ensued in the east enabled the empire to face a new German challenge with success. When Jovian died in 364 a council of leading military and civilian officers chose as emperor Valentinian, a devoutly Christian Pannonian soldier of humble origin, who promptly appointed his brother Valens as co-emperor, with responsibility for the east. Valentinian (364–375) and Valens (364–378) were animated by the provincial egalitarianism of the soldiers who were the support of their power. Senators were once again ousted from high office and persecuted in the west, while in the east there was a witch hunt of pagan intellectuals. The theological disputes of the age were treated with benevolent, if uncomprehending, indifference. Valentinian was succeeded in the west on his death in 375 by his sons Gratian and Valentinian III, still children. Meanwhile the Germanic world was more and more disturbed by pressure from the Huns, as they moved westwards through the steppe zone. In the west Alamans, Saxons and Franks attacked Gaul by land and sea, while the Picts and Scots joined with the Saxons in invading Roman Britain. Valentinian offered successful resistance. In the east matters took a more serious turn. The Ostrogoths and Visigoths, long settled between Don and Dnieper rivers, together with a number of lesser Germanic tribes, were rolled westward by the Huns. By 376 the Visigoths were on the Danube frontier, demanding to be allowed to settle in the empire. Valens admitted them as federates to the region between the Danube and Thrace. Many barbarian groups had been so settled in the past, but never before a whole people with its political structure intact: the dangers were manifest. Mistreated and exploited by local officials and others, the desperate Visigoths revolted in 377, and were joined by many runaway slaves, some of Germanic stock. Valens decided to destroy the rebels. In the outcome, on 9 August 378, it was the Roman army that was destroyed and its emperor killed, as the Gothic cavalry mowed down the Roman infantry at Adrianople. The Balkans were at the mercy of the Visigoths, and the Roman empire leaderless.

The German problem, with which the empire had to contend henceforth, had three aspects. First, more and more Germanic peoples pressed across the frontiers, pillaging as they went. Second, many of these invaders had to be allowed to settle in the empire as federates, dividing the land with the original owners and forming autonomous enclaves. Finally, the defence of the empire came to depend on military leaders, often of German origin, whose authority depended on the loyalty of their barbarian troops. The problem was handled with very different success in east and west.

Theodosius (AD 379 to 395)

In 379 Gratian appointed as co-emperor and effective ruler a Spanish officer with a good military record, Theodosius. His reign was marked by growing unity in the east and growing chaos in the west. By a combination of military pressure and negotiation he brought the Visigoths under Roman control; a treaty of 382 allowed them to settle in the Balkans as federates under their own leaders. Similar agreements with other Germanic bands helped to fill the gap in civilian and military manpower and to turn an armed attack into a 'peaceful invasion'. But there were dangers; Theodosius' army consisted largely of Germans. In 384 peace with Persia freed the emperor's hands in the east. In the west he had to deal with a series of usurpers enjoying some support from the senatorial aristocracy, which more and more opted out of imperial politics and concentrated on extending its already vast estates, some of which provided an income equal to one-sixth of the fiscal revenue of Egypt. The Germans in the west made the most of Roman disarray. Theodosius was a devoted believer in Nicaean doctrine. His reign saw increasing intolerance, persecution of heretics, and oppression of pagan worship (though never of pagan belief). In 382 the altar of Victory was removed from the Senate House. Temples were closed all over the empire. The Olympic games were suppressed in 393 and the Eleusinian Mysteries in 396. Many of the pagan senators in the west became openly or covertly hostile to the Christian government and were ready to support usurpers who promised restoration of paganism, even when they were clearly the tools of Gothic war leaders. Other senators threw in their lot with the Church, which developed a more independent stance in the disturbed west than in the peaceful and well-organized east. In 395, after defeating the usurper Eugenius who had controlled the west for three years, Theodosius died, leaving two juvenile sons, Arcadius and Honorius, to reign in east and west respectively. The Roman empire remained divided until Justinian's reconquest of Italy in the mid-sixth century brought a part of the west briefly under eastern control.

After Theodosius: the German problem in the east

On news of Theodosius' death the new leader of the Visigoths, Alaric, rampaged through the central Balkans and Greece, and in 397 settled in Epirus, where an impotent government in Constantinople had to recognize him as military commander of Illyricum. Gainas, a Gothic officer long in the Roman service, revolted in 400 and for a time was in control of Constantinople. There was danger that he and his band might make common cause with Alaric, a development that would not have been unwelcome to a faction in the eastern court who preferred to fill Thrace with peasants rather than corpses. But an anti-German group prevailed, Gainas was ousted from Constantinople and his forces dispersed, and in 401 Alaric, despairing of finding a home for his people in the east, marched into Italy. Gradually an indigenous army with indigenous leaders was built up in the east, while peace reigned with Persia and the Danube frontier was relatively untroubled. Parallel to this went a growing Hellenization of public life and a cultural as well as a political break between east and west. When Arcadius died in 408 power passed without dispute to his son Theodosius II.

The German problem in the west: the sack of Rome

In the west things took a different course. The Romanized Vandal general Stilicho, appointed by Theodosius as guardian to the youthful emperor Honorius, met as best he could revolt in Africa in 395–6, the menacing arrival of Alaric and his Visigoths in Italy in 401, an invasion from the north by a mixed group of Germans under Radagaisus in 405, the collapse of the Rhine frontier and a devastating invasion of Gaul in 406, and a series of revolts in Britain in 407. More and more the western government had to buy off its enemies rather than meet them in battle, and Stilicho could never count on the support of the senatorial aristocracy, who despised him as a barbarian. In 408 Alaric, who had been plundering Noricum, returned to Italy, and demanded 4000 pounds of gold. A court faction had Stilicho assassinated, suspecting him of complicity with Alaric. The Visigoths were soon at the gates of Rome. Interminable negotiations went on with the court at Ravenna, during which Alaric forced the Senate to proclaim a rival emperor, Attalus. Finally Alaric's patience was exhausted, and on 24 August 410 his Gothic soldiers broke into and looted Rome. Three days later they left, taking with them Galla Placidia, the emperor's sister. Alaric hoped to find a home for his people in Africa, but died in Calabria on the way there. The sack of Rome seemed a portent of doom, and set men to questioning their deepest beliefs, whether in the destiny of Rome or in the providence of God.

The Visigoths were now led by Alaric's brother-in-law, Athaulf, who saw the most promising future for his countrymen in cooperation with the Romans. In 412, at Roman instigation, he crossed into Gaul and overthrew a short-lived usurper, Jovinus. As the Romans were unable to provide the supplies he demanded, he and his Visigoths settled in Provence and Aquitaine, in theory federates, in practice independent. Many of the Gaulish landowners threw in their lot with the Goths. Athaulf, pursuing his goal of peaceful coexistence, married Galla Placidia in 414. Much of Spain fell under control of the Germanic Vandals and Suevi and the Iranian Alans, who spent much energy feuding with one another.

The Huns

Meanwhile the Huns pressed forward into eastern Europe, building a great empire of subject peoples, of whom the most notable were the Ostrogoths. In 422 the first Hun invasion of Thrace took place, but was repulsed easily. The pressure grew. The Huns, controlling as they did many other aggressive groups, were able to put into the field a larger force than any single Germanic people. In 430 the government in Constantinople agreed to pay them tribute. In 434 the tribute was doubled at the demand of the new king of the Huns, Attila.

The west in the early fifth century

Honorius died in 423 and was succeeded by Valentinian III after a period of anarchy at Ravenna. What real power there was in the west belonged to the military leaders. Crushed between the warlords, the barbarians and the great landowners, the Roman state became a façade. For a time there was rivalry between the military men, until in 433 Aetius became dominant leader. He had spent many years as a hostage at the court of the Huns, and owed his position to his ability to recruit Hun contingents to fight for Rome. He installed the Huns in Pannonia (433) and with their aid held at bay for a time the Franks, Burgundians and other peoples who poured into Gaul. Yet Armorica had to be abandoned, and a treaty with the Visigoths in 439 ceded more territory to them. Caught between the conflicting interests of the Roman landlords and Attila, Aetius lost Hun support, and was unable to prevent Attila's invasion of Gaul in 451. In 454 he was assassinated.

Roman troops had been withdrawn from Britain at the beginning of the fifth century by a locally proclaimed emperor. There was some kind of Roman presence there in the first half of the fifth century, but links with Rome gradually became more tenuous as local leaders took over defence against invaders and recruited their own Germanic federates. In Spain the Vandals moved southwards, devastating the country as they went, and in 429 crossed to Africa. A Roman army from Constantinople vainly tried to contain them (431–432). A treaty of 435 failed to stop their advance. In 439 they took Carthage and in 442 a new treaty granted them the status of federates; in fact Roman Africa had become an independent state ruled by a Vandal aristocracy. Anxious to forestall a Roman counterattack by sea, the far-seeing Vandal king Gaiseric seized Sardinia and Corsica and built a powerful fleet which put an end to Roman control of the Mediterranean. In 455 he captured and pillaged Rome. Then, as earlier, the government at Ravenna showed itself powerless. When Attila had invaded Italy, it was Pope Leo I who had negotiated with him and obtained his withdrawal. In 455 Valentinian III, the last of the dynasty of Theodosius, was assassinated, as was his successor, Petronius Maximus, a few months later.

Collapse in the west

A period of total disintegration began in the west. The only effective power was that of the Suevian general Ricimer, who, often in collusion with the Gaulish aristocracy, appointed a series of short-lived and impotent emperors: Majorian (457–461), Libius Severus (461–465), Olybrius (April–November 472). Avitus (455–456) was supported by the Visigoths and the Gaulish nobility. Anthemius (467–472) and Julius Nepos (472–474) were nominees of the eastern emperor Leo I. Glycerius (473–474) was creature of the Burgundian king Gundobad, the nephew of Ricimer. Romulus (475–476) was thrust on to the throne by his father Orestes, a Roman official in Pannonia who had once been secretary to Attila. Finally, on 23 August 476, the soldiers in Milan mutinied and proclaimed as their king a Scirian officer, named Odoacer. Odoacer declared himself king of Italy, sent the imperial insignia to Constantinople, and was rewarded by the eastern emperor Zeno with the rank of patrician.

The Roman empire had ended in the west, but few at the time noticed its passing. Its last twenty years had seen the capture of Narbonne by the Visigoths, and their expansion into Auvergne and all the country south of the Loire, while the Burgundians occupied eastern Gaul from the Loire to the Jura and the Alps, and the Franks relentlessly pressed in from the north. By 476 only a small area round Soissons was technically Roman territory; in 486 it was taken over by the Franks. All over Gaul the great landowners made their own accommodations with the new Germanic rulers. In Spain the Visigoths pushed south from the Pyrenees, drove the Suevi into Galicia, and established control over all the rest of the peninsula. Rhaetia was lost to the Alamans and Noricum and Pannonia to the Ostrogoths, who had shaken off the Hun yoke. The western Mediterranean was a Vandal lake.

Survival in the east

In the eastern half of the empire the crisis was weathered. Much of the internal history is unknown. A series of civilian ministers headed the government under Theodosius II, and great influence was wielded by the emperor's sister, Pulcheria, and his Athenian wife, Eeudocia. In 425 public higher education in Constantinople was reorganized. In 429 work was begun on a collection of all surviving imperial legislation since Constantine. The result, the Theodosian code, was published in 438. Though firmly Nicaean, the eastern church became sharply divided on the relation of the human and divine natures in Christ. An ecumenical council held at Ephesus in 431 condemned the Nestorian doctrine of two entirely separate natures. A second Council of Ephesus in 449, which was dominated by the powerful Egyptian church, declared in favour of a single divine nature which entirely took over Christ's human nature. Two years later the Council of Chalcedon decided that the two natures coexisted eternally and inseparably, a doctrine that was acceptable to the western church but alienated many eastern Christians, especially in Egypt and Syria. The principal military danger in the east came from the Hun empire of Attila. By careful diplomacy, payment of tribute, and the gradual creation of an indigenous army an all-out clash with the Huns was avoided, though in 447 they raided as far south as Thermopylae. Finally Attila lost interest in the east and turned his attention to the feebler west.

In the early fifth century there was deep distrust of Germanic and other foreign military leaders. Later, as the Huns became the common foe of Romans and Germans alike, men able to command a military following came to the fore again, but they never held a monopoly of power as in the west. When Theodosius II died in 450 it was the Alan general Aspar and the emperor's sister Pulcheria who put Marcian (450–467) on the throne. And again in 467 Aspar was able to secure the succession for his henchman Leo I (467–474). Frightened by the power of Aspar, Leo began mass recruitment to the army of Isaurian mountaineers from the Taurus mountains. As 'internal barbarians' these tough highlanders made good soldiers but they were unlikely to make common cause with potential invaders.

Relations between east and west

Throughout the fifth century the empire remained in theory one and indivisible, and relations were in general cordial between the courts of Constantinople and Ravenna. Western emperors sought and usually obtained recognition from their eastern colleagues. Eastern emperors such as Marcian sometimes dispensed with western recognition. The promulgation of the Theodosian Code in 438 ended the duality of legislation that had grown up since the death of Theodosius, and provided a basis for the law governing Romans in the new Germanic kingdoms of the west.

Occasional military intervention by the eastern rulers in the affairs of the west took place: in 410 an eastern army was sent to help Honorius deal with Alaric, in 424–425 an eastern force secured the western throne for Valentinian III; in 431 an eastern army was sent to Africa to confront the Vandals; in 441 an eastern force occupied Sicily to prevent it falling to the Vandals; in 452 Marcian sent an expeditionary force to attack Attila in Italy; in 470 Leo I put an easterner, Anthemius, on the western throne. But such intervention was spasmodic and of limited effect. The two halves of the empire drifted apart. The east survived the great movement of peoples, the west was torn asunder by it. In the east the state, the court and the administration strengthened their hold on society, in the west they were replaced by local centres of power, barbarian, Roman or both. The eastern church became closely associated with the state, the western church had to deal with a multiplicity of states and developed a taste for independence. Eastern theologians were preoccupied with Christological problems of great philosophical complexity, western theologians were concerned with grace and salvation. In the east knowledge of Latin became less widespread, while the intellectual leaders of the west often knew little or no Greek. The common culture of the high Roman empire was breaking up into its constituent parts. Western cities were often rebuilt after the invasions on a small fraction of their former area; in the east city life still flourished, though city autonomy was withering and churches were replacing temple and agora as the centre of urban complexes. In the east a new Christian Greek civilization was being shaped which lasted right through the Middle Ages; in the west the future peoples of Europe were shaking themselves free of the political trammels of a Mediterranean empire whose culture they esteemed but scarcely understood.

The fall of the Roman empire: causes and symptoms

The nature and cause of the collapse of the Roman empire have been the object of lively discussion since the fifteenth century, and especially since the publication of Edward Gibbon's *Decline and Fall of the Roman Empire* (1776–88). Gibbon summed up his conclusion in the phrase 'the triumph of barbarism and religion'. Others have sought explanations in climatic changes, underpopulation, disease, racial mixture, the extermination of an intellectual élite, the decline of slavery, failure of civilization to reach the masses, and slackening of personal morality. Some of these explanations rest on misleading biological analogies. All are probably oversimplified. The decline was not a cataclysmic event, but a slow process of transformation and adaptation. And every level of human activity and organization was involved, from price inflation to religious belief. No single factor is likely to provide a sufficient explanation for so complex a set of changes. It is not easy in a continuous process to distinguish between causes and symptoms of change. For instance it is clear that in late antiquity a larger proportion of the population was withdrawn from direct productive activity than in the early empire, either as soldiers, as officials, or as clergy. Is this a cause of decline, as some have thought, or a sympton?

External and internal causes

Certain factors in the transformation of late Roman society have already been alluded to. Here space permits only a brief survey. First, the barbarians. Their pressure, the origins of which are to be sought in demographic and political changes far from the Roman frontiers, was certainly serious. But was it more serious than in the past? Recent studies have suggested that no Germanic people could muster more than 20,000–25,000 fighting men, hardly a serious threat to a state with a population of at least 25 millions. But the continuity of barbarian attacks and the coincidence of attacks at many points on the frontier were new. Though not the prime cause of Roman collapse, the barbarian onslaught probably accelerated processes already under way, and triggered off disastrous chain reactions. Some internal changes had begun long before the crisis became acute: for example, there had been a slow, steady rise in prices since the Antonine age, and the inability of cities to manage their own affairs was occasionally evident even earlier. In general the stable economic and social balance between city and countryside, between central authority and local initiative, between Greek east and Latin west began to be ruptured in the late second century, and the ensuing wave of external pressure brought out the political consequences of these economic and social changes. Some scholars today emphasize changes in men's perception of and attitude to the second. This is an important but difficult field of research, in which proof is not easy. These changes, whose reality is not disputed, seem more likely to be symptoms than prime causes of radical change.

It is important to bear in mind the difference between the course of events in east and west. A careful study of this difference in all its concrete detail may well throw light on the causal links in this most complex historical process. Finally, it should be remembered that words like 'decline', 'fall', and 'collapse' embody value judgments. Late antique society had its own essence, and was not just a degenerate form of classical society. To many Romans, particularly in the eastern part of the empire, it may have offered greater opportunities for personal fulfilment than did the world of Augustus and Trajan and Marcus Aurelius.

Early Christianity

R. A. Markus

Beginnings: Judaism and Christianity

In its beginnings Christianity was the religion of a Jewish sect: one of a great many groups into which Judaism was divided, especially in its Palestinian homeland. Among their fellow Jews, Christians were distinguished by their belief that the promised Messiah who would deliver his people and inaugurate the kingship of God had already come in the person of Jesus, the Christ. In his person and in his work, his life, suffering and death, the God of their fathers had brought to a fulfilment the promises made of old to Abraham and the prophecies of the Old Testament. If the Jews were God's chosen nation, the Christians saw themselves as the true Jews. Among them God had brought to a conclusion the saving work accomplished among the people of the Old Covenant.

The whole structure of Jewish society in Palestine was shaken by the flare-up of Jewish nationalism in the 60s of the first century AD, and the conflict with the Roman government that ended with the fall of Jerusalem in AD 70. Long before this, however, the Christians–or 'Nazarenes', as they were called in Jewish circles–had begun to spread beyond the Jewish milieu in which they originated. They had adherents not only among the Jewish communities in the Hellenistic cities around the eastern Mediterranean, but also among Gentiles. Within the lifetime of the first generation of Jesus's followers, such as the apostles Paul, Peter and James, questions of agonizing urgency began to agitate the new religious group: how far were Jewish traditions to be held binding on converts? Beneath the immediate problems of religious practice, communal life and observance, the fundamental question was whether Christianity was a way of being a Jew, or something else. The divergence on this question between Paul and James in the first generation of apostolic Christianity remained a feature

Fragment of a papyrus codex of a gospel, second century AD. The message of the Christians was crystallized in written form early on.

of Christianity for a long time to come. While Christianity spread in the Gentile world and rapidly discarded many of the forms of Jewish ritual and observance, there were also places, and not only in Palestine, where Christianity remained very closely linked with the local Jewish community, with its synagogue and its traditions. These 'Jewish Christians', or 'Ebionites' as they also came to be called, were increasingly anomalous in the Christian church as it took shape in the second and third centuries and were widely regarded as heretical sects.

The paths between traditional Judaism, especially as represented after AD 70 by the rabbis, and Christianity on its way to becoming a universal religion, were diverging. With their distinctive belief that the Messiah had already come in the person of Jesus and inaugurated the reign of God, Christians came to see the Jewish nation as having rejected the Messiah, and the Jews regarded Christians as traitors to their traditions and aspirations. For Christians, the kingdom of God would be established in its full, visible reality only with the Lord's return in glory to gather his faithful from the ends of the world; and that was not yet, and no man could tell when it would be. Meanwhile, Christians had to continue living in the world, the realization of their ardent hope indefinitely postponed, disowned by the Jewish people, called to convert the whole of mankind to their Lord's message.

The Roman state and the Christians

In their attitudes to collaboration with the Roman authorities or resistance to them, the Jewish sects of the first century had been deeply divided. The Christians avoided identifying themselves with the more fanatical resistance movements, or with sects that withdrew from society into a separated mode of existence. They had a stake in the continuance of the order secured by Roman government; their leaders readily subjected themselves to Roman law; they prayed for emperors and magistrates and saw them as agents of the divine justice in maintaining public order and restraining crime. The kingdom that Jesus had established among men was not, as he was reported to have said, 'of this world', and their subjection to his kingship was no threat to their loyalty as citizens of an earthly empire. Nevertheless, for nearly 300 years, they came into frequent conflict with non-Christian society.

The reasons for such conflict were varied. Until the third century, at any rate, Christian groups were widely distrusted as cliquish, close-knit, inward-looking groups. Late in the second century it was still plausible to represent them as composed largely of the uneducated, the lower orders of urban society, the easily led and misled. Their communal life and religious practices became the subject of rumours; the worst was always easy to believe about them. In urban riots they were the natural victims of pogroms; they could easily be made the scapegoats for disasters such as the great fire in Rome under the emperor Nero in AD 64. The authorities were not, generally, very interested in them, except

when trouble had already flared up locally; and they were more concerned to satisfy themselves on the score of their obedience and loyalty than their religious beliefs or practices.

Loyalty tests inevitably led to collision between the Christians' uncompromising monotheism and the Roman state's traditional religious foundations. In the third century, when the state came close to disintegration in the course of political instability, military and economic crises and social upheavals, the refusal of Christians to rally to the traditional Roman cults was seen as a threat to the moral homogeneity of Roman society. The persecutions from Decius (249–251) to Diocletian (284–305), now instituted by government initiative and systematic in intention, were aimed at eliminating a dangerous subversive group in society. But by this time the nature and composition of the Christian church had changed almost out of recognition: it could no longer be regarded as a Jewish sect disowned by its progenitors; nor could it be seen as small, close-knit and cliquish groups, provoking the suspicions and dislike of outsiders by their outlandish ways. Christian communities had become cross-sections of Roman society, their members ranged at all levels of the social scale, with a culture, values and tastes corresponding to those of their non-Christian fellows. Their unpopularity was now a measure of their nascent respectability and the threat it was seen to pose to the traditional religious roots of Roman civilization and to a society in the grips of a crisis that was shaking its foundations.

Principal developments in the first three centuries

During these centuries Christianity became 'the Church' as we have come to know it in its subsequent history. In every important aspect of its being, its life and its mind, the foundations were laid for its subsequent development.

From the beginning, the belief of Christians was centred on the lordship of Jesus. In him the God of the Old Testament, the God of Abraham, Isaac and Jacob and of the Jewish people, had brought to completion his saving work among men. In professing loyalty to him, however, many facets of their belief remained to be defined subsequently. The lively sense of an imminent end to history with the second coming of the Lord, though liable to be revived sporadically in places down to our own day, was generally eclipsed within the first two apostolic generations. Christians came to see their group as a permanent feature of the world; and with the sense of permanence came institutional development, greater crystallization of belief and standardization in worship.

Christian communities were established in Jerusalem, and very soon, Antioch, Ephesus, Alexandria and the other cities around the eastern Mediterranean. Before the end of the first apostolic generation the movement had reached Rome, and the travels of apostolic missionaries and their successors ensured that it was to reach most of the major cities, especially where there were established Jewish communities, first around the

Mediterranean, then in the whole Roman empire. The pattern of this missionary enterprise gave the Christian church a strongly urban stamp, which it retained long after it began to penetrate into the countryside. The centres of Christianity remained the Graeco-Roman towns. It was around them that the organization of the Church took shape. The origins of leadership and organization in the earliest Christian communities are not easily discernible in the period after the apostolic generation; there are traces of a variety in the development. Well before the end of the third century, however, the pattern had become remarkably uniform: everywhere urban churches were governed by 'bishops' who had general charge of their communities, to whom priests, deacons and minor functionaries as well as lay people were subject. The areas under their charge, their 'dioceses' were, generally speaking, the territories subject to the Roman *civitas*. The network of bishoprics of which the Church consisted thus came to reduplicate the administrative geography of Roman municipal government with considerable fidelity.

Growing uniformity and increasing definition also characterized the development of belief during the first three centuries. By the early third century a body of early Christian literature generally accepted as 'canonical' had come into being. A variety of doctrinal, devotional and other traditions were still comprised within this canon, the New Testament, as it came to be distinguished from the scriptures of the Old Testament. But the canonization of a body of scriptures, though it enshrined a variety of early and divergent traditions, was nevertheless a landmark in restricting once and for all the range of doctrinal options regarded as allowable within the Church. The tradition handed down from the apostles was henceforth thought to be located within the canonical scriptures. Other alleged 'revelations' often claiming the authority of the Lord or of one or other of his disciples, became 'apocryphal' and could not be invoked to justify teaching at variance with that of the bishops. In interpreting this body of canonical material the authority of the bishops was decisive. The teaching of individual bishops was legitimized by their communion with the bishops of the apostolic sees, whose occupants could claim descent in unbroken succession from the apostles themselves. Here and there these doctrinal traditions came to be formulated in 'rules of faith' and perhaps in precursors of the creeds.

Through these various means the Church came to possess a coherent and homogeneous structure and a body of more or less identifiable belief. These served to distinguish the 'great' or, as it came to be called 'Catholic' Church from various other claimants. Among these those that posed the greatest threat to the identity of Christianity, especially in the second century, were the various religious movements generally grouped together under the label 'gnostic'. In the third century, the organized, official Church of the bishops could face the challenge of prophetic religious movements, such as the Montanists, who rejected the institutionalized structure claiming direct inspiration by the Holy Spirit.

The Constantinian revolution

To all intents and purposes the main lines along which the Church was to develop had become clear by the end of the third century; some of them well before. Many areas of uncertainty, tension and even conflict remained, and many more were to be brought to light, and sometimes resolved, later. The foundations, however, had been laid. Christianity entered the fourth century with an identifiable system of belief, an organizational structure and a rudimentary mechanism for resolving doubts and disputes. Though beginning to spread into the countryside, for instance in Africa, it was still very largely an urban church; but it now numbered among its adherents a wide cross-section of Roman society. No longer an outlandish sect of underprivileged, uneducated outcasts of no social standing, Christian communities had come to represent the whole variety of Roman society from the high aristocracy to the flotsam of the uprooted and displaced persons among the urban proletariat.

The advent of the first Christian emperor was, nevertheless, a major landmark in the history of the Church. Constantine (proclaimed emperor in 306, achieved control of the western part of the empire in 312, sole emperor 324–337) favoured the Christians, with the aid of whose God he believed he had achieved victory, from 312. Privileges were granted to the Church and imperial patronage allowed a greatly increased number of Christians to achieve status in public life, wealth and prestige. Under his successors, despite a short-lived reversal under the emperor Julian (sole emperor 361–363), imperial legislation soon began to outlaw pagan worship, heresy and schism. By the end of the century, especially during the reign of Theodosius I (379–395) Christianity had become the official religion of the empire.

The new conditions of the Church's existence in this post-Constantinian period both accentuated some developments already established, and brought new tensions. Christianity was becoming a way to social advancement: conformity could pay. The Church became rich through imperial and other benefactions; large church buildings, elaborately decorated, were being built in cities throughout the empire. By the end of the century that began with the persecution of Christians, Christianity had become the religion of the majority and had the backing of laws enforcing orthodoxy. The majority of churchmen came to accept the new order of things with alacrity. The established order of Roman society was sanctioned as a God-willed embodiment of Christian society. Roman imperial ideology was reinterpreted in Christian terms. The emperor was widely seen as God's representative, with a mission to safeguard the unity and well-being of the Church and a duty to supervise its affairs. The Church came to identify itself very closely with the established social and political order. The Roman empire became a Christian empire, often seen as an image of the heavenly kingdom.

There were, however, groups among the Christians who resisted this widespread movement of identification with the established order. Chief among such were the various Christian groups dissenting from the imperial orthodoxy, such as the representatives of the teaching defined by the Council of Nicaea (325) under emperors with Arian sympathies. More important among movements of dissent was the Donatist church in Africa, upholding ancient African traditions and aspirations to ecclesiastical autonomy. It resisted domination both by imperial orthodoxy and the ecclesiology of Italian and Gallic churchmen. Its traditions of independence remained characteristic of the African church right through its history, until its extinction by the Muslim conquest in the seventh century.

The ascetic and monastic movement was not, as such, a movement of protest against a Christianity too closely identified with the Roman establishment. Its roots lay in the third century, when hermits began to seek Christian

Above: San Giovanni in Laterano, the cathedral church of Rome, built during the reign of Constantine (AD 307–337).

Below: Plan of San Paolo Fuori le Mura, Rome, one of a series of great fourth century churches.

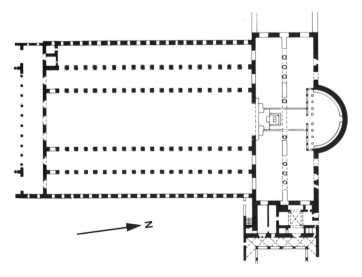

perfection in the deserts of Egypt. By about 400, it had spread widely into other parts of the empire, including the west. Varied forms of organization of monastic life in communities came into being. The aim, always, was to live the life of prayer and to seek Christian perfection, rather than to question the established order of society. It stood, however, for a style of life and of Christian observance dramatically different from that of conformist lay society, often different also from that of the bishops and clergy whose status was approaching that of public officials. In spreading its influence in society, the monks came frequently into conflict with the episcopal order.

The problem of classical culture

Almost from the beginning, Christians had been divided in their attitudes towards secular learning and culture. St Paul had contrasted the wisdom of this world which is foolishness with the foolishness of God which is wiser than men (I Cor. 1: 18–25). The problem of relating secular education, literature, philosophy and the whole culture of Graeco-Roman antiquity to their religious convictions became serious in the course of the second century, when men of learning were beginning to be found among the Christians. It was during the second half of this and in the early third century that a sharp divergence appeared between men such as Justin Martyr, Clement and Origen (the last two both at Alexandria), who took a favourable view of classical learning at its best, and others such as Tatian and the African Tertullian, who took the opposite view. For Justin, Clement and Origen, the best achievements of secular thought had paved the way for Christianity. Christianity could be regarded as the crown of secular culture, summing up in its teaching all the fragmentary truth and value anticipated by Graeco-Roman paganism. It was the task of Christian thinkers and writers to make use of this heritage for the purpose of deepening their scriptural faith and nourishing their Christian spiritual life. As against this accommodation with classical culture, other writers, for instance, Tertullian (fl. 196–212), saw an unbridgeable gulf fixed between Christianity and all the intellectual achievement of pagan antiquity, which they saw as irredeemably infected with idolatry.

The two attitudes co-existed during the third and much of the fourth centuries. With the growing number of educated Christians, who had undergone the same education as their pagan contemporaries, shared their tastes and many of their attitudes, it was inevitable that hesitations about the right of Christians to take an interest in classical literature should fade. In the generation following Constantine, as Christianity became more prestigious and socially more acceptable, secular education came to be generally valued among Christians. It was not until after the 360s that the old conflicts broke out once again. The issue was revived by the pagan reaction under Julian, and the slightly later movement of aristocratic paganism in the west. Classical learning was now becoming identified with the values that pagan traditionalists tried to maintain. It was drawn into the conflict between pagan and Christian religion, and caused Christian scholars and thinkers like St Jerome (?331–420) and St Augustine (354–430) to hesitate about its value. This conflict was resolved after a generation or so, when the confrontation between the last aristocratic pagans and the Christian establishment had passed. Classical philosophy, literature and art came to be cultivated by Christians without inhibition, and moulded many of the forms of their thinking and expression.

The fourth and fifth centuries were the great age of Christian literature. Theological writings of many forms, ecclesiastical history and biography, poetry and sermons, were thriving, encouraged, among other things, by the great doctrinal debates of the time. It was also the creative period of Christian art and architecture, now flourishing on a scale that could not have been dreamed of in the pre-Constantinian era.

On the threshold of a new Europe

By the early fifth century Christianity had come to identify itself in very large measure–apart from the solitary protest of St Augustine in his *The City of God*–with the Roman order, its destiny, its culture, and many of its values. The centuries that followed, the fifth and sixth, saw the dissolution of the Roman empire under the invasions and settlements of Germanic barbarians in its western provinces. Western Europe became a mosaic of new barbarian kingdoms, while the empire survived in the east. Henceforth Christianity came to assume different forms, related in different ways to the societies in which it existed.

To the new barbarian peoples in the west the Church was one of the principal vehicles for the transmission of classical civilization. Aristocratic bishops from Roman families had made the heritage of their pagan predecessors their own. Education in western Europe came to depend increasingly on their activities in their own households. The Church also played a key role in the development of institutions in these societies. Everywhere, by the end of the sixth century, the Germanic nations had accepted or were on the way to accepting Catholic Christianity and, along with it, many of the forms of Roman culture and Roman traditions of public life.

In the east Roman, or Byzantine, empire Christianity continued to be all-pervasive in every part of life. Society was wholly Christianized; the Byzantine empire was seen by its inhabitants as the heir of classical antiquity, as well as the one true embodiment of a civilized Christian social order. It defined many aspects of public life and ritual, without ever giving foothold to the dualism of the clerical and the lay elements in society, to sacred and secular in its activities, that came to characterize the simpler societies of western Europe. Without dominating society through a clerical élite, Christianity came to pervade Byzantine society and its culture at every level. The fifth and six centuries saw the beginning of this parting of the ways.

The Graeco-Roman City

R. F. Willetts

Planned and unplanned

The concept of the Graeco-Roman city connotes, in the broadest sense, those numerous urban centres, set in the midst of a basic agricultural economy, established in the Greek-speaking world, in Italy and around the Mediterranean littoral in the early centuries of the Iron Age and eventually incorporated within the far-flung boundaries of the Roman empire, at least until such time as the empire was sundered into two separate regions–an eastern or Byzantine empire centred upon Constantinople and a western centred upon Rome. In historical terms this means roughly a time span of rather more that 1000 years, from the Archaic period of Greece (say the eighth or seventh centuries BC) until the foundation of Constantinople in AD 330. (That city was in fact founded originally as Byzantium by the Megarians in 658 BC. It remained a Greek city for 2000 years, until it was captured by the Turks in AD 1453; and it was ideally situated to be a centre of sea power and of control of seaborne commerce.) Such geographical factors motivated the siting and development of many of the famous cities of ancient Greece and then those of the Roman empire, with its vast territories in Asia and Africa, as well as Europe, from Britain to the Sudan, from Portugal to the Euphrates. Rome itself was traditionally founded in 753 BC and the western empire endured until AD 476 when its last emperor was deposed.

The multifarious cities of the Graeco-Roman world had their individual histories and their local traditions, but it is possible to make a broad distinction between those that developed haphazardly without deliberate planning and those that, for one reason or another, were established by design. Both Athens and Rome were conspicuous examples of the first category. So too was Sparta, formed out of five villages before the end of the ninth century BC. Compared with most Greek cities Sparta even had no real acropolis, lacked fortification until the time of the tyrant Nabis (207–192 BC), and had no real walls until Roman times.

Alexandria belongs in the second category. It was

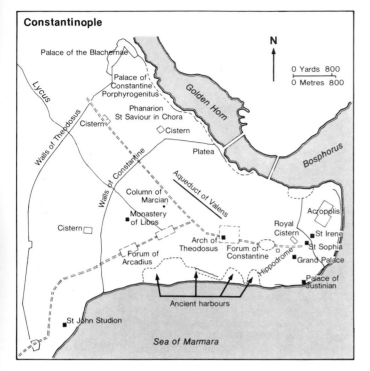

Constantinople

founded by Alexander the Great in 331 BC, to replace Tyre as the principal trading centre of West Asia and the eastern Mediterranean. He recognized the potentiality of the site of a fishing village called Rhacotis; and the city named after him was planned by the Rhodian architect Dinocrates between Lake Mareotis and the sea. The great natural harbour was protected to the north by the island of Pharos, soon to have the lighthouse that became one of the seven wonders of the world. This island was connected to the mainland by an artificial causeway about 2000 yd (1830 m) long. The new city was fashioned geometrically, with wide streets on a rectangular grid. Alexander himself was reputed to have marked the ground plan, marketplace, wall circuit, temples of Isis and the Greek gods.

The Greeks had had a long previous experience of planning cities on new sites, frequently following a rectangular or grid-iron or Hippodamian system—after Hippodamus of Miletus, the celebrated architect of the fifth century BC. Such planned cities were to be found in the west but are most commonly associated with Ionia and especially with Miletus, the great maritime state, which was the most southerly of the 12 cities of the Ionian confederacy.

The Greek city state
The *polis*, the city state of Greek antiquity, was the characteristic social unit of the Iron Age. It was so characteristic indeed that, for Aristotle (384–322 BC), it seemed to be an ideal completion for civilized life. He considered that the partnership finally composed of several villages is the city state, which has at last attained the limit of virtually complete self-sufficiency and which, while it comes into existence for the sake of life, exists for the good life. Therefore every city state exists by nature, inasmuch as the first partnerships so exist. For the city state is the end of the other partnerships, and nature is an end, since that which each thing is when its growth is completed we speak of as being the nature of each thing. The city state is a natural growth and man is by nature a *politikon zoon*, a city state creature.

It is true that the Hellenistic monarchs, including Aristotle's former pupil, Alexander the Great (d. 323 BC), were soon to put an end to this ideal conception of self-sufficiency of the independent city state as the basis of civilized good living. Nevertheless, when the Romans had brought this whole sphere of Mediterranean-based civilization under their sway, the city remained as a local centre of government for several centuries. When this ceased to be the case, the Roman empire had also ceased to be an enduring historical reality.

The basic features of the *polis* were fashioned in the early part of the first millennium BC, after the collapse of the preceding great Bronze Age civilizations. The techniques of the Bronze Age had been normally monopolized by minority ruling groups. By comparison, the techniques of the Iron Age were at once more widespread and also more localized as iron, eventually to be cheaper and more efficient than bronze, became more and more plentiful, causing fresh innovations in industry and commerce. Division of labour and of labour skills gradually became more varied in the spheres of handicraft industry, agriculture and trade. Differentiation became steadily more marked, between urban centres and the villages of the countryside, as also between various occupation groups who shared common interests. Former tribal or semi-tribal forms of social organization were superseded by city state institutions with their new kinds of officialdom.

Initially these city states, with their satellite villages of peasants, were controlled by a landed nobility. In due course this ruling aristocracy became increasingly privileged, socially and economically; and thus also there developed, in addition to the settled peasants, a landless population which migrated overseas in the colonization period of the eighth and seventh centuries BC. By the sixth century BC Greeks had settled over a very wide area, with colonies on the shores of Thrace and the Black Sea, in Italy and Sicily, Spain and Gaul. Significantly there was a general trend toward the codification of law in the Greek world, accompanied by the diffusion of alphabetic writing, in the course of the seventh century BC. This remarkable innovation began, not on the mainland of Greece, but in Greek colonies—and in the western colonies first of all, at once more distant and less accessible than those in the east. It may be that a primary stimulus stemmed from the need to provide a single code of law for colonists originating from different cities with varying systems of customary law. This helps to account for the appearance of famous lawgivers who included, for instance, Zaleucus in Achaean Locris,

Charondas in Ionian Catana, and Diocles in Dorian Syracuse. The laws of Zaleucus and Charondas were generally supposed to be the oldest written Greek laws, probably announced in the first half of the seventh century BC. Some of these western codes became familiar in eastern Greece, including that of Charondas in the island of Cos. Some cities of Asia Minor and the islands produced lawgivers such as Pittacus of Mytilene. Some others, like Lycurgus of Sparta, Dracon of Athens and Philolaus of Corinth produced codes for mainland cities—but unwritten in Sparta.

Social and economic developments

Throughout this period there was, naturally, a considerable expansion of trade and of commodity production; and coined money replaced barter to facilitate the exchange of goods. Social conflicts ensued in many of the cities, which culminated in the establishment of the first forms of democratic government in human history. The first stirrings of this democratic movement began in Ionia, then spread to the Greek mainland and along the trade routes even as far as the Greek colonies in Italy and Sicily.

There were hundreds of Greek city states which went through their various phases of uneven historical development. Although our detailed knowledge of regions and of individual cities steadily advances, as a result of archaeological investigation and fresh examination of old sources or the discovery of new inscriptions or papyrological evidence, our information about most of these cities, their siting, causes of foundation and their vicissitudes, is still but partial. We happen to be relatively well-informed about Athens and we also possess enough historical sources about Sparta to lend plausibility to a still widely accepted but over-simplified view, dramatized by the prolonged conflict of the Peloponnesian War, that the states of Athens and Sparta represented rather extreme contrasts. Because of its political and cultural achievements, the published material about ancient Athens, its situation and its monuments, is prolific. The same is true of ancient Rome, which became the metropolitan centre of a huge empire. But, although Athens and Rome, at various times, shared common features with other Mediterranean cities, it would obviously be incorrect to regard them as typical.

It had been quite usual for Bronze Age urban centres to have harbour towns; and such continued to be the case in historical times. Piraeus, still the port of Athens, was planned by Hippodamus after the Persian Wars. Ostia, founded in the late fourth century BC as a military colony, at the mouth of the river Tiber, became the flourishing port of Rome, some 16 miles (26 km) away by land. Its old walled nucleus was but 5 acres (2 ha) in size, of rectangular plan, divided into four equal areas by two intersecting streets; as it developed, its later streets were flanked by storeyed blocks of dwellings.

The *acropolis*, the 'upper' or 'higher city', in comparison with the *asty*, the lower town, was a regular feature of Greek city states, a place of refuge in times of

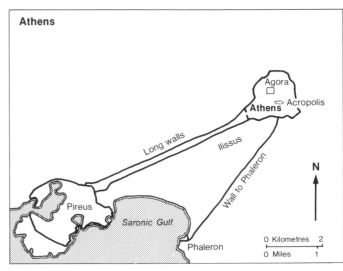

danger and often with religious associations. The story of Rome's origin affords a parallel in terms of pious memory. According to tradition, confirmed by archaeology, Rome began as a settlement on the Palatine Hill by herdsmen from the Latin hinterland. Here a round hut, known as the 'House of Romulus' was long preserved as a national monument. Temples, shrines and sanctuaries were ubiquitous in pagan antiquity, and much detailed study has been applied to their architecture as well as their function in the social life of cities. Equally important in everyday affairs was the marketplace, the *agora* of the Greek city, formerly also a place of assembly for citizens. Public buildings for various purposes were erected in these areas. For example, the *stoa*, a sort of open colonnade, was a familar architectural feature of the *agora* and similar

The Maison Carrée, Nîmes, the best-preserved Roman temple in existence (*c*16 BC).

public places. Theatres were of considerable importance in the social life of Greek cities. Their cultural role is matched by the high level of engineering skills that went into their construction, often on hillside slopes below an acropolis, resulting in admirable acoustic achievements. Athletic pursuits, though denied to rapidly increasing slave populations, were cultivated by the male, free citizen classes. Hence the appearance of the gymnasium, another characteristic institution of the city state. Large cities had two or more gymnasia. When formal educational systems had been established in the principal Greek mainland cities, the gymnasium, focus of athletic activity, was closely associated with them. The architecture of the gymnasium reflected an abiding relationship in education between athletics, music and philosophy.

The Roman city

The Roman *forum* is the equivalent of the Greek *agora*, and naturally, with the expansion of the city, these places multiplied in Rome. There were no theatres in early Roman times, but they began to be constructed in the first century BC. The theatre of Pompey (55 BC) could seat 40,000. Of the circuses, where chariot and horse races took place, the Circus Maximus had capacity for 300,000 spectators.

For historical reasons, Roman construction of cities within the geographical boundaries of their empire drew upon a mixture of theory and practice. In fact, it has been well said that the differences between Greek and Roman cities lie rather in the introduction of new constructional techniques, new types of building, and new amenities, such as improved water supply and drainage, than in new principles of planning. The consequence was that the new cities of the western provinces of the Roman empire had a regular street plan, good drainage and water supply and impressive public buildings. Theatres, baths, hotels, libraries and colonnades became customary amenities of urban life. Some houses even had central heating, wall paintings and mosaics.

The Greek Mind

John Gould

In the middle of the fourth century BC at Athens, two of the most brilliant and original of ancient Greeks, Plato and Aristotle, worked together in close association as teacher and pupil, over a period of some 20 years. Yet as thinkers they could not have been more different: Plato aristocratic, inclined to puritanism, deeply mistrustful of any empirical approach to philosophical problems and committed, emotionally and intellectually, to a belief in the reality only of transcendental, absolute and immutable patterns of what we take as real in the world around us; Aristotle, the son of a court doctor from distant Macedon and the creator of formal logic, inclined by temperament to begin any enquiry by recalling what 'we say', and the instigator of programmes of research into the history of medicine, into biology and into the political history and current workings of every Greek community (*polis*). This episode should warn us against any too-ready generalizations about 'the Greek mind'. But it also points to a recurring theme in ancient Greek thinking and feeling about the world of their experience, a creative co-existence of quite opposite tendencies. For it repeats a pattern that we can see, for example, a hundred years earlier, in the divergent imaginations of Herodotus and Thucydides, between them the founders of Western historical writing, or among the anonymous authors of the fifth-century BC writings that we call Hippocratic, a tension between specific, concrete observation, meticulous and sharp-eyed in its perception, and general theories of a high degree of abstraction and formalization.

Aristotle (384–322 BC), philosopher and tutor of Alexander the Great, was the son of a Macedonian doctor and pupil of Plato.

Consider the following two quotations from the Hippocratic corpus. The first is from a series of case histories called *Epidemics*:

'The woman who suffered from sore throat, who lived near Aristion's place, started first with her voice becoming indistinct. Her tongue was red and parched. First day: shivering; high fever.

Third day: rigor, high fever; a hard reddish swelling on either side of the neck down to the chest, extremities cold and livid, respiration superficial. What she drank was regurgitated through the nostrils and she was unable to swallow. Stools and urine suppressed.

Fourth day: all symptoms more pronounced.

Fifth day: died.'

The second is from a work called *The Nature of Man*:

'Children suffer from stones owing to the warmth of the whole body and of the region about the bladder in particular. Adult men do not suffer from stones because the body is cool; it should be thoroughly appreciated that a person is warmest the day he is born and coldest the day he dies. So long as the body is growing and advancing towards strength it is necessarily warm; but when it begins to wither and fade away to feebleness, it cools down. From this principle it follows that a person is warmest the day he is born because he grows most on that day; he is coldest the day he dies because on that day he withers most.'

We can recognize both these passages as in some sense quintessentially 'Greek', and yet they quite evidently stem from wholly divergent ways of approaching experience. If there are continuities in ancient Greek thought and feeling, they are as much continuities of difference as continuities of sameness.

Tension between co-existing opposites is already present at the level of values. We may think of the Delphic commandments 'know thyself' or 'nothing to excess' as characteristic expressions of the coolness of Greek moral attitudes, or of *sophrosyne* (self-restraint and discipline) as a classically Greek virtue, bearing the mark of the calm equilibrium valued by the culture that produced the Parthenon frieze. But the same culture was attuned to thinking of men's relations with one another and with their environment in terms of unremitting conflict, to judging human behaviour by standards that approved the ruthless defence of 'honour', of social status and 'face', against any slight or attempted humiliation (real or fancied), and to responding, in its theatre, with passionate understanding to play after play that centred on the values of violent revenge and requital, supernatural as well as human: 'hurt thy enemies' was accepted as as much a positive moral imperative as 'benefit thy friends', and the most absolute of evils was 'any appearance of failure, weakness or dependency'. These values constitute an interpretation of human existence as self-assertion against which Socrates (and later Plato) rebelled with outright re-jection, but they form a link between the majority of Socrates' contemporaries and the heroes of the Homeric poems, the earliest products of the Greek imagination, some four centuries earlier.

Yet there too conflicting strands stand side by side. The values by which a Hector or an Achilles live (and will die) are consciously juxtaposed with the values of an Andromache, saying to Hector in the sixth book of the *Iliad*:

'Dearest,
your own great strength will be your death, and you have no pity
on your little son, nor on me, ill-starred ...
... for me it would be
far better to sink into the earth when I have lost you, for there is
no other consolation for me after you have gone to your destiny–
only grief';

and with the image of Hector's son in tears, terrified by his father's towering helmet and horsehair plume. No attempt is made by the poet to deny or write down one set of values in the interests of the other or to soften the conflict between them: they co-exist.

This capacity to give equal recognition to divergent, even opposed aspects of human experience has been described as 'isonomic'. It is prominent also in ancient Greek explanations of human behaviour, where we see used side by side human and 'superhuman' frameworks of explanation. The Persian decision to attack Greece in 480 BC, for example, is presented by Herodotus, writing only a generation or so later, as a decision reached only after several changes of mind and as the outcome simultaneously of a variety of political pressures on the Persian king (the sense of a mission inherited from his father and predecessor, the presence in his court of influential advisers with private motives for wishing to see Greece absorbed into the Persian empire, and so on), and of a series of supernatural visitations, in the form of a recurring god-sent dream.

Indeed the religion of ancient Greece, considered as an explanation of human experience, is characterized throughout by the same multiplicity of statement. It is a religion of many divine powers, some localized, others 'free' but recognized by their particular spheres or kinds of activity: any human experience may be the result of the actions of any one of a number of such powers. The powers, as they are interpreted in Greek myth, are imagined as having the same diversity of loyalties, obligations and enmities as any plurality of human individuals, so that conflicting, seemingly contradictory experiences, that threaten to make no sense, may be understood as the outcome of conflict among the powers themselves. Yet at the same time the divine powers are conceived on the model of a human social group, a family with a head, Zeus, the 'father of gods and men', so that in the last resort there is a guarantee of some ultimate unity and order in experience, a shield against the possibility of total and meaningless chaos.

Other aspects of ancient Greek religion suggest how pervasive is this mode of thinking. Oracular utterances at cult centres, dreams, 'ominous' occurrences, even cases of human 'psychic' seizure and abnormal behaviour–all are imagined as forms of communication between gods and men, but they are also assumed to be systematically ambiguous, constantly in need of interpretation by men and constantly misinterpreted by them. There are obvious connections again between this way of looking at relations between divine powers and men, and the double-sided imagery that expresses, in Greek art and myth alike, the appearance of the divine powers, who are seen sometimes as superhumanly 'human' in their physical perfection, sometimes as animal, as bulls and snakes and birds. It may be possible to explain these two strands in religious imagery as the product of different periods in the history of Greek culture; nevertheless the fact that such imagery survives into the fifth century BC is evidence that it retains its meaning and still says something of significance to the contemporaries of Thucydides and Socrates.

Tension and double-sidedness in ways of seeing the world men live in, and what they themselves offer as patterns of human conduct, is a source of creative vitality in the tradition of ancient Greek literature from its very beginning. The fact that the *Iliad* takes the 'wrath of Achilles' as its central theme is due perhaps before all else to the ambiguity of Achilles' role. Humiliated, as he sees it, in the public quarrel with Agamemnon at the beginning of the poem, he responds with a violent, if negative, assertion of his honour by withdrawing from the Greek attack on Troy. In doing this, he is asserting the validity of the code which not only he but the audience of the poem also accept as overriding, and behaving as the paradigm of the heroic man of honour. Yet as the story proceeds, his position comes to seem more and more open to question, until, by allowing his closest comrade, Patroclus, to enter the fighting to avert total Greek defeat and the burning of the ships, he indirectly brings about Patroclus' death. Achilles' stand, in achieving the humiliation of the Greeks, has become a mockery of the values it seeks to underwrite and has lost its meaning, as he himself acknowledges in preparing to avenge Patroclus by seeking out his Trojan slayer, Hector, and pursuing him to his death:

'But what pleasure is this to me, since my dear companion has perished,
Patroclus, whom I loved beyond all other companions . . .
        the spirit within does not drive me
to go on living and be among men, except on condition
that Hector first be beaten down under my spear.'

The story of Achilles' 'wrath', and of its outcome, focuses with an almost overpowering sharpness of vision on the contradictions latent in the traditional code of Greek values: as a hero he is unforgettably ambivalent, as, in quite another way, is the 'resourceful' Odysseus, re-sourceful, diplomatic, but also devious, dissembling, a purveyor of false tales, a man who waits and waits for his revenge.

Greek tragedy

There is something characteristically 'Greek' about the fascination of the ambiguous story, the ambivalent hero. All three of the great tragic poets of Athens in the fifth century BC dramatized the story of Orestes' revenge, a story that is alluded to already in the *Odyssey*, but as a tale with a simple moral, a son's duty to avenge a murdered father. That is not at all the source of its fruitfulness as a theme for Aeschylus, Sophocles and Euripides. The earliest dramatic treatment of the story that we have, Aeschylus' trilogy of plays, the *Oresteia* (458 BC), systematically explores the multiple contradictions embedded in the story of Agamemnon's return from Troy: the festering memory of his sacrifice of his daughter, Iphigeneia, to appease the gods and gain a fair wind; his murder by his wife, Clytaemnestra, and her lover, Agamemnon's cousin, Aegisthus, the inheritor of a family blood feud between his father and Agamemnon's; and the revenge taken for that killing by Agamemnon's son, Orestes, on Aegisthus and on his mother.

The story of Oedipus, killer in ignorance of his own father and subsequently husband of his mother and father of children by her, is another story dramatized by each of the three fifth-century dramatists: it too is a story without simple moral or transparent meaning, but one in which the inscrutability of the divine powers, the fragility of human achievement and the gap between human intention and result are prominent themes. As it is handled by Sophocles, in *King Oedipus*, its function is not so much (as it is in the Old Testament story of Abraham and Isaac, for example) the reinforcement of traditional wisdom or of traditional morality but the exploration of ambiguity and ambivalence in a traditional story. Sophocles returned to the story of Oedipus in his last play, *Oedipus at Colonus* (c406 BC), which deals with the last hours of Oedipus' life: now an outcast, old and blind, he is given protection from his enemies by the king of Athens, Theseus, and goes to his death on Athenian soil with promises to Athens of future supernatural protection, which he will exercise from his grave as a 'hero' (rather as the relics of a Christian saint may offer protection from his grave). Sophocles is clearly fascinated by the multiple contradictions of this story: between the frailty of a blind and feeble old man, needing to be guided at his every step by his two faithful daughters, and the supernatural power that comes to him in dying; between the seeming passivity of the victim of the gods and the awful violence of his curse upon his warring sons. The play says much about the gulf that divides the physical and the spiritual but it denies neither.

At almost the same time as Sophocles was writing *Oedipus at Colonus*, Euripides was writing his last group of plays, one of which is *Bacchae*. Here Euripides too goes back to a theme that had occupied him in earlier plays,

The playwright Aeschylus (525–456 BC) who fought against the Persians at Marathon and Salamis. In the *Persae*, produced in 472 BC, he ascribed the Greek victory to divine will, not native prowess.

the double-sidedness of human experience as imaged in the double-sidedness of divinity. The god Dionysus, whose divinity and power have been denied by men, takes his revenge upon Thebes, the community of his birth which has denied him, by taking possession of the women of the city and causing them to abandon Thebes for the mountains that loom over it. Dionysus comes to Thebes in the guise of a stranger and with a band of female worshippers of the god; his human adversary, Pentheus, king of Thebes, takes him for a handsome gigolo whose purpose is to spread sexual depravity through the community. The central movement of the play brings descriptions of Dionysiac miracles (an earthquake in the city and on the mountains miraculous springs of honey, milk and wine breaking from the earth at the touch of the possessed women), and a song celebrating the sense of release and peace given by the god to his worshippers. The play reaches its climax with Pentheus, now in the hold of the god's psychic power, seeing him momentarily with bull's head and horned, before being led by the god in women's clothes to view the women on the mountain. There he is pulled from the top of a tree, which he is using as his hide, and torn to death by the women, incited by his own mother, Agave, who fails to recognize him and takes him for a young lion. At the end of the play, she is brought, step by step to

recognition of what she has done by Cadmus, Pentheus' grandfather, who turns to Dionysus, now revealed as true divinity, to acknowledge human wrong but also to assert that gods should be unlike men in their response to slight. Dionysus says only that 'Zeus has agreed these things long since': they are inevitable, and it makes no sense to ask 'why?'. The failure in imagined understanding between man and god is complete. But *Bacchae* says, of course, more than this: Euripides' recognition that human experience of divinity embraces both unequalled peace and unequalled violence is brilliantly, hauntingly conveyed. The cruelty of the god is no bar to acceptance of his reality, nor does recognition of the reality of divinity require any denial of his cruelty: the two truths are kept in balance, and that is very Greek.

Religious beliefs

Though the Greeks learned much from their contacts with other cultures round the eastern Mediterranean, they were never tempted by the myth of the righteousness of power, as it is expressed in the royal inscriptions of Assyria or Persia, justifying human violence as expressions of the will of divinity, or in the stories of the Old Testament, justifying the ways of god to men and explaining human suffering in terms of human failure to 'obey the voice of the Lord': 'Now therefore stand still, that I may reason with you before the Lord, of all the righteous acts of the Lord, which he did to you and your fathers' is not an injunction that many ancient Greeks would have understood. Nor is there any central myth of 'original sin' in Greek tradition. True, the story of Prometheus' cheating of Zeus over the sacrificial meat, and of his theft of fire from Zeus, is made the occasion for Zeus' creation both of the present agricultural order, in which men live and must win their food by working the land, and, through the making of Pandora, of the present social order, of male and female, sex, marriage and property inheritance. Both are punishments, but Prometheus is a god, not a man, and neither is the source of any deep-seated human sense of guilt, nor is the story of Prometheus ever invoked to explain other aspects of human experience, for example death, war or human wrongdoing. Moreover, the story of Prometheus, unlike the story of Adam, is at the same time the story of a culture hero, the benefactor of mankind and their saviour from primitive misery, even from destruction at the whim of Zeus, by the creation of technology.

There is another Greek story of original sin, which concerns the death of Dionysus himself, torn apart by the Titans who then fed on his dismembered body: the Titans were destroyed by Zeus' thunderbolt for this crime, and men were born from their ashes, thus inheriting, as part of their nature, some share in the responsibility for Dionysus' death. This myth *is* used to explain human proclivity to evil, and is associated both with ideas of an afterlife in which men are punished for wrongdoing in this world, and with ideas of a cycle of rebirth from which men can escape only by leading a life of ritual purity and abstinence. But significantly this

myth figures in the beliefs and practices of cult associations (connected with Pythagoras and the mythical
singer Orpheus) that are marginal to the mainstream of
Greek religious tradition, and is not part of the central
body of Greek myth.

We have to remember that ancient Greek religion is
not a revealed religion: the stories of the gods and their
relations with men that we encounter in Greek literary
tradition are never the 'word of God', but are understood
always as the products of human imagination, which, it
is accepted, may or may not succeed in describing the
realities of the human condition. Hence they are not
revelations of divine truth, rather matrices of possible
interpretations of human experience, fluid in form and
variable in meaning. If Plato was extreme in rejecting
almost all of Greek mythical traition as a systematic
falsification of the truth about divinity, he was altogether representative in his assumption that there was
no supernatural authority guaranteeing the authenticity of the traditional stories: almost 200 years before
him, the Ionian traveller and geographer Hecataeus, in
proclaiming that he would write what seemed to him to
be 'the truth', had described the traditional stories as
'ridiculous'. It was perhaps above all this absence of
supernatural authority that permitted, even encouraged, an empirical approach to interpreting the
experience of men, and led both to the historical writing
of a Herodotus and to the beginnings of scientific
thinking. Indeed the word *historiē*, used by Herodotus of
his own enquiries and the origin of our word 'history',
meant originally no more than a questioning, and could
be used as readily of scientific enquiry or theory as of
history, in our sense of an investigation into the past: the
word continued, indeed, to be used of scientific investigation and of the knowledge acquired by it long
after Herodotus.

The era of philosophical speculation
Scientific questioning of the world of human experience
had begun in the sixth century BC, a hundred years
before Herodotus, particularly on the fringes of the
Greek-speaking world, on the Asia Minor seaboard and
in southern Italy, where contact with other cultures had
perhaps encouraged a loosening of the hold of traditional modes of understanding. It too developed upon
quite divergent lines. One approach, best represented in
the work of Parmenides of Elea, south of Naples in Italy,
at the end of the sixth century BC and foreshadowing the
work of Plato, rejected altogether the evidence of the
senses and constructed a model of reality, perfect,
without variation, unchanging, which derived, not from
observation but from an *a priori* logic of predication.
Another tradition, seen in the work of the Sicilian
Empedocles (early fifth century BC), combined theories of
the basis of physical reality and the powers that control it
with the pursuit of spiritual salvation through mystical
beliefs and rituals of purity: in Empedocles, philosophical
'truth' is treated as a secret revelation, not to be divulged
to the uninitiated. A third, diametrically opposed approach is that of the Ionian tradition of Anaximander

(sixth century BC) and Anaxagoras (fifth century BC),
which attempted, by inference from observed phenomena and by argument from analogy, to reduce reality to
its ultimate constituents and to its origins in time: it
reached its ultimate development in the highly *a priori*
atomism of Democritus and Leucippus (fifth century BC),
which described the world in terms of irreducible
particles of matter forming chance conjunctions to
produce the physical world of our experience.

This ferment of speculative thinking, argument and
counterargument, was characteristically the product of
the century and a half between 550 and 400 BC. The last
few decades of the fifth century were marked by a certain
shift of interest, away from cosmological speculation to
human experience and human society itself, its origins,
forms and values. This is the age of the sophists,
professional teachers of the leisured class in rapidly
developing societies such as Athens, teachers mainly of
the skills and techniques of persuasion, masters of public
argument and debate. It is a heady period of Greek
intellectual activity and its most characteristic representative is Protagoras, from Abdera on the north coast
of the Aegean. Protagoras was sceptical of the possibility
of penetrating to any absolute knowledge of the world or
of divinity: 'concerning the gods,' he wrote, 'I have no
means of getting to know either that they exist or that
they do not': he gave as his reasons 'the lack of evidence
and the shortness of human life'. For him, man was 'the
measure of all things': his tone is confidently pragmatic
and humanist, in its assumption that men possess the
capacity to solve almost all the problems that experience
presents to them; like Herodotus, he was ready to accept
what one writer has called the 'irreducible variety of
human behaviour and character'.

Two things, finally, should be said about the variety of
Greek intellectual endeavour. The first is that, for all its
passionate curiosity about man's experience, there were
some areas of the human predicament that it never
illuminated. Those aspects of human existence, for
example, where posing technological questions and
finding answers to them might have made great advances possible were barely touched on. Technological
skills, certainly, went into the design of buildings such as
the great fifth-century temples, but they, precisely, were
buildings not for human use but for divinity. Specifically
human problems, of transport or food production, for
example, were left in a state that had changed little, if at
all, since the end of the Greek dark age in the ninth
century BC. Nothing like the industrial revolution of
eighteenth-century England, with its ever-renewed
ingenuity in the harnessing of new forms of energy, new
means of communication, new methods of production,
is imaginable within the horizon of ancient Greek
intellectual activity. The explanation may lie in part in
the ready provision of slave labour from the margins of
the Greek world, the result of which was that a labour-
intensive economy and subsistence farming were no bar
to the intellectual development of a leisured class. But we
must also feel that for ancient Greeks to have turned
their creativity and curiosity in that direction would

have represented a development for which nothing that we know of the Greek mind had prepared us.

The second point concerns the underlying tenor of Greek thought. It is often described as pessimistic, and its clear-sighted perception of human mortality and of the fragility and incompleteness of human achievement may dispose us to call it so. Certainly when Achilles, in the last book of the *Iliad*, describes to Priam the nature of the human condition in his image of the two urns on Zeus' threshold, 'an urn of evils, an urn of blessings', from which Zeus bestows on men their experience of life, the one possibility that he passes over is an experience of unmixed blessings:

'such is the way the gods span life for unfortunate mortals,
that we live in unhappiness, but the gods themselves have no sorrows.'

But for all their awareness of the precariousness of human achievement, the vision of an Aeschylus or a Protagoras is essentially optimistic and affirmative. An account of the rise of human culture that perhaps goes back to Democritus in the fifth century BC makes the point well. After asserting that 'the first men to come into existence lived an unsettled and animal life', without clothes, fire, settled habitation or agriculture, the writer goes on: 'as a general rule, it was always necessity that taught men better, by giving them appropriate instruction; and man received the instruction, since he was an animal with natural ability, who had, as his assistants in all he tackled, his hands, his reason, and his quickness of wit.'

Better terms to describe Greek thought would be realism; an unwavering regard for fact; an absence, in large measure, of escapism or sentimentality; a passion for accuracy and precision of statement. The last word can be left to Thucydides, the fifth-century Athenian historian who recorded the long, bitter and finally fatal conflict between his city and Sparta. In 427 BC the Athenian assembly debated whether to revoke its own decision on how to react to an attempt by Mytilene, a city within the Athenian empire, to break away during the war with Sparta, with Spartan help. The attempt was defeated and the original decision was to execute the entire adult male population, and enslave the women and children. Here is part of the speech that Thucydides gives to Diodotus, an Athenian who is urging the assembly to rescind its decision:

'No man has ever yet risked committing a crime which he did not think he could carry out successfully. The same is true of states. None has ever yet rebelled in the belief that it did not have sufficient resources ... to make the attempt. Cities and individuals alike are by nature disposed to do wrong, and there is no law that will prevent that, as is shown by the fact that men have tried every kind of punishment, constantly adding to the list, in the attempt to find greater security from criminals. It is likely that in early times punishments even for the greatest crimes were not as severe as they are now, but the laws were still broken, and in time the death penalty became generally introduced. Yet even with this, the laws are still broken. Either, then, we must discover some fear more potent than the fear of death, or we must admit that we have clearly not got an adequate deterrent. So long as poverty forces men to be bold, so long as the insolence and pride of wealth give food to their ambitions ... so long will their impulses drive them into danger.'

The Roman Mind

Kenneth Quinn

The chief evidence for the Roman mind and character is provided by the Romans themselves. Greek testimony is limited in scope and superficial. Thus Polybius (second century BC) was a good historian who saw, and participated in, the first beginnings of a new Graeco-Roman culture, but the extraordinary cultural development to which these led belongs to the centuries after his death; Plutarch (second century AD), was a diligent popular biographer and antiquarian—both are openly pro-Roman. But their values are those of the Greek-speaking Hellenistic world; their understanding of the human condition is warped by naïve, sentimental conventions of analysis (the early event in life that reveals a man's future character, the single great event that marks the turning point in his career).

The evidence the Romans provide about themselves is subject, however, to qualifications.

First, much of the evidence is *retrospective*—an attempt to bridge the gap between the legendary foundation of the city (traditional date 753 BC) and the beginnings of systematic reconstruction in the middle of the third century BC. Cato (second century BC) is already a mythologizer. A natural tendency to depict themselves as the descendants of a tough, rustic people was encouraged by Hellenistic historians. By the Augustan age, the habit of retrospection is firmly ingrained in the urban intelligentsia of a city already merging its cultural identity in the standardized, international high culture

The stage-building, as seen from the audience, at Sabratha, North Africa. Gestures were important to Roman actors because of the size of theatres and the use of masks.

of the Hellenistic world. In its more sophisticated form, the myth reaches back into the remote past, as in the word picture of primitive Italy put by Virgil on the lips of Romulus in *Aeneid* 9 (a patriotic Italian's reformulation of Lucretius' picture of primitive nomad life in Book 5 of the *De Rerum Natura*):

There are no Atrid brothers here, no false-tongued Ulysses. A tough race by birth, we take our sons down to the river and toughen them in the harsh chill of its waters. Tireless hunters, our boys do not let the forests rest; horsemanship is their play and the practice of archery. They become men able to endure work and live on little, who rake and tame the land, strike fear into towns in war. We at no time quit our swords, with spears reversed we belabour the oxen's backs. Old age does not slow us, weakens not our strength of spirit nor our vigour; we press our grey hairs into the helmet, ever glad to bring home the freshly-won prize and to live by pillage.

(*Aeneid* 9. 602–13)

It extends down into historical times at least as far as the Second Punic War (218–202 BC), as in Horace:

Not from parents such as these were sprung
the men who stained the sea with Punic blood,
overthrew Pyrrhus, beat back Antiochus
and grim Hannibal:

they were virile soldier-farmers' sons,
taught to till the fields
with Sabellian hoe and to fetch
the cut fire logs

at their stern mother's bidding, when the Sun-god
stretched the shadows of the hills and took
the yokes from the tired oxen as his chariot sped
away,
at the welcome evening hour.

(*Odes* 3. 6. 33–44)

The myth serves as the basis for a simple polarity: urban life is corrupt, loaded with frustrations; rural life simple and wholesome. It is only a step from Horace's pseudo-realism of *Satires* 2. 6 ('O rus, quando ego te aspiciam?') and the *Odes* to the out-and-out pastoral daydreaming of Virgil's *Eclogues*–and, in the opposite direction, to the satirist's picture of city life as utterly loathsome, which we find in Juvenal.

The Romans came to see themselves as a people different from the Greeks, with a role of their own to play in the world, a people that instinctively looked to the past for its standards. Take Anchises' famous words to Aeneas:

Others will force on breathing bronze a softer line,
I well believe, tease from marble the living face,
plead cases better, plot with rod orbits
in the sky, predict the planets' rise.
You, Roman, remember that to govern nations
will be your culture, to add to peace a way of life:
mercy for the conquered; with the proud, unending war.

(*Aeneid* 6. 847–53)

This is not a prophecy of the Augustan Age: by then, Romans were doing all these things as well as almost any Greek; it is a vision of the Roman mission in the world, upon the actual accomplishment of which Virgil's contemporaries could look back with pride, as some consolation for the steady degeneration which they believed to be their destiny. The Romans of the Augustan Age were a nation who live in the past. Horace puts that view more brutally than most:

What has ruinous time not diminished?
Our parents, not their parents' match,
produced our more corrupt generation, soon to bear
sons and daughters more degenerate still.

(*Odes* 3. 6. 45–8)

Livy speaks as an intellectual, not a moralist; he presents a possible view of Roman history, but it is the view of a conservative and a Roman:

Afterwards, as their discipline began gradually to weaken, one notices first the decline in moral standards; next the progressive collapse and decay, until we come to our own times, when we can endure neither the ills of our society nor the cures for them.

(*Preface*)

A second qualification we must apply to the evidence

provided by the Romans about themselves is that much that is revealed about the Roman mind and character is revealed *involuntarily*. The view of history that the habit of retrospection evolved is contradicted by evidence from other sources. Cato's old Romans have to be reconciled with the evidence of Cato's elder contemporary Plautus (*c*254–184 BC). Plautus' plays are more than a parody of foreign ways, for an audience that appreciated such talk and such dealing cannot have been out of sympathy with the way of life the comedies depict; they correct the one-sided picture too often accepted by modern scholars of the Roman mind and character. Sentimental retrospection, pessimism, loyalty to the rural way of life, hostility to progress–these are only one side of the Roman character. The other is represented by wholehearted acceptance of progress and a way of life characterized by urban sophistication. The respect traditionally accorded *gravitas* (moral seriousness) by Cicero and his contemporaries has to be reconciled with the ideal–as consciously cultivated by Cicero, in his public as well as his private way of life–of *urbanitas* (sophistication).

Language

This dogged sense of inherited identity, stubbornly opposed to a new, irresistibly attractive international culture, has almost as much to do with language as with character. Latin has been described, with some truth, as a language of peasants; but it is a language of peasants who had greatness thrust upon them–and the peasants proved themselves as equal to the linguistic challenge as they proved equal to the political challenge to survive and expand.

The vowel system of Latin resembles that of modern Italian; Latin, however, is characterized by heavy combinations of consonants; it has a complex system of inflexion to express the relationships between the words in a sentence; there is neither a definite nor an indefinite article; the vocabulary is limited (adequate for the needs of a nation of farmers, weak in abstractions). In all these respects, Latin was unlike Greek–at first sight, no match for Greek. It was a language more like modern Russian in character than modern French or English, and closer than Greek to its Indo-European origin.

The Romans liked to think of themselves as aphoristic, pragmatic; their history is studded with the short, blunt, memorable phrases of their political leaders (for example Caesar's famous '*Veni, vidi, vici*'). For as long as it remained the speech of the Roman people, Latin never lost its rugged compactness. But that quality had to cope with new problems of expression. Forced to undertake new tasks, Latin evolved (following Greek models) an architectural masterpiece: the Ciceronian periodic sentence. The elaborate sentence remained, however, a showpiece of the Senate House and the law courts. Those who designed their prose to be read preferred the old, short, pungent directness; the cult of *urbanitas* produced the elegant simplicity of a Catullus, or of Cicero in his letters: even those who welcomed the new international culture preferred a way of writing and talking that showed a respect for reticence, a dislike for wasting words. In the hands of a craftsman like Virgil or Tacitus, apparently simple statement becomes the expression of compact thought; the best Roman poetry is characterized by a densely allusive structure of words, a solid edifice of deceptively simple statement, in which little is said and much implied. Where Greeks were voluble, endowed with a language that permitted the most complex expression of thought, the nicest qualifications of meaning, a Roman preferred statement laden with implication.

Periods

The time span involved is of the order of a thousand years. If we adopt a division into five periods, we have a useful framework for discussion. The periods are:

(i) an *archaic period*, extending from the foundation of Rome to the First Punic War (say 750–250 BC);

(ii) a *pre-classical period*, extending over the next 150 years (say 250–100 BC)–the period of the first surviving texts, the plays of Plautus and Terence, the fragments of half a dozen other dramatists and the fragments of early narrative poetry (especially the *Annals* of Ennius: about 500 lines have come down to us), the beginnings of historical, oratorical and didactic prose (represented only by fragments, except for the *De Agricultura* of Cato, a handbook for prospective landowners);

(iii) the *classical period* (roughly the last century BC), in some respects better regarded as two distinct periods, (a) the *Age of Cicero* (106–43 BC)–the last 60 years or thereabouts of the Roman republic (the period of Lucretius and Catullus, the immense corpus of Cicero's surviving writings, the two surviving monographs of Sallust), and (b) the *Augustan Age* (32 BC–AD 14)–the period of the poets Horace, Virgil, Propertius, Tibullus, Ovid, the great history of Livy (the longest work ever written in Latin);

(iv) a *post-classical period*, from the accession of Tiberius to the middle of the third century (14–250 AD): the first half of the first century AD is notable for a handful of writers (Lucan, Petronius, Seneca) grouped around the emperor Nero (the 'Age of Nero'); the second half of the century is represented by the prose of the younger Pliny and the verse of the poetasters Statius, Valerius Flaccus and Silius Italicus; the turn of the century brings two major figures, the satirist Juvenal and the historian Tacitus; the end of the period is represented by the biographer Suetonius and the 'novelist' Apuleius;

(v) the period from AD 250 to the fall of Rome in AD 476, sometimes called the later Roman empire–a transitional period represented on the one hand by a lapse into mediocrity and a cult of the past (Aulus Gellius, and the grammarians and commentators–the best known is Servius), save for one interesting figure, the satirist and scholar Macrobius, and, on the other hand, by the beginnings of Christian Latin.

The archaic period

The Romans of subsequent periods liked to think of the archaic period (especially the time of Rome's first struggles with its Italian neighbours) as a heroic age during which the Roman cast of mind and character took shape. The Augustan age inherited a mass of legendary material which had been tidied up by Hellenistic historians; like Greek tales of the Trojan War and the 'Age of Heroes', this material had come to occupy a position midway between myth and what might pass for things that had actually happened. Livy allotted the first 20 books of his *History* to this period. About the earlier legends he displays the scepticism appropriate to an intellectual able to distinguish between history and poetry; the scepticism of modern historians is apt to cover the whole of the period. ('In the beginning', said a cynic, 'was the Second Punic War.') Documentary evidence is confined to a few religious and legal texts (the Salic and Arval hymns, the Laws of the Twelve Tables) and a handful of religious formulae and notable sayings (all preserved by later writers, and probably corrupted as much by sham archaism as by unconscious modernization); the only authentic evidence for what archaic Latin looked like—or what Romans thought it should look like when carved on stone—is provided by a few brief inscriptions. Given such material, it is almost impossible to disentangle worthwhile evidence about the Roman character from what Romans of the pre-classical and classical periods liked to think about their origins.

The pre-classical period

The pre-classical period represents a coming to terms with more historically definable cultural pressures: those of tradition and those brought to bear through increasing contact with the Hellenistic world, first in southern Italy and Sicily (Magna Graecia) and then in Greece itself and the eastern Mediterranean. It is a period of a growing awareness in the Romans of their own character, and a period of excitement stimulated by contact with a culture more sophisticated than their own. As always, awareness of individuality meant resistance, to, as well as acceptance of, change. The myth of the old Roman and the traditional way of life he symbolized became the expression of attitudes opposed to change. Cato's *De Agricultura*, though ostensibly a practical handbook for practical men, is laden with value judgments, implicit and explicit, representative of this resistance to outside ideas.

The Romans of the pre-classical period were no longer what we must suppose they long had been: a largely peasant community grouped around a tiny city to which they could retreat under attack and which provided a centre of religious, legal and administrative life. Their readiness to repel invasion, to carry the attack into their neighbours' territory, to establish a workable relationship with those they had defeated in battle, brought about an expansion and a restructuring of that original community. The new structure was based on the personal wealth and established political power of a conservative aristocracy forced to open its ranks to a largely urban proletariat and to share the reins of power with those who had won power and influence by their

Bust of Cato (second century BC), spokesman of traditional and conservative Roman values, despite his use of Greek oratory.

own efforts within a system that permitted social mobility.

Cato, himself a *novus homo* (the first of his family to achieve high political office) recognizes three ways in which a man can make money: as a moneylender, as a *mercator* (the buyer and seller of goods), and as a landowner. For Cato, the superiority of the last is beyond question: the dominance of the class he speaks for (the proprietor of the large estate worked by a labour force composed chiefly of slaves—originally, men enslaved for debt, later increasingly prisoners of war) was challenged in Cato's own lifetime. Attempts were made, a generation after his death, at agrarian reforms. But though these resulted in some distribution of political power, the prestige of the way of life of the landed proprietor active in public life at Rome, possessed of large estates, remained unshakable throughout the classical period. To emulate his way of life became the ambition of others, whether on a modest scale (like Horace), or on a shamelessly immodest scale, the sterile ostentation of which (elaborate *villae*, ornamental grounds overlooking what had once been productive land) Horace attacks in *Odes* 2. 15.

No doubt the values of the majority of the ruling class remained throughout the pre-classical period as doggedly pragmatic and conservative as Cato's. But Cato's down-to-earth, no-nonsense forthrightness is the immediate reaction to imminent change. By the end of the classical period, Rome had become the capital of an Italy accustomed to the idea of itself as a single nation, no longer needing to sustain itself by its own agricultural output, in a position to rely on foreign corn. As a result, Rome became increasingly dependent on the *mercator*, now no longer a small-time trader living by his wits but often a man of wealth, if never quite socially respectable–he is always a butt for ridicule in Horace. The moneylender, for Cato little better than a usurer and a rogue, became the banker, a figure of power and sometimes a man of culture and undeniable social status in an increasingly capitalistic society in which the immense wealth of individuals is the dominant factor. They were joined by the *publicanus* (the entrepreneur capitalist who made his money by bidding for government tax contracts). All were in a position to buy estates of their own, as proof of status. In the post-classical period, the old-style aristocratic landowner will be no more than a memory, his austere way of life a theme for the moralist (Seneca, *Epist.* 86).

The comedies of Plautus need to be put in the context of a rapid development of a new popular culture, of which they are both the product and the stimulus: this is seen in their exuberance of language, their reversal of accepted social values (supposedly respectable citizens depicted as of doubtful moral integrity, the dupes of their wives; slaves allied with sons to outwit their fathers). The audience to which these plays appealed was a popular audience, an audience of young men, many of whom had fought in the campaigns in southern Italy and Sicily; an audience quick to appreciate the boisterous fun, the scintillating wordplay of these remarkably funny plays and willing to see them, despite their Greek settings, as depicting the world of their own experience and opposing to conventional values a system of values that were their own. These are the values of the new, less rigidly structured, sophisticated, individualistic urban culture of the Hellenistic world. But there is something genuinely Roman, too, in the boisterous surrender to the absurd. No other writer appeals like Plautus to a popular audience; Roman writers after Plautus prefer a more exclusive audience; Ovid is perhaps the only exception.

Terence's comedies, written half a century after those of Plautus, represent the adoption of the new culture by a new internationally minded élite. His plots depict elegant young men out to have their fling, determined to marry the girls they fall in love with rather than those chosen for them by their fathers. His audience, we can imagine, were not displeased to see young men about town depicted as a little stupider than they thought themselves so long as they could regard the play as a vindication of a way of life they had themselves espoused.

The classical period

The flow of intellectuals from the Greek-speaking east began in the pre-classical period; by the middle of the classical period it had become a flood. Some came as prisoners of war (technically slaves), some as honoured guests. Some came merely as visitors. The traditional structure of Roman society was modified to cope with this influx. Those who came as prisoners of war were incorporated into the household (the *familia*) of their master. Freed slaves (*liberti*) retained their attachment to a former master, who now became their *patronus*; by the end of the classical period, they represented an important force in Roman cultural and administrative life. Those who came as free men attached themselves on their own initiative to a *patronus* who could protect their interests, make the right contacts, or appear in court on his client's behalf if the need arose.

The step from the traditional structure of the Roman ruling class (a group of powerful *patroni* and their *clientes*) to that specialized form that we call 'patronage' was easy and inevitable; the case we happen to know most about, the relationship of Horace to his patron Maecenas, seems in all essential respects typical. It was a significant, perhaps a crucial, step towards the transformation of Roman cultural life. That it should have been taken shows the vulnerability of Roman society to such a cultural fifth column.

While the smart young set were cultivating Terence, their elders were listening to Ennius' resounding hexameters and, in their more relaxed moments, to the satiric comment in verse on the contemporary scene of Lucilius, a gentleman like themselves, if only a Campanian gentleman. By the middle of the classical period (around 50 BC), the number of leading Roman *patroni* whom we hear of as opening their houses to Greek intellectuals and teachers is remarkable–teachers of the art of public speaking (*rhetorici*), professors of literature and literary critics (*grammatici*), philosophers (Stoics, Epicureans, Peripatetics, adherents of the New Academy and of lesser sects).

We must assume there were also Roman *patroni* who remained the austere, laconic philistines of our history books. Doubt might be permitted as to whether these old Romans ever existed, if it were not for the gaunt, deep-chiselled, unsmiling faces recorded for posterity by Roman portrait sculpture. Once again we must be on our guard: this is how the Romans liked to see themselves; the evident realism of the portrait in stone is limited by conventions that have their origin in the wax death mask. Yet everything points to a sombre god-fearing pessimism as characteristic of the Roman mind–a pessimism made tolerable by relaxation into the simple joys of the rustic festival. With the transformation from a rustic to an urban culture the better-off, more leisured, more travelled upper-class Roman turns increasingly to the new high culture of the Hellenistic world.

At the height of the boom there were 20 *grammatici* teaching in Rome, each with a 'school' of his own. Equally impressive is the number of distinguished Romans said to possess their own libraries. Leading statesmen were also acknowledged followers of philosophical schools and many had studied like Cicero at Athens. The *De Rerum Natura* of Lucretius is a sophisticated poem written for an audience interested in ideas.

The library, the collection of papyrus rolls, became an indispensable basis for a new, distinctively Roman organization of the intellectual life: books give access to those who wrote in another time, in another place and in another language; expert interpreters are on hand, themselves scholars, eager to promote the habit of scholarship in others; a poet like Catullus or Horace needs books or he cannot work; if he leaves Rome, he must take books with him. Catullus probably borrowed volumes from a wealthier person's library; in the Augustan Age there were public libraries.

For the Greeks, the basis of the cultural life, whether it was poetry or philosophy, was the spoken word. At Alexandria the written text acquired a new authority, as the authentic record, the basis for a performance that could be no more than a reconstruction. The great poets and thinkers were dead, there was no public to sustain an oral culture; the library was the repository of a past culture, which was preserved and studied by professional scholars, and reshaped by bookish poets for bookish readers. Rome followed Alexandria and the intellectual life became based upon the written text; the term *litterae* recognized the new reality.

The concept of *litterae* denoted not just poetry, or even what we call literature, but the bookish life in general: philosophy, history, science, as well as poetry, *litterae* came to symbolize, not merely entertainment (that which makes life more agreeable), but also a preparation for life; a rational basis for the conduct of one's life (with obvious practical advantages), as well as a consolation for life's frustrations. *Litterae* became a *studium* (an activity, implying active participation), not a consumer product. It is an attitude of mind that was to have interesting consequences: the pervasion of a ruling class by a common culture; the evolution, based on rational argument, of a pragmatic humanitarianism which gave Rome goals almost adequate for her expanding role as an imperial power; and the limitation of that culture to a social élite (the ruling class and their associates, politely termed their *amici*)–*litterae* remained something to be involved in, to be talked about, within a series of groups, each gathered round a *patronus*, not something shared with a wider audience.

The number of such groups cannot have been large. Their activity, however, was prodigious. They produced, or supported, first-rate writers, and a host of lesser talents. The world came to be seen, however, through the eyes of the members of a cultural élite–well read, in its own opinion humane and open-minded, but limited in its interests and expectations.

The post-classical period and the late Roman empire

The order restored by Augustus was a sterile order. Its sterility can be sensed during the second half of Augustus' long reign; in the post-classical period, it becomes apparent. The great *patroni* retained their social trappings: men aspired to be elected consul, and were elected, but office carried no significance; independence of action, the capacity to function as an intellectual catalyst, were gone. Devotion to *litterae*, if concerned at all with serious thought, became a private consolation for impotence (Seneca, Tacitus; on a more trivial level, the younger Pliny). What we call literature became an empty repetition of traditional forms: the writers of Flavian epic had nothing to say; the *recitatio*, the formal performance by the author before an invited audience of his own work, became as meaningless a social ritual as election to the consulship.

No doubt during much of the first century AD writers and their friends were haunted by the thought that it is safer to have nothing to say. The fate of a handful of talented writers at the court of Nero foolish enough to believe that association with an emperor who proclaimed himself a patron of the arts granted freedom of thought (or permitted technical brilliance, should the protégé outshine his patron) was warning enough. But the lapse into sterility was the result also of a failure to find a new social status for literature.

One major writer, Ovid, seems to have attempted to free himself from the old structures, in order to communicate directly with a new kind of audience. To achieve that end he had been prepared to make literature what it had not been since Plautus: an entertainment. Not a popular entertainment, as it had been with Plautus, but highbrow entertainment in a city large enough and materially comfortable enough to provide such a public, a public that appreciated wit, that could be flattered by an appeal to its cynicism about traditional values and even about its own way of life–a way of life dominated by pleasure. Ovid's hero is a kind of Don Juan figure, the witty light-hearted womanizer, for whom the only woman who is chaste is the one who has never been propositioned ('*Casta est quam nemo rogavit*'). Ovid went too far. The fact that once again literature was not imitating life, but giving the lead by representing the pursuit of love as the smart way to behave in the new, frankly amoral urban culture, did not help; it was necessary for Augustus to dissociate himself from a picture of society that openly conflicted with his own much-publicized (and wholly unrealistic) campaign for a return to the old Roman morality.

The conflict between the urban culture of the Hellenistic world (optimistic, hedonistic, materialistic, sophisticated) and inherited Roman feelings of belonging to a simpler, more austere world doomed to disappear continued throughout the post-classical period. The same feelings eventually generated a new myth, the cult of a more recent Roman past, that of the high culture of the Augustan Age, when in its turn, in the third and fourth centuries AD, that past is irretrievably lost and Horace, Virgil, Livy and Ovid rank as *antiqui scriptores*.

It is easy to feel that after Tacitus and Juvenal nothing matters (except, perhaps, Apuleius–a wholly exotic figure), and depressing to be forced to the conclusion that in the third and fourth centuries AD the Roman mind sank into vacuity; but it is a conclusion impossible to escape. From the fourth to the fourteenth century AD much survives that is interesting; the best is infused with a *naïveté* as attractive as it is unexpected. But this is the voice of a culture that was wholly un-Roman. However limited the vision of the Roman mind, what a Roman says is the product of reflection; we feel the care exercised to reduce thought to the right words. Whether archaic and simple or witty and sophisticated, what a Roman says rarely sounds naïve.

China

Shang bronze ritual cauldron, *ting*, used in ceremonies connected with ancestor worship. The faces serve as reminders of the Shang custom of human sacrifice (fourteenth to eleventh centuries BC).

Shang

Arthur Cotterell

The Shang dynasty (c seventeenth century BC to 1027 BC)

According to the *Shu Ching* (Book of Documents) the first Shang king was T'ang, a virtuous nobleman whom Heaven called upon to overthrow the corrupt Hsia dynasty. He was endowed 'with valour and prudence to serve as a sign and direction to the myriad regions and to continue the old ways of Yu.' The event, it is said, took place in 1766 BC.

Of the Hsia dynasty there is no certain archaeological trace. This is not the case with Shang China, though until quite recently our knowledge came chiefly from excavations conducted at Anyang in northern Honan. Since 1950 archaeological activity has been more widespread in that province—possibly two other Shang capitals have been identified, Po at Erh-li-t'ou and Ao at Cheng-chou. In all the Shang, or Yin, are supposed to have occupied nine capitals between 1766 and 1027 BC.

If, as many Chinese archaeologists are now convinced, the Shang settlement at Erh-li-t'ou was Po, we have located the seat of T'ang. Build on a tributary of the Yellow River, Erh-li-t'ou boasted a palace erected on an earthen platform, houses, storage pits, wells, kilns, and a cemetery. Among the artifacts recovered there are ceremonial bronze vessels, the prototypes of containers used throughout antiquity by the Chinese in the rites of ancestor worship. It would seem from current findings that Erh-li-t'ou represents a stage of cultural development intermediate to the neolithic Lung-shan culture and the more advanced Shang civilization of later sites. Clearly inherited from the Lung-shan culture was scapulimancy: divination by observing the cracks that resulted from heating the shoulder blades of oxen or sheep. But at Erh-li-t'ou no elaborate preparations or inscriptions are in evidence.

Cheng-chou and Anyang

Whereas the settlement at Erh-li-t'ou marked the break with neolithic traditions in terms of urban development and bronze metallurgy, the fortifications of Cheng-chou dating from around 1650 BC established beyond doubt that under the Shang kings Chinese civilization emerged. Over 25 yd (23 m) wide at the base, the city wall ran for more than 1 mile (1.6 km) enclosing nearly 600 acres (243 ha). The ubiquity of walls in China has often been remarked. In fact the Chinese use the same word, *ch'eng*, for a city and a city wall: town planning always commenced with the external fortifications. Work continues on the Shang remains at Cheng-chou, but the sequence of cultural development appears to conform to the Erh-li-t'ou pattern, except that its final phases were more splendid.

Within the walled enclosure were sited the administrative and ceremonial buildings. Structures of palatial proportions have been traced as well as the outline of an altar made of compressed earth. Beneath the floor of one of these buildings a ditch was discovered in 1974, containing about a hundred human skulls, mostly sawn

Chronology of Ancient China

Prehistory	Yang-shao culture (after c 5000 BC) Lung-shang culture	(Hsia dynasty c 2205-1766 BC?)	NEOLITHIC
Historical period begins	Shang dynasty (c 17th century-1027 BC) Chou dynasty (1027-256 BC)	Western Chou (1027-771 BC) Ch'un Ch'iu period (722-481 BC) Warring States period (481-221 BC)	BRONZE
The early empire	Ch'in dynasty (221-207 BC) Former Han (207 BC-AD 9) Hsin dynasty: Wang Mang's usurpation (AD 9-23) Later Han (AD 24-220)		(Steel?) IRON
Age of disunity	Three Kingdoms (AD 221-65) Western Chin dynasty (AD 265-316)	Shu kingdom (AD 221-64) Wei kingdom (AD 220-65) Wu kingdom (AD 220-80)	
	Fall of the northern provinces to Tartar peoples (AD 316)		

off across the eyebrow and ear portions. The nearest parallel at Erh-li-t'ou would be burials of victims with heads or parts of the limbs missing. The finds indicate a highly stratified society in which slaves or prisoners of war, possibly both, could be used in religious ceremonies and even as raw material for bone manufacture. Only the royal family and the nobility along with personal retainers would have dwelled inside the walls. Outside the people lived either about workshops or in farming villages. The two bronze foundaries so far excavated show the relative social importance of bronze-casters; their workshops and dwellings were more commodious than any other section of the ordinary population.

Although three pieces of inscribed oracle bone have been found at Cheng-chou, it is argued that they were introduced from the last Shang capital, Anyang. Excavated from 1928 to 1937 and again after 1950, Anyang is the chief site of Shang civilization. Notable features are the royal graves at nearby Wu-kuan-ts'un and the deposits of inscribed oracle bones. It was commerce in oracle bones—considered in the late nineteenth century AD by Chinese apothecaries to have strong medicinal powers—that first drew scholars' attention to the site. The 'dragon bones', as they were called, provide invaluable details of Shang life and culture, and their inscriptions bear witness to the advent of literacy. The origins of the Shang script, the pictograms from which derive Chinese characters, may be the marks of ownership or manufacture inscribed on neolithic pottery. Actual inscriptions on the oracle bones or tortoise shells usually comprise a question and an answer. The ancestral spirits were looked upon as powerful guardians; descendants zealously sought their goodwill by means of offerings, such as food cooked in bronze vessels, and asked their advice by means of scapulimancy and plastromancy.

Ancient China.

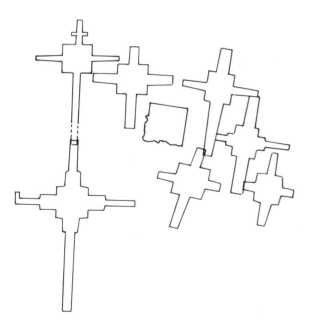

Entirely familiar in the Bronze Age was the funeral megalomania of Shang kings. The ten or eleven 'royal tombs' at Wu-kuan-ts'un were built and furnished on the grand scale. Oriented north–south, they were approached by long ramps on two or four sides. One of these graves has a burial pit about 15 by 20 yd (14 by 18 m) deep. A ramp leads from the ground to the bottom of the pit on each of the four sides; the southern ramp measures more than 35 yd (32 m). A wooden chamber in the burial pit itself contained the deceased ruler, while placed on adjacent ledges and on the ramps were human and animal sacrifices. In sum the number of victims is 131: 52 animals and 79 human beings.

Economy and society

Behind this bloody tribute stood a body of religious ideas and cultic practices which were later transformed by Confucius (551–479 BC) and his followers into the state religion of China. Human sacrifice declined sharply after the end of the Shang dynasty. The continuity of Shang and the rest of ancient Chinese civilization lies in the rites of ancestor worship performed by the priest-king.

Anyang 'royal' tombs.

The Shang nobles were a closely knit kinship group, whose chief member, the king, traced his line of descent from their supreme god, Shang Ti, the founder-ancestor of their people and the present ruler of the natural world. Shang Ti was thought of as ruling on high, and his realm extended beyond the world of their ancestors to include control of the great natural phenomena–sun, moon, stars, rain, wind and thunder. When a king died, he went up to heaven to join his great ancestor, bequeathing to his eldest son the role of chief worshipper in the ancestor cult. Upon the benevolence of Shang Ti and the honoured dead everything depended: they received the appropriate sacrifices for the seasons and major events, besides providing guidance when governmental decisions were necessary. The king was the Son of Heaven, and his terrestrial authority inextricably bound up with divine approval. Thus the usurpation of T'ang was justified by such signs as eclipses and floods.

Affairs of state were in the hands of the king. He decided policy, fixed tribute, commanded the army, now equipped with the chariot and the bow, and oversaw hydraulic conservancy schemes. Water-control works were always fundamental to Chinese civilization, and probably the earliest projects in the Yellow river valley underpinned the first social structure there. The legendary Yu–commended to T'ang on his accession–had 'mastered the waters of the Great Deluge' by deepening channels and conducting the streams to the sea. For this singular achievement Yu earned the privilege of founding China's first dynasty, the Hsia. The mobilization of labour in the corvée permitted not only irrigation and flood prevention on an increasingly larger scale but even more it confirmed the position of the ruler at the top of a feudal society.

'Water benefits' greatly assisted the Shang farmers. Crops were millet, wheat and rice, and known animals

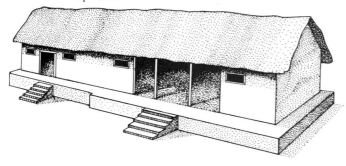

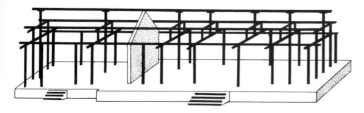

A representative 'palace' building at Anyang, one of the Shang capitals.

included oxen, sheep, horses, goats, dogs, chicken and pigs. Hunting and fishing would have contributed protein, too. The agricultural surplus, the result of irrigation and hard work, supported the nobility and their retainers as well as the craftsmen, who may have formed a hereditary group. Handicrafts comprised work in clay, bronze, bone, leather, stone, jade, wood, silk and wool. Outstanding in quality and style are Shang bronze casting and jade carving.

Architecture

The chief method of wall construction was tamped or rammed earth. Wooden shuttering was used, dry earth being rammed until solid. Then, the shuttering would be removed and the process repeated at a higher level. Bamboo or another wooden material might be placed between each layer to absorb moisture. Earthen walls must have determined the two characteristic features of Chinese architecture, namely that walls were not in general weight-bearing, and that buildings were furnished with generously overhanging eaves.

At Anyang there are several palatial buildings erected on stamped earthen terraces. One of these raised floors is more than a yard thick. Stone pillar bases were placed on the earth foundation, and from ash deposits we can assume that pillars, cross beams and ridgepoles were made of wood. A representative building with 31 pillars was divided into two sections: each section had a hall onto which opened rooms, in one case seven, in the other four. The entire structure was finished with earthen walls, finely plastered, and a roof composed of a mixture of grass, thatch, rushes and bamboo. It is quite likely that some of the Anyang palaces had a second storey. During the laying of foundations both human beings and animals were ritually killed and interred.

Two other kinds of structure are identified. First, there are the homes of ordinary people. Most of these were semi-subterranean buildings, with floors as much as 9 ft (2.7 m) below ground level. Their underground location may be seen as a protection from the bitter, dust-laden winds blowing off the Gobi desert. Usually 14 ft (4.3 m) in diameter, they had outer earthen walls and stone-based centre columns as well as subsidiary posts that supported overhanging thatched roofs. The earthen steps down into these humble dwellings and those giving access to the terraces on which stood the houses of nobles appear to have determined the everyday usage for visiting and movement: the Shang Chinese said 'ascend and descent' for 'come and go'. The second kind of structure, likewise underground, is connected with economic activity. Some of these functioned as small workshops, others as storage pits. At Anyang we can confidently say that the deep-sunken pits were used as granaries, except in one case where thousands of fragments of inscribed bones and hundreds of tortoise shells divulge an archive.

The extent of the Shang cultural area

By the beginning of the second millennium BC the Lung-shan cultures of northern China were approaching the threshold of civilization. In Honan, as we have seen, the earliest known phase of Chinese civilization emerged under the Shang dynasty. When P'an Keng founded Anyang about 1384 BC, a mature cultural stage was already in existence, marked by city life, writing, metallurgy and impressive art. Though the power of the ruler of Anyang was centred in the Yellow river valley, the traditional area of authority, the Shang state may have exercised suzerainty over the incipient civilizations in the Huai river valley, on the northern bank of the Yang-tze river, and in the Shantung peninsula. Recent excavation suggests a widely spread cultural influence. The fall of the Shang dynasty itself was connected with the rise of one of these tributary areas, the Wei river valley, upstream from Anyang. From there the Chou people descended to overthrow the last Shang king, the tyrannical Chou Hsin. That the new Chou dynasty took over the apparatus of Shang state largely as it was points to the formative role of the Shang kings in establishing Chinese civilization.

A tamped or rammed earth wall under construction.

Chou

Arthur Cotterell

Historical outline

The overthrow of the last Shang king, wicked Chou Hsin, by Wu-wang of Chou was seen by later Chinese as a justified rebellion. Ancient historians perceived events as moving in cycles, whereby a new cycle began when a new hero-sage toppled the worthless tyrant of the old house and set up a new rule. From the fall of Chou Hsin the philosopher Mencius (c390–305 BC) even constructed a theory of the right of rebellion against unjust rulers.

The historical circumstances of the collapse of the Shang dynasty were more complex and obscure. Shang rulers appear to have weakened themselves with ceaseless campaigns in the Huai river valley. Possibly their rule became oppressive, especially if tributary peoples were expected to furnish victims for sacrifice. Neglect of the western approaches to their kingdom may account for the rise of the Chou people, who in the generation before Wu-wang remained half nomadic and half agricultural. Ch'ang, the predecessor of Wu-wang, established the first capital at Hao in the Wei valley. The date for the capture of Anyang is uncertain, but Wu-wang's attack can be said to have occurred some time between 1122 and 1027 BC. The issue of the struggle was for some time in doubt. It was the fourth son of Ch'ang, Tan, the duke of Chou, who finally established the new dynasty when, after the death of Wu-wang, he acted as regent for the young king, Ch'eng. This elder statesman was credited with great wisdom by Chinese historians. Looking back on these early years from the confusion at

the end of the Chou dynasty, many scholars, the philosopher Confucius (551–479 BC) among them, regarded this period as a lost ideal. The duke of Chou had shown proper respect for the fallen house–one of the remaining Shang princes was invested with the fief of Sung in order that the ancestral sacrifices might be continued–and his treatment of the state officials was a sign of the value he attached to peace. They were found employment under the new dynasty. The relative backwardness of the Chou people may have inclined them to this policy of assimilation. Their early bronze vessels were less fine than late Shang, but not for long, and their contributions in both religion and politics brought the feudal system to full maturity. The country was partitioned into fiefs, held by the great nobles, who were liable to render war services at the king's behest. The nobility was divided into grades, duke, count and baron; the gentry, 'sons of lords', served both the king and the feudal lords. Supporting the whole system was the labour of the peasant farmers; they sustained society by producing an agricultural surplus and by providing unpaid labour in the form of the corvée. The slave class in evidence under the Shang kings largely disappeared.

The period of the Chou, the longest dynasty in Chinese history, lasted till 256 BC. It witnessed fundamental changes in society and mental outlook, so that conditions were prepared for the unification of China in 221 BC and the establishment of an imperial system that was to last two thousand years. The Middle Kingdom, as the territories in northern China by now termed themselves, enjoyed stability till 771 BC, when the feudal system broke down as a result of an alliance of barbarian tribesmen with the relatives of the queen, who had been set aside because of the king's infatuation with a favourite concubine. Hao was sacked and the monarch slain. The house of Chou recovered from this catastrophe, though a new capital had to be established in a safer place at Loyang, far downstream. Royal authority was broken and power transferred to the nobles holding great fiefs, soon independent states in all but name.

The Spring and Autumn period (722–481 BC), called after annals of the same name, demonstrated the weakness of the Chou kings. They gradually lost their power and authority, retaining undisputed only a religious function in the small and impoverished royal domain surrounding Loyang. With the decay of feudal obligations and the undermining of central authority, the emergent states fought each other for land and competed to attract technicians and peasant farmers. In the west primitive Ch'in encouraged immigration from rival states by offering houses and exemption from military service. Incessant warfare, either between the Chinese themselves or with invading barbarians from the northern steppes, brought about a substantial reduction in the number of states. In the eighth century BC 200 feudal territories existed; by 500 BC less than 20

states could boast their independence. The climax of the internecine struggle happened in the Warring States period (481–221 BC). The chief competitors for supremacy were the states of Ch'in and Ch'u.

The rise of Ch'in seemed phenomenal. Its hard-bitten rulers cut their way to power so decisively that they were compared to silkworms devouring a mulberry leaf. In 316 BC the conquest of Shu and Pa, modern Szechuan, had added valuable resources and outflanked Ch'u on the upper Yang-tze river. An extensive irrigation scheme near Cheng-tu quickly turned the area into a granary. More important still was the digging of the Chengkuo canal, which connected the Ching and Lo rivers north of the Wei valley. This massive project, finished in 246 BC, transformed what is now central Shensi into the first key economic area, an area where agricultural productivity and facilities of transport permitted a supply of grain so superior to that of other areas, that the people who controlled it could control all China.

The construction of large-scale hydraulic conservancy schemes strengthened the authority of the Ch'in rulers at the expense of the nobility, and a more streamlined state emerged, the predecessor of the bureaucratic system that later comprised the Chinese empire. The court ceased to be the preserve of the highborn. Ch'in princes attracted the able and rewarded those who would advance their ambitions. Such a man was Shang Yang, who served Ch'in from 350 to 338 BC. His settled policy was outright aggression, in true fascist manner the subservience of everything to the will of the warlike ruler. He said that it should be made worse for people to fall into the hands of the police than to fight the forces of an enemy state. This philosophy, known as the School of Law, legitimized the authoritarianism of the Ch'in state. Possibly its semi-barbarian population accounts for the un-Chinese outlook. Without doubt the Legalist principle assisted Ch'in war aims, though economic factors were of crucial influence. Apart from the improvement in agricultural output, the state foundries appear to have developed strong cast-iron or possibly steel weapons – the means of the overwhelming victories that eclipsed all rival states. In 246 BC the last Chou ruler was deposed and within 25 years Prince Cheng could title himself Ch'in Shih-huang-ti, 'the First Ch'in Emperor'.

Alongside the process of centralization that led to the foundation in 221 BC of a unified empire organized by bureaucratic officials, an equally significant social revolution was taking place. In place of the old feudal structure, with its sharp division between a hereditary nobility and a peasantry, a more complex community evolved, so that all sections of society became the First Emperor's subjects, likewise divided, but by less insurmountable barriers than birth. The twin pillars of imperial society were to be a progressively more privileged bureaucracy closely connected with the landown-

The duke of Chou addressing the officials of the deposed Shang dynasty in the new city of Lo.

ing class, and the great multitude of farmers, no longer tied to a feudal lord but now liable to taxation, labour on public works, and military service.

During the Warring States period the four famous estates of Chinese society were first recognized. These classes, in order of precedence, were *shih*, the lesser nobility, that is the gentry, knights and scholars; *nung*, the peasant farmers; *kung*, the artisans; and *shang*, the merchants. The low social position of the merchants—a prevailing feature in Chinese history—was the natural outcome of economic development down to 221 BC, because princes assumed most of the responsibility for industry and water-control works. Metallurgy tended to be under state supervision, as in the Shang dynasty, and the distribution of metal weapons and implements was held to be a matter of important policy.

Out of the conflict between states and within states arose a new social class, just below the feudal hierarchy. This was the *shih*. With the blurring of feudal distinctions and the disappearance of so many states the rights of birth seemed to count for less than ability and talent. A growing surplus of younger sons, educated but without rank, took advantage of whatever opportunities offered themselves. These usually were service with a state or a noble family. During the turmoil of the Warring States period itinerant members of this class were willing to sell their skills to the highest bidder. Mencius noted sadly that princes only welcomed those with destructive projects. Military service itself of course offered another, if socially less distinguished, career.

The *nung*, the peasant farmers, were always highly regarded and overworked. Their poverty was a continual complaint, though successive rulers sought to protect honest countryman. Moreover, the introduction of private ownership of land in Ch'in, a policy of Yang Shang, led to the impoverished selling out and becoming tenants or sharecroppers. The lot of the *nung* was eased by the rapid strides in iron technology and it is arguable that improved tools put an end to the Shang legacy of slavery. As decisive an influence on the social structure was the crossbow, another early technical achievement. The feudal levies fired these weapons from the numerous defensive walls. At a time when armour was rudimentary these powerful weapons gave the nobles no tactical advantage, such as that of the armoured knight in the West, and Mencius could reasonably talk about the right of the people to overthrow tyrants.

Whereas the *kung*, the artisans, continued to work in foundries and workshops close by cities, the *shang*, the merchants, who traded in the products they made, as well as raw materials, were less fixed in their places of habitation. Taking advantage of improved communications, both road and canal, the merchants plied their trade the length and breadth of the Middle Kingdom. Commodities exchanged were iron, salt, fish, lacquer, silk, wood, precious stones, bronze vessels, cloth, and musical instruments. The minting of coins in copper and gold denominations occurred well before the Warring States period. The *shang* gathered wealth and not prestige, since their sons were debarred from official

Peasant farmers, *nung*, at work in the fields with iron implements. A rubbing from a Han stone relief.

appointments and their property subject to heavy taxation.

'A hundred schools contend'

The turmoil of the Warring States period was unprecedented in ancient China. The confusion and uncertainty of the age jarred with an increasing prosperity as cities grew in size, technology advanced, and trade flourished. Rulers appeared indifferent to anything but personal gain. Only the glibbest advisers could expect to make careers for themselves and avoid miserable ends. Even a successful policy-maker like Shang Yang could find that execution awaited him at the end of his service in 338 BC. The political troubles were lamented by scores of philosophers who keenly felt their own marginal influence on contemporary events. Their frustration called forth an intellectual ferment unmatched in the later monolithic unity of the Chinese empire. They were compelled to write books because kings would rarely listen to their advice; they were obliged to sigh for the order of the Early Chou period (1027–771 BC) because conditions were not immediately suited to an alternative to feudalism. Not until 221 BC did the king of Ch'in complete his conquest of the other states, unite the Middle Kingdom under his rule, and impose a bureaucratic empire that left room for neither feudal sentiment nor local variation. Everything was standardized, including thought. The reaction toppled the second Ch'in emperor in less than a generation and inaugurated the compromise of the Han dynasty.

The Warring States period was the time of the Hundred Schools, when roving philosophers offered advice to any lord who would listen to them or collected followers in order to establish a body of teachings. Apart from Han Fei-tzu (c280–233 BC), who was a prince of the royal family of the small state of Han, the philosophers seem to have been *shih*, members of the scholar-gentry. Their social position entitled them to a freedom of thought and movement that was denied to the noblemen above them, as it was also to the peasant farmers beneath them. Four main philosophies evolved:

Confucianism (*ju chia*), Taoism (*tao chia*), Mohism (*mo chia*), and Legalism (*fa chia*). Because of the lasting importance of Confucianism and Taoism, two mutually opposed systems of thought, we shall discuss each separately, but first a word is required on Mohism and Legalism, the most heatedly debated philosphies of the period.

Mo-tzu (*c*479–438 BC), we are told, once served as a minister in the state of Sung. Yet he would appear to have travelled extensively, visiting one state after another in an attempt to spread his doctrine of universal love and to dissuade feudal rulers from attacks on each other. On one occasion Mo-tzu succeeded in persuading the king of Ch'u to disband an expedition against Sung. In his own native state of Lu he ran a school or academy like Confucious before him, and from there his followers intervened in political squabbles, offering both ethical exhortation and practical aid. Moists hastened to the relief of beleaguered states, and since many of these men were artisans skilled in the art of military defence, their arrival was often timely.

Above all Mo-tzu attacked the abuses of the feudal aristocrats and the scholar-gentry. He was filled with compassion for the common people. 'The man of Ch'u is my brother', he said to his disciples, lest they restrict affection to family, clan or even the purely Chinese feudal states north of the Yang-tze river. The chief target of Mo-tzu was filial piety, so dear to the Confucians, though he stopped short of the condemnation of feudalism enunciated in Taoism. 'The Confucians', Mo-tzu complained, 'corrupt men with their elaborate and showy rites and music and deceive parents with lengthy mournings and hypocritical grief. They propound fatalism, ignore poverty, and behave with tremendous arrogance.' Mencius regarded such views as the greatest threat to the Confucian concept of unselfish but carefully graded benevolence and kindness towards others. But he had to agree with Mo-tzu over the need for moderation in funerals, especially when the families of princes filled tombs with 'those who are chosen to accompany the dead'. Human sacrifice was anathema to both philosophers. The decline of Moist philosophy under the Han emperors may have been the result of the affluence then enjoyed by educated men. Stable political conditions led to a growing sophistication and rationalism, which had little interest in vengeful ghosts. Mo-tzu had argued: 'If the fact that the ghosts and spirits reward the worthy and punish the evil can be made a cornerstone of policy in a state and impressed upon the people, it will provide a means to bring order to the state and benefit to the people.' Popular Taoism was to absorb the ancient beliefs in the spirit world that Mo-tzu had so fervently affirmed.

The teacher of Han Fei-tzu, the chief exponent of Legalism, was the heterodox Confucian philosopher Hsun-tzu (320–235 BC), who believed that the nature of man was basically evil. This initial thesis led Hsun-tzu to place tremendous emphasis upon the need for education and moral training. It contrasts sharply with orthodox Confucianism as propounded by Mencius, who saw man

as naturally inclined to goodness. To Hsun-tzu the spiritual realm was a polite fiction and he poked fun at ceremonies devised to obtain heavenly favours like rain. 'They are done', he wrote, 'merely for ornament. Hence the gentleman regards them as ornaments, but the common people regard them as supernatural.' Rites and ceremonies were considered necessary for society, not heaven. 'The ancient kings hated disorder (resulting from the self-seeking of men), and so they established ritual practices in order to curb it, to train men's desires and to provide for their satisfaction.' The ruler, a man whose intelligence and knowledge had outstripped his fellows, governed fairly and used the best abilities of his subordinates. Hsun-tzu visited Ch'in, and recognized the military and economic accomplishments of its rulers, yet he deplored their reliance on naked force and terrorism.

Legalism addressed itself exclusively to the feudal rulers. Neither the hallowed customs of the past nor the private lives of individuals were its concern, except to the extent they effected the interests of the ruling class. The only goal was to teach the ruler how to survive and prosper in the present world. Crucial to this aim was *fa*, positive law. Following the precepts of Shang Yang, Han Fei-tzu held that an elaborate system of laws backed by inescapable punishments was necessary for a strong state. 'If the laws are weak,' he wrote, 'so is the kingdom.' Above the law himself, the ruler kept a tight rein on his bureaucratic subordinates and their activities. 'He does not let cities grow too large', nor powerful families too rich. 'The ruler alone should possess the power,' Han Fei-tzu insisted, 'wielding it like lightning or like thunder.' Obedience to the letter of the law was demanded. As a consequence the ordinary relations that exist between people were proscribed by the Legalists. It was this lack of mercy in daily life, an intolerable social trait to the ancient Chinese, that helped to engineer the downfall of the Ch'in empire. The success of Liu Pang, the usurping first Han emperor, was due in part to an overestimation of the amount of bullying and oppression the people of the Middle Kingdom would stand.

Taoism

The first of the 'irresponsible hermits', according to the Confucians, was Li Er, the 'madman of Ch'u', but it has become usual to refer to the founder of Taoism as Lao-tzu, the Old Philosopher. He may have been keeper of the royal archives at Loyang, the Chou capital, but few details are known of his life. Even his birthdate, 604 BC, is disputed. There is no doubt, however, concerning the seminal influence of the book associated with his name, the *Tao Teh Ching* (*The Way of Virtue*). Its five thousand or so characters have been read and reread by every generation of Chinese. The lapidary and paradoxical style has defied successive translations, not least because the content represents an esoteric wisdom. 'Those who know don't tell,' Lao-tzu coyly remarked, 'and those who tell don't know.' Taoist quietism was not something to be bruited from the rooftops. On the contrary, the masters kept silent in the presence of strangers; in regard to their disciples, they took into account their readiness for wisdom. Fables and anecdotes were always favoured in teaching.

The Way of Virtue contains many apt comments on the Warring State period. The senseless rivalry of princes is placed in a cosmic perspective, though the delight in humour is perhaps the notable difference from Confucian seriousness. 'He who feels punctured must have been a bubble.' And 'He who feels unarmed must have been armed.' What exercised Lao-tzu's mind was man's rootedness in Nature, the inner power that made all men wiser than they knew. 'Knowledge studies others; wisdom is self-known.' The artificial demands of feudal society had disturbed the innate abilities of men. Instead of following the natural way (*tao*), codes of love and honesty were invented to provide people with a new social ethic. Learning became necessary and charity was prized because kindness could not be expected from everyone. Most unfortunate was the Confucian emphasis on the family, the preoccupation with benevolent fathers and dutiful sons. To the Taoists social evolution had taken a wrong course with feudalism. They harked back to the primitive collectivist society that was supposed to have existed prior to the Hsia dynasty. Reluctance to take office or to attempt reform sprang from the belief that things were best left alone. It was summed up in the concept of *jang*, or yieldingness. 'The wise man keeps to the deed that consists in taking no action and practises the teaching that uses no words.' The sign of the sage is effective non-assertion. He gives up in order to get; he relinquishes control in order to understand–he welcomes a relationship that is mutual, he is moved by a sense of profound non-possessiveness. The historical origin of this fundamental Taoist idea could have been the potlatch, a ceremony of largesse common in primitive collectivist societies. During the Warring States period it caused Chuang-tzu (350–275 BC), the most distinguished follower of Lao-tzu, to turn down the premiership of the state of Ch'u.

According to Hsun-tzu, the Taoists were entirely misguided in their concentration on Nature. He marvelled that they devoted themselves to study and contemplation without ever trying to exploit their findings. He was baffled by their interest in 'things the knowledge of which does not benefit men, and ignorance concerning which does no harm to men'. In fact this detached outlook proved to be important for the development of science in China, since it has been plausibly argued that Taoist observation and experiments in alchemy equal the dim beginnings of scientific method. Furthermore, Hsun-tzu's scepticism was not generally shared where alchemical research was involved. The Taoist pursuit of an elixir of life, a way to longevity, attracted feudal rulers and later emperors. The persistent belief in a chemical means of immortality is revealed in an incident recorded in the ninth century AD. The chance excavation of a long-buried stone box filled with silk disturbed a grey-haired man of dignified mien who arose, adjusted his clothing, and then disappeared. Not for nothing was another root of Taoism the magic of the *wu*–female and male thaumaturges. Their sympathetic magic eased the lot of the hard-pressed peasant farmers by placating malignant spirits and invoking those more kindly disposed. Details of a ceremony of exposure survive; it suggests that the drops of sweat shed by the sorcerer, dancing within a circle under the blazing sun, were expected to induce drops of rain. The psychic powers of the *wu* also enabled contact to be made with departed spirits, though their abilities in this direction were unappreciated by the nobility. In opposition to Confucian ethics, Taoism drew upon the primitive strength of these thaumaturges, whose shamanism was later reinforced by invaders from the northern steppes, and in the process the philosophy of Lao-tzu and his followers was eventually subsumed in Taoist religion. During the crisis of the early empire after AD 220 Taoism became the indigenous religion of personal salvation. It provided solace for the *nung*.

Confucianism

Referring to the Taoists, Confucius said: 'They dislike me because I want to reform society, but if we are not to live with our fellow men with whom can we live? We cannot live with animals. If society was as it ought to be, I should not be seeking change.' It was a point constantly made by the Confucians: their doctrine rested on this worldly social-mindedness.

Kung Fu-tzu, Confucius himself, accepted feudalism wholeheartedly. The abuses prevalent during his lifetime (551–479 BC) set his mind on a course of reform. He strove for justice within the framework of the feudal, or feudal-bureaucratic social order. 'I am a transmitter and not a creator,' he said, 'I believe in the past and love it.' Yet Confucius failed to obtain any official appointment of note, probably because he was disinclined to flatter or conduct intrigues. Temperamentally a teacher rather than a politician, he found that through his followers an influence could be exerted on the feudal courts, once kings appreciated the value of officials who prized loyalty to principles, not factions. The students of Confucius were never chosen on grounds of birth. The only criteria for admission to this school were virtuous conduct, intelligence, and a willingness to study. Confucius commended in his teachings the renowned rulers of former days, kings and princes whose benevolence (*jen*) and propriety (*li*) had led their subjects to prefect lives. Tan, the duke of Chou, was held up as a prime example of the aristocratic sage. The very character for *li* tells us a little about Confucius' original idea. The strokes represent a sacrificial vessel in which precious objects have been placed as a sacrifice to the ancestral spirits. The rites of ancestor worship, elevated into a moral code by his philosophy, were the meeting point of two worlds, the spiritual and the temporal. Here heavenly benefits were bestowed on the dutiful descendant, the preserver of traditional values.

The attitude of Confucius to religion was practical. 'I stand in awe of the spirits,' he told his students, 'but keep them at a distance.' This is neither the thoroughgoing rationalism of Husn-tzu nor even a sceptical point of

Confucius (551–479 BC) founded a school of philosophy that was to influence the development of Chinese civilization for two thousand years.

help in introducing a sense of balance in the supernatural world as well as on the earthly level. In Chinese civilization 'holy wars' were conspicuous by their absence. Though Confucius died a disappointed man, apparently ineffectual against feudal decline, the later influence of his philosophy was so immense that he has been acclaimed the 'uncrowned emperor' of China.

Instrumental in advancing the fortunes of Confucianism was Meng-tzu, or Mencius, who lived in the fourth century BC. He dealt with opposing philosophies, especially Moism, and developed the doctrine of mankind's natural goodness. He was also the archetype of the filial son, the upholder of the family against the encroaching state. Whenever a ruler lost the goodwill of his subjects and resorted to oppression, the heavenly mandate was said to be withdrawn and rebellion justified. This constitutional safety valve was to prove of tremendous value to the Chinese empire. It was a democratic theory which Mencius elaborated from the famous saying in the *Shu Ching* (*Book of Documents*) that 'Heaven sees according as the people see, heaven hears according as the people hear.' Speaking of the callousness of some feudal rulers, he said: 'A benevolent man extends his love from those he loves to those he does not love. A ruthless man extends his ruthlessness from those he does not love to those he loves.' Kindness was the sign of the real man, unkindness and cruelty being explained in the surprisingly modern terms of social deprivation. Proper upbringing was essential. To a disciple Mencius once remarked, 'A trail through the mountains, if used, becomes a path in a short time, but, if unused, becomes blocked by grass in an equally short time. Now your heart is blocked by grass.' This accords with the accepted model for the Confucian scholar-official, who staffed the imperial civil service after the founding of the Han dynasty in 207 BC. He was a man firm in principle and benevolent in outlook; he served the throne and protected the ordinary people.

view, but an intimation that the celestial realm was far above men's comprehension: something not readily plumbed by scapulimancy and star-gazing. Nor could natural phenomena, like earthquakes and floods, be so readily interpreted as the will of heaven. Nevertheless, the reluctance of Confucius to pronounce on religion did

Imperial Unification

Arthur Cotterell

Four issues dominate the history of the early Chinese empire, its administration, the direction of the economy, the intrigues of powerful families and the northern frontier. Ch'in and Han emperors struggled with the problems these threw up, and the deposition of the usurping Hsin emperor, the reformer Wang Mang, was caused in AD 23 by a combination of them all.

The Ch'in dynasty (221 to 207 BC)
By 221 BC all resistance from other feudal rulers had ended and Prince Cheng could style himself Ch'in Shih-huang-ti, 'the First Ch'in Emperor'. The new title was

adopted to show his supremacy over the kings (*wang*) whom he had dethroned. It may have contained the notion of divinity, or divine favour. Although the Ch'in dynasty was of short duration, such was the energy and determination of its founder that this period represents a turning point in the history of Chinese civilization. The bureaucratic type of government developed under the centralized Ch'in monarchy became the model for future Chinese political organization, lasting until modern times. The significance of the revolutionary change that Ch'in Shih-huang-ti began and Liu Pang, the founder of the following Han dynasty, completed cannot be underestimated. Ancient Chinese civilization flowered within the framework of a unified empire.

Ch'in Shih-huang-ti preferred precept to example. He issued edicts intended to control his subjects, harness their strength, and exploit natural resources in order to enrich and strengthen the state. In his drive for uniformity he became one of the great destroyers of history. Lacking any degree of economic integration, the Ch'in empire was insecure in two main directions—the east and the north. The deposed aristocracy of the old feudal states posed an internal threat, especially in the lower Yellow river valley, and on the northern steppes there was danger from the Hsiung Nu nomads, probably the Huns who invaded the Roman empire in the fifth century AD. Military strength seemed the best answer. Feudal holdings were abolished and the nobles compelled to live in the west, away from their supporters; peasant farmers received greater rights over their land, but became liable for taxes; the empire was divided into new administrative districts and garrisons were planted at strategic locations; there was standardization of weights and measures, currency, written language, vehicle axles; a national road network was built and canals improved for the supply of the army. When Ch'in Shih-huang-ti discovered that these innovations drew criticism from the scholar-gentry, he ordered that all schools of philosophy were to shut and all books were to be burned, except for the writings of the authoritarian Legalists and useful works on medicine, divination and agriculture.

Folk song records the equal dislike of ordinary people for the severity of the Ch'in dynasty. Their discontent was focused on the construction of the Great Wall, started in 214 BC. Thousands toiled on the line of fortresses designed to contain the Hsiung Nu, suffering and dying in the cold mountains and desert lands of the northern frontier. Casualties remain unknown, yet apparent is the acceleration of social change brought about by the almost continuous use of the corvée. Surnames began to appear for the first time. There was room in the administrative hierarchy for a new man literally to make name for himself. Ch'in Shih-huang-ti refused to invest any of his own sons or relatives with fiefs, arguing that the existence of such local ties was the prime cause of the divisions and wars that had plagued China for the previous five hundred years.

A court intrigue on the death of Ch'in Shih-huang-ti in 210 BC gave the oppressed Chinese an opportunity to revolt. That the imperial armies were not then concentrated in the west near the Ch'in capital but were dispersed in garrisons all over the empire played into the hands of the rebels. Some of these troops, led by their commanders, also revolted. A complicated struggle ensued between several insurgent groups and the second Ch'in emperor until in 202 BC Liu Pang gained overall control.

The Great Wall of China near Peking, as rebuilt under the Ming dynasty (AD 1368–1644).

Former Han (207 BC to AD 9)

The social origins of Liu Pang, the first Han emperor Kao-tzu, were extremely humble. The *Ch'ien-Han Shu* (History of the Former Han) recalls the remarkable physiognomy of Liu Pang, his prominent nose, 'dragon forehead' and the 'seventy-two black moles' on his left thigh, as well as the scaly dragon that appeared to his mother at his conception, but it cannot disguise the historical fact of a peasant background. Han Kao-tzu was almost certainly illiterate and not a little intolerant of scholars. His accession represents a popular movement. On the throne he neither aped aristocratic manners nor slackened his compassion for ordinary people, and his habit of squatting down, coupled with an earthy vocabulary, unsettled polite courtiers. Yet Han Kao-tzu had the wit to appreciate the value of learned and cultivated advisers and assistants. His chamberlain was commissioned to write a treatise on statecraft and another official arranged a court ceremonial for his boisterous personal followers. The emperor's only instruction on the latter was 'Make it easy'.

The early Han emperors ruled carefully and skilfully. Han Kao-tzu (207–195 BC) settled for a compromise after the oppression of Ch'in; he granted fiefs to close relatives and allowed the restoration of certain feudal houses, but their diminished holdings were intertwined with districts ruled by imperial officers. A rebellion among the eastern landholders in 154 BC was used by emperor Han Ching-ti (156–141 BC) to alter the laws of inheritance. Thereafter all sons were co-heirs to their father and land was divided between them. This amendment did much to quicken the breakdown of large units into little more than substantial country estates. The emperor Han Wu-ti (141–87 BC) completed the

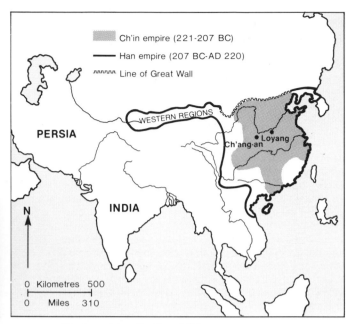

Ch'in empire (221-207 BC)

Han empire (207 BC-AD 220)

Line of Great Wall

PERSIA

WESTERN REGIONS

Ch'ang-an • Loyang

INDIA

N

0 Kilometres 500

0 Miles 310

The imperial unification of China.

dispossession of the old aristocracy by means of harsh officials (*k'u-li*) who moved against powerful families, whether of ancient lineage or recent origin.

The retention of the administrative structure of the Ch'in empire made possible the revival of scholarship. The Han emperors needed a civil service and they soon found in Confucian scholars excellent administrators. There were strenuous arguments between officials who favoured a Ch'in-like approach to government and those who looked back to the less involved rule of the Chou kings, but by the usurpation of Wang Mang (AD 9–22) the tenor of thought was primarily Confucian. Han Kao-tsu first summoned to the capital Chang-an, 'men of wisdom and virtue' and 'men of letters'. The first emperor known to have set examination questions was Han Wu-ti in 130 BC. When the grand minister of ceremonies advised the emperor on the grading of the answers from the hundred recommended candidates, Han Wu-ti could not accept the poor mark awarded to a certain Hung Kung-sun, who was so poor he supported his family by breeding pigs. Hung Kung-sun impressed the emperor with his honesty, erudition and Confucianism, eventually rising in 125 BC to the highest post in the civil service, that of imperial chancellor. The questions (*ts'e*) and answers (*tui-ts'e*) were the first steps towards the regular examination system established after AD 600. During the Han period such tests were only held when the emperor deemed them necessary. In 130 BC Han Wu-ti clearly took advantage of the practice to recruit officials inclined to his own view of administration.

In 124 BC the Imperial University (*Poh Shih Kuan*) was founded. There were separate departments for each of the great books of tradition: the *I Ching* (*Book of Changes*), the *Shu Ching* (Book of Documents), the *Shih Ching* (Book of Odes), *Ch'un Ch'iu* (*Spring and Autumn Annals*), the *Li Chi* (*Book of Rites*), the *Chou Li* (*Book of Ceremonial Usage*), and the *I Li* (*Book of Ceremonies*). History fascinated the Han Chinese, the most distinguished historian being Ssu-ma Ch'ien (*c*145–90 BC) His *Shih Chi* (*Records of the Historian*) marks a watershed in historical thought because Ssu-ma Ch'ien included social and economic considerations in the study of the past. Not lost on him was the importance of the Chengkuo canal in the rise of Ch'in. No account, however, is given of the reign of Han Wu-ti. In 99 BC a memorial Ssu-ma Ch'ien wrote about the wars with Hsiung Nu was misunderstood by the throne and manipulated by his opponents; the result was the charge of attempting to deceive the emperor, a perfunctory trial, and castration. Presumably the missing section contained all the historian's venom over his unjust humiliation.

Han Wu-ti himself was a forceful ruler, chiefly occupied with the direction of the economy and the security of the northern frontier. He seems to have avoided the court intrigues that beset other emperors by the desperate expedient of slaughtering his wife's relations. Political complications tended to arise in the imperial palace with plots centred on the consort family, the relations of the empress. Early imperial China had no civilized neighbours to provide royal brides for the emperor and so the ennoblement of the empress's family led to a power struggle with the old consort family, the relatives of the emperor's mother. The family of Wang Mang had been influential at court through marriage for two decades before his usurpation of the throne (AD 9).

Action in the economic sphere was forced on Han Wu-ti by mounting difficulties in the production and distribution of basic commodities. Inflation was encouraged by the private minting of coin. The emperor called in these copper coins by issuing treasury notes made from the skin of a white stag. He also declared in 120–119 BC a state monopoly over the iron and salt industries. At first he gave charge to leading courtiers but their incompetence compelled the recruitment of salt boilers and ironmasters, merchants expert in the key industries. The *Yen-t'ieh lun* (Discourses on Salt and Iron) record the philosophical debate over this extension of public control. Despite the opposition of the Confucianists the arrangement became a fundamental part of imperial policy, though the monopoly on the production of alcoholic spirits declared in 98 BC was later dropped. To counter speculation in foodstuffs Han Wu-ti established public granaries and ordered provincial officials to buy grain when prices were low and to sell in times of shortage. This was known as the levelling system (*p'ing chang*), which even Ssu-ma Ch'ien had to admit was effective in stabilizing prices.

Equally vigorous was the action of Han Wu-ti in dealing with the Hsiung Nu. The Great Wall of Ch'in Shih-huang-ti only gave partial protection to the northern frontier. Annual gifts to the nomadic Hsiung Nu were necessary from 200 BC, when Han Kao-tsu was almost captured on the battlefield. By the 130s BC nomad incursions and the flight of Chinese rebels to the steppes necessitated a change of approach. The emperor dispatched an envoy westwards to stir up the enemies of the Hsiung Nu there: to the amazement of the Chinese court he reported that another civilization existed in Afghanistan, the recently conquered Graeco-Buddhist kingdom of Bactria. What interested Han Wu-ti, however, were the large horses bred by these westerners, since they could be used to carry heavily armed men against the Hsiung Nu who rode the smaller Mongolian pony. Expeditions by 102 BC had secured enough horses for stud purposes and given China suzerainty over a number of peoples in the 'Western Regions'. Although the new cavalry helped increase Chinese military mobility, the northern frontier remained a constant source of anxiety. No emperor could afford a prolonged war lest the burden on the ordinary people cause a rebellion like the one against the Ch'in dynasty. Chinese foreign policy was always dictated by the need to contain nomad pressure, never by any ambition for foreign acquisitions.

The usurpation of Wang Mang (AD 9 to 23)

Recurring difficulties with the economy and renewed activities by the Hsiung Nu were behind the brief Hsin dynasty. The fall of Wang Mang, the usurping emperor, was similarly connected with the more radical reforms he proposed to solve these problems. A controversial figure, the elder statesman Wang Mang sought to limit the wealth of powerful families, whose holdings of land had increased considerably. Emperor Han Ai-ti (7–1 BC) had tried unsuccessfully to stem this quasi-feudal revival some years before Wang Mang banned the purchase of land and slaves and ordered small families owning large estates to surrender part of their holdings for distribution to those who had none. Re-allocation was justified by reference to land tenure under the early Chou kings, when private property hardly existed. Government loans at low interest rates were offered to peasants for the purchase of tools and seeds. Finance for this regeneration of the countryside was derived from the state monopolies on salt and iron.

Resistance to Wang Mang's measures was aided by the lukewarm attitude of officials, often the relatives of important landowners. It became irresistible when famine and mismanaged relief drove the poorest people into open rebellion. A huge expedition against the Hsiung Nu, a shift in the course of the Yellow river, and severe droughts toppled Wang Mang.

Later Han (AD 24 to 220)

The Later Han emperors were much less independent because in the restoration of the imperial house the first one, Han Kuang-wu (AD 23–58), had to rely on support from the big landowners. In AD 39 he found it impossible to conduct a survey of cultivated land for the purpose of reassessing the land tax. As a result of this central weakness there occurred a gradual resurgence of feudalism. The *nung*, the peasant farmers, became tenants on large estates, sharecroppers, or just wage labourers. Soon artisans (*kung*) and scholars (*shih*) associated themselves with local magnets strong enough to offer protection against bandits or rebellious soldiers. After the abolition of conscription (AD 46) the government was dependent on regular troops and the retainers of powerful families. Underlying military weakness explains too the less aggressive policy adopted on the northern frontier in the second century AD. The Later Han emperors achieved victories with the aid of friendly barbarians. Later, the Western Chin dynasty (AD 265–316) was unable to resist pressure from nomadic and semi-nomadic peoples who had been allies in civil disturbances. By AD 316 everything north of the Yangtzu watershed had fallen to the Tartars.

The decline of the imperial model during Later Han was brought about by factors other than the growth of large estates. The economic pattern of China was undergoing a significant change. When Han Kuang-wu moved the capital downstream from Ch'ang-an, in the Wei river valley, to Loyang, in the lower Yellow river valley, he acknowledged the shift of the key economic area eastwards and southwards. The lower Yellow river valley and the Huai river valley had overtaken Shensi as the most developed region in the empire. The break-up of China in the Three Kingdoms period (AD 221–280) can be seen as a continuation of the same process. Two southern kingdoms–Shu based on the Red river basin of Szechuan and Wu on the lower Yang-tze valley–were sufficiently powerful to challenge for many years the northern state of Wei, the rump of the Han empire. Perhaps the conflict can be attributed to something deeper than economic rivalry. The Ch'in empire had been regarded as an alien imposition throughout China, but the people who lived in the old state of Ch'u (Wu) had more reason to dislike its northwestern austerity. They were heirs to a quite different cultural tradition, one that contained strong maritime and southern elements. Though the compromise of the Han settlement had worked for centuries, the possibility of economic independence in southern China may have been seized upon not so much by an ambitious family as by a people in cultural reaction to the north.

Another contributory factor was the political conflict between the rival factions within the imperial palace. In AD 92 there occurred a bitter dispute between the consort family and the palace eunuchs, who were in league with merchants and the *nouveaux riches*. Han Kwang-wu had first promoted eunuchs so as to check the influence of officials sponsored by the wealthy and well-placed. In the second century AD these men intimidated courtiers and officials alike, till at last their machinations drew the army into politics. The assassination of a renowned general at court brought in AD 189 an immediate response from his troops, who stormed the imperial palace and slaughtered all the eunuchs in sight. The beneficiary of the coup was another general, the soldier-poet Ts'ao Ts'ao (died AD 220). He assumed authority in all but name: the Later Han dynasty was continued as long as politically useful. In AD 220 Ts'ao Ts'ao's son, Ts'ao Pi, could force the puppet emperor to abdicate in his favour.

The Crisis of the Early Empire

Arthur Cotterell

The Three Kingdoms (AD 221 to 65)

Popular discontent against the tyrannical adminis-tration of the eunuchs under the Later Han flared in AD 184 in the rebellion of the Yellow Turbans, a movement with strong Taoist associations. A faith healer and magician found himself the centre of the uprising in the eastern provinces; the movement started in modern Hopeh but quickly spread north, west and south. The rebellious peasants were as convinced that the Han emperors had lost the heavenly mandate as that their own leader had powers capable of restoring to life those who fell on the battlefield. Though by AD 190 the insurgents had exhausted themselves in looting and squabbling, the impact on the tottering empire was overwhelming and the aftermath was a prolonged struggle between the rebels and a number of contending generals. From AD 189 the soldier-poet Ts'ao Ts'ao (AD 150–220) became the dominant figure in northern China. Having demonstrated his military abilities

The Three Kingdoms (AD 221–265).

Division of China during Tartar partition (AD 316-589)
The Three Kingdoms

against the Yellow Turbans, Ts'ao Ts'ao obliged the shaken throne to let him eliminate other military leaders. In AD 208 he felt strong enough to tackle the Sun family, a rival dynasty established on the Yang-tze river valley. The superior nautical skills of the southern-ers discomforted Ts'ao Ts'ao at Ch'i-pi and he had to accept the division of China for the time being. On the accession of his son Ts'ao P'i as the first Wei emperor, after the deposition of Han Hsien-ti in AD 220, the country split into three kingdoms. There was northern Wei, controlled by Ts'ao P'i; Wu south of the Yang-tze under the Sun; and Shu, modern Szechuan, proclaimed by the Liu family, originally allies of the Sun.

The rivalry of the Three Kingdoms (*san kuo*) is celebrated in the famous novel *The Romance of the Three Kingdoms*. To the Chinese the period appears romantic and legendary. From one of the generals they have even derived Kuan Ti, the Confucian god of war. He is not, however, a Mars figure, warlike and implacable, but rather the deity or genius who prevents war. He is regarded as the antithesis of Ts'ao Ts'ao, whose famous epigram was 'I would rather betray the whole world than allow the world betray me.'

The long struggle between the Three Kingdoms was ended in AD 280 by the Western Chin dynasty, which had displaced the Ts'ao line (the Wei house) 15 years earlier. The first Western Chin emperor, Ssu-ma Yen, was another northern general, but he outdid Ts'ao Ts'ao by briefly achieving the reunification of the whole country. Under his direction Wei, the ancient heartland of China, the Middle Kingdom, reasserted its authority over the southwestern and southern regions, two newly developing areas of economic activity. What stood behind the triumph of Wei was its greater concentration on agricultural productivity and water transport as a means of strengthening military power. From AD 241 50,000 men were permanently settled in the Huai river valley as state colonists, to defend the southern frontier and to contribute grain for stockpiling against future campaigns. Local magnates were stripped of their re-tainers but the tendency of the age quickly transformed the officials planted in their place into new magnates themselves. However, by avoiding pitched battles and waging an economic war of attrition Wei was able to reduce Shu (AD 264) and Wu (AD 280).

Western Chin (AD 265 to 316)

The Western Chin dynasty lasted only until AD 316. In that year the northern provinces passed into the hands of peoples from the steppes and the remnants of the Ssu-

A section of the vast underground pottery army of Ch'in Shih-huang-ti, the first emperor of China.

ma house fled southwards to Nanking, on the Yang-tze river, where they managed to set up the diminished Eastern Chin dynasty (AD 317–420).

A combination of pressures brought down the Western Chin and ensured that China should be divided for 273 years. Encroachment from nomads had worried the empire from the reign of Han Kao-tzu (207–195 BC) onwards, but it was the more conciliatory policy inaugurated during Later Han (AD 23–220) that opened the northern frontier to invaders. The price of employing friendly barbarians as allies was the settlement of large numbers within the empire itself. That these people posed an internal threat was not fully appreciated, though Ts'ao Ts'ao had contrived to disperse the largest tribes into smaller groups, each under the supervision of a Chinese official. Periods of civil strife were the most dangerous because opposing groups were tempted to call upon friendly barbarians for aid. This occurred in AD 304. The Hsiung Nu backed one prince and the Hsien Pei, Tartar tribesmen, were enlisted by another. In AD 311 Loyang was sacked and the emperor captured; then in AD 316 the next, and last, Western Chin emperor was also taken prisoner on the fall of Ch'ang-an.

Ssu-ma Yen himself must bear some responsibility for the collapse of the northern provinces. He made a fatal error when he allowed his 25 sons to govern separate areas. It weakened the central government of the restored empire and encouraged fragmentation into quasi-feudal holdings. The family conflict after his death was the nomad opportunity. But it would be wrong to suppose that ferocious invaders conquered an enfeebled China. They did not. In AD 383 the better discipline and equipment of the small Eastern Chin army gave it a decisive victory at Fei Shui over a force reputed to have included 270,000 nomad cavalry. This engagement confirmed the independence of the Chinese living south of the Huai river valley. The nomad threat only became serious when the tribesmen adopted Chinese civilization. One Hsiung Nu chief knew by heart parts of the *Shu Ching* (Book of Odes) and *I Ching* (Book of Changes). His people were equally versed in applied technology. After AD 316 northern China was a battleground of competing barbarian princes, who found themselves exposed to fresh invasion from the steppe lands. In AD 439 a new people, the Toba Tartars, succeeded in subduing the various principalities and uniting all the northern provinces.

Taoist religion

In the first century AD Taoism was converted into a popular faith. It absorbed the magical rites and practices of the countryside, making an appeal to the peasant farmers which Confucianism could not match. The sceptical tenor of Confucian orthodoxy–clearly articulated in the work of Wang Ch'ung (AD 27–97)–kept the rural gods and spirits out of the mainstream of educated

belief, so that Confucianism was the preserve of the scholar-gentry. Though the mass of the people agreed with Confucius on the fundamental importance of the family and respect for ancestors, they wanted something less austere and intellectual. This Taoism provided through the ministry of men like Chang Tao-ling (alleged dates, AD 34–156). He was the first heavenly teacher (*t'ien shih*) of the Taoist church. For a time Chang Tao-ling was able to establish a small, semi-independent state on the borders of Szechuan and Shensi provinces. His organization of the peasants living there into a quasi-religious, quasi-military movement was the first of many such rural ventures. The Yellow Turban rebellion (AD 184–90) drew on Taoist revolutionary doctrines. But Chang Tao-ling was also a precursor of the popular alchemist, since he experimented to find the elixir of immortality. Even the practical and forceful emperor Han Wu-ti (141–87 BC) had not been able to resist the vogue for alchemy, but it was only later that the enthusiasm of ordinary people was aroused. Longevity of course had always been desired by the Chinese, as the ancient ideal of 'five generations beneath one roof' indicates.

Alchemical theory was systematized by Ko Hung (AD 283–343), who saw in the myriad metamorphoses (*i*) of natural phenomena the possibility of transforming metal into gold and men into immortals (*hsien*). According to legend, Ko Hung succeeded in preparing pills of immortality. He gave one to a dog, which dropped down dead; he then took one himself with the same result. Yet in the midst of preparations for the funeral, both Ko Hung and the dog came back to life. The most dramatic exit was that of Chang Tao-ling: he merely left behind his empty clothes. The heavenly teacher had raised himself, body and soul, to the airy void. Archaeological testimony of the elaborate methods used to delay physical corruption was found in 1968. A tomb in Hopei disclosed the funeral suit of princess Tou Wan, who was buried during the reign of Han Wu-ti: it comprised 2160 pieces of jade, wired together with gold and silk-wound iron. The Taoist church liked to recall that Lao-tzu had no grave–he simply disappeared westwards. Under pressure from the newly imported Buddhist faith it even claimed that the new doctrines were a debased form of Lao-tzu's teaching among the western barbarians.

Philosophical Taoism enjoyed a last flowering in the third century AD. Wang Pi (AD 226–249) wrote commentaries on the *I Ching* (Book of Changes) as well as on the writings of Lao-tzu (born 604 BC) and Chuang-tzu (350–275 BC). He emphasized mystical elements, paying little attention to the observation of Nature. In this shift of interest scholarly Taoists paralleled the popular trend towards religious belief. It was something that boded ill for the future development of science in China.

The coming of Buddhism

The first known reference to Buddhism was made in AD 65. Emperor Han Ming-ti (AD 58–75) addressed his nephew prince Liu Yang as one who 'recites the subtle words of Huang-lao, and respectfully performs the gentle

The Buddha at Yunkang, northern China. During the Tartar partition (AD 383–589), rock-cut shrines and monasteries were commissioned by the invaders.

sacrifices of the Buddha'. There is also mention of monks. In this accolade we find the characteristic Chinese mixture of Taoist and Buddhist elements. Eclecticism was born of the circumstances of the new religion's arrival as well as the ability of the Chinese mind to hold simultaneously without apparent distress a number of different propositions. The earliest Buddhist converts had few texts, depended on the testimony of foreigners, and had scant idea of the society in which the Buddha had preached. *Mahayana* (the Great Vehicle) was the form carried to China and this more evolved version of the faith had already more than a dozen opposing schools. To overcome uncertainties a Chinese pilgrim like Fa-hsien (who left China in AD 399 and returned AD 414) travelled to India in order to receive instruction and collect manuscripts. Translation of such texts as were available quickly drew criticism from Confucian scholars, who accused the new teachings of being unfilial. But they were not immune themselves from Buddhist speculation, once translations of high literary quality came into general circulation. An Indo-Scythian, Chih Ch'ien, and a Sogdian, K'ang Seng-hui, both born in Chinese territory and both recipients of a Chinese education, made a considerable impression by their teaching and translations. The ruler of Wu, one of the Three Kingdoms, appointed Chih Ch'ien as a scholar of wide learning (*po-shih*), and charged him with the education of the crown prince.

To counter the charge of filial impiety scriptures were translated that showed concern for the family. One text relates how a *bodhisattva*, or 'being who is possessed of the essence of the Buddhahood', chose to be reborn as the son of a childless, blind couple who wanted to retire into the forest to lead a life of contemplation. During the T'ang dynasty (AD 618–906) the Buddha was transformed into the epitome of the dutiful son and the *Sangha*, community of monks, accommodated itself to a position within the Confucian state.

By AD 500 the Buddhist faith had penetrated all the provinces of China. The many-sided struggle for power at the end of Later Han and during the short-lived dynasties down till AD 316 undermined confidence in Confucian orthodoxy. While Taoism recovered much ground, the years of crisis really prepared educated Chinese for the spread of Buddhism. After the Tartar partition of the country (AD 316) there was an increasingly favourable social and intellectual climate for the Indian faith.

Imperial reunification

The battle of Fei Shui (AD 383) halted the southward movement of the invaders from the steppes. The line of partition was in fact almost identical to the northern boundary of the wet-rice growing area, countryside unsuited to the military tactics of nomad cavalry. The reverse at Fei Shui also disturbed the balance of power in the northern provinces, which succumbed to a fresh barbarian invasion by the Toba Tartars, a branch of the Hsien Pei that was already urbanized. These people founded a new dynasty, the Toba Wei (AD 386–554), which through a succession of able rulers defeated all rival princes. Modelled on Chinese principles and sustained by intermarriage, the Toba kingdom was eventually sinicized. In AD 500 a decree prohibited the use of the Tartar language, costume and customs.

The sinicization of the ex-nomads, a consequence of settlement and the remarkable absorptive power of Chinese culture, left the way open for imperial reunification. This happened in AD 589, when general Yang Chien, a man with Hsien Pei blood, seized the northern throne and then conquered the southern provinces. Unlike the western half of the Roman empire, no province in China was lost forever after the disaster of AD 316. The empire weathered the crisis and under the T'ang rulers, the Chinese heirs of reunification, produced a brilliant cultural renaissance.

Early Science and Technology

Ho Peng Yoke

Prehistory

The earliest known primitive man in China, discovered in Yunnan province in 1965, is known to us as the Yuan-mou Man and lived 1.7 million years ago. Possible use of fire by the Yuan-mou Man is suggested by the presence of ashes and charred bones at the site of discovery of fossil teeth belonging to this primitive people. Crude stone implements were also found together with fossil teeth of other primitive men in later excavations, such as in the Lung-ku Cave in Yun-hsien and the Pai-lung cave in Yun-hsi, both in Hupeh province and dating to 0.5 million to 1.0 million years ago. These two sites were excavated in 1975 and 1976

respectively. Then there were the Lan-t'ien Man (0.6 million years ago) in Shensi province and the Peking Man (about 0.5 million years ago) at Chou-k'ou-tien near Peking. Evidence of the use of fire from burnt earth, charred bone and charred stones and a variety of stone tools, such as hammers and flint scrapers, have been found at the site of the latter. Chou-k'ou-tien was also inhabited in the late paleolithic by the Upper Cave Man (about 19,000 years ago), who definitely knew how to make fire.

In 1952 the earliest known culture in the Neolithic Age in China was discovered at the Pan-p'o site in Shensi. Carbon-dating of samples of charcoal and fruit seed at various layers of the site gives dates ranging from 3635 ± 105 BC to 4770 ± 110 BC, taking a C14 half-life of 5730 years; and comparison with growth rings of ancient bristle-cone pines gives a range from 4290 ± 200 BC to 4770 ± 135 BC. Evidence was found of the cultivation of plants, farming with the use of stone axes and spades for loosening earth; and animal husbandry. The agriculture was mainly based on millet and the animal husbandry mainly on pigs. Stone whorls for spinning thread and bone needles provide evidence of weaving and sewing. Craft tools in the form of stone chisels and stone edges, fishing tools in the form of bone harpoon heads and hunting tools in the form of bone arrowheads were also found at the site. One of the most interesting discoveries in Pan-p'o is the variety of pottery, some with textile impressions, testifying to the use of weaving; some with patterns, suggesting a primitive form of Chinese script and numerals.

Pan-p'o represents an early phase of the Yang-shao culture (sixth millennium BC until about 3000 BC). Other phases of this culture have been found in Kansu, Shensi, Shansi, Honan and Shantung provinces. This culture, first discovered in Honan in 1921, is characterized by its red painted pottery which took many forms, such as bowls, basins, vases and tripods.

Other cultures developed in east China before the

Reconstruction of a neolithic house at Pan-p'o. This Yang-shao site was discovered in 1952.

Yang-shao culture had run its course. One of them was the Ho-mu-tu culture (5000 BC to 4000 BC), named after the Ho-mu-tu site in Chekiang province excavated in 1973, when rice grains and ploughs made of animal bones were found. In the Ch'ing-lien-kang culture (c3000 BC) discovered in 1951 at Huai-an in Kiangsu province the people engaged mainly in agriculture, growing paddy rice and rearing domestic animals like cattle, dogs, pigs and sheep, and also in hunting and fishing. Specimens of rice grains were also found in south China at Shih-hsia in Kwangtung province (2500 BC).

Chronology of Science and Technology in Ancient China

1.7 million years ago	Yuan-mou man discovered in 1965
0.6 million years ago	Lan-t'ien man found in 1963
0.5 million years ago	Peking man discovered in 1927
c4800 BC–3600 BC	Pan-p'o culture gives evidence of agriculture, pottery, weaving and primitive writing
5000 BC–4000 BC	Rice grains found at Ho-mu-tu site, Chekiang province, in 1973
1700 BC	China already entered the Bronze Age
21st to 16th centuries BC	Existence of the Hsia culture now being searched after by Chinese archaeologists
17th to 11th centuries BC	Shang dynasty noted for its bronze vessels, oracle bones which contain the earliest known Chinese written records
	Evidence of a luni-solar calendar and astronomical records of eclipses and a nova
11th century BC–711 BC	Weapons with iron plates from meteorite source found in 1949
840 BC	Earliest absolute date in Chinese history
613 BC	Earliest recorded sighting of Halley's comet
5th century BC	Double-edged steel sword unearthed in Ch'ang-sha in 1976
4th century BC	Earliest Chinese star catalogues produced by Kan Te, Shih Shen and Wu Hsien. Yu Hoi discovered precession of the equinoxes
c300 BC	Tsou Yen's application of the *yin* and *yang* concept and the 'Five elements' theory
2nd century BC	Earliest existing Chinese astronomy book written on silk found in Ma-wang-tui. Earliest existing Chinese medical treatise *Huang Ti Nei Ching* and earliest Chinese pharmacopoeia *Shen Nung Pen Tsao Ching* written
134 BC	Nova sighted in Scorpio
1st century BC	Earliest Chinese mathematical book, the *Chou Pei Suan Ching* took its final form
	Paper came into use in China
cAD 100	Chang Cheng constructed first seismoscope
2nd century AD	Wei Po-yang wrote the earliest book on alchemical theory extant, the *Ts' an T'ung Ch'i*
early 4th century AD	Ko Hung, the systematizer of Chinese alchemy, wrote the *Pao P'u Tzu Nei P'ien*

The Bronze Age

In the late neolithic period, between the late fourth and early third millennia BC, there existed the Lung-shan culture; first discovered in Ch'eng-tzu-yai, Shantung in 1928, it has since been found distributed along the upper and lower reaches of the Yellow river. This culture is characterized by its black and white pottery, most of which was made on the potter's wheel. The Lung-shan culture was followed by the Erh-li-t'ou culture, discovered after 1974 in Yen-shih in Honan. The discovery of bronze vessels in Erh-li-t'ou shows that China had entered the Bronze Age not later than about 1700 BC.

Bronze ritual vase used in ancestor worship. In Shang China bronze was seldom employed for tools or weapons.

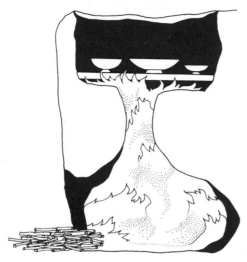

Pottery kiln at Pan-p'o. Many varieties of pottery were discovered at Pan-p'o, some with textile impressions and some with patterns suggesting Chinese script and numerals.

The dawn of history

Erh-li-t'ou could have been one centre of the Hsia culture which is now being searched after by Chinese archaeologists. According to later Chinese written records the Hsia dynasty existed between the twenty-first and the sixteenth centuries BC, but so far archaeological evidence is still lacking. The existence of the Shang dynasty (from about the seventeenth to eleventh century BC) is substantiated by excavations in Cheng-chou and Anyang, both in Honan. Bronze vessels, pottery moulds for casting bronze, crucibles for refining ore, and fragments of charcoal in the ruins of a bronze foundry were found in Cheng-chou, the site of an important city in early Shang (c sixteenth to fourteenth centuries BC). Other bronze artifacts together with foundry sites have also been discovered at Erh-li-kang in Honan (c 1400 BC). Analysis of an early Shang bronze wine vessel shows a content of 91.29 per cent copper, 7.1 per cent tin and 1.12 per cent lead. Bronze objects in Shang China were used for ceremonial purposes, or as containers, but seldom as tools or weapons. It was also in Cheng-chou that the earliest proto-porcelain ware in China was found. It takes the form of a *tsun* (a wine container with a large mouth), made of kaolin clay, and having a yellowish-green glaze on the surface about the mouth and translucent deep-green glaze on the inner and other surfaces.

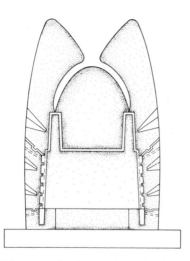

Clay mould for casting bronze ritual vessels. Shang period.

Oracle bones

The ruins at Anyang are the remains of the capital of the last Shang dynasty (fourteenth century to 1207 BC), also known as Yin. Many bronze artifacts, including inscribed bronze vessels, bronze seals and bronze mirrors, have been excavated in Anyang besides oracle bones, gold, jade, pottery, shell objects, wooden artifacts with traces of lacquer, traces of silk fabric, and a chariot. Oracle bones are carapaces of tortoises and shoulderblades of oxen used by the Yin kings for divination. They contain the oldest known Chinese written records. More than 5000 different Chinese characters have been found in the oracle bones studied so far. Among them we can find epigraphical evidence for the use of the writing brush by the Yin people. Archaeologists even consider it a possibility that the writing brush was used by the Pan-p'o people to do the designs on their pottery. The mention of wine in the oracle bones and the large number of wine vessels suggest the wide use of alcohol, at least by the aristocrats, during the Yin period. The characters for silk and mulberry indicate the practice of sericulture at that time.

The oracle bones show that the Yin people were already using a luni-solar calendar, with each year consisting of 12 lunar months of either 29 or 30 days each and a 13th lunar month added about once in every 2 or 3 years. They also used a decan of 10 days. A cycle of 10 ordinals, called the 'celestial stems' (t'ien-kan), and another cycle of 12 ordinals called the 'terrestrial branches' (ti-chih) were already used for naming the days and probably also the months, and these two cycles formed a sexagesimal cycle. Traditionally the Chinese luni-solar calendar has always been known as the Hsia calendar (Hsia-li), attributing its origin to the Hsia dynasty. The oracle bones also contain records of eclipses, novae, and names of stars and constellations that made up a few of the 28 groups of stars along the Ecliptic known to the Chinese as 'lunar mansions' (hsiu).

Beginning of written books

The Shang dynasty gave way to the Chou dynasty. The latter has been divided by historians into three periods, i.e. Western Chou (1027–771 BC), Spring and Autumn period (770–476 BC), and Warring States period (475 BC–221 BC). It is in Western Chou that we find the earliest absolute date in Chinese history in the year when King Li was deposed (841 BC). This early period of the Chou dynasty is noted for its bronze vessels, many of which have inscriptions. Proto-porcelain wares of Western Chou have also been unearthed in several cities in Shensi, Honan, Kiangsu provinces and in Peking.

Astronomy

The Shu Ching (Book of Documents)–consisting of 29 Chin wen (modern documents) chapters, 13 of which are considered to date back to the tenth century BC, 10 to the eighth century BC, and the rest to not earlier than the fifth century BC–is the earliest existing Chinese historical text. It attributes the placing of the meridian passages of certain stars in relation to the seasons and the fixing of

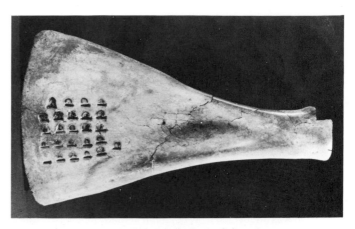

Shang oracle-bone. Divination took the form of observing cracks that resulted from heating the shoulder bones of oxen and deer.

the intercalary lunar month during the time of the legendary emperor Yao, believed to have reigned for 70 years half-a-century before the Hsia dynasty. Names of some of the 28 lunar mansions are also mentioned in the Shih Ching (Book of Odes), compiled from materials from the twenty-first to the sixteenth century BC. These have given rise to a protracted debate among Sinologists, Indianists, Assyriologists, and astronomers since the eighteenth century over the issue of the antiquity and origin of Chinese astronomy, but of course, recent Chinese archaeological finds were not available then. There has also been a division of opinion for the last two thousand years concerning another passage in the Shu Ching on some kind of an astronomical instrument used by the legendary emperor Shun, who was supposed to have reigned for 50 years immediately before the Hsia dynasty.

The Ch'un Ch'iu (Spring and Autumn Annals), a chronicle of the state of Lu kept between 722 BC and 481 BC, contains records of solar and lunar eclipses, comets and meteor streams. For example, it mentions a comet in 613 BC, which is now regarded as the earliest sighting of Halley's comet. Earliest records on the shadow measurements of the sun using the gnomon at the winter solstices are found in 655 and 522 BC. Towards the end of the Spring and Autumn period, in the fifth century BC, the Chinese used the so-called Quarter-Remainder Calendar (ssu-fen-li), which was based on the equivalent of $365\frac{1}{4}$ days to one tropical year and 237 lunations to 19 tropical years.

The earliest Chinese star catalogues were produced by Kan Te, Shih Shen and Wu Hsien (fourth century BC). Their original star catalogues are now lost, but Ch'en Cho (fl. late third century AD) constructed a star map from them. Shih Shen gave positions of stars in terms of polar distances and distances from the determinant stars of the 28 lunar mansions. Many important discoveries were made in 1973 in an excavation in Ma-wang-tui (second century BC) in Hunan, including the ephemerides of Jupiter, Saturn and Venus for a period of 70 years from 246 BC to 177 BC, and a book written on silk describing the various shapes of comets with illustrations. The accuracy of the observations suggest the use of an armillary sphere, predating the one made by Lohsia Hung during the first century before the Christian era. In 1972 a calendar for the year 134 BC was discovered in the excavation of a Han tomb at Lin-i in Shantung. A study of this calendar shows that in 134 BC the Chinese were still using the calendar system of the Ch'in dynasty (221–207 BC), which began the year with the tenth lunar month. Recently a bronze clepsydra was discovered at the excavation of Liu Sheng's tomb (died 113 BC) in Hopeh. Excavations in 1974 and 1975 in Honan have uncovered the ruins of a Han observatory built in AD 56. A bronze sundial of about the same period was discovered in a Han tomb in Kiangsu in 1965. More recently a Han diviner's plate was also found.

The nova of 134 BC in Scorpio, sighted by Hipparchus in Europe, was also observed by Chinese star clerks, who gave the exact dates of its appearance. Sunspots were first mentioned in the *Huai Nan Tzu* (*c*140 BC) and the earliest records on sunspots, dated 43 and 28 BC, are recorded in the *Ch'ien Han Shu* (History of the Former Han). The *Huai Nan Tsu* also mentions that sailors knew the directions of east and west by looking at the Northern Dipper and Pole Star. Yu Hsi discovered the precession of the equinoxes early in the fourth century AD.

The earliest Chinese cosmological theory was that of *kai-t'ien*, which imagined the heavens as a hemispherical cover and the earth as an inverted bowl. It could have been as archaic as the beginning of the Chou dynasty, or even earlier. A second theory was that of *hun-t'ien*, postulating the earth to be like a spherical pellet or the yolk of an egg floating on water in the centre of a spherical heaven. Exponents of this theory included Lohsia Hung (first century BC), Chang Heng (second century AD) and Ko Hung (AD 283–343). A variant of the *hun-t'ien* theory was given by Yao Hsin (third century AD). A third theory was that of *hsuan-yeh*, which regarded the heavenly bodies floating in an infinite space. The philosopher Chuang-tzu (350–275 BC) had alluded to this, but a clear statement of this theory was made only by Ch'i Meng (second century AD).

The Iron Age

By the Spring and Autumn period China had entered the Iron Age. A double-edged steel sword dating back to the late Spring and Autumn period was unearthed from a tomb in Ch'ang-sha in 1976. Two weapons with iron plates from a meteorite source dating back to the Western Chou period were discovered before 1949. Many iron implements and iron mines of the Warring States period were found in Hupeh in 1974. Since then further discoveries of iron objects of the fifth century BC have been discovered in Kiangsu and Honan provinces. A striking characteristic of the Chinese iron industry lies in the early knowledge of cast iron about the fifth century BC, soon after iron was found to be used by the Chinese. This contrasts with the much later development of cast-

Iron mould for casting sickle-blades dating from the fifth or fourth century BC in the Warring States period; excavated at Hsing-lung, Hopei, in 1953.

iron technology in Europe, in spite of the apparent earlier use of iron there. Another interesting feature is that although iron weapons were used in China much earlier than once thought, it was not until the Former Han dynasty (207 BC–AD 9) that they replaced bronze weapons on a large scale.

The 'hundred schools' of philosophical teachings

The period between the sixth and fourth centuries BC has been known to Chinese scholars as that of the 'hundred schools' of philosophical teachings. Some of these schools played an important role in the early history of Chinese science and technology. Confucius (551–479 BC) himself edited the *I Ching* (Book of Changes) which embodies a system of 64 hexagrams, believed by some to hold the secrets of not only the future of human affairs but also the riddles of the universe. Mo-tzu, who was born around the time of the death of Confucius and whose school of philosophy taught universal love, utilitarianism, pacifism, and awareness of the other-worldly, wrote the *Mo-tzu* (The Book of Master Mo) in which he gives a qualitiative discussion of the focus and the image produced by concave as well as convex mirrors, the inverted image produced by a pinhole, and the balance. The book also has something to say about logic.

Lao-tzu, an elder contemporary of Confucius, has been claimed by the Taoists to be the founder of Taoism. Besides deriving their philosophy from other writers like Chuang-tzu and Lieh Yu-k'ou of about the fourth or the third century before the Christian era, the Taoists also inherited the teachings of the Naturalists, the greatest name among whom was Tsou Yen who lived about the year 300 BC in the eastern seaboard state of Ch'i in modern Hopeh province.

The 'Yin and Yang' and the 'Five-Element' theories

The Naturalists (*yin-yang chia*) taught and applied the concept of the *yin* and *yang* and the theory of the five 'elements' (*wu hsing*) to explain not only natural phenomena but also all mundane affairs including political events. *Yin* and *yang* are the two opposite yet complementary components of the cosmological force of nature, called *ch'i*, in a way corresponding to the Greek *pneuma* or our modern concept of matter-energy. *Yin* represents the moon, night, earth, water, coldness, dampness, darkness, cloudiness, softness, what is feminine, and so on; *yang* represents the sun, day, heaven, fire, heat, dryness, brightness, sunshine, hardness, what is masculine and so forth. When *yin* is on the ascendancy *yang* moves in the opposite direction until *yin* reaches its maximum height when *yang* is at its corresponding lowest position, and then *yin* will gradually decline while *yang* becomes dominant in a continuous cyclic process. In the system of the *I Ching* (Book of Changes) *yin* is represented by a broken line and *yang* by a full line; taken 6 at a time there are 64 different combinations giving us the 64 hexagrams. In the theory of the five elements, *yin* and *yang* each breaks down to form fire, water, wood, metal and earth.

Unlike the elements of the modern chemist these five 'elements' suggest motion rather than rest and are perhaps more appropriately called 'agents' or 'phases'. They have been known as elements probably because of the convenience of using the same term as the Four Elements of the Greeks, who had fire, air, earth and water. However, the Chinese elements do not correspond exactly with their Greek counterparts. The Chinese have an order of mutual conquest in which earth conquers water, water conquers fire, fire conquers metal, metal conquers wood and wood conquers earth, and an order of mutual production in which earth produces metal, metal produces water, water produces wood, wood produces fire and fire produces earth. They also have worked out two principles, one of which is the principle of control (*hsiang chih*) by which a process of mutual conquest may be controlled by the elements that conquer the conqueror, as for example, fire conquers metal, but the process may be controlled by water, which conquers the conqueror. The other is the principle of masking (*hsiang hua*), by which a process of mutual conquest may also be controlled by the element that produces or generates the element under subjugation, as for example, fire conquers metal, but the process may be controlled by earth which replenishes the supply of metal.

Alchemy

The beginnings of alchemy in China are connected with the School of the Naturalists, particularly its founder Tsou Yen. By that time the concept of the elixir of immortality had already crystallized. The Taoists began to seek ways and means of preparing the elixir by alchemical means, and these methods included aurification, although what the alchemist succeeded in doing was to make imitation gold. During the third century before the Christian era the first Ch'in emperor, Shih-huang-ti, enlisted the service of shamans, magicians and alchemists and sent several expeditions to the eastern sea in search of the medicine of immortality. During the second century before the Christian era Liu An, the prince of Huai-nan, produced a book on magic and alchemical recipes with the help of some alchemists living in his household, but only fragments of this book survive. By that time aurification had become so common that an imperial edict was issued in 144 BC to ban it.

In about the year 60 BC the Han emperor ordered Liu Hsiang to make gold for him and put the latter in prison when it was discovered to be only artificial gold.

The earliest book on alchemical theory extant, entitled *Ts'an T'ung Ch'i* (Kinship of the Three), was written about the middle of the second century AD by Wei Ao, better known by another name or style Wei Po-yang. For this reason Wei has been called the 'father of alchemy'. However, it was Ko Hung (AD 283–343) whom we should regard as the systematizer of Chinese alchemy through his work the *Pao P'u Tzu Nei P'ien* (Book of the Preservation-of-Solidarity Master: Esoteric Chapter *c* AD 320).

Mathematics

The oracle bones show that the Shang Chinese were already using the decimal place-value system. The earliest Chinese mathematical book extant is the *Chou Pei Suan Ching* (The Arithmetical Classic of the Gnomon and the Circular Paths of Heaven), which contains material between the fourth and sixth centuries BC and was put in its final form in the first century BC. It is also a book on astronomy explaining the theory of *kai-t'ien*. It attributes the knowledge of a special case of the Pythagoras theorem to a mathematician named Shang Kao in the eleventh century BC, that in a triangle with sides in the ratio 3:4:5 the square of the longest side equals the sum of the squares of the other two sides.

The ancient Chinese used counting rods to perform their calculations. In 1971 bone counting rods of the first century BC and in 1975 bamboo counting rods of the second century BC were excavated. By about that time the most important and influential early Chinese mathematical work, the *Chiu Chang Suan Shu* (Nine Chapters of the Mathematical Art) was in formation. The 246 problems in this book deal with (a) rules for the area of rectangles, trapeziums, triangles, circles, arcs and annuli; (b) percentages and proportions; (c) partnership problems and rules of three; (d) finding the sides of figures given the areas and single sides, using square roots and cube roots; (e) finding volumes of solid figures, like prisms, cylinders, pyramids, circular cones, frustums of a cone, tetrahedrons, wedges, and so on; (f) pursuit and alligation; (g) a Chinese algebraic invention known as the 'rule of false position', used mainly for solving the equation $ax = b$; (h) simultaneous linear equations involving both positive and negative numbers; and (i) properties of the right-angled triangle expressed algebraically. The earliest available text of the *Chiu Chang Suan Shu*, or *Chiu Chang Suan Ching* contains a commentary by Liu Hui, (*fl.* third century AD), who also wrote the *Hai Tao Suan Ching* (Sea–Island Mathematical Manual) dealing exclusively with measurements of heights and distances.

There were other mathematical writings in Han China, but all are now lost with the exception of the *Shu Shu Chi I* (Memoir on Some Traditions of Mathematical Art) written by Hsu Yo (*fl.* AD 190). This book refers to magic squares, arithematical series, different forms of the abacus, very large numbers, divination methods, and the magnetic compass. Lastly, an interesting work that gives the earliest example of a worked-out problem in indeterminate analysis appeared between AD 280 and 473 in the *Sun Tzu Suan Ching* (Master's Sun's Mathematical Manual).

Medicine

Between the Spring and Autumn and the Warring States periods the first Chinese medical treatise was in its formation stage. It finally took the title *Huang Ti Nei Ching* (The Yellow Emperor's Manual of Corporeal Medicine) during the Former Han dynasty (207 BC to AD 9). The earliest Chinese pharmacopoeia, the *Shen Nung Pen Ts'ao Ching* (Pharmacopoeia of the Heavenly Husbandman) also appeared during the same period. We do not know the actual authorship of these two books–the names of the legendary heroes Huang Ti and Shen Nung were used to give prestige. Both these books bear the influence of Tsou Yen's teachings on the *yin* and *yang* and the 'Five-Element' theory.

The excavation of the Ma-Wang-tui site at Ch'ang-sha in 1973 brought to light a Former Han medical treatise hitherto unknown. Specimens of some Chinese herbal medicine were also found. In the tomb of Liu Sheng (died 113 BC) in Hopeh province gold and silver needles used for acupuncture were recovered.

At the end of the second century AD two medical treatises, one on fever and the other on dietetics, were written by Chang Chi, more often known by his style Chang Chung-ching. In the early third century AD Hua T'o was said to have produced general anaesthesia by the use of a wine called *ma-fei-san*, which is now supposed to contain Indian hemp. Much development of Chinese medicine took place from the time of the Chin dynasty (after AD 265). At the beginning of this period Wang Shu-ho wrote the first book on pulse-reading, which has become and still remains an important technique used by Chinese physicians for diagnosis. An important work on acupuncture was also written at about the same time by Huangfu Mi. Finally, the alchemist Ko Hung wrote two medical books dealing with infectious diseases, giving prescriptions for the treatment of various types of sickness, including eye trouble and beri-beri.

Writing material

The ancient Chinese wrote on pottery, bronze, bones, carapaces of tortoise, bamboo, wood and silk. In the case of bronze the writings were either engraved or printed from moulds. As mentioned earlier the writing brush seemed to have been used by the Pan-p'o people (fifth and fourth millennia BC) for making the designs on their pottery. Black ink and vermillion were used for writing with the brush on the Yin oracle bones. Modern excavations have uncovered many documents written on bamboo, wood, and silk. Paper came into use in China not later than the first century BC. A specimen of paper dating back to 49 BC was discovered in Sinkiang in 1933, and another dating back to the reign of the

Early characters as used on vessels in ancestor worship. It is possible that the people of Pan-p'o used the writing brush for making designs on their pottery.

emperor Han Wu-ti (141 to 87 BC) was discovered near Sian in 1957. The technique of paper-making was improved by Ts'ai Lun (*c*AD 105).

Further science and technology after the Ch'in period (221–207 BC)

In 1976, the ruin of a large shipbuilding site of the Ch'in period was found in Kuang-chou, Kwangtung province. According to estimation wooden ships measuring 90 ft (27 m) in length and 18 to 24 ft (5.5 to 7 m) in width and with a laden weight of between 50 and 60 tons could have been built on this site. Between 1973 and 1975 models of wooden ships were found in two Former Han tombs at the Feng-huang-shan mountain in Chiang-ling, Hupeh province.

The earliest Chinese maps drawn on silk were discovered at the Ma-wang-tui site in Ch'ang-sha (second century BC). Earthquakes were recorded, and Chang Heng the astronomer constructed the first seismoscope used for detecting the direction of earthquakes (*c* AD 100).

The Chinese could recognize ice crystals (second century BC). We can find this in a description given in the *Han Shih Wai Chuan* (Moral Discourses Illustrating the 'Book of Odes', 135 BC). A few centuries earlier they made observations on the haloes and the parhelic phenomena.

Obviously it is impossible to cover every aspect of Chinese science and technology within a limited space. We conclude this brief survey by giving an interesting example of the practical sense of the Chinese in their development of the breast-strap harness, which showed far better knowledge of mechanics and the horse than the throat-and-girth harness of the Roman chariot adopted in Europe. The breast-strap harness was used in China in the early days of the Former Han dynasty (*c*200 BC). It later went to Europe and developed into the modern collar harness in AD 600–1000.

Chinese Art

William Watson

Neolithic styles in the fourth and third millennia BC

The history of pre-Han China is largely concerned with the expansion of the state from the middle course of the Yellow river (Honan and eastern Shensi) towards the east and south. In the evolution of artistic style a similar expansive unity can be seen in material that has survived in the tombs of the Shang dynasts, and, after the Chou conquest in 1027 BC, in the tombs of the notables of the central Chou state and of the chief feudal principalities. Since the establishment of the People's Republic more systematic archaeological excavation has illustrated the progress of the arts in regions other than the centre, as well as adding much to our knowledge of the metropolitan tradition.

With this greater knowledge of the Bronze Age art it is possible to turn more critically to the question of the preceding neolithic traditions, which were so rapidly superseded upon the introduction of bronze-working and of the city-state polity that depended on it. In economy and technology Chinese neolithic culture fits into the wider Asian scheme embracing West Asian civilization, while showing features peculiar to East Asia. It divides broadly into two traditions. On the primary loess soil (the yellow earth) in Honan and Shensi, and later in Kansu west of the river, Yang-shao culture flourished in populous and pacific farming communities whose art is preserved in pottery painted in black and purplish-red. The designs consist in the earlier phase of geometric figures exclusively: triangles, segments of circles, eyed sworls and similar linear figures. There are rare and tentative examples of birds' heads and fish. The latter, known at the village of Pan-p'o in Shensi, are given a geometric treatment that anticipates the main trend of the succeeding Bronze Age styles. An extremely stylized human face or monster mask is combined with the other figures.

In the later Yang-shao phase of Kansu (which descends into the second millenium BC and so marches with the bronze period) zoomorphic elements are even rarer and linear figures are elaborated. The splendid decoration of spirals and other abstract designs, the imitations of net and basket, all executed with unsurpassed zest and spontaneity, rank this pottery with the best of the wide-flung Asian tradition of painted wares. Only three or four examples of modelled subjects—a human face and dubious phalloi—can be traced. This strange absence of a pottery plastic art is repeated in the later neolithic tradition termed the Lung-shang culture, which succeeded Yang-shao in Honan some time after 3000 BC. Here the finest pottery is plain black, burnished and sometimes only two or three millimetres in thickness. Its distinguishing feature is the care bestowed on the profile and proportions of the vessels. Unlike the hand-made and merely rounded pottery of Yang-shao,

these display structural features deriving from the use of the potter's wheel, with sharply ridged sides and contrasting planes.

The Shang dynasty (*c* **seventeenth century** BC **to 1027** BC)

The art of the Shang and Chou dynasties survives most fully in bronze. From the start, in the earlier phase of Shang represented by the walled city built near modern Cheng-chou, the bronze sacrificial vessels combined the predilection for elaborate linear design seen in the later Yang-shao pottery with the attention to balance and proportion of shape more characteristic of the Lung-shan tradition; but the evolution which connected these styles in the transition from neolithic to metal-using civilization is not well understood. The explicit themes of Shang art appear to be original inventions. They are small in number, centring on the *t'ao-t'ieh* (monster mask), and show great variety of detailed elaboration. The mask has uniform features throughout the Shang period, as something between tiger and bull, generally horned, with large eyes and a fanged upper jaw but no lower jaw. At the side of the earlier masks as they appear at the neck of the vessels are horizontal linear elements fringed with spurs, composing a compact zone of flat ornament above which only the eyes protrude.

In later treatments the mask is so arranged that each half resembles a one-legged dragon seen in profile (the so-called *kuei* dragon), the original lateral extensions being shaped briefly into a body, and parts of the design are raised in relief. Apart from this ubiquitous motif, which seems to have had an evil-averting function, Shang ornament seen in the production of the later city at Anyang adds more or less stylized animal motifs, such as long-tailed birds, silkworms, an occasional bucranion and deer head, and various small rectilinear spiral figures filling the interstices of the main ornament. The artificiality of this style has been termed hieratic, as denoting the conventions of ornament used on vessels associated with priestly rite and sacrifice to ancestral spirits. This manner coexisted, however, with an undercurrent of more naturalistic representation that emerges occasionally in the hieratic context, particularly in certain bird and tiger motifs.

Sufficient of Shang art in other materials—jade, wood and pottery—survives to show how completely the hieratic style dominated in all forms of artistic production associated with the ruling class and its ceremonial. Nowhere in the ancient world can be found better examples of powerful and sombre expression achieved by the manipulation of a few precise motifs, in which figurative and abstract linear elements are inseparably combined. A similar discipline is seen in the vertical build of the later elaborate vessels, which have

311

White pottery tripod jug *kuei*, an early Chinese vessel, Shang or Chou period.

been found chiefly at the Shang city site of Anyang. These often have fantastic relief, and a delicate poise that denies their weighty substance. A few masks and figures carved in jade, and even rarer examples of masks cast on the vessels, are the only hint of interest in the human form. The faces, somewhat brutal and expressionless, may be intended to show prisoners of war, or sacrificial victims.

The Western Chou period (1027 to 771 BC)

Following the Chou federal establishment imposed at the end of the eleventh century BC, versions of the hieratic style prevailed at the city courts of the chief subordinate rulers. In contrast to the close-knit and delicate schemes of Shang the new decoration favours more explicit animal ornament, and concurrently the abstraction of animal forms into larger anonymous shapes. A crested long-tailed bird now tends to replace the *t'ao-t'ieh* as the central item of the sacrificial iconography. This motif, as well as the broader treatment of the whole decoration, must derive from the practice of the Chou people in their homeland of Kansu and west Shansi, although it has not yet been possible to date any piece of their style in this area to a time preceding the fall of Shang.

Bronze *kuang*, or wine mixer, cast as a monster, with the blunted horns of a sacrificial victim. Shang period, *c*1000 BC.

The tenth-century style is ideally represented by the bronze vessels excavated recently at Fu-feng in Shensi. The *t'ao-t'ieh* are in higher and softer relief, the dragons more varied, and a peculiar effect is sought by lining the vertical angles of the vessels with projecting hooks of characteristic shape. In the Western Chou period (1027–271 BC) the *ting* tripod and *kuei* bowl known to the Shang are still manufactured, but more heavily ornamented and with the loss of the tense silhouette of their predecessors.

In the later eleventh and early tenth centuries BC there is notable concentration on the wine mixer called *kuang*, whose sides may bear *t'ao-t'ieh* while its lid imitates a kind of bovine tiger, and, at Fu-feng, such a fanciful addition as a peacock's tail. The concluding stage of the first phase of Chou is reached in the ninth century when tripod legs assume cabriole curves and the reduction of birds, dragons and masks issue in zones of recumbent G-like figures or in broad undulating schemes of concave bands. Tall vases, of round or square body, are characteristic of the period around 800 BC. On them various items, the *disjecta membra* of the former repertoire, are apt to appear with new detailed heraldry, a development that was due to transform the hieratic style in the course of the next few centuries. The chief of these features is the production of continuous ornament by intertwining serpentine elements and aligning complex linear units in which only a projecting beanlike eye betrays an origin in the dragons, birds and masks of the early Chou bronze founders.

The Shang bronze vessels had been cast from ceramic multi-part moulds, and there is no evidence to hand which suggests that this method was abandoned, in the case of vessels, before about 400 BC. Soon after 800 BC, however, means were found of manufacturing mould

parts by the use of a stamp giving a succession of identical figures which combined into continuous uniform ornament.

Secularization of style in the middle and late Chou periods (seventh to third centuries BC)

In the course of the mid-Chou development, lying between the ninth and seventh centuries BC, the Honan foundries were the most inventive and exercised the greatest influence on China as a whole. The reduction to linear diaper of the hieratic animal scheme, as instanced above, and illustrated notably from the finds at Hsincheng in Honan, never wholly excluded the allusion to a dragon form, although this may be detected only by an eye familiar with older more explicit versions. A second cycle of hieratic style begins around 600 BC, heralded by the ornament cast on ritual vessels (*ting*, *kuei*, and the *yi* resembling a sauceboat) found at Li-yü in Shansi. Here the principle of interlocking repeated units is continued, but now yields broader zones of interlacing bands. Each band is filled with repeats of a spiral-and-triangle unit that was destined to have a dominant structural role at a later stage of the hieratic logic.

The Li-yü bands in some instances suggest a movement to one side or the other, but in most redactions form static symmetrical panels. Here and there among the interlacery is a scatter of rolled snouts and spurlike wings, while the anonymity of the design is relieved at intervals by fully drawn frontal ram masks. All this ornament forms a smooth uninterrupted surface. As if to remind the viewer that the artist was capable of more than rich arabesque, the vessel lids often carry small figures of duck, buffalo or sheep modelled with a realism startling in its context. Similar feeling for animal form in the round appears in vessels that themselves imitate whole animals, such as an unspecific tapir-like figurine included in the Li-yü group. The exact dating and the diffusion through China of bronzes of the Li-yü type remain unsolved problems, especially since the discovery of a highly productive foundry at Hou-ma in Shansi where elements of Li-yü design appear to have survived until the late fifth or fourth century BC.

Meanwhile there had been launched in Honan a fresh version of hieratic which (with the preceding Shang and mid-Chou styles) constitutes the third Honan style. From the large finds of bronze vessels made nearly half a century ago near Shou-hsien in Anhui this phase was termed Huai style, in western literature, after the main river of Anhui. Its characteristic feature is the ubiquitous employment of a diaper consisting of two parts: a whorl joined to a brief wing reducing in the course of time to a spiral-and-triangle reminiscent of the Li-yü convention and better justifying the conventional name of hook-and-volute. On the series of great bells from Honan tombs, which exemplify the earliest stage of this style, the hook-and-volute diaper was raised in considerable

Bronze monster mask and loose-hanging ring p'u shou, *with writhing animal forms, a phoenix and a precisely formed dragon. Chou dynasty, period of the Warring States, fifth century* BC.

relief imparting unprecedented animation to panels of the ornamental scheme. In the chief places the scatter of the motifs is organized again to suggest the *t'ao-t'ieh*, and the bodies of tigers and dragons forming the handles of bells and tall vases are interpreted in the whole silhouette and in detail in terms of the same briefly spiralling movements. These *ronde-bosse* animals, and the interlacery of serpents and dragons in relief, introduce a fresh body of animal design into the hieratic discipline. Compared with the art as it was known in earlier centuries, the new ornament wears a more secular air, on the sacrificial vessels and particularly in its adaptation to all manner of utilitarian objects. The decoration of weapons, harness pieces and belt hooks shows that the style held a universal sway in decorative art. Nowhere does the ingenuity and closely disciplined invention of the artist appear to greater advantage.

From 500 until almost 200 BC the hieratic style evolves through a further three phases. Already in the early fourth century BC the first *élan* is passed, the basic hook-and-volute is reduced in size and relief, and the splendid invention of the bell ornament no longer appears. The bronzes of the tomb of the marquis of Tsai typify this stage. A greater boldness of design replaces

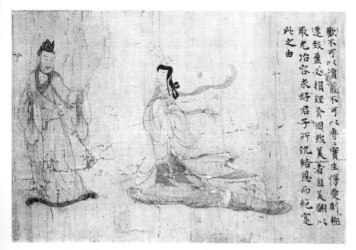

Detail from the *Admonitions of the Instructress to the Court Ladies* attributed to the famous Ku K'ai-chih (*c*334–406).

the subtler graphic of the earlier phase, with much projection of more or less zoomorphic handles, flanges and crowns. In principle the earlier cycle is repeated, the tendency towards linear reduction produces a pattern that is at first rectilinear, repeating without symmetry, then forming symmetric units in heraldic fashion. Finally a milder curvilinear arabesque emerges to replace, or accompany, the stiffer versions. From this last phase the spirit of hieratic tradition has all but departed, and the first great cycle of Chinese style approaches its close.

Viewed, as it must mainly be, in the terms of grave goods, the hieratic style begins in Shang clearly under ritual dictate and acquires more general secular currency. Jade carving follows a comparable course. *Pi* rings, the *tsung* and *huang* symbols and bird plaques of the twelfth and eleventh centuries BC contrast in function as much as in technique of production with jades attributed to the later centuries of the Chou period. Around 400 BC jade carving was revived, evidently stimulated by the introduction of rotary saws and drills. The finest work was destined for personal adornment, as for the dress pendants and ornaments for swords and scabbards. Within the limits set by the intractable material the jade carver in his turn was imitating styles first established by his contemporaries in bronze.

New themes and realism in the Former Han period (207 BC to AD 9)

The artistic consequences of the unification of China that took place under Ch'in Shih-huang-ti in 221 BC are not apparent before the beginning of the Former Han dynasty at the opening of the second century BC. With centralized economy and officialdom went an increasing uniformity of art, promoted in large measure by the

Leopard in parcel-gilt bronze with inlay of silver and garnets. Found in the tomb of princess Tou Wan at Man-ch'eng, Hopei, in 1968. Western Han dynasty, late second century BC.

activity of official workshops. The decoration of the backs of bronze mirrors is a notable case. Previously, from the fourth century BC, this had excerpted elements of the late hieratic style, with added animal figures and with lozenge effects taken from twill weaving. Under the Han these schemes were replaced, in the second century BC, by compact and more static scrollery in which fragmented dragons and lozenges are interspersed with the frilly Han 'cloud motif'.

In the following century these designs survive in an altered form as the painted decoration of lacquer cups and toilet boxes, and archaistic prolongation of the earlier manner, while the mirror decoration turns to a variety of more or less abstract schemes alluding to astronomy and cosmology. Of these the most intriguing is the TLV diagram in which a square earth is symbolized at the centre of a circular heaven and the cardinal points are occupied by the so-called sacred animals: the tortoise and serpent at the north ('the dark warrior'), the green dragon of the east, the red bird of the south and the white tiger of the west.

Our knowledge of this period is greatly expanded by two recent discoveries. The tombs of the prince Liu-sheng and his wife at Man-ch'eng in Hopei were replete with decorative bronzes in which animal forms predominate and the newly acquired technique of fire-gilding is much in evidence. Gilding is used with consummate skill in small figures of crouched leopards and on a tall vase covered with cloud scrollery. On such a piece as the domed openwork censer (*po shan-lu*, 'vast mountain censer') the sacred animals around the base of the mountain have the sinuous vivacity associated with the animal art of the Asian steppes, and we are reminded that work in the pure steppe style was being produced contemporaneously in the Ordos region of northwest China. On the sides of the censer bears and tigers, and a woodman with his cart, are examples of a vein of narrative realism, which now enters Chinese art for the first time.

The contents of the tomb of the mummified Lady Tai, the Ma-wang-tui at Chang-sha in Hunan, include a well-preserved painting on silk in which mythology and terrestrial life are combined. Unusual dragons and

demons inhabit the upper and lower quarters, soaring through space and bearing up the scene, while two human scenes occupy the middle of the picture: the Lady herself in conversation with servants, and a scene at her death. In the first the figures show easy mastery of profile posture and of the adaptation of line to the representation of volume; in the second the rows of kneeling mourners receding from the viewer towards the coffin, which stands at the back of the scene, are evidence of settled principles of perspective painting. The art of Man-ch'eng reflects the taste and ideas of a courtly milieu, in which motifs taken from earlier tradition accompany new themes in which the growing attachment of the ruling class to Taoist cosmology and alchemy is revealed. The jade suits encasing the occupants of the tombs, intended to prevent putrefaction, are items inspired by the same ideology. The pictorial art is chiefly concerned with other-world myth and posthumous destinies of the human soul.

To these chief divisions of the earlier Han art can be added a third, that of the Tien kingdom of Yunnan, which may stand for a provincial tradition as yet little influenced by the artistic conformity of the empire. Until

109 BC the kings of Tien were independent under Chinese tutelage. To their tombs were consigned bronze figurines of persons and animals modelled convincingly in the round with a mastery of realistic detail and a sense of genre that place them quite outside the metropolitan tradition. The most accomplished pieces are plaques in high relief showing leopards attacking more pacific animals. Beautifully modelled birds and felines adorn axes and other weapons. Crowded scenes of village festival and ceremony, and a procession of the representatives of various tribes, are fascinating portrayals of real persons and events.

The art of the official class in the Later Han period

The Later Han (AD 24–220) saw the abandonment in official art of the archaism that preserved elements of Chou style, and great reinforcement of realistic style in all the arts. In the decoration and furnishing of the tombs of the now dominant official class figurines and reliefs representing a governor's progress are standard features. The modelling of horses shows much closer approximation to real anatomy than had ever been thought necessary before, although a degree of stylization, for example in the head and jaws, was still found to be compatible with this three-dimensional realism. As

Figure of a flying horse with one hoof on the back of a swallow. Bronze figure excavated at Wu-wei, Kansu, in 1969. Eastern Han dynasty, second century AD.

appears also in other art, the notion of reality is often sought by imparting a sense of movement. In the case of animal sculpture the bronze horse called Flying Swallow excavated from a second-century tomb at Wu-wei, Kansu, is the ideal example. We are now fortunate in possessing fuller documentation of painting in various forms, and here movement and poise in attitude and in gesture are increasingly captured by the manipulation of the painter's brush–the instrument, used equally for writing, that has remained unchanged until modern times. The figures of officials in conversation painted in black and colour on some tomb bricks well demonstrate this new technique of conveying the mass and volume of the forms by the inflexion and varying breadth of the contour line. At the end of the Western Han similar subjects had been represented chiefly by areas of colour with a line less suggestive of calligraphic movement.

While greater realism is found in scenes of men, animals and buildings wherever they were portrayed, it is not unexpected to find that the style of the northeast, where civilized practices were longest established, should reflect a particular formalism. The classic instances of this art are found in scenes carved in shallow relief on stones of the funeral shrine of Wu-liang (the Wu-liang-ts'u) in Shantung, which date to the second quarter of the second century. The subjects are shown in silhouette: processions of carriages and horses; scenes taken from recent history (for example the attempted assassination of the Ch'in emperor); incidents from the Confucian Analects and from the biographies of famous exponents of filial piety. The last subject, as befitting Confucian teaching, became ubiquitous in tomb decoration.

At the Wu-liang-ts'u recession in depth is shown by oblique arrangements, the depiction of figures in three-quarter view. In general the representation of gesture and energetic movement suggests that while the artist had at his command considerable means for conveying the illusion of the third dimension in his work, he was restrained from bringing them all into play by an archaic convention of mural painting. In the decoration of the hypogeum at Yi-nan, also in Shantung, this restraint is relaxed and we gain the impression of a fully developed technique of spatial design. The latter murals are engraved in line on the stone surface. Behind all the tomb reliefs we may imagine larger-scale murals depicted in bright colour and, like the tomb decoration, including culture-heroes, monsters, revelries and hobgoblins along with officials and their servants.

With this northeastern art we may compare the corresponding tomb pictures of Yunnan in southwest China. In these the conventions of spatial design are more fully accepted and the repertory is greatly widened. Scenes of feasts show dancers and jugglers attended by guests and musicians whose receding place in the composition is indicated by oblique arrangements and greater height of the field of the picture. The themes are less concerned with the court and with Confucian literature, taking in hunting, harvesting and even salt mining.

A revival of mirror ornament occurs in the later second century in the Shou-hsing area of Kiangsu. The crowded arrangements of Taoist deities, carriages and horsemen here make a singular contrast with the order and significant spacing which prevailed in pictorial art as a whole. On these mirrors occur the figures of Hsi-wang-mu, Queen Mother of the West in Taoist myth, and her winged attendants. This personage had figured in a minor way in the Shantung murals together with Fu-hsi, Nü-wa and other culture heroes more prominent in the Confucian reconstruction of myth and legend. Taoist and Confucian elements are blended in the Confucian ideology and iconography, the result of the intellectual movement whose origins are traced from the first century BC.

The age of the Three Kingdoms and the Western Chin dynasty (AD 221 to 316)

In the troubled times that followed the collapse of the Later Han dynasty the course of art, in so far as it was influenced by the cultivated class and by government patronage, was interrupted to a degree that leaves many of the historian's questions still unanswered. Before AD 316 the earliest Buddhist images must have been manufactured in China, although only the merest hint of them, as in the decoration of bronze mirrors, seems to be preserved. A major movement dated to this period was, however, destined to have the greatest influence in conditioning many aspects of craft. In the region of Chekiang the so-called proto-Yüeh porcelain launched the tradition of porcelain manufacture. Purity of feldspathic glaze was the goal of the makers of this celadon ware, and with it went an increasing feeling for the purity of ceramic form. Meanwhile the intellectual tradition was finding an accommodation with Buddhist philosophy, whose quietistic element matched the nature of Taoist thought. From this conjunction arose the art of the philosophized landscape which was due to dominate painting through its whole later history; but this movement took productive shape only at the turn of the fourth and fifth centuries, when, among artists, it is associated with the great Ku K'ai-chih.

America

Temple I, Tikal in the Petén, Guatemala. Maya architecture of the Classic period was carried out in stone and rubble with dressed masonry facings.

The Olmecs

Ignacio Bernal

The name

The term Olmec means, in Nahuatl, 'inhabitant of rubber country'. This name has therefore been used to describe various groups that originated at different times in these parts, or rather in areas south of what is now Veracruz and the north of Tabasco. Because of their origin, we have given this same name to the people who lived there long before their historically known Olmec successors. Sometimes they are called 'archaeological Olmecs to differentiate them from the Olmecs proper; other names have also been suggested for them but have not been widely accepted.

Although these areas were already inhabited, the history of the Olmecs, as encountered by the archaeologist (there are no written dates), began about 1200 BC and ended about AD 400. Olmec influence, however, continued for some time after this, and elements appeared for several centuries after AD 400. The same happened to the people we will call Olmecoids, to whom reference will be made later.

The homeland

The metropolitan area of the Olmecs occupies about 690 sq miles (1790 km²). Except for the vast mountainous area of the Tuxtlas, it is a large alluvial plain with an average height of 325 ft (99 m) above sea level. It is crossed by innumerable slow-running rivers. During the rainy season the heavy rainfall, which reaches an average amount of nearly 100 in (254 cm) per year, and the water carried down by the rivers cause continuous flooding, thus forming several more or less permanent marshes and lakes. The dry area consists of high mountains inhabited by the usual tropical animals: jaguars, monkeys, serpents—none of them of much nutritional value. On the other hand, fish and shellfish are very abundant and we have evidence that they were much used. The same is true of numerous aquatic birds. Wild animals and fish certainly played an important part in the limited diet of the Mesoamerican labourer.

Agriculture had been practised in Mesoamerica for some years before the advent of the Olmec civilization, but little is known about it in this area. No doubt it was what is called the slash-and-burn or swidden type of cultivation whereby part of a mountain is cleared, and the trees and fallen branches are burned to provide space for seed to be sown in the cleared areas. This system is laborious, especially as land used in this way without fertilizer becomes unproductive within a few years and eventually has to be abandoned to the underbrush that spreads across it. This gives rise to the need to clear new ground for agriculture every four or five years and to be continually moving from one such patch of cultivated land to another, never staying long. It has been calculated that this system only allows for 20 per cent of the available area to be fully exploited each year.

It also stresses the need for the labourer to move ever farther away from home over a cycle of very many years. As a result this tends to prevent any great increase of population in any one place and therefore the development of reasonably populous villages. This is how we know that Olmec population centres were small: it is hardly possible to talk of towns. These only developed in later years and in other areas. However, the total population in the area was sufficiently large—it has been calculated that there were approximately 350,000 inhabitants—to occupy several localities most probably linked to one another in various ways. Thus, based on the archaeological finds the assumption has arisen that there were what we would call scattered towns, in which the structures of the towns are not crowded together to make a whole but are dispersed, forming isolated units, each with its own centre where the authorities and the buildings dedicated to religion could be found. Put together, the scattered habitations would show certain characteristics indicative of a town, such as are necessarily at the base of any civilization.

The people

We can only speculate as to the language the Olmecs spoke. They lived in a region where at one time a proto-Mayan dialect was spoken from the Huasteca to the Yucatán. It is thus possible that they spoke a proto-Mayan-Huastecan dialect. We do not even know what name they gave themselves.

Nor can we establish their physical appearance from the remains excavated in the area. Due to the extreme dampness and salinity of the soil in the graves that have been discovered, the bones they contain are so decomposed that they do not allow us to form a clear picture of what the Olmecs looked like. On the other hand, we have numerous portrayals of individuals, especially in stone, which have led us to the conclusion that they are, as has been defined: 'People of small stature with well-formed bodies inclined to plumpness, rounded heads and faces, chubby-cheeked with thick napes, slanting and heavy-lidded eyes with epicanthic folds, short wide noses, mouths slanting downwards at the corners and thick lips, strong jaws and short and thick necks.' This description fits pretty well most of the present inhabitants of the region, especially when young, which seems to suggest that though they do not share the same culture they are descendants of the ancient Olmecs. Many sculptures, however, represent men with certain jaguar features, confusing the issue as they obviously relate to mythical figures only partly based on reality.

Pisac, near Cuzco, Peru. One of the better-known Inca sites. Although some of the Inca sites are fairly large and imposing, the Inca settlement pattern was not truly urban.

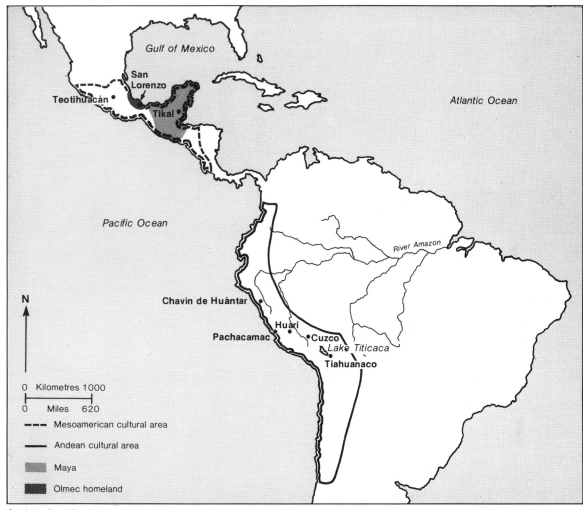

Ancient America.

Olmec culture

With this background established it is possible to concentrate on what is known for certain about the Olmec culture. There is no clear evidence of planning in the Olmec centres except for the main one: La Venta, at the southern Veracruz site of San Lorenzo. It is situated on an island 2 sq miles (5.22 km²) in area formed by rivers and estuaries, but only the ceremonial part has been explored. Here we have a clearly defined layout which was obviously worked out even before construction took place. A central north-south line with an 0° 8′ deviation to the west divides it in half. San Lorenzo's central group of structures is located to the north. This central axis in La Venta is characterized not only by certain of the buildings and the most important

The great oval Maya pyramid, 'Temple of the Dwarf', at Uxmal, Yucatán. Its oval plan is unusual in Maya architecture.

pyramid in the area, but also for features that are sometimes hidden, such as splendid mosaics formed by stone slabs representing very stylized jaguar heads: curiously, these were covered over with earth after being carved. Some of the large sculptures also formed integral parts of the planning.

But the Olmecs could not develop their architecture in an area without stone. Thus their buildings are made of clay, sometimes coloured, which does not allow for architecture in the true sense. The main pyramid of La Venta rises to a height of 100 ft (30.5 m) and has a distinctive shape which, according to one of the explorers, was intentional. It is the forerunner of the innumerable pyramids that were later built in Mesoamerica. There are also buildings backing on to other monuments; this idea was to be copied frequently, for example in the great pyramids of Teotihuacán.

Occasionally, so as to enclose a particularly important area, great columns of natural basalt brought down from the Tuxtlas were erected all around it. Tomb A in La Venta, the most important of many that have been found in this area, was also built with these columns.

Chronology for Ancient America

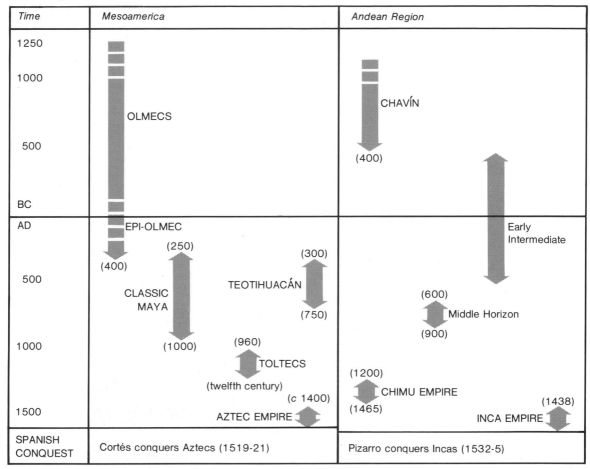

Time	Mesoamerica	Andean Region
1250	OLMECS	CHAVÍN
1000		
500		(400)
BC		
AD	EPI-OLMEC (250)	Early Intermediate
	(400)	
500	CLASSIC MAYA	TEOTIHUACÁN (300) / (750)
		(600) Middle Horizon (900)
1000	(1000)	TOLTECS (960)
	(twelfth century) (c 1400)	(1200) CHIMU EMPIRE (1465)
1500	AZTEC EMPIRE	(1438) INCA EMPIRE
SPANISH CONQUEST	Cortés conquers Aztecs (1519-21)	Pizarro conquers Incas (1532-5)

This tendency to utilize basalt columns seems to have originated in the earlier use of tree trunks, which is explained by the abundance of wood and the lack of stone in the region. It did not prove to be a successful method nor was it copied later. The other Olmec towns also do not boast any very remarkable monuments and their organization, as yet understudied, is still not clear.

If, with the exception of the La Venta layout, the architecture of the Olmecs is relatively poor, their sculpture is outstanding; in fact these people achieved some of the most notable pieces in all the history of Mesoamerica. Dealing firstly with monumental sculptures in stone, we can divide the works into four categories.

1. *Giant heads* We know of 15 of these and one fragment. They range from about 5 ft to 10 ft (1.60 to 3.00 m) in height. They are all heads without bodies. They depict relatively fat, young men with fleshy facial features wearing helmets similar to those worn by American football players. There has been much speculation as to

Colossal Olmec head (c AD 600). The Olmecs excelled both in colossal statuary and in the most delicate carvings.

who they could be—chiefs, gods?—but it is clear that they all form part of the same complex culture. The differences between them are minor and are most likely attributable to the time lag between the first and last carving—we do not exactly know how long this was—and to the fact that they were carved in different towns. It is difficult to guess their chronological order.

2. *Large rectangular monoliths, called altars* It has been suggested that these were not really altars but huge thrones. Their sides are frequently embellished with scenes or figures, both in high and bas relief. A favourite theme is that of a figure rising from a niche with a child in its arms. Frequently, also, the niche resembles the open mouth of a jaguar whose eyes and eyebrows are shown above. The altar of Potrero Nuevo, which is an earthenware block supported by two Atlantean figures in high relief, is very different. This idea of using Atlantean figures endured and it is encountered in a very different style in, for example, Tula, 1500 years later. Eleven Olmec altars and five fragments are known.

3. *Stelae* These slabs, sometimes of irregular shape, are very varied in appearance as well as in size and each one represents something different. The most interesting are those of Tres Zapotes, where two great stelae depict scenes with various human forms, and stela C contains the oldest complete date in the Mayan calendar system as yet discovered. (This will be considered below.) On some there are hieroglyphics which demonstrate without doubt that there was already an alphabet. Unfortunately, because of their scarcity, these hieroglyphics have not been properly deciphered. Some 18 stelae are known but, as some have been entirely effaced, there is doubt as to their classification.

4. *Giant or medium-sized statues* portraying human figures sometimes resembling animals, particularly the jaguar or the serpent. These are very numerous and it is sometimes difficult to be certain that some of them do not postdate the Olmecs. However, among them are some of the most beautiful and advanced pieces of Olmec sculpture. They always depict men standing or sitting in the oriental fashion, or half-kneeling, as in monument 34 at San Lorenzo. Almost alone at this time in Mesoamerica there is an attempt to show the beauty of the human body. Among the subjects portrayed is the so-called wrestler of Uzpanapa, or the figure of a man carrying a boy, who is perhaps dead, from the Limas. Although all these latter pieces are in high relief, at times they are embellished by very fine incisions representing human or animal forms, hieroglyphics or scrolls. In some cases the human figure has feline features, or there are hieroglyphics such as those that have been interpreted as indicating the skin of the jaguar.

Some important Olmec works do not fall into any of the categories mentioned above—such as a large lidded sarcophagus in La Venta decorated with a jaguar mask, or a stone box covered in bas relief with numerous

scrolls, which lead us to conclude that it is a late piece of Olmec art. Others represent animals and there are some that show the mating of a woman with a jaguar, though this interpretation is uncertain: reference may be made to the history of the jaguar men so typical of this culture.

The smaller Olmec sculpture is no less valuable. The Olmecs used many varieties of stone; prominent among them is the bluish jade so typical of this people. There are small figurines depicting men standing or crouching, sometimes with monstrous or dwarfish features, comparable to the familiar association of a man with a jaguar, or a bird such as the duck or the eagle. Large or small masks depicting men or deified jaguars are fairly common. At times they are hollow on the back and are covered with fine perforations or incisions supplementing the design.

There are many anthropomorphous axes with the characteristic Olmec mouth with (as in other pieces) the triangular cut-out in the centre of the head that continued right into the beginnings of the Teotihuacán epoch. Some of these axes are veritable works of art and they come in various sizes and in different materials. It is

Olmec sculpture from Veracruz. The art of the Olmecs is unique—simple, direct, forceful.

presumed that they were ceremonial axes and not used for any practical purpose. In the same way, many pieces made for personal ornament, carved in stone or sometimes in bone, have also been found: necklace beads, pendants, earrings and a wide variety of ornaments representing different objects. Of the many other types of objects found, some are practical, such as spatulas, punches, spindles; others simply seem to be symbolic like the jade canoe of Cerro de las Mesas. Also very interesting are the bloodstone mirrors, though these apparently come most probably from Oaxaca and were then brought to the Olmec region for commercial purposes.

Olmec religion and influence

It has been suggested that some Olmec figures already represent anthropomorphous gods such as those worshipped by later Mesoamerican cultures. Some of these gods have even been identified with divinities otherwise known to us only in the later Mexican pantheon. In a few such cases the evidence is conclusive, but in others there is still doubt. The importance of the investigation lies in the fact that if these gods were already represented at this date, this not only indicates a very long tradition extending back to the sixteenth century BC, but also justifies our referring to these manifestations as Olmec religion and not merely as magic related to natural phenomena. Evidently the Olmecs were, in their religion as in so many things, at the base of each subsequent culture of Mesoamerica. Hence the name of 'mother culture' awarded to them.

When the superior culture of the Olmecs began, it had behind it thousands of years of American development. The people of Mesoamerica were already farmers, and settlers, they worked in ceramics and were fairly advanced in their organization. But city life hardly originated with the Olmecs, though they had planned towns. However, we have various indications of their extensive commerce. Objects brought from other parts of Mesoamerica have been found in the metropolitan area. Likewise in various regions, namely Oaxaca, Chiapas, Guatemala and in the rest of Veracruz there are clear examples of the influence exercised by the Olmecs on other peoples. Most probably because of their geographical position, and because the rivers in the area obviously flowed from the mountains to the sea, we note how the Olmecs imported large and heavy objects–as well as certain smaller items–such as the great stones for their monoliths, and how in exchange they exported easily transportable articles such as their jades. Above all else they exported their own particular life style. Thus extensive trading was set in motion and was inherited by later cultures.

We cannot ascertain whether commerce was already linked to war and to the imposition of taxes, as happened much later, nor do we know anything about Olmec armies or possible military triumphs. There are no certain representations of soldiers carrying arms nor do we know of any arms or defensive weapons that they might have had.

The Olmecoids and the colonial Olmecs

We come across the presence of the Olmecs, or at least the influence of their style, in several regions. These can be divided into two groups which may be termed the Olmecoids and the colonial Olmecs. The Olmecoids are those people already reasonably advanced on the path to civilization and who at a given point in time allow the archaeologist to catch a glimpse of the Olmec world in its midst. The colonials are those still backward people who received Olmec influence which, having no comparable local rival, was virtually a unique manifestation with no important cultural style for it to mix with.

This second group is especially notable in the valleys of the high Mexican plain in places like Tlatilco where there are no other characteristic features except for the marvellous ceramics, the style of which is very much like Olmec work. In certain areas scattered across Mesoamerica where there are no planned centres, nor any large sculpture in stone, some features are found that are missing from the metropolitan area. There are two in particular: first, *petroglyphs* representing scenes with many Olmec figures. The most famous are in such different places as Chalcatzingo in Morelos, Piedra Parada in Guatemala, Batchatén in Chiapas and Las Victorias in El Salvador. Their absence from the metropolitan zone could be due to the lack there of rocks that would allow this type of bas relief; secondly, *wall paintings*, also done on natural rock, often inside caves such as the very interesting ones discovered in the state of Guerrero. They are the oldest paintings that we know of in Mexico with designs that are at times very complicated.

The world of the Olmecoids, whose main centres were in Oaxaca, Chiapas, Guatemala and Veracruz, was much more advanced. We have already found at least the beginnings of planned towns of which Monte Albán is the most famous, although somewhat later in relation to the central zone. For the first time a true architecture emerged in stone and not in clay, which gave scope for considerable improvements. One new structure was the pyramid that ascended in vertical-walled terraces, each smaller than the one below. The slope and the slab so typical of Mesoamerican architecture do not appear until the end of the period of the Olmec civilization, in part when Teotihuacán was at its height. Moreover, many stelae which undoubtedly came from the Olmecs have been found.

The advent of literacy

With the stelae–although not only on them–appeared the most advanced feature of Olmec civilization in general: the calendar and the alphabet. They appear at a late stage in the development of Olmec civilization–in the period that has been called Olmec III–and in fact when some of the important towns were beginning to disappear or to be abandoned. The most famous monument is stela C of Tres Zapotes. Part of it was discovered by Dr Matthew W. Stirling. This explorer correctly read the date–which at the time was incomplete. Many years later the other half of the monument was found. This amply corroborated Stirling's assumption and gave the date of 2 September AD 31. This date is represented in the Mayan system which was probably invented by the Olmecs at a later stage of their development. The oldest date in Guatemala corresponds to 6 December 35 BC. Other stones also in Guatemala or Chiapas show dates close to these. There is no doubt that all precede the earliest dates discovered up till now in the Mayan region but they are written according to the same system. All this constitutes a final contribution, a late bloom of the Olmec civilization, to its successors in Mesoamerica. Thus there already existed the clearest indication of a civilized world: the alphabet and an established calendar.

Teotihuacán

Robert S. Santley

The ancient city of Teotihuacán is located approximately 25 miles (40 km) northeast of modern Mexico City in the Basin of Mexico, Mexico. At the time of the Spanish conquest the site was the capital of a small territorial state tributary to the Aztec capital, Tenochtitlán, but during the period from 100 BC to AD 750 Teotihuacán was a huge sprawling urban centre covering some 8 sq miles (20 km²) with an estimated population of 100,000–200,000 persons. During the Classic period (c AD 300–750) Teotihuacán was also able to exert widespread 'influence' throughout Mesoamerica. Indeed, this 'influence' is so widespread and pronounced that several prehistorians have proposed using evidence of Teotihuacán 'contact' as a pan-Mesoamerican chronological marker.

The site of Teotihuacán
Surface survey and excavation at Teotihuacán indicate that the city was laid out on a grid orient 15° 30′ east of

Ruins of the ancient city of Teotihuacán: temples and pyramids. The ceremonial centre covers 8 sq miles (20 km²).

astronomic north. The main axes of this grid are three main avenues: the Street of the Dead, which ran 3 miles (5 km) south from the Pyramid of the Moon, and East and West avenues, which ran east-west intersecting the Street of the Dead at the Ciudadela-Great Compound complex. Branching off from these thoroughfares are a great number of secondary streets and small alleys which permitted access to all parts of the city. The city as it now stands–the urban grid, its great civic-ceremonial edifices, and the several thousand apartment compounds–represents construction activity that occurred largely after AD 300. The precise plan of the city during previous time periods is still in dispute, though a number of of constructions, the pyramids of the Sun and Moon and the Street of the Dead, were originally built on the same plan several centuries earlier.

Architecture
The heart of the urban zone is totally dominated by the Pyramid of the Sun and the Pyramid of the Moon. The Sun Pyramid, with a volume of about 1,296,000 cu yd (1,000,000 m³), is the largest single-period building

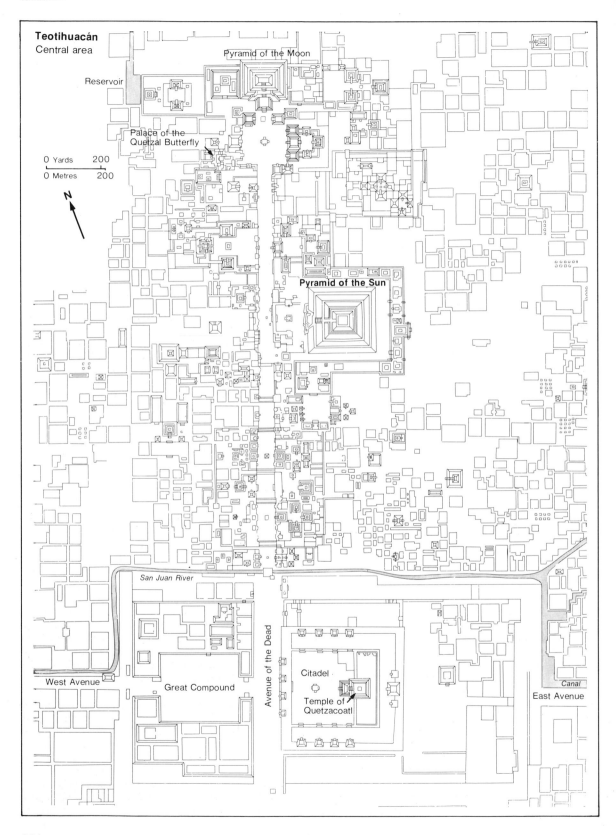

Teotihuacán
Central area

Reservoir

Pyramid of the Moon

Palace of the
Quetzal Butterfly

0 Yards   200
0 Metres   200

N

Pyramid of the Sun

San Juan River

West Avenue

Great Compound

Avenue of the Dead

Citadel

Temple of
Quetzacoatl

Canal

East Avenue

effort in the precolumbian New World. The Sun Pyramid is a four-stage truncated platform, 220 × 220 × 75 yd (200 × 200 × 70 m), which supported a small temple on top. Its interior was formed entirely of sun-dried mud bricks held in place by exterior walls of stone set in lime mortar and faced with lime stucco and plaster. Access to the summit is by a broad, balustraded stairway bifurcated on the lower terrace because of the later construction of a small apron. In front is a small plaza-altar complex flanked on both sides by residential compounds, all of which, including the Sun Pyramid, were built on an enormous platform roughly 300 × 395 yd (280 × 360 m) in dimensions. The Pyramid of the Moon, the northern terminus of the Street of the Dead, was constructed similarly although smaller in size. Hundreds of smaller temple platforms, occasionally arranged around small plazas in tripartite fashion, also occur throughout the city. All platform architecture at Teotihuacán was built using the talud-tablero motif: a rectangular panel with inset (the tablero) placed over a sloping batter (the talud). The talud-tablero motif is a hallmark of Teotihuacán architecture, not only within the urban zone itself but also about the Basin of Mexico at large.

In the geographic centre of the city is the Ciudadela-Great Compound complex. The Ciudadela, probably the royal palace, consists of a large raised platform about 330 yd (300 m) on a side surrounding a sunken interior enclosure. Within the enclosure on its eastern side is the Pyramid of Quetzalcóatl: a six-stage, talud-tablero platform temple with façades of sculptured Feathered Serpents and Rain God effigies. Flanking the temple to the north and south are two room complexes, presumably the residence(s) *per se* of the ruler of Teotihuacán. Directly to the east are a number of large apartment compounds which may have housed administrative functionaries associated with the palace. The entire complex, including the presumed administrative compounds, was enclosed by a large stone wall, suggesting that the Ciudadela was not for general access.

Immediately across the Street of the Dead is the Great Compound, a building complex comparable in size to the Ciudadela. In actuality, the Great Compound consists of two enormous, low U-shaped platforms with the remains of small apartment compounds on top, arranged around a vast central plaza. Access to the plaza was by two broad ground-level entrances: one to the Street of the Dead to the east, the second to West Avenue directly to the west. Excavations on the platforms uncovered little evidence of a domestic or residential function, implying to the excavators that the compounds atop both platforms may have formed the city's bureaucratic centre. In addition, the Great Compound is surrounded by great numbers of craft workshops, many devoted to obsidian working. These lines of evidence, combined with the plaza's high accessibility, imply that the Great Compound may have served as Teotihuacán's principal marketplace.

Distributed about Teotihuacán are several thousand apartment compounds, the standard unit of residence for the bulk of the city's population. Each compound contains a complex of rooms, patios, porticoes, light wells, small temple shrines and passageways, all enclosed by thick stone exterior walls. Individual rooms, perhaps family apartments, are arranged around small patios, and these in turn are oriented to one or more main entryways. Sometimes, the main entrance opens on to a larger patio with a central altar flanked by several shrines, as at Yayahuala, indicating construction following a preconceived plan. In other cases like Tlamimilolpa growth appears to be by accretion; rooms seem to be crowded without apparent planning, and the well-planned entryway/compound shrine complex is absent. Although compound size varies greatly, from 16–22 yd (15–20 m) on a side to 55 × 165 yd (50 × 150 m), most appear to fall into the 65 × 65 yd (60 × 60 m) size range. Consequently, while many compounds are similar in size and external appearance, there is considerable variability in the internal partitioning of rooms, hallways and courts. Population estimates range from 60 to 100 persons on average, based on the frequency of 'potential' sleeping rooms. Investigations of anomalies in bone structure of burials from several compounds indicate that males were more closely related genealogically than females. Post-marital residence, as a result, may have been virilocal, whereas descent may have been reckoned patrilineally, to judge from ethnohistoric analogues. Thus, each compound may have been occupied by a local lineage segment, each room cluster by an extended family and each room or two by a nuclear family, all related in unilineal fashion.

Social differentiation

A city as a large as Teotihuacán was undoubtedly characterized by marked social differentiation. Based on size and quality of residential architecture and associated artifacts, three social levels are indicated: élite, intermediate and low. High-status residences are largely confined to the heart of the city, along the Street of the Dead between the Moon Pyramid and the Ciudadela-Great Compound complex, and were probably occupied by the Teotihuacán's top-level political, administrative, religious and commercial personages. The proximity of temples and élite residences, moreover, indicates intimate involvement on the part of high status individuals with the city's religious organizations. In addition, élite residences are situated close to obsidian workshops, workshops using high quality obsidian from the Navajas source and producing tools mainly for export. High status, therefore, may have had an important economic base.

Intermediate status residences comprise the bulk of the city's population. Such residences, generally apartment compounds of the sort previously described, are distributed throughout the city in a relatively uniform manner. Members of this status level appear to have been agriculturalists, farming lands in the lower Teotihuacán valley, or craft specialists of various kinds, producing a wide variety of tool types to meet local domestic needs.

Low status residences occur either in pockets around intermediate status residences or on the city's periphery. In many instances the apartment compound was not the unit of residence. Rather, structures appear to have been built using more impermanent materials; one excavated building, for example, was constructed entirely of adobe bricks. On the other hand, the Tlamimilolpa compound, with its crowded cluster of rooms, may be one example of an apartment compound of low status. Low status individuals doubtlessly accounted for a substantial segment of the city's farming population, and there is evidence to suggest that they formed the social stratum from which Teotihuacán's military was drawn. Evidence of organization of the indigenous population into barrios, or local wards, is meagre. In several cases compounds group spatially, suggesting the presence of an organizational level above that of the individual compound, and these occasionally associate with small temples. Likewise, at least two foreign groups are represented in localized areas: the Oaxaca Barrio and the Merchant's (or Gulf Coast) Barrio.

Economic differentiation
Craft specialization at Teotihuacán was also highly developed and internally differentiated. To date, 842 Classic period workshops have been discerned within the confines of the city: 126 figurine workshops, 213 pottery workshops, 105 ground stone workshops and 398 obsidian workshops, in addition to 13 marketing facilities. Add to these workshops for which there is no easily recognizable material evidence, and some 25–30 per cent of Teotihuacán's resident population may have been full-time craft specialists. Figurine workshops closely parallel the distribution of temples, occurring largely in the city's core. Pottery workshops, in contrast, manifest a high correlation with population density, following the distribution of intermediate status residences. Ground stone workshops pattern in yet another way, being located away from the city's main axes and near its periphery. Markets also tend to be situated away from the city's main avenues but are highly accessible in terms of workshop locations. Different kinds of workshop activity are therefore distributed in different ways about the city, and marketing locations appear to have been selected to maximize access to the greatest number of different kinds of specialized activities.

Perhaps the greatest fund of information pertains to obsidian working, the city's principal craft. Nearly 400 Classic period obsidian working loci have been discovered thus far, representing at least 12 per cent of the city's total population. Obsidian workshop sites can be divided into local areas, workshops responsible for satisfying the technological requirements of Teotihuacán itself, and export areas, workshops devoted to producing tools for exchange beyond the city. A large proportion of all workshops, some 60 per cent, appear to have manufactured a few specialized implements for long-distance exchange: bladelets, point blanks, figurines and eccentrics–while another 20–25 per cent

produced the full range of tools for use about the Basin of Mexico and Teotihuacán dependencies on the Central Plateau. Roughly 25 per cent of all workshop activity appears to have been devoted to blade tool production, with an equal amount to point and/or knife blank manufacture. Export workshops, moreover, generally produced tools of a certain type, prismatic blades in particular, whereas local areas processed tools of several different types. Export workshops, especially those involved in blade manufacture, are tightly clustered near the Great Compound. Local workshops, on the other hand, are more evenly distributed about the city. Navajas obsidian, the principal obsidian medium channelled into blade tool and export workshops, appears to have entered the city via a single conduit, perhaps regulated by the Teotihuacán state. Local workshops, in contrast, appear to have developed their own independent procurement systems, some obtaining obsidian from the source region while others collected or traded for waterworn nodules carried in rivers from the source. Clearly, the obsidian craft was a major component, perhaps the dominant component, in the economy of the ancient city.

Regional settlement patterns
Unquestionably, Teotihuacán was an urban centre of the first magnitude, unparalleled in size and in complexity in Classic period Mesoamerica. Not only is the city's civic-ceremonial precinct one of the most impressive architectural achievements in the precolumbian New World but also Teotihuacán appears to have been characterized by considerable social and economic diversity. Such sites, the capitals of large, politically centralized and socially stratified socio–cultural systems, exert powerful effects on surrounding rural landscapes. The rural area dominated by ancient Teotihuacán included the Basin of Mexico, southern Hidalgo, and parts of the modern states of Puebla, Tlaxcala and Morelos. Within this area the landscape may be divided into three spatial components: a core area, which funded Teotihuacán with the bulk of its basic energy needs; a hinterland area, which was subordinate politically but relatively self-sufficient in terms of basic grains, providing the urban zone with specialized food and raw material resources; and a number of exchange corridors, colonized by Teotihuacán to provide the city with permanent lines of exchange to vend craft goods.

The core area includes all that space within a 12–mile (20 km) radius of the urban zone. The size distribution of rural communities in this zone is bimodal, with large villages commonly occurring. Because locational rents were high, virtually all settlements were tightly nucleated, many duplicating Teotihuacán in layout and residential pattern. In comparison with the hinterland, rural settlements are relatively infrequent and widely spaced, since a substantial proportion of the population of the urban zone appears to have been farmers. The lower Papalotla and Teotihuacán valleys appear to have been the primary agricultural resource areas available to farmers resident in the city. This land was probably intensively cultivated, most likely under permanent irrigation and, if contemporary patterns of hydraulic land use can be used as a guide, this area would have been capable of furnishing the urban zone with a major proportion of its basic energy needs. Since provincial administrative centres do not occur in the core, the general pattern of political and economic integration with Teotihuacán was probably highly dendritic, with most exchanges in energy, information and craft goods transpiring directly between the urban centre and rural villages, and horizontal exchanges between dependent villages of equivalent rank being relatively few in number.

The hinterland includes all that area within a 12–60 mile (20–100 km) radius of Teotihuacán. Communities in this zone exhibit a more normal rank-size distribution, and the site hierarchy includes at least four tiers, due to the appearance for the first time of second-order provincial centres and great numbers of small unobtrusive hamlets. Moreover, as distance from Teotihuacán increases, settlements become smaller in size and more dispersed in character.

Different parts of the Basin are variations on this theme. Sites elsewhere in the central Basin, in the Cuautitlan, Tenayuca, and Temascalapa regions in particular, are reasonably large and highly nucleated, largely following the pattern just described, and their consistent orientation to prime irrigable land suggests that they also supplied Teotihuacán with basic grain

staples. Communities in the northern Basin are also highly nucleated but interestingly in close proximity to major lime deposits, not prime irrigable land, implying a very specialized function. This general pattern extends into southern Hidalgo where sites appear to have been politically dependent on the large Teotihuacán centre, Chingu. Given the extensive use of lime plaster and stucco at Teotihuacán, it seems likely that the northern Basin and the Tula Region, nearly uninhabited previously, were colonized directly from Teotihuacán for the explicit purpose of mining and exporting processed lime to the burgeoning urban centre. In contrast, settlements in the southern Basin are more dispersed and much smaller in size on the average, though a distinct site hierarchy is again in evidence. Sites in the southern Basin prefer three distinct loci for settlement: the shore of Lake Chalco-Xochimilco, the upper segment of the alluvial plain, and the middle part of the piedmont. Settlements on the lakeshore and in the piedmont appear to have specialized in the exploitation of lacustrine and forest products respectively, furnishing Teotihuacán with important hunted, gathered and fished food supplements, and basic construction materials.

A number of these communities, especially sites at higher elevations, seem to have been seasonally occupied, perhaps by individuals who resided permanently in apartment compounds at Teotihuacán itself. Sites on the alluvial plain, on the other hand, appear to have been year-round agrarian communities. Northeast of the Basin is another area colonized by Teotihuacán.

Valley of Teotihuacán, ecological divisions.

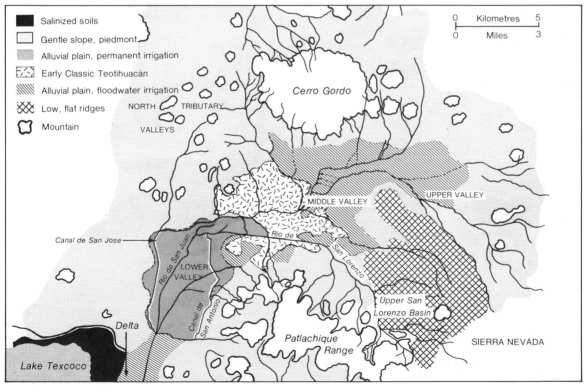

Settlements in this area are also large and tightly nucleated, again frequently mimicking the urban centre in plan. Residential sites in this area are either located near obsidian deposits (for example, Huapalcalco) or are situated in localties to maximize access to raw obsidian procured from several sources (for example, Tepeapulco). Great numbers of small obsidian quarrying, processing and trans-shipment sites also occur, suggesting that rural settlements in this area were closely tied in with Teotihuacán's main craft industry, obsidian working.

Beyond the hinterland are a number of corridors of Teotihuacán settlement which extend outward from the Basin of Mexico in pseudopod-like fashion. The site distribution in this zone is largely bimodal, with most of the population nucleated in a few large sites due to proximity to the political frontier. These sites are generally located along established routes of communication and exchange about the Central Plateau. Either such areas were unoccupied previously or commensurate with the Teotihuacán presence there was a major reorganization in settlement pattern, implicating colonization directly from the Basin of Mexico. Included here are the corridor of Teotihuacán settlement running southeast from the Teotihuacán valley to the Gulf Coast escarpment and the apparent ribbon of Teotihuacán sites in the Amatzinac Region immediately to the south of the Basin of Mexico. The recently reported Teotihuacán occupations in the valley of Toluca may belong to yet another band of Teotihuacán settlement outside of the Basin of Mexico proper. Teotihuacán 'influence' has also been documented beyond the Central Plateau. Sites displaying evidence of contact with Teotihuacán generally fall into two categories: occupation at ports-of-trade, which are typically situated on the boundaries between rival trading systems (for example, Matacapan on the south of Gulf Coast and Kaminaljuyú/Solano in the valley of Guatemala); or occupation at large established centres far removed from the urban zone, which may have served as distributional nodes for Teotihuacán commodities.

The basic configuration, then, is of a densely settled core area in the Teotihuacán valley surrounded by at least four areas of varying economic importance which comprise the hinterland. The central Basin appears to be the agricultural area which funded Teotihuacán with basic grain staples. The southern Basin may have provided lake and forest products plus some cultivated foodstuffs. The northern Basin/Tula region appears to have been the major locus of lime manufacture, whereas the area directly to the northwest of the Basin seems to have specialized in obsidian exploitation. Beyond the Basin proper are a number of areas quite distant from Teotihuacán, colonized to secure exchange routes. This general pattern represents a complete departure from previous settlement configurations, when the southern Basin was the main nucleus of settlement with a population in the neighbourhood of 90,000 and the central and northern parts of the Basin were virtually unoccupied, implying quite strongly that Classic Period rural settlements in the Basin of Mexico were direct extensions of the state authority resident at Teotihuacán. Indeed, it is very difficult to escape the conclusion that the political system centralized at Teotihuacán had completely expropriated the Basin of Mexico as its own private domain, wholly rearranging local populations to suit state needs.

The rise and fall of Teotihuacán civilization

A variety of arguments have been advanced to explain the origins of civilization in prehispanic Mesoamerica. Most scholars, however, feel that economic stratification is a major component in the evolutionary process leading to early states. Thus, differential control over capital resources is viewed as the mechanism stimulating the ability to amass private wealth. Once the ability to stockpile wealth becomes concreted, the germ is laid for the development of specialized institutions whose function is to preserve the differentiated economic order. As pronounced social distinctions based on wealth emerge, political privilege becomes the prerogative of those with economic advantage, with the evolution of the state rapidly following suit.

In central Mexico investment of control of water resources in the hands of a select group of individuals is considered as the principal factor effecting economic stratification and centralized decision-making. Organizational control is necessary not so much physically to construct canal systems but to quell disputes arising from inequities in water distribution, the proverbial upstream-downstream dichotomy. In the Teotihuacán valley cultivation on the alluvial plain requires irrigation before the start of the rainy season, due to great variations in the date of its inception and in the total amount of precipitation. Cultivation without irrigation, therefore, generally results in total crop failure. Spring-fed perennial streams, however, are few in number, but when found, they are surrounded by reasonably large areas of low risk, high water table land. Such lands, usually situated in upstream localities, consequently have a higher population support capacity when cultivated using extensive techniques. These areas will be colonized early in the occupational sequence, but with population growth downstream communities must form: communities that because of the lack of access to high water table land must engage in hydraulic agriculture. These conditions impose stress on traditional institutions as upstream communities begin restricting access to water resources. Although irrigation agriculture can permit other societal arrangements, the most efficient type in semi-arid settings is the stratified social system, with its hierarchy of formal status positions, frequently based on wealth differences, and their delegated powers and centralized authority.

The conditions that select for this development are (1) great variety in the degree of agricultural risk, with low risk crop land being highly restricted in amount and distribution, (2) a water course long enough to permit the formation of downstream communities, (3) a relatively low amount of perennial water discharge so that not all users of the system can irrigate simultaneously, (4) a reasonably large area of high agricultural productivity having a demographic support capacity minimally in the tens of thousands, (5) high levels of environmental and/or social circumscription which effectively inhibit populations from fissioning into adjacent areas, and (6) comparable sets of events occurring in neighbouring regions. These factors are most satisfied in the Teotihuacán valley.

The advent of hydraulic agriculture, however, is the end product of the process of agricultural intensification: a process brought about by population growth in an environmentally or socially circumscribed region. Population growth in the Basin is rapid and sustained throughout the Formative period (c1500–300 BC). The conditions that favour demographic growth are: reduced female mobility, which relaxes the cultural checks regulating growth commonplace previously in more mobile societies; a balanced diet, relatively rich in raw protein, essential amino acids and carbohydrates; and relatively low population density. These conditions stimulate shorter birth intervals and inhibit the role of infectious disease in curbing growth. In the Basin of Mexico, moreover, the absolute rate of population growth increases as more northerly parts are colonized; in dietary terms this is reflected by increased carbohydrate consumption, due to the greater contribution of wild seeds, and increased protein intake, since the problem of animal protein capture is the least severe on the frontier of an expanding agricultural population. Thus, not only are the necessary local environmental conditions provided in the Teotihuacán valley but also populations inhabiting that region appear to have been growing unchecked at the fastest rate.

Prior to Teotihuacán's emergence as an urban centre the southern Basin was the favoured locus of settlement, with a well developed hierarchy of regional centres, villages and hamlets distributed in distinct clusters, but during the Tzacualli phase (100 BC–AD 150) the Teotihuacán polity was able physically to subdue the south, forcibly relocating upwards of 90 per cent of the population of the Basin at the urban centre. By Miccaotli times (AD 150–300) the Basin is recolonized, and these settlements, especially in the central Basin, are repeatedly associated with prime irrigable land, a dramatic rearrangement in settlement pattern. The internal plan of the urban zone is restructured during the succeeding Tlamimilolpa phase (AD 300–500); the apartment compound becomes the basic unit of urban residence, with all civic-ceremonial and residential architecture incorporating the talud-tablero motif in construction design. Tlamimilolpa phase rural villages about the Basin also follow this design. In every way, shape, and form, this reorganization of Teotihuacán's settlement system appears to have been a state-directed project.

Coeval with this dramatic change in settlement and residential pattern is a massive increase in the incidence of obsidian working at Teotihuacán. The amount of workshop activity at Teotihuacán is considerable: sufficient to provide for the annual domestic needs of some 3–6 million consumers. Great numbers of export workshops cluster near the Great Compound, Teotihuacán's presumed main marketplace and administrative centre, and this, combined with the spatial structure of Teotihuacán obsidian exploitation and processing sites northeast of the Basin of Mexico, suggests that the export trade was a state-subsidized enterprise. Why Teotihuacán was able to monopolize access to the obsidian raw material may be linked to its geographic position close to the source deposits and to its emergence as a pre-eminent centre in a comparative socio-political vacuum. Why Teotihuacán was so preoccupied with producing goods for long-distance trade certainly relates to the capital gain returned to the urban zone from the exchange process. How Teotihuacán was able to attract such a large consumer clientele may be attributed to the implementation of a highly discriminatory pricing policy: a policy under which the producing node absorbs some of the costs involved in transshipping goods over great distances, thereby underbidding potential or extant rival manufacturing centres.

The obsidian trade, as a result, may have provided Teotihuacán with an important source of unearned income. Such an unearned resource base was largely unavailable to any other early civilization in prehispanic Mesoamerica. This implies that Teotihuacán's unique ability to restructure its settlement pattern on such an unprecedented scale can be explained in terms of surplus revenue from the exchange process. Thus, to live in the city may have meant economic advantage, an advantage made possible largely from imported energy. This capital gain may have also furnished the state with an effective means of solidifying its political position at home, for surplus energy could be returned to the local populace, either as rebates in subsistence produce or in the form of government-sponsored building projects.

Economic strategies of this sort work only as long as rival production nodes are underdeveloped. Once these centres arise, undoubtedly for the same reasons as at Teotihuacán but at a slower pace, production and distributional systems become highly competitive. In response, the exchange system should contract spatially, and reduced numbers of consumers mean less surplus energy returned to Teotihuacán. Craftsmen, given changing economic conditions, would be expected to gravitate towards new centres of production. As predicted, near the end of the Classic period there is a decline in the frequency of workshop activity at Teotihuacán, a period when rival competing states like Tula, Cholula, and Xochicalco were gaining stature. During the succeeding Early Toltec period (AD 750–950) each of these centres maintained independent production and distribution systems, utilizing obsidian from a different subset of sources. Teotihuacán, however, still exercised firm control over the Basin of Mexico. The Early Toltec site itself covers some 45 sq miles (10 km²), with rural communities conforming to the pattern previously described. Domination of international markets, on the other hand, had severely waned. Ecological theory predicts that diversification is the adaptive norm in mature ecosystems. In economic terms, production centres should be redundant, distributed near marketing areas. This being the case, the 'collapse' of Teotihuacán's monopolistic economy can be viewed as a step leading to a more mature, certainly a more balanced adaptive plateau.

The Toltecs

Richard A. Diehl

Introduction

The Toltecs were the dominant society in northern Mesoamerica during the Second Intermediate or Early Post-classic period (about AD 900 to 1200). Their capital was Tollan, today called Tula, about 35 miles (56 km) north of modern Mexico City. For a century or two they dominated much of north-central and west Mexico and perhaps a portion of the Gulf coast tropical lowlands. They also conquered the Maya of northern Yucatán and established economic ties extending into northern Central America. By AD 1200 the Toltec empire or state fell into pieces and Tollan lay in ruins.

This article summarizes current knowledge about the Toltecs, emphasizing new archaeological data rather than the more traditional historical approach to Toltec studies.

Mesoamerica was occupied by several highly developed civilizations in the centuries after Christ; those of Teotihuacán and the Maya are the best known but others existed in Oaxaca, Veracruz and the Guatemalan highlands. Political, social and economic systems evolved that lasted for many centuries; however, radical changes took place after AD 700. Teotihuacán's decline was followed shortly by the complete disintegration of Classic Maya culture. The economic and political dislocations which accompanied the Teotihuacán decline formed the matrix out of which the Toltecs emerged.

We are fortunate to have both documentary and archaeological information on the Toltecs. The documentary materials were recorded by Spaniards and literate Indian-Spanish Mestizos in the sixteenth century AD; these accounts relate the historical legends of the Aztecs who considered themselves the cultural heirs of the Toltecs. They contain a wealth of information on Toltec dynastic history, political events and culture, but care must be exercised to separate facts from fables and to resolve the many conflicting accounts. The archaeological data comes from excavations and surveys at Tollan; virtually no excavations have been undertaken on other Toltec sites. Surface surveys have been done in the area around Tollan and in the Basin of Mexico to the south, and most of the Toltec communities which existed in these areas have been located.

Toltec history and chronology

The Toltec dynastic lists, migration legends, and other 'histories' handed down by the Aztecs are so confused that experts in these materials have been unable to resolve many of the basic conflicts. There is near consensus that Tollan was the Toltec capital and that it flourished between c AD 900 to 1200. Both points have been confirmed by archaeology, although radiocarbon dates suggest that Tollan was abandoned by AD 1100 or 1150. The documents also tell of a time of civil war or internal strife culminating with either the flight of the losers or the complete abandonment of the city. Some sources place this conflict at the time of Tollan's collapse, others put it several centuries earlier when the city was just beginning to attain prominence. Some archaeological evidence supports the latter position but the entire episode is still shrouded in mystery.

The Toltec occupation of Tollan is divided into several archaeological phases. The community was first settled in the Prado phase (AD 700–800). The Corral phase (800–950) was a time of considerable growth, by its end the community covered at least two sq miles (5 sq km). The Tollan phase (950–1150 or 1200) marks the time when the city grew to its maximum size and played its major role in pan-Mesoamerican affairs. By the end of the phase the city was abandoned and the empire had disintegrated.

Tollan, the Toltec capital

Tollan is located in the southeastern section of Hidalgo state on a ridge overlooking the confluence of the Tula and Rosas rivers. Remains of the ancient city cover the ridge and extend into the alluvial plain and up the nearby hillslopes. Tollan's status as a true urban centre is indicated by its five sq mile (13 sq km) settlement area, its estimated population of 32,000 to 37,000 inhabitants, and the evidence for marked social and economic stratification among its inhabitants.

The centre of the city was a large architectural complex, known as the Main Civic Precinct, and located at the highest point of the ridge. The Main Civic Precinct contained numerous public buildings such as temples, colonnaded halls, 'palaces', ballcourts, a skull rack and other structures. This was the secular and religious administrative centre of the city and the ruler and other high dignitaries probably lived in nearby but yet undiscovered palaces. The largest and most impressive buildings occupy the edges of an open plaza approximately 130 yards (119 m) on a side. Many architectural details of the buildings are questionable because the Aztecs systematically looted the sculptures and carved facing stones for re-use in their own buildings.

Virtually all the buildings of any size were placed on solid, rubble-filled platforms, the temple platforms being stepped pyramids much taller than those of other buildings. The largest temple, known as Structure C, has been too badly destroyed to recover much information on its exterior appearance. Structure B, located north of C, is in a similar state of destruction but intact friezes of bas relief facing tablets were found on the north and east platform sides. The friezes depict pumas, jaguars, eagles and vultures eating human hearts, and a creature with human, feline, reptilian and avian characteristics. The temple on top of the platform was completely destroyed but evidence indicates that its doorway was framed with feathered serpent sculptures and the roof was supported by large Atlantean columns depicting Toltec warriors. It is thought that this building was dedicated to Tlahuizcalpantecuhtli, the god Quetzalcóatl (the Feathered Serpent) in his guise as Venus, the Morning Star. Structure B is flanked by two large multiroomed buildings. Though termed palaces, they apparently did not function as residences. The building on the west (the Palacio Quemado or Burnt Palace) had three large rooms with benches built against the interior walls and a

The temple of Quetzalcóatl at Tollan (today called Tula), the Toltec capital, was completely destroyed. Four warrior columns have been re-installed on the platform of the temple.

multitude of stone columns supporting the roof. Carved tablets on the benches depict processions of elaborately dressed dignitaries and may symbolize actual ceremonies and activities conducted in the rooms.

The west end of the plaza is closed off by a large ballcourt consisting of two long platforms that enclose a playing field shaped like a capital I. Here teams competed with each other in attempts to drive a solid rubber ball through holes in two stone rings placed into the court walls. A similar ballcourt is found north of Structure B and several others remain to be excavated. A *tzompantli* or skull rack was located in front of the first-mentioned ballcourt, where the skulls of sacrificial victims were displayed in a visual reminder of Toltec power and of the debt of human life and blood owed to the gods.

A smaller civic precinct called Tula Chico was located half a mile north of the Main Civic Precinct. It predates the latter and was abandoned by the beginning of the Tollan phase.

Tollan residences have not been excavated in great numbers but surface surveys show that closely packed houses covered at least four sq miles (10 sq km) of the five sq mile (13 sq km) urban zone. The best information on residential architecture comes from excavations in the northern part of the city. The houses were rectangular buildings with stone foundations, adobe block walls, flat roofs and compacted earth or white plaster floors. Variations in house size, complexity and construction quality reflect wealth and status differences among the occupants. Houses occur in clusters of three

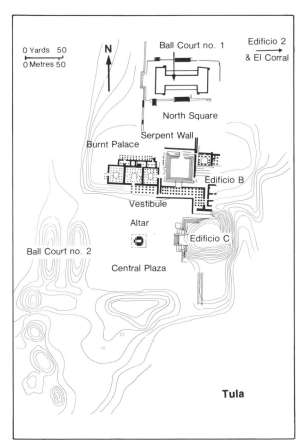

or four arranged around open courtyards; the courtyards were the *loci* of much daily activity and the rooms were primarily used for sleeping and storage. Cluster residents were probably kinsmen, perhaps members of extended families. The courtyards contained small rectangular altars with burials inside them. The burials were probably the remains of elder kinsmen, while other cluster residents were buried under house floors.

Tollan's economy

Agriculture, craft production and trade were the basic economic activities at Tollan. Numerous rural village sites near the city suggest that most of the land was cultivated by villagers rather than city dwellers. The basic agricultural techniques included irrigation, hillside terracing, and rainfall-based, non-irrigation farming. Planting was done with a digging stick; the absence of large domestic animals precluded the use of ploughs and fertilizer. The main crops were maize, beans, squash, chilli peppers, amaranth and prickly pear. A mildly alcoholic beverage called *pulque* was fermented from the sap of the mature maguey cactus. Meat consumption was limited; the dog and turkey were the only domestic food animals, but wild game included deer, rabbits, small rodents and birds.

A substantial portion of the urban dwellers were specialists involved in craft production of one sort or another. Obsidian processing was a major industry, at least one sq mile (2.5 sq km) of the city being littered with workshop debris. This volcanic glass was used for making razor-sharp blades, scrapers, projectile points and other artifacts. The raw materials came from quarries up to 40 miles (64 km) away.

The initial processing was done at the quarries by removing useless waste, and the material was then shipped to Tollan where craftsmen prepared cores and tools. Cores were the most common product of the Tollan workshops; they were sold to consumers who removed blades from them as they were needed. The shimmering green-gold obsidian from the quarry at Pachuca was highly prized for its beauty and workability, and the Toltecs appear to have monopolized its exploitation and distribution.

Extensive workshop zones for other craft products have not yet been identified at Tollan but ceramics, textiles, wood implements, and ground and polished stone tools and ornaments may have been produced in substantial quantities. Extensive lime deposits near Tula were probably exploited for construction materials and for lime to soak maize during its preparation into tortillas.

The Toltec trade and exchange system had local, regional and 'international' components. The local component probably emphasized marketplace exchanges at Tollan and in provincial centres. The regional system integrated the Toltec heartland area, described later, and presumably included markets, tribute paid to the Toltec government by politically subordinate peoples, and gifts from the Toltec rulers to the local élite.

The goods which circulated in the local and regional systems included foodstuffs, textiles, tools, pottery, and speciality items.

The international trade was probably handled by élite merchants analogous to the Aztec *pochteca*; these merchants travelled beyond the frontiers of the state and brought back exotic luxury goods. Such goods are known to include pottery from Guatemala, northern Central America and north Mexico; and turquoise from New Mexico, USA. Other imports may have included skins, feathers, shells, cacao beans, peyote, hallucinogenic mushrooms, fine textiles, and a host of other exotica.

Jaguar: the fanged god of precolumbian religion in the New World. A Toltec carving.

The Toltec heartland

The Toltec heartland was a relatively small and compact territory occupied by peoples directly under Tollan's political control. Although boundaries are not precisely known and in all likelihood changed constantly, it included modern Hidalgo, the northern portion of the Basin of Mexico, and sections of Michoacan, Queretaro, Guanajuato, and San Luis Potosí. The effectiveness of Toltec control over this area must have varied with time and distance; it would have been most effective at about AD 1100 and increasingly weaker the further away from the city.

Archaeological data on the heartland zone is very scanty and virtually no excavations have been undertaken outside Tollan. Settlements pattern surveys around Tollan and in the Basin of Mexico provide information on the number, size and distribution of communities at this time. Tollan was surrounded by numerous villages and the total Tollan phase occupation in a 386 sq mile (1000 sq km) area is estimated to have been 60,000 people. Most of the villagers were peasant-farmers. In the Basin of Mexico, the population was dispersed in hundreds of small villages and hamlets. These were administered at the local level by a few provincial centres that were in turn subject to Tollan. Some evidence suggests that Cholula in Puebla controlled portions of the Basin and that an east-west belt of deserted terrain in the Basin constituted a political boundary or no man's land between the Toltec and Cholulan polities.

The Toltec heartland was a distinctly marginal zone from an agricultural point of view. The aridity made rainfall-based farming a risky venture at best and crop failures must have been recurrent. Except for the Tollan area and the northern Basin of Mexico, the irrigatable zones were small and widely dispersed and could not be counted on to provide sufficient foodstuffs in times of drought. In addition, much of the area was covered with prairie-like grasslands that could not be cultivated without ploughs and draft animals. The overall agricultural insecurity and marginality of the heartland must have placed a considerable strain on the stability of the Toltec state and may have played a significant role in its collapse.

Toltec contacts outside the heartland

The Toltecs interacted with societies in virtually all parts of Mesoamerica. Most of the relationships with other societies were probably commercial ties concerned with exchanges of luxury goods but in at least one instance, that of Yucatán, the native peoples were conquered. Archaeological evidence shows contact with local groups in west and north-west Mexico as far north as Sinaloa. The communications route apparently followed the Lerma-Santiago river drainage to the Pacific coast. This area provided Tollan with Pacific coast shells, semi-precious stones and copper ornaments. The Toltecs maintained fairly intensive relationships with people on the Gulf coast from whom they obtained shells, feathers, animal skins, rubber, cacao and cotton in exchange for

The pyramid-temple of Kukulcán, the largest building of Chichén Itzá. The Toltec overlords erected buildings at Chichén Itzá identical to structures at Tollan (Tula).

obsidian, pottery, and other goods. The strength of the ties between these two areas is shown by the presence of a temple at Tollan dedicated to Ehecatl, the wind god; Ehecatl was a Huastec diety whose cult originated on the north Gulf coast.

Large quantities of Plumbate pottery at Tollan indicate well-developed commercial ties with the Pacific coast and the piedmonts of Guatemala and Chiapas, and the documentary sources contain tantalizing hints of Toltec conquest of the area. Toltec interest in this area may have been due to the fact that it was the prime cacao producing zone in Mesoamerica; cacao beans were not only used for a chocolate drink but also served as a pan-Mesoamerican medium of exchange or money.

The best documented case of Toltec activity in foreign lands is found in Yucatán where they conquered the Maya centre of Chichén Itzá and established a regional capital. This conquest is verified by both historical references and archaeological data. The Toltec overlords erected buildings at Chichén Itzá identical to structures at Tollan, introduced Toltec cults and dieties, and recorded their conquest in mural paintings. They were apparently every bit as quarrelsome as their relatives at Tollan because their conquest state disintegrated in the midst of a civil war among the élite.

The rise and fall of the Toltecs

The factors and processes involved in the Toltec rise and collapse are still open to question. Many of the ideas presented here are reasoned guesses rather than proven facts, nevertheless a fairly coherent picture emerges from the data at hand. Prior to AD 700 the locale of Tollan was not occupied, but a Teotihuacán-controlled regional centre existed a few miles away at Chingu. Chingu was abandoned at about AD 750, the inhabitants probably migrated to Tollan where they established the Tula Chico civic precinct.

As Teotihuacán's power waned and it lost control over its lands outside the Basin of Mexico, Tollan expanded its hinterland and the city grew. Much of its growth was the result of immigration because the urban and areal population expanded far too rapidly to be accounted for by natural internal growth alone. The immigrants appear to have come from two sources, Teotihuacán and the Mesoamerican frontier zone north of Tollan. The Teotihuacanos were probably craftsmen taking advantage of the expanding markets offered by Tollan. The motivations of the northern frontiersmen are not so apparent. There is evidence for southward emigration out of this zone by farming peoples as early as AD 600. The causes may include agricultural problems related to declining rainfall in this arid marginal zone. The disruptions engendered by this southward trek of displaced persons may have been a major factor in Teotihuacán's demise. Both archaeological and documentary evidence suggest that Tollan's population included many recently arrived northerners.

By the Tollan phase the Toltecs had gained control of the Pachuca obsidian sources and set out to replicate Teotihuacán's mercantile empire. They were unable to do so prior to this time because of competition by epigonal Teotihuacán, Cholula, Xochicalco, El Tajin, and perhaps other communities. Teotihuacán, Xochicalco and El Tajin had all ceased to be power centres by the time of the Tollan phase, and the Toltecs had a clear field in most of northern Mesoamerica. The Toltec role in these collapses is not clear but it may be assumed that at the least they took best possible advantage of the situation. However they were unable to consolidate their position for any length of time and by AD 1150 or 1200 Tollan lay in ruins.

The reasons for the Toltec collapse are unclear. The legends emphasize internal conflict and civil war but the timing of these events is open to question. Even if these accounts do apply to Tollan's abandonment, the conflicts were an immediate rather than a basic cause of the Toltec collapse. The basic causes probably included agricultural problems, continued immigration from the north, power struggles among different ethnic groups in the Toltec heartland, disruption of trade and commerce, and a fundamental inability of the Toltec rulers to resolve these problems.

Whatever transpired, Tollan was abandoned and the area experienced one or two centuries of political and social chaos in which petty states vied with each other for power. The Aztecs, or Mexica, emerged as the winners in this power struggle and inherited the civilization that both astounded and horrified the Iberian *conquistadores*.

The Maya

Gordon R. Willey

The Maya area subsumes all of Guatemala, portions of the Mexican states of Chiapas and Tabasco on the west, all of the peninsula of Yucatán to the north, the country of Belize, and the fringes of Salvador and Honduras on the east. This geographical definition pertains to the territory occupied by peoples of Maya speech at the time of the Spanish conquest in the early sixteenth century AD, but it also applies to a Maya occupation that extends well back into the precolumbian past.

The Maya language family includes several branches, languages, and dialects. The major division is between the Quichean Maya of the Gutemalan highlands and the Maya proper (Chorti, Chol, Yucatec) of the Petén-Yucatecan lowlands. This major linguistic division corresponds approximately with a division in precolumbian culture types. Both highlands and lowlands had long, complex, and rich precolumbian cultural developments. Their culture histories were linked to a degree, but it is the spectacular achievements of the lowlands–the hieroglyphic writing, the architecture, and the sculptural arts–that will be the primary concern in this discussion of what is generally known as Classic Maya civilization.

The roots of this civilization lie well back in the prehistoric past, and reference will be made to the following chronological framework:

Pre-classic Period
Early	2000–1000 BC
Middle	1000–300
Late	300 BC – AD 1

Proto-classic Period . . . . AD 1–250

Classic Period
Early	250–600
Late	600–800
Terminal	800–1000

Post-classic Period
Early	100–1250
Late	1250–1540

In general, the Pre-classic and Proto-classic periods saw the first settlement of the lowlands by sedentary farming peoples and the subsequent gradual development of the Classic Maya civilization; the Classic period was the time of its florescence; and the Post-classic the period of decline, foreign influences, and radical restructuring. The dates for this chronology are derived from radiocarbon determinations, especially for the Pre-classic era, from Maya Long Count calendrical dates for the Classic period, and from various historical estimates for the Post-classic period.

This chronology has an approximate application for all of precolumbian Mesoamerica. Mesoamerica may be defined as a 'culture area with time depth'. It comprises the southern two-thirds of Mexico and adjacent upper Central America. The Maya area is a part of this greater Mesoamerican culture sphere in which peoples of various ethnic and linguistic groups shared many common culture traits such as similar domesticated plants, a common ritual 260-day calendar, and mutual religious concepts; at the same time, the cultures of the several areas or regions of the greater Mesoamerican area developed somewhat differently in arts, crafts, specifics of religion, and political organization. It is, however, important to keep in mind that the culture history of any area or region within Mesoamerica may be understood only with some reference to what was going on in other parts of the Mesoamerican entity; and this pertains to the Maya.

The earliest human history of Mesoamerica, like that of North or South America, is known from scattered lithic finds left by very ancient hunters and gatherers. Some of these finds date back to 10,000 BC and before. There are hints of such antiquity for man in the Maya highlands; for the lowlands nothing of such great age has appeared as yet, although recent excavations in Yucatán indicate that man as a hunter and forager was present here several thousands of years ago. These glimpses of early occupation precede the Pre-classic period.

The Pre-classic period

The Pre-classic period of the Maya lowlands is defined by the first appearances of sedentary farming and pottery-making communities. The evidences for this have come from recent excavations made in northern Belize (formerly British Honduras). It is a moot point whether or not these early farmers were immigrants from nearby areas, such as the Guatemalan highlands or the Gulf coastal country of Tabasco and Veracruz to the west, or whether they were descendants of earlier resident hunters and gatherers who had adapted to agriculture and pottery through contacts with more advanced neighbours. But whatever their antecedents, we know that they were established in the Maya lowlands by 2000 BC. Their houses were of poles and thatch with prepared clay floors. Their pottery was competently made, simple in form and ornamentation, and can be related to other Early Pre-classic and Middle Pre-classic wares from other regions of southern Mesoamerica. The linguistic

Maya ceramic sculpture: one of thousands of remarkable portraits found on the island necropolis of Jaina, Classic period (AD 700–800).

337

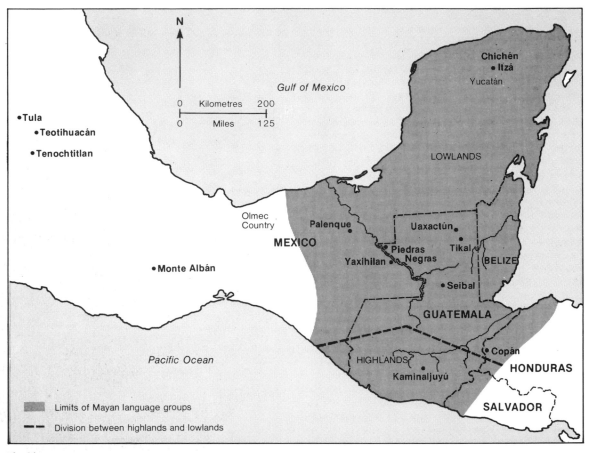

The Maya.

identity of these early farmers must remain a matter for speculation, but it is probable that they were of Mayan speech.

Towards the end of the Early Pre-classic period changes occur in the simple farming communities which suggest the beginnings of a more complex social order. Some structures–perhaps temples or chiefs' houses–are built on raised earth and mortar-covered platforms, indicating corporate labour activities under centralized authority. It is significant that at this same time similar changes were appearing in other Mesoamerican regions; and, in one region in particular, that of the Olmecs of the Tabasco-Veracruz coast, these changes had assumed quite notable proportions. In 1200 BC the Olmecs appear to have been the most advanced and sophisticated people of Mesoamerica. This is attested to by the big mound constructions and monumental stone sculpture at the southern Veracruz site of San Lorenzo. San Lorenzo was clearly the political and religious centre of a non-egalitarian society. This type of society, one featuring the construction and maintenance of centres or 'capitals' supported by satellite village and hamlet populations, was soon to become the standard one for much of Mesoamerica during the Pre-classic period. The Olmecs undoubtedly contributed

to its propagation. At the same time, the Pre-classic, as a period of population growth, provided the conditions for the widespread acceptance and development of social and political complexity; and the peoples of the Maya lowlands, as those of other regions of Mesoamerica, responded.

This cultural and social evolution continued in the Maya lowlands throughout the Middle Pre-classic and into the Late Pre-classic. By the latter period a number of major centres had been established. These were marked by large pyramid and platform constructions of dressed stone and lime-mortar masonry, often ornamented with stucco reliefs. Late Pre-classic burial practices give evidence of distinctions between élite and commoner classes. The volume of foreign trade, especially with the Guatemalan–Salvadoran highlands, increased. This is registered in obsidian and jadeite and in ceramic innovations that can be traced back to the highlands. Painted pottery decoration began to appear. At first this was either as a direct import or in imitation of highland styles; but slightly later the new technique of multi-colour painting was adapted to conform to local styles. The synthesis of foreign stimuli and in situ development that was to lead to Classic Maya lowland civilization was well under way in the Late Pre-classic and was to continue at an increasing tempo.

The Proto-classic period

The Proto-classic period saw the completion of the synthesis of Classic Maya civilization. The very essence of that civilization, or at least its élite segment, is its art and iconography and the linking of these to its systems of hieroglyphic writing and calendrics. All of these together compose a unique expression of an ideology and world view. Undoubtedly, this ideology had a long history on the Maya lowland scene, but its formulation and presentation in artistic symbols, writing, and recorded time-counting seem to have taken place in a relatively short time just before the Classic period threshold. Many of the elements of Maya religious iconography can be traced back to much earlier Olmec art—feline, serpent, and saurian forms, moon and day symbols—but the continuity of these still remains to be traced in the archaeological record. There are no sequences in the lowlands that document such an evolution, but there are clues to an Olmec-Maya transition in certain art styles and monuments that have been found on the Pacific slopes of Chiapas and Guatemala and in the Guatemalan highlands. Sculptures from the Proto-classic period site of Izapa provide one such possible link; those from Abaj Takalik and Kaminaljuyú are others. But whatever the original sources of the ideas, or the course of development which they followed, they appear to have had a refocalization and regeneration in a purely lowland Maya setting for it is in the northeastern sector of the Petén lowlands, at some distance from the Guatemalan highlands, that we see their first full-blown manifestation in what has been called the Classic Maya 'stelae cult'. It is with this stelae cult that we have the final synthesis of Maya culture that marks the beginning of the Classic period.

The Classic period

The stelae cult refers to the practice of setting up and carving columnar stone monuments to commemorate rulers, political events, and the passages of periods of time. The earliest such dated monuments are known from Tikal and Uaxactún in the northeastern Petén, and from the data now at hand it would appear that the practice spread from here to other Late Pre-classic centres until it covered the entire southern lowlands. As so much of Maya hierarchical life was bound up in these stelae dedication practices, it seems appropriate to begin discussion of the Classic period with them.

Politics, religion, and prophecy were expressed in the stelae carvings; and the skills of writing, time-counting, astronomy, and mathematics were attendant upon these. An individual ruler or dignitary was usually depicted on the face of a stela while the sides and back of the monument bore hieroglyphic inscriptions. Such inscriptions identified the person and offered information on his genealogy and accomplishments. The Maya hieroglyphic writing system was the most complex and advanced in precolombian Mesoamerica. Dates and glyphs referring to rulers and cities, plus some others, can be read and translated, but most of the glyphs remain undeciphered. The system, however, appears to

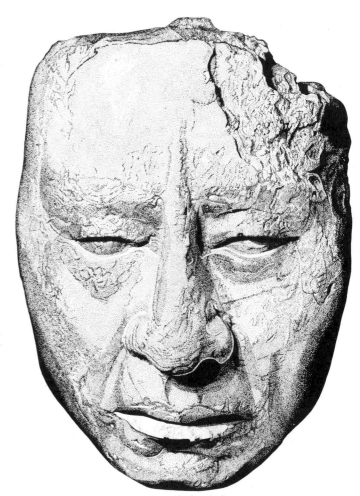

Maya stucco portrait head from Palenque, Classic period (AD 700–800).

be at least partly phonetic so there is hope for further progress. Most probably it relates to the lowland Maya languages, and these are still spoken today. The Maya had several calendars running concurrently, including a 365-day solar calendar, a 260-day ritual calendar, and, most importantly in connection with the stelae, a Long Count system of day tabulations. These tabulations were reckoned in a series of descending units of the *baktun* (144,000 days), *katun* (7200 days), *tun* (360 days), *uinal* (20 days), and *kin* (one day). This counting of days began at a mythical starting point in 3113 BC; however, all known Maya Long Count dates pertain to the eighth, ninth, and tenth *baktuns*, a period, in the case of the dates available, extending from about AD 270 to 910. It is these Long Count dates, most frequently recorded at *katun* (approximately 20-year) intervals, that are carved on the stelae. This was done with appropriate hieroglyphs indicating the time period units and with bar (for five) and dot (for one) numerals in a system of place enumeration. The Maya had the concept of zero and a sign for it. In addition to dates and historical material,

The signs of the months from the Maya calendar. The Maya hieroglyphic writing system was the most complex and advanced in the precolumbian Mesoamerica.

astronomical observations, both solar and lunar, were frequently recorded on the stelae; and these and solar and lunar calendars were integrated with Long Count notations in what seems almost an obsession with the phenomenon of time.

The carved stelae, executed in varying degrees of relief, were works of art as well as political, calendrical, and astronomical memoranda. Rulers were either deified or were represented as being surrounded by symbols of supernatural sanctions. These symbols, as represented on the stelae, on wall or lintel carvings, in stucco relief ornamentation, as well as in small artifactual carvings or in pottery painting, are the recurring subjects of Maya art, either as central themes in themselves or as embellishments to human and animal scenes. A full repertory of them is extensive. Some are serpent-dragons or saurian-dragons. This particular motif is a representation of the all-powerful deity Itzamna. Other deity motifs include sun-god and death-god representations. Animals, including deer, jaguars, and monkeys, as well as various birds and fish, are often portrayed quite naturalistically. The use of water-lily motifs or garlands is also typical of Maya art. Wall-panel scenes, where a large flat surface is carved or painted, often depict scenes of ritual or political import with dignitaries seated on thrones or benches interviewing persons seated or standing before them. A set of famous

wall paintings from the Classic period site of Bonampak, in Chiapas, appears to relate to an arraignment of captives before a great lord and the subsequent sacrifice of some of the prisoners. Lavish costuming, of brightly painted textiles, feathers, and jade ornaments, is typical of such art.

Care and artistry were bestowed on crafts, and the polychrome painting of the finest pottery is closely related to the portraiture and ornamentation of stelae and other monuments. The Classic Maya were great workers in jade, or jadeite, carving necklaces, pendants, and figurines. The Maya lapidary also worked in other stones, shell, and bone. Metals, however, were not known during the Classic period.

The stelae and the other monuments were found in the political and religious centres. These were the seats of the governing élite, and they are marked by tall pyramids capped by temples and by somewhat lower and more oblong platforms which were the bases of long, multi-roomed palace buildings used as aristocratic residences. Such temples and palaces were often placed around open courts or plazas. Small centres might consist of only one such plaza arrangement, but the major Maya Classic centres often covered upwards of 250 acres (1 km²) of ground and were composed of numerous plazas. Examples of the latter would be Copán, in Honduras, which consists of a multi-plaza acropolis and an attached great enclosure, all within a space of something less than 250 acres (1 km²), or Tikal, in the Petén, whose central core of great buildings is spread over $1\frac{1}{2}$ sq miles (4 km²). Maya architecture was carried out in stone and rubble. Dressed masonry facings covered and retained the earth and rubble fills of platforms and pyramids. The palaces and temples on these bases were similarly laid up of dressed and carefully coursed masonry. Some buildings had flat beam-and-mortar roofs; others had corbelled, or false-arch, roofs. Because of the inherent weakness of this type of vaulting walls tended to be very thick in proportion to room widths. Some Maya vaults are still standing, but a great many of them have, through the ages, collapsed. In addition to temples and palaces, the other major public construction in the Maya centres was a prepared ball court, consisting of two long parallel mounds or platforms flanking a playing alley in which a game was played between two teams with a rubber ball. There are sixteenth-century ethnohistoric accounts of this game, and it is also depicted in Maya art. The ball game was a Mesoamerican trait which the Mayas shared with other nations of the area.

The degree to which the Maya centres were true cities has long been a debatable point in Maya archaeology; but recent surveys around several of them indicate residential areas of populations of urban proportions. As to their functions there can be little doubt but that many of these were of a city-like nature. They were the foci of political and religious activities, marketplaces, and, in some instances, they were fortified defensive strongholds.

Viewing settlement more widely, we can say with

certainty that virtually all of the Maya lowlands were quite densely settled, especially in the Late Classic period. Not all of the land was suited for cultivation, but over 50 per cent of it was, and this portion shows settlement evidence. Unsuitable lands, poorly drained or with poor soils, tend to be distributed throughout the lowlands; and this also applies to good lands. Speaking broadly, all the lowlands show precolumbian settlement. Throughout the Pre-classic period there was a steady increase in settlement and, presumably, population. Although there is regional variation, the Proto-classic and Early Classic saw settlement and population rather levelling off; but, again, in the Late Classic there was another settlement and population boom. Decline set in rapidly after this in the terminal Classic and Post-classic, with many regions being markedly depopulated. Settlement arrangement—and this pertains primarily to the Classic period for which we have the most information—was integrated through a system of major centres and minor centres. These tended to be more or less equidistantly spaced, with major centres averaging 18 miles (29 km) apart and lesser ones distributed within this larger network. From present information, there would appear to have been a tiered hierarchy of settlement, with at least three tiers or levels in most Maya lowland regions. Each centre, major or minor, was surrounded by outlying residential units. In some places these were most thickly placed immediately around the centres and less so further out; in other regions rural populations seem to have been evenly distributed between centres. These wide-scale settlement patterns carry not only ecological and subsistence implications with reference to the land but political implications. It is possible to construct, although not document, a model of a major centre with a paramount ruler presiding over a considerable territory; under him would be minor chiefs and subchiefs governing from lesser centres.

One of the indirect results of intensive Maya lowland settlement studies has been a reconsideration of ancient Maya subsistence economy. These settlement surveys forced the conclusion that there were just too many inhabitants of the Maya lowlands for them to have been supported by a system of long-term slash-and-burn or swidden cultivation, the former standard assumption about Maya farming practices. A number of new lines of inquiry were pursued. One of these concerned the possibility of agricultural terracing, and studies in the Rio Bec region of southern Campeche revealed extensive terrace systems clearly indicative of more intensive precolumbian cultivation methods. Another discovery lead to the realization that the Maya practised artificial raised-field cultivation, a highly intensive form of farming for which there were extensive evidences in both Campeche and Belize as well as elsewhere. Added to these is the high probability that Maya crops were highly diversified and that root starches were grown in household garden plots to provide a dietary supplement to maize and beans.

Olmec and Izapan contacts and influences on lowland Maya culture development have been mentioned in

Monument from Copán, in Honduras, one of the major Maya Classic centres.

connection with the Pre-classic and Proto-classic rise of Maya civilization; and it should be emphasized that outside or foreign contacts did not cease after these. Undoubtedly, one of the most important influences impinging on the Maya was that of the Central Mexican Teotihuacán civilization during the Early Classic period. This is seen not only in the presence of Central Mexican green obsidian in Maya lowland sites but in strong ceramic influence and, at Tikal, in the major arts. A stela at that site portrays a ruler who is presented with Teotihuacán symbols, and the burial of this individual is similarly accompanied with Teotihuacán-style luxury goods as well as with other artifacts that link him with Kaminaljuyú in the Guatemalan highlands. There is also hieroglyphic evidence at Tikal to suggest that this personage, known to archaeologists by his hieroglyphic cognomen of 'Curl-Snout', came to Tikal as a foreigner and married a daughter of the then ruling lineage, founding, as it were, a new dynasty. This took place in the fourth and fifth centuries AD; and this glimpse into Maya dynastic history, imperfect as it still may be, holds out exciting possibilities for further hieroglyphic and iconographic research on the precolumbian Maya. It also gives us some idea of the closeness and complexity of relationships between ancient Mesoamerican cultures. Teotihuacán-Kaminaljuyú influence waned in the Maya lowlands after AD 450 although its residual impress on Maya culture—in ceramics, architecture, and religious inconography—continued to be felt throughout the Classic period.

Between about AD 550 and 600 the lowland Mayas appear to have undergone some sort of a crisis. For a half-century or so there was a marked slackening or cessation of high ritual activity. Few buildings were put up, few stelae dedicated. The nature and causes of this crisis are unknown. After it had passed, however, there was a return to building activities in the centres. Many new centres were founded; and the period of 600–800 was, throughout the entire lowlands, one of marked population increases. It was also a period of regionalization of styles; and from this, and from what can be deciphered in the hieroglyphic inscriptions, it would appear that the Maya political scene consisted of a number of small regional states who formed changing alliances, engaged in intermittent warfare, and whose aristocratic classes were linked by dynastic marriages. It is in the Late Classic that we see the most striking regional differences in architectural and ceramic styles with the Petén styles and their variations in the south, the Rio Bec and Chenes styles of the central regions, and the Puuc styles of northern Yucatán. One notable difference between the south and the other regions is that hieroglyphic inscriptions and the stelae cult were much more developed in the south. The northern regions, on the other hand, excelled in palace and temple architecture and especially in the façade ornamentation of buildings.

In about 800 a decline set in in the Maya lowland centres. Again, as at the close of the Early Classic, there was a marked falling off in construction and stelae dedication. This time, however, the crisis was a more profound one, or, at least, the Maya did not recover in the same way as before. By 900 virtually all of the major centres or cities of the south had been abandoned, and in the succeeding century this decline and abandonment moved northward through the Rio Bec-Chenes and Puuc regions. While this collapse of the Classic is most dramatically underscored by the cessation of élite centre activities, there is also evidence that residential areas were similarly deserted. Its causes remain one of the great precolumbian mysteries. Invasion and disruption by peoples from Central Mexico, including the Toltecs, is a possibility, and in northern Yucatán there is evidence that they planted a colony in an old Classic period centre at Chichén Itzá; however, for the most part there is little evidence of conquest or invasion by foreigners. Crop failures, overpopulation, natural disasters, epidemics, and the like have all been advanced as explanations; but none is fully satisfactory. Viewing the Mesoamerican scene at large, we do know that after about AD 700–750, with the fall of the Central Mexican metropolis of Teotihuacán the era of relative peace of the Classic period came to a close. The Terminal Classic and Post-classic periods were times of new state formations, and these new states were militaristic and aggressive. The most powerful ones, such as the Toltecs and, later, the Aztecs, were Central Mexican empires. Eventually, they pushed south. Perhaps in this new political environment of the conquest state the Maya were unable to adapt and compete, at least in a major way. When Europeans first entered the Maya lowlands in the 1520s they found small town-states and petty chiefdoms in the north, and the area of the southern lowlands was almost entirely deserted. All over, the old great centres or cities had long been abandoned to the jungle.

The Aztecs

H. B. Nicholson

'Aztec' is now commonly employed to designate the culture of the late pre-Hispanic peoples of Central Mexico in general. It is sometimes construed more narrowly to apply only to the people of Mexico Tenochtitlan (modern Mexico City), the largest and politically most powerful city in North America at the time of the Spanish conquest. Both uses of the term are somewhat anachronistic, for in AD 1521 the inhabitants of this metropolis were known among themselves and to their neighbours as Tenochca, Mexica, and Colhua Mexica rather than Azteca, which, strictly speaking, applied only to their ancestors during their migratory period before the founding of Mexico Tenochtitlan. However, since Alexander von Humboldt (1769–1859) and William Prescott (1796–1859) popularized the word Aztec in their immensely influential writings during the last century, it has achieved such wide acceptance that it would probably be futile to try to discard it. It is most usefully employed as a generic cultural label for the Late Post-classic Central Mexican groups in the aggregate, rather than as a specific ethnic appellation, for Mexica and Tenochca are clearly preferable when referring to the inhabitants of Mexico Tenochtitlan as a social and political entity.

History

Like most politically prominent groups in world history, the ruling élite of Mexico Tenochtitlan had developed an 'official' tradition concerning their origins, according to which their ancestors had migrated from a place to the northwest called Aztlan (thus, Azteca, 'people of Aztlan'), which their patron god, Huitzilopochtli, had commanded them to leave in the twelfth century AD. After a long period of wandering, they entered the Basin of Mexico and established themselves at Chapoltepec sometime in the second half of the thirteenth century AD. Driven from here c1300 by a coalition of enemies, for about a generation they were under the control of Colhuacan—settling near this major power of this period, which had most directly inherited the Toltec political-dynastic tradition. They eventually escaped by moving a few miles to the north, to islands in a swampy area in the western arm of the great saline lake that covered much of the floor of the Basin of Mexico. The most popular version of the end of their long migration was that they chose the site of Mexico Tenochtitlan after they encountered an eagle with a rattlesnake in its beak perched on a nopal cactus growing from a stone (the name of the city meant 'Place of the Mexica/Next to the Stone Nopal Cactus'). The traditional date for its founding was the year Two House (2 Calli), 1325, though some scholars would place it a generation or two later.

The first ruler, or *tlatoani*, of Mexico Tenochtitlan, Acamapichtli–who, in most accounts, acceded in 1376–was a scion of the royal dynasty of Colhuacan, which claimed direct descent from Topiltzin Quetzalcoatl, the traditional founder of Toltec power. Thus, Mexico Tenochtitlan considered itself to have inherited the mantle of Toltec political pre-eminence, which certainly contributed significantly to the driving force of Mexica imperialism. At first, the city was subservient to Azcapotzalco, just to the west, capital of the Tepaneca, who, starting in the mid-fourteenth century AD, carved out a sizable Central Mexican empire under the dynamic leadership of a remarkable ruler, Tezozomoc. After his death in 1426–7, one of his sons, Maxtla, usurped the throne, resulting in a period of civil strife and general revolt. By 1433–4 Tepanec power was completely broken, and most of its former tributaries had passed under the control of Mexico Tenochtitlan, now ruled by its fourth *tlatoani*, Itzcoatl, a son of Acamapichtli, and of Tetzcoco, capital of a large province, Acolhuacan, comprising much of the eastern Basin of Mexico and ruled by the famous 'poet-king' Nezahualcoyotl.

A new political order was formalized by the creation of the 'triple alliance' of the Mexica (Mexico Tenochtitlan), Acolhuaque (Tetzcoco), and Tepaneca (much weakened but by no means destroyed, with a new capital, Tlacopán). The Triple Alliance generated great military power, steadily bringing under its control all areas formerly under Tepanec domination and soon expanding far beyond, principally to the south and east. Under the first Motecuhzoma (ruled 1440–1469), a nephew of Itzcoatl, Mexico Tenochtitlan clearly forged ahead of its partners in power. Three of his grandsons, Axayacatl (1469–1481), Tizoc (1481–1486), and Ahuitzotl (1486–1502), followed him in succession, and all successfully continued his policy of aggressive expansionism. By the death of the third, at the opening of the sixteenth century, the Triple Alliance was receiving tribute from hundreds of communities scattered from San Luis Potosí to the borders of Guatemala. The powerful Tarascan empire of Michoacan, however, blocked its westward thrust; and Tlaxcallan, a potent Nahuatl-speaking state to the east, although entirely surrounded, managed to maintain its independence

until the coming of Cortés.

When Motecuhzoma II, the son of Axayacatl, acceded in 1502–3, the power of Mexico Tenochtitlan was near its zenith. Although a substantial portion of western Oaxaca remained to be conquered–and Motecuhzoma succeeded in subduing most of it during his reign–the era of spectacular Triple Alliance imperialist expansion was almost over. His was essentially a period of consolidation and integration of past gains. According to tradition, Motecuhzoma II created a much more opulent and aristrocratic court than those of his predecessors, which greatly impressed the Spaniards. This was a clear reflection of the power and wealth of an imperial capital

Stone image of Xochipilli, the Aztec god of flowers, feasting and music, wearing a mask and adorned with floral blossoms.

that controlled, with its two allies, an area perhaps over 116,000 sq miles (300,000 km²) and was extracting a rich tribute from millions of subjects.

Subsistence

Intensive agriculture, which seems to have become well established in Mesoamerica by the third millennium BC, constituted the mainstay of the subsistence system. A wide variety of crops was cultivated, with maize the outstanding staple. Other important crops were beans, squash, sweet potato, grain amaranth, manioc, avocado, tomato, and various fruits, including the pineapple and papaya. Cotton and maguey provided the bulk of fibre for weaving. The fermented saccharine exudation of the latter plant also yielded the only significant intoxicating beverage, *octli* (pulque). Various hallucinogenic plants, which were gathered wild, were taken mainly for divinatory rituals, especially certain species of mushrooms (*teonanacatl*), the seeds of a morning glory (*ololiuhqui*), and the 'buttons' of a type of cactus (*peyotl*). Cacao (*cacahuatl*), the source of chocolate, a luxury drink of the upper classes, was an important crop in parts of the tropical lowlands. Here also grew the trees tapped for rubber, from which the balls used in the ritual ball game were manufactured—and which were also burned as incense.

The simple digging stick was the basic agricultural tool. In the heavily vegetated lowlands a shifting, slash-and-burn (swidden) technique of farming was typical. In the semi-arid highlands more intensive methods, such as repeatedly cultivating the same fields or letting them lie fallow at fairly lengthy intervals, depending on the types of soils and the availability of moisture, could be employed. Floodwater farming, terracing, and irrigation were practised where local conditions permitted. A specialized type of irrigation, the *chinampa* or 'floating garden' system, was of great importance in shallow freshwater lakes, especially in the southern Basin of Mexico. An intricate network of small rectangular islands of mud scooped up from the lake bottoms was gradually constructed. Constantly replenished with fresh mud, these lacustrine plots yielded extraordinarily productive crops of food staples and flowers. Food storage facilities were well developed, with large, sturdily constructed granaries of both quadrangular pole and adobe vasiform (*cuezcomatl*) form.

The preferred method of preparing maize for consumption was to mix the ground kernels with water, forming a thick paste from which the thin round *tlaxcalli* (Spanish: *tortilla*) was shaped and toasted on a griddle. The tortilla often served as a utensil for scooping up other foods or for a wrapper for bits of meat and vegetables (the original taco). Aztec cuisine, in general, was rich and variegated, featuring various hot sauces spiced with chilli. Hunting, especially deer, rabbits, peccary, and waterfowl, provided much of the meat in the diet, although the turkey was also a significant source of protein. The only other important domesticated animal was the dog, whose flesh was also occasionally consumed.

The economic system

Commensurate with the great size and social and political complexity of the empire, economic institutions were well developed but appear to have been dominated more by political institutions than by genuine market mechanisms *per se*. At least three major economic subsystems stood out: market exchange, at both the local and regional level; the local and imperial tribute-taxation system; and 'foreign commerce'. The point at which they interacted and were integrated into the overall economic system was the formal, community-regulated market, which was also a central focus of social interaction. The greatest New World market at the time of the Conquest was in Tlatelolco, Tenochtitlan's twin city. This huge, colourful emporium—which tremendously impressed the *conquistadores*, especially Cortés himself who estimated that 60,000 attended it daily—featured well-arranged displays of virtually every type of merchandise available in the Aztec world. It was closely supervised by appointed officials, some of whom held court in a building in the centre of the vast marketplace to settle disputes on the spot. Lesser versions of this famous market flourished throughout the empire. Some daily business was transacted in all of the leading markets, but every fifth day was the official market day, especially devoted to commercial activity.

The professional merchants, *pochteca/oztomeca*, were highly organized into socio-political structures somewhat resembling medieval guilds. They lived in their own wards in the big communities under their own leaders, propitiated their own deities, and conducted far-flung trading expeditions—for both state and private ends—throughout the empire and even beyond, perhaps as far to the east as Panama. Especially prized by the highlanders were the products of the lush tropical lowlands; those living here were, in turn, eager to obtain certain goods only available on the cool, semi-arid plateau. Although barter was the chief means of exchange, the precious cacao beans and cotton mantles of standardized sizes were most often used as fixed units of value in commercial transactions.

Urbanism

There were many sizable towns throughout the empire, especially in the highlands. The largest, Mexico Tenochtitlan, with its northern twin city, Tlatelolco, boasted a population probably well over 100,000, perhaps even double or triple that size. At the time of the Conquest it was a spectacular New World Venice interlaced by numerous canals and linked to the shore by four principal causeways. As the imperial capital, it was studded with large palaces, temple precincts, and market squares, amid countless *chinampas*. The steady evaporation of the lake since the early colonial period has left Mexico Tenochtitlan's even greater urban successor, Mexico City, high and dry, with an entirely different appearance and situation.

Dress

In the highland zones the typical female costume was

the shift, *huipilli*, and wrap-around skirt, *cueitl*. Men normally wore a loincloth, *maxtlatl*, and mantle, *tilmatli*, knotted over one shoulder, plus sandals, *cactli*. In the warmer lowlands women often went topless, wearing only a skirt. The richness of fabric (maguey fibre for the lower classes, cotton for the upper) and design depended on the wealth and social status of the wearer.

Shelter

Housing was generally simple and utilitarian. In the highlands most homes were built of adobe brick (sometimes with stone foundations), with flat or sloping roofs; in the lowlands, with wattle-and-daub walls and peaked thatched roofs. The layout of most households was a compound, comprising the main dwelling, storage structures, and sweathouse. The establishments of rulers and wealthier members of the nobility were often rambling, multi-roomed plastered adobe structures of considerable size, arranged around patios.

Family and society

The minimal social unit was the nuclear family. However, the typical household normally included additional persons, particularly agnatic relatives and in-laws. All members of these extended families cooperated closely in their economic support. Girls normally married quite early, boys somewhat later, after a period of military service. Polygyny was standard among the aristocracy, whereas most commoners' marriages were–probably mainly because of economic reasons–monogamous. The husband's chief responsibility was family support, usually as a farmer or craftsman. The wife's role centred on her domestic duties, which included cooking, weaving her family's clothing, and child-rearing. By the age of ten most boys separated from their families to attend either their wards' military schools, *telpochcalli*, or, particularly if they belonged to the nobility, schools connected with the temples, *calmecac*, where they received a more religiously oriented education that explicitly trained them for the priesthood or to be leaders in their communities. Some girls also attended temple schools, but the majority were instructed in domestic skills by their mothers and other female relatives.

Numerous, usually blood-related families were grouped, in turn, into larger dwelling units which constituted either small separate dependencies or subdivisions, wards, of sizable towns. They were known as *calpolli* (*tlaxilacalli, chinamitl* etc.) and apparently exercised various corporate functions, including jurisdiction over some communal property and the supervision of all transactions involving the landholdings of its members, the *calpoleque*. Most free members of the community–nobility and commoners–seem to have belonged to these units, each of which maintained a cult to its own patron deity; the commoners provided corvée labour for public works and military service within the framework of their *calpolli* affiliation. Some *calpolli* were composed primarily of specialized craftsmen or of other occupations such as merchants.

Aztec society was sharply stratified, with two major classes: nobles, *pipiltin*, and commoners, *macehualtin*, with various rank distinctions within each stratum. Most members of the former class, the majority affiliated with various recognized aristocratic houses, *tecalli*, possessed their own patrimonial lands and were often additionally supported by lands granted to them during their terms as community officeholders. These properties were normally worked for them by commoners, including tenants who were attached to them and paid no other tax. All other commoners had to fulfil tax obligations to their rulers and, if their communities were subject to outside powers, to contribute to the collective tribute. The nobles were usually free from local tax obligations but were expected to serve their communities in various official and leadership positions, especially military service. Slaves, *tlacotin*, were owned mainly by the nobility, but they possessed definite legal rights and were not considered mere chattels.

Political structure

A multitude of communities of greatly varying sizes studded the Central Mexican landscape at the advent of Cortés. They were inter-related in various ways. The commonest pattern was that of a dominant large town, *altepetl* (Spanish: *cabecera*), which exercised political control over a cluster of surrounding lesser communities. These city states or chiefdoms usually shared a common history and considered themselves and were considered by their neighbours to constitute distinctive ethnic units. They were typically politically autonomous. Even if subordinate members of a larger imperial system–as was the case with most of them at the time of the Conquest–they retained a high degree of internal control and authority.

The imperial capital, Mexico Tenochtitlan, was governed by a succession of Toltec-descended rulers, *tlatoque*, selected from a single royal lineage–and this system was typical of all major centres at the core of the empire. The rulership normally passed from brother to brother, father to son (or grandson), or uncle to nephew. The *tlatoani* possessed great power as the earthly representative of the city state's patron deity, but he was expected to consult with an advisory council composed of the highest-ranking nobles, often his close relatives, before making important decisions. The Triple Alliance empire had been created by conquest and was effectively maintained by military force, including the establishment of imperial garrisons in strategic locations, usually commanded by a great noble who also frequently served as provincial governor. An extensive bureaucracy, its top positions often virtually hereditary in certain aristocratic families, had evolved to conduct the essential business of local and imperial administration, especially the collection of taxes and tribute. Many of the higher administrative officials appear to have also exercised judicial functions, as *tecuhtlatoque*, functioning within a complex, hierarchically organized system of local and imperial courts. They applied a rich corpus of traditional law based both on formal codes–particularly that promulgated by Nezahualcoyotl of Tetzcoco

Aztec stone sacrificial knife, with anthropomorphic wood handle decorated with turquoise mosaic, used to rip out the hearts of war captives and slaves as offerings to the gods.

(1431–1472)–and on recognized precedents, especially famous decisions of Nezahualcoyotl.

Communication and learning

The dominant language of Central Mexico in AD 1519 was Nahuatl, the southernmost representative of a widespread North American linguistic stock, Uto-Aztecan, which extended from Montana to Panama. Other unrelated languages were also spoken, the most important of which were Totonac, Popoloca, and, especially, various members of the Otomian family (Otomi, Matlatzinca, Mazahua, Ocuilteca, and so on). The Spanish missionaries adapted the Roman alphabet to Nahuatl, and there emerged a considerable literature in this rich, expressive language. Before the Conquest, an embryonic writing system was employed, essentially pictographic but with some phonetic elements, utilizing the principle of the rebus or 'phonetic transfer', in place and name signs. In addition to extensive treatment of religious themes, histories, genealogies, maps and plans, and administrative records such as tribute lists, censuses, and cadastres were typical of Aztec 'writings' on paper (manufactured from the inner bark of a fig tree), tanned animal skin, or cotton sheets. Aztec knowledge of astronomy and mathematics (*see below* for calendrics) was rudimentary by modern standards. However, their ability successfully to treat various diseases with an extensive repertoire of medicinal plants even impressed the Spanish physicians, who borrowed some of their pharmacopoeia and therapeutic techniques.

Religion

Religion played a particularly pervasive role in Aztec culture. From birth to death, the individual was immersed in his religious obligations and few of his daily activities escaped the influence of religious concepts and ritual practices.

Cosmogony

Four great cosmic eras, or 'suns', were believed to have preceded the present age. The inhabitants of each (giants flourished in the first) were destroyed at their ends–with the exception of single male-female pairs which survived to continue the race–by different types of cataclysm: respectively, swarms of ferocious jaguars, hurricanes, rains of fire, and a great deluge. The present, or fifth, sun was to have been terminated by violent earthquakes. At

the beginning of this final period, two major deities, Tezcatlipoca and Quetzalcoatl, dispersed the waters and raised the sky. Fire was produced, then a new generation of mankind: Quetzalcoatl travelled to the Underworld, Mictlan, to obtain from the death god, Mictlantecuhtli, bones and ashes of previous humanity, from which the assembled gods created the primeval human pair, following which they provided their sustenance, above all, maize. A new sun and moon were created by means of the cremation in great ovens at Teotihuacán of two gods, one a diseased but courageous pauper and the other rich but cowardly, who were transformed thereby into the solar and lunar orbs. The gods then sacrificed themselves to provide sustenance (blood and hearts) for the new sun. However, his terrible food had constantly to be supplied to satisfy his insatiable appetite, and to this end war, for the primary purpose of obtaining victims for sacrifice, was instituted–and this perpetual obligation was laid on man.

Cosmology

The earth was conceived as a quadrangular land mass surrounded by water. At each vari-coloured cardinal direction stood a sacred tree upon which perched a sacred bird. The earth was also visualized in a more metaphoric manner, as a great crocodilian monster, *cipactli*, or a gigantic, crouching toadlike creature with gaping, teeth-studded mouth, Tlaltecuhtli, who devoured the blood and hearts of sacrificed victims and the souls of the dead. The heavens consisted of thirteen differently coloured tiers, in the uppermost of which dwelled the supreme creative deities. Beneath the earth's surface were nine levels, the lowermost the ultimate resting place of most of the deceased.

Deities

A remarkably crowded pantheon of individualized supernatural personalities was believed to control the various spheres of the universe. Nearly every major natural and human activity was embodied in at least one god or goddess. This multitude of deities can be considered to have expressed different aspects of three fundamental, and overlapping, cult themes: first, celestial creativity; second, agricultural fertility; last, war, sacrifice, and the sanguinary nourishment of the sun and earth. Included within the first theme were Ometeotl, the bisexual creator; Tezcatlipoca, the omnipotent 'supreme god'; and Xiuhtecuhtli, the old god of fire. Prominent within the second theme were Tlaloc, the pre-eminent fertility deity, the producer of rain; Ehecatl-Quetzalcoatl, the wind god; Centeotl-Chicomecoatl, the maize deity (with both male and female aspects); Ometochtli, the *octli* (pulque) deity; Teteoinnan-Tlazolteotl, the earth mother; and Xipe Totec, the macabre 'flayed god'. The third theme featured Tonatiuh, the solar deity; Huitzilopochtli, the special patron of the Mexica with predominant martial associations; Mixcoatl-Camaxtli, the Chichimec hunting and war god; Tlahuizcalpantecuhtli, the Venus god; and Mictlantecuhtli, the death god. Space does not allow the mention of numerous other major deities. Many minor deities presided over various crafts and occupations, the most important of which was Yacatecuhtli, the god of the merchants. A major, complex deity who defies neat categorization was Quetzalcoatl, whose creative function stands out and with whom was blended in tradition a semi-legendary Toltec ruler who bore the same name.

Ritualism-Calendrics

The richness and intricacy of the Aztec ceremonial system was remarkable. The Spanish missionary chroniclers, influenced by Christian ritualism, divided the major public ceremonies into those that were 'fixed' (geared to the 365-day year) and 'movable' (regulated by the 260-day divinatory cycle). The latter was the most basic count, consisting of 20 named days combined with 13 numerals to produce a permutation cycle of 260 days, the *tonalpohualli*, which was employed mainly for divination. Each day possessed a favourable or unfavourable connotation, which had to be determined by a diviner, *tonalpohuqui*, particularly when casting the horoscope of a newborn child as determined by the day of his birth. Another calendric cycle, the *xihuitl*, grouped the *tonalpohualli* days into 18 named periods of 20 days, plus 5 extra days to equal the vague tropical year of 365 days. The years were further grouped into cycles of 52 years, each designated by the *tonalpohualli* day on which it ended (360th day) or began. The greatest of all Aztec public rituals, *toxiuhmolpilia*, 'Binding Up of the Years', or 'New Fire Ceremony', was celebrated at the expiration of one 52-year cycle and the beginning of another.

Many of the 'fixed' ceremonies, in line with their close connection with the annual agricultural cycle, were concerned with promoting fertility and involved propitiation of deities most clearly expressing the agricultural fertility theme. They were normally performed at

the close of each of the 18 *veintenas*, or 20-day periods. Human sacrifice (usually war captives or condemned slaves) often accompanied the principal ceremonies—and portions of the bodies were sometimes eaten by the worshippers in ritual after-feasts. The *tonalpohualli*-geared ceremonies were generally more modest in scope but some were quite impressive, particularly the 4 Ollin ceremony dedicated to the sun, which consisted of a strict fast and ritual bloodletting on the part of the entire community. There were numerous other ceremonial occasions: dedications of new structures and monuments, before and after battles, triumphs, and coronations—as well as considerable daily domestic ritual, centred on the hearth fires and household shrines. Funerals were also highly ritualized, especially those for the rulers and great nobles; the dead were usually cremated.

Various games and sports were popular, but the most important, characteristically with strong religious associations, was the rubber-ball game, *ollamaliztli*. Played on a formal, capital I-shaped court, *tlachtli*, the sport involved opposing teams whose players, among other methods of scoring points, sought to propel a solid rubber ball through the apertures in stone rings mounted vertically on the side walls of the court without use of hands or feet.

Temples

Religious activities were especially focused on the temples, *teocalli*. They were usually situated within walled precincts, which might also contain sacerdotal dormitories and schools, sacred pools for purificatory ablutions, skull racks, platform altars, giant braziers for sacred fires, gardens and artificial forests, arsenals, ballcourts etc. The typical *teocalli* consisted of a solid staged substructure, with balustraded stairway on one side, on the top of which was a shrine containing the image of the deity to which the temple was dedicated.

Priesthood

The profession of full-time priest, *teopixqui*, supported by the community, was highly important. These religious

Relief carving on the Huehuetl of Malinalco, a cylindrical upright wooden drum, featuring a dancing jaguar and eagle, flanking the date 4 Ollin, symbol of the current sun, and a dancing human figure wearing the costume of a bird.

practitioners usually lived together, practising sexual abstinence, in *calmecac*, monastic-style establishments in the ceremonial enclosures, where they performed a rigorous daily programme of offerings and sacrifices. In addition to the priest who served his community as a whole, the practitioner of white and black magic, *nahualli*, who mainly served individuals, also played an important role, particularly in curative medicine. The priests of late pre-Hispanic Central Mexico, as the intermediaries between their communities and the supernatural forces believed to control the universe – especially through their management of all 'higher education', in the temple schools–wielded tremendous power and authority.

Arts and crafts

Late pre-Hispanic Central Mexico can boast of some outstanding aesthetic achievements, particularly in monumental stone sculpture, one of the high points in the history of art. Superb wood carving, precious stone mosaic, the lapidary craft, featherworking, and ornamental metalwork were other major Aztec arts. Most pottery was merely competently mass-produced, but some superior pieces were manufactured for ceremonial use. Weaving, exclusively a feminine craft, was also highly developed, although almost no specimens have survived. Architecture, if not outstanding, was often impressive, particularly the temples and the rulers'

palaces. An oral literature of considerable expressive power and variety flourished, especially historical sagas and lyric poetry. Music, if perhaps rudimentary by European Renaissance standards, was important in ceremonial and was performed on numerous instruments, principally of the wind and percussion type. Dancing was almost entirely ritual; some dancing, often involving many sumptuously clad individuals of both sexes, accompanied nearly all of the major ceremonies.

The Aztec heritage

Aztec civilization, the inheritor and synthesizer of the results of millennia of intensive cultural development in Mesoamerica, was in full flower at the time of the Conquest. It was being carried by millions of Indians inhabiting hundreds of communities of differing sizes, some of them metropolitan centres considerably larger than any city of Spain in the early sixteenth century. Although overrun, ravaged, and dominated for well over four centuries by an alien civilization structured on very different lines, much survives of that remarkable, blood-soaked yet beauty-loving culture that greeted the dazzled but uncomprehending eyes of the *conquistadores*. Certainly no satisfactory understanding of modern Mexico can be acquired without full appreciation of the persisting Indian component of the complex cultural mosaic that gradually emerged out of the smoking ruins of Mexico Tenochtitlan.

The Incas

Geoffrey W. Conrad

Few ancient civilizations had as dramatic a history, or played their parts upon as rugged a stage, as the Inca empire (AD 1438–1532). From its first military victory to its final defeat by a few hundred Spanish adventurers, the empire flourished for only a century. Yet within that brief span the Incas rose from rustic obscurity in the southern Peruvian highlands, conquered every major state and tribe in the Andean world, extended the boundaries of South American civilization, and created the largest empire ever formed in the precolumbian New World. Superimposed on a map of modern South America, the Inca realm begins on the southern frontier of Colombia, stretches southward along the coast and highlands of Ecuador and Peru, sprawls across highland Bolivia into northwestern Argentina, and extends down into central Chile.

When the Incas began their expansion, this vast territory, over 2600 miles (4200 km) long and inhabited by at least six million people, was a land of incredible ethnic diversity. We do not know the exact number of groups involved–in fact, we do not even know the names of many of the smaller tribes–but in AD 1532 the

empire contained approximately 100 administrative provinces, some of them encompassing more than one ethnic unit, in Peru and Bolivia alone. Building upon a Peruvian civilizational tradition that was already some 4000 years old, the Incas began, but never completed, the task of moulding their extremely heterogeneous subjects into one nation with one language, one religion, and one culture.

Geography

The Incas themselves called their domain Tawantinsuyu, or 'Land of the Four Quarters'. The lines separating the four quarters ran approximately north-south and east-west, intersecting in Cuzco, the imperial capital. The division of the empire into four parts was a basic principle of Inca social and political organization, but it was also a rough reflection of geographical reality. The geography of Tawantinsuyu was as richly varied as its peoples, but in a general sense the former imperial territory is composed of two longitudinal belts. In the west, along the Pacific, is a narrow coastal plain. At its northern and southern ends this lowland plain is moist and forested, but for much of its length it is a rainless desert interrupted by a series of fertile river valleys. Behind the coastal lowlands the towering wall of the Andes rises abruptly to an average elevation of over 9840 ft (3000 m): several peaks exceed 21,000 ft (6400 m). Much of this rugged terrain is uninhabitable, but intermontane valleys and high, grassy plateaus are suitable for human occupation.

If the Inca world was characterized by this coastal-highland division, it was also cross-cut by a north–south distinction. The greatest concentrations of agricultural land and population in the highlands were south of Cuzco, in the Lake Titicaca basin and the adjacent high plain now known as the Bolivian *altiplano*. These extensive flatlands formed part of Collasuyu, the largest and southernmost of the quarters. In contrast, the richest coastal regions lay to the north of Cuzco in the Chinchaysuyu quarter, along what is today the north coast of Peru. Here the coastal desert plain is at its widest, lowest, and flattest; both river valleys and intervalley deserts were farmed with the aid of extensive irrigation networks. The eastern and western quarters, Antisuyu and Cuntisuyu respectively, were neither as productive nor as populous as the core areas of Collasuyu and Chinchaysuyu.

A great variety of plants and animals, all of them domesticated long before the establishment of the Inca empire, were raised within the borders of Tawantin-suyu. The most important highland food animals were the guinea pig and muscovy duck. Two camelids, the llama and alpaca, were herded: llamas provided wool and meat and served as beasts of burden; alpacas were bred only for wool. Coastal peoples also raised guinea pigs but obtained most of their animal protein from wild marine resources: fish, shellfish, sea mammals, and birds. Dogs were kept as pets throughout the empire.

A list of the most important domesticated plants

The four quarters of the Inca empire.

includes maize, common beans, lima beans, various squashes, chilli peppers, potatoes, sweet potatoes, manioc, other tubers such as oca and olluco, quinoa and other grains, avocados, peanuts, gourds, cotton, and coca. These plants grew in widely varying altitudinal ranges reflecting, among other things, their different temperature and rainfall requirements. In general, most highland plants could be grown on the coast, but the reverse was not true.

As a result, parts of the Inca world, especially the southern highlands, were characterized by a phenomenon known as the 'vertical archipelago'. In order to insure an adequate food supply a community situated in one altitudinal ecological zone maintained a chain of satellite settlements in other zones. The vertical archipelago was an ancient subsistence pattern adopted by the Incas for imperial purposes, and the Inca nobility were quick to tell Spanish chroniclers that their citizens were dependent on state-controlled redistribution of foodstuffs. This statement was purest propaganda, much

The mountain-top fortress of Pisac, near Cuzco, Peru: a provincial administrative centre of the Inca empire.

349

more of a long-term goal than an immediate reality. At the time of the Spanish conquest most of Tawantinsuyu's villages were still largely self-sufficient.

Pre-Inca Andean civilizations

In Cuzco imperial dogma held that the entire Andean world had been in a state of savagery before the coming of the Inca empire. This claim was the most flagrant fiction. The truth of the matter is that the Incas did not establish Andean civilization; they inherited a tradition that was already some 4000 years old and built upon it. The history of Andean civilization is long and complex, and only some of the highlights can be given here.

Although human populations entered the Andes before 10,000 BC, the story of Andean *civilization* really starts in the period known as Preceramic VI (2500–1800 BC). The best data on this epoch come from the Chinchaysuyu coast, which saw the establishment of permanent settlements with populations ranging as high as several thousand inhabitants. The social and

Chavín de Huántar, Peru. Ceremonial centre and settlement.

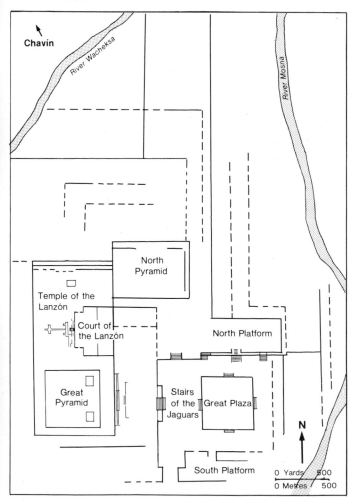

political organization of these settlements became increasingly complex during Preceramic VI. Some of the coastal sites dating to the later part of the era–for example, Aspero, Rio Seco, and El Paraiso–have impressive public architecture that reflects the presence of some sort of higher authority able to mobilize and coordinate large work forces. The data from the highlands are much scantier, but evidence from the site of Kotosh indicates that comparable phenomena were occurring, albeit on a somewhat smaller scale. The first flowering of coastal cultures may have been underwritten by the rich marine resources of the near-shore waters; similar developments in the highlands were undoubtedly supported by an emerging agricultural economy.

The Initial period (1800–1400 BC), which followed Preceramic VI, is again best known from the Chinchaysuyu coast. Throughout this region the Initial period was characterized by a general shift of settlements away from the shoreline; in particular, new centres of social and political organization and public architecture were established in the interior reaches of the coastal valleys. This change in settlement pattern is interpreted as indicating the rise of an economy based on irrigation agriculture.

The Post-Initial period history of Andean civilization is one of epochs of widespread cultural similarity or unification alternating with epochs of regional diversification. Three times in the preconquest era the Andean world was swept by great unifying movements whose manifestations–disseminations of iconographic elements or art styles–define the so-called horizons of Andean archaeology. Each of these horizons had strong religious overtones and was associated with a major cult figure. Each embraced more territory, but endured for a shorter time, than the preceding one.

The first extensive diffusion of distinctive iconographic elements, that of the Early Horizon (1400–400 BC), is generally seen as reflecting the spread of a religious cult. The principal cult centre seems to have been the site of Chavín de Huántar in the northern highlands of Peru. Here a major temple with elaborately carved stone sculptures was founded around 1500 BC and remained in use until about 600 BC. Modifications of this temple, along with concomitant changes in iconography, argue that there were several episodes of religious innovation at Chavín. The last and most important of the cult figures depicted in Chavín art is a deity known as the 'Staff God'; we cannot identify him precisely, but he seems to have been some sort of a sky-god.

During the Early Intermediate period (400 BC–AD 600) a number of distinctive cultures and art styles emerged out of the Early Horizon base. In most parts of the Andean world there was a trend towards greater differentiation of architecture and burial patterns; the implication is one of increased social complexity. In several areas archaeologists have traced sequences of development culminating in elaborate regional civilizations. Among the latter are Moche of the northern coast, Nasca of the southern coast, Recuay of the

600–900). The diffusion of Middle Horizon iconography involved two major centres: Tiahuanaco on the Bolivian shore of Lake Titicaca and Huari in the south-central Peruvian highlands. The prevailing opinion holds that Tiahuanaco was the centre of a religious cult. The focus of this cult was a multi-faceted sky-god whose most famous depiction is found on a carved stone gateway at Tiahuanaco; for this reason he is often called the 'Gateway God'. According to the standard interpretation, early in the Middle Horizon individuals from the Huari area made religious pilgrimages to Tiahuanaco and brought back ideological concepts connected with the Gateway God. As these new ideas became established at Huari, they were modified in unspecified ways, grew aggressively proselytizing, and were carried outwards by military conquest. Huari itself became the capital of an empire that expanded in several stages. This empire eventually collapsed during the latter half of the Middle Horizon, the site of Huari was abandoned, and cultural unification was once again replaced by regional diversity.

There are a number of problems with this interpretation; most of them concern the postulated Huari empire. Huari itself has been only minimally investigated, but its architectural planning is very different from that of its supposed satellite administrative centres in the highlands: the former cannot have provided a model for the latter. Furthermore, sites on the Chinchaysuyu coast that were once thought to be intrusive Huari administrative centres have invariably proved to be something else. Hence at the very least the extent of the Huari empire has been exaggerated. Finally, on the Chinchaysuyu coast the most marked difference between the Middle Horizon and earlier epochs is a change in burial practices, and it may well be that Middle Horizon unification was much more religious than political.

In any case, the breakdown of Middle Horizon coher-

One of a number of large, flat, unshaped stone slabs carved with human figures, found in the valley of Casma; contemporary with Chavín culture.

northern highlands, and Huarpa of the south-central highlands, along with Pucará and Tiahuanaco in the Titicaca basin. Some of these archaeological cultures have settlement patterns characterized by a hierarchy of ceremonial and administrative centres headed by one predominant site; such cultures seem to represent political states or kingdoms. Fortifications and strongholds speak of competition and warfare among these regional states.

The second great unifying movement of Andean prehistory occurred during the Middle Horizon (AD

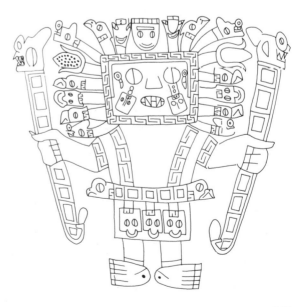

The sky-god of Tiahuanaco: a version of the Gateway God on a large jar from Pacheco, Río Grande de Nazca, Peruvian coast.

ence shifted the focus of Andean civilization from the highlands to the Chinchaysuyu coast. During the later half of the Middle Horizon and the first part of the Late Intermediate period (AD 900–1476) the most influential site in the Andean world was probably Pachacamac, the seat of a famous oracle and a centre for religious pilgrimages, near modern Lima, Peru. Eventually, however, the balance of power swung to the northern coast, which witnessed the rise of the Chimú empire (c AD 1200–1465). At its zenith the Chimú empire controlled the northernmost 600 miles (965 km) of the Peruvian coast and was the largest, most powerful state in the Andean area.

Most of the Late Intermediate period was an era of political fragmentation in the highlands. No single state achieved a predominant position until the very end of the period, when a previously obscure kingdom began an abrupt rise to power, challenged the Chimú, defeated them, and established the last great epoch of Andean cohesion. That last epoch is known as the Late Horizon (AD 1476–1532), and its unifying force was the Inca empire.

Inca history

Both archaeology and ethnohistory have contributed information on the Inca empire. The Incas themselves had no writing, and Inca oral history was a mixture of fact, myth, legend, and imperial propaganda. Hence the sixteenth- and seventeenth-century chronicles in which Inca traditions were recorded can be interpreted in different ways. For example, the Inca king list names 13 rulers from the inception of the dynasty to the Spanish conquest. Of the first eight kings, as many as half may have been mythical figures. Alternatively, it has been suggested that most of the supposedly early rulers were actually members of a subordinate dynasty that existed simultaneously with a principal dynasty containing the 'later' and better known emperors. Until varying modern interpretations of the chronicles can be reconciled, archaeology will continue to provide the most reliable, albeit least detailed, information on early Inca history.

The first archaeological manifestation of Inca culture is the Killke phase (c AD 1200–1438) of the area around Cuzco in the southern Peruvian highlands. The Incas' origins were certainly humble: excavated sites portray the Killke Inca nation as a small, rustic, and entirely undistinguished kingdom that controlled only the immediate vicinity of Cuzco. At this time the Incas were merely one of many such polities in the southern highlands, and the area was in a chronic state of petty warfare.

The more trustworthy portion of Inca history, as well as the imperial expansion itself, began with Pachakuti, who ruled from 1438 to 1471, according to the most widely accepted chronology. Tawantinsuyu was born, not in a campaign of aggression, but from a defensive victory. The Chanka, a hostile people who lived to the northwest of Cuzco, besieged the Inca capital. Pachakuti, who was only a son of the reigning king and not even the designated heir to the throne, assumed military command, defeated the Chanka, had himself crowned as ruler, and set out to build an empire. After consolidating the area around Cuzco he turned south into Collasuyu, annexing the rich Titicaca basin to his domain.

In about 1463 Pachakuti entrusted control of the army to his son Topa Inca (ruled 1471–1493) and began to devote most of his time to the reorganization of his realm. One of his most far-reaching reforms was the establishment of Quechua, the Inca language, as the administrative lingua franca of Tawantinsuyu. The fact that Quechua is today the most widely spoken Indian language in the Americas is part of Pachakuti's legacy.

While Pachakuti was still ruling, Topa Inca led the army north into Chinchaysuyu. He conquered the highlands up to Quito, Ecuador, but his most valuable prize was the fertile north coast of Peru. This area had been the heartland of the Chimú empire, which before its defeat by the Incas had been the predominant political power in Andean civilization. With its strongest rival destroyed and the most productive areas in the Andean world under its control, Tawantinsuyu became an irresistible force.

After ascending the throne in 1471, Topa Inca ruled for some 22 years. During his reign he enlarged the empire by conquering the south coast of Peru, southern Bolivia, northwestern Argentina, and Chile as far south as the Rio Maule. His victories were eventually halted, probably by overextension of the empire's supply lines rather than by superior military force. In any case, his son and successor, Huayna Capac (ruled c1493–1525), subjugated some areas along the northern frontiers of the empire but added relatively little territory.

The seven years between Huayna Capac's death (1525) and the Spanish conquest (1532) were marked by a bitter power struggle between the legitimate heir, Huascar, and his half-brother Atahualpa. This fratricidal conflict climaxed in a disastrous civil war that devastated the empire. In one of the supremely ironic moments of history, Atahualpa achieved final victory just in time to be captured by 168 Spaniards under the command of Francisco Pizarro. Within less than a year Atahualpa had been executed, a puppet ruler had been installed in his place, and Tawantinsuyu had ceased to exist as an independent realm.

Social and political organization

If the nuclear family is excluded, the basic unit of Inca social organization was the ayllu, a theoretically endogamous kin group tracing descent in the male line from a common ancestor. The ayllus of any given province were grouped into larger units called saya. Ideally the partitioning of provinces into saya was a system of dual division; that is, there were two saya per province, and they functioned as moieties. Apparently, however, especially large and populous provinces were separated into three saya to promote governmental efficiency. Two or three saya, then, constituted an administrative province (wamañ), corresponding more or less to an indigenous ethnic group, although some provinces contained more than one tribe. Finally, the provinces were combined to form the four quarters (*suyu*) that gave the empire its name.

At the head of Tawantinsuyu's governmental hierarchy sat the emperor, who claimed descent from the sun-god Inti and was treated as a divine being. (Among the emperor's titles were *Sapa Ĩnka*, or 'Unique Inca', and *Intip Cori*, 'Son of the Sun'.) Upper-class polygyny allowed the emperor to have a large number of secondary wives, but from the reign of Topa Inca on each ruler's principal wife (*qoya*) was his full sister. The emperor was supposed to choose as his successor his most competent son by his principal wife, thereby keeping intact the divine bloodline of the ruling dynasty.

The emperor owned vast amounts of personal property–lands in all the provinces of the realm, buildings, herds, precious metals, elaborate textiles, and so on–and one of the distinctive features of the imperial succession was the fact that no ruler could inherit any of his predecessor's possessions. A dead king's property remained under his ownership and was used solely to maintain his mummy in state and perpetuate his cult. Therefore, each ascending emperor was forced to amass his own holdings in order to sustain himself in the correct style, solidify his power by rewarding his supporters, and insure the proper continuation of his cult after his death. In the author's opinion, this peculiar form of inheritance law was the major cause of the unrelenting Inca drive for conquest.

The emperors' kinsmen were grouped into ten or eleven *panaqas*, or royal *ayllus*. (Interpretations of the exact number and nature of the *panaqas* differ.) These lesser members of the ruling dynasty constituted the social class termed the 'Incas by blood'. Pachakuti instituted another class known as the 'Incas by privilege', composed of all the tribes around Cuzco who spoke Quechua as their native language; those who lived in the immediate vicinity of Cuzco were organized into ten noble *ayllus* that were paired with the *panaqas* for ceremonial purposes. Together the Incas by blood and by privilege formed the pool from which Tawantinsuyu's highest civil and religious functionaries were drawn.

Directly beneath the emperor in the government were the prefects (*apo*) of the four quarters; below them were the governors (*tokrikoq*) of the individual provinces. Each governor supervised an administrative hierarchy of hereditary officials known as *curacas*; ideally there was a *curaca* in charge of every group of 10,000, 5000, 1000, 500 and 100 families. Beneath the *curacas* were non-hereditary foremen (*kamayoq*) responsible for groups of 50 and 10 families. Census and tax records, along with the authorized version of Inca history, were kept on *quipus*, mnemonic devices of knotted strings that were interpreted by trained specialists.

The decimal system described above was largely an approximation for administrative purposes. The actual organization of Tawantinsuyu's provinces depended on circumstances. If a newly conquered area was already characterized by centralized authority, the Incas simply co-opted the local leadership into the imperial government and maintained the existing political organization. Recalcitrant members of the local aristocracy were replaced with Incas by privilege if necessary. Where strong indigenous leadership was lacking, decimal organization was imposed by decree.

Likewise, in their provinces the Incas took over established administrative centres or constructed new ones. Among the better-known Inca sites are Ollantaytambo, Pisac, Machu Picchu, Vilcashuamán, and Huánuco Pampa in the highlands, and La Centinela, Tambo Colorado, and Chiquitoy Viejo on the coast. Although some of these sites are fairly large and imposing, the Inca settlement pattern was not truly urban. Most citizens of the empire lived in villages and hamlets. The typical Inca administrative centre had a relatively small permanent population consisting of governmental and religious officials, along with a supporting staff. Even Cuzco proper had a comparatively small number of permanent inhabitants, although the surrounding area was densely settled.

Communications throughout the empire were maintained along a system of roads that was, for its time, one of the finest in the world. Two main highways ran the length of the empire, one through the highlands and the other along the coast, connecting all the major administrative centres to Cuzco. A network of roads and paths linked these highways to one another and to all the lesser centres and settlements of Tawantinsuyu. Traffic

Quipu-keeper, an important member of the administrative hierarchy of the Incas. Drawing by Felipe Guamán Poma de Ayala, sixteenth century AD.

along the road system was restricted to persons carrying out official business. The most renowned travellers were the Inca armies and the *chaskis*, trained relay runners who conveyed messages up and down the administrative hierarchy.

Economic organization

Although official dogma held that all land was owned by the emperor and allotted to the citizenry through his generosity, the *ayllu* was basically a self-sufficient unit. Each *ayllu* had a parcel of land appropriate to its size and raised the crops from which it derived its support. *Ayllus* received food from the state only in times of poor harvests or other disasters and under the circumstances described below.

The economy of the empire, as opposed to that of the local kin group, was a system of labour taxation supervised by the administrative hierarchy and regulated by a set of reciprocal obligations between state and taxpayer. The taxpayer, or able-bodied adult male head of household, was required to contribute a certain amount of labour to the state and its official personnel on a yearly basis. In return, citizens had to be fed, sheltered, and equipped by the beneficiary of their work while they were engaged in fulfilling labour obligations. Taxpayers also had to be entertained during their periods of service, and one of the most important products distributed to them was *chicha*, the native Andean maize beer.

The taxpayers' specific duties were of several kinds. One of the most important labour services was the cultivation of state-owned farmlands. Scattered throughout the empire were agricultural tracts belonging to the state, its official religion, and individual rulers. Taxpayers farmed these lands and deposited their produce in extensive state-controlled storage complexes, from which it was redistributed to support civil and religious functionaries, fulfil reciprocal obligations to taxpayers, and sustain citizens in times of need.

Another of the taxpayers' major duties was the *mita*, or service on public-works projects. *Mita* labourers increased the state's arable acreage by constructing hillside agricultural terraces and networks of irrigation canals; they also built and repaired roads, bridges, storehouses, palaces, government buildings, temples, and other edifices. All of the structures viewed today as examples of 'typical' Inca architecture (which is characterized by finely dressed, polygonal stone masonry with trapezoidal doors, windows, and wall niches) were actually special-purpose state buildings erected through the *mita*.

The last important obligation of Inca taxpayers was service in the armies that assembled the empire in the first place. Tawantinsuyu's victories were achieved through superior numbers, organization, and discipline, rather than through more sophisticated armament. Inca soldiers carried the same weapons as their enemies: spears, clubs, maces, slings, and bolas; bows and arrows were used only by natives of provinces along the eastern slopes of the Andes. Citizens who distinguished themselves in battle were rewarded with prestige and highly prized gifts. The most outstanding warriors were even granted positions in the administrative hierarchy, and military prowess was one of the few avenues of social mobility in the otherwise rigidly stratified Inca society.

Some groups were exempted from these normal forms of taxation. The nobility paid no taxes at all. Positions requiring specialized knowledge, such as the posts of the *quipu* interpreters, were filled by trained individuals who worked only at their appointed tasks. Skilled crafts were also delegated to full-time specialists. The empire obtained common cloth through taxation, but certain grades of fine cloth were woven by state personnel. Metalworking was another tax-exempt profession. (Bronze was the most technologically advanced metal used in Tawantinsuyu; in the terminology of Old World archaeology the Incas would be a Bronze Age civilization.) In addition, certain tribes were excused from the general *mita* in return for distinctive services; for example, the Rukana provided litter-bearers for the imperial court.

Two other social groups merit special mention. The first is the *mitmaqkona*, or resettled colonists. One of the *mitmaqkona*'s functions was to increase Tawantinsuyu's internal security: some colonists were rebellious peoples removed to more docile provinces, and some were loyal subjects installed in newly conquered territory. However, other *mitmaqkona* served an economic purpose; they were farmers skilled in growing certain crops who were resettled in areas where those crops had not been raised before. These latter *mitmaqkona* were a mechanism through which the Incas were attempting to replace the old kin-based vertical archipelago with an institution imposed by the state.

Finally, the *yanakona* constituted a class of full-time retainers that was supposedly created by Topa Inca. Among the tasks turned over to *yanakona* in later Inca times was the cultivation of royal and noble estates. This replacement of regular taxpayers by retainers may have been the first step toward a fundamental change in the relationship between state and citizen. The state had reciprocal obligations to taxpayers in return for their labour, but not to *yanakona*. The Incas' ultimate goal may have been to transform all of their subjects into one vast yanaconate, but they had not progressed very far in this direction by the time of the Spanish conquest.

Religion

In essence, Inca religion was a form of ancestor worship. The local *ayllu* looked to its ancestors for protection, treated their bodies and tombs as sacred objects, and renewed burial offerings to the dead on a regular basis. Deceased emperors were especially honoured ancestors in Tawantinsuyu; their mummies were maintained in state, consulted in times of stress, and brought out to attend important ceremonies, in which they played a major role. Finally, the official imperial religion itself, the cult of the sun-god Inti, was simply the worship of the ruling dynasty's divine ancestor.

Inca doctrine recognized a number of supernatural beings besides Inti. There was a creator known as

Procession of the dead with a corpse being carried on a litter: an expression of ancestor worship. Drawing by Felipe Guamán Poma de Ayala, sixteenth century AD.

Wiraqocha and a host of celestial divinities, including the moon (Killa) and thunder (Illapa), as well as a number of stars and constellations. Most of these sky-gods seem to have been male, with the exception of Killa, who was Inti's wife. Other female supernaturals belonged to a terrestrial group whose most important figures were the Earth (Pachamama) and water (Mamaqocha). The Spanish chroniclers and modern scholars have usually treated all of these beings as discrete deities, but this interpretation may represent the forcing of a rigid Graeco-Roman framework on to a more fluid Andean concept of godhead.

In any case, the Incas established temples of the state religion throughout their empire. The most important shrine was the Qorikancha in Cuzco. This building is commonly called the 'Temple of the Sun,' but it actually housed images of Wiraqocha and all the important members of the sky-god complex. The Qorikancha and other temples were tended by a graded hierarchy of priests roughly paralleling the civil administration; the high priest was a close relative of the emperor. In addition, temple staffs contained *mamakona*, consecrated women who were members of a larger group of females selected for their beauty (the *aklla*, or chosen women). *Mamakona* wove cloth of high quality for sacerdotal garments and ritual sacrifices; they also brewed *chicha* for use in festivals and distribution to taxpayers cultivating the fields assigned to the state religion.

Inca ceremonies were numerous, elaborate, and regulated by a lunar calendar. (This festival calendar was reconciled, in a manner not entirely clear, with an agricultural calendar based on solar observations.) Nearly every ceremony involved the sacrifice of one or more of the following items: llamas, guinea pigs, food, *chicha*, coca, and fine cloth. Human sacrifice occurred, but on a small scale, and even then only on the most solemn occasions or in times of terrible distress.

Inca religion also emphasized oracles, divination, ritual curing, and the veneration of *huacas*. *Huaca* was a general term for any person, place or object with supernatural associations. Besides the bodies and tombs of the dead mentioned earlier, *huacas* included anything odd or unusual: certain mountains, caves, springs, boulders, and buildings; persons born feet first or with six-fingered hands; strangely shaped or coloured stones and plants; etc. There were multitudes of *huacas* in Tawantinsuyu; the vast majority were of strictly parochial interest and were probably connected with the local *ayllus'* ancestors. Three hundred and twenty-eight of the most sacred *huacas* lay in the capital district around Cuzco and were conceived of as lying along imaginary lines (*ceques*) radiating outward from the Qorikancha. Each *ceque* was under the care of one of the social groups into which Cuzco's population was divided.

The Incas' eventual goal was to impose a uniform creed throughout their domain, but they were careful not to provoke newly conquered peoples by effecting radical changes hastily. In provincial areas immediate Inca policy was to tolerate native beliefs as long as sun worship and the veneration of the ruling dynasty were grafted on to them. Usually the Incas merely added a sun temple to the principal local religious centre and left other matters untouched, trusting that future generations raised as citizens of Tawantinsuyu would complete the transformation for themselves. (The most famous example of this policy of limited interference was the erection of a sun temple at Pachacamac, the long-established and highly prestigious oracular centre near present-day Lima.) In fact, many provincial religions were probably easy to tolerate because, like Inca beliefs, they were derived from an ancient, widespread, and deeply conservative Andean tradition of ancestor worship.

Epilogue

The Spanish conquest brought an end to Tawantinsuyu, but not to its peoples. Today there are perhaps 13 million Indians in Andean Peru, Ecuador, and Bolivia. To be sure, their lives have been greatly affected by events of the Spanish colonial and modern eras, but many elements of Inca culture have endured. Approximately five-sixths of all Andean Indians speak Quechua. In remote farming villages people still view their world as being divided into four parts, while herders count their flocks on *quipus*. Worship of the ancestors persists in amalgamation with Christian beliefs. The list of survivals could go on and on. After 450 years of alien domination the Inca heritage is still strong.

Further Reading

Prehistory

Barash, D., *Sociobiology and Behaviour*, Oxford and New York, 1977

Bender, B., *Farming in Prehistory: from Hunter-Gatherer to Food Producer*, London and New York, 1975

Daniel, G., *The Idea of Prehistory*, London and Cleveland, Ohio, 1962

Geertz, C., *The Interpretation of Cultures*, New York, 1973; London, 1975

Harnard, S., Steldis, H., and Lancaster, J. (ed.), 'Origins and evolution of language and speech', *Annals of the New York Academy of Sciences*, Vol. 280, New York, 1976

Jerison, H., *Evolution of the Brain and Intelligence*, New York, 1973; London, 1974

Leakey, R. E., and Lewin, R., *Origins*, London and New York, 1977

The Emergence of Civilization

Adams, R. M., *The Evolution of Urban Society*, London and Chicago, 1965

Cassirer, E., *An Essay on Man*, London and New Haven, Conn., 1944

Cherry, J. F., 'Generalisation and the archaeology of the state', in *Social Organisation and Settlement*, ed. D. R. Green, C. C. Haslegrove and M. J. T. Spriggs, British Archaeology Reports, Supplementary Series 47, pp. 411–38, London, 1978

Childe, V. G., 'The urban revolution', *Town Planning Review*, 21, no. 1, p. 3, London, 1950

————, *Social Evolution*, London and Cleveland, Ohio, 1951

Feibleman, J. K., *The Institutions of Society*, London, 1956

Flannery, K. V., 'The cultural evolution of civilizations', *Annual Review of Ecology and Systematics*, 3, pp. 399–426, Palo Alto, Cal., 1972

Fried, M. H., *The Evolution of Political Society*, New York, 1967

Friedman, J., and Rowlands, M. J. (ed.), *The Evolution of Social Systems*, London and Pittsburgh, Pa., 1978

Kluckhohn, C., 'The moral order in the expanding society', in *City Invincible: an Oriental Institute Symposium*, ed. C. H. Kraeling and R. M. Adams, Chicago, 1960

Mumford, L., *The City in History*, London and New York, 1961

Renfrew, C., *The Emergence of Civilization : the Cyclades and the Aegean in the Third Millennium BC*, London, 1972; New York, 1979

————, *Before Civilization: the Radiocarbon Revolution and Prehistoric Europe*, London and New York, 1973

Wittfogel, K. A., *Oriental Despotism, a Study of Total Power*, London and New Haven, Conn., 1957

EGYPT

Ancient Egypt

Adams, W. R., *Nubia—Corridor to Africa*, London and Princeton, N.J., 1977

Aldred, C., *The Egyptians*, London and New York, 1961

————, *Akhenaten—Pharaoh of Egypt*, London, 1968; New York, 1969

Badawy, A., *History of Egyptian Architecture*, Cambridge and Berkeley, Cal., 1954–68

Baines, J., and Málek, J., *An Atlas of Ancient Egypt*, London, 1980

Cambridge Ancient History, 2nd edn, Vols I and II, Cambridge and New York, 1970–5

Edwards, I. E. S., *The Pyramids of Egypt*, Harmondsworth and New York, 1970

Emery, W., *Archaic Egypt*, London and New York, 1961

Erman, A., *The Ancient Egyptians—a Sourcebook*, London and New York, 1966

Gardiner, Sir A., *Egyptian Grammar*, Oxford, 1978

————, *Egypt of the Pharaohs*, Oxford and New York, 1966

Harris, J. E., and Weeks, K., *X-Raying the Pharaohs*, London and New York, 1973

Harris, J. R. (ed.), *The Legacy of Egypt*, Oxford and New York, 1971

Hayes, W., *Most Ancient Egypt*, London and Chicago, 1965

Iversen, E., *Canon and Proportions in Egyptian Art*, Warminster, 1975; Forest Grove, Ore., 1976 (with Y. Shibata)

James, T., *The Archaeology of Ancient Egypt*, London, 1972; New York, 1973

————, *An Introduction to Ancient Egypt*, London, 1979

Kees, H., *Ancient Egypt—a Cultural Topography*, London and Chicago, 1979

Lichtheim, M., *Ancient Egyptian Literature*, 2 vols, Berkeley, Cal., 1973–6

Lucas, A. (ed.), *Ancient Egyptian Materials and Industries*, rev. and enlarged edn, London and New York, 1962

Mekhitarian, A., *Egyptian Painting*, London and New York, 1978

Michalowski, K., *The Art of Ancient Egypt*, London, 1969; New York, 1977

Ruffle, J., *Heritage of Ancient Egypt*, London, 1977

Schäfer, H., *The Principles of Egyptian Art*, ed. E. Brunner-Traut, tr. J. Baines, Oxford and New York, 1974

Trigger, B., *Nubia Under the Pharaohs*, London and Boulder, Colo., 1976

Wilson, J., *The Culture of Ancient Egypt*, Chicago, 1956

The Sea Peoples

Breasted, J. H., *Ancient Records of Egypt*, Vols III and IV, Chicago, 1906

Casson, S., *Ships and Seamanship in the Ancient World*, Princeton, N. J., 1971

Desborough, V. R. d'A., *The Last Mycenaeans and Their Successors*, Oxford and New York, 1964

Guido, M., *Sardinia*, London and New York, 1963

Karageorghis, V., *Kition*, London and New York, 1974

Luce, J. V., *Homer and the Heroic Age*, London and New York, 1975

Macqueen, J. G., *The Hittites and their Contemporaries in Asia Minor*, London and Boulder, Colo., 1976

Nelson, H. H., *The Earliest Historical Records of Ramesses III, Medinet Habu*, Chicago, 1930–2

Pritchard, J. B. (ed.), *Ancient Near Eastern Texts Relating to the Old Testament*, Princeton, N. J., 1969

Sandars, N. K., *The Sea Peoples, Warriors of the Ancient Mediterranean, 1250–1150 BC*, London and New York, 1978

Vaux, R. de, *Histoire ancienne d'Israël des origines à l'installation en Canaan. 2, la période des Juges*, Paris, 1971–3

Wiseman, D. J. (ed.), *Peoples of Old Testament Times*, London and New York, 1973

Wreszinski, W., *Atlas zur Altägyptischen Kulturgeschichte*, Leipzig, 1935

Ptolemaic, Roman and Byzantine Egypt

Badawy, A., *Coptic Art and Archaeology*, London and Cambridge, Mass., 1978

Beckwith, J., *Coptic Sculpture*, London, 1963

Bell, H. I., *Egypt from the Reign of Alexander the Great to the Arab Conquest*, Oxford, 1948

Bourguet, P. du, *Coptic Art*, London, 1971

Roberts, C. H., *Manuscript, Society and Belief in Early Christian Egypt*, Oxford and New York, 1979

Shore, A., *Portrait Painting from Roman Egypt*, London, 1972

Walters, C., *Monastic Archaeology in Egypt*, Warminster, 1974

The Religion of Ancient Egypt

Breasted, J. H., *The Dawn of Conscience*, London and New York, 1933

Černý, J., *Ancient Egyptian Religion*, London and New York, 1952

Frankfort, H., *Ancient Egyptian Religion*, New York, 1948

Kaster, J., *The Literature and Mythology of Ancient Egypt*, London, 1970

Morenz, S., *Egyptian Religion*, London and Ithaca, N.Y., 1973

Shorter, A. W., *The Egyptian Gods*, London, 1937; Ann Arbor, Mich. (University Microfilms)

WEST ASIA

Sumer and Akkad

Cambridge Ancient History, 2nd edn, Vols I and II, Cambridge and New York, 1970–5
Falkenstein, A., and Soden, W. von (ed. and tr.), Sumerische und Akkadische Hymnen und Gebete, Zürich, 1953
Jacobsen T., Towards the Image of Tammuz, ed. W. L. Moran, Cambridge, Mass., 1970; London, 1971
Jacobsen, T., and Wilson, John A., Most Ancient Verse, Chicago, 1963
Kramer, S. N., History Begins at Sumer, London, 1958; New York, 1959
————, The Sumerians, Chicago, 1963
————, From the Poetry of Sumer, Berkeley, Cal., 1979
Pritchard, J. B. (ed.), Ancient Near Eastern Texts Relating to the Old Testament, Princeton, N.J., 1969
Sollberger, E., and Rupper, J., Inscriptions royales sumériennes et akkadiennes, Paris, 191

Babylon

Bottéro, J., et al, The Near East: The Early Civilizations, tr. from French, New York, 1967; London, 1968
Brinkman, J. A., A Political History of post-Kassite Babylonia, Rome, 1968
Driver, G. R. and Miles, J. C., The Babylonian Laws, 2 vols, Oxford and New York, 1952–5
Grayson, A. K., Assyrian and Babylonian Chronicles, Locust Valley, N. Y., 1975
————, Babylonian Historical-Literary Texts, Toronto, 1975
Hallo, W. W. and Simpson, W. K., The Ancient Near East, London and New York, 1971
Lloyd, S., The Archaeology of Mesopotamia: From the Old Stone Age to the Persian Conquest, London and New York, 1978
Neugebauer, O., The Exact Sciences in Antiquity, London and New York, 1962
Oates, J., Babylon, London and New York, 1979
Oppenheim, A. L., Ancient Mesopotamia, 2nd edn, London and Chicago, 1977
Postgate, J. N., The First Empires, Oxford, 1977
Saggs, H. W. F., Everyday Life in Babylonia and Assyria, New York and London, 1965

Assyria

Barnett, R. D., Assyrian Sculpture, Toronto, 1975
Driver, G. R. and Miles, J. C., The Assyrian Laws, Oxford, 1935
Grayson, A. K., Assyrian Royal Inscriptions, Wiesbaden, 1972 onwards
Layard, A. H., Nineveh and Its Remains, ed. H. W. F. Saggs, London and New York, 1970
Mallowan, M. E. L., Nimrud and Its Remains, 2 vols, London and New York, 1966
Olmstead, A. T., History of Assyria, London and Chicago, 1923
Rogers, R. W., A History of Babylonia and Assyria, 2 vols, 6th edn, Cincinnati, 1915
Smith, S., Early History of Assyria to 1000 BC, London and New York, 1928; Vol. 3 of A History of Babylonia and Assyria, (Vols 1 & 2 L. W. King)

Mitanni

Gelb, I. J., Hurrians and Subarians, Chicago, 1944
O'Callaghan, R. T., Aram Naharaim: A Contribution to the History of Upper Mesopotamia in the Second Millennium BC, Rome, 1948

The Hittites

Bittel, K., Die Ruinen von Boğazköy, Berlin and Leipzig, 1937
Breasted, J. H., The Battle of Kadesh, Chicago, 1903
Garelli, P., Les assyriens en Cappadoce, Paris, 1963
Garstang, J., The Land of the Hittites, London, 1910
————, The Hittite Empire, London, 1929; New York, 1930
Gurney, O. R., The Hittites, Harmondsworth and New York, 1952
Guterbock, H. G., The Song of Ullikummi, New Haven, Conn., (American Schools Oriental Research), 1952

Urartu and Armenia

Burney, C., and Lang, D. M., The Peoples of the Hills—Ancient Ararat and Caucasus, London and New York, 1971
Der Nersessian, S., The Armenians, London and New York, 1969
Lang, D. M., Armenia, Cradle of Civilization, London and Boston, Mass., 1978
Piotrovsky, B. B., Urartu: the Kingdom of Van and its Art, tr. P. S. Gelling, London and New York, 1967

Syria

Bermant, C., and Weitzman, M., Ebla, London and New York, 1979
Buccellati, G., The Amorites in the Ur III Period, Naples, 1966
Dossin, G. et al., Archives royales de Mari, Paris, 1950–60
Gelb, I. J., Hurrians and Subarians, Chicago, 1944
Liverani, M., Storia di Ugarit nell' eta degli archivi politici, Rome 1960
Malamat, A., The Aramaeans in Aram Naharaim and the Rise of their States, Jerusalem, 1952 (in Hebrew)
Montet, P., Byblos et L'Egypte, Paris, 1929
Nougayrol, J., Le Palais royale d'Ugarit III–IV, Paris, 1955–6
O'Callaghan, R. T., Aram Naharaim, Rome, 1948
Wiseman, D. J., Chronicles of the Chaldaean Kings, London, 1956
————, The Alalakh Tablets, London, 1953

Phoenicia

Bikai, P. M., The Pottery of Tyre, Warminster and Forest Grove, Ore., 1978
Culican, W., The First Merchant Adventurers, London, 1964
Harden, D. B., The Phoenicians, London and New York, 1962
Karageorghis, V., Kition, London and New York, 1974
————, Salamis in Cyprus, London, 1970
Moscati, S., The World of the Phoenicians, tr. A. Hamilton, London and New York, 1968
Winter, I. J., 'Phoenician and North Syrian ivory carving in historical context etc.', Iraq, 38, 1976, pp. 1–22

Israel

Bright, J., A History of Israel, London and Philadelphia, Pa., 1952
Herrmann, S., A History of Israel in the Old Testament Times, tr, J. Bowden, London and Philadelphia, Pa., 1975
May, H. G., and Hunt, G. H., Oxford Bible Atlas, 2nd edn, Oxford and New York, 1974
Noth, M., The History of Israel, tr. S. Godman and P. R. Ackroyd, London and New York, 1960
Pedersen, J., Israel, Its Life and Culture, Oxford, 1959
Ringgren, H., Israelite Religion, tr. D. Green, London and Philadelphia, Pa., 1966

Troy

Bittel, K., Kleinasiatische Studien, Istanbul, 1942
Blegen, C. W., Troy and the Trojans, London and New York, 1963
Cook, J. M., The Troad: an Archaeological and Topographical Study, new edn, Oxford and New York, 1973
Dorpfeld, W., Troja 1893, Leipzig, 1894
————, Troja und Ilion, Athens, 1902
Leaf, W., Troy: a Study in Homeric Geography, London, 1912
Lloyd, S., Early Anatolia, Harmondsworth and New York, 1956
Schliemann, H., Troja, London and New York, 1884
Schmidt, H., Heinrich Schliemann's Sammlung trojanischer Altertümer, Berlin, 1902

Phrygia and Lydia

Akurgal, E., Ancient Civilizations and Ruins of Turkey, Ankara, 1973
————, Die Kunst Anatoliens von Homer bis Alexander, Berlin, 1961
Bean, G. E., Aegean Turkey: an Archaeological Guide, London and New York, 1966
Cambridge Ancient History, 3rd edn, Vol. II, Part 2, Cambridge and New York, 1975
Hanfmann, G. M. A., 'Excavations at Sardis', Publications of the American Society for the Excavation of Sardis, Leiden, 1924
Mellink, M., 'The city of Midas', Scientific American, 201, 1959
Ramsay, W. M., The Cities and Bishoprics of Phrygia, Oxford, 1895; New York, 1908

Persia and After Alexander

Bevan, E. R., The House of Seleucus, London, 1902
Bickerman, E., Institutions des Séleucides, Paris, 1937
Cambridge Ancient History, Vols IV and VII, Cambridge and New York, 1926–8

Colledge, M. A. R., *The Parthians*, London and New York, 1968
Ghirshman, R. *Iran*, Harmondsworth, 1954; New York, 1955
Frye, R. N., *The Heritage of Persia*, London and Cleveland, Ohio, 1963
Millar, F., *The Roman Empire and its Neighbours*, London and New York, 1967
Runciman, S., *Byzantine Civilization*, London and New York, 1948
Tarn, W. W., *The Greeks in Bactria and India*, Cambridge and New York, 1951
Tarn, W. W., and Griffith, G. T., *Hellenistic Civilization*, 3rd edn, London and New York, 1952
Ziegler, K. H., *Die Beziehungen zwischen Rom und dem Partherreich*, Wiesbaden, 1964

Mesopotamian Religion
Dhorme, P., *La Religion assyro-babylonienne*, Paris, 1910
Hooke, S. H., *Babylonian and Assyrian Religion*, London and New York, 1953
————. *Middle Eastern Mythology*, Harmondsworth and New York, 1963
Jacobsen, T., *Towards the Image of Tammuz*, ed. W. L. Moran, Cambridge, Mass., 1970
————. *The Treasures of Darkness: a History of Mesopotamian Religion*, London and New Haven, Conn., 1976
Kramer, S. N., *Sumerian Mythology*, revised edn, London and New York, 1961
Pritchard, J. B., *Ancient Near Eastern Texts Relating to the Old Testament*, Princeton, N.J., 1950
Ringgren, H., *Religions of the Ancient Near East*, tr. J. Sturdy, Philadelphia, Pa., 1972; London, 1973

The Evolution of the Alphabet
Diringer, D., *The Alphabet*, London, 1975
Driver, G. R., *Semitic Writing from Pictograph to Alphabet*, Oxford, 1944; new edn, ed. S. A. Hopkins, Oxford and New York, 1977
Gelb, I. J., *A Study of Writing*, London and Chicago, 1952
Naveh, J., *The Development of Aramaic Script*, Jerusalem, 1970
Peckham, J. B., *The Development of Late Phoenician Scripts*, Cambridge, Mass., 1960

INDIA

The Indus Civilization
Allchin, B. and R., *The Birth of Indian Civilization*, New York, 1971
Fairservis, W. A., Jnr, *The Roots of Ancient India*, New York and London, 1971
Gordon, D. H., *The Prehistoric Background of Indian Culture*, Bombay, 1958
Kosambi, D. D., *The Culture and Civilization of Ancient India in Historical Outline*, London, 1965
Mackay, E., *The Indus Civilization*, London, 1935
Marshall, Sir John, *Mohenjo-Daro and the Indus Civilization*, London, 1931
Piggott, S., *Prehistoric India to 1000 BC*, Harmondsworth, 1950
Rao, S. R., *Lothal and the Indus Civilization*, Bombay, 1973
Wheeler, Sir Mortimer, *The Indus Civilization*, 3rd edn, Cambridge and New York, 1968; supplementary vol. to *Cambridge History of India*, 7 vols.
————. *Early India and Pakistan to Ashoka*, London and New York, 1959

The Aryan Invasion
Burrow, T., 'The early Aryans', in *A Cultural History of India*, ed. A. L. Basham, Oxford and New York, 1975
Childe, V. G., *The Aryans: a Study of Indo-European Origins*, London and New York, 1926
Mayrhofer, M., *Die Indo-Arier in alten Vorderasien*, Wiesbaden, 1966
Piggott, S., *Prehistoric India*, Harmondsworth, 1950; New York, 1962

Early Imperial India
Basham, A. L., *The Wonder That Was India*, London, 1954; New York, 1955
Kosambi, D. D., *The Culture and Civilization of Ancient India in Historical Outline*, London, 1965

Majumdar, R. C. (ed.), *The Gupta-Vakataka Age*, Lahore, 1946
Narzin, A. K., *The Indo-Greeks*, Oxford, 1957
Smith, V. A., *Aśoka, the Buddhist Emperor of India*, Oxford, 1901
Thapar, R., *Aśoka and the Decline of the Mauryas*, Oxford, 1961
Warmington, E. H., *Commerce Between the Roman Empire and India*, Cambridge, 1928

Hinduism
Bhattacharji, S., *The Indian Theogony*, Cambridge and New York, 1970
Bouquet, A. C., *Hinduism*, London, 1947; New York, 1948
Eliade, M., *Yoga: Immortality and Freedom*, tr. W. R. Trask, London and New York, 1958
Farquhar, J. N., *An Outline of the Religious Literature of India*, Oxford, 1920
Keith, A. B., *The Religion and Philosophy of the Veda and Upanisads*, London and Cambridge, Mass., 1925
Kramrisch, S., *The Hindu Temple*, Calcutta, 1946
Nikhilananda, S. (tr.), *The Bhagavad Gita*, New York, 1944
O'Flaherty, W. D., *Hindu Myths*, Harmondsworth, 1965
————. *The Origins of Evil in Hindu Mythology*, Berkeley, Cal., 1976
Zimmer, H., *Philosophies of India*, ed. J. Campbell, New York, 1951; London, 1952
————. *Myths and Symbols in Indian Art and Civilization*, ed. J. Campbell, London and New York, 1956

Buddhism
Babbitt, I. (tr.), *The Dhammapada*, London and New York, 1936
Conze, E., *Buddhism: Its Essence and Development*, London and New York, 1951
————. *Buddhist Thought in India*, London, 1962; Ann Arbor, Mich., 1967
Cowell, E. B. (tr.), *The Jataka Tales*, Cambridge, 1895–1907
Davids, T. W. Rhys, *Buddhist India*, 9th edn, Delhi, 1970
Dutt, S., *Buddhist Monks and Monasteries of India*, London and New York, 1962
Keith, A., *Buddhist Philosophy in India and Ceylon*, Oxford, 1923
Ling, T., *The Buddha: Buddhist Civilization in India and Ceylon*, London and New York, 1973
Mookerji, R., *Aśoka*, 3rd edn, Delhi, 1962

Jainism
Basham, A. L., *History and Doctrines of the Ājivikas*, London, 1951
Jaini, J. L., *Outlines of Jainism*, ed. F. W. Thomas, Cambridge, 1940
Jaini, P. S., *The Jaina Path of Purification*, Berkeley, Cal., 1979
Mehta, M. L., *Jaina Psychology*, Amritsar, 1956

EUROPE

The Minoans
Evans, Sir Arthur, *The Palace of Minos*, London, 1921–35
Graham, J. W., *The Palaces of Crete*, Oxford and Princeton, N.J., 1962
Hood, S., *The Minoans*, London and New York, 1971
Hutchinson, R. W., *Prehistoric Crete*, Harmondsworth and New York, 1962
Nilsson, M. P., *Minoan-Mycenaean Religion*, Lund, 1950
Willetts, R. F., *Cretan Cults and Festivals*, London and New York, 1962
————. *The Civilization of Ancient Crete*, London and Berkeley, Cal., 1977

Mycenaeans
Carpenter, R., *Discontinuity in Greek Civilization*, Cambridge, 1966; New York, 1968
Chadwick, J., *The Mycenaean World*, Cambridge and New York, 1976
Desborough, V. R. d'A., *The Last Mycenaeans and their Successors*, Oxford and New York, 1964
Dietrich, B. C., *The Origins of Greek Religion*, Berlin, 1974
Dickinson, O. T. P. K., *The Origins of Mycenaean Civilization*, Gothenburg, 1977
Hood, M. S. F., *The Arts of Prehistoric Greece*, Harmondsworth, 1978
Hooker, J. T., *Mycenaean Greece*, Boston, Mass., 1976; London, 1977
Schliemann, H., *Orchomenos*, Leipzig, 1881
Scoufopoulos, N. C., *Mycenaean Citadels*, Gothenburg, 1971
Taylour, Lord William, *The Mycenaeans*, London and New York, 1964

Archaic and Classical Greece

Anderson, J. K., *Military Theory and Practice in the Age of Xenophon*, Berkeley, Cal., 1970
Andrewes, A., *The Greek Tyrants*, London, 1956; New York, 1966
Boardman, J., *The Greeks Overseas*, Harmondsworth and Magnolia, Mass., 1973
Burn, A. R., *Pericles and Athens*, London and Mystic, Conn., 1948
————, *Persia and the Greeks*, London and New York, 1962
Davies, J. K., *Democracy and Athens*, Glasgow, 1978
Finley, M. I., *The Ancient Economy*, London and Berkeley, Cal., 1973
Forrest, W. G., *A History of Sparta*, London and New York, 1968
————, *The Emergence of Greek Democracy*, London, 1966; New York, 1967
Frankel, H., *Early Greek Poetry and Philosophy*, tr. H. Moses and J. Willis, Oxford and New York, 1975
Guthrie, W. K. C., *A History of Greek Philosophy*, 3 vols, Cambridge and New York, 1962
Jeffery, L. H., *Archaic Greece: the City-states, c. 700–500 BC*, London and New York, 1976
Kirk, G. S., and Raven, J. E., *The Presocratic Philosophers*, Cambridge and New York, 1957
Lawrence, A. W., *Greek Architecture*, Harmondsworth, 1973; rev. edn., New York, 1975
Lesky, A., *A History of Greek Literature*, tr. J. Willis and C. de Heer, London and New York, 1966
Oxford Classical Dictionary, ed. N. G. L. Hammond and H. H. Scullard, 2nd edn, Oxford and New York, 1970
Meiggs, R., *The Athenian Empire*, Oxford and New York, 1972
Robertson, C. M., *A History of Greek Art*, 2 vols, Cambridge, 1975; New York, 1976
Robertson, D. S., *A Handbook of Greek and Roman Architecture*, Cambridge, 1929
Usher, S., *The Historians of Greece and Rome*, London, 1969; New York, 1970
Webster, T. B. L., *Greek Art and Literature, 700–530 BC*, London, 1959; New York, 1968

Macedon

Cawkwell, G. L., *Philip of Macedon*, London, 1978
Ellis, J. R., *Philip II and Macedonian Imperialism*, London, 1976; New York, 1977
Hammond, N. G. L., *A History of Macedonia, Vol. I*, [to 550 BC], Oxford and New York, 1972
————, *Alexander the Great: King of Macedon, Commander and Statesman*, Princeton, N.J., 1980
Hammond, N. G. L., and Griffith, G. T., *A History of Macedonia, Vol II* [550–336 BC], Oxford and New York, 1979
Lane Fox, R., *Alexander the Great*, London, 1973; New York, 1974
Tarn, W. W., *Alexander the Great*, 2 vols, Cambridge, 1946; Vol. I, new edn, Vol. II, new impr., Boston, Mass., 1979
————, *Antigonos Gonatas*, Oxford and New York, 1913
Tarn, W. W., and Griffith, G. T., *Hellenistic Civilization*, London, 1952; rev. edn New York, 1961
Walbank, F. W., *Philip V of Macedon*, Cambridge and Hamden, Conn., 1940
Wilcken, U., *Alexander the Great*, ed. E. N. Borza, tr. G. C. Richards, London, 1932; New York, 1967

Carthage

Finley, M. I., *Ancient Sicily*, revised edn, London and Totowa, N.J., 1979
Harden, D. B., *The Phoenicians*, London and New York, 1962
Moscati, S., *The World of the Phoenicians*, tr. A. Hamilton, London and New York, 1968
Picard, G. and C., *Daily Life in Carthage*, London and New York, 1961
————, *The Life and Death of Carthage*, London and New York, 1968
Scullard, H. H., *Scipio Africanus and the Second Punic War*, Cambridge, 1930

Sicily and Magna Graecia

Dunbabin, T. J., *The Western Greeks*, Oxford and New York, 1948
Finley, M. I., *Ancient Sicily*, revised edn, London and Totowa, N. J., 1979
Talbert, R. J., *Timoleon and the Revival of Greek Sicily, 344–317 BC*, Cambridge and New York, 1974
Tillyard, H. J. W., *Agathocles*, Cambridge, 1908
Woodhead, A. G., *The Greeks in the West*, London and New York, 1962

Etruscans

Banti, L., *The Etruscan Cities and Their Culture*, Berkeley, Cal., 1973; London, 1974
Dennis, G., *The Cities and Cemeteries of Etruria*, London, 1878, 1907; New York, 1907
Heurgon, J., *Daily Life of the Etruscans*, tr. J. Kirkup, London and New York, 1964
Pallottino, M., *The Etruscans*, Harmondsworth and New York, 1955
Scullard, H. H., *The Etruscan Cities and Rome*, London and Ithaca, N.Y., 1967
Strong, D., *The Early Etruscans*, London and New York, 1968

Rome Before the Republic

Alföldi, A., *Early Rome and the Latins*, London and Ann Arbor, Mich., 1965
Bloch, R., *Les Origins de Rome*, Paris, 1959
Ogilvie, R. M., *Early Rome and the Etruscans*, London and Atlantic Highlands, N.J., 1976
Trump, D. H., *Central and Southern Italy before Rome*, London and New York, 1966
Whatmough, J., *The Foundation of Roman Italy*, London, 1937

The Roman Republic

Badian, E., *Roman Imperialism in the Late Republic*, 2nd edn, Oxford and Ithaca, N.J., 1968
Brunt, P. A., *Social Conflicts in the Roman Republic*, London, 1971; New York, 1972
Crawford, M. H., *The Roman Republic*, Cambridge and Atlantic Highlands, N.J., 1978
McDonald, A. H., *Republican Rome*, London and New York, 1966
Masson, G. A., *A Concise History of Republican Rome*, London, 1973
Scullard, H. H., *From the Gracchi to Nero*, 4th edn, London and New York, 1976
Sherwin-White, A. N., *The Roman Citizenship*, 2nd edn, Oxford and New York, 1973
Syme, R., *The Roman Revolution*, Oxford and New York, 1939

The Early Roman Empire

André, J. M., *Le siècle d'Auguste*, Paris, 1974
Kienast, D., *Augustus*, Darmstadt, 1977
Grant, M., *The World of Rome*, London and Cleveland, Ohio, 1960
————, *The Climax of Rome*, London and Boston, Mass., 1968
MacMullen, R., *Roman Social Relations, 50 BC–AD 284*, London and New Haven, Conn., 1974
Millar, F., *The Roman Empire and its Neighbours*, London, 1967; New York, 1968
————, *The Emperor in the Roman World*, London and Ithaca, N.Y., 1977
Petit, P., *Histoire générale de l'empire romain*, Paris, 1974
Scullard, H. H., *From the Gracchi to Nero*, 4th edn, London and New York, 1976
Starr, G. G., *Civilization and the Caesars*, Oxford and Ithaca, N.Y., 1954

The Later Roman Empire

Bowder, D., *The Age of Constantine and Julian*, London, 1978; New York, 1979
Brown, P., *The Making of Late Antiquity*, Chicago, 1978; London, 1979
————, *The World of Late Antiquity, From Marcus Aurelius to Muhammad*, London and New York, 1971
Browning, R., *The Emperor Julian*, London, 1975; Berkeley, Cal., 1976
Bury, J. B., *History of the Later Roman Empire from the death of Theodosius to the death of Justinian*, vol. 1, London, 1923
Gagé, J., *Les Classes sociales dans l'empire romain*, Paris, 1969
Geffcken, J., *The Last Days of Greco-Roman Paganism*, Amsterdam, 1978
Jones, A. H. M., *The Later Roman Empire, AD 284–602*, 2 vols, Oxford and Norman, Okla., 1964
Marron, H. -I., *Décadence romaine ou antiquité tardive? IIIe–IVe siècle*, Paris, 1977
Mazzarino, S., *The End of the Ancient World*, tr. G. Holmes, London and New York, 1966
Momigliano, A. D. (ed), *The Conflict between Paganism and Christianity in the Fourth Century*, Oxford and New York, 1963
Piganiol, A., *L'Empire chrétien*, 2nd edn, Paris, 1972
Stein, E., *Histoire du Bas-Empire*, vol. 1, Paris, 1959

Vogt, J., *The Decline of Rome*, tr. J. Sondheimer, London, 1967; New York, 1969

Walbank, F. W., *The Awful Revolution. The Decline of the Roman Empire in the West*, Liverpool and Toronto, 1969

Early Christianity

Chadwick, H., *The Early Church*, Harmondsworth, 1967; Grand Rapids, Mich., 1969

Cochrane, C. N., *Christianity and Classical Culture*, London and New York, 1940

Dodds, E. R., *Pagan and Christian in an Age of Anxiety*, Cambridge and New York, 1965

Frend, W. M. C., *Martyrdom and Persecution in the Early Church*, Oxford and New York, 1965

Grabar, A., *The Beginnings of Christian Art*, London, 1967

Kelley, J. N. D., *Early Christian Doctrines*, London, 1958

Laistner, M. L. W., *Christianity and Pagan Culture in the Later Roman Empire*, new edn, London and Ithaca, N.Y., 1968

Markus, R. A., *Christianity in the Roman World*, London, 1974; New York, 1975

Nock, A. D., *Conversion: The Old and the New in Religion from Alexander the Great to Augustine of Hippo*, 2nd edn, London, 1952

Pelikan, J., *The Christian Tradition: a History of the Development of Doctrine*, vol. I *The Emergence of the Catholic Tradition, AD 100–600*, London and Chicago, 1971

Stevenson, J., *A New Eusebius*, London, 1959; New York, 1963

Volbach, W. F., *Early Christian Art*, London, 1961; New York, 1962

The Graeco-Roman City

Jones, A. H. M., *The Greek City from Alexander to Justinian*, Oxford and New York, 1940

Ward-Perkins, J. B., *Cities of Ancient Greece and Italy*, London and New York, 1974

Willetts, R. F., *The Civilization of Ancient Crete*, London and Berkeley, Cal., 1977

Wycherley, R. E., *How the Greeks Built Cities*, 2nd edn, London and New York, 1962

The Greek Mind

Barnes, J. *et al.* (ed.), *Articles on Aristotle, I–IV*, London and Atlantic Highlands, N.J., 1975–9

Boardman, J. B., *Greek Art*, new edn, London and New York, 1973

Bowra, C. M., *Pindar*, Oxford and New York, 1964

———. *Homer*, London and New York, 1972

Coulton, J. J., *Greek Architects at Work*, London, 1977

Dover, K. J., *Aristophanic Comedy*, London and Berkeley, Cal., 1972

Gosling, J. C. B., *Plato*, London and Boston, Mass., 1973

Guthrie, W. K. C., *A History of Greek Philosophy*, Cambridge and New York 1962–79 (5 vols)

Kirk, G. S., *The Songs of Homer*, Cambridge, 1962; abridged edn: *Homer and the Epic*, New York n.d.

Lesky, A., *A History of Greek Literature*, tr. J. Willis and C. de Heer, London and New York, 1966

Long, A. A., *Hellenistic Philosophy*, London and New York, 1974

Norwood, G., *Greek Tragedy*, New York, 1960

Page, D. L., *Sappho and Alcaeus*, Oxford and New York, 1955

The Roman Mind

Altheim, F., *A History of Roman Religion*, tr. H. Mattingly, New York, 1937; London, 1938

Balsdon, J. P. V. D., *Roman Women: Their History and Habits*, London, 1962; New York, 1963

Brunt, P. A., *Social Conflicts in the Roman Republic*, London, 1971; New York, 1972

Clarke, M. L., *The Roman Mind: Studies in the History of Thought from Cicero to Marcus Aurelius*, London and Cambridge, Mass., 1956

Crook, J. A., *Law and Life of Rome*, London and Ithaca, N.Y., 1967

Daube, D., *Forms of Roman Legislation*, Oxford and New York, 1956

Earl, D., *The Moral and Political Tradition of Rome*, London and Ithaca, N.Y., 1967

Fowler, W. W., *Religious Experiences of the Roman People*, London, 1922

Fraenkel, E., *Horace*, Oxford and New York, 1957

Gelzer, M., *The Roman Nobility*, tr. R. Seager, Oxford and New York, 1969

Grimal, P. *et al.*, *Hellenism and the Rise of Rome*, London, 1968; New York, 1969

Ogilvie, R. M., *The Romans and their Gods in the Age of Augustus*, New York, 1969; London, 1970

Otis, B., *Virgil: a Study in Civilized Poetry*, Oxford, 1963; New York, 1964

Quinn, K., *Catullus: an Interpretation*, London, 1972; New York, 1973

———. *Texts and Contexts: the Roman Writers and their Audience*, London and Boston, Mass., 1979

———. *Virgil's Aeneid: a Critical Description*, London and Ann Arbor, Mich., 1968

Rist, J. M., *Epicurus: an Introduction*, Cambridge and New York, 1972

———. *Stoic Philosophy*, New York, 1969; Cambridge, 1970

Taylor, L. R., *Party Politics in the Age of Caesar*, Berkeley and Los Angeles, Cal., 1949

Williams, G., *Tradition and Originality in Roman Poetry*, Oxford and New York, 1968

CHINA

Shang and Chou

Bynner, Witter (tr.), *The Way of Life according to Lao Tzu*, London and New York, 1962

Chang, Kwang-chih, *The Archaeology of Ancient China*, 3rd edn, London and New Haven, Conn., 1977

Cotterell, Y. Y. and A. B., *The Early Civilization of China*, London and New York, 1975

Creel, H. G., *Confucius and the Chinese Way*, London and New York, 1960

Dubs, H. H., *Hsün tzeu: the Moulder of Ancient Confucianism*, London and New York, 1927

Herrmann, A., *An Historical Atlas of China*, ed. N. S. Ginsburg, Edinburgh and Chicago, 1966

Lau, D. C., (tr.), *Mencius*, Harmondsworth and New York, 1970

Li Chi, *Anyang*, Seattle, 1977; Folkestone, 1978

Waley, A., (tr.), *The Book of Songs*, London, 1937

Watson, B., (tr.), *The Basic Writings of Mo Tzu, Hsün Tzu, and Han Fei Tzu*, London and New York, 1967

Watson, W., *Cultural Frontiers of Ancient East Asia*, Edinburgh, 1971; Totowa, N.J., 1972

Imperial Unification and the Crisis of the Early Empire

Ch'en, K. K. S., *Buddhism in China: A Historical Survey*, Princeton, N.J., 1964; Oxford, 1965

Chi Ch'ao-Ting, *Key Economic Areas in Chinese History, as Revealed in the Development of Public Works for Water-Control*, London, 1936; New York, 1970

Chu T'ung Tsu, *Han Social Structure*, Seattle, 1972; London, 1973

Cotterell, Y. Y. and A. B., *The Early Civilization of China*, London and New York, 1975

Elvin, M., *The Pattern of the Chinese Past*, London and Stanford, Cal., 1973

Fitzgerald, C. P., *China. A Short Cultural History*, 3rd edn, London and New York, 1961

Groot, J. J. L. de, *The Religions of China*, Leiden, 1892

Loewe, M., *Crisis and Conflict in Han China*, London and Totowa, N.J., 1974

Watson, B., (tr.), *Records of the Historian* (Ssu-ma Chien), New York, 1969; London, 1970

Wright, A. F., *Buddhism in Chinese History*, London and Stanford, Cal., 1959

Yu Ying-Shih, *Trade and Expansion in Han China; a Study in the Structure of Sino-Barbarian Economic Relations*, Cambridge and Berkeley, Cal., 1967

Early Science and Technology

Chang, Kwang-chih, *Early Chinese Civilization*, London and Cambridge, Mass., 1976

Chang Tzu-kao, *Chung-kuo ku-tai hua-hsueh-shih* [*History of Chemistry in Ancient China*], Hong Kong, 1977

Ho Peng-Yoke, *The Astronomical Chapters of the Chin Shu*, Paris, 1966

Ho Ping-ti, *The Cradle of the East*, Hong Kong, 1975; London and Chicago, 1976

Needham, J., *Science and Civilization in China*, 7 vols so far published, Cambridge and New York, 1954–76

———. *Clerks and Craftsmen in China and the West*, Cambridge and New York, 1970

Ware, J. R., (ed.) *Alchemy, Medicine and Religion in the China of AD 320; the 'Nei P'ien' of Ko Hung*, London and Cambridge, Mass., 1966

Chinese Art

Medley, M., *A Handbook of Chinese Art*, London, 1973; New York, 1974
Watson, W., *The Genius of China*, London, 1973 (Catalogue of the Chinese Exhibition)
———, *Style in the Arts of China*, Harmondsworth, 1974; New York, 1975
Weber, G. W., *The Ornament of Late Chou Bronze*, New Brunswick, 1953
Willetts, W., *Chinese Art*, Harmondsworth and New York, 1958

AMERICA

The Olmecs

Adams, R. E. W., *Prehistoric Mesoamerica*, Boston, Mass., 1977
Bernal, I., *El mundo olmeca*, Mexico City, 1968
———, *A History of Mexican Archaeology*, New York, 1979; London, 1980
Marquina, I., *Arquitectura prehispánica*, Mexico City, 1951

Teotihuacán

Millon, R. (ed.), *Urbanization at Teotihuacán, Mexico*, Vol. I, Parts 1 & 2: *The Teotihuacán Map*, Austin, Tex., 1973; London, 1975
Sanders, W. R., Parsons, J. R., and Santley, R. S., *The Basin of Mexico: Ecological Processes in the Evolution of a Civilization*, New York, 1979
Wolf, E. R. (ed.), *The Valley of Mexico: Studies in Prehispanic Ecology and Society*, Albuquerque, N. Mex., 1976

Toltecs

Acosta, J. R., 'Interpretación de algunos de los datos obtenidos en Tula relativos a la época Tolteca', *Revista Mexicana de Estudios Antropológicos*, 14: 75–110, Mexico, 1956–7
Davies, N., *The Toltecs: Until the Fall of Tula*, Norman, Okla., 1977; London, 1978
Diehl, R. A. (ed.), 'Studies of ancient Tollan', *University of Missouri Monographs in Anthropology*, 1, Columbia, Mo., 1974
———, 'Tula, Hidalgo', *Supplement to the Handbook of Mesoamerican Indians*, ed. J. Sabloff, Austin, Tex. 1980
Matos, E. M. (ed.), 'Proyecto Tula: primera parte', *Colección Científica 15*, Instituto Nacional de Antropología e Historia, Córdoba, Mexico, 1974
——— (ed.), 'Proyecto Tula: segunda parte', *Colección Científica 33*, Instituto Nacional de Antropología e Historia, Córdoba, Mexico, 1976

The Mayas

Adams, R. E. W., *Prehistoric Mesoamerica*, Boston, Mass., 1977
——— (ed.), *The Origins of Maya Civilization*, Albuquerque, N. Mex., 1977
Culbert, T. P. (ed.), *The Classic Maya Collapse*, Albuquerque, N. Mex., 1973
Hammond, N. (ed.), *Social Process in Maya Prehistory*, London and New York, 1977
Hammond, N., and Willey, G. R. (ed.), *Maya Archaeology and Ethnohistory*, Austin, Tex., 1979
Harrison, P. D., and Turner, B. L., *Pre-Hispanic Maya Agriculture*, Albuquerque, N. Mex., 1978
Thompson, J. E. S., *The Rise and Fall of Maya Civilization*, Norman, Okla. 1966
———, *Maya History and Religion*, Norman, Okla., 1970; Folkestone, 1971

The Aztecs

Katz, F., *The Ancient American Civilizations*, tr. K. Lois Simpson, London and New York, 1972
Vaillant, G. C., *The Aztecs of Mexico*, 6th edn, London and New York, 1960
Weaver, M. P., *The Aztecs, Maya, and Their Predecessors*, London and New York, 1972

The Incas

Bingham, H., *Lost City of the Incas: the Story of Machú Pichú and its Builders*, New York, 1948; London, 1951
Brundage, B. C., *Lords of Cuzco: a History and Description of the Inca People in their Final Days*, Norman, Okla. 1967; Folkestone 1969
Hemming, J., *The Conquest of the Incas*, London and New York, 1970
Lumbreras, L. G., *The Peoples and Cultures of Ancient Peru*, tr. B. J. Meggers, Washington 1974
Moore, S. F., *Power and Property in Inca Peru*, London and New York, 1958
Willey, G. R., *An Introduction to American Archaeology*, Vol. 2: *South America*, Englewood Cliffs, N.J., 1971; Hemel Hempstead, 1972
Zuidema, R. T., *The Ceque System of Cuzco: the Social Organization of the Capital of the Inca*, Leiden, 1964

List of Maps

Illustration Acknowledgments

The producers of this book would like to thank the following for granting permission to reproduce illustrations. Every effort has been made to trace all copyright owners. The producers apologize if the acknowledgment proves to be inadequate; in no case is such inadequacy intentional. Page numbers in **bold** denote colour plates.

Ashmolean Museum. Oxford: 35, 43, 204
By kind permission of The Athlone Press. University of London: 257 from *A History of Architecture*. 18th edition. page 288 by Sir Banister Fletcher
BBC Hulton Picture Library: 296
Barnaby's Picture Library: 40, 118
By kind permission of Book Club Associates: 205 (drawing by Andrew Kay)
Courtesy of the Trustees of the British Museum. London: 14 right, 15, 42, 71, 74, 93, 96, 98, 100, 104, 109, 110, 114, 120, 144, **150**, 156, 162, 169, 187, 213 top, 238, 243, 251, 252 top, 261 top, 269, 314 top, 346 top; and from Robert Harding Associates: 28, 160, 232
By kind permission of Cambridge University Press: 291, 292 both from *Science and Civilization in China*. volume 3 by Joseph Needham
Ny Carlsberg Glyptotek. Copenhagen: 47
The J. Allan Cash Photolibrary: 119, 175, 178, 193, 199, **218, 236**, 241, 257 top, 265, 282, 297, 325, 335, 349
Bruce Coleman Ltd: 9 (photo R. I. M. Campbell)
Dr William Culican: 133
By kind permission of Deutsche Orient-Gesellschaft. Berlin: 112
By kind permission of The Estate of Sir Arthur Evans: 16
Mary Evans Picture Library: 19, 143
Alison Frantz (from Robert Harding Associates): 208 below, 215
Government of India. Department of Archaeology (from Robert Harding Associates): 190
Robert Harding Associates: 145 (photo Josephine Powell). 287, 306, 307, 308, 312, 313, 314 below (Harding/Times)
The John Hillelson Agency: **301** (photo Marc Riboud)
Hirmer Verlag/Fotoarchiv. München (from Robert Harding Associates): 32, 34, 209
Michael Holford: **149** (British Museum). **167** (Musée Guimet, Paris)
By kind permission of the Director of the India Office Library and Records: 186, 192

Institut d'Ethnologie. Paris: 353, 355
By kind permission of The Institute of History and Philology. Academia-Sinica, Taipei, Taiwan. The Republic of China: 289, 290, 306
Michael Kelly: title-page illustration. 6, 24, 62/63, 181, 182, 222, 231, 239, 252, 315, 322, 323, 333, 334, 337, 339, 340, 343, 346, 347, 351
By kind permission of Seton Lloyd: 13 below, 73 top
MacQuitty International Collection: 293
Mansell/Alinari: 132, 245, 248, 261 below, 264, 276, 279
The Mansell Collection Ltd: 21, 36, 53, 81, 85, 88 below, 91 top, 107, 116, 123, 166, 180, 208 top, 212, 221, 226, 272 top, 275
Mansell/Giraudon: 88 top, 115 and 142 (from Robert Harding Associates)
By kind permission of Methuen & Co. Ltd: 20 (from *The Emergence of Civilisation* by Colin Renfrew. drawing by Mr H. Walkland)
Metropolitan Museum of Art, New York. Rogers Fund, 1961 (from Robert Harding Associates): 103
Middle East photographic Archive. London (Photos Alistair Duncan): 49, 50, 67 (Cairo Museum)
By kind permission of the MIT Press. Cambridge, Massachusetts: 56 (from *Coptic Art and Archaeology* by Alexander Badawy)
Museo di Villa Giulia, Rome (from Robert Harding Associates): 244
National Archaeological Museum, Athens (from Robert Harding Associates): 213 below
Oriental Institute. University of Chicago: 45
Popperfoto: 202, 256, 341 (from Robert Harding Associates)
Rainbird Publishing Group Limited: 141 and 235 (from Robert Harding Associates). 217 (photo Tim Mercer)
Museo di Villa Giulia. Rome (from Robert Harding Associates): 244
Ronald Sheridan: 13, 29, 130, 140, 152
Spanish National Tourist Office: 259
Staatliche Museum. Berlin (from Robert Harding Associates): 91 below

John Topham: 126, 148, 151, 203
Victoria and Albert Museum, London Crown copyright: **168**, 189, 194, 195, 201
Dr Colin Walters: 38, 57 above
ZEFA: **68** (photo G. Sirena), **302** (photo J. Bitsch), **317** (photo Joop Grijpink), **319** (photo Janoud), **320** (photo U. Bagel)

Index